Sex and Character

An Investigation of Fundamental Principles

Otto Weininger

Translated from German by Ladislaus Löb
Edited by Daniel Steuer with Laura Marcus
With an introduction by Daniel Steuer
Research assistant: Audrey Hartford

Indiana University Press
Bloomington and Indianapolis

We are grateful to the British Academy for awarding a research grant that allowed us to employ a research assistant. We would also like to thank Ritchie Robertson (Oxford) and David Stern (Iowa) for their prompt support when needed.

This book is a publication of

Indiana University Press
601 North Morton Street
Bloomington, IN 47404-3797 USA

http://iupress.indiana.edu

Telephone orders 800-842-6796
Fax orders 812-855-7931
Orders by e-mail iuporder@indiana.edu

The paper used in this publication meets the minimum requirements of American National Standard for Information Sciences—Permanence of Paper for Printed Library Materials, ANSI Z39.48-1984.

Manufactured in the United States of America

Library of Congress Cataloging-in-Publication Data

Weininger, Otto, 1880–1903.
[Geschlecht und Charakter. English]
Sex and character : an investigation of fundamental principles / Otto Weininger ; translated from German by Ladislaus Löb ; edited by Daniel Steuer and Laura Marcus ; with an introduction by Daniel Steuer.
p. cm.
Includes bibliographical references and index.
ISBN 0-253-34471-9 (cloth : alk. paper)
1. Sex. 2. Sexual ethics. I. Löb, Ladislaus. II. Steuer, Daniel. III. Marcus, Laura. IV. Title.
HQ21.W413 2005
306.7—dc22

2004006423

1 2 3 4 5 10 09 08 07 06 05

Contents

A Book That Won't Go Away: Otto Weininger's Sex and Character xi
Daniel Steuer
Translator's Note xlvii
Ladislaus Löb

Preface 3

First (Preparatory) Part: Sexual Diversity

Introduction 9

On the development of concepts in general and in particular. Man and Woman. Contradictions. Fluid transitions. Anatomy and endowment. No certainty in morphology?

Chapter I: "Men" and "Women" 12

Lack of differentiation in the embryo. Rudiments in the adult. Degrees of "gonochorism." Principle of intermediate forms. M and W. Evidence. Necessity of establishing types. Summary. Oldest inklings.

Chapter II: Arrhenoplasm and Thelyplasm 16

Location of sexuality. Support for Steenstrup's view. Sexual characteristics. Internal secretion. Idioplasm — arrhenoplasm — thelyplasm. Oscillations. Proofs from unsuccessful castration. Transplantation and transfusion. Organotherapy. Individual differences between cells. Cause of intermediate sexual forms. Brain. Surplus of boys born. Determination of sex. Comparative pathology.

Chapter III: Laws of Sexual Attraction 27

Sexual "taste." Probable existence of laws. First Formula. First interpretation. Proofs. Heterostyly. Interpretation of same. Animal kingdom. Further laws. Second formula. Chemotaxis? Analogies and differences. "Elective affinities." Adultery and marriage. Consequences for the offspring.

Chapter IV: Homosexuality and Pederasty 41

Homosexuals as intermediate sexual forms. Innate or acquired, healthy or pathological? Special case of the law. All humans pre-

A Book That Won't Go Away: Otto Weininger's *Sex and Character*

DANIEL STEUER

Otto Weininger's Life and Work

The shorter a life the more difficult it can be to give an adequate account of it. In the case of the Viennese Otto Weininger, who was born in 1880 and died in 1903, this difficulty is further complicated by the fact that his writings—produced, not to be forgotten, in the short space of three years between the ages of 20 and 23—do not allow for a straightforward and simple reading. Neither his contemporaries nor those after him, including ourselves a hundred years later, agree on the merits of his work. The evaluations range from readings of Weininger as a pathological misogynist and antisemite who paved the way toward National Socialism, to those that see him as a critic of alienation in the modern age, and an agent of human emancipation. Both parties have very good, some may say almost conclusive arguments. Thus, Weininger is still able to divide the minds and to provoke debate among scholars from a wide range of fields; perhaps not such a surprise, given the extent of his popularity at the time and his influence on other writers and thinkers who are central to that best-selling academic product called the fin-de-siècle, and to the mainstream of twentieth-century European culture in general.

The text we present here for the first time in its entirety in English was first published in May 1903 as *Geschlecht und Charakter. Eine prinzipielle Untersuchung* [*Sex and Character: An Investigation of Fundamental Principles*]. Weininger, much to his dismay, had been asked by one of his doctoral supervisors, Friedrich Jodl, as early as December 1901, to change the original title, *Eros und Psyche. Eine biologisch-psychologische Untersuchung* [Eros and psyche: A biological and psychological investigation]. In a letter to Jodl he says: "As far as the title is concerned, 'Geschlecht und Charakter, biol.-psychol. Studie' does not sound as nice as 'Eros und Psyche,' but it fulfills the purpose of a title as good as the original name."[1] As we shall see, this re-christening of the book can be taken as a useful point of reference for structuring Weininger's life, as it marks his turning away from empirical science (biology and psychology) toward questions of principle (logic and ethics); note that he eventually changed not only the main title but the subtitle as well. The rupture which this intellectual re-orientation produced in his thoughts is translated into various fault-lines which run through the book, adding further to the difficulty of coming to terms with it.

Weininger's only other publication is a posthumous collection of essays, *Über die letzten Dinge*, now also available in English as *On Last Things*.[2] In these, Weininger has shed his empirical skin, and we are faced with the beginnings of a metaphysics which may have led Weininger, with equal likelihood, to develop an interesting philosophy of culture or an obscure form of symbolism. Therefore, in all that follows it will be wise to bear in mind that we are faced with a life and work which were left "jagged & incomplete," cut short by a decision of the author himself, who took his own life in October 1903.[3]

Otto Weininger was born on 3 April 1880 in Vienna, the son of Leopold and Adelheid Weininger, and the eldest of seven children, two of whom did not reach a mature age. It seems, according to Richard and Rosa, two of his siblings, that Otto and his father shared a number of features: strict moral ideas, a love of music (in particular that of Wagner), a talent for languages, and also antisemitic convictions. With respect to the last, Rosa wrote to David Abrahamsen: "My father was highly anti-Semitic, but he thought as a Jew and was angry when Otto wrote against Judaism."[4] Somewhat similarly, the father opposed his son's intention to convert to Protestantism when they first discussed the issue in the summer of 1900, but later claimed he would never have done so had he noticed any "traces of the wonderful transformation" that was to come: "Back then, there was no question of a Christian spirit in my son, and I believed that he wanted to convert for material reasons."[5] Otto finally adopted the Protestant faith and was baptized on 19 July 1902, the day of his doctoral graduation. In so doing, he joined the religion of Kant. What this meant to him is articulated most clearly in an earlier letter to his friend Hermann Swoboda: "The choice is yours. If only you were less of a Catholic! You are just as Catholic in your wanting-to-believe in Avenarius as you were in your wanting-to-believe in the Holy Trinity. Can you not see that your fanaticism about breeding is the same fanaticism you invested in the conversion of your family to the apostolic faith? You may be the last important materialist. And the last important materialist must end up in a monastery!!"[6]

The period of Weininger's short life saw the end of a long phase of social and political stability, and the rise of a modernity which seems to be identical with its own crisis. Weininger's work, like so many others, reflects this complex crisis and is, like so many others, an extreme reaction to it. But in Weininger's case the extremism, somewhat paradoxically, follows from his insistence on the autonomous individual and on the faculty of reason. While others around him wrote eloquent lamentations about their loss of trust in language and discussed Mach's unsalvageable self, Weininger postulated the necessary conditions for establishing concepts, for having a self, and for making clear judgments. While Viennese culture indulged in circular sexual affairs, and, in some cases, advocated prostitution as a wonderful means to foster male genius, Weininger wrote a 600-page reminder of how the value of human dignity demands that no individual be treated as a means to an end, and claimed in a short essay on the theme of time that everything circular is immoral—such as, for example, the Viennese waltz.[7]

Clearly, the Weininger family belonged to the assimilated Jewry of the late and dying Habsburg monarchy, who were part of the German middle class and who shared the values of the Austrian political tradition, which Steven Beller has labeled as "antitolerant liberalism," that is, a liberalism which allows "strangers" to change and become members of the community, but not to continue existing as a separate culture within a pluralist framework.[8] Otto's father was a fairly well-known goldsmith. He produced jewelry for the aristocracy, had exhibits in the Metropolitan Museum in New York, and was recognized as an authority in his field. But he had never experienced higher education, and therefore his son was the first to enter that world. He did so with verve. At the age of 16 he sent his first article on the etymology of a word in Homer to a journal in Leipzig (it was not accepted, but Weininger kept arguing his case with the editor, see Hirsch 1997, pp. 239–242); at 18 he began his university career; at 21 he submitted his first manuscript, *Eros und Psyche,* to the Archive of the Austrian Academy of Science (this was common practice as a means to secure an author's priority); at 22 his second manuscript, *Zur Theorie des Lebens* [On the theory of life]; and in the same year he submitted his doctoral thesis, *Geschlecht und Charakter. Eine biologische und psychologische Studie* [Sex and character: A biological and psychological study], and passed his doctoral examinations. The titles already suggest that Weininger had no taste for questions of detail within a limited field (despite his almost obsessional collating of evidence from a wide-ranging literature); rather, he preferred to tackle big questions and to attempt a synopsis of knowledge from many different areas.

It is no over-simplification to say that Weininger's biography is essentially the story of his education. From Hannelore Rodlauer's introductory essay to the two documents Weininger deposited at the Academy of Science,[9] together with the very useful chronology, incorporating excerpts from Weininger's correspondence and from the literature on Weininger, provided in Hirsch (1997), a reasonably consistent picture of that education emerges. An influence that links Weininger's time at grammar school, ending in July 1898, and the beginning of his university career in the autumn of the same year, is his teacher Wilhelm Jerusalem. Jerusalem was not only a classical philologist but also a *Dr. habil.* in philosophy, the author of a book on evolutionary epistemology, *Die Urteilsfunktion. Eine biologische und erkenntnistheoretische Untersuchung* (1895; The function of judgment: A biological and epistemological investigation), and a member of the "Philosophical Society at the University of Vienna." Upon registering as a student at the Faculty of Philosophy and joining the Philosophical Society, Weininger became acquainted at first hand with the liberal, anticlerical, and empirically minded school of thought that dominated Vienna and was represented by figures like Ernst Mach (a friend of Jerusalem's), Friedrich Jodl (to become, with Laurenz Müllner, the supervisor of Weininger's dissertation), Ludwig Boltzmann, Franz Hillebrand, Sigmund Exner, Wagner-Jauregg, and Krafft-Ebing.[10] Here he met Hermann Swoboda, Moriz Rappaport, and Oskar Friedländer (later Ewald) who become friends, and he heard papers presented by, among others, Heinrich Obersteiner, Houston Stewart Chamberlain, Josef Breuer, Christian Ehrenfels, and Alois Höfler.[11] Typically philosophical themes like solipsism and Zeno's paradox were discussed at the society's meetings, but there was also a strong preponderance of more scientific topics such as the psychology of sense perception, the experimental investigation of musical phenomena, and Darwinism. One of Breuer's papers, for example, is on Fechner's ideas about the evolution of organic beings. Weininger took courses in zoology and botany, in mathematics, physics, and chemistry, and in a number of medical subjects as well as in the history of philosophy and in logic,[12] and it is fair to say that he "spent his first university years in the sciences more than in philosophy" (Burns 2001, p. xix).

Weininger's youthful academic self-confidence during the first phase of his studies—his "empiriocritical phase"—already shows a pronounced skeptical tendency toward theoretical positions when he writes to Swoboda: "I put a bee (in empiriocritical terms: a vital sequence) in Müllner's bonnet. It is called Avenarius."[13] Müllner, who followed Franz Brentano and Franz Hillebrand to the second Chair of philosophy, had been appointed in order to shift the balance toward the clerical and conservative side, whereas Jodl, who edited Feuerbach's writings, was clearly a liberal and secular philosopher who saw himself in the tradition of the Enlightenment. However, despite Weininger's harsh criticism of purely secular science it was Jodl who showed more understanding for *Sex and Character,* while Müllner was by far more condemning of it. Both, however, distanced themselves from Weininger's radical claims concerning women and Jews.

On 25 October, a "clarification" by Jodl appeared in the *Neues Wiener Journal.*[14] While Jodl points out that Weininger's academic teachers had no influence on most of the second part of *Sex and Character,* he does not distance himself altogether either from the person, or the book. On the contrary he goes on to say that he expects the book to fulfill the role of the "whipping boy, who gets publicly beaten, while secretly being made to work for his tormentors,"[15] and that he is therefore pleased to have the opportunity to do justice to a dead person and to defend his work against the worst kinds of misinterpretation. He begins by stating that Weininger's dissertation was an exceptional achievement. Müllner, in his report on the dissertation, agrees that Weininger's exceptional talent is beyond doubt, but ultimately judges the work to be a metaphysics without any foundation. The tone of his remarks is decidedly ironic; the insults which the author continuously heaps on women, he says, produce an almost comical effect because in the end he is forced "to declare those women who cannot be denied ethical and logical thought for men, and thus to perform a deed of which, as is well known, not even the mighty English parliament is capable."[16]

On 26 December 1899 Weininger called on Ernst Mach, but apart from the exact length of his visit—47 minutes according to a letter to Swoboda (see Weininger 1990, p. 62)—nothing is known about the nature of their conversation. In any case, it was to take Weininger less than a year to become critical of Mach's philosophy, and less than two to abandon empiriocriticism altogether. In August 1900, together with Swoboda, he attended the International Psychological Congress in Paris and made a contribution, in French, to the discussion of Joire's presentation on new methods in psychological studies, which was subsequently included in the proceedings.[17] In this he points out that psychology cannot do without introspection as a source of information. Self-observation and the physiological approach would need to be developed simultaneously. This as yet balanced attitude was later to give way to a far more polemical stance toward the emerging branch of experimental psychology. On 4 December 1901 Weininger ended a letter to Swoboda by exclaiming: "Therefore, farewell empiriocritical phase!"[18] This was neither said whimsically, on the spur of the moment, nor was it a wholesale rejection of Avenarius's position. The preceding letter qualifies the categorical judgment by singling out Avenarius's lasting achievements. The decisive farewell is based on the rejection of what Weininger perceives as "naïve realism," and his arguments for this rejection are themselves empirical in nature, i.e., the Weber-Fechner law and the process of the gradual clarification of thoughts. A naïve and monist concept of the world cannot account for the fact that there is no simple representational relationship between the (internal) mind and the (external) world. Weininger is aware that sense perception and subsequent mental processes are transcriptional in nature, and this creates the justification for a science of psychology as separate from physics. Nineteenth-century physiology depended to a large extent on the technical possibility of producing graphs with the help of recording devices.[19] Weininger realized that, logically, the correspondence between recorded graphs and mental processes depends on a recourse to inner experience, and therefore the latter cannot be explained by the former.[20] In the last instance he was to extend this insight and draw the conclusion that the possibility of all knowledge depends on the ability of a self to make coherent judgments on the sensations in the process of experience. His notion of the genius as a monadic individual with perfect memory was then to turn the tables on all science which treats the individual as determined by causal factors.

Around the same time (27 December 1901), Weininger, in the letter to Jodl mentioned above, cautiously set out his theory of the "ethical dualism" between M and W, his abbreviations for the ideal (Platonic) types of Man and Woman. He talks of "ethical phenomenology" which he perceives as "a kind of biology of ideals" (Weininger 1990, p. 101). This phase in his development is worth noting for two reasons, firstly because it shows that his criticism of experimental psychology grew out of empirical considerations and was not a case of a sudden transition from a scientific position to a speculative one; secondly, as the letter to Jodl shows, his typology of M and W was not as black-and-white to begin with as it then turned out in *Sex and Character*.[21]

Eros und Psyche was submitted to the Academy on 8 June 1901, and *Zur Theorie des Lebens* on 27 March 1902, only four months before Weininger's doctoral examination on 19 July 1902. Unfortunately, the dissertation has not survived in the form in which it was submitted,[22] but Jodl's and Müllner's reaction to the published version bear witness to the vast changes and additions Weininger made to the text (including the final two chapters, probably not finished before May 1903, and the theory of hysteria developed in the autumn of 1902). Alongside these revisions and extensions he worked on various of the essays in *On Last Things* (including those on

Ibsen's *Peer Gynt,* finished by 25 October 1902, and on "Science and Culture," finished by 22 January 1903). His full adoption of a version of Kantianism and his rejection of Mach and Avenarius must have been completed by 2 March 1902, when he writes: "Most importantly, I have given up the epistemology of Mach-Avenarius completely. The self *is,* and it is not at all necessary to salvage it."[23] However, this turn from empiriocriticism to a Kantian idealism was in many ways a return to the educational world with which Weininger had been most familiar since his days at school through the influence of Wilhelm Jerusalem. As Rodlauer points out, he was deeply influenced by Plato and Socratic ethics both in *Sex and Character* and in *On Last Things* (see Rodlauer 1995, p. 15); in fact, his ethical turn was a return from a deviation which, as he himself saw it, had been caused by the influence of his friend Swoboda: "Now my turning away from this psychology, my return to myself makes you angry. Perhaps, the blame for this falls more on me than on you, because I even intensified the influence which you exerted on me in this respect since our first conversation about psychology (Western corner of the Votivkirche, beginning of June 1899)."[24]

Weininger's friendship with Swoboda, and his empiriocritical interlude, goes a long way toward explaining the division of *Sex and Character* between a first empirical-physiological and a second philosophical and psychological part, with the former proceeding in a more inductive, the latter in a more deductive manner. In the former he demonstrates a full awareness of methodological questions. His theory of gender identity, based on two different kinds of cytoplasm, is set up in conscious analogy to the normal scientific procedure followed, for example, in physics, which constructs ideal cases in order to measure empirical cases against these standards.[25] Some of the conclusions of this part must certainly be considered as progressive for the times.[26] Weininger views sexuality as not simply to be identified with certain anatomical features, but distributed across all parts of the body; he establishes continuous bisexuality as the normal case, explaining homosexuality as the natural sexual inclination of those individuals situated in the middle of the male/female spectrum (so-called intermediate forms), and arguing against an unnatural morality which only credits part of the spectrum with social acceptability. Even his law of sexual attraction, formulated in arithmetical terms and suggesting that individuals with complementary distributions of male and female cytoplasm are attracted to each other, provides an interesting framework for thinking about a notoriously untidy issue; nor does Weininger fail to add that events in real life are subject to many further influences. Such scruples are absent in much of the second part. There Weininger re-interprets his scientific ideal cases of M and W as ideal cases for a normative ethic, increasingly confusing a metaphysical and a transcendental use of these types. This is the origin and source of the notorious Weininger. However, some of the discussions in the second part, for example those of memory and genius, and the criticism of empirical psychology, can be read independently of Weininger's gendered superstructure. In this context, it is interesting to point out that *On Last Things* contains far fewer misogynist or antisemitic remarks. Of course, the strong presence of both elements in *Sex and Character* cannot be overlooked. But it would be equally wrong to consider them as integral, or even central, to Weininger's thought. In any case, the thinker who seems to emerge in the posthumous collection of essays is even more decidedly a cultural critic and a conservative critic of modern alienation than the author of *Sex and Character.*

The second part of *Sex and Character* contains, among other things, a theory of hysteria which assumes that the conflict in afflicted women results from a projection, and adoption, of male (ascetic) values. The symptoms of hysteria become manifest when the true (sexual) nature of a woman can no longer be suppressed. It was Swoboda who suggested to Weininger that he might ask Freud for support in publishing his book. Weininger called on Freud in the autumn of 1901 (probably October); his remarks on this meeting in two letters to Swoboda testify yet again to a surprising degree of self-assurance: "He said many nice, even praising, things, but, he said, the world doesn't want ideas, it wants proofs! Well, that I can't understand. What kind of thinking is that? How am I supposed to *prove* facts, when all I can do is *point* to this and that."[27] Weininger's intellectual surprise is genuine and worth considering from a philosophical point of view—it anticipates Wittgenstein's saying-showing dichotomy, and his lifelong interest in the limits of verifiability—but it is not the only reason why he did not follow Freud's advice. In another letter to Swoboda he reports the following conversation with Freud: "[He said] I should take my time and prove everything, everything, e.g. that M is most likely to go bald. I told him that I don't want to be bald myself by the time E.u.P. [Eros and psyche] finally appears; in 10 years I would much rather write ten more books like it; and, frankly, my scientific interest is not strong enough for me to guarantee that I have the patience of a census statistician in the civil service."[28]

The Swoboda-Freud-Weininger connection was also instrumental in Fließ's accusations of plagiarism leveled against Weininger with respect to the ideas of bisexuality and periodicity. Swoboda had known Freud, probably as a patient, in the autumn of 1900 (Rodlauer in Weininger 1990, p. 33). Fließ claimed that Swoboda had learned of his idea of bisexuality (and periodicity) through Freud (who conceded as much) and had passed the idea on to Weininger, while Swoboda himself went on to write his book on periodicity, which was published in 1904.[29] In both instances, the accusation of plagiarism is difficult to support. In the case of bisexuality, "even though Weininger presumably had taken the central idea from Fließ, he nonetheless worked it out in such idiosyncratic fashion, that the accusation of plagiarism does not seem justified" (Schröter 2002, p. 342), and Swoboda discusses Fließ's work on the same topic extensively in his own book (see Schröter 2002, pp. 351–355).[30]

During the last one and a half years of his life, Weininger, traveling on his own, undertook two long journeys, one to Norway from July to September 1902, and one to Italy in July and August of 1903. Artur Gerber reports that after the first journey, having been contacted by Weininger's worried father, he had persuaded Weininger not to commit suicide (20 November 1903);[31] and after returning from the second journey, Weininger was again in a depression. As early as 13 February of that year, he had written a will which meticulously sets out the details of who is to receive which of his belongings, of some payments still to be made, etc. On 21 August he sent a second will from Italy to Rappaport. Having returned to Vienna on 29 September, he amended the will on 3 October, and shot himself in the chest that same night. He died on the morning of the 4th. The place of his suicide, a room he rented in the same house in which Beethoven had died (Schwarzspanierstraße 15), is unfailingly mentioned in every report on his death, and in most later writings on him. Jean Améry, in his long essay on suicide, is an exception.

Weininger provides a recurrent point of reference throughout Améry's phenomenological essay on suicide. In the first part, Améry establishes that his theme cannot usefully be approached by applying the logic of life. A suicidal person cannot be persuaded by reason, nor, ultimately, can a suicide be explained by psychology. Améry is far from invoking self-hatred, or any other psychological category, as an explanation for Weininger's suicide; rather, he could be said to employ Weininger's own argument about the impossibility of a scientific psychology of the self.[32] If the self with its *weltanschauung* exists it does not follow communal values and worldly logic but establishes its own world and values. Thus, any "logotherapist" who tried to dissuade Weininger from suicide might have been right "in the global system of life," but crucially, only within the system of life. "Since Weininger, as I assume, was already poised on the threshold when those soothing, luminous words reached him, such wisdom, to him, would only have carried the fool's sceptre" (Améry 1976, p. 28).

Weininger's last aphorisms, written on his journey through Italy, seem to become more and more fantastic, especially where he elaborates on his peculiar form of symbolism: "The swamp is the false completion of the river, and a merely apparent triumph over itself" (Weininger 2001, p. 149).[33] "Fear of midges is the reverse side of the love for birds."[34] However, they are also more radically honest in their self-reflexivity: he identifies the hatred of women with hatred of one's own sexuality insofar as one has not yet overcome it (see Weininger 1980, p. 626), and he labels the person who fails in his attempt to commit suicide the perfect criminal "because he wants life in order to take revenge" (Weininger 1980, p. 624). He regards suicide to be cowardly, "even if it is the least of the cowardly acts" (Weininger 2001, p. 157), and he considers the possibility that it might depend on the shallowness or depth of an individual whether he or she considers suicide permissible in certain circumstances or not permissible in any (Weininger 1980, p. 602).

"There is *only* psychotherapy," he writes, and in proper psychotherapy everyone is his own diagnostician and thus his own therapist: "Everyone must cure himself and be his own doctor. If that is what he wants, God will help him. If not, nobody will help him" (Weininger 1980, p. 602). The idea of autonomy can hardly be pushed any further than this. Yet, Weininger does not stop there. Finally, he seems to have begun to move from an ideal of autonomy to one of fusion, as the last attempt at overcoming vanity: "The stars symbolize people who have conquered everything but vanity. . . . There are many stars, for the problem of vanity is the problem of individuality. . . . There is no ego, there is no soul. Only *the good,* which encloses all *particulars* within itself, is of the *highest, most perfect reality*" (Weininger 2001, p. 148).[35]

Weininger's Influence and Reception

Almost every year between 1903 and 1932 a new edition of *Sex and Character* appeared, including a popular edition ("Volksausgabe") in 1926, followed by another in 1947.[36] Finally, there is the 1980 reprint by Matthes and Seitz which reproduces the first edition and does not include Weininger's changes to the text as implemented by Gerber for the second edition, which appeared as early as November 1903 (and on which all subsequent pre-1980 editions, as well as the "beastly" English translation of 1906, are based).[37]

While the number of editions and copies sold does not necessarily reflect the cultural and intellectual significance and influence of a book, with *Sex and Character* this is undoubtedly the case. The list of literary and philosophical writers who were influenced by Weininger in some form—whether they welcomed and adopted his ideas or felt obliged to criticize and reject them, or whether they simply used some of his stereotypes—ranges from Karl Kraus, Elias Canetti, Robert Musil, Heimito von Doderer, and Thomas Bernhard to August Strindberg, Gertrud Stein, Italo Svevo, E. M. Cioran, James Joyce, and—to return to the Austrian context—Ferdinand Ebner and Ludwig Wittgenstein. In fact, every selection of names in this context will be arbitrary, while providing a comprehensive list is next to impossible. In light of this, the following remarks will attempt to charter the territory along the fault-line of antagonisms which continues to inform Weininger reception and scholarship.[38]

But first a remark from Wittgenstein's *Culture and Value* may be quoted as a reminder of how difficult it is to assign Weininger a place in cultural and intellectual history:

> In Western Civilization the Jew is always being measured according to calibrations which do not fit him. That the Greek thinkers were neither philosophers in the western sense, nor scientists in the western sense, that those who took part in the Olympic Games were not sportsmen & fit into no western occupation, is clear to many people. But it is the same with the Jews too. . . . In this context Spengler is quite right not to classify Weininger with the western philosophers. (Wittgenstein 1998, p. 23e)

This passage raises a number of questions concerning Wittgenstein's attitude toward his own Jewishness and the position of Jews and Jewry in the society of his time.[39] However, leaving these aside, it points toward a feature of Weininger's thought that is otherwise easily lost. We may call it his "Manicheism," but a Manicheism of a pre-Socratic, certainly pre-Christian, nature. Ultimately, elementary and anonymous forces or principles are at work in the cosmos, as we have seen in his very last notes in which Weininger forsakes even Kantian individuality, and pronounces it to be a form of "vanity." Only the good is real. This fits in well with Spengler's claim that Weininger's moral dualism was a "purely Magian conception," and his death ("a spiritual struggle of essentially Magian experience") one of the most sublime moments of late religiosity, putting him next to Spinoza and the Baalshem as representatives of a Jewish mysticism that can only be recognized as such if one views it "through a colour-wash of Western thought-forms."[40] All of this points to a subterranean flow of thought in Weininger that gradually works its way out into the open, although the sense in which it may be called religious needs further qualification, as we shall see when we discuss Ebner.

Early Reactions to *Geschlecht und Charakter* and *Über die letzten Dinge*

It has sometimes been said that *Sex and Character* owed its notoriety to the fact that the author committed suicide shortly after its publication. Whatever the impact of the suicide, the long-term interest in Weininger's work certainly cannot be explained by it. Even before his suicide the book had sparked off an energetic response from at least one public figure, the German doctor and phrenologist Paul Julius Möbius. Möbius, well-known for his work on the "physiological feeble-mindedness of women" (*Über den physiologischen Schwachsinn des Weibes,* 1900, with nine editions between 1900 and 1908) and various others, was first to accuse Weininger, at least implicitly, of plagiarism in his review of the book for *Schmidts Jahrbücher der gesamten Medizin* (August 1903). Weininger had called Möbius's views on sexual intermediacy "homespun"; this dismissal, Möbius wrote, had been motivated by fear of being accused of plagiarism.[41] Weininger then had written to him from Italy asking him to publicly renounce the accusation, but Möbius did something quite different. He wrote a short pamphlet called *Geschlecht und Unbescheidenheit* [Sex and presumption], in which he took the young man to task. His strategy is quite clever. He claims that he had never accused Weininger of plagiarism, but had rather said that Weininger must have been afraid of being called a plagiarist. The ideas in question had in any case been in circulation since time immemorial, and were too general to be the subject of a priority dispute. In contrast, the title of Weininger's book, Möbius claimed, was modeled on a series of his own publications (such as *Geschlecht und Entartung* [Sex and degeneration], which was followed by further contributions to the differences between the sexes from *Geschlecht und Mathematik* [Sex and mathematics] to *Geschlecht und Alkohol* [Sex and alcohol]). The level at which he engages with Weininger's ideas, by and large, does not warrant a detailed discussion. In other respects, however, the text reveals some interesting points. What motivates Möbius apart from protecting his own glory, seniority, and authority,[42] is an insistence on disciplinary boundaries, based on a purely rhetorical reference to experience as the basis and touchstone for science. In his review, he had replied to Weininger's suggestion that sexual intermediacy, contrary to Möbius's understanding of it as something degenerate, is the norm: "So a man dressed in the philosopher's coat wants to decide what is normal and what is pathological!" (Möbius 1904, p. 4). In a similar vein, he exclaims later on: "The other day, a newspaper editor reviewing my work said that he also knew what degeneration was. No, journalists and philosophers have no say in this matter" (ibid., p. 14). Of course, it is legitimate for an expert to insist on his (or her) competence; what is worrying is the circular argument on which Möbius establishes his authority. He simply knows what is normal and what is not: "A number of steps lead from the normal human being to the distinct hermaphrodite; the more normal a human being is the more clearly he is man or woman, and the closer he is to the hermaphrodite the more abnormal he is" (ibid., p. 13). This follows a passage in which Möbius rubbishes the empirical evidence Weininger has collected on intermediate forms from the scientific literature and natural history. But what are the empirical arguments for his own views? He immediately continues: "All experts have long since agreed that this is true of the physical; to understand that those deviations from the sexual type which seem purely mental are also pathological symptoms, such understanding is real progress. Those who can think clearly do not really need proofs" (ibid.). My point is not to turn the tables on Möbius, rather it is to point out that the invocation of "experience," or "empirical evidence," without proper methodological reflection on the notion of the empirical, when faced with the need to draw the line between what is and what is not science, is a common phenomenon in nineteenth-century science. And whereas the "best" of positivists, like Mach, turn this "openness" of the concept into a critical instrument, the worst use it in order to prove their preconceptions. Thus, Weininger's criticism of Möbius's ideas as "homespun" hits the mark. Möbius must have felt it, and it must have hurt him, particularly coming from a callow youth, a "philosophical clown," from Vienna![43] But this philosophical clown at least made a distinction between his constructed ideal and empirical diversity, whereas Möbius simply regards a certain ideal as normal.

Another factor that clearly plays a part in Möbius's attack is the relation between Germany and Austro-Hungary. With heavy-handed humor, he writes: "Finally, something light-hearted: On page 193 he says: 'A man feels unscrupulous and immoral if, at any point in his life, he hasn't reflected for some time.' What wonderful men must be found in Vienna's lecture halls and coffee houses."[44]

We find the same attitude in Dr. Ferdinand Probst's psychiatric study *Der Fall Otto Weininger* (The case of Otto Weininger, a title later to be adopted by Le Rider), also published in 1904. Probst fully agrees with Möbius's view on the question of priority, but he attempts to do more: he wants to show that Weininger wrote what he wrote because he was insane. Thus Probst's text is divided into an introduction, an anamnesis, a discussion of Weininger's works, and a diagnosis (entitled "The illness"). It is an exercise in reductive pathologizing which apparently was not even enjoyed by its author, who was a junior doctor at the Munich psychiatric hospital and had been charged with this task by his superior, Professor Leopold Loewenfeld. Writing later than Möbius, Probst is able to refer to some positive reactions to Weininger, such as Strindberg's praise of *Sex and Character.* Probst has no difficulty finding an explanation for such evaluations in the current climate of decadence and religious irrationality. "In Vienna, the centre of modern decadence," he writes, "the home town of the 'philosopher,' Weininger even seems to have some kind of a community of religious followers" (Probst 1904, p. 2). He goes on to quote from Rappaport's introduction to *On Last Things* (one of his main sources): "I would like to add that at the time of his funeral a partial eclipse of the moon, which could only be seen in Vienna, took place. It ended exactly the moment his body was lowered into the ground" (ibid.). Probst not only quotes Rappaport out of context, he misquotes him as well. Rappaport did not refer to a partial eclipse that could "only" be seen in Vienna, but simply to an eclipse that "was visible in Vienna" (Rappaport 1904, p. xx). This may seem like a trivial detail, but it illustrates again how important it was to empiricists, or men of positive science, who considered themselves committed to reason and common sense, to show that their opponents were irrational and could not be taken seriously. Rappaport anticipates objections to his description from people who may say "But there wasn't a partial eclipse where I was," whereas Probst's insertion of "only" turns it into a claim of supernatural intervention.[45]

Another of Probst's targets is supplied by the examples of Weininger's musical sensitivity which Rappaport quotes. However, when looked at in their totality as expressions of aesthetic experience, they are far from irrational.[46] Like his (largely undeveloped) symbolism in which every empirical phenomenon of the macrocosm was meant to stand for a possibility of the human microcosm, they evoke a system, albeit an aesthetic one, that expresses through analogies what cannot be said in a conceptual form. For Probst—and it is important to see that this is not malice on his part—these analogies are nothing but symptoms of a hysterical psychosis which grew out of the cultural climate of Vienna.[47] This climate exercises Probst a great deal in the context of his diagnosis: he repeats, with an interesting adjectival addition, his initial characterization of Vienna as the "center of the most sublime decadence" and continues,

> which has already produced so many precocious literary saviors, and of which it is said that its truest sons are born with a pessimistic frown on their forehead, realize at the age of ten that Michelangelo was a nitwit, before they feel in their early twenties that they are the microcosmic center of the universe. Next to the peculiarity of Weininger's personality, which adds the unique individual aspect to his psychosis, the significance of this breeding ground cannot be overestimated. In contact with many different elements in this society of "mattoids" (Lombroso), and on the basis of his psychopathic degeneration, Weininger seems to have developed a mental illness.[48]

While Probst does not explicitly say that Weininger is one of those true sons of Vienna, it takes careful reading to see that he allows for the influence of Weininger's individual endowment having played a part, and arguably one which left him with the alternative, given Möbius's understanding of "degeneration" (as a neutral term, meaning a deviation from the mean) referred to by Probst (see p. 35), of becoming a genius or an idiot. However, the study in its entirety—with its increasingly hostile qualifications of Weininger's thought as "great nonsense" (p. 17), "a wild sea of crude claims and the wildest nonsense" (p. 18), "straight madness" (p. 32), "hair-raising" (p. 34), and "bottomless idiocy" (p. 34), and of Weininger himself as a "conjurer of logic" (p. 20) performing his sleights of hand (see p. 25)—leaves little doubt in the reader that Weininger was meant to be one of these Viennese half-wits.

Little wonder then if Weininger's father, who had provided Loewenfeld with information on his son, felt betrayed and did whatever he could to rehabilitate him.[49] For this purpose he turned once again to Karl Kraus, who had helped him before to contradict the suggestion made by Rappaport in his preface (without any bad intention) that Weininger suffered from bouts of epilepsy.

Weininger's Early Defenders: Karl Kraus and *Die Fackel*[50]

Probably the best known statement by Kraus on Weininger is his—apparent—reversal of Weininger's evaluation of women: "An admirer of women enthusiastically agrees with your arguments for despising women" (F 229, 1907, p. 14).[51] The confusion between ideal types and empirical women, implicit in this statement, not only confirms Weininger's analysis, but also glorifies women's position as sexualized inspirational accessories for creative men. Whereas the theories of Möbius and Freud aimed to establish for women a biological character that showed them as opposed to, or at least not inclined to be active in, the process of civilization and the creation of culture, Kraus pretends to take a morally neutral position. In fact, he falls back on a view of gender relationships that may almost be called medieval: the gallant knights are inspired to perform by the presence of the ladies.

Kraus later wrote that he had sympathized with Weininger from a distance (F 251/2, 1908, p. 39), and he was clearly impressed by his book once it had been published. From a letter by Weininger to Kraus, written on 20 June 1903 (F 568/571, 1921, p. 48), we know that Kraus had sent him a telegram the same day asking for permission to quote from it, and suggesting a meeting.[52] Weininger, on and off, remained a presence in *Die Fackel* (at least into the early 1920s), as well as an influence on both the content and style of Kraus's writing, although Kraus was loath to acknowledge this.[53]

Two weeks after Weininger's suicide (17 October 1903), *Die Fackel* opened with Strindberg's homage: "Idolatry and Gynolatry (An obituary by August Strindberg)," and devoted a further six pages to Weininger, including, apart from a letter by Emil Lucka, a long piece by Kraus himself in which he attacks the *Neue Freie Presse* for its inaccuracies in reporting on Weininger and his death. The notice on his suicide had wrongly claimed that Weininger had wanted to use his book to acquire the right to teach as a *Privatdozent* at the university, and that his supervisors had distanced themselves from the work (see F 144, 1903, p. 18). Not surprisingly, Kraus seized the opportunity to highlight the immoral and mediocre behavior of Austrian journalism, in particular against Austrians, whereas abroad "the life-work of the Viennese [Weininger] is acknowledged in the form of serious reflections in extensive obituaries."[54] The intellectual nature of this "clan" of journalists, as he calls them, is such that one can easily use them as a kind of dowser for genius; where they condemn, originality and genius are likely to be found, and we should only criticize them "where they want to condemn to silence" (ibid., p. 19).

In the issue of 23 December 1903, Kraus published a counter-statement by Weininger's father to Rappaport's claim that his son suffered from bouts of epilepsy. In the issue of 16 January 1904, he printed a very short letter in which Rappaport simply says that he had repeatedly witnessed what he describes in his biographical sketch, and that his description of Weininger's health was based on Weininger's own repeated statements. This was followed by a commentary from Kraus, which incorporates the reaction of Weininger's father (to whom Kraus had shown Rappaport's letter) and a letter from the Weininger family's doctor, certifying that there was no reason whatsoever to assume that the son had suffered from epilepsy. Kraus, in effect, adds little himself, but expresses the hope that this is the end of the sad story, and repeats his attack on the press. He calls it a "clown's joke" that Weininger was not mentioned in any Austrian list of famous people who died in 1903, whereas he was routinely included in the lists published in Germany: "Now these idiotic megalomaniacs even believe they can condemn to life by silence! This, they certainly can't do!"[55]

As well as taking sides for Weininger, Kraus used his work for polemical purposes. On 23 November 1904, he gave Leopold Weininger an opportunity to defend his son against Probst (F 169, 1904, pp. 6ff.). In 1905 (28 February) he referred to a hostile review in the *Frankfurter Zeitung* ("The Munich snooper [Probst] has received enthusiastic support from a certain Hugo Ganz, who goes in for an orgy of common sense in the *Frankfurter Zeitung*.," F 176, p. 22), quoting a long letter from a reader in Berlin who calls Probst's study "one of the most ridiculous products of medical dogmatism of all times" (p. 24). Later, in October 1906 and January 1907, he commented on the charges of plagiarism brought forward by Fließ (see F 210, F 216). On Karl Lueger's death in 1910, Kraus brilliantly opens *Die Fackel* with a long series of quotations from chapter V (part 2) ("Endowment and Memory," pp. 121–122) and chapter X ("Motherhood and Prostitution," pp. 200–203; with some omissions) of *Sex and Character.* These passages describe the affinity between the great men of action (politicians, tribunes, emperors, military commanders) and prostitutes. What they share is the will to power and ambitions in the empirical world. Ambition comes from "ambitio"; these types amble around like prostitutes. The relation between the politician and the plebeian mass mirrors that between the prostitute and her customers. Both live for the moment and do not create anything that lasts. These empirically minded types do not even make history because in order truly to make history one has to stand outside history: "*The exceptional individual has a history, the leader is had by history*" (p. 122). Thus the empirical type of a "great man" is the opposite of a genius. The headline Kraus uses is simply: "Lueger. After Otto Weininger: . . . ," followed by the quotations without any further commentary.

When we move beyond controversies and polemics, the problematic side of

Weininger reception becomes apparent. It is often easy to agree with, or at least understand, Weininger's and Kraus's attacks on cynicism and hypocrisy in sexual matters, but it is less clear what should replace that which is being attacked. This is already apparent in Karl Bleibtreu's review in *Die Fackel* of 1904 (see F 157, pp. 12–20), which pays Weininger the double-edged compliment of regarding him—like his Jewish "tribesman" Heine—as a better German than those chauvinistic "beer-swilling, card-playing roughnecks" (ibid., p. 20), and in which Weininger's arguments concerning women, Jews, and asceticism are used to express Bleibtreu's own dislike of his age of "breeding and fornication" ("Zucht- und Unzuchtwahl," ibid., p. 19). It is at this point in Bleibtreu's text that Kraus inserts a footnote of his own, praising Weininger for freeing "the urge" (i.e., the sexual drive) of all ethical ballast and for ascribing it to women's nature in a higher degree than to men's. The footnote sits oddly between a criticism of a sexualized age and a summary of Weininger's work as a warning against the female as custodian of the natural drives and the Jew as the priest of everything sexual and anti-transcendent—all of which does not do Weininger any favors.

In 1907 an article by Stanislaw Przybyszewski, entitled "Das Geschlecht" (Sex) and dedicated to Weininger's soul, appeared in *Die Fackel* (F 239/40, 31 December, pp. 1–11). The author celebrates "sexus" as the universal moving principle, in a Nietzschean style and Schopenhauerian vein, ending with a utopian vision of mankind considering sexuality as something beautiful and practicing it accordingly. He seems to be saying that Weininger was right, not because sexuality as such was evil, but because of what mankind at the time was making of it. This is a valid point, but it provides no clues to the factors involved in leading mankind either astray or in the right direction, and as a result it comes close to Kraus's simple re-evaluation of female sexuality.

Der Brenner: Dallago and Ebner

Moving on from Kraus's *Die Fackel* to Ludwig von Ficker's *Der Brenner* we find two further—sympathetic—attempts at correcting Weininger. One is Carl Dallago's *Otto Weininger und sein Werk* [Otto Weininger and his work], published in three parts in 1912.[56] Dallago interprets Weininger as an author who failed to come to terms with the truth of his own diagnosis, and he opposes his own Rousseauistic views on the original perfection of man to it. In short, overcoming the decadence of the time would mean a return to nature, rather than moving toward Weininger's utopian ideal of genius. Dallago understands Weininger's case for asceticism; however, he believes that he can circumvent Weininger's arguments by assuming that in the natural state there is nothing nauseating or immoral about sexual relations between men and women. Dallago, like so many others, feels that Weininger suffered from the same symptoms of the spirit of his age, but he wants to replace the life-denying side of Weininger's case by an affirmation, and glorification, of unadulterated nature.

The second example, Ferdinand Ebner, is by far the more important one. Ebner was highly impressed when he first read Weininger (and was certainly also influenced by him), but later found it difficult to understand his original fascination. His major work, *Das Wort und die geistigen Realitäten* (The word and the realities of the spirit; originally published by the Brenner Verlag in 1921), includes a critique of *Sex and Character* which forms the sixteenth of the book's eighteen "fragments," and which had already been published separately in *Der Brenner* two years earlier (October 1919, Jg. 6, H. 1, pp. 28–47). Here, and in another of the fragments published as "Kultur und Christentum" [Culture and Christianity] in the following issue of *Der Brenner* (December 1919), Ebner formulates his theological position, which did not at all coincide with the view of many artists and authors in the Brenner circle, although Ebner was later to meet and establish very amicable relationships with some of them (see Methlagl 2002). The crucial point in which Ebner differed was his notion of "Geist" (spirit) which for him was distinct from any form of intellectual activity or any manifestation of such activity in the empirical world. Therefore, though he was by no means a philistine, in his view, no art was capable of expressing, rendering, or even hinting at, Christian truth. He summed up the tradition of Western culture after Christ as a long "dream of the spirit" which would never become a reality. Ebner saw every kind of philosophy as ultimately feeding off some form of idealism, and he believed that once all forms had been tried and found to be wanting, the solution of philosophical problems would appear as the suicide of philosophy, the end of the dream of the spirit and the true encounter with the reality of the spirit (see Ebner 1921, p. 85). The end of philosophy would at the same time be the end of aesthetics: "When life begins in all seriousness, all dreaming is over, and beauty becomes irrelevant" (ibid., p. 328).

Ebner's perspective on Weininger follows directly from his view on the relation between (compensatory) Western idealism and genuine Christian faith. He sees Weininger as the last, and rather desperate, sign of life shown by idealism before its historical demise (see Ebner 1921, p. 284). He claims that in Weininger the general inability of idealism to understand the reality of the spirit takes the form of a concoction of spirit and sexuality, and that Weininger, confusing the spiritual and the sensual, fails to see that spirit is neither male nor female but neuter (see ibid., p. 285). He sees the true importance of Weininger's work in the fact that Weininger drew a consequence from idealism which had previously gone wholly or at least largely unnoticed, and which was its intrinsic anti-feminism. Idealist anti-feminism, just as Weininger's antisemitism, was based on a fundamental misunderstanding of the spirit, which it confused with merely empirical intellectuality. Genius is "a fact of nature" (ibid., p. 290) like any other,[57] and it is Weininger's greatest mistake to consider Jesus as belonging to any particular category—the founders of a religion—and therefore as a genius.[58] For Ebner this flies in the face of what constitutes the essence of Christianity: God becoming human in Jesus Christ as an irreducible article of faith, and the words of Jesus—but also language in general, the relation between I and Thou in particular—as the evidence of the spirit. Nor does Ebner agree with

Weininger's identification of Judaism with the modern age. He argues as follows: the Jews, by and large, do not contribute to Western culture, but are rather, thanks to their talent for concepts, the born critics of idealism and may thus help to destroy humankind's false dream of the spirit. They are the chosen people, to whom God, in his spiritual reality, once revealed himself directly. Though their faith, since the time of Christ, has been untrue, they themselves are still being carried by the spirit (how else would they have survived for two thousand years without being a nation?). Their spiritual stature may have diminished as a consequence of not accepting Jesus as the Messiah, but that is no worse than most of Christianity's failure to take into account the fact that the Savior has appeared, and to abandon its false dream of the spirit. Whereas the Jews have denied Christ, the Christians keep dreaming of the spirit—both reactions fall short of the truth of the reality of the spirit.

Ultimately, all of Ebner's criticism is directed against Weininger's confusion—in various forms and instances—of the purely empirical with what is not to be explained empirically. Even without this ongoing confusion in his writings, Weininger's insistence on the ineffability of the self would not have sufficed to save him from Ebner's criticism. Weininger's self that can neither be proved nor disproved is still a fact, and as such part of the empirical world, not of the reality of the spirit. Nevertheless, Weininger played an influential role in the formation of Ebner's thought, as can be gleaned from the following remark on the relation between spirit and sexuality: "Sexuality, exactly in its fractured form in human beings, is, and will remain, the abyss in which spirituality threatens to be lost" (ibid., p. 288). It is philosophically less crucial, but perhaps more telling of Weininger's influence, when Ebner calls the Jew the "most unmusical" human being, to whom music is most alien. Here the tone is reminiscent of Weininger: "He [the Jew]—despite all the contemporary singing, music-making and composing—is the most unmusical human being. Music is alien to him, and only once Western music, beginning with Beethoven, had moved away from its spiritual origin, and, abandoning its 'inwardness,' approached the externals of noise and sound, finally to be totally alienated from that origin in Wagner and Strauss (and thus totally unmusical)—only then did he pluck up the courage to compose and practice music" (ibid., p. 292). If we ignore the judgment on Weininger's hero Wagner, this passage could come straight from *Sex and Character.* In general, however, Stieg (1984) is right in praising Ebner for overcoming Weininger's tendency to create scapegoats (though he holds on to the fundamental diagnosis of modern decadence): "Ebner, though influenced by Kraus and Weininger (Weininger, indeed, is his deepest intellectual wound), develops a strategy for overcoming antifeminism and anti-Semitism—in a much more reflected way than Dallago with his 'closeness to nature'—and I want to give it my full admiration" (pp. 66–67). In other words, for Ebner, as for Weininger (and various others like Musil and Doderer; see Luft 2003), the crisis of modernity found an expression in the domains of gender, race, and sexuality. But for Ebner, unlike Weininger and, after him, Wittgenstein, who sought secular solutions, the answer was religious in nature. All three, however, may be subsumed under Janik's term "*kritische Moderne*" (critical modernism), denoting "one peculiar response to this situation of being alienated with society, which seems to be the destiny of Western society," though their position in relation to religious thought seems to run parallel to their position in relation to the basically "uncritical fixation on culture with its extreme fondness for theatricality as well as an obsession with one's identity in a social situation where one's public persona often had precious little in common with one's private thoughts."[59] Even the "theologians," like Ebner or Theodor Haecker, did not steer clear of polemics (as a form of theatricality),[60] and Wittgenstein, as his private diaries reveal, considered all forms of theatricality—hypocrisy, inauthenticity, vanity—as so many forms of sin which need to be fought off.[61] A theme that links them all (and Janik includes even Karl Popper in this) is a "notion of self-mistrust [. . .] and deep-seated tendencies to self delusion" that stem from Weininger.[62]

David Luft's most recent intervention in his *Eros and Inwardness* (2003) fits in well with this. He reads Weininger's work as an attempt to navigate his way between "philosophical irrationalism and modern science" (p. xi), with the former, in the tradition of Schopenhauer and Nietzsche, rejecting "the idea of thinking of the self as a rational soul" (p. 9), and the latter reducing the self to an object of science. At the same time Weininger criticized "the division of labour between men and women, their sexual as well as their social and spiritual relations" (pp. 67–68). Luft demonstrates that a coherent reading of Weininger as a critic of alienation—setting "the terms for his generation's exploration of philosophical themes in terms of metaphors of sexuality and gender" (p. 3)—can be backed up by close textual evidence, while making clear that his "preoccupations with science, modernity, and the crisis of traditional values are obscured by his insistence on labeling issues in terms of what was feminine or Jewish" (p. 214 n. 96). This fact, and his refusal to give up absolute polarities in favor of balancing opposite ends (see p. 85), sets the limits to Weininger's project. However, Luft concludes, "[t]he sense of loss in Weininger about the Western tradition is not so much about gender and race as it is about the possibility that there is some coherent sense to reality and human experience—and that these are related through the mind. . . . Weininger was aiming at the possibility of meaningful, ethical existence in a world dominated by inauthenticity and manipulation" (p. 86). And this world, of course, in important respects is, and is not, still ours.

Thus, we have already arrived at contemporary scholarship on Weininger, where, in many ways, he becomes a paradigmatic case for discussing historiographical questions.

Contemporary Scholarship: How to View the Past

In 1981, Allan Janik published an article on William Johnston's study *The Austrian Mind* (1972), and more specifically on Johnston's wide-ranging application of the term "therapeutic nihilism," which plays a crucial role in it, and which Weininger is said to have epitomized (see Janik 1981, p. 263). The subtitle of Janik's article —"How Not to Write about Otto Weininger"—is directed against a form of historiography which tends to transpose onto the object under investigation values which are either culturally or temporally removed from it. Johnston, Janik argues, takes a form of liberalism as a paradigm for what is healthy and opposes it to what he, less than clearly, terms "therapeutic nihilism," an attitude associated in the first place with the Vienna medical school, and in particular Carl von Rokitansky. In Johnston's metaphorically extended use the term comes to signify a defeatist view of social and other ills, which does not even share the medical profession's trust in nature's healing powers as the only hope available but is content with lamenting suffering and society's unethical behavior in the face of it.

Underlying Janik's argument, there is an important general point concerning the nature of rationality whose validity is not limited to Weininger's work, but which applies to any work sufficiently distant in time (or cultural context) from the observer-interpreter. However, to the extent that Weininger discusses the relationship between belief and truth, between an individual's *weltanschauung* and the judgments of that individual, in the context of an implied "absolute perspective" (or "perspective outside time"), he is not only an example in the debate about the subjectivity of truth claims, but he also attempts to formulate his own solution.[63]

Janik sees the identification of rationality with truth as always in danger of assuming "that the present state of knowledge has normative value in assessing rationality, that those beliefs which are currently taken to be normal are the very substance of rationality. On the account that I am criticising here, to reject the contemporary view of something or other or its legitimate precursor is to be 'anti-modern' and consequently irrational" (Janik 1981, pp. 270–271). Once the notion of an absolute truth (dogmatism) is rejected there are, however, still two alternatives. One is a version of strong verificationism (e.g., that of the Vienna Circle: "substantive meaning must be tied to sensible experience," ibid., p. 272), where truth, in the final analysis, is a true content. This, in a sense, reintroduces an absolute perspective. The other alternative concentrates on procedure and defines rationality by the way an agent, be it an individual or group, reacts when confronted with counter-evidence to the beliefs currently held. This second alternative also grants that there may be different forms of verification for different types of claims. In this perspective, scientific theories are still of interest even if they no longer agree with current knowledge, and the history of science becomes the "history of scientific communities and their projects" (ibid., p. 277), and of the way "scientists actually operate with concepts" (ibid., p. 276).

Of course, the argument applies not merely to the history of science but to intellectual and cultural history as such; in many ways it addresses the same problems as Continental hermeneutics from an Anglo-Saxon angle: "When we judge a thinker solely by reference to his political views or by reference to his role or that of his type of thought in political developments without examining the reasoning that went into his views, then there is so little chance of obtaining any genuine understanding of those views that come to be identified as 'anti-modernist' that we are constrained to adopt the hypothesis that the segment of intellectual life to which he belonged was, in some sense or other, *sick*" (ibid., p. 276). In other words, when writing about Weininger, the paradox emerges that even, or particularly if, we wish to criticize his views, we are bound to repeat the exclusionist gesture.

Contrary to an ahistorical condemnation of Weininger as a monomaniac and misogynist, Janik suggests an evaluation of his work "by reference to the state of biological science, psychology and humanistic social reform circa 1903," and in addition puts forward the thesis that there is "a strong dialectical element in Weininger's thinking which actually renders his conclusion that the argument turns against men less paradoxical than it appears at first glance" (ibid., p. 280).[64]

Janik's article, written as a response not just to Johnston but to the kind of intellectual history he practices, can easily be read in conjunction with Jacques Le Rider's monograph on Weininger, originally published one year later, 1982, in French, and in a German edition in 1985. Le Rider, in retrospect, characterized his approach as follows: "Weininger's works may be interpreted as symptoms of a repressive and authoritarian civilization, founded on the principle of male superiority" (Le Rider 1995, p. 21). This assumption, he says, informed his book. Implicit in Le Rider's work, as in Stieg (1984), are certain values of emancipation and of scientific rationality as well as an opposition between Enlightenment values and progressive modernism on the one hand, and the Western philosophical tradition of idealism and regressive anti-modernism on the other. Weininger, Le Rider recapitulates, was not a scientific genius, nor did he provide solutions, but was rather "a brilliant symptom" [*ein geniales Symptom*]. In his time no one had internalized the spirit of the age as comprehensively, and his writings are the pandemonium of an epoch, the Viennese turn of the century, whose status nowadays is raised wholesale under the term "Viennese modernism" (Le Rider 1984, p. 96).[65] In Le Rider's interpretation, the various forms of cultural criticism which belong to this period are characterized by an anti-modern turn which sets up the female and ornamental, a principle of sensuous pleasure, against the male and functional, a principle of strong will, and sees the latter as properties of the redeemer. This construction of Le Rider's replaces an investigation of actual history with a mythology (see ibid., p. 97). "What Loos and Weininger have in common," Le Rider concludes, "is an inability to think in dialectical terms, and thus not only to criticize but also to save. . . . Loos condemns the ornament just as Weininger condemns woman" (ibid., p. 99).[66]

Gerald Stieg, an Austrian living in Paris, is even more critical about the historical place of Weininger's work. For him, *Sex and Character* is one of "the greatest defeats of reason at the beginning of the 20th century; it is the psychological-metaphysical prelude for National Socialism including its variants" (Stieg 1984, p. 60). Stieg, consciously, employs medical metaphors in his argument: "Where Weininger and Kraus become virulent in combination, anti-feminism and anti-Semitism rage without limits" (ibid., pp. 62–63), and he sees them both as "excessively eurocentric, they are Westerners from top to bottom" (ibid., p. 66).[67] From this perspective, the way one reacts to Weininger therefore becomes an indication of one's energy in fighting off the temptations of exclusionary thinking and discriminatory politics. Canetti and *Der Brenner,* in particular Carl Dallago and Ferdinand Ebner, are seen as anti-idealistic (therefore anti-Kant and anti-Weininger) forces (see ibid., p. 62). Stieg reads Canetti's *Die Blendung* (*Auto da Fe*) as a satire on Weininger,[68] and as we have seen above, he commends Ebner for resisting the temptation to follow Weininger's train of thought.

Progressive Anti-modernism?

> One age misunderstands another; and a petty age misunderstands all the others in its own ugly way. (Wittgenstein, *Culture and Value,* p. 98e)

Le Rider's classification of *Sex and Character* as an "experimental novel," in the chapter of the same title, points in an interesting direction, even if Le Rider (1985, pp. 59–77) uses the term, by and large, as a metaphor for reductive positivism and naïve sociobiology. In fact, he does not interpret the book as an experimental novel, but rather accuses it of being pseudo-scientific, due to a confusion of metaphysics, literature, and science. In the next chapter, Freud, Fließ, and Swoboda are included in the charge of not being able to tell science from pseudo-science.[69]

If we take the notion of the experimental novel as defined by Zola—i.e., a novel built on "knowledge of the mechanism of the phenomena inherent in man" which shows "the machinery of his intellectual and sensory manifestations, under the influences of heredity and environment, such as physiology shall give them to us" (Zola 1964, pp. 20–21)—and the conclusion he reaches from this—i.e., that "metaphysical man is dead; our whole territory is transformed by the advent of the physiological man" (ibid., p. 54)—it immediately becomes apparent that Weininger may have been operating in the same context, but certainly would not have subscribed to Zola's program. Zola is indeed arguing at an exclusively positivist level. Following Claude Bernard, his reasoning is, as he himself admits, "the simplest; if the experimental method can be carried from chemistry and physics into physiology and medicine, it can also be carried from physiology into the naturalistic novel" (ibid., p. 14). If the body of man is only a machine to be taken apart and re-assembled at will, "then we can pass to the passionate and intellectual acts of man. . . . We have experimental chemistry and medicine; we shall have an experimental physiology, and later on an experimental novel" (ibid., p. 16). In this context, Zola quotes Bernard's distinction between the external and internal, or "interior," conditions, with the latter complicating the task of the physiologist as compared with that of the physicist; yet, "the complexity due to the existence of an interior organic condition is the only reason for the great difficulties which we encounter in the experimental determination of living phenomena" (Bernard, quoted from ibid., p. 15). It is characteristic of nineteenth-century science, indeed of much of science, to interpret qualitative difference—here that between inner and outer—as basically quantitative, i.e., to understand it as levels of complexity in fundamentally atomistic structures. Zola continues this train of thought onto the moral and social plane: "we take man from the hands of the physiologist solely, in order to continue the solution of the problem, and to solve scientifically the question of how men behave when they are in society" (ibid., p. 21).

In contrast to this, and from the very beginning, even in his early, still largely empiricist, draft "Eros und Psyche," Weininger is aware of qualitative differences as differences *sui generis.* One example is his discussion of differential psychology, or characterology, as opposed to universal psychology. The latter may go a long way through introspection (though, at this time, Weininger still regards physiology as the ultimate foundation of psychology), whereas the former, for methodological reasons, must be conceived in analogy to animal psychology: "the one and only method by which characterology can be practiced, is very close to that of animal psychology" (Weininger 1990, p. 159). The background to this is the philosophical problem of other minds and of solipsism, which Weininger will explore further, and more radically, in *Sex and Character* and *On Last Things.*

Another qualifying remark in the early draft, written in the first half of 1901, concerns culture: "Contrary to Nietzsche [in *Thus Spake Zarathustra,* III, "Old and New Tables"], man may be something final; the *necessity* of further *empirical* [*immanente*] development may no longer exist in the light of the absolute novelty mankind has introduced into the history of the earth: in the light of his specific nature being projected onto the earth, of the fact of culture, of 'objective' spirit" (ibid., p. 178).

The second draft, "Zur Theorie des Lebens," has a very different genesis; it was written down within the space of five days in March 1902, and consists of three rather heterogeneous segments. It starts by characterizing the nature of life as being inextricably bound up with "individuation," which is equated with the "structure of the organic," and this, in turn, is seen as identical with Hering's idea of memory as a property of organized matter. However, Weininger, whether he is aware of it or not, goes much further than Hering's Lamarckism. His general point is that all science of the inorganic (chemistry and physics) can only be understood within the context of biology "as borderline cases of biological events" (Weininger 1990, p. 194, "Grenzfälle biologischen Geschehens"). At the very end of the draft, Weininger suggests the term "biography" as the name for the one science which, he claims, biology and psychology ultimately are (p. 208). In between we find a defense of the existence of the self as well as some highly speculative passages on the duration of individual lives and characterological types.

If we take these hints together with their development in Weininger's arguments concerning organic unity, the self of the genius, and the role of the principle of identity and memory in *Sex and Character,* as necessary preconditions for any apperception and cognition, and memory as that faculty which elevates human beings above temporal transience,[70] what emerges is not the idea of the experimental novel, but Weininger's quest for "a science of the human mind," a science which "would have to account for the *mental life as a whole* as it progresses from the birth of an individual to his death according to certain laws, just as it does for the coming into being and passing away, and all the discrete phases in the life of a plant. And it is to be called *biography,* not *biology,* because its task is to explore the unchanging laws of the *mental* development of the *individual.* So far the history of all species has only known individuals, βίοι. But here the task would be to develop general points of view, to establish types. *Psychology would have to make a start at becoming* ***theoretical biography***" (p. 114). Later this quest for a theoretical biography is further complicated by the following argument from the "Wissenschaft und Kultur" ("Science and Culture") section in *On Last Things:*

> Likewise my own existence, the 'I', if it is to have *value, cannot* be proven; and likewise the 'you', when it is not the consequence of a reason and is not to be used as the means to an end, cannot be demonstrated. *The refutability of solipsism* is no more *compatible* with *ethics,* than is the possibility of *proving* the existence of one's own ego.[71]

This train of thought leads to what is arguably the central aporetic point in both the early and the later Wittgenstein, where it re-appears as an investigation of the limits of language and of fundamental language-games, i.e., the distinction between what can be justified by reasons and arguments, and what can at best be demonstrated. It also points toward one of the central motifs in the modern-postmodern landscape: the inexpressible or ineffable as the hinge on which discourses can swing from dogmatism to relativism. Weininger's argument concerning the autonomous individual puts the finger on the question of identity; it can be applied not only in psychology, but also to questions concerning academic disciplines and the limits of theory, and to the relationship between the general and the individual, between individual and public (or cultural) memory. The role he gives to "biography"—as noted above, his term for a new form of biological psychology—has not lost its relevance, and the contradictions of his theory of a double life, between empirical and intelligible self, are not just a last neo-Kantian flowering of Western idealism before its final demise, but also a consequence of a cultural split that is still very much with us. Freed of its metaphysical application to gender and to race, it can be seen as a philosophical plea against the exclusion of phenomena which lie outside an instrumental and functional conception of the world.

Thus, the program of the experimental novel was, for Weininger, part of the problem, not the solution. This problem was, roughly, the materialist vision of the nineteenth century which, in the form of an all-pervasive Darwinism and physicalism, and associated, perhaps paradoxically, with liberal politics, left no space for the dignity and freedom of the individual. Work, or labor power (*Arbeitskraft*), had become a central category, and all nature, including the human body and mind, was perceived in analogy to a working machine: "The metaphor of the human motor lent credibility to the ideals of socially responsive liberalism, which could be shown to be consistent with the universal laws of energy conservation: expanded productivity and social reform were linked by the same natural laws. The dynamic language of energy was also central to many utopian social and political ideologies of the early twentieth century: Taylorism, bolshevism, and fascism" (Rabinbach 1990, p. 2). Against this rule of exploitation on the basis of a thermodynamic cosmology, be it with "good" or "evil" intentions, Dostoevsky's "underground man" had been an early rebel, insisting on his right to act against his own best interest, and to hold that 2 plus 2 may well be 5. Oscar Wilde made the point with aphoristic elegance: "A truth ceases to be true when more than one person believes in it."[72] What I would like to suggest is that Weininger's work can be seen within the tradition of such a protest of subjectivity. He argues for the inseparability of the self and truth in order to resist any possible instrumentalization of either. But he also insists on the coherence of the self, in parallel to the organic coherence of the body, against all causal or teleological conceptions of the organism. This allows him to avoid the implicit pessimism of the naturalist writer in the face of scientific optimism. The world might be made up of a vast amount of energy, but any joy over that "was rapidly undercut by the pessimistic doctrine of the irreversibility of heat flow" (Rabinbach 1990, p. 47). In other words, the age of progress was at the same time the age of entropy, and ideas about cultural decline, decadence, and degeneration were firmly tied up with the facts of science. Fatigue in the human body and mind followed from the same laws as entropic exhaustion in nature. Zola's "science," in this context, has been said to express the "essential epistemological issues of his age" (Baguley 1990, p. 222; paraphrasing Michel Serres):

> The contours of the organisation of material reality fade; its ordered arrangements are perceived to degenerate into disorder; the continuity of the laws regulating it breaks down; matter becomes energy—and the spectre of its dissipation looms. . . . At the heart of the naturalist vision, then, there is a poetics of disintegration, dissipation, death, with its endless repertory of wasted lives, of destructive forces, of spent energies, of crumbling moral and social structures, with its promiscuity, humiliations, degradation, its decomposing bodies, its invasive materialism. (Ibid.)

It should at least be clear that, if anything, Weininger was an anti-naturalist writer. While many aspects and details of his protest and the form it takes are specific to fin-de-siècle Vienna, with its multifarious attempts at creating a coherent *weltanschauung* (see Fischer 1999), Weininger's radicalism finally leads him to formulate ideas concerning the basis and legitimacy of truth claims which are of general significance, and which also go beyond a purely subjectivist philosophy.[73] The theoretical foundations are given in the "philosophical" chapters of *Sex and Character* (IV–VIII), and the most advanced attempt at applying them in the service of cultural criticism and psychological analysis can be found in the first and last chapter of *On Last Things* (on "Peer Gynt and Ibsen" and "Science and Culture").

Weininger's criticism of the criminal mind (of which the typical scientist of his day would be a prime example) and his regard for the autonomous individual as the absolute value on which all other values depend, stands in an uncanny relation to the post-war diagnosis of Germans having depended on a narcissistic vision of community in which there was no gap between self and other. "This," Santner writes, "was a world where the mournful labor that opens up the space between 'I' and 'Thou', 'here' and 'there', 'now' and 'then', could be banished as degenerate (entartet) and Jewish" (Santner 1990, p. 6). Whether or not this analysis, which follows the Mitscherlichs' earlier diagnosis of the Germans' inability to mourn, is correct, it puts the blame on the same lack of sensitivity toward the other person that Weininger had in mind when he wrote:

> The fundamental psychological precondition for all practical altruism is a theoretical individualism. Only those who feel that the other person is also a self, a center of the world, will automatically be protected from using and considering another human being purely as a means to an end, as is the way of the Jew: because usury implies the same attitude toward one's fellow humans as that of the tick toward the dog. Thus, the self is a condition for any altruistic ethics. In the face of a pure knot of "elements" I would never act ethically. (Weininger 1990, p. 201)

Here, as in many other places, the offensive—and, of course, indefensible—passages could be omitted without even changing the grammar, leaving behind a perfectly valid argument. This suggests that the obsessional and prejudiced side of Weininger was something that operated almost as an independent part of his thought in parallel to his other reflections; at least, such an independence can be traced at the level of language.

If Weininger accuses the "Jews" (to him, a type and not a race) of the same condition the "Germans" are being blamed for in the wake of Auschwitz (a de-individualizing, narcissistic sense of community, no regard for the other), one obvious way to interpret this is to say that antisemitism and misogyny have always been based on the projection onto other groups of one's own undesired and rejected characteristics. This, in turn, leads to the question of how to distinguish between such a projection and diagnosis: while Weininger's argument seems, to us, a clear case of projection, the Mitscherlichs' argument is seen as a diagnosis. The fact that despite the blatant difference in the amount of evidence available for the two arguments there remains something problematic in this parallel, can be seen in Santner's discussion of Paul de Man and the reactions to the discovery of his war-time writings. What is problematic here is the basis on which legitimacy of tradition may be determined. If Derrida, a philosopher who is certainly free of any suspicion of revisionist tendencies, is inclined to exculpate de Man by pointing out the inevitable taintedness of all legacies, he performs the move that characterizes postmodern, decentered critical theory, as understood by Santner, in order to stabilize his own intellectual identity. At the same time, he shifts the argument from the level of representational artifacts (theory) to the level of historical facts (in this case de Man's biography), just as the Mitscherlichs apply psychoanalytic theory to the psychohistory of an alleged collective. In what conditions is such a shift acceptable?

What is problematic can now be further pinned down to the question of the general relation between ethics and theory, or the relation between moral and theoretical judgments. At a formal level, the procedure followed by Weininger and that followed by the Mitscherlichs (and Santner) are identical. The legitimacy of the transition from theory to object of theory is not, and perhaps cannot be, based on argument. Rather, the transition produces a vision of the object which identifies it with general and abstract concepts. Most importantly, no evidence could contradict this vision of the object within the parameters of the theory.

Santner's description of postmodern critical theory as a form of Western collective intellectual mourning points to the fact that this tradition of Western thought has, perhaps understandably, so far failed to address the moral and ethical legacy of Auschwitz at any level other than on the level of theory. The danger is that this may create the illusion of a moral righteousness of the present over the past; we know the crimes, we know the culprits. But so did Weininger. Nor does the inconceivable vastness of a crime make it any easier either to understand its social, political, and historical causes, or to formulate the knowledge on which the moral condemnation of it could be based. In short, the dilemma in Weininger's writing between the employment of reason in the pursuit of genuine philosophical and ethical concerns and irrational conclusions abandoning any rational limitations of thought is still with us today, except that it now takes the form of intellectual practice as detached, to all intents and purposes, from political and social reality. Reflective thought itself, the human capacity both to view a situation from the outside and to participate in it—in Weininger's terminology, the hyper-empirical self outside time, as opposed to the self that indulges in the temporal and empirical play of things—has become a "stranded object." The "facilitating environment" (Santner 1990, p. 26) necessary for the development of a self that would perceive itself as sufficiently independent to respect others has become rare, and consequently the mourning necessary to overcome symbiotic, and narcissistic, continuity in favor of interpersonal contiguity has become more and more dangerous to the mourner, ironically, at a time which, on the surface, celebrates diversity and individualism. Santner sums it up thus: "Mourning without solidarity is the beginning of madness" (ibid.). This recalls Weininger's aphorism, quoted against him, by Probst (of all people), "But he who negates logic has already been deserted by logic, and is on his way to insanity" (Weininger 2001, pp. 32–33). This aphorism at once reopens the dilemma of existence in the conditions of fragmented modernity—a situation where the lack of solidarity is compensated for by narcissistic gratification (or, in Marcuse's term, repressive de-sublimation)—and may help to explain why some contemporary readers of Weininger found traces not only of madness but also of themselves—and, most of all, of their own times—in his work.

To make the same point from yet another side, while postmodernism may appropriate Benjamin's analysis of the baroque *Trauerspiel*, by shifting the emphasis from "mourning" to "play" (see Santner 1990, p. 12), this in no way removes, or even diminishes, the difficulty of mourning, or recovering stranded objects. Even if such a shift were successful at the theoretical level, the difference between the loss of intellectual certainties and the reality of human suffering and death, cannot be eradicated. Postmodernism may teach the people at large to raise their level of tolerance for nomadic, non-rooted, non-organicist living conditions, but this in itself does not address the question of balance, and mutual dependence, between individual autonomy and social cohesion. After all, the fascist, pseudo-organicist version of community could only emerge because there seems to be a genuine need for community and groundedness as a precondition of genuine individuality and mutual respect. Assuming that this is the case, the binary logic of regressive nostalgia for rootedness and the certainties of monolithic community on the one hand, and a progressive acceptance of "nomadic playfulness" (Santner 1990, p. 11) within an open semiotic field and the uncertainties of an increasingly absent social cohesion in modern conditions on the other, helps to reproduce the situation that has led to totalitarian solutions.

Auschwitz is neither only an aspect, nor simply the climax, of processes of modernization aiming at the eradication of difference, and thus of the individual, nor is it separate from these processes. This makes a progressive anti-modernism possible. The extent to which Weininger should be seen as part of such a progressive anti-modernism is debatable. The way in which he mobilized the resources of Kantian and idealistic philosophy, but also of organicism and physiognomy, against the decentering tendencies of modern science suggests that this debate should take place apart from the (un-)certainties of postmodern theory and its criticism of "logocentrism" (in all its variants). Rather, the question seems to be whether his notion of genius and self inevitably falls into the opposite mistake of postulating a dogmatic absolute self that is incapable of negotiating its boundaries, and thus ultimately represents a case of "transcendental narcissism" (see Stern's contribution in Stern and Szabados), or whether his analysis of the intricate play of projection between individuals and his concept of love and redemption allow for a less radical, and more communicative, interpretation. In either case, it would be wrong to view his work as a monument to a kind of prejudice which is by now a thing of the past, rather than a reminder of the costs and dangers of the continuing process of modernization and the strain it puts on human selfhood—a selfhood which seems to be happy neither with an utterly monadic, nor with an utterly nomadic self.

Notes

1. Letter to Jodl, 27 December 1901, in Weininger (1990), p. 100. This volume, edited, with a lengthy introductory essay (see n. 9) by Hannelore Rodlauer, contains the two early manuscripts which Weininger deposited at the Austrian Academy of Science, unabridged letters to Swoboda and Jodl, and documents relating to Weininger's doctoral examination, including Jodl's and Müllner's reports. An early draft of Jodl's report, showing some interesting deviations, can be found in Gimpl (1990), pp. 224–226. E.g., one half-clause Jodl leaves out in the final version concerns the limits of experimental psychology, confirming Weininger's criticism of it in a rather ironic mode: "and certainly the times where all blessings were expected to come from it are already in decline" (ibid., p. 225; "und sicherlich ist die Zeit, da man von ihr allein schon das Heil erwarten zu dürfen

glaubte, schon im Niedergange"). On Jodl's attitude to Weininger, see also n. 14. All translations from German material in the introduction are mine (D.S.).

2. Weininger (2001). This volume includes a very balanced and informative introduction by the translator Steven Burns (Burns 2001).

3. Wittgenstein (1998), p. 53e: "When people have died we see their life in a conciliatory light. His life looks well-rounded through a haze. For *him* it was not well-rounded however, but jagged & incomplete. For him there was no conciliation; his life is naked & wretched." (The remark does not refer to Weininger.)

4. Abrahamsen (1946), p. 204. Letter of 27 August 1938 from Budapest. Abrahamsen's *The Mind and Death of a Genius* is still one of the best sources on Weininger's life. On the family background, see also Le Rider (1985), pp. 16–20.

5. Hirsch (1997), p. 21 n. 15. In a letter of 1908 (a reply to a certain Georg Bamberger, Berlin, who had inquired about a plagiarism charge, Otto's family, and his health), Leopold Weininger writes about his family: "We are Jews by descent but not by conviction, and in his father's house Otto W. certainly did not acquire hatred against Judaism" (Hirsch 1997, p. 257). This seems to contradict Rosa's perception of her father. He also speaks of his wife's inclination toward lying which, he says, exceeded the normal extent to which we find it in women, and had a "pathological side to it" (ibid.).

6. Letter to Swoboda, 2 June 1902, in Weininger (1990), p. 122. In a postscript to the letter he recommends the reading of Kant's *Religion within the Limits of Pure Reason;* this, he says, is what Swoboda lacks.

7. See "On the Unidirectionality of Time," in Weininger (2001), pp. 82–94.

8. See Beller (1995): "Otto Weininger as Liberal?" on this tradition of which Weininger, Beller says, was a part.

9. "Fragmente aus Weiningers Bildungsgeschichte 1895–1902," in Weininger (1990), pp. 13–51. English version: Rodlauer (1995): "Fragments from Weininger's education (1895–1902)."

10. See the introduction in Kurt Rudolf Fischer (no date), pp. ix–xix, and Erna Lesky (1976).

11. See Rodlauer's introductory essay ("Fragmente aus Weiningers Bildungsgeschichte") in Weininger (1990), pp. 11–51, here pp. 17–19, for the full program which was omitted in the English version (Rodlauer 1995).

12. See his "Rigorosenakt" (documents relating to his doctoral examination) in Weininger (1990), pp. 210–211.

13. Letter to Swoboda, 1 July 1899, in Weininger (1990), p. 59.

14. The full text can be found in Gimpl (1990), pp. 232–237, and in a brochure published by Braumüller (1905) containing early reviews of *Geschlecht und Charakter,* pp. 6–10. In his piece on Jodl and Weininger ("Friedrich Jodl über Otto Weininger und die Biologie der Ideale" [Friedrich Jodl on Otto Weininger and the biology of ideals]) Gimpl argues convincingly that Weininger followed many of the ideas of his liberal mentor and that his liberal mentor recognized his own ideas in Weininger. This corrects substantially the received view that Jodl met Weininger mainly with incomprehension—a view largely based on some statements made by Jodl in a letter to Loewenfeld in which he says: "I disliked him as a person to the highest degree, and I can not pride myself of a direct influence on his thought. . . . His soul is a riddle to me" (Gimpl 1990, p. 209; also quoted in Le Rider 1985, p. 36). His defense in the *Neue Freie Presse* speaks a different language.

15. *Neues Wiener Journal,* 25 October 1903, pp. 10–11. Le Rider (1985), p. 53. Gimpl (1990), p. 233.

16. Weininger (1990), p. 214; Gimpl (1990), p. 231.

17. An excerpt can be found in Le Rider (1985), p. 28.

18. Letter to Swoboda, 4 December 1901, in Weininger (1990), p. 99.

19. See de Chadarevian (1993). At the same time the general application of recording

devices, such as Marey's chronophotography, led to a disintegration in the way space and time were perceived, a development with strong repercussions in philosophy as well as in the arts. See Rabinbach (1990), esp. chapters 4–6 ("Time and Motion: Etienne-Jules Marey and the Mechanics of the Body," "The Laws of the Human Motor," "Mental Fatigue, Neurasthenia, and Civilization"). Worries about decadence and degeneration were by no means limited to cultural pessimists populating Viennese coffee-houses.

20. Wittgenstein will later make the same point in the *Blue Book* where, in order to eliminate the transcriptional step, he imagines an experiment in which the experimenter and the subject of the experiment are the same person. Even then, he concludes, all we could gain is a new criterion for the occurrence of a thought etc., but not an explanation of it. See Wittgenstein (1960), pp. 7–8. In the *Tractatus,* Wittgenstein, by and large, seems to accept Weininger's stance toward solipsism and the self. Later, he may still have held on to the idea of solipsism as a philosophical position that can neither be proved nor refuted. However, by then his arguments on questions of privacy and private language were an attempt to fend off any isolationist conclusions to be drawn from this: "Now if it is not the causal connection which we are concerned with, then the activities of the mind lie open before us. . . . We are most strongly tempted to think that here are things hidden, something we can see from the outside, but which we can't look into. And yet nothing of the sort is the case" (ibid., p. 6).

21. The letter talks, for example, of women's "good-naturedness," and, in general, of moral characteristics as tertiary sexual characteristics. The emphasis is not on good or bad properties but on the phenomenon of projection: "Always the same old story: what one is lacking becomes the ideal" (Weininger 1990, p. 102). In line with this, he does not ascribe falseness to women (or W) as such; rather he says that whether a woman lies or not doesn't interest men. It can, of course, not be ruled out that Weininger presents his ideas in a more neutral form so as to make them more acceptable to his supervisor.

22. Based on Weininger's letter to Jodl, Jodl's report on the dissertation, and the changes to the first edition, Hirsch suggests that it comprised chapters I–VI of part 1, and chapters I–III and V–VIII of part 2 of the published version (Hirsch 1997, p. 25 n. 19).

23. Letter to Swoboda, 2 March 1902, Weininger (1990), p. 107.

24. Letter to Swoboda 19 May 1902, Weininger (1990), p. 118.

25. "By classifying the majority of living things in the most general terms and simply calling them male or female, man or woman, we can no longer do justice to the facts" (p. 12). *"Between Man and Woman there are* ***innumerable gradations****, or 'intermediate sexual forms.' Just as physics talks about ideal gases*—i.e. those that precisely follow Boyle-Gay-Lussac's law (in reality none obeys it)—before proceeding to note divergences from this law in concrete cases, *we can also posit an ideal Man M and an ideal Woman W, neither of whom exists, as sexual types.* These types not only *can* but *must* be constructed. *The type, the Platonic idea, is not only the 'object of art' but also that of science"* (p. 13). In effect, Weininger's procedure establishes the distinction between biological sex and gender, neither of which—as a scientific category—is naturally given: "But if there are no males and females in the strict sense, what can it mean to assert that individuals are bisexual? That term would in fact be meaningless until an abstract theoretical account of 'male' and 'female' was provided. This is the goal of Weininger's characterology. His vehicle for attaining it was the Ideal Type, which does not refer to a Platonic essence [however, cf. quotation above], but to what he termed idealized limiting cases that establish a spectrum along which the significance of empirical data can be evaluated for their cultural significance, that is, to what we would today call 'models'" (Janik 2001, pp. 48–49). In this sense, the discussions of the first part uncover the conventionality of sexual stereotypes, and raise the problem of where to draw the line between nature and culture. The second part attempts to solve this problem, and thus the two parts reflect on each other. However, it is "the tragedy in Weininger's work that in combating one set of stereotypes, that is, the

Virile Male and the Devoted Wife, he created another, that is the omnicompetent Male and the irrational Female" (Janik 2001, p. 49). Put another way, Weininger's work is critical in its form (and in this sense constitutes an advance over both positivist science and the modern dissipation of epistemological categories), but not in its content.

26. Janik (2001) argues that *Sex and Character* was "an effort to provide a critical theory of sexuality by giving Kantian foundations to Lombroso's view of actual and ideal relationships between the sexes" (p. 51). Sengoopta (2000), weighing each part of Weininger's scientific patchwork independently, reaches the conclusion that parts of the text "were malignantly prejudiced, parts merely dull and tedious, and yet other parts 'modern,' or indeed, more 'modern' than the most radical statements on gender that one could find in fin-de-siècle Europe. . . . As far as gender and sexuality were concerned, fin-de-siècle debates were far too complex to be reified with anachronistic labels such as 'modern' or 'reactionary,' and there exists no better example of such discursive complexity than *Geschlecht und Charakter*" (p. 102).

27. Undated letter to Swoboda, October 1901 (Weininger 1990, p. 87).

28. Letter to Swoboda, presumably 6 November 1901 (Weininger 1990, pp. 91–92).

29. *Die Perioden des menschlichen Organismus in ihrer psychologischen und biologischen Bedeutung* [The periodicity of the human organism and its psychological and biological significance], Vienna: Deuticke.

30. We shall come across another charge of plagiarism below. And again it will seem more interesting to ask why individuals around that time were so concerned about priority, rather than to wonder whether or not what happened actually constituted a case of plagiarism.

31. See his account in Gerber (1919), pp. 16–21.

32. This may be the point where Weininger differed most sharply from the psychology of his day and from Freudian psychoanalysis. Freud has no trouble, within the space of a footnote, in explaining Weininger's ideas, and by implication his suicide, as the result of an unresolved castration complex: "The castration complex is the deepest unconscious root of anti-semitism; for even in the nursery little boys hear that a Jew has something cut off his penis—a piece of his penis, they think—and this gives them a right to despise Jews. And there is no stronger unconscious root for the sense of superiority over women. Weininger (the young philosopher who, highly gifted but sexually deranged, committed suicide after publishing his remarkable book, *Geschlecht und Charakter* [1903]), in a chapter that attracted much attention, treated Jews and women with equal hostility and overwhelmed them with the same insults. Being a neurotic, Weininger was completely under the sway of his infantile complexes; and from that standpoint what is common to Jews and women is their relation to the castration complex." Freud (1909), p. 36 n. 1.

33. "Der Sumpf ist eine falsche Allheit des Flusses, und sein Scheinsieg über sich selbst." Weininger (1997), p. 186.

34. "Die Furcht vor Mücken ist die Kehrseite der Liebe zum Vogel." "Otto Weininger's Taschenbuch," in Weininger (1980), pp. 602–626, here p. 622.

35. Weininger's changing conceptions of the self are discussed in a paper by Louis Sass, which was presented at a conference to mark the present publication and to reevaluate *Sex and Character* (University of Sussex, June 2003). A volume based on the contributions to this conference and to a similar event organized by Allan Janik at the Brenner Archive in Innsbruck (May 2003) is in preparation.

36. For details in chronological order see Hirsch (1997), pp. 300–313; for the textual differences between editions, see Hirsch (1997), pp. 314–354. See also the translator's note in the present edition.

37. "Beastly" is Wittgenstein's characterization of the translation in a letter to George Edward Moore: "I can quite imagine that you don't admire Weininger very much, what

with that beastly translation and the fact that W. must feel very foreign to you. It is true that he is fantastic but he is great and fantastic. It isn't necessary or rather not possible to agree with him but the greatness lies in that with which we disagree. It is his enormous mistake which is great. I.e. roughly speaking if you just add a '~' to the whole book it says an important truth." Wittgenstein (1997a), p. 250. On Wittgenstein and Weininger see Burns's introduction in Burns (2001), pp. xxii–xxvi, and Stern and Szabados (2004).

38. For a first orientation on the ramifications of Weininger's influence the reader can be referred to the volumes edited by Harrowitz and Hyams (1995), esp. the editors' "critical introduction to the history of Weininger reception" (pp. 3–20), and by Le Rider and Leser (1984). The following also contain chapters on Weininger's influence: Le Rider (1985), chapter 10, pp. 220–243 and Sengoopta (2000), chapter 8, pp. 137–156. Sengoopta covers not only Weininger's presence in literary writing, but also in philosophy, feminism, and, shortly, among scientists and physicians.

39. See, e.g., Stern (2001), which also contains a passage on Wittgenstein and Weininger, and McGuiness (2001).

40. Spengler (1928), pp. 321–322. Incidentally, Spengler was born the same year as Weininger.

41. Möbius (1904), p. 4. In this publication, Möbius quotes his earlier review in *Schmidt's Jahrbücher der gesammten Medicin* (August 1903) *in extenso.*

42. A task he sets about with endearing naïveté, bordering on self-irony: "In reading through all this [Weininger's book] once again, manfully suppressing all rising feelings of nausea, I feel impelled to take my hat off to myself." Möbius (1904), p. 23.

43. "I was a doctor of philosophy when he [Weininger] was not even born, I witnessed the enthusiasm for Büchner, for Strauss, for Du Bois-Reymond. No, these are not proper philosophers, these are philosophical clowns." Möbius (1904), p. 18.

44. Ibid., p. 22.—The joke rebounds on Möbius himself as he misquotes Weininger. What Weininger really says, is: "Man regards himself as unscrupulous and immoral if he finds that he has not thought of any one point of his life for a long time" (p. 131). This is at least an interesting suggestion in the context of Weininger's attempt to demonstrate the morality of memory. Möbius's misreading is not untypical of those who only look out for Weininger's prejudice, and thus miss the psychological and philosophical points.

45. Rappaport wanted to find a suitable and poetic ending to his biographical sketch, which is far from hagiographic, is very understanding of Weininger's mind, and thus opted for this parallel to Schopenhauer's report on a cloud rising at Kant's funeral.

46. He describes the overture to the 3rd act of *Sigfried* as "the battle between the totality and nothingness, between cosmos and chaos, the greatest choice in the world; and the turmoil in the whole of nature in this battle"; another Wagner motive is called "the resorption of the horizon," some Beethoven melodies are associated with "salvaged joy," and Solveig's song is styled "the most extreme dilution of air ever achieved." Rappaport (1904), pp. 8–9. As far as verbal descriptions of musical emotions go, these seem as good as any.

47. "These absolutely unique sensations he experienced when listening to music are hysterical, and nothing but hysterical. There could be no better expression of the modern degenerative element in a hysterical psychosis." Probst (1904), p. 37.

48. Probst (1904), p. 36. It does not seem altogether unlikely that passages such as these are partly a response to Weininger's remark in a letter (of 29 July 02) sent from Munich to Gerber, and reprinted at the end of Rappaport's preface: "Munich, so far, has not produced any great men: it attracted them all, but kept none of them."

49. Loewenfeld's explanatory footnote at the beginning of Probst's study makes it clear that it was he who approached Leopold Weininger, not, as Le Rider (1985) implies—"Dieser sollte den 'Fall' Weininger genauestens untersuchen, . . . " (p. 14; "He was meant

to investigate the 'case' of Weininger in the greatest detail, . . . ")—Weininger who approached Loewenfeld. His motivation for doing so is not clear.

50. The section on Kraus and *Die Fackel* is greatly indebted to information provided by Dr. Gilbert Carr, Trinity College Dublin. All interpretations, and any errors and inaccuracies, are my own. *Die Fackel*, quoted as F.

51. See also F 169, 1904, p. 7: "It is possible to imagine someone who frowns upon Weininger's conclusions (inferiority of women), and is jubilant about his insights (the different nature of women's value)."

52. It is not clear whether the meeting took place.

53. See F 372/373, 1913, pp. 38–39. For Kraus and the sexual politics of his time, see Nike Wagner (1982); on Kraus and Weininger esp. part 3, pp. 132–181.

54. F 144, 1903, p. 17. Kraus is right as far as the number of articles on Weininger are concerned; their seriousness is a more difficult issue. See Hirsch (1997), pp. 358–363 for a list of reviews. Weininger's publisher, Braumüller, in 1904 compiled a brochure containing 22, mostly positive, reviews with a more balanced distribution between Austrian and German sources. One foreign source which certainly gave substantial space to Weininger, and which formed the background to Kraus's attack on the *Neue Freie Presse*, was the Swiss writer J. V. Widmann, who had first published what he called a "feuilletonistic joke" in the *NFP* of 18 August under the title "Der Philosoph in Champex" [The philosopher in Champex], but who subsequently wrote six pieces on Weininger for his newspaper *Der Bund* and forced the *NFP* to publish a correction to its claim that his "feuilletonistic joke" was an adequate account of the book. His series of articles, quoted by Kraus, begins by stating that Weininger's work cannot be laughed off by a piece of journalism, and ends by calling Weininger's death "a true philosopher's end of the kind known in the world of antiquity" (F 144, p. 21).

55. F 152, p. 20. "Nun glauben diese größenwahnsinnigen Schwachköpfe bereits, daß sie—lebendigschweigen können! Und das können sie schon gar nicht!"

56. *Der Brenner*, III. Jahr, 1 and 15 October, 1 November 1912 (Heft 1–3).

57. It is difficult here not to be reminded of Wittgenstein's *Tractatus* and his *Lecture on Ethics*.

58. Ebner (1921), p. 295: "The worst mistake in Weininger's idealism, though it is rooted in idealism as such, is his conception of the life and personality of Jesus."

59. See Janik (2001), p. 13, and chapters 2 ("Weininger's Critique of a Narcissistic Culture"), 3 ("Weininger, Ibsen, and the Origins of Viennese Critical Modernism"), and 4 on Ebner ("Ebner contra Wagner: Epistemology, Aesthetics, and Salvation in Vienna, 1900"); see also Methlagl (2002), p. 8.

60. See the preface to Ebner (1921), and the biographical sketch by the editor in Haecker (1989).

61. See Wittgenstein (1997b; an English translation is forthcoming, in James C. Klagge and Alfred Nordmann, eds., *Ludwig Wittgenstein: Public and Private Occasions*). In this context, Wittgenstein comes close to Weininger's ultimate renunciation of individuality by renouncing his own power to judge: "One might say: It is God's decision what is a farce and what is not" (ibid., p. 82).

62. Janik (2001), p. 83. Janik sees the Peer Gynt essay, and therefore "Ibsen's dramatic analysis" (ibid.) of self-delusion as crucial in this context: "Weininger's legacy to fin de siècle critical modernists was to pose the problem of the limits of the self and *a fortiori* self-expression. He was the 'theorist' of a critical modernism inasmuch as he laid the groundwork for the immanent critique of our tendencies to self-deception in his essay on Ibsen" (ibid.).

63. In the chapter "Endowment and Memory," Weininger argues that memory is proof of the fact that something timeless exists, in fact that we can only think of the very concept of time if we partake in the timeless: "One must *somehow* have *overcome* time in

order to be able to *reflect* on it, somehow *stand outside time* in order to be able to *contemplate* it." He further relates this to the theme of value: "In order to explore this timeless entity, let us first reflect on *just what* is released from time by memory. We have seen that it is anything that is *of any interest or has any significance* to the individual or, to put it briefly, *anything that has a* ***value*** *for the individual.* One remembers only those things that have had a ***value,*** albeit often for a long time an unconscious one, for a person: ***it is this value that makes them timeless.*** *One forgets everything that has not somehow, albeit often unconsciously, been* ***attributed value*** *by the person*" (pp. 115–116). And this, in turn, will form the basis of the notion of genius and of the relationship between "the event of the self" and *weltanschauung* in chapter VIII of the second part ("The Problem of the Self and Genius"), once Weininger has established the principles of logic as something outside time, and logic as the basis for all empirical judgments which are made with the help of concepts: "*This* is the true function of the principle of contradiction and the principle of identity. *They constitute conceptuality*" (p. 135). For a more detailed exposition of the argument, see my contribution in Stern and Szabados (2004).

Wittgenstein will later, among others, take up the theme of duality between time and timelessness: "But now it seems to me too that besides the work of the artist there is another through which the world may be captured sub specie aeterni. It is—as I believe—the way of thought which as it were flies above the world and leaves it the way it is, contemplating it from above in its flight" (Wittgenstein 1998, p. 7e; stress omitted).

64. These demands have since mostly been met, partly by Janik himself, partly by others. Sengoopta's recent study (Sengoopta 2001), while not uncritical, has embedded Weininger firmly within the scientific culture of his day. Janik has worked out the details of Weininger's psychological projectionism (Janik 1995), establishing at the same time that Weininger's thought contains a very strong social component. A recent paper by Janik on Weininger and Viennese middle-class feminism (to appear in the volume mentioned in note 35), and Gimpl's contextualization of *Sex and Character* with Jodl's liberalism (Gimpl 1990) further confirm that Weininger was not out of line with the political discussions of his day. Finally, Le Rider (1993) places Weininger in the center of the most general trends of modernity and their effect on subjectivity.

65. See his *Modernity and Crises of Identity* (where Weininger is again a central figure) for a detailed discussion of his view of Viennese modernism. The conclusions he reaches in this book are far less polemical and provide evidence of thematic similarities between the "modern" and our "postmodern" present: "However, the pessimism of Broch or Wittgenstein, faced with the vacuum of modern culture and the difficulties of the individual, forced to seek a footing without any collective norm to hold on to, must not blind us to the fact that the general destruction of identities, felt with dizzying and anxious intensity in modernist Vienna, also carried within it the utopias which could regenerate the human race" (Le Rider 1993, p. 298). Utopias, the reader may conclude, that are available "so long as no new reaction comes to cut short our postmodern game of self-invention" (ibid., p. 301). But what if someone sees this game as precisely in the service of universal repression? We are back with the paradoxes of liberalism.

66. It should be noted here that the German original does not allow us to decide with certainty whether Le Rider claims that Weininger condemned women, or his ideal type of Woman. My English version opts for the much more defensible second possibility.

67. "Kraus und Weininger sind eurozentrisch bis zum Exzeß, sie sind mit allen Fasern Abendländer."—It is interesting to see the polar opposition between this perspective and that of Spengler/Wittgenstein.

68. Stieg (1984), p. 61 on *Die Blendung:* "Weininger's 'experimental novel,' however, long before Bernhard found its perfect aesthetic realization; but not by way of confirmation, rather by way of 'precise' satirical exaggeration." Le Rider (1985), in his chapter on Weininger's influence, calls Thomas Bernhard one of the endpoints of twentieth-century

literature which relentlessly deepened the theme of "irreversible loneliness" [*das Thema der unaufhebbaren Einsamkeit*] (p. 243). For a different view on *Die Blendung* as straightforwardly Weiningerian, see Tyler (1996).

69. Le Rider (1985), p. 100: "The controversy over plagiarism between Weininger, Fließ, Freud and Swoboda is interesting because it throws light on the incredible confusion concerning scientific criteria of rationality, method and concepts at the time. . . . The level at which this whole controversy is played out proves how difficult it was for Weininger's contemporaries to distinguish between science and pseudo-science, and how tentative psychoanalysis still was in its beginnings."

70. See, e.g., pp. 38 and 134 on organisms as indivisible totalities, pp. 115–117 on the connection between memory, time, and value, and pp. 128–130 on logic and memory.

71. Weininger (2001), p. 118. For a detailed discussion of the role of solipsism in Weininger see Burns's contribution to Stern and Szabados (2004), and Gabriel (1990).

72. Oscar Wilde, "Phrases and Philosophies for the Use of the Young," in Wilde (1966), pp. 1205–1206, here: p. 1205.

73. It is worth keeping in mind that Weininger's work could be called "the first great attempt at dialogical philosophy in Vienna, long before Martin Buber and Ferdinand Ebner." Gimpl (1990), pp. 156–157.

Bibliography

Abrahamsen, David. 1946. *The Mind and Death of a Genius.* New York: Columbia University Press.

Améry, Jean. 1976. *Hand an sich legen. Diskurs über den Freitod.* Stuttgart: Klett-Cotta.

Baguley, David. 1990. *Naturalist Fiction: The Entropic Vision.* Cambridge: Cambridge University Press.

Beller, Steven. 1995. "Otto Weininger as Liberal?" In Harrowitz and Hyams, eds., pp. 91–101.

Braumüller, Wilhelm, ed. 1905. Publisher's brochure containing an introduction and early reviews of *Geschlecht und Charakter.* Vienna, Leipzig: Braumüller.

Burns, Steven. 2001. "Introduction." In Weininger (2001), pp. xiii–xlii.

de Chadarevian, Soraya. 1993. "Die 'Methode der Kurven' in der Physiologie zwischen 1850 und 1900." In Jörg Rheinberger and Michael Hagner, eds., *Die Experimentalisierung des Lebens,* pp. 28–49. Berlin: Akademie Verlag.

Ebner, Ferdinand. 1921. *Das Wort und die geistigen Realitäten. Pneumatologische Fragmente.* In Ferdinand Ebner, *Schriften,* 3 vols., ed. Franz Seyr, vol. 1, pp. 75–342. Munich: Kösel (1963).

Fischer, Kurt Rudolf. 1999. "Zur Theorie des Wiener Fin de siècle." In Kurt Rudolf Fischer, *Aufsätze zur angloamerikanischen und österreichischen Philosophie,* pp. 33–47. Frankfurt/M.: Peter Lang.

Fischer, Kurt Rudolf, ed. n.d. *Österreichische Philosophie von Brentano bis Wittgenstein.* Vienna: Wissenschaftlicher Universitätsverlag.

Freud, Sigmund. 1909. *Little Hans.* In *The Complete Psychological Works of Sigmund Freud,* trans. James Strachey, vol. X. London: Hogarth Press.

Gabriel, Gottfried. 1990. "Solipsismus: Wittgenstein, Weininger und die Wiener Moderne." In Helmut Bachmaier, ed., *Paradigmen der Moderne,* pp. 29–47. Amsterdam, Philadelphia: John Benjamins.

Gerber, Artur. 1919. "Ecce Homo!" Preface to *Otto Weininger: Taschenbuch und Briefe an einen Freund,* ed. Artur Gerber, pp. 5–24. Leipzig, Vienna: E. P. Tal.

Gimpl, Georg. 1990. *Vernetzungen. Friedrich Jodl und sein Kampf um die Aufklärung.* Oulu: Veröffentlichungen des Historischen Instituts der Universität Oulu. Ideen-und Wissenschaftsgeschichte (Jg. 1990, Band 2).

Haecker, Theodor. 1989. *Tag- und Nachtbücher.* Ed. Hinrich Siefken. Innsbruck: Haymon.

Harrowitz, Nancy A., and Barbara Hyams, eds. 1995. *Jews and Gender. Responses to Otto Weininger.* Philadelphia: Temple University Press.

Hirsch, Waltraud. 1997. *Eine unbescheidene Charakterologie. Geistige Differenz von Judentum und Christentum; Otto Weiningers Lehre vom bestimmten Charakter.* Frankfurt/M.: Peter Lang.

Janik, Allan. 1981. "Therapeutic Nihilism: How Not to Write about Otto Weininger." In Barry Smith, ed., *Structure and Gestalt. Philosophy and Literature in Austria Hungary and Her Successor States*, pp. 263–292. Amsterdam: John Benjamins.

——. 1995. "How Did Weininger Influence Wittgenstein?" In Harrowitz and Hyams, eds., pp. 61–71.

——. 2001. *Wittgenstein's Vienna Revisited.* New Brunswick, N.J.: Transaction Publishers.

Johnston, William. 1972. *The Austrian Mind: An Intellectual and Social History 1848–1938.* Berkeley and Los Angeles: University of California Press.

Klagge, James C., ed. 2001. *Wittgenstein: Biography and Philosophy.* Cambridge: Cambridge University Press.

Klagge, James C., and Alfred Nordmann, eds. Forthcoming. *Ludwig Wittgenstein: Public and Private Occasions.* Lanham: Rowman and Littlefield.

Kraus, Karl, ed. 1977. *Die Fackel.* Vienna, 1899–1936. Reprint, 12 vols., Frankfurt/M.: Zweitausendeins.

Le Rider, Jacques. 1984. "Nachwort zum Fall Otto Weininger." In Le Rider and Leser, eds. (1984), pp. 96–105.

——. 1985. *Der Fall Otto Weininger. Wurzeln des Antifeminismus und Antisemitismus.* Vienna, Munich: Löcker.

——. 1993. *Modernity and the Crises of Identity.* New York: Continuum.

——. 1995. "'The Otto Weininger Case' Revisited." In Harrowitz and Hyams, eds. (1995), pp. 21–33.

Le Rider, Jacques, and Norbert Leser, eds. 1984. *Otto Weininger. Werk und Wirkung.* Vienna: Österreichischer Bundesverlag.

Lesky, Erna. 1976. *The Vienna Medical School of the Nineteenth Century.* Baltimore: Johns Hopkins University Press.

Luft, David. 2003. *Eros and Inwardness in Vienna: Weininger, Musil, Doderer.* Chicago, London: University of Chicago Press.

McGuiness, Brian. 2001. "Wittgenstein and the Idea of Jewishness." In Klagge, ed., pp. 221–236.

Methlagl, Walter. 2002. *Bodenproben. Kulturgeschichtliche Reflexionen.* Ed. Forschungsinstitut Brenner-Archiv, Innsbruck: Haymon.

Möbius, Paul Julius. 1904. *Geschlecht und Unbescheidenheit.* Halle: Verlag von Carl Marhold.

Probst, Ferdinand. 1904. *Der Fall Otto Weininger. Eine psychiatrische Studie.* Wiesbaden: Verlag von J. F. Bergmann.

Rabinbach, Anson. 1990. *The Human Motor: Energy, Fatigue and the Origins of Modernity.* New York: Basic Books.

Rappaport, Moriz. 1904. "Vorrede." In Otto Weininger, *Über die letzten Dinge.* Vienna, Leipzig: Braumüller.

Rodlauer, Hannelore. 1995. "Fragments from Weininger's Education." In Harrowitz and Hyams, eds., pp. 35–58.

Santner, Eric. 1990. *Stranded Objects: Mourning, Memory, and Film in Postwar Germany.* Ithaca, London: Cornell University Press.

Sengoopta, Chandak. 2000. *Otto Weininger: Sex, Science, and Self in Imperial Vienna.* Chicago, London: University of Chicago Press.

Schröter, Michael. 2002. "Fließ vs. Weininger, Swoboda und Freud: Der Plagiatsstreit von 1906 im Lichte der Dokumente." *Psyche—Z Psychoanal* 56, pp. 338–368.

Spengler, Oswald. 1928. *The Decline of the West. Perspectives of World-History.* London: George Allen & Unwin.

Stern, David. 2001. "Was Wittgenstein a Jew?" In Klagge, ed., pp. 237–272.

Stern, David, and Béla Szabados, eds. 2004. *Wittgenstein Reads Weininger.* Cambridge: Cambridge University Press.

Stieg, Gerald. 1984. "Otto Weininger's 'Blendung.' Weininger, Karl Kraus und der Brenner-Kreis." In Le Rider and Leser, eds., pp. 59–68.

Swoboda, Hermann. 1904. *Die Perioden des menschlichen Organismus in ihrer psychologischen und biologischen Bedeutung.* Vienna: Deuticke.

Tyler, Simon. 1996. "Homage or Parody? Elias Canetti and Otto Weininger." In *Gender and Politics in Austrian Fiction,* ed. R. Robertson and E. Timms, pp. 134–149. Austrian Studies VII. Edinburgh: Edinburgh University Press.

Wagner, Nike. 1982. *Geist und Geschlecht: Karl Kraus und die Erotik der Wiener Moderne.* Frankfurt/M.: Suhrkamp.

Weininger, Otto. 1980. *Geschlecht und Charakter. Eine prinzipielle Untersuchung.* München: Matthes & Seitz.

———. 1990. *Eros und Psyche. Studien und Briefe 1899–1902.* Ed. with a preface and introduction by Hannelore Rodlauer. Vienna: Verlag der österreichischen Akademie der Wissenschaften.

———. 1997. *Über die letzten Dinge.* Munich: Matthes & Seitz.

———. 2001. *On Last Things.* Trans. and with an introduction by Steven Burns. Lewiston, Queenston, Lampeter: Edwin Mellen Press.

Wilde, Oscar. 1966. *Complete Works of Oscar Wilde.* London and Glasgow: Collins.

Wittgenstein, Ludwig. 1960. *The Blue and Brown Books.* Oxford: Basil Blackwell.

———. 1997a. *Cambridge Letters. Correspondence with Russell, Keynes, Moore, Ramsey and Sraffa,* ed. B. McGuiness and G. H. v. Wright. Oxford: Basil Blackwell.

———. 1997b. *Denkbewegungen. Tagebücher 1930–1932/1936–1937.* Ed. Ilse Somavilla. Innsbruck: Haymon.

———. 1998. *Culture and Value.* Ed. Georg Henrik von Wright, in collaboration with Heikki Nyman, trans. by Peter Winch. Oxford: Basil Blackwell.

Zola, Émile. 1964. *The Experimental Novel and Other Essays.* New York: Haskell House.

Translator's Note

Ladislaus Löb

The only English translation of *Sex and Character* until now was published in 1906 by William Heinemann, London, and G. P. Putnam's Sons, New York: a reprint was issued in 1975 by AMS Press Inc., New York, and in 2003 by Howard Fertig, New York. The title page refers to an "Authorised Translation from the sixth German Edition," although there is no indication as to who authorized it or who the translator was. The volume further contains a "Note to the Sixth German Edition (By the German Publisher)" and an index of people and subjects which does not appear in the German editions. A substantial selection, by Kevin Solvay, from the 1906 translation is also available on the Internet. One may therefore ask why it was considered necessary to produce a new translation. The simple answer is that the old one is totally inadequate.

In an essay entitled "'26. unveränderte Auflage.' Bemerkungen zur Textgeschichte von Otto Weinigers *Geschlecht und Charakter*" ["'26th unaltered edition.' Notes on the textual history of Otto Weininger's *Sex and Character*"] Waltraud Hirsch traces the various German editions of the book.[1] *Geschlecht und Charakter* was first published by Wilhelm Braumüller, Vienna and Leipzig, in May 1903. Shortly before his suicide Weininger undertook a thorough revision, and a second edition—incorporating Weininger's amendments, and overseen by his friend Artur Gerber, who also contributed a preface—was published by Braumüller in the autumn of 1903. The third edition (1904/1905) was identical to the second, except that it no longer contained Gerber's preface. All subsequent editions, up to and including the 26th in 1925, were identical to the third. The 27th and 28th "popular editions," of 1926 and 1947 respectively, were slightly cut. After a long interval, the latest edition (Matthes & Seitz, Munich 1997) reverted to the text of the first edition and is about 10 pages shorter than the second and subsequent editions. The present English translation is based on the text of the second edition, without Gerber's preface.

It is no exaggeration to say that the anonymous 1906 translation is totally inadequate. Ludwig Wittgenstein called it "beastly"[2] and Chandak Sengoopta, the author of one of the most recent books on Weininger, explains that when quoting in English he could follow it "rarely without significant emendations."[3] The picture presented by this version of a major document of intellectual history is indeed full of distortions and highly misleading.

Weininger's own 600-page volume contains a 130-page "appendix" with additions and references to a wide range of scientific, philosophical, and literary works that underpin his own. Not only do these notes demonstrate an astonishing degree of learning for a young man of 23, but they also provide important insights into many central issues and personalities in *fin-de-siècle* Austrian, German, and European intellectual life. The 1906 translation omits them all.

The main text itself is significantly shorter in the 1906 translation than in the original. Again numerous references to people, works, and ideas which firmly place Weininger's argument in the broad intellectual context of his time are missing, as are single words, clauses, sentences, and whole paragraphs in which the argument is explained, refined, amplified, and carried further. In a surprising number of cases the 1906 translator simply did not understand the most elementary German vocabulary, grammar (including tense, case, gender, and number) and idiomatic usage. There are literally hundreds of mistranslations, ranging from slight inaccuracies, through substantial mistakes, to downright howlers, at times saying the very opposite of Weininger's own statements.

Given the limitations of space it is not possible here to analyze the inadequacies of the translation in detail, but a number of illustrations—taken, for convenience's sake, from the first part of the book, with the correct translations in square brackets preceding the 1906 version in each case—should enable the reader to gauge the extent to which they oversimplify, blur, twist, or actually contradict the meaning of the original.

Mistranslations of single words or phrases include:

Übersicht (5) [overview (10)]: superficial view (3)
in dieser Form (10) [in this form (14)]: in another respect (7)
den umfassendsten Beweis (11) [the most comprehensive proof (14)]: the most striking proofs (8)
noch gar nicht angestrebt (11) [so far not attempted (15)]: by no means striven against (9)
es ist klar (25) [it is clear (23)]: it does not follow (21)
sexuelle Vereinigung (33) [sexual union (28)]: marriage (27)
gerade in der Mitte (36) [exactly in the middle (30)]: nearly midway (36)
rein-ästhetisch untadelige Frauen (37) [aesthetically impeccable women (31)]: aesthetically beautiful women of blameless character (31–32)
mit annähernder Vollständigkeit (37) [almost completely (31)]: most accurately (32)
jedoch (41) [however (33)]: moreover (35)
einen weiteren Faktoren (43) [one other factor (34)]: a few factors (36)
Ehebruch (48) [adultery (35)]: divorce (41)
beiderseitige sexuelle Erregung beim Geschlechtsakte (52) [mutual sexual arousal during intercourse (40)]: mutual participation in the sexual act (44)
körperlich eitler (68) [more physically vain (50)]: physically lazier (56)
kunstübende Frauen (86) [women artists (61)]: women-workers (69)
wenn von Motiven der Eitelkeit . . . abgesehen wird (87) [disregarding the motives of vanity (62)]: from various motives, such as vanity (70).

Some fuller examples may represent more complex forms of mistranslation:

daß . . . beliebig vertauschte Ovarien . . . nie die Verkümmerung der sekundären Charaktere . . . aufzuhalten vermögen (24) [that ovaries exchanged arbitrarily . . . will never be able to prevent the secondary characteristics . . . withering away (22)]: that when an exchange of the ovaries has been made . . . there is no failure of the secondary sexual characters (20).

ebenso ziehen aber auch . . . die ganz jungen Mädchen . . . ältere Männer oft jüngeren vor, um später wieder mit ganz jungen Bürschlein die Ehe zu brechen (43) [quite young girls . . . equally often prefer . . . older men to younger ones, but later frequently commit adultery with quite young lads (35)]: quite young girls . . . generally prefer much older men, but, later in life, may marry striplings (37).

der Grundgedanke der Goetheschen "Wahlverwandtschaften," wie er . . . von denen entwickelt wird, die seine tiefe schicksalsschwere Wahrheit nachher an sich selbst erfahren sollen (48) [the fundamental idea of Goethe's *Elective Affinities,* developed . . . by those who will later learn its profound fateful truth through their own experience (37)]: the fundamental idea in Goethe's . . . Elective Affinities . . . the full force of which he was fated himself to experience in later life (41).

Prozeduren, die man vornimmt, um Weibchen durch männliche Zuchttiere auch dann belegen zu lassen, wenn diese an jenen wenig Gefallen gefunden haben, . . . sind . . . stets von irgend welchen üblen Folgen begleitet (51) [procedures undertaken to have females served by male breeding animals, even when the latter do not much like the former . . . always have some bad consequences (39–40)]: methods . . . to secure the serving of mares by stallions unattractive to them . . . are followed by indifferent results (43).

Der Sinn dieser Empfehlung kann aber nur der sein, . . . die Befolgung der . . . Gesetze gegen homosexuelle Akte . . . zu deren Abschaffung diese Zeilen ebenfalls beitragen wollen, möglichst leicht zu machen (60) [the purpose of this suggestion can only be to make it as easy as possible . . . to obey the laws banning homosexual acts . . . to the abolition of which these lines are also intended to make a contribution (45)]: knowledge of such a solution should lead to the repeal of the . . . laws . . . directed against homo-sexuality, so far at least as to make the punishments the lightest possible (51).

Weibliche Männer haben oft ein ungemein starkes Bedürfnis zu heiraten, mögen sie . . . materiell noch so glänzend gestellt sein (67) [feminine men often have an exceptionally strong need to marry, even if . . . they are themselves extremely wealthy (50)]: womanish men are usually extremely anxious to marry, at least . . . if a sufficiently brilliant opportunity offers itself (56).

Two longer extracts may exemplify how substantial omissions in the 1906 version misrepresent Weininger's sophisticated arguments. In the first extract a lengthy passage of the original is rendered by two short sentences, in which Weininger's crucial references to Kantian philosophy and Kant himself are completely ignored:

In dieser Zeit der hochflutenden Literatur über das Verhältnis des Physischen zum Psychischen . . . wäre es von Nutzen gewesen, auf diese Verhältnisse zu reflektieren. Man hätte sich dann freilich die Frage vorlegen müssen, *ob nicht die Setzung einer wie immer gearteten Korrespondenz zwischen Physischem und Psy-*

> *chischem eine bisher übersehene, apriorische, synthetische Funktion unseres Denkens ist* —was mir wenigstens dadurch sicher verbürgt scheint, daß eben jeder Mensch die Physiognomik *anerkennt,* insoferne jeder, *unabhängig* von der *Erfahrung,* Physiognomik *treibt.* So wenig Kant diese Tatsache bemerkt hat, so gibt sie doch seiner Auffassung recht, daß über das Verhältnis des Körperlichen zum Geistigen sich *weiter* wissenschaftlich nichts beweisen noch ausmachen läßt. Das Prinzip einer gesetzmäßigen Relation zwischem Psychischem und Materiellem *muß daher als Forschungsgrundsatz heuristisch acceptiert werden,* und es bleibt der Metaphysik und der Religion vorbehalten, über die Art dieses Zusammenhanges, *dessen Tatsächlichkeit a priori für jeden Menschen feststeht,* noch nähere Bestimmungen zu treffen (73)

> [At a time like the present, when we are being flooded by writings about the relationship between the physical and the psychic . . . it would have been useful to reflect upon these circumstances. However, in that case one would also have had to ask *whether or not the assumption of any kind of correspondence between physical and psychic elements is an a priori synthetic function of our thought that has so far been overlooked*—which seems to me to be firmly established at least through the fact that every human being *recognizes* physiognomy simply by *practicing* physiognomy, *regardless* of *experience.* Although Kant did not notice this fact it confirms his view that nothing *more* can be scientifically proven or ascertained about the relationship between the physical and the psychic. A relationship, governed by laws, between the physical and the psychic *must therefore be accepted as a heuristic principle of scientific inquiry,* and the further determination of the nature of this relationship, *which is a priori regarded as a fact by everybody,* remains the privilege of metaphysics and religion (53)]:

> It is certainly the case that every one believes in physiognomy and actually practices it. The principle of the existence of a definite relation between mind and body must be accepted as an illuminating axiom for psychological research (60).

In the second extract the four short sentences standing in for some 1600 words of the original (not quoted in full here) omit Weininger's important philosophical reflections and his acknowledgment of the thought of Hume and Mach:

> *Warum* zieht der eine die Katze vor, der andere den Hund? Warum? Warum?
>
> Diese Fragestellung scheint jedoch gerade hier nicht sehr fruchtbar. Ich glaube nicht, daß Hume, und besonders Mach recht haben, wenn sie keinen besonderen Unterschied zwischen *simultaner* und *succedaner* Kausalität machen. Gewisse zweifellos formale Analogien werden da recht gewaltsam übertrieben . . . man könnte, eine lehrreiche Ausführung Machs benützend, verlangen, daß auch die organische Welt, sofern sie wissenschaftlich begreifbar und darstellbar, eine solche sei, in der zwischen n Variablen eine Zahl von Gleichungen bestehe, die kleiner sei als n (und zwar gleich n-1, wenn sie durch ein wissenschaftliches System *eindeutig* bestimmbar sein soll: die Gleichungen würden bei geringerer Zahl zu unbestimmten Gleichungen werden, und bei einer größeren Zahl könnte der durch eine Gleichung ausgesagten Abhängigkeit von einer zweiten ohne weiters widersprochen werden).
>
> Dies ist die logische Bedeutung des Korrelationsprinzipes in der Biologie: es enthüllt sich als die Anwendung des *Funktionsbegriffes* auf das Lebendige,

> und darum liegt in der Möglichkeit *seiner* Ausbreitung und Vertiefung die Hoffnung auf eine theoretische Morphologie hauptsächlich begründet (74–77)
>
> [*Why* does one person prefer cats, the other dogs? Why? Why?
>
> This question, especially in the present context, does not seem very fruitful. I do not believe that Hume and, in particular, Mach are right in failing to make an explicit distinction between *simultaneous* and *succedaneous* causality. Some undeniable formal analogies are thereby rather forcibly exaggerated . . . using an instructive explanation of Mach, one could stipulate that the organic world too, insofar as it is to be scientifically intelligible and representable, should be one in which the number of equations between n variables is smaller than n (and equal to n-1 if it is to be *unmistakably* definable by a scientific system: given a smaller number, the equations would become indefinite, and given a larger number, the dependence indicated by one equation could easily be contradicted by another).
>
> This is the logical significance, in biology, of the correlation principle, which reveals itself as the application to living beings of the *concept of function* (54–55).]:
>
> Why are cats attractive to one person, dogs to another? Why? I do not think that this is the most fruitful way of stating the problem. I believe it to be more important to ask in what other respects lovers of dogs and of cats differ from one another (61).

The illustrations could be multiplied over and over again.

The aim of the present English translation is to reproduce Weininger's complete text, including his notes, as fully and as faithfully in both substance and tone as possible. No attempt was made to produce a pastiche of English as written around 1900. Nor was this necessary, as Weininger's own language, for all its idiosyncrasies, does not seem overly archaic today. While much of his science is obviously out of date, the English equivalents of most of the terms he uses are still current, and the same applies to his philosophical vocabulary. It cannot be denied that his writing is clumsy, pedantic, and verbose, but these features reflect the intricacies and subtle nuances of his thought and the personality behind them. Occasionally it was necessary to break up his long hypotactical periods into shorter English sentences, but generally his phrasing was adhered to as far as was feasible, so as to convey the flow of his reasoning and the flavor of his mode of expression.

In some cases Weininger's indiscriminate use of several words for the same concept had to be replaced by one English word for the sake of clarity or for want of alternatives. An outstanding example is his oscillation between "Weib" and "Frau." While "Weib" in today's German usually has derogatory connotations, in Weininger's time it could be a value-free synonym of the purely descriptive term "Frau." For all his questionable views on women, Weininger's text offers no evidence that he ever intended to use "Weib" in itself as a disparagement, and therefore the translation "woman" for both "Weib" and "Frau" seemed appropriate. Where he uses "Weib" and "Frau" in the singular to denote the type rather than the individual the capitalized spelling "Woman" was adopted—as was the capitalized spelling "Man" where he uses the singular "Mann" for the same reason.

In other cases it was necessary to substitute a variety of English words for the same German word. The prime example here is "Mensch." Although the most handy translation would have been "man," as a neutral term to include both sexes, this would often have run the risk of being confused with "man" in the sense of the male of the species. Therefore "human being" was generally chosen as the most appropriate English equivalent. However, where the repetition of "human being" would have seemed too cumbersome, it was replaced with "individual," and occasionally with "person" or "people." Where Weininger refers to "der Mensch" by the masculine pronoun "er," which is the only grammatically correct one in German, the best solution seemed to be to resort to "he" or "she" where the sex of the human being in question was clearly identifiable, and to "he" or the plural for either sex where it was not. The same method was employed for pronouns referring to "individual" or "person." One of Weininger's favorite phrases is "ein bedeutender Mensch," which is very close in meaning to "a great man," but the phrase "an exceptional individual" was chosen to reflect the fact that, for whatever reason, he insists on writing "Mensch" rather than "Mann" in the passages concerned.

In analogy to "Weib," "Frau," or "Mann" in the singular, Weininger often uses "Prostituierte" to describe a certain psychological type of woman rather than one actually engaged in prostitution. While it is possible that he avoided the broader term "Hure" for reasons of propriety, the present translation opted for "prostitute," not "whore," in order to keep as closely as possible to his own wording.

For "das Ich" three different alternatives offered themselves, but of these "the ego" would have had too many Freudian associations and "the I" would have sounded too un-English. Therefore the term was translated throughout as "the self."

There were also three possible equivalents for "Judentum": "Judaism," "Jewishness," and "Jewry." Weininger's own explanation that he had not a race or a religion but a certain human constitution in mind obviated "Jewry" in most places and might have argued for "Jewishness." However, in order to convey the abstract and general, rather than personal, quality that Weininger intended, "Judaism" seemed most appropriate.

As to the very first word of Weininger's title, "Geschlecht" in German has never had the secondary meaning of "sexual intercourse," as English "sex" has today. Rather, it has always carried the main connotations of "gender," as used by those who wish to avoid the ambiguities of "sex." A strong case could thus have been made for choosing "gender," but given that "gender" has late-twentieth-century—and to some extent ideological—connotations, and that the English-speaking world has known Weininger's book for a century as *Sex and Character,* it was decided to keep the same title for the present translation.

Both in his main text and in his appendix Weininger quotes copiously from sources in a variety of languages. His quotations from texts originally written in English, whenever he uses a German version rather than the English wording, are reproduced from the English originals. For his quotations from German works existing English translations were used whenever they could be found: otherwise they were translated by the present translator. The editions of existing English translations listed are those most readily available today. Quotations in French, Greek, Latin, and Italian were left in those languages, partly in order to preserve the exact appearance of Weininger's original volume and partly to prevent this volume becoming even larger. However, English titles and details of publication are included for the works in question as far as possible.

Where Weininger supplies only page references, rather than actual quotations, bibliographical details of an existing English version of the work concerned are provided, but no attempt is made to identify the matching English pages.

Where the English titles given are those of existing translations, they are printed in italics and placed in square brackets after the complete reference supplied by Weininger: if no translator is named, the translator is not known. Where no existing English translations could be discovered, titles translated by the current translator appear in square brackets immediately after the title of the original, and are not italicized.

Throughout the appendix Weininger's own somewhat inconsistent method of referring to his sources is reproduced, with the exception of "vol.," "part," "ed.," "p.," and certain place names, which are provided in a standardized English form.

A name index, not contained in Weininger's original, has been added to the volume.

The translator's warmest thanks are due to his research assistant, Audrey Hartford, for all the diligence, determination, ingenuity, and good humor that she brought to the task of ferreting out a large amount of often remote and recalcitrant material. He is particularly indebted to one of the editors, Daniel Steuer, for his extremely painstaking reading of the manuscript and a wealth of helpful suggestions.

Weininger's work has been interpreted in many conflicting ways—as that of an idealist or nihilist, a reactionary or a progressive, a fanatical misogynist or a champion of women's true role, a rabid antisemite or a Jewish mystic, a proto-fascist or an advocate of the free self, a conspicuous representative of his own age or a thinker of perennial value, a genius or a madman. As far as English-speaking readers are concerned, it is hoped that this new translation will enable them, if any translation can, to make up their own minds on the basis of what Weininger really wrote in German a century ago.

Notes

1. In Waltraud Hirsch, *Eine unbescheidene Charakterologie. Geistige Differenz von Judentum und Christentum. Otto Weiningers Lehre vom bestimmten Charakter* [An immodest characterology: The spiritual difference between Judaism and Christianity. Otto Weininger's theory of fixed character] (Frankfurt/M., Bern, New York, Paris: Peter Lang, 1997), pp. 314–354.

2. Ludwig Wittgenstein, *Cambridge Letters,* ed. Brian McGuinness and Georg Henrik von Right (Oxford: Blackwell, 1995), p. 250.

3. Chandak Sengoopta, *Otto Weininger: Sex, Science, and Self in Imperial Vienna* (Chicago, London: University of Chicago Press, 2000), p. 160.

Sex and Character

Preface

THIS BOOK ATTEMPTS to throw a new and decisive light on the relationship between the sexes. It is not intended to list the largest possible number of discrete characteristics or to compile the results of the scientific measurements and experiments carried out so far, but tries to trace all the contrasts between Man and Woman back to a single principle. Consequently it differs from all other books of its kind. It does not linger on this or that idyll, but advances to a final goal; it does not pile observation upon observation, but places the intellectual differences between the sexes within a system; it is not about women, but about Woman. It takes the most common and superficial things as its starting point, but only in order to *interpret* all the single, concrete experiences. This is no "inductive metaphysics," but a gradual progression to ever deeper psychological layers.

My investigation is not concerned with specifics, but with principles; it does not despise the laboratory, although it regards the laboratory's resources as limited in comparison with the work of analytical self-observation when dealing with deeper problems. An artist portraying a woman can also convey typical features without demonstrating his legitimacy by presenting figures and serial numbers to a guild of experimental judges. The artist does not spurn experience but, on the contrary, regards gaining experience as his *duty*. However, experience, to him, is only the starting point for delving into himself, which in art seems like delving into the world.

The psychology used in my account is thoroughly philosophical, although its particular method, which is justified only by its particular topic, is to start out from the most trivial experiences. However, the difference between the philosopher's and the artist's task is only a formal one. What is a symbol for the latter becomes a concept for the former. The relationship between expression and content is the same as that between art and philosophy. The artist has inhaled the world in order to exhale it: for the philosopher it has been exhaled and he must inhale it again.

However, there is of necessity something pretentious about all theory, and thus the same content that appears like nature in a work of art may appear much harsher and indeed offensive when it is put forward within a philosophical system as a condensed generalization, as a thesis that is subject to the principle of sufficient reason and that sets out to provide proofs. Where my account is anti-feminist—which it is almost everywhere—men will also be reluctant to agree readily and whole-heartedly: their sexual egotism always makes them prefer to see Woman as they want her to be and as they want to love her.

How could I then be unprepared for the reply women will have to my judgment of their sex?

The fact that the investigation finally turns against *Man,* placing the largest, and indeed the real, share of the blame on *him* in a deeper sense than the feminist can imagine, will do the author little good and is least likely to help rehabilitate him in the eyes of the *female* sex.

My analysis arrives at the problem of guilt because it rises from the simplest and most obvious phenomena to those high points which not only offer an insight into the nature of Woman and her significance in the world as a whole but which also open up a vista of her relationship with humanity and its highest and ultimate tasks. It is from these points that a stance can be taken on the problem of culture and the contribution of femininity to the totality of higher aims. Where the problems of culture and humanity coincide I will therefore try not only to explain but also to evaluate: indeed, here explanation and evaluation coincide of their own accord.

My investigation is, so to speak, forced to such a high vantage point without aiming for it from the outset. It gradually recognizes the inadequacy of all empirical psychological philosophy on the very grounds of empirical psychology. This does not diminish its respect for experience, which, rather than being destroyed, is always more appreciated if we recognize in the phenomena—in fact the only things that we can experience—any components which assure us that the phenomena are not the *only* things that exist, and when we perceive those signs that point to something higher, situated *above* the phenomena. That there *is* such a primary source can be asserted even if no living human being will ever reach it. And this book will not rest until it has led its reader close to that source.

I would not have dared to aspire to such a high goal in the narrow space in which the different opinions about Woman and the Woman Question have clashed so far. However, the problem involves all the most profound mysteries of existence. It can be resolved, practically and theoretically, morally or metaphysically, only with the firm guidance of a *weltanschauung.*

A *weltanschauung*—that is, one worthy of this name—is not something that could ever prove to be a hindrance to particular discoveries. On the contrary, it is the motive force of every particular discovery that conveys a deeper truth. *Weltanschauung is productive in itself,* and can never be synthetically generated, as every age that subscribes to merely empirical science believes, from a sum of specific knowledge, however large this may be.

Only the germs of such a comprehensive outlook become visible in this book. This outlook is most closely related to the views of Plato, Kant, and Christianity, although I was to a large extent obliged to create the scientific, psychological, and philosophical, logical and ethical foundations for myself. There are many things that I have been unable to discuss in detail and that I intend to explain fully in the near future. If I nevertheless draw attention to those parts of the book in particular, it is because I am even more concerned that what it says about the most profound and most general problems is taken to heart than with any applause that its specific application to the Woman Question might expect.

Should the philosophical reader be embarrassed by the fact that the discussion of the most elevated and ultimate questions seems, as it were, to be pressed into the *service* of a specific problem of no great dignity, I would share this unpleasant feeling with him. However, I may say that here the specific problem of the opposition of the sexes is the starting point rather than the goal of a more penetrating study. Thus I have derived great profit from the examination of this problem with regard to the cardinal questions of logic concerning judgments and concepts and their relationship with the axioms of thinking, to the theory of the comic, of love, of beauty and of value, to issues such as solitude and ethics and the connections between the two, and to the phenomenon of genius, the longing for immortality, and Judaism. Naturally such broad discussions in the end also benefit the specific problem, which enters into more and more varied relationships the more the field of investigation increases. And if, in this broader context, the nature of Woman proves to offer little hope for culture, if the final results completely devalue, indeed negate, femininity, they are not intended to destroy anything that *is,* to disparage anything that *has* a value *in itself.* I would be somewhat horrified by my own action if I were really only a destroyer and nothing were left standing! Perhaps the affirmative statements in the book have been orchestrated less forcefully, but those who can hear will nevertheless be able to hear them everywhere.

The book is divided into two parts: the first biological and psychological, the second psychological and philosophical. Some may think that it would have been better if I had divided the whole into two separate books, one purely scientific and the other purely introspective. However, I had to free myself from biology in order to become a psychologist through and through. My treatment of certain psychological problems in the second part is quite different from the approach of a present-day scientist, and I realize that this also puts the reception of the first part by many readers at risk. Nevertheless, the entire first part demands to be noted and judged by science, which the second part, with its greater concentration on internal experience, can demand only in a few places. Because the second part emanates from a non-positivist outlook, many will regard both parts as unscientific (however firmly positivism is refuted in that part). For the time being I must learn to live with this in the conviction of having given biology its due and vindicated the rights of a non-biological, non-physiological psychology for all times.

Perhaps I shall be accused of not supplying enough *proofs* at certain points. However, this seems to me to be the smallest weakness of my investigation. What could "prove" mean in this context? What is discussed here is neither mathematics nor epistemology (the latter only in two places), but matters of empirical science, where the most one can do is to put a finger on what *is*. In these areas what is normally called *proof* is merely an agreement between the new experiences and the old, and it does not matter whether the new phenomena are experimentally produced by a human being or given in a finished state by the creative hand of nature. Of the latter kind of proof this book supplies plenty.

Finally, as far as I can judge, the main part of the book is not one that can be understood and absorbed after a single superficial reading. I wish to state this for the information of the reader and for my own protection.

The less I repeated old and well-known things in both parts (particularly in the second), the more I wanted to point out all concurrences when I found myself in agreement with what had been said before and what was generally recognized. That is the purpose of the references in the appendix. I tried to reproduce the quotations accurately and in such a form as would be of use to both lay readers and experts. Because of their exhaustiveness, and in order to prevent the reader stumbling at every step, these references have been relegated to the end of the book.

My thanks are due to Professor Laurenz Müllner for his effective support, and to Professor Friedrich Jodl for the kind interest he has taken in my work from the outset. I feel specially indebted to the friends who assisted me in correcting the book.

First (Preparatory) Part:

Sexual Diversity

Introduction

All thinking begins with *intermediate generalizations* and then develops in two different directions, one toward concepts of ever higher abstraction, which encompass ever larger areas of reality by registering properties shared between ever more things, the other toward the intersection of all conceptual lines, the concrete complex unit, the individual, which we can only approach in our thought with the help of an infinite number of qualifications and which we define by adding to the highest generalization, a "thing" or "something," an infinite number of specific distinguishing features. Thus fish were known as a class of animal separate from mammals, birds, and worms, on the one hand long before distinctions were made between osseous and cartilaginous fish and on the other hand long before it was felt to be necessary to include fish with birds and mammals within a larger complex through the concept of the vertebrate, and to distinguish that larger complex from worms.

This self-assertion of the mind over the innumerable similarities and differences that make reality so confusing has been compared to the struggle for life among all beings.[1] We *fend off* the world through our concepts.[2] Slowly and gradually we bring the world under the control of our concepts, just as we first restrain a madman's whole body in a rough and ready fashion in order at least to impose some limits on his ability to be a danger, and only restrain his individual limbs once we feel comparatively safe.

Two concepts are among the oldest used by mankind to eke out a makeshift intellectual existence. They have often undergone minor corrections and been taken to the workshop in order to be patched up, after a fashion, when a wholesale reform was needed. Odd bits have been removed or added, reductions made in some cases and enlargements in others, just as new needs gradually assert themselves against an old electoral law, which is forced to unfasten one leash after another. On the whole, however, we believe that we can still manage along

1. Spencer's model of the world, based on differentiation and integration, can also be readily applied at this point.

2. This is true of concepts, but only as objects of a psychological, not a logical way of looking at things. Despite all modern psychologism (Brentano, Meinong, Höfler), the two cannot be lumped together without damage to both.

familiar lines with the concepts that I have in mind here, the concepts of *man* and *woman.*

We talk about lean, thin, flat, muscular, energetic "women," "women" of genius, "women" with short hair and deep voices, and about beardless, garrulous "men." We even accept that there are "unwomanly women," "masculine women," and "unmanly," "feminine" "men." Concentrating on one characteristic alone that is used to assign a person to a sexual category at birth, we even dare to combine some concepts with attributes that actually negate them. Such a state of affairs is logically untenable.

Who has not listened and contributed to heated discussions about "men and women" or "the liberation of women" in a circle of friends or in a salon, at a scientific or public meeting? In such conversations and debates "men" and "women," with dreary regularity, were placed in total opposition to each other, like white and red balls, as if there were not the slightest difference between balls of the same color. There was never any attempt to discuss individual issues as such; and since everybody had only his own individual experiences to go by there was naturally no possibility of agreement, as is always the case when different things are described by the same word, when language and concepts do not coincide. Is it really the case that all "men" and all "women" are totally different from each other, and that all those on either side of the divide, men on the one hand, women on the other, are completely alike in a number of respects? This is assumed, of course most of the time unconsciously, in all discussions about sexual differences. Nowhere else in nature are there such glaring discontinuities. We find continuous transitions between metals and non-metals, chemical compounds and mixtures, and intermediate forms between animals and plants, phanerogams and cryptogams, mammals and birds. Initially it is only because of a very general practical need for an overview that we create divisions, set up boundaries by force, and distinguish separate arias within the infinite melody of all things natural. But "Sense becomes nonsense, good deeds a nuisance" is as true of the old intellectual concepts as it is of the inherited rules of social behavior. In view of the analogies cited we may be permitted to consider it unlikely that in nature a clean *cut* was made between masculinis on the one hand and femininis on the other, and that a living being can be simply described as residing on this side or that side of such a gulf. Even grammar is not that strict.

In the controversy about the Woman Question *the anatomist* has often been called upon to act as arbitrator and carry out the controversial demarcation between those qualities of the masculine and feminine cast of mind that are *unalterable* because they are *innate,* and those qualities that are acquired. (In any case it was a strange idea to make the answer to the question of the natural capability of man and woman dependent on the anatomist's findings: as though, if all other kinds of experience were *really* unable to establish any difference between them, an excess of a hundred and twenty grams of brain on one side could have disproved such a result.) However, sober anatomists, when asked for criteria that apply without exception, whether in respect of the brain or of any other organ of the body, will always answer that it is not possible to demonstrate *constantly recurring* sexual differences between *all* men on the one hand and *all* women on the other. Although, they will say, the skeleton of the hand in the majority of men is different from that in the majority of women, it is not possible to determine the sex of a person from (isolated) parts, either in skeletal form or preserved together with muscles, ligaments, tendons, skin, blood, and nerves. The same holds for the thorax, the sacrum, and the skull. And what about that part of the skeleton which, if anything, should show strong sexual differences, the pelvis? After all, the pelvis is generally believed to be adapted for the act of birth in one case and not in the other. But even the pelvis cannot serve as a certain criterion. As every man in the street knows—and anatomists know little more in this respect—there are enough "women" with a narrow masculine pelvis and enough "men" with a broad feminine pelvis. Are there no sexual differences then? Might it perhaps be wiser in the end not to distinguish between men and women at all?

How do we resolve this question? The old answers are insufficient, but we cannot do without them. Accordingly, where the traditional concepts do not suffice we shall abandon them, but only in order to seek new and better bearings.

I "Men" and "Women"

BY CLASSIFYING THE majority of living things in the most general terms and simply calling them male or female, man or woman, we can no longer do justice to the facts. The inadequacy of these terms is felt more or less clearly by many. The first objective of this study is to get matters straight in this respect.

Joining other authors who have recently written about phenomena related to this topic, I take as my starting point *the absence of sexual differentiation at the earliest embryonic stage* of humans, plants, and animals, as established by developmental history (embryology).

In a human embryo aged less than five weeks, for example, it is impossible to recognize the sex into which it will develop later. Not until the fifth fetal week do those processes begin which will, toward the end of the third month of pregnancy, develop the primitive genitalia, originally shared by both sexes, in one particular direction and in due course produce an individual that can be *sexually defined in precise terms.*[1] I will not describe these processes in detail here.

It is easy to see a connection between the *bisexual predisposition* of all organisms, including the highest, and the fact that *even in the most monosexually developed* individual plant, animal, or human the characteristics of the other sex *persist without exception* and never completely disappear. In other words, sexual differentiation is never complete. *All the characteristics of the male sex, however weakly developed, can somehow also be detected in the female sex; and equally all the sexual characteristics of a woman, however retarded, are somehow present in a man.* They are present in what is commonly called "rudimentary" form. For example, among humans, on whom we shall almost exclusively concentrate, even the most feminine woman has a delicate growth of unpigmented down called "lanugo" in the place where men have beards, and even the most masculine man has a complex of incompletely developed glands under his nipples. These things have been investigated in particular in the area of the sexual organs and their exits,

1. Naturally—as our need for continuity forces us to believe—sexual differences, albeit anatomically and morphologically invisible and unascertainable by the eye even with the utmost microscopic magnification, must *somehow* be "pre-formed," i.e., formed before the first phase of differentiation. But just how this happens is the greatest conundrum of the entire history of evolution.

the "urogenital tract" proper, where it has been possible to demonstrate in both sexes all the characteristics of the other, in a rudimentary form but in complete parallel.

These observations of embryologists, placed side by side with others, can be interrelated within a system. If we follow Häckel in calling the separation of the sexes *"gonochorism"* we shall first have to distinguish between different *degrees* of gonochorism among the different classes and species. The different species, not only of plants, but also of animals, will contrast with each other according to the *quantity of latent characteristics* of one sex in the other. In this broader sense the most extreme case of sexual differentiation, that is, the highest degree of gonochorism, is *sexual dimorphism.* This is a peculiarity, for instance, of some species of isopods in which the difference in external appearance between males and females is as great as, and sometimes even greater than, that between members of two different families or genuses. Thus gonochorism among vertebrates is never as highly developed as, for instance, among crustaceans or insects. In their case there is not such a complete separation between males and females as in sexual dimorphism, but rather countless sexual mixtures, including so-called "abnormal hermaphroditism"; and among fish there are even families with exclusive, or "normal hermaphroditism."

It must be assumed from the outset that there are not only extreme males with the smallest residues of femininity on the one hand, extreme females with totally reduced masculinity on the other hand, and a concentration of those hermaphroditic forms in the middle, with nothing but empty spaces between these three points. We are particularly concerned with humans. However, almost everything that can be said about them in this respect may also be applied, with greater or lesser modifications, to most other creatures that reproduce sexually.

In the case of humans the following is undoubtedly true:

Between Man and Woman there are ***innumerable gradations****, or "intermediate sexual forms." Just as physics talks about ideal gases*—i.e., those that precisely follow Boyle-Gay-Lussac's law (in reality none obeys it)—before proceeding to note divergences from this law in concrete cases, *we can also posit an ideal Man M and an ideal Woman W, neither of whom exists, as sexual types.* These types not only *can* but *must* be constructed. *The type, the Platonic idea, is not only the "object of art" but also that of science.* The science of physics explores the behavior of *completely* rigid and *completely* elastic bodies, in full awareness that reality will never supply it with either the one or the other for confirmation. The intermediate stages that are empirically established as existing between the two serve merely as a starting point in this search for typical forms of behavior and, on returning from theory to practice, are treated and exhaustively described as mixed forms. *And, equally, there are any number of intermediate stages between the complete Man and the complete Woman,* which may both be approximated but which are never experienced as such in reality.

It should be noted that I am not talking merely about a bisexual *predisposition* but about *permanent* bisexuality, nor merely about those stages *midway* between the sexes, the (physical or psychical) hermaphrodites, to whom all studies of this kind have been restricted until now for obvious reasons. In this form, then, my idea is entirely new. For until today the term "intermediate sexual stages" has been applied only to the *midway* stages between the sexes, as if, mathematically speaking, these constituted a particular *point of concentration and were something* ***more*** *than just one small stretch along a connecting line between two extremes which is* ***equally*** *densely occupied at every point.*

Man and Woman, then, are like two substances divided between the living individuals in different proportions, without the coefficient of one substance ever reaching zero. One could say that *in empirical experience there is neither Man nor Woman, but only male and female.* Thus one must no longer call an individual A or an individual B simply a "man" or a "woman," but each must be described in terms of the fractions it has of *both,* for instance:

$$A \begin{cases} \alpha M \\ \alpha' W \end{cases} \qquad B \begin{cases} \beta W \\ \beta' M \end{cases}$$

where always

$$0 < \alpha < 1, \quad 0 < \beta < 1,$$
$$0 < \alpha' < 1, \quad 0 < \beta' < 1.$$

This view—as suggested in the introduction in the most general terms—can be supported by innumerable precise pieces of evidence. One may remember all those "men" with a feminine pelvis and feminine breasts, missing or scant beards, a distinct waist, overlong hair, all those "women" with narrow hips[2] and flat breasts, thin nates and subcutaneous fat on their femurs, deep hoarse voices and a moustache (for which there is a much more abundant predisposition than is generally noticed because it is of course always removed: I am not speaking of beards, which so many women develop after menopause), etc., etc. All these things, *which typically are almost always found together in the same person,* are known to every clinician and every practical anatomist from his own experience, although so far they have not been collected anywhere.

The most comprehensive proof of the view being advocated here is provided by the wide range of variations in the figures referring to sexual differences that are found invariably both within individual studies and between various anthropological and anatomical surveys devoted to the measurement of the same.

2. A fairly safe and generally applicable physical criterion of the W content is not the absolute width of the pelvis measured as the distance in centimeters between the heads of the femurs or the spines of the ilium but the relative breadth of the hips in comparison to that of the shoulders.

In all these cases the figures given for the female sex never begin where those for the male end, but there is always a central area in which both men and women are represented. However much this uncertainty benefits the theory of intermediate sexual forms, it must be sincerely regretted in the interests of true science. So far professional anatomists and anthropologists have not attempted any scientific representation of the sexual types but have only ever wanted to establish equally valid general characteristics, which, time and again, they have been prevented from doing through the greater number of exceptions. This explains the vagueness and diversity of all measurements in this area.

Here, as elsewhere, the urge for statistics, which distinguishes our industrial era from all earlier ones and which—obviously because of its distant relationship with mathematics—leads this era to regard itself as being eminently scientific, has greatly inhibited the progress of knowledge. What was sought after was the *average*, not the *type*. It was not understood at all that in a system of pure (not applied) science the latter is the only thing that matters. That is why those concerned with types are completely let down by the information supplied by current morphology and physiology. To satisfy their needs all the measurements and other detailed investigations have yet to be carried out. What exists is entirely useless to science even in the looser (let alone Kantian) sense of the word.

Everything depends on knowing M and W, on correctly establishing the ideal Man and the ideal Woman (ideal in the sense of typical, without implying any evaluation).

Once it has been possible to recognize and construct these types their application to the individual case and its representation by quantifying the proportions in the mixture will be as easy as it will be fruitful.

I will sum up the contents of this chapter. There are no living beings that can bluntly be described as being unisexual and of one definite sex. Rather, reality fluctuates between two points at neither of which an empirical individual can be encountered, but *between* which every individual has its place *somewhere*. It is the task of science to determine the position of every single being between these two morphological blueprints. These blueprints must not be attributed any metaphysical existence beside or above the world of experience, but it is necessary to construct them for the heuristic purpose of representing reality as perfectly as possible. — —.

An inkling of this bisexuality of all living things (as a result of sexual differentiation which is never complete) is as old as time itself. It may not have been alien to Chinese myths and it was certainly very much alive in Greek antiquity. This is demonstrated by the personification of Hermaphroditos as a mythical figure; the story of Aristophanes in Plato's Symposium; and even in a late period the Gnostic sect of Ophites regarded the primeval human being as being simultaneously male and female, ἀρσενόθηλυς.

II Arrhenoplasm and Thelyplasm

THE FIRST THING expected from a work designed to be a universal revision of all the relevant facts would be a new and complete representation of the anatomical and physiological qualities of the sexual types. However, since I have not undertaken any of the independent investigations required for that comprehensive task, and do not in any case regard the answers to those questions as necessary for the *ultimate* objectives of this book, I must renounce that enterprise right at the outset—quite apart from the question whether such an enterprise would not far transcend the powers of one individual. Compiling the results set out in the existing literature would be superfluous, as this has been excellently done by Havelock Ellis. A derivation of the sexual types by means of probable inferences from the results collected by him would remain hypothetical and would not spare science one single new labor. The discussions in this chapter will therefore be of a more formal and general nature. They will be concerned with biological principles, although they are also intended to recommend the consideration of certain specific points in the course of the work that needs to be carried out in future, and thus to be beneficial to that work. The biological layman may skip this section without greatly impairing his understanding of the rest.

So far the theory of different degrees of masculinity and femininity has been developed in purely anatomical terms. However, anatomy will ask not only in what forms but also in what places masculinity and femininity express themselves. The examples, given earlier, of sexual differences in other parts of the body make it clear that sexuality is not restricted to the reproductive organs and gonads. But where can one draw the line? Is sex confined exclusively to the "primary" and "secondary" sexual characteristics? Or is its range much wider? In other words, where is sex situated and where is it not?

Many facts brought to light in recent decades now seem to force us to revive a theory which was first put forward in the 1840s but which acquired few adherents because, both to its founder and to its opponents, its consequences seemed to contradict a number of research results that the latter, albeit not the former, regarded as indisputable. The theory which, with some modification, experience once more compels us to face is that of the Copenhagen zoologist, J. J. S. Steenstrup, who maintained that *sex is present everywhere in the body.*

The results, excerpted by Ellis, of numerous examinations of almost all the tissues of the organism demonstrate the ubiquity of sexual differences. I note that the typically male complexion is very different from the typically female, which allows us to assume sexual differences in the cells of the cutis and the blood vessels. However, such differences have also been discovered in the quantity of hemoglobin and in the number of red blood corpuscles per cubic centimeter of blood fluid. Bischoff and Rüdinger have observed differences between the sexes in respect to the brain, and most recently Justus and Alice Gaule have also found such differences in the vegetative organs (liver, lungs, spleen). In fact *everything* about a woman, albeit more strongly in some zones and less in others, has an "*erogenous*" effect on a man, and similarly *everything* about a man has a sexually attractive and stimulating effect on a woman.

We may thus arrive at the following notion, which is hypothetical from the point of view of formal logic, but which is raised almost to the level of certainty by the sum total of the facts: *every cell of the organism* (as we will provisionally say) *has a sexual character, or a certain sexual emphasis.* According to our principle of the generality of intermediate sexual forms we hasten to add *that this sexual character can be of different degrees.* The prompt assumption of different degrees in the development of the sexual characteristics would make it easy for us to incorporate in our system pseudo-hermaphroditism and even genuine hermaphroditism (the occurrence of which among many animals, albeit not with certainty among humans, has been established beyond doubt since Steenstrup's time). Steenstrup said: "If the sex of an animal really only had its seat in the sexual organs one could imagine the presence of two sexes in one animal, of two such sexual organs side by side. But sex is not something that has its seat in any particular place or that manifests itself through any given organ; it pervades the whole being and is developed at every point of it. In a male every part, even the smallest, is male, however much it may resemble the corresponding part of a female, and in the latter, likewise, even the smallest part is exclusively female. Therefore the joint presence of both sexual organs would make a being bisexual only if the natures of both sexes were able to dominate the whole body and assert themselves at every point—something that, owing to the diametrical opposition of the sexes, could only result in the two sides canceling each other out and all sex disappearing in such a creature." If, however, as all empirical facts seem to dictate, *the principle of innumerable transitional forms of sexuality between M and W is extended to all cells of the organism* the difficulty that troubled Steenstrup is removed and bisexuality no longer runs counter to nature. Based on this principle it is possible to imagine *an infinite number of different sexual characteristics* ***of every single cell,*** from total masculinity through all intermediate forms down to its complete absence, which would coincide with total femininity. It would be wise to refrain from any assumptions as to whether this gradation in a scale of differentials should be conceived in the image of *two* *real* substances coming together in different proportions or of a *uniform* protoplasm in an infinity of modifications (e.g., a different spatial arrangement of the atoms in large molecules). The first assumption would be difficult to apply physiologically—if one thinks of a movement of a male or female body and the consequent need for duplication of the conditions determining its real manifestation, which ultimately is always physiologically uniform. The second assumption is too reminiscent of some less than successful speculations about heredity. Perhaps both are equally remote from the truth.

At present our empirical knowledge does not enable us to determine, even as a mere probability, what may actually constitute the masculinity or femininity of a cell, what histological or molecular-physical or indeed chemical differences may distinguish every cell of M from every cell of W. Without preempting any future investigation (which is most likely to recognize the impossibility of deriving specifically biological qualities from physics and chemistry) a good case can be made in defense of the assumption of *variously* strong sexual emphases in all the *individual cells* and not only in their sum total, the *whole* organism. Feminine men usually have an altogether more feminine skin, and in their case the cells of the male organs have a weaker tendency to divide, as suggested beyond doubt by the slighter development of their macroscopic sexual characteristics, etc.

The sexual characteristics must be classified in accordance with the varying degrees of their macroscopic development, and their arrangement, on the whole, coincides with the strength of their erogenous effect on the other sex (at least in the animal kingdom). To avoid any confusion I will follow John Hunter's commonly accepted nomenclature, applying the term *primordial sexual characteristic* to the male and female gonads (testis, epididymis, ovary, epoophoron) and *primary* to both the inner adnexes of the gonads (spermatic cord, seminal vesicle, tuba, uterus, whose sexual characteristics experience has sometimes shown to differ widely from those of the gonads) *and* the "external sexual organs," which alone are used to establish the sex of human beings at birth and which, to a certain extent, determine their destiny in later life (often incorrectly, as will be seen). What all the sexual characteristics that follow the primary ones have in common is that they are not directly required for the purposes of copulation. As for the first group of *secondary sexual characteristics* we can most clearly distinguish those that do not become externally visible until *the time of puberty* and which, according to a view that has almost reached the level of certainty, cannot develop without the "inner secretion" of certain substances from the gonads into the blood (growth of beards in men and hair in women, development of breasts, breaking of the voice, etc.).

The use of the term *tertiary sexual characteristics* is suggested, by *practical* rather than theoretical reasons, for certain innate qualities which can only be deduced from utterances or actions, such as muscular strength or independence of mind in men. Finally, as a result of relatively accidental customs, habits, or occupations, there are the accessory or *quaternary* sexual characteristics, such as smoking and drinking among men or needlework among women. These too do not fail to have an occasional erogenous effect, which already suggests, much more than is perhaps assumed, that they may be derived from the tertiary characteristics and sometimes even have a profound connection with the primordial ones. This classification of the sexual characteristics is not intended to prejudge an *essential* sequence or to decide whether mental qualities precede bodily qualities or conversely are determined by, and derived from, the latter in a long causal chain. It is likely, however, to correspond in the majority of cases to the strength of the attraction,[1] the temporal sequence in which the qualities in question strike the opposite sex and the degree of certainty with which they are recognized by the opposite sex.

In the context of the "secondary sexual characteristics" I referred to the inner secretion of material from the gonads into the blood. The effects of this secretion, or the artificially induced lack of it due to castration, have been studied mainly in connection with the development, or failure to develop, of the *secondary* sexual characteristics. However, "inner secretion" without doubt exerts an influence on *all* the cells of the body. This is proved by the changes that occur at the time of puberty in the *whole* organism and not only in those areas distinguished by secondary sexual characteristics. In fact, right from the start, it would be difficult to understand the inner secretion of all glands affecting all the tissues in any way other than *equally*.

It is, then, only the inner secretion of the gonads that completes the sexuality of the individual. Accordingly, we have to *assume in each cell an original sexual characteristic,* which must, however, be joined *to a certain extent* by the inner secretion of the gonads *as a complementary condition in order to produce a definite, finished male or female.*

The gonad is the organ in which the sexual characteristics of the individual appear most *visible* and in whose elementary morphological units they can most readily be demonstrated. However, we must also assume that the genus-specific, species-specific, and family-specific qualities of an organism are represented most completely in the gonads. While Steenstrup rightly taught that sex extends over the whole body and is not localized only in the specific "sexual organs," Naegeli, de Vries, Oskar Hertwig, et al. developed the extremely instructive theory, solidly based on weighty arguments, that every cell of a multicellular organism carries in it *all* the qualities of the ***species*** and that in the gonads these are only concentrated in a particularly marked form—as will perhaps appear

1. The various "fetishisms" must of course be ignored here; and the primordial characteristics are equally irrelevant to the erogenous effect.

obvious to all researchers one day, in view of the fact that every living being comes into existence through the cleavage and division of *one* single cell.

Based on many phenomena that have been multiplied since then by numerous experiences of regeneration from any given parts, and by observations of chemical differences in homologous tissue from different species, the researchers named above were entitled to assume the existence of *idioplasm* as the *totality* of the particular properties of the ***species***, even in all those cells of a metazoon that no longer directly serve the purpose of reproduction. Similarly *we* too can, and must, create the concepts of *arrhenoplasm* and *thelyplasm as the two modifications in which any idioplasm can appear in sexually differentiated beings,* bearing in mind that these concepts, according to the views advocated in this study as matters of principle, again stand for *ideal cases,* or boundaries, *between* which empirical reality resides. Thus the protoplasm which exists in reality increasingly departs from the ideal arrhenoplasm and, passing through a (real or imaginary) point of indifference (= true hermaphroditism), turns into a protoplasm which is closer to thelyplasm and from which it is finally only distinguished by a small differential. This is nothing more than a logical conclusion from the sum of what has already been said before, and I apologize for the new names: they have not been invented merely in order to increase the novelty of the matter.

The proof that every single organ and indeed *every single cell* possesses a sexuality located at some point between arrhenoplasm and thelyplasm, i.e., that, originally, every elementary part is sexually determined in a certain way and to a certain degree, can easily be supplied through the fact that even in the *same* organism the sexual characteristics of the different cells are not always identical and very often differ in strength. It is by no means the case that all the cells of a body show the same M or W content, i.e., the same approximation to arrhenoplasm or thelyplasm, and some cells of the same body may even be situated on different sides of the point of indifference between these poles. If, instead of always spelling out masculinity and femininity as such, we choose different algebraic signs for each and allocate, without any deeper and underhand ulterior motives at this stage, a plus to the male and a minus to the female, the proposition can be rephrased thus: the sexuality of the cells in the same organism may not only differ in absolute quantity but may also be positive or negative. There are some *otherwise* fairly distinctive males with quite weak beards and muscles, or almost typical females with small breasts, and, on the other hand, rather feminine men with strong beards and women who have abnormally short hair and a clearly visible beard but at the same time well developed breasts and a spacious pelvis. I also know people with a masculine thigh and feminine lower leg, or a feminine right hip and masculine left. In general local differences between sexual characteristics exist most frequently between the two sides of the body right and left of the median plane, which in any case are symmetrical in ideal circumstances only: here one finds an enormous number of asymmetrically developed sexual characteristics, e.g., in respect of beards. However, as I have already said, this lack of uniformity (and absolute uniformity never exists among sexual characteristics) can hardly be attributed to uneven inner secretion. The mixture, albeit not necessarily the amount, of the blood that reaches all organs must always be the same, that is, in non-pathological cases, of both the quality and the quantity needed for survival.

If these variations were not caused, as we must assume, by an original sexual characteristic which is fixed from the beginning of embryonic development and which is generally different in every single cell, it would be possible to describe the sexuality of an individual fully by simply indicating how closely, for example, his or her gonads approach the sexual type, and the situation would be a great deal simpler than it really is. However, sexuality is not, as it were, spread out over the whole individual in a fictitious standard measure, where the sexual definition of *one* cell also applies to all others. Although there will rarely be *wide* gaps between the sexual characteristics of the different cells or organs of the *same* living organism, the *general* rule must be the *specificity* of the sexual characteristics of every single cell. At the same time the fact remains that approximations to a complete uniformity of sexual characteristics (throughout the body) are found much more frequently than, apparently, substantial differences in degree between the individual organs, let alone the individual cells. In order to determine the maximum range of possible variations, a detailed investigation would be required.

According to a popular belief which dates back to Aristotle and which is also held by many doctors and zoologists, the *castration* of an animal regularly entails a sudden change in the direction of the opposite sex, and the emasculation of a male animal, for instance, *eo ipso* results in complete effemination. If this were so the presence in every cell of a primordial sexual characteristic independent of the gonads would again become doubtful. But the most recent experiments of Sellheim and Foges have shown that there is a type of castrate which is entirely different from the female, and that emasculation is not simply identical with effemination. However, in this respect also it will be wise to avoid too far-reaching and radical conclusions, and one must not rule out the possibility that, after the removal or atrophy of a first gonad, a second gonad of the opposite sex, which has been latent, will come to dominate an organism whose sexual characteristics fluctuate to a certain degree. The best known examples, even though they are perhaps generally interpreted too boldly (as the complete adoption of male characteristics), would be those numerous cases where, after the involution of the female sexual organs during menopause, a female organism begins to show external secondary characteristics of the male: the "beard" of human "grandmothers," the short bumps sometimes developing on the foreheads of old does, the "cock feathers" of old hens, etc. But such changes also seem to occur without any senile atrophies or the impact of external surgical interventions. They have been established beyond doubt as the *normal* development in some representatives of the genuses of cymothoa, anilocra, and nerocila among the cymothoidae, a family of parasitic isopods found on fish. These animals are hermaphrodites of a peculiar kind: in them the male and female gonads are permanently and simultaneously present, but they never function simultaneously. This is a kind of "protandry": each individual functions first as a male, later as a female. At the time of their male function they have entirely male sexual organs, which are discarded when the female exits and postvaginal lamellas have developed and opened. The fact that such things also exist among humans seems to be proved by those extremely peculiar cases of "eviratio" and "effeminatio" in mature male adults, reported by sexual psychopathology. Thus we shall be even less entitled to deny categorically that effemination can occur in reality if it is granted favorable conditions such as the extirpation of the male gonad.[2] However, the fact that the connection is not a general and necessary one, and that castration does not *with any certainty* turn an individual into a member of the opposite sex, is yet another proof of the general necessity of assuming that the whole body is made up of originally arrhenoplasmic and thelyplasmic cells.

The existence of original sexual characteristics in every cell and the powerlessness of the gonadic secretions when entirely thrown back on their own resources are further proved by the total failure of transplantations of male gonads to female animals. If these experiments were to serve as conclusive evidence it would be necessary to implant the extirpated testicles in the most closely related female, possibly a sister of the castrated male, so that *at least* the *idioplasm* was not too different. Here as elsewhere much would depend on isolating the decisive conditions for the success of the experiment in the purest form in order to obtain the most unambiguous results. Experiments at Chrobak's clinic in Vienna have shown that ovaries exchanged arbitrarily between two randomly selected female animals will atrophy in the majority of cases and will never be able to prevent the secondary characteristics (e.g., the mammary glands) withering away: alternatively, if the gonad is removed from its natural location and implanted in a different place in the *same* animal (which thus retains its own tissue), in ideal circumstances the *complete* development of the secondary sexual characteristics is *as* possible as it is where no operation at all takes place. The reason why transplantations to castrated members of the same sex fail is, perhaps, the lack of family relationship: it would be most important to pay attention to the idioplasmic aspect.

All this closely recalls the experiences gained from the *transfusion* of hetero-

2. Just as it is not possible categorically to *deny* masculinization in the opposite case of the castration of a female animal.

logous blood. It is a practical rule among surgeons that (in order to avoid the risk of serious complications) any replacement of blood lost must come not only from the same species and a related family but also from the same sex. The parallel with the experiments in transplantation is unmistakable. However, if the views advocated here are correct any surgeon who carries out transfusions, and does not prefer saline infusions, would not only have to ensure that the substitute blood is taken from a phylogenetically closely related animal, but it might also not be too much to demand that the degree of masculinity or femininity of any blood used should be as similar as possible.

Just as these conditions pertaining to transfusion supply proof of the sexual characteristics of blood corpuscles, the total failure of all transplantations, mentioned before, of male gonads to females or female gonads to males further proves that inner secretion *can only have an effect on an arrhenoplasm or thelyplasm adequate to it.*

In this context something should be said about organotherapeutic procedures. From the above it is clear that, and why, if the careful transplantation of relatively intact gonads to individuals of the other sex was unsuccessful, the injection of ovarial substance into the blood of a male, for example, could also do nothing but harm. On the other hand many objections to the *principle* of organotherapy are invalidated by the fact that organic preparations from *non*-members of the species, naturally, cannot always have a full effect by their very nature. In ignoring a biological principle of such importance as the theory of idioplasm the medical representatives of organotherapy may have forfeited many successful cures.

The theory of idioplasm, which attributes the particular characteristics of the species even to those tissues and cells that have lost their reproductive ability, is not yet generally recognized. But everybody must at least accept that the characteristics of the species are collected in the gonads and that, in the case of preparations from the gonads in particular, the shortest possible distance between relatives must be the prime requirement, if this method is meant to achieve more than just supplying a good tonic. It would perhaps be useful to carry out parallel experiments involving the transplantation of gonads and injections of their extracts: for instance, one could compare the effect on a rooster of a testicle, taken from himself or from a closely related individual and transplanted, for instance, to his peritoneal cavity, with that of intravenous injections of testicular extract into another castrated rooster, the extract again being taken from the testicles of related individuals. Such experiments might also provide instructive information as to the most appropriate quantities and methods of producing the organic preparations and individual injections. It would further be desirable from a *theoretical* point of view to establish whether the inner secretions of the gonads form a chemical compound with substances in the cell, or whether their effect is merely catalytic and essentially independent of their quantity. Given the investigations carried out so far, the latter assumption cannot yet be ruled out.

I had to outline the limits of the impact of inner secretion on the formation of the definitive sexual character in order to ward off any objections to the assumption that every cell contains original sexual characteristics that *generally* differ in degree and are determined from the outset.[3] Although in the overwhelming majority of cases such characteristics may not be particularly different in degree in the various cells and tissues of the same individual, there are some striking exceptions which reveal the possibility of great amplitudes. Thus the individual ova and spermatozoa, not only of different organisms, but also in the follicles and the sperm mass of the *same* individual, will show differences in the degree of their femininity and masculinity, both at the same time and even more at different times: for example, the sperms will be more or less slender, more or less fast. So far we know very little about these differences, but only because nobody has as yet examined these matters with the same intention as the present study.

Nevertheless—and this is the interesting thing—in the testicles of some amphibia actual, and well developed, *ova* were found side by side with the normal developmental stages of spermatogenesis, not only by one observer on a single occasion but by several on many different occasions. This interpretation was contested and there were those who admitted for certain only the existence of abnormally large cells in the sperm canal, but subsequently the above fact was established beyond doubt. Hermaphroditic forms are indeed extremely common among the amphibia in question, but this fact alone is sufficient proof of the necessity of *caution* in assuming the relative uniformity of arrhenoplasm or thelyplasm in *one and the same* body. It seems remote from the matter under discussion, and yet a similar kind of rash judgment, to describe and continue to regard a human individual as a "boy," just because he was born with a very short or indeed epispadic or hypospadic male organ, let alone with double cryptorchism, when other parts of his body, e.g., the brain, are much closer to thelyplasm than to arrhenoplasm. No doubt, we must try to learn how to diagnose more subtle shades of sexuality at birth.

As the result of these lengthy inductions and deductions we may now consider as firmly established that the original sexual characteristics must not be regarded as identical or even roughly identical in all the cells of the same body. Every cell, every complex of cells, every organ has a certain index that shows its position between arrhenoplasm and thelyplasm. In general, *one* index for the *whole* body will be sufficient to satisfy any moderate demands for exactitude. However, we would be committing disastrous theoretical errors and grievous

3. That such limits exist is also shown by the existence of sexual differences *before* puberty.

practical sins if we seriously thought that with such an incorrect description we had done everything possible for individual cases.

The occurrence of intermediate sexual forms is **determined** *by the different degrees of original sexual characteristics in conjunction with the inner secretions* (which probably *vary* in quality and quantity in each individual).

Arrhenoplasm and thelyplasm, in their infinite gradations, are the *microscopic agencies* which, jointly with "inner secretion," create those *macroscopic* differences which were the sole subject of the previous chapter.

Assuming that the explanations given so far are correct, there is a need for a whole series of anatomical, physiological, histological, and histo-chemical investigations into the differences between the *types M and W* in the structure and function of *all* individual organs, and into the way arrhenoplasm and thelyplasm are differentiated in the various tissues and organs. Our present knowledge of averages in these matters is hardly enough even for the modern statistician, and its scientific value is very small. One reason why all studies about sexual differences in the brain, for example, have been able to produce so little of value is that researchers did not examine the *typical* conditions, but were satisfied with what a certificate of baptism or the most superficial aspect of a dead body revealed about the sex of a person, and thus accepted every Jack or Jill as complete representatives of masculinity or femininity. If they did not believe that they needed any psychological data they should at least have ascertained some other facts in the make-up of the body which may determine masculinity or femininity, such as the distance between the great trochanters, the *spinae iliacae ant. sup.*, etc., etc. After all, harmony between the sexual characteristics of the various parts of the body is more common than great leaps of the same between different organs.

Incidentally, the same source of errors—the unthinking acceptance of intermediate sexual forms as individuals providing the norm—has been left open in other investigations, and this carelessness may slow down the discovery of tenable and provable results for a long time ahead. For instance those speculating about the causes of the *surplus of boys being born* should not entirely ignore these circumstances. However, those who dare to try to solve the *problem of the causes determining sex* without taking them into account will have to pay particularly dearly for their failure to do so. Until they examine the position between M and W of every living being that is born and becomes the object of their studies, their hypotheses or indeed their methods of experimental manipulation may be distrusted with good reason. For if they continue to classify the intermediate sexual forms being born as male or female in the same superficial way as before, they will be claiming *for* themselves some cases that testify *against* them if examined in greater depth, and regard other cases as counter-examples, which in fact they are not. Without the ideal Man and the ideal Woman they will lack a firm standard to apply to reality and stumble in uncertain superficial illusions.

For example the results achieved by Maupas, who succeeded in experimentally determining the sex of the rotifer hydatina senta, still contained 3–5 percent deviations. Although at lower temperatures he expected the birth of females, that percentage of births was male; and, equally, at high temperatures, counter to the rule, roughly the same percentage of females emerged. It must be assumed that these were intermediate sexual forms, very arrhenoplasmic females at a high temperature, very thelyplasmic males at a low. Where the problem is much more complicated, e.g., in the case of cattle, not to mention humans, the percentage of cases supporting the theory will hardly ever be as great as here, and the correct interpretation will therefore be much more heavily impaired by irregularities due to the intermediate sexual forms.

A comparative *pathology* of sexual *types,* just like their morphology, physiology, and developmental biology, for the time being, remains merely a desideratum. However, both in this area and in the others, we may draw some conclusions from statistics. If statistics demonstrate that a certain illness is found much more often in the "female sex" than in the "male" we may generally assume that this is an "idiopathic" affliction peculiar to thelyplasm. Thus myxoedema, for example, is probably an illness of W, while hydrocele is naturally an illness of M.

Nevertheless, even the most telling statistical figures cannot with any certainty prevent theoretical errors until an indissoluble functional connection is established between a particular illness and masculinity or femininity. The *theory* of the illnesses concerned will also have to explain *why* they "appear almost exclusively in one sex," that is (in the terminology developed here), they belong either to M or to W.

III | Laws of Sexual Attraction

Carmen:
"L'amour est un oiseau rebelle,
Que nul ne peut apprivoiser:
Et c'est bien en vain qu'on l'appelle
S'il lui convient de refuser.
Rien n'y fait; menace ou prière:
L'un parle, l'autre se tait;
Et c'est l'autre que je préfère;
Il n'a rien dit, mais il me plaît.
. . . .
L'amour est enfant de Bohême
Il n'a jamais connu de loi."

EXPRESSED IN THE old terms, among all sexually differentiated organisms there is an attraction between males and females, Man and Woman, the objective of which is copulation. However, since Man and Woman are only types, not found in a pure form in reality, we can no longer say that sexual attraction seeks to bring together an out-and-out male and an out-and-out female. Nevertheless, the theory being advocated here must take account of the sexual effects if it is to be complete, and the new methods must be able to represent the area in which they occur better than the old if they are to maintain their advantage over the latter. In fact the discovery that M and W are *distributed* among the organisms in all possible *different* proportions has led me to the discovery of an unknown *natural law,* which has been suspected only once by a philosopher, a *law of sexual attraction.* I gleaned this law from my observation of human beings and will therefore start with them here.

All human beings have their own specific "taste" as far as the opposite sex is concerned. If, for example, we compare the portraits of the women who are known to have been loved by any famous man in history, we almost always find that there is an almost constant likeness between all of them. In their external appearance this is most marked in their *build* (in the narrow sense of the *figure*) or in their *face,* but, on closer inspection, it extends to the smallest details—*ad unguem*—down to the fingernails. The same, however, also applies elsewhere. Thus every girl who strongly attracts a man immediately reminds him of all those girls who earlier had a similar effect on him. Further, everybody has numerous acquaintances whose taste in respect of the opposite sex has caused him to exclaim: "It's beyond me how anybody can fancy her." Darwin (in *The Descent of Man*) collected a great number of facts that make it impossible to doubt that among animals also each individual has its own specific taste. It will soon be shown that there are clear analogies to this fact of specific taste even among plants.

Almost without exception sexual attraction, like gravitation, is reciprocal. Where there seem to be exceptions to this rule it is almost always possible to demonstrate some more differentiated factors which prevent the pursuit of *immediate*—almost always reciprocal—liking, or which create a desire if that immediate first impression has not been present.

Common sayings, such as "the right person will come along" or "these two are completely unsuited to each other," also suggest a dim awareness of the *fact that in all human beings there are certain qualities that make it appear less than completely fortuitous* ***which*** *individual of the opposite sex is suited to sexual union with them; and that it is not possible for every "man" or "woman" to stand in for every other "man" or "woman" without it making a difference.*

Everybody also knows from personal experience that certain members of the opposite sex may downright *repel* him, others leave him cold, others again appeal to him, until finally (perhaps not always) one individual arrives who arouses in him such a desire for union that *in comparison* he may come to regard the whole world as worthless and non-existent. Which individual is this? What qualities must this individual possess? If—and this is so—every type of man really has as his correlate a corresponding type of woman who has a sexual effect on him, and vice versa, then, at least, a certain law seems to be at work here. What kind of law is that? How can it be formulated? "Opposites attract," I was told when, already in possession of my own answer, I stubbornly pressed various people to pronounce such a law, assisting their capacity for abstraction with examples. This is also acceptable in a certain sense and for a minority of cases. But it is too general, it runs through the fingers that try to grasp something concrete, and admits no mathematical formulation whatsoever.

This book does not presume to uncover *all* the laws of sexual attraction—for there are many—and thus by no means claims to be in a position at this stage to supply every individual with reliable information as to which individual of the opposite sex would best correspond to his taste, although a complete knowledge of the relevant laws would indeed make this possible. Only one of these laws will be discussed in this chapter, because it is organically related to the other discussions of the book. I am on the trail of a number of further laws, but this was the first that I became aware of, and what I have to say about it is, relatively speaking, most complete. The imperfections of the evidence may be forgiven in view of the novelty and difficulty of the subject matter.

However, in a certain sense it is, fortunately, unnecessary to list here either the facts from which I originally gleaned this law of sexual affinity, or the large number of people who have confirmed it to me. Everybody is requested to test it first on himself and then look around the circle of his acquaintances: in particular I would advise him to recollect and pay attention to those cases where he did not understand their taste or even denied that they had any "taste," or where the same was done to him by others. The minimal knowledge of the external forms of the human body that is needed for this scrutiny is at everyone's disposal.

It was in the same way, which I thought I had to point out here first, that I myself also arrived at the law that I will now formulate.

The law runs thus: "*It is always a* ***complete*** *Man (M) and a* ***complete*** *Woman (W) who strive to join in sexual union,* ***although they are distributed in different proportions between the two different individuals in every single case.***"

To put it differently: if in an individual μ, described according to common understanding simply as a man, m_μ is the male element and w_μ the female, and in a person ω, otherwise superficially described simply as a "woman," w_ω expresses the degree of the female element and m_ω the male, then in every case of *complete affinity,* i.e., of the *strongest* sexual attraction,

(Ia) $m_\mu + m_\omega = C(\text{onstant})_1$ = the ideal Man

and therefore, at the same time, naturally

(Ib) $w_\mu + w_\omega = C_2$ = the ideal Woman.

This formulation should not be misunderstood. It describes *one* case, *one single sexual* relationship, for which both formulae are valid, but where the second formula follows directly from the first, without adding anything new to it. For we are working on the assumption that all individuals have as much femininity as they lack masculinity. If they are *completely* male they will desire a *completely* female counterpart, and if they are completely female, a completely male. If, however, they contain a somewhat larger proportion of Man and another, by no means negligible, proportion of Woman, they will demand an individual who will complement them and their fragmentary masculinity to form one whole; *at the same time,* their proportion of femininity will be complemented in the same way. Let us assume, for instance, that an individual has

$$\mu \begin{cases} \tfrac{3}{4}\,\text{M}, \\ \text{therefore} \\ \tfrac{1}{4}\,\text{W}. \end{cases}$$

Then, according to our law, that individual's best sexual complement will be one that can be sexually defined as follows:

$$\mu \begin{cases} \tfrac{1}{4}\,\text{M}, \\ \text{therefore} \\ \tfrac{3}{4}\,\text{W}. \end{cases}$$

This formulation already shows the advantage of greater generality over the common view. That Man and Woman, as sexual types, attract each other is contained in it only as a *special case* in which an imaginary individual

$$X \begin{cases} 1.\ M \\ 0.\ W \end{cases}$$

is complemented by an equally imaginary

$$X \begin{cases} 0.\ M \\ 1.\ W. \end{cases}$$

Nobody will hesitate to admit the fact of a definite sexual taste. In so doing, however, the justification of asking about the *laws* of this taste, and about the functional relationship between sexual preference and the other physical and psychological qualities of an organism, is also recognized. The law established here has nothing obviously improbable about it, nor does it *conflict* in the slightest with ordinary or scientifically calibrated experience. But in itself it is certainly not "self-evident" either. It could *conceivably*—since the law itself cannot as yet be further deduced—also run thus: $m_\mu - m_\omega$ = Const., i.e., the *difference*, and not the sum, of the M content could be a constant quality and therefore even the most masculine man would be as far removed from his complement, which would then be located exactly in the middle between M and W, as the most feminine man from his, which would in this case have to be regarded as extreme femininity. It would, as I say, be *conceivable*, but this does not mean that it exists in reality. If, remembering that we are dealing with an empirical law, we follow the dictate of moderation, we shall not, for the time being, talk about a "force" pulling two individuals toward each other like puppets, but consider the law only as the expression of a relationship that can be detected in every instance of the strongest sexual attraction in the same *manner:* it can only reveal an "invariant" (Ostwald) or "multiponible" (Avenarius), which in this case is the always constant sum of the masculine and the feminine in the two organisms that attract each other most strongly.

Here the "aesthetic" or "beauty" element must be completely ignored. For how often does one man happen to be completely enraptured by a certain woman, and be beside himself over her "extraordinary," "enchanting" beauty, while another man "would like to know what he can see in her" because she is not also *his* sexual complement. Without assuming the position of some normative aesthetic or wishing to collect examples for a relativism of evaluations, one may say that a person in love will regard as beautiful something that from the purely aesthetic point of view is not merely *indifferent* but downright *ugly*, where "purely aesthetic" means not something absolutely beautiful but only *the beautiful*, i.e., that which is *aesthetically pleasing* once all the "sexual apperceptions" have been deducted.

I have found the law itself confirmed in several hundred cases (to cite the lowest figure), and all the exceptions merely apparent. Almost every courting couple one meets in the street supplies a new confirmation. The exceptions were instructive insofar as they strengthened the clues for the other laws of sexuality and invited further investigation. Incidentally, I myself have carried out a number of experiments by conducting a survey based on a collection of photos of aesthetically impeccable women, each of whom corresponded to a certain W content, that I presented to a number of acquaintances, whom I deceitfully asked to "choose the most beautiful." The answer I received was regularly the same as I had expected from the outset. Conversely, I had myself tested by others, who already knew what was at stake, by showing me pictures from which I had to choose those that they would find most beautiful. This I always succeeded in doing. To others again, who had not previously presented me with any random samples, I was able to describe their ideal of the opposite sex, occasionally almost completely and, at any rate often, with much greater accuracy than they themselves were able to specify. Sometimes they also became aware of what they *disliked*—which people generally know much better than what attracts them—only after I had told them.

I believe that the reader, with some practice, will soon acquire the same skill, which some acquaintances of mine chosen from a close scientific circle of friends, stimulated by the ideas advocated here, have already gained. Admittedly, it would also be very desirable to know the other laws of sexual attraction in this context. As a test of the proportions in a really complementary relationship many special constants could be identified. For instance, one could maliciously say that the total length of two lovers' hair is always equal. However, if only for the reasons discussed in the second chapter, this would not always be the case, since not all parts of the same organism are equally male or female. Moreover, such heuristic rules would soon multiply and then soon descend to the level of bad jokes, which is why I would rather refrain from putting them forward here.

I am not ignoring the fact that the way this law was introduced here was somewhat dogmatic, which becomes it even less well in the absence of exact proofs. However, here too I was less concerned to put forward finished results than to stimulate the search for such, since the means at my disposal for verifying those propositions according to a scientific method were extremely limited. If therefore many details remain hypothetical I nevertheless hope that I shall be able, in what follows, to prop up the individual beams of the building with one another by indicating some remarkable analogies that had not been noticed until now: even the principles of analytical mechanics may not be able to do without "retrospective reinforcement."

A most striking confirmation of my law is initially provided by a group of facts from the plant kingdom, which have so far been studied in complete isolation and which therefore seemed to be extremely strange. As any botanist will immediately have guessed, I mean the phenomenon of *heterostyly,* the presence of styles of unequal length, discovered by Persoon, first described by Darwin, and given its name by Hildebrand. This is as follows: Many dicotylous (and some monocotylous) species of plants, e.g., primulaceae and geraniaceae, but especially many rubiaceae, all of them plants in whose flowers both the pollen and the stigma are able to function albeit only in response to products of alien flowers, and which therefore appear androgynous from a morphological point of view, but dioecic from a physiological perspective—all these have the peculiarity of *developing their stigmas and anthers to different heights in different individuals.* One specimen develops exclusively flowers with a long style and therefore a high stigma and low anthers: this, in my opinion, is the more female one. The other specimen produces only flowers with a low stigma and high anthers (because of its long stamens): the more male one. Apart from these "dimorphous" species, however, there are also "trimorphous" ones, such as lythrum salicaria, with three different lengths of the sexual organs: among these, the flowers with long styles and those with short styles are joined by the "mesostylous" variant, i.e., one with styles of medium length. But although only dimorphous and trimorphous heterostyly has found its way into the compendia, it still does not exhaust all the variations. Darwin suggests that "if smaller differences are taken into account, *five* distinct positions of the male organs are to be distinguished." Here too, then, the discontinuity which undeniably exists, the separation of different degrees of masculinity and femininity on different storeys, is no *general* rule, and in this case too we are sometimes faced with *more continuous intermediate sexual forms.* On the other hand, these discrete categories also have some striking analogies in the animal kingdom, where the phenomena in question were regarded as equally isolated and miraculous because heterostyly was not even *thought of.* In many genera of insects, i.e., the forficulidae (earwigs) and lamellicorns (lucanus cervus, the stag beetle, dynastes hercules, and xylotrupes gideon) there are *on the one hand* many males in whom the antennae, the secondary sexual characteristic that separates them most visibly from the females, are very long, while the *other* main group of males has relatively short antennae. Bateson, who provided a fairly detailed description of these conditions, therefore distinguishes "high males" and "low males" among them. These two types are linked through continuous transitions, but the intermediate forms between them are rare, and most specimens are situated at one extreme or the other. Unfortunately Bateson was not interested in exploring the sexual relations of these two groups with the females, because he mentions these cases only as examples of discontinuous variation, and thus it is not known whether there are also two groups of females within the species in question that have different sexual affinities to the different forms of males. Therefore these observations can be used only as a morphological parallel to heterostyly, but not as physiological instances of the law of sexual attraction, *for which heterostyly can indeed be utilized.*

The heterostylous plants may actually hold a complete confirmation of the belief in the general validity of that formula for all living beings. Darwin demonstrated, and many other observers have also noted since, that in heterostylous plants fertilization hardly ever has any prospect of success, or indeed is impossible, unless the *pollen of a macrostylous flower,* i.e., from the lower anthers, is transferred to the *microstylous stigma* of another individual, which has long filaments, or unless *pollen* from the high anthers of a *microstylous flower* is transferred to the macrostylous stigma of another plant (with short filaments). Therefore in one flower the length of the style, i.e., the development of the female organ in the female direction, must equal the length of the male organ, i.e., the filament, in the other flower, which is to succeed in fertilizing it, and in the latter the style, whose length measures the degree of femininity, must be correspondingly shorter. Where there are three different lengths of style, fertilization, according to the same expanded rule, turns out best if pollen is transferred to a stigma of the same height in another flower as the anther from which the pollen derives. If this is not observed and, for example, artificial fertilization is carried out with inadequate pollen, the procedure, if at all successful, almost always results in sickly, stunted, dwarfish, and totally infertile offspring with an extreme resemblance to hybrids of different species.

All those authors who have discussed heterostyly are perceptibly dissatisfied with the customary explanation of this diversity of behavior in the process of fertilization. The customary explanation is that this remarkable effect is caused by the fact that insects visiting plants touch sexual organs positioned at the same height with the same part of their body. However, Darwin himself admits that bees carry all kinds of pollen at each point of their body, so that the *elective* procedure of the female organs in the course of pollination with two or three different kinds of pollen still remains unexplained. Moreover, that explanation, appealing and magical though it sounds, seems somewhat superficial if it is to make clear why artificial pollination with inadequate pollen, so-called "*illegitimate fertilization,*" is destined to have so little success. If this were so, such an exclusive contact with "legitimate" pollen would have made the stigmas receptive *through habit* for pollen of this one provenance alone. However, according to Darwin's own testimony, the absence of contact with other pollen is totally illusory, since the insects employed here as marriage brokers are in fact much more likely to favor *indiscriminate cross-breeding.*

It therefore seems a much more plausible hypothesis that the reason for this peculiar selective behavior is something different, deeper, and originally inherent in the flowers themselves. The point is that here, as among humans, sexual attraction is greatest between those individuals *of whom one possesses as large a quantity of M as the other does of W,* which is of course just another way of expressing the above formula. The probability of this interpretation is greatly increased by the fact that in the more masculine flower with the shorter style the pollen grains in the anthers, which are higher, are always larger, and the papillae of the stigma smaller than in the homologous parts of the more female ones with the long styles. This shows that we can hardly be dealing with anything other than different degrees of masculinity and femininity. And on this assumption the law of sexual affinity established here is brilliantly verified because in fact in the animal and plant kingdoms—we shall have to return to this later—fertilization is *always* most successful *where the parents had the greatest sexual affinity to each other.*[1]

That the law is entirely valid in the *animal kingdom* will only become highly probable when we come to discuss "sexual inversion." For the time being I would only like to note how interesting it would be to examine whether or not the larger and less mobile ova may attract the more nimble and slimmer spermatozoa more strongly than do the smaller, polylecithal and at the same time less inert ova, while the latter may not attract precisely the slower and more voluminous zoosperms. Perhaps a correlation will really come to light here between the rates of movement or kinetic energies of the two sexual cells, as L. Weill presumed in a short speculative piece about the factors determining sex. After all, so far it has not even been established—and it is very difficult indeed to establish—whether the two sexual cells would move toward each other with increasing or uniform speed if frictions and currents in the liquid medium were eliminated. These and many other questions could be asked here.

As already emphasized on several occasions, the law of sexual attraction in humans (and probably also in animals) discussed so far is not the only one. If it were, the fact that it was not discovered long since would seem quite incomprehensible.

Cases of *irresistible* sexual attraction are so *rare* precisely because so many factors contribute, because a number, possibly a substantial one, of other laws must be complied with.[2] As the relevant research is not yet complete I will not talk about those laws here and will only indicate, by way of illustration, one other factor that could play a part and that probably cannot be formulated easily in mathematical terms.

The particular phenomena to which I am alluding are rather well known.

1. For the special purposes of breeders, whose intention is usually to modify natural tendencies, this principle must often be abandoned.
2. Generally, when talking about a constant in the sexual taste of men or women, one thinks first of a preference for a favorite hair color in the opposite sex. It really seems that, where a particular hair color is at all preferred to all others (which is not the case with all people), the preference is rather deep seated.

When one is quite young, less than 20 years old, one is most attracted to older women (of over 35), while with advancing age one loves younger and younger women; on the other hand, quite young girls in their teens equally often (reciprocity!) prefer older men to younger ones, but later frequently commit adultery with quite young lads. The whole phenomenon may be more deeply rooted than it would seem, given the anecdotal way in which it is mostly reported.

Despite the unavoidable restriction of this study to the one law, in the interest of correctness, I will now attempt a better mathematical formulation, which does not feign an untrue simplicity. Even without introducing all the contributing factors and all the other laws that could play a part, we shall achieve this formal accuracy by adding a proportional factor.

The first formula was only an "economical" summary of the *uniform elements* of all cases of sexual attraction of *ideal* strength, insofar as the sexual relationship is at all determined by the law. Now I will write down a formula for the *strength of sexual affinity* in any conceivable case. Incidentally, this formula, because of its indefinite form, could *at the same time* provide *the most general description of the relationship between any two living beings, even of different species and of the same sex.*

If any two living beings are sexually defined as

$$X \begin{cases} \alpha\, M \\ \alpha'\, W \end{cases} \quad \text{and } Y \begin{cases} \beta\, W \\ \beta'\, M \end{cases}$$

where again

$$0 < \begin{matrix} \alpha \\ \beta \\ \\ \alpha' \\ \beta' \end{matrix} < 1$$

then the strength of attraction between them is

$$A = \frac{k}{\alpha - \beta}\,.f(t) \quad \ldots\ldots\ldots\ldots (II)$$

where f (t) stands for any empirical or analytical function of the time the individuals are able to act upon each other, that is, the "*reaction time*," as we might call it; while k is that proportional factor—to be specially established in each case—in which we accommodate all the known and unknown laws of sexual affinity, which, in addition, depends on the degree of species, race, and family relationship as well as on the health and the absence of deformities in the two individuals, and which, finally, decreases with increasing distance in space.

If in this formula $\alpha = \beta$, then $A = \infty$. This is the most extreme case: it is sexual attraction as an elementary force, as presented with uncanny mastery in Lynkeus's story "In the Post Chaise." Sexual attraction is something that follows a natural law, just as roots grow toward the center of the earth and bacteria migrate toward the oxygen at the edge of the specimen slide. Admittedly one must first get used to such a view of the matter. I will return to this point presently.

When $\alpha-\beta$ reaches its maximum value

$$\lim (\alpha-\beta) = \text{Max.} = 1$$

then $\lim A = k.f(t)$. Thus, as a specific *borderline case,* the result is all the sympathetic and antipathetic relationships between human beings (which, however, have nothing to do with the *social* relationships that constitute society's legal system) insofar as they are not regulated by *our* law of sexual affinity. Since k increases with the strength of family relationships in general, A has a greater value, for example, among members of one nation than among those of different nations. The reasonableness of f(t) can readily be observed where two domestic animals of different species live together: their first impulse is often bitter enmity or mutual fear (with A becoming a negative value), later frequently replaced by a friendly relationship, in which they seek each other out.

If I further posit

$$A = \frac{k.f(t)}{\alpha-\beta} \quad \ldots\ldots. \quad k = 0$$

then $A = 0$, i.e., between two individuals of too different origins no noticeable attraction will take place at all.

Since the penal codes are unlikely to contain the sodomy law for nothing, and sexual acts have been observed even between a human and a hen, it can be seen that k is larger than zero within very *wide* limits. Therefore we must not restrict the two individuals in question to the same species, or even the same class.

That all encounters of male and female organisms are ruled by certain laws, rather than being a matter of chance, is a new view, and its strangeness—which was touched upon earlier—forces us to discuss the profound question of the mysterious nature of sexual attraction.

The well-known experiments of Wilhelm Pfeffer have shown that the spermatozoids of various cryptogams are attracted not only by the female archegoniae under natural conditions but also by some substances that are either excreted by these in customary conditions, or are artificially produced, and often even by substances that do not occur in nature and would therefore never have the opportunity to come into contact with the spermatozoids, unless mediated by the specific experimental conditions. Thus the spermatozoids of ferns are attracted not only by the malic acid secreted from the archegoniae, but also by synthetically produced malic acid, and even by malonic acid, while those of funaria are attracted by cane sugar. The spermatozoon affected, we do not know how, by differences in the concentration of the solution moves toward the higher concentration. Pfeffer called these movements *chemotactic* and coined the term *chemotropism* for all these phenomena, as well as for other cases of asexually stimulated tropical movements. There seem to be many indications that among animals the attraction exercised by the female when perceived by the male from a distance through the sense organs (and vice versa) is in some respects analogous to chemotactical attraction.

Chemotropism is most probably the cause of that energetic and persistent movement also undertaken by the sperms of mammals, independently, without any external support, for whole days *in opposition* to the direction of the cilia of the uterus's mucous membrane, which oscillate from the interior toward the exterior, from the body toward the neck of the womb. With incredible, almost mysterious, assurance, despite all mechanical and other obstacles, the spermatozoon is able to find the ovum. Most peculiar in this respect are the enormous migrations of many fish: salmon migrate without any nourishment for many months from the sea upstream against the waves of the Rhine in order to spawn in a safe place with copious stocks of food near its source.

On the other hand it is worth recalling P. Falkenberg's pretty description of the fertilization process among some low algae of the Mediterranean. Just as we talk about lines of force pulling two magnetic poles with different denominations toward each other, here too we are faced with a natural force that drives the spermatozoon toward the ovum with irresistible power. The main difference will be that the movements of *inorganic* matter require shifts in the conditions of stress in the *surrounding* media, while the forces of *living* matter are localized in the organisms themselves as veritable *power centers.* According to Falkenberg's observations the spermatozoa in their movement toward the ovum overcame even that force which would otherwise have led them toward the incoming light. Thus the ***chemo**tactical effect, called sexual urge,* is stronger than the ***photo**tactical.*

If two individuals who, according to our formulae, are badly matched form an association and the real complement of one subsequently appears, the inclination to leave the earlier makeshift arrangement will follow immediately with the inevitability of a natural law. *Adultery takes place,* as an elemental event, a natural phenomenon, just as when $FeSO_4$ is brought together with 2 K OH, and the SO_4 ions at once abandon the Fe ions in order to cross over to the K ions. Whoever tried to approve or disapprove in moral terms when such a leveling out of potential differences is about to take place in *nature* would appear to many to be playing a ridiculous part.

This is, of course, also the fundamental idea of Goethe's *Elective Affinities,* developed in the fourth chapter of the first part as a playful prelude full of unsuspected future significance by those who will later learn its profound fateful truth through their own experience. I am proud of being the first to return to this idea in the present study. In so doing, however, I wish as little as Goethe to defend adultery, but rather to make it understandable. In *human beings* there are motivations that can successfully counteract adultery and prevent it. This will be discussed in the second part. One sign that in human beings even the low sexual sphere is not as strictly governed by natural laws as in other organisms is that human beings are sexually active in *all* seasons and that in them the remnant of a special rutting season in the spring is much less pronounced than in domestic animals.

The law of sexual affinity further shows, albeit alongside radical differences, analogies to a well-known law of theoretical chemistry. Our law is analogous to the "law of mass impact" insofar as, for example, a stronger acid primarily unites with a stronger base just as the more male being does with the more female. Nevertheless we have here more than one new quality as compared to inorganic matter. Above all, a living organism is no homogeneous and isotropic substance capable of being split into any number of qualitatively equal parts: the "principium individuationis," the fact that whatever lives lives as an individual, *is identical with the fact of structure.* Therefore in the latter case it is not possible, as it is in the former, for a larger part to enter into one association and a smaller part into another, thus generating a by-product. Further, chemo*tropism* can also be *negative.* Beyond a certain size of the difference $\alpha-\beta$ in formula II we obtain a negative attraction, i.e., one in the opposite direction, and *we are faced with sexual repulsion.* It is true that in inorganic chemistry, too, the *same* reaction may occur at *different speeds.* However, at least according to the latest views, if a reaction is totally absent (or, in our case, present in the form of its opposite) it can never be induced, for example by means of a catalyst, whether over a longer or a shorter period of time. On the other hand it is possible to create a compound that forms at a certain temperature and decomposes at a higher temperature, and vice versa. In the latter case the *direction* of the reaction is a function of the temperature, in the former frequently one of time.

The last analogy of sexual attraction to chemical processes probably rests in the significance of the t factor, the "reaction time," if such comparisons are not rejected out of hand right from the outset. Here too one could think of a formula for the *speed of the reaction,* the different degrees of speed at which the sexual reaction develops between two individuals, and perhaps actually try to differentiate A according to t. However, nobody should allow pride in "mathematical pomp" (Kant) to lead him to tackle such complicated and difficult circumstances, such functions of very doubtful constancy, with a differential quotient. The point will be taken in any case: like a chemical process which takes a very long time to become noticeable, sensual desire can develop between two individuals who are together or, preferably, *locked up together,* for a lengthy period, even where it did not exist beforehand or where there was actually repulsion. This is probably one reason for the comfort commonly given to those marrying without love: that would come "later"; it would happen *"in the course of time."*

It is clear that no great store should be set by the analogy with affinity in inorganic chemical processes, although I thought it *enlightening* to engage in such reflections. Even the question whether sexual attraction should be subsumed under tropisms is as yet undecided, and even if this were *certain for sexuality* it still would not *implicitly* decide anything with regard to *erotic* matters. The phenomenon of love needs further treatment, which the second part of my book is intended to provide. Nevertheless, there are some undeniable analogies between those chemotropisms and the forms in which the most passionate attraction occurs even between humans: note the account of the relationship between Eduard and Ottilie in the *Elective Affinities.*

At the first mention of this novel the problem of marriage was already briefly dealt with, and some practical applications deriving from the theoretical discussions of this chapter will initially also be related to the problem of marriage. The one law of sexual attraction which I have established, and to which the others seem to be very similar in structure, teaches that there are innumerable intermediate sexual forms and that as a result there will always be *two* beings that are *best* suited to each other. *In this respect,* then, marriage is justified, and "free love," from this biological point of view, should be rejected. However, the question of monogamy becomes extremely complicated, and finding a solution less simple, owing to other circumstances, such as the periodicities that I will mention later and the changes of taste with advancing age that I discussed earlier.

A second conclusion follows if we remember heterostyly, and in particular the fact that "illegitimate fertilization" almost always produces germs incapable of development. This already suggests that the strongest and healthiest offspring of other organisms will issue from unions in which there is a high degree of reciprocal sexual attraction. Accordingly, people have long spoken of "love children" in a special way, believing that these will turn out more beautiful, better, more magnificent people. That is why, for the sake of hygiene alone, even those who do not feel that they have a special vocation for the breeding of humans will disapprove of marrying merely for money, which may be very different from marrying for purely rational reasons.

I would like to mention in passing that observing the laws of sexual attraction could also have a considerable influence on animal husbandry. From the outset more attention than before will be paid to the secondary sexual characteristics and the degree of their development in the two individuals that are to be mated. The artificial procedures undertaken to have females served by male breeding animals even when the latter do not much like the former may not entirely miss their purpose in individual cases, but as a general rule always have some bad consequences. These procedures, for example, are surely the ultimate cause of the tremendous nervousness of young stallions, sired on the wrong mares, that need feeding with bromide and other medicines, like any modern young man. Similarly, the physical degeneration of modern Jewry may not least be caused by the fact that among Jews, much more often than anywhere else in the world, marriages are made by marriage brokers and not by love.

In his works, which are as fundamental in this respect as in others, Darwin established through very extensive experiments and observations something that has since been generally confirmed, i.e., that both very closely related individuals and individuals of overly unequal species characteristics have less sexual attraction for each other than certain "insignificantly different" individuals. If fertilization does take place regardless, the germ either dies in the preliminary stages of development or turns out to be sickly and usually incapable of reproduction, just as in heterostylous plants "*legitimate* fertilization" produces *more* and *better* seeds than any other combination.

Thus those germs whose parents have shown the greatest sexual affinity will always thrive best.

From this rule, which can probably be regarded as generally valid, follows the correctness of the conclusion drawn from what has gone before: if there must be marriage and if children must be produced, at least they should not result from an effort to overcome sexual repulsion, which could not happen without sinning against the child's physical and mental constitution. Certainly a high proportion of sterile marriages are marriages without love. The old experience that mutual sexual arousal during intercourse is supposed to enhance the prospects of conception is probably connected with this and will be more easily understood as a consequence of the greater intensity, from the outset, of the sexual urge between two individuals who complement each other.

IV | Homosexuality and Pederasty

The law of sexual attraction, which has just been discussed, also contains the—long sought—theory of sexual inversion, i.e., sexual inclination toward one's own (and not, or not only, to the opposite) sex. Apart from one distinction, which will be made later, it can boldly be claimed that every sexual invert also exhibits the anatomical characteristics of the opposite sex. There is no such thing as purely "psychosexual hermaphroditism." Men who feel sexually attracted to men are partly feminine in their external appearance and behavior and women who have a sensual desire for other women show partly masculine physical characteristics. On the assumption of a strict parallelism between physical and psychic properties this view is *self-evident*, but in order to demonstrate it in detail attention must be paid to the fact, which I mentioned in the second chapter, that not all parts of the *same* organism are situated in the same position between M and W but different organs may be male or female in different degrees. *Thus a sexual invert always shows an anatomical approximation to the opposite sex.*

This alone would suffice to refute the opinion of those who regard sexual inversion as a property acquired by the individuals concerned in the course of their lives and covering normal sexual feeling. That such a property is acquired through external stimuli in an individual's life is believed by respected scientists such as Schrenck-Notzing, Kräpelin, and Féré, who regard abstaining from "normal" intercourse and, particularly, "seduction" as such causes. But where does that leave the first seducer? Was he taught by the god Hermaphroditos? To me this whole idea has always seemed no different from thinking of the "normal" inclination of typical men toward typical women as something artificially acquired, and from claiming, even more absurdly, that this attraction was invariably the result of instruction by older companions who had discovered the pleasure of sexual intercourse *by chance.* Just as a "normal person" discovers by himself "what a woman is," in the "sexual invert" too the sexual attraction exercised on him by persons of the same sex probably appear of their own accord through the mediation of those ontogenetic processes that continue after birth and throughout life. Naturally an *opportunity* must arise if the desire for homosexual acts is to emerge, *but the opportunity can only actualize* what, to a larger or smaller degree, has long been present in the individuals and has only been waiting to be released. *What the acquisition theorists would have to explain is the fact that in the event of sexual abstinence* (to bear in mind the second alleged cause of sexual inversion) *it is possible to resort to something other than masturbation;* however, for *homosexual* acts to be aimed for and carried out, a natural predisposition must already exist. After all, heterosexual attraction could also be called "acquired" if it was felt to be necessary, for example, to spell out that a heterosexual man must have seen a woman, or at least a picture of a woman, in order to fall in love with her. But those who treat sexual inversion as an acquired property seem to be reflecting on nothing but that one notion, excluding the entire predisposition of an individual, which alone can provide a framework for a specific cause to have its specific effect: they seem to make an external event of minor importance, a final "complementary condition" or "partial cause," the sole factor producing the entire result.

Sexual inversion is no more *inherited* from parents or grandparents than it is acquired. Admittedly nobody seems to have made that precise claim—which would be contradicted at first sight by all experience—but it has been suggested that the precondition of sexual inversion is a thoroughly neuropathic constitution, a general hereditary deficiency, which expresses itself in the offspring, among other things, through an inversion of the sexual instincts. The whole phenomenon was allocated to the realm of psychopathology. It was considered a symptom of degeneration and those afflicted by it as sick people. Although this view now has fewer adherents than it did some years ago, before its former main advocate Krafft-Ebing himself tacitly dropped it in the later editions of his *Psychopathia sexualis,* it is still worth remarking that sexually inverted people can otherwise be perfectly healthy and, apart from accessorial social factors, do not feel worse than all the other healthy people. If one asks them whether they have any wish to be different in this respect, one quite often receives a negative answer.

All these attempts to explain homosexuality were misguided because the phenomenon was entirely isolated and no attempt made to connect it with other facts. Those who regard "sexual inversions" as something pathological or as a ghastly and monstrous anomaly in mental development (the latter being the view sanctioned by philistines), or indeed as a vice acquired by habit or the result of a monstrous seduction, should stop to think *that there is an infinity of transitions from the most masculine male, through the feminine man and finally the male sexual invert, to* hermaphroditismus spurius *and* genuinus, *and from there, through the tribade and the virago, to the female virgin. According to the view advocated here, sexual inverts* ("of either sex") *must be defined as individuals in whose case the fraction* α *fluctuates around 0.5,* that is, does not widely differ from α' (cf. p. 11), and who therefore have in them roughly the same quantity of the male element as of the female, and indeed often more of the female even when they are considered men, and perhaps more of the male even when they are considered women. Since the sexual characteristics are not always distributed uniformly across the whole body, it is certain that some individuals are often enough allocated, without further thought, to the male sex simply on the basis of a male primary sexual characteristic, even if the *descensus testiculorum* appears late, epispadia or hypospadia is present, or azoospermia occurs at a later stage, or even if (in females) *atresia vaginae* is observed. Therefore such individuals are educated as males and recruited for military service, etc., *even if in their case* $\alpha < 0.5$ and $\alpha' > 0.5$. Accordingly, their sexual complement will apparently be located on that side of the divide which belongs to the primary characteristic, where, however, they merely *seem* to be, while in reality they are already on the other side.

Incidentally—and this not only supports my theory but is actually explained by it—there is no sexual invert who is *just* an invert. From the outset all are *bisexual,* that is, capable of sexual intercourse with both men and women. It is possible that they later actively promote their own unidirectional development toward one sex, pushing themselves toward unisexuality, and finally causing heterosexuality or homosexuality to prevail in them, or allowing themselves to be influenced by external causes to move in one of those directions. However, this can never extinguish their bisexuality, which continues to reveal its temporarily suppressed existence again and again.

A connection between homosexual phenomena and the bisexual predisposition of every embryo in the animal or plant kingdom has been recognized repeatedly and, in recent times, with increasing frequency. The novelty of *my* account is that, unlike those investigations, it does not see homosexuality as a regression or an incomplete development, i.e., a defect in sexual differentiation, and that it no longer regards homosexuality at all as an anomaly that stands in isolation, intruding into the otherwise complete separation of the sexes as a remnant of an earlier undifferentiated condition. Rather, it includes homosexuality as the sexuality of intermediate sexual forms within the continuity of intermediate sexual forms, *which it regards as the only forms occurring in reality, while the extremes are only ideal cases.* According to this theory, just as all organisms are also *heterosexual* they are *all also homosexual.*

Corresponding to the *more* or *less* rudimentary development of the *opposite* sex, the predisposition for homosexuality is still present, however faintly, in every human being. This is particularly clearly proved by the fact that at the age *before* puberty, when a relative lack of differentiation still prevails and the inner secretion of the gonads has not yet finally determined the degree of unidirectional sexual development, those rapturous "juvenile friendships" that are never entirely devoid of a sensual aspect are the rule among both the male and the female sex.

People *beyond* that age who go into extreme raptures over "friendship" with their own sex carry a strong element of the opposite sex in them. However, a much more advanced intermediate form is represented by those who enthuse about companionship between the "two sexes," who, without having to keep guard over their own feelings, are able to have comradely relations with, and become confidants of, the opposite sex, which is, after all, their own, and who try to impose such a "pure" and "ideal" relationship on others who find it less easy to remain pure.

Nor is there such a thing as a friendship between men that completely lacks an element of sexuality, although, far from representing the essence of friendship, the very thought of sex is *embarrassing* to friends and *opposed* to the *idea* of friendship. That this is correct is sufficiently proved by the mere fact that there can be no friendship between men if their external appearance has not aroused any sympathy at all between them and they will therefore never come closer to each other. A great deal of "popularity," protection, and nepotism among men derives from such relationships, which are often unconsciously sexual in nature.

A phenomenon analogous to juvenile sexual friendship is perhaps the reappearance in older men of latent amphisexuality alongside the senile atrophy of the sexual characteristics that developed unidirectionally in their prime. This may be the reason why so many men aged 50 and upward are prosecuted for committing "indecent acts."

Finally, a large number of homosexual acts have also been observed among animals. F. Karsch has made a commendable (albeit incomplete) compilation of cases from the literature. Unfortunately the observers hardly ever report anything about the degrees of "masculinity" or "femininity" in these animals. Nevertheless, there can be no doubt that here we also have a proof of the validity of our law for the *animal kingdom.* If bulls are locked up and not allowed near a cow for a lengthy period, acts of sexual inversion can be observed between them after a while: some, the more feminine ones, take to this sooner, others later and some, perhaps, not at all. (The large number of intermediate sexual forms has already been established for cattle in particular.) This proves that they have the predisposition, except that previously they were able to satisfy their need in a better way. The behavior of captive bulls is no different from that of human beings in prisons, boarding schools, and monasteries. Among animals too there are intermediate sexual forms, and the fact that they know not only onanism (which occurs among them as it does among humans) but also homosexuality seems to me one of the strongest confirmations of the law of sexual attraction formulated above.

Thus, for this theory, sexual inversion is not an exception from the natural law, but only a special case of the same. According to this same law, an individual who is half Man and half Woman desires another individual with roughly the same proportions of both sexes. This is the reason for the phenomenon, which of course also demands an explanation, whereby sexual "inverts" almost always practice their kind of sexuality solely *among themselves* and—sexual attraction being reciprocal—those who do not seek the same form of satisfaction are rarely found in their circles; and *this* is also the powerful factor that always causes homosexuals to recognize each other instantly. However, this is also why "normal" people generally have no idea of the enormous incidence of homosexuality and even the worst "sexually normal" lecher believes himself fully entitled to condemn "such monstrosities." As late as 1900 a professor of psychiatry in a German university seriously recommended that homosexuals should simply be castrated.

The therapeutic method used today to combat sexual inversion (if it is attempted at all) is less radical than that advice, but its practical application reveals the total inadequacy of many theoretical ideas about the nature of homosexuality. Today the people concerned are treated—mainly by the acquisition theorists, as one would expect—with hypnotism: attempts are made, through hypnotic suggestion, to introduce and accustom them to the idea of Woman and "normal" active sexual intercourse with her. As the practitioners admit, the success is minimal.

From our point of view this is obvious. The hypnotist presents his subject with the *typical* picture of Woman, that is, with something abhorrent to his entire innate nature, and especially to the unconscious part of it, which is not easily accessible to hypnotic suggestion. His complement is not W, and the doctor must not send him to the first available prostitute, who will let him have his way with her merely for the money, as the crowning achievement of the treatment, which will generally have made his abhorrence of "normal" sexual intercourse even greater. Rather, if we ask our formula about the complement of the sexual invert, the reply will be: the most masculine woman, the lesbian, the tribade. *She, in fact, is almost the only woman who attracts the sexual invert, and the only woman who is attracted to him.* If there must be a "cure" for sexual inversion, and if we cannot do without developing one, this theory recommends that one sexual invert should be guided to another sexual invert, the homosexual to the tribade. However, the purpose of this recommendation can only be to make it as easy as possible for *both* to obey the laws banning homosexual acts still in existence (in England, Germany, Austria), which are ludicrous, and to the abolition of which these lines are also intended to make a contribution. The second part of this book will explain *why* the active prostitution of one man through a sexual act carried out with him, and the passive participation of another man in such an act, is felt to be so much greater a disgrace, while sexual intercourse between a man and a woman seems to degrade both less. *In ethical terms, however, there is no difference whatsoever between the two acts in themselves.* Despite all the popular drivel of today about the different rights of different personalities there is only one universal ethic, which is the same for all human beings, just as there is only one logic and not several logics. It is utterly reprehensible and, moreover, entirely *incompatible* with the principles of the penal code, which punishes crime but not sin, to forbid homosexuals to pursue their way of sexual intercourse while allowing heterosexuals to pursue theirs, if both do so equally without creating a "public nuisance." The only *logical* thing (totally disregarding, in these reflections, the perspective of pure humanity and a penal code that is more than a "deterrent" purposive system of social education) would be to let "inverts" find their satisfaction where they seek it: among each other.

This theory seems to be entirely without contradictions and complete within itself, providing a wholly satisfactory explanation for all the phenomena. But now I must face up to some facts with which it will certainly be countered and which really seem to invalidate the subsumption of this sexual "perversion" within the intermediate sexual forms and the law of their sexual relations. While the above explanation may perhaps suffice for inverted women, there are certainly and beyond doubt men who are hardly feminine and on whom nevertheless persons of their own sex have a very strong effect. Indeed this effect may be stronger than that made on men who are much more feminine than they; it may also emanate from masculine men; and, finally, it may often be stronger than the impression that any woman is able to make on those men. Albert Moll is right in saying: "There are psychosexual hermaphrodites who feel attracted to both sexes, but who love in each sex only the typical qualities of that sex, and on the other hand there are psychosexual [?] hermaphrodites who do not love in either sex the typical properties of that sex, but regard those properties with indifference and partly even with revulsion." It is to this difference that the *distinction between homosexuality and pederasty* in the title of this chapter refers. The distinction can be justified as follows: a homosexual is that type of "pervert" who, according to the law that has been discussed, prefers very theloid men *and* very arrhenoid women; *the pederast, on the other hand, can love very masculine men and, equally, very feminine women,* the latter ***insofar*** *as he is* ***not*** *a pederast. Nevertheless, his inclination toward the male sex will be stronger and deeper than that toward the female.* The question about the cause of pederasty is a problem in its own right and will remain completely unresolved in this study.

V | Characterology and Morphology

GIVEN A CERTAIN correspondence between physical and psychic phenomena, the wide range of the principle of intermediate sexual forms, as demonstrated in the morphological and physiological context, may from the outset be expected to yield at least a similarly rich psychological harvest. There is certainly also a psychic type of Woman and of Man (at any rate the results obtained so far make it our task to search for such types), even though they are never reached by reality, which is as replete with successive intermediate forms in the mental domain as it is in the physical. My principle therefore has every prospect of proving itself also in relation to *mental* properties and of throwing some light into the confused darkness that still hides from science the psychological differences *between human individuals.* For in the process a step forward has also been taken toward a differentiated understanding of the mental disposition of every human being, and in scientific terms also we shall no longer speak of the *character* of a person as if it were *simply male* or *simply female.* Instead, we shall observe and ask *how much Man and how much Woman* there is in a person. Was it *he* or *she* in the individual concerned who did, said, or thought this or that? This will facilitate an *individualizing* description of all human beings and all human issues, and bring the new method into line with the development of all scientific research, as explained at the beginning of this study: from time immemorial all human knowledge, setting out from intermediate generalizations, has diverged in two directions, i.e., not only toward the most general aspect common to all single entities, but also toward the most singular, most individual phenomena. Therefore there is every reason to hope that the principle of intermediate sexual forms will provide the strongest support for the, as yet, unfulfilled scientific task of a characterology, and there is every justification for trying to raise it, as a method, to the rank of a *heuristic principle* in the "psychology of individual differences" or "differential psychology." And the application of the principle to the field of characterology, which has so far almost exclusively been ploughed by literary figures and rather neglected by scientists, is perhaps to be welcomed all the more warmly because it can immediately accommodate all the quantitative gradations, so that nobody, so to speak, will any longer be permitted to back away from seeking the percentage of M and W that an individual also possesses in the psychic domain. Bearing in mind my explanations in the second chapter concerning the differences in *degree* between the masculinity and femininity even of the single *physical* parts and properties of the same individual, it seems clear that this task is not fulfilled through an *anatomical* answer to the question of the sexual location of an individual between Man and Woman, but *in general* demands further special study, even if this were to bring to light a much greater frequency of similarities than dissimilarities in the *particular* cases.

In this context the coexistence of masculine and feminine elements in the same person should not be understood as either a complete or an approximate *simultaneity*. The important addition which is now called for is not only a direction for the correct psychological use of the principle but also an important extension of points made earlier. *All human beings oscillate between the Man and the Woman in them.* These oscillations may be abnormally large in one person and almost imperceptibly small in another, but *they always exist* and, if they are substantial enough, they also reveal themselves through the changing physical appearance of the individuals concerned. These *oscillations of the sexual characteristics* can be divided, like the oscillations of the earth's magnetism, into regular and irregular ones. The regular oscillations are either small: for example, some people feel things in a more masculine way at night than in the morning; or they follow the major *periods* of organic life, which have hardly begun to be noticed and the exploration of which seems bound to throw some light on what is so far an incalculable number of phenomena. The irregular oscillations are probably triggered by external factors, primarily the sexual character of the person next to oneself. To some extent they are certainly the cause of those remarkable phenomena of *attitude* which play the greatest part in the psychology of a *crowd,* although they have not yet received the attention they deserve. In short, *bisexuality* will not manifest itself at one single moment but can do so only *in succession,* regardless of whether this difference between sexual characteristics in time obeys the law of periodicity, or whether the amplitude of the oscillation toward one sex is different from that toward the other, or whether the antinode of the male phase is equal to the antinode of the female phase (which need not necessarily be the case but, on the contrary, is only one case among innumerable equally possible ones).

One may therefore be inclined to admit in theory, even before it is tested by experiment, that the principle of intermediate sexual forms makes possible a better characterological description of individuals by demanding the assessment of the proportions in which male and female elements are mixed in every organism, and by insisting on the determination of the elongations of the oscillations, toward either side, of which an individual is capable. But *here* we reach a question which forces us to make a choice, because the further progress of our investigation almost entirely depends on the answer. The question is whether we should initially cross the whole infinitely rich field of intermediate sexual forms, or *sexual diversity in the psychic domain,* while trying to observe, as accurately as possible, the conditions that prevail at particularly suitable points, or whether we should start by planning and completing the construction of the psychology of the "ideal Man" and the "ideal Woman," before investigating the various possibilities of their empirical combination *in concreto* and examining the extent to which the pictures reached by deduction coincide with the reality. The first way corresponds to the common view of the psychology of the thinking process, according to which ideas are always drawn from reality and the sexual types can be gleaned only from sexual diversity, which alone is real: this is the inductive and analytical method. The second way would have the advantage of rigorous formal logic over the first: this is the deductive and synthetic method.

I did not want to take the second route for two reasons. One reason was that anybody can easily apply two clearly defined types to concrete reality on his own, since this only requires that the *proportions in the mixture* of the two (which must at any rate be specifically ascertained in each new case) be known to create the possibility of matching up the theory and the practice. The other reason was (assuming the choice of an investigative approach which, being simultaneously historical and biographical, would be beyond the competence of the author) that all the benefits of these ramifications would be reaped by the interest in individuals and none at all by the theory. The first, inductive, route is impracticable because in this case it would be necessary constantly to repeat what had been said before and the bulk of repetitions would occur in that part devoted to a table of contrasts between the sexual types, and furthermore because the preliminary study of the intermediate sexual forms and the preparation of the types accompanying it would be lengthy, time-consuming, and unprofitable for the reader.

The classification, therefore, had to be determined by a different consideration.

Since a morphological and physiological investigation of the sexual extremes was not my concern, I only dealt with the principle of intermediate forms, but this I did in relation to every aspect that it seemed likely to elucidate, including the biological. That is how the present work as a whole obtained its shape. While its first part is constituted by the examination of the intermediate forms, the second part will embark on, and try to carry as far as possible, the purely *psychological analysis of M and W.* As for concrete cases, anybody will easily be able to assemble them by applying the insights attained here, and to represent them with the aid of the experiences and concepts gained in the second part.

The second part will receive very little support from the familiar and commonly held views about the mental differences between the sexes. Nevertheless, if only for the sake of completeness and without attributing any particular importance to the matter, I will take this opportunity to illustrate very briefly the intermediate sexual forms of mental processes by means of a few commonly known peculiarities and some of their modifications, although they will not yet be submitted to closer analysis at this point.

Feminine men often have an exceptionally strong need to marry, even if (to avoid any misunderstanding) they are themselves extremely wealthy. If they can, they will almost always do so at a very young age, and they will often be particularly flattered by having a famous woman, a poet or painter or possibly a singer or actress, as their wife.

Feminine men, in accordance with their femininity, are also more physically vain than other men. There are "men" who stroll along the promenade simply in order to feel that their face, which is a woman's face and therefore usually amply betrays the intention of its wearer, is admired, and then they go home satisfied. Narcissus was modeled on such "men." These same persons, of course, also take extreme care over their hairstyle, clothing, shoes, and underwear. Their consciousness of their momentary physical posture and of their external appearance on any particular day, of the smallest details of their attire, and of the most fleeting glances from other people is almost equal to W's constant awareness of such things, and their walk and gestures are downright coquettish. Viragos, on the other hand, often display a flagrant neglect of dress and a lack of personal hygiene, and they often complete their toilet much faster than many feminine men. All "foppery" and "dandyism," as well as part of women's emancipation, derives from the current increase in the number of such hermaphroditic creatures. This is more than "mere fashion." The question is always *why* something can become a fashion, and there is probably altogether less "mere fashion" than the spectator who goes in for superficial *criticism* believes.

The more of W a woman has in her, the less she will *understand* a man, but the more he will *affect* her *through his sexual peculiarity,* that is, the more he will impress her as Man. This is not only explained by the law of sexual attraction, but is also due to the fact that the more purely feminine a woman is, the more she will be able to grasp her opposite. Conversely, the more a man has of M, the less he will be able to *understand* W, but the more *urgently* women will *present* themselves to him in their entire *external* nature, their femininity. Therefore the so-called "connoisseurs of women," i.e., those who are nothing more than mere "connoisseurs of women," are themselves to a large extent women. Consequently, the more feminine men often know better how to treat women than do complete men, who only learn this after a great deal of experience and who, apart from a few exceptions, probably never learn it fully.

To these few illustrations, which were intended to demonstrate the applicability of the principle to characterology by means of examples deliberately chosen from the *most trivial* sphere of the tertiary sexual characteristics, I would like to add the obvious applications that seem to me to result from it with regard to pedagogy. In so doing I hope that the general acceptance of the common element that underlies these and many other facts will have *one* result above all: *a more individualizing education.* Every shoemaker who measures feet must know more about individuality than today's educators, both at school and in the home, who cannot be brought to a living awareness of such a moral obligation. For up to now the education of the intermediate sexual forms (particularly among women) has aimed to achieve as close an approximation as possible to a conventional ideal of maleness and femaleness, which has been tantamount to psychological orthopedics in the full meaning of torture. This has not only deprived the world of a great deal of variety, but has also suppressed many things that are embryonically present and could take root, while twisting other things into an unnatural position and breeding artificiality and pretence.

For a very long time our educational system has had a standardizing effect on all those born with male and all those born with female genitals. From an early age "boys" and "girls" are forced into different clothes and taught to play different games. Even primary education is entirely separate, with all the "girls" learning handicraft, etc., etc. *The intermediate forms are given less than their fair share.* Nevertheless, one often sees, even *before* puberty, how strong the instincts, the "determinants" of the natural disposition, of these ill-treated people can be: some boys are happiest playing with dolls, learn crocheting and knitting from their little sisters, are fond of wearing girls' clothes and enjoy being called by female forenames; and some girls mingle with boys, in whose wilder games they want to participate and who often treat them as complete equals and "buddies." However, in all cases a nature suppressed from outside through education comes to light *after* puberty: masculine women crop their hair, prefer gowns reminiscent of frock coats, study, drink, smoke, climb mountains, become passionate hunters; feminine men grow their hair long, wear corsets, and empathize with women's worries over their attire, with whom they are able to have companionable conversations about shared interests; indeed, they often sincerely enthuse over friendship between the two sexes, as do, for example, effeminate male students over being "colleagues" with female students, etc.

Girls and boys suffer equally from the vice-like pressure of an education that forces them into line, although at a later stage the latter suffer more from being subjected to the same *law* and the former from being stereotyped through the same *moral norm.* I fear therefore that in people's *heads* the demand articulated here will encounter more passive resistance with regard to girls than to boys. In this context it is essential to recognize the utter untruth of the widespread and endlessly reiterated belief, passed down by the authorities of the day, in the *sameness of all "women"* ("there are no differences, no individuals among women; if you know one woman you know them all"). It is true that *those individuals closer to W than to M* (i.e., "women") *show far fewer differences and possibilities than the rest*—the greater diversity of "males," not only among humans but in the entire area of zoology, is a general fact, thoroughly appreciated by Darwin in particular—*but there are still enough differences.* The psychological genesis of the widespread erroneous belief to the contrary is largely conditioned by the circumstance that (cf. chapter III) every man in his life makes the *relatively intimate* acquaintance of only *one* group of women, all of whom, *in accordance with natural law,* have a great deal in common. Women too, for the same reason and with even less justification, are often heard to say: "one man is like another." This *also* explains some, to say the least, *risky* statements by feminists about Man and his allegedly untrue superiority, which again derive from the *kind* of men with whom *they* as a rule become more closely acquainted.

Thus the *variously graded coexistence of M and W,* which we have recognized as one of the *main principles of all scientific characterology,* proves to be a fact that must also be taken to heart by special pedagogy.

The relationship between characterology and that kind of psychology which alone should really be valid according to a psychological "theory of actuality" corresponds to that between anatomy and physiology. Since there will always be a theoretical and practical need for characterology, it must be permissible to practice the psychology of individual differences regardless of its epistemological foundations and its demarcation against the subject matter of general psychology. Those who adhere to the theory of psycho-physical parallelism will agree with the basic principles of our approach so far, since they believe that *characterology must have morphology as a sister science,* just as psychology in the narrower sense and physiology (of the central nervous system) are parallel sciences. Indeed there is reason to hope for great things in the future from the connection between anatomy and characterology and the stimulus they can receive from each other. At the same time such an alliance would provide an invaluable aid to *psychological diagnostics,* which is the prerequisite of all *individualizing education.* The principle of intermediate sexual forms, and even more the method of assuming a *parallelism between morphology and characterology* in its *wider* application, afford us a view of a time when *physiognomy,* a task that has so powerfully attracted and so persistently repulsed the most outstanding minds, will at last be honored with the title of a scientific discipline.

The problem of physiognomy is the problem of a constant relationship between the psychic element *in repose* and the physical element *in repose,* just as the problem of physiological psychology is that of a regular relationship between the psychological element *in motion* and the physical element *in motion* (which is not to advocate a special *mechanics* of neurological processes). One is to some extent *static* and the other more purely *dynamic,* but in principle neither enterprise is more, nor less, legitimate than the other. It is therefore very wrong, both methodologically and factually, to regard the study of physiognomy, because of its enormous difficulties, as something extremely *dubious,* which is what happens, unconsciously rather than consciously, in scientific circles today, and which occasionally comes to light, as it did, for example, in the reactions to Moebius's revival of Gall's attempts at discovering the physiognomy of the born mathematician. If it is possible to say many correct things about the character of a person one never knew, merely on the basis of his external appearance and an immediate sensation unsupported by a wealth of conscious or unconscious experiences—and there are people who possess this ability in a high degree—then it cannot be impossible to arrive at a scientific system of these matters. All that is needed is the conceptual clarification of certain strong feelings, the laying of a cable to the speech center (to put it very crudely), although it is true that this task is often exceedingly difficult.

In any case it will be a long time before official science ceases to regard the study of physiognomy as something highly *immoral.* Scientists will continue to swear by psycho-physical parallelism as they have done up to now, and yet at the same time regard physiognomists, just as they regarded researchers into hypnotism not very long ago, as lost souls or charlatans, even though there is no human being who is not an unconscious, and no outstanding human being who is not a conscious, physiognomist.

The saying "You can tell by his nose" is also used by people who have no regard for physiognomy as a science, and the picture of an eminent person or a murderer is of great interest even to those who have never heard the word "physiognomy."

At a time like the present, when we are being flooded by writings about the relationship between the physical and the psychic, when the call "Psychological parallelism!" uttered by a compact majority is countered by the call "Reciprocity!" uttered by a small but courageous and growing group, it would have been useful to reflect upon these circumstances. However, in that case one would also have had to ask *whether or not the assumption of any kind of correspondence between physical and psychic elements is an a priori synthetic function of our thought that has so far been overlooked*—which seems to me to be firmly established at least through the fact that every human being *recognizes* physiognomy simply by *practicing* physiognomy, *regardless* of *experience.* Although Kant did not notice this fact, it confirms his view that nothing *more* can be scientifically proven or ascertained about the relationship between the physical and the psychic. A relationship, governed by laws, between the physical and the psychic *must therefore be accepted as a heuristic principle of scientific inquiry,* and the further determination of the nature of this relationship, *which is a priori regarded as a fact by everybody,* remains the privilege of metaphysics and religion.

Whether or not characterology is considered to be related to morphology, it may be true of either of them on its own or of the coordinated practice of both, i.e., physiognomy, that the almost complete failure so far of the attempts to create such sciences is due not least to the lack of an adequate method, even though it is also deeply rooted in the nature of that difficult enterprise. The proposal that I will now develop in order to fill that gap has guided me safely through many a maze. I therefore feel that I must not hesitate to submit it to general scrutiny.

Some people like dogs and cannot stand cats, others only enjoy watching kittens at play and regard dogs as revolting animals. In such cases the question asked with great, and justifiable, pride has always been: *Why* does one person prefer cats, the other dogs? Why? Why?

This question, especially in the present context, does not seem very fruitful. I do not believe that Hume and, in particular, Mach are right in failing to make an explicit distinction between *simultaneous* and *succedaneous* causality. Some undeniable formal analogies are thereby rather forcibly exaggerated in an attempt to prop up the swaying edifice of the system. It will simply not do to identify the relationship between two phenomena that regularly follow each other in time with a regular functional relationship between different *simultaneous* elements. Nothing in reality warrants talking of *sensations* of time, and even less assuming the existence of a sense of time alongside the other senses. Anybody who believes that he has solved the problem of time by merely considering time and the hour angle of the earth as one and the same thing, to say the least, overlooks the fact that even if the earth were suddenly to start revolving round its axis at an uneven speed we would still make the a priori assumption of an even lapse of time. Where cause and effect occur *one after the other* in a *chronological* sequence it is entirely legitimate and fruitful to distinguish time from the material experiences on which the distinction between succedaneous and simultaneous dependence is based and thus to ask the question about the *cause* of *changes,* that is, the question *Why.* However, in the case cited above as an example of the kind of questions asked in individual psychology, empirical science, which as such does not *explain* the regular coexistence of individual features in a complex by means of the metaphysical assumption of a *substance,* should not search for the Why but rather start by examining *what* ***else*** *distinguishes cat lovers from dog lovers.*

I believe that the habit of constantly asking this question about any corresponding *other* differences, where *one* difference between elements in repose has been identified, will benefit not only characterology, but also pure morphology and will therefore become the obvious method of combining them, physiognomy. The fact that many characteristics of animals never vary in isolation already occurred to Aristotle. Later it was, of course, first Cuvier and then Geoffroy St. Hilaire and Darwin who studied these phenomena of "correlation" in detail. The existence of constant relationships can sometimes easily be understood as the result of a common purpose. Thus, where the digestive tract is adapted for a meat diet, an obvious teleological expectation will be that a masticatory apparatus and organs for seizing the prey must also be present. But why all ruminants have cloven hoofs and, if they are male, horns, why in some animals im-munity against certain poisons is always accompanied by a specific hair color, why the varieties of pigeons with short beaks have small feet and those with large beaks have large feet, or indeed why white cats with blue eyes are almost invariably deaf—such regular concurrences cannot be explained either by one obvious reason or with reference to a uniform purpose. This is, of course, not to say that as a matter of principle science will have to be satisfied in all eternity with merely establishing a constant coexistence. After all, that would be as if somebody claimed for the first time to be proceeding scientifically by *restricting* himself to *finding* that if he puts a coin in a slot machine a box of matches will come out, while anything that went beyond this was metaphysics and an evil, and the criterion of a genuine scientist was resignation. Problems like how it comes that long hair and two normal ovaries are almost always found together in the same person are of the utmost importance, but they fall within the remit of *physiology* and not of *morphology.* One *aim* of an *ideal morphology* may be usefully outlined by suggesting that *a deductive and synthetic part* of it should not crawl into holes in the ground or dive to the bottom of the sea in pursuit of every single existing species—which is the scientific approach of a stamp collector—but should be able to construct the *whole* organism from a *given number* of qualitatively and quantitatively accurately determined parts. Nor should this be based on an intuition, as a man such as Cuvier was able to do, but on a rigorous process of proof. For this science of the future, any organism of which one property has been accurately indicated should be qualified by another property which is no longer arbitrary but capable of being determined just as accurately. In the language of the thermodynamics of our own day this could equally well be expressed by demanding that for such a *deductive* morphology the organism should have only a finite number of "degrees of freedom." Or, using an instructive explanation of Mach, one could stipulate that the organic world too, insofar as it is to be scientifically intelligible and representable, should be one in which the number of equations between n variables is smaller than n (and equal to n–1 if it is to be *unmistakably* definable by a scientific system: given a smaller number, the equations would become indefinite, and given a larger number, the dependence indicated by one equation could easily be contradicted by another).

This is the logical significance, in biology, of the correlation principle, which reveals itself as the application to living beings of the *concept of function,* and that is why the possibility of its expansion and refinement provides the main foundation of the hope for a theoretical morphology. Thus causal research is not excluded but directed, for the first time, to its proper province. It will probably have to seek the causes of the facts underlying the correlation principle in the *idioplasm.*

The possibility of a *psychological* application of the principle of correlative variation exists in "differential psychology," or the *theory of psychological variety,* and the clear correlation of anatomical appearance and mental character becomes the task of *static psychophysics or physiognomy.* However, research in all three disciplines will have to be guided by the question how two living beings that have behaved differently in one respect will differ *further.* To ask this question seems to me to be the only imaginable "methodus inveniendi," as it were, the "ars magna" of those sciences, and to be well placed to penetrate the entire technique of their operations. Now people will no longer labor to dig up the hard earth in a hole, in order to fathom a psychological type by just nagging away at the question Why in the most hermetic isolation possible. They will cease to bleed to death like Jacques Loeb's stereotropic worms in their triangular vessel, or to blinker their own view of what they could easily reach if they looked sideways, in their struggle to find the cause, which is inaccessible to any merely *empirical* science, by nosing deeper and deeper in a straight line. If, whenever *one* difference becomes visible, it is resolved to avoid all negligence and spare no effort in paying attention to the *other* differences which, according to our principle, must unavoidably *also* be present, and if in every instance "a watcher in the intellect is appointed" for the unknown properties that have a functional connection with the one property that has already been identified, then the prospect of discovering new correlations will be significantly increased. Once the question is asked the reply will come sooner or later, depending on the stamina and vigilance of the observer and the suitability of the material chosen for his examination.

In any case, through the conscious use of this principle one will no longer be reduced to waiting until somebody, through the lucky whim of an intellectual constellation, is *struck* by the constant coexistence of two things in the same individual. Rather, one will learn *to ask at once* about the *second thing,* which will also be present. How long have all discoveries been restricted to the mere chance of a favorable conjunction of ideas in one man's mind! How great a role has been played by arbitrary circumstances, which may, at the appropriate moment, lead two heterogeneous groups of ideas to that crossing point where alone the child, which is the new insight and experience, can be born! The new question, and the will to pursue it in every individual case, is eminently capable of reducing this role. Given the succession of cause and effect, the psychological stimulus for asking a question appears sooner because any violation of the stability and continuity of an existing psychological state has an immediately disturbing effect and "makes a vital difference" (Avenarius). *However, where the dependence is simultaneous this motive force no longer applies.* That is why the method advocated here could do the researcher the greatest service, even if he were already in the middle of his work, and indeed speed up the progress of science as a whole. The recognition of the heuristic applicability of the correlation principle would be a discovery that could assist the birth of further new discoveries in a continuous process of creation.

VI | Emancipated Women

Following directly from the application of the principle of intermediate sexual forms in differential psychology, I must now deal for the first time with the question that this book is above all else intended to solve in theoretical and practical terms, insofar as it is not a theoretical question of ethnology and political economy, i.e., social science in the broadest sense, or a practical question of the legal and economic order, i.e., social policy: the *Woman Question.* However, the answer given to the Woman Question in this chapter will not solve the problem for my whole investigation. Rather, it is only a provisional answer, since it is unable to deliver more than can be concluded from the principles I established so far. Moving exclusively in the lowly sphere of individual experience, it makes no attempt at rising to any general concepts of deeper significance. The practical instructions supplied by it are not maxims of moral behavior that should, or could, regulate future experience, but only rules for technical social use, abstracted from past experience. The reason is that I make no attempt as yet to examine the male and female type, a task which I leave to the second part. This provisional examination is designed to present only those characterological *results of the principle of intermediate forms that are of importance for the Woman Question.*

How this application of the principle will turn out is rather obvious in the light of what I have said so far. It culminates in the notion that *a woman's need for emancipation, and her capacity for emancipation, derives exclusively from the proportion of M in her.* However, the concept of emancipation is *ambiguous,* and those who, with the help of this word, have pursued practical intentions that could not stand up to theoretical insights have often had a vested interest in increasing its lack of clarity. By the emancipation of a woman I mean neither the fact that it is she who gives the orders in her house while her husband no longer dares to contradict her, nor her courage to walk in unsafe areas at night without the protection of an escort; neither her disregard of social conventions, which all but forbid a woman to live on her own, which do not allow her to visit a man, and which prohibit any reference to sexual topics either by her or by others in her presence, nor her desire to earn an independent living, whether she chooses to attend a commercial school or a university, a conservatory or a college of education for that purpose. There may be many other things hiding behind the large shield of the emancipation movement, but these will not be discussed for the time being. Further, the emancipation that I have in mind is not a woman's desire for external *equality* with a man. The *problem* that I wish to solve in my search for clarity in the Woman Question is that of a woman's *will* to *become internally equal* to a man, to attain his intellectual and moral freedom, his interests and creative power. And what I will argue now is *that W has no need and, accordingly, no capacity, for this kind of emancipation. All those women who really strive for emancipation, all those women who have some genuine claim to fame and intellectual eminence, always display many male properties, and the more perceptive observer will always recognize in them some anatomically male characteristics, an approximation to the physical appearance of a man.* Those women of the past and present whom the male and female champions of the emancipation movement constantly name as proof of the great achievements of *women* come exclusively from the ranks of the *more advanced* intermediate sexual forms, one might almost say, from the ranks of those intermediate sexual forms which are barely classified as "women." To start with, the very first of them in historical order, Sappho, is a sexual *invert,* from whom the designation sapphic or lesbian love, for a sexual relationship between women, is derived. Here we see how we can benefit from the discussions of the third and fourth chapters to arrive at a decision concerning the Woman Question. The characterological material at our disposal with regard to so-called "eminent women," that is, women who are de facto emancipated, is so scanty, and its interpretation subject to so many contradictions, that we cannot use it with any hope of providing a *satisfactory* solution. We lacked a principle enabling us to establish unambiguously a person's location between M and W. Such a principle was found in the law of sexual attraction between men and women. Its application to the problem of homosexuality led to the discovery that a woman attracted to another woman is half man. This, in fact, is almost all the evidence that we need in order to prove, with reference to individual historical cases, the thesis that the degree of a woman's emancipation is identical to the degree of her masculinity. Sappho was *only the first* on the list of female celebrities who had homosexual or at least bisexual feelings. Scholars have tried very hard to clear her of the suspicion that she conducted real love affairs, beyond mere friendship, with women, as if such an accusation, if true, were necessarily a great slur on a woman's moral character. That this is by no means so, that a homosexual love honors a woman, in particular, more than heterosexual relationships, will be shown clearly in the second part. Here it may suffice to remark that a woman's inclination to lesbian love is precisely a *product of her masculinity, which is in fact the prerequisite of her superiority.* Catherine II of Russia and Queen Christina of Sweden, as well as reportedly the highly gifted deaf, blind, and dumb Laura Bridgman and surely George Sand are partly bisexual, partly exclusively homosexual, as are all those women and girls with any abilities worth considering, whom I have personally had the opportunity to meet.

In the case of the many emancipated women for whose lesbian leanings we have no evidence there are almost always some other clues which prove that I am neither making an arbitrary assertion nor indulging in a bigoted and greedy egoism that desires to claim *everything* for the male sex, if I speak of the masculinity of all those women who are generally summoned, with some justification, as witnesses to women's aptitude for higher things. Just as bisexual women have sexual relations either with masculine women or with feminine men, heterosexual women will still manifest their content of masculinity through the fact that their male sexual complement will never be a genuine man. The most famous of George Sand's many "affairs" were those with Musset, the most effeminate lyrical poet known to history, and with Chopin, who was so effeminate that he could actually be described as the only female musician.[1] Vittoria Colonna owed her fame less to her own poetic production than to being admired by Michelangelo, who otherwise only had erotic relationships with men. The authoress Daniel Stern was the mistress of the same Franz Liszt whose life and work always contain a thoroughly feminine element, and whose friendship with Wagner, another far from completely masculine individual and indeed something of a pederast, involved almost as much homosexuality as the effusive veneration of King Ludwig II of Bavaria for Wagner. Mme. de Staël, whose treatise on Germany should perhaps be regarded as the most significant book written by any woman, probably had sexual relations with the homosexual tutor of her children, August Wilhelm Schlegel. Klara Schumann's husband, to judge by his face alone, would be taken for a woman rather than a man at certain times of his life, and in his music there is also a large, albeit not always the same, amount of femininity.

Where no information of any kind is available about the people with whom famous women had sexual relations, or where such individuals are not mentioned at all, the gap is often enough amply filled by brief comments that have been handed down to us about the women's exterior. They show how the masculinity of these women is expressed in the physiognomy of their faces and figures, and they thus confirm, as do the surviving portraits of the women, the correctness of the view advocated here. We read that George Eliot had a broad, massive forehead and that "her movements and her facial expressions were sharp and determined but lacked the grace of feminine softness"; and we are informed about the "sharp, intelligent face of Lavinia Fontana, which seems strange to us." The features of Rachel Ruysch "bear a character of almost mas-

1. This is also clearly shown by his portrait. Mérimée calls George Sand "maigre comme un clou." At her first meeting with Chopin "she" was obviously the male and "he" the female: *he* blushes when she fixes her eyes on him and begins to pay *him* compliments in a *deep* voice.

culine resolution." The biographer of Annette von Droste-Hülshoff, the most original poetess, notes her "elfishly slim, delicate figure"; and the face of this female artist has an expression of austere masculinity that distantly recalls Dante's features. The authoress and mathematician Sonja Kowalewska, like Sappho before her, had an abnormally sparse head of hair, even sparser than is common among the female poets and students of today, who regularly mention her first when the question of the intellectual achievement of women is raised. Anybody who might claim to recognize *one* feminine trait in the face of the most eminent female painter Rosa Bonheur would have been misled by the sound of her name, and the famous Helena Petrovna Blavatsky was also very masculine in appearance. Of the productive and emancipated women still alive, I have deliberately mentioned none. I have kept silent about them even though it was *they* who provided not only the incentive for many of the ideas that I have put forward, but also the most general confirmation of my view that genuine Woman, W, has nothing to do with the "emancipation of women." Historical research is obliged to agree with the popular saying which has long since anticipated its discovery: "The longer the hair, the smaller the brain." This saying is correct, except for the reservations voiced in the second chapter.

And as for emancipated women: *it is only the man in them who wants to be emancipated.*

There is a deeper reason than is generally assumed why women writers so often adopt a male name: they feel almost as if they were men, and with persons such as George Sand this is in full accord with their preference for masculine clothes and masculine activities. Their motive in choosing a male pseudonym must be the sense that nothing else corresponds to their own nature, and it cannot be rooted in the desire for greater public attention and recognition. After all, women's productions have always attracted more interest than, *ceteris paribus,* the creations of men, because of the sexual piquancy associated with them; and, if they were good, they have always received more lenient treatment and incomparably higher praise than anything equally good achieved by men, because of the lower expectations attached to them right from the outset. This is particularly the case today, when women are still constantly achieving high reputations thanks to products that would hardly be noticed if they originated from men. It is time to exercise some discrimination and to separate the wheat from the chaff here. If one takes the established creations of men in the history of literature, philosophy, science, and art as a standard, the not inconsiderable number of women described time and again as significant minds will shrink pitifully at the first blow. Indeed it takes a great deal of charity and laxness to attribute the tiniest title of *significance* to women like Angelika Kaufmann or Mme. Lebrun, Fernan Caballero or Hroswitha von Gandersheim, Mary Somerville or George Egerton, Elizabeth Barrett-Browning or Sophie Germain, Anna Maria Schurmann or Sibylla Merian. I will not talk about the degree to which earlier female individuals cited as models of viraginity (e.g., Droste-Hülshoff) are overestimated, nor criticize the measure of fame won by some living female artists. Suffice it to say in general that not one among *all* (even the most masculine) women in intellectual history can truly bear comparison *in concreto* with even fifth- and sixth-rate male geniuses, for example, Rückert among poets, van Dyck among painters, or Schleiermacher among philosophers.

If, for the present, we eliminate hysterical visionaries such as the Sibyls, the Pythiae of Delphi, Antoinette Bourignon and Susanna von Klettenberg, Jeanne de la Mothe-Guyon, Joanna Southcott, Beate Sturmin or St. Theresa,[2] we are left with cases like Marie Bashkirtseff. Her physique (as far as I can tell from my memory of her picture) was indeed decidedly female, apart from her forehead, which gave me a somewhat masculine impression. But anybody who sees her pictures hanging in the Salle des Étrangers in the Luxembourg Palace in Paris beside those of her beloved Bastien-Lepage will know that she adopted his style no less accurately and completely than Ottilie did Eduard's handwriting in Goethe's *Elective Affinities.*

The large residue is formed by the numerous instances in which a *talent* owned by all members of a family accidentally emerges most strongly in a *female* member, who need not in the slightest be a genius. For only talent, and not genius, is hereditary. Margaretha van Eyck and Sabine von Steinbach, merely provide the paradigm for a long line of female artists about whom Ernst Guhl, a writer who is uncommonly well-disposed toward women artists, writes: "It is explicitly reported that they were taught an art by their father, mother or brother, in other words, that they received the impulse to become professional artists within their own family. There are two or three hundred of them, and how many hundred more may have become artists through similar influences without being mentioned by history!" To appreciate the significance of these figures one must bear in mind that a little earlier Guhl speaks "of the approximately thousand names of female artists known to us."

This concludes my historical review of emancipated women. It has *confirmed* the assertion that a genuine need, and a real capacity, for emancipation in a woman presupposes masculinity. The vast majority of women certainly never *lived* for art or for knowledge, which they only pursued, in place of the usual "handicraft," as a mere *pastime* in the undisturbed idyll of their lives, while many others engaged in intellectual or artistic activities only in an enormously strained form of *coquetry* in front of more or less specific persons of the male sex. For the sake of clarity, I was able, and indeed obliged, to exclude these two

2. Hysteria is one of the main causes of the higher aspirations of many outstanding women. However, its common meaning, restricted to pathological excesses of the body, is too narrow, as the second part (chapter XII) will attempt to explain.

large groups from my examination. All the rest, looked at more closely, prove to be intermediate sexual forms.

On the other hand, if the need for liberation and equality with men shows only in masculine women, we are *justified* in concluding, *per inductionem,* that *W feels no need whatsoever for emancipation.* This conclusion is correct even though, for the time being, it has been derived solely from specific historical observation and not from an examination of the psychic properties of W herself.

Accordingly, if we adopt a hygienic (not ethical) point of view as to what practice would be most appropriate to a natural predisposition, we arrive at this judgment concerning the "emancipation of woman." The *nonsense* of the emancipatory efforts lies in the *movement,* the *agitation.* Given women's great propensity for imitation, and disregarding the motives of vanity and the desire to catch men, these are the things that seduce some of them into taking up studying, writing, etc., even if they never had an original desire to do so, and in these women the striving for education is *induced* by the large number of others who really seem to have a certain inner need for emancipation. As a result, studying becomes a *fashion* among women, and finally a ridiculous agitation of women among themselves makes *all* of them believe in the authenticity of something that good housewives so often use only as a means of demonstration against their husbands, and daughters only as a pointed manifestation against the authority of their mothers. The practical answer to the whole question would therefore have to be as follows, although this rule (if only because of its fluid character) cannot and must not be treated as the basis of any legislation: *Unrestricted access to everything for, and no obstacles anywhere in the way of, those whose true psychic needs, always in accordance with their physical constitution, impel them to masculine activities, that is, women with male characteristics. But away with the formation of* ***parties****, away with any* ***untrue*** *revolutionizing, away with the whole women's* ***movement****,* which in so many women creates an artificial aspiration that runs counter to nature and is fundamentally false.

And away, likewise, with the platitude of "complete equality"! Even the most masculine female probably never contains more than 50 percent of M, and it is to *this* ***fineness*** that she owes her entire significance, or rather, everything that she *could* perhaps signify. Many intellectual women seem to draw general conclusions which would demonstrate not the parity but indeed the superiority of the female sex, based on the particular experiences with men that they have had the opportunity to gather (which, as indicated earlier, are not typical in any case). One must on no account do this but rather, as Darwin suggested, compare the outstanding individuals on one side with the outstanding individuals on the other: "if two lists were made of the most eminent men and women in poetry, painting, sculpture, music (inclusive both of composition and performance), history, science, and philosophy with half-a-dozen names under each subject, the two lists would not bear comparison." If one further considers that, on close inspection, the persons on the female list too would only bear witness to the *masculinity of genius*, the desire of feminists to venture on the compilation of such a catalogue would probably become even less ardent than it has been hitherto.

The usual objection, which will again be voiced now, is that history proves nothing, because the movement must first create space for the full and uninhibited intellectual development of women. This objection fails to recognize that at *all* times there have been emancipated women, a Woman Question, and a women's movement, although their liveliness has varied in the different epochs. It immensely exaggerates the difficulties that men have created at any time, and are allegedly creating now in particular,[3] for women intent on an intellectual education. Finally, it ignores the fact that today again it is not the real Woman who demands emancipation, but invariably only the more masculine women, who misinterpret their own nature and who fail to recognize the motives of their own actions, in the belief that they are speaking in the name of Woman.

Like all other movements in history, the women's movement too was convinced that it was unique, new, unprecedented. Its pioneers taught that previously women had languished in darkness and chains, and were only now beginning to recognize and claim their natural rights. As with all other historical movements, for the women's movement too it has been possible to find earlier and earlier analogies: not only was there a Woman Question in the *social* sense in Antiquity and in the Middle Ages, but *intellectual* emancipation was also being pursued in days long past, both by women through their own achievements and by male and female apologists of the female sex through theoretical arguments. Therefore the belief, to which the feminists' struggle owes so much enthusiasm and freshness, that up to recent times women never had the opportunity to develop their intellectual potential unobstructed, is totally false. Jacob Burckhardt writes about the Renaissance: "The highest praise that was given at that time to the great Italian women was that they had a masculine mind and a masculine disposition. We have only to observe the thoroughly masculine bearing of most of the women in the heroic poems, especially those of Boiardo and Ariosto, to realize that we are dealing with a particular ideal. The title 'virago,' which is regarded as a very equivocal compliment in our century, at that time implied nothing but praise." In the sixteenth century the stage was opened to women and the first actresses were seen. "At that time women were considered able to reach the highest degree of culture, no less than man." It is the age

3. Incidentally, there have been many totally *uneducated great* male artists (Burns, Wolfram von Eschenbach), but no comparable female artist.

when one panegyric on the female sex appears after another, when Thomas More calls for complete equality between women and men, and when Agrippa von Nettesheim actually exalts women high above men. And those great successes of the female sex were lost again, as the whole age sank into oblivion, from which it was not retrieved until the nineteenth century.

Is it not very striking that attempts at the emancipation of women seem to appear in world history at constant intervals, always with the same amount of time between them?

By all estimates, there have been considerably more emancipated women and a stronger women's movement in the tenth, in the fifteenth and sixteenth, and now again in the nineteenth and twentieth centuries, than in the intervening epochs. It would be rash to build a hypothesis on this alone, but one must at least envisage the possibility of a powerful periodicity at work here, with more hermaphrodites, or intermediate forms, being regularly born during certain phases than in the intervals between them. Such periods have been observed in related matters among animals.

According to our view, at such times there would be less gonochorism, and the fact that in certain periods more masculine women are born than in others would have to be counterbalanced, on the opposite side, by the birth of more feminine men in the same periods. This indeed is seen to apply in a surprising measure. The entire "taste of the Vienna Secession," which awards the prize for beauty to tall, slim women with flat chests and narrow hips, can perhaps be traced back to this. The enormous increase of dandyism, as well as homosexuality, in recent years can only be a consequence of the greater femininity of the present era. And it is not without a deeper reason that both the aesthetic and the sexual taste of this age seeks support from the Pre-Raphaelites.

The existence in organic life of periods which resemble the oscillations in the lives of individuals, but which cover several generations, offers a broader prospect of understanding many obscure points in human history than the initiatives of the pretentious "historical conceptions" that have multiplied so rapidly in recent times, in particular the economic-materialist. For human *history* a *biological* approach is sure to yield an infinite number of insights in the future. However, I will restrict myself here to seeking its practical application to the case under study.

If it is true that at certain times more hermaphroditic people are born and at other times fewer, one might anticipate that the women's movement would largely *disintegrate of its own accord* and would not reappear for a long time, continuing to submerge and resurface in a rhythm without end. Women *wanting* to emancipate themselves would be born in larger numbers in some periods and in considerably smaller numbers in others.

Economic conditions, which can force even the highly feminine wife of a proletarian with many children into the factory or onto the building site are, of course, not the issue here. The connection between industrial and commercial development on the one hand and the Woman Question on the other is much looser than it is made out to be, particularly by social-democratic theoreticians, and a causal connection between aspirations to intellectual and to economic competitiveness exists even less. In France, for example, which has produced three of the most eminent women, a women's *movement* has never really taken root, and yet in no other European country do as many women work independently in business as there. Thus the struggle for material existence has nothing to do with the struggle for an intellectual purpose in life, if such a thing is really being pursued by any group of women, and the two must be clearly distinguished.

The prognosis that has been made for the second movement, the intellectual, is not encouraging. It is probably even more dreary than it would be if one could assume, as some authors do, a *progressive* development of mankind toward *complete* sexual *differentiation,* that is, toward downright sexual dimorphism.

The latter view seems to me to be untenable because in the more highly developed members of the animal kingdom no commensurate increase in the separation of the sexes can be demonstrated. Certain gephyrea and rotatoria, many birds and, among monkeys, the mandrill reveal much stronger gonochorism than can be observed, from the morphological point of view, in humans. But while this assumption predicts a time when at least the perceived *need* for emancipation would have ceased to exist *for ever* and there would be only complete males and complete females, the assumption of a periodic recurrence of the women's movement most cruelly condemns the entire undertaking of the feminists to painful impotence, revealing all their activities as a labor of the Danaids, whose successes, in the course of time, will automatically vanish in the same nothingness.

This could be the dismal lot of women's emancipation if it steadily continued to pursue its aims solely in the *social* area, in the historical future of the *species,* blindly imagining its enemies lurking among men and in the legal institutions created by men. If this were so it would indeed be necessary to form an Amazon corps, and nothing permanent would be gained as it dissolved again and again long after its creation. In that respect the Renaissance and its complete disappearance provides a lesson to feminists. The true liberation of the mind cannot be sought by an army, however large and however savage, but must be fought for by the single individual alone. Against whom? Against that which opposes it in the individual's own soul. *The greatest, the only, enemy of the emancipation of women is Woman.*

To prove this is the task of the second part.

Second or Main Part:

The Sexual Types

I | Man and Woman

All that a man does is physiognomical of him
—Carlyle

The way is cleared for the exploration of all the real contrasts between the sexes when we recognize that Man and Woman can only be understood as types, and that the confusing reality, which will forever supply the familiar controversies with new fuel, can only be reproduced by a mixture of these two types. The only really intermediate sexual forms were dealt with in the first part of this study and, as I must now emphasize, in a somewhat schematic manner. This was the result of the need to consider the general biological validity of the principles I was developing. Now that *the human being* is to become the object of consideration even more exclusively than before, and the psycho-physiological alignments are about to give way to introspective analysis, the universal claim of the principle of intermediate sexual stages must undergo a significant qualification.

Among plants and animals the occurrence of genuine hermaphroditism is a fact established beyond any doubt. But even among animals hermaphroditism often seems to signify a juxtaposition of the male and female gonads, rather than a balance of the two sexes, in the same individual, a co-existence of the two extremes, rather than a totally neutral condition in the middle between them. Of *human beings,* however, it may be said with the greatest certainty that *psychologically* a person *must necessarily be* ***either*** *male* ***or*** *female,* at least initially and at one and the same time. This unisexuality is not only in keeping with the observation that all those who regard themselves simply as male or female believe their complement to be "Woman" or "Man" pure and simple.[1] It is also most powerfully demonstrated by the fact, the theoretical importance of which can *hardly be overrated,* that within the relationship of two homosexuals, whether

1. I once heard a bisexual man exclaim at the sight of a bisexually active actress with a slight hint of a beard, a deep sonorous voice, and almost no hair on her head: "What a gorgeous woman!" To every man "woman" means something different and yet the same; in "woman" every poet has celebrated something different and yet identical.

male or female, one always plays the physical and psychological role of the man and, in the course of a prolonged relationship, keeps or assumes a masculine first name, while the other plays that of the woman, keeping or assuming a feminine first name or—even more frequently and characteristically—being given one by the former.

In the sexual relations between two female or male homosexuals, then, one always performs the function of the male and the other that of the female, which is a fact of the greatest significance. The man-woman relationship, at the *decisive point,* proves to be something *fundamental* and inescapable.

All intermediate sexual forms notwithstanding, a human being ***is*** *ultimately one of two things,* ***either*** *a man* ***or*** *a woman.* This most ancient empirical duality (which is not merely anatomical and which in concrete cases does not correspond at all regularly and precisely to the morphological findings) contains a profound truth that is not neglected with impunity.

By recognizing this, a step of the greatest consequence has been taken, which could prove equally beneficial or disastrous for all further insights. Such a view establishes a *being.* The task set for the entire investigation which follows is to investigate the *meaning* of this *being.* But as this problematic *being* touches directly on the main difficulty of characterology, it will be advisable, before beginning the work naïvely and boldly, to attempt a brief orientation about this most delicate problem, at the very threshold of which all audacity falters.

The obstacles facing any characterological investigation are enormous, if only because of the complicated nature of the material. Again and again the path that one believes to have found through the forest is lost in the dense undergrowth, and the thread can no longer be unraveled from the infinitely tangled mass. The worst thing, however, is that as the interpreter tries to derive general principles, even from successful beginnings, time and again the gravest doubts arise concerning the method for a systematic presentation of any disentangled material, forming a formidable obstacle in particular to the establishment of types. In respect of the contrasts between the sexes, for example, so far only the assumption of a certain kind of polarity and of innumerable intermediate forms between the extremes has proved to be of use. Similarly, in most other characterological matters—some of which I myself shall discuss later—there seems to be such a thing as a polarity (already suspected by the Pythagorean Alcmaion of Croton); and in this area Schelling's philosophy of nature will perhaps one day reap much greater rewards than the resurrection which a physical chemist of our time believes it owes him.

But are we justified in hoping ever to exhaust the individual as such by fixing him to one particular point along the lines connecting any two extremes, or even by accumulating an infinity of such connecting lines, a system of coordinates with an infinite number of dimensions? Shall we not relapse, only in a more concrete area, to the dogmatic skepticism of self-analysis as practiced by

Mach and Hume, if we expect a complete description of the human individual in the form of a *recipe?* And shall we then not be led by a kind of Weismannian atomism of determinants to a "mosaic physiognomy" when we are only just beginning to recover from "mosaic psychology"?

Here we are faced with a new version of the old fundamental problem which, as it turns out, is still full of tenacious life: Is there a unified and simple being in humans, and how does it relate to the multiplicity that undoubtedly exists alongside it? Is there a psyche? And what is the relationship between the psyche and the psychic phenomena? We now understand why there is still no characterology: because the existence of the object of this science, character itself, is a problematic one. The problem of all metaphysics and epistemology, the cardinal question of psychology, is also the problem "facing any characterology that will be able to present itself as a science." Or at least of any characterology that strives for insight into the differences in the *essential nature* of human beings in full critical awareness of the epistemological status of its own postulates, claims, and objectives.

This, let it be said, immodest characterology aims to be more than the "psychology of individual differences" that L. William Stern has restored as an aim of psychological science, which was nonetheless a commendable deed: it aims to offer more than the particulars of the motor and sensory reactions of an individual, and it should therefore not immediately descend to the low level of all other modern research in experimental psychology, which is in fact nothing but a strange combination of a statistical seminar and laboratory practice in physics. It hopes to remain in close contact with the abundance of psychic reality, unlike the lever-and-screw psychology whose self-assurance can only be explained by its total oblivion of this reality, and it does not worry about having to satisfy psychology students thirsting for enlightenment about themselves by carrying out investigations into the learning of words of one syllable and the influence of small doses of coffee on doing sums. It is a sad sign of the basic inadequacy of the work of modern psychology, which, incidentally, is vaguely felt everywhere, that, in view of the prevailing desolation, respected scientists who imagined that psychology was more than a theory of sensations and associations understandably arrive at the conviction that reflective science must forever leave problems such as heroism or self-sacrifice, madness or crime, to art as the only organ capable of understanding them, and abandon all hope, not of understanding them better than the artists (which would be an insult to a Shakespeare or a Dostoevsky), but at least of comprehending them in a systematic way.

No science is bound to become shallow as quickly as psychology if it parts with philosophy. The true cause of the decline of psychology is its emancipation from philosophy. Psychology should have remained philosophical, certainly not in its assumptions, but in its ultimate aims. The first insight that it would then have reached is *that the study of sensory perceptions bears no direct relation whatsoever to psychology.* The empirical psychologies of today begin with the sense of touch and the sensations in general and conclude with the "development of a moral character." However, the analysis of sensations is part of the physiology of the senses, and any attempt to relate its special problems more deeply to the other concerns of psychology is bound to fail.

It was the misfortune of scientific psychology that it was most strongly influenced by two physicists, Fechner and Helmholtz, and thus failed to recognize *that the internal world, unlike the external, is not made up of sheer sensations.* The two most sensitive empirical psychologists of recent decades, William James and Richard Avenarius, are the only two who have felt, at least instinctively, that one must not begin psychology with the sensations of the skin and the muscles, while all the rest of modern psychology is more or less sensationalist humbug. *This* is the reason, not expressed precisely enough by Dilthey, why today's psychology *completely fails to reach* those problems normally described as eminently psychological, the analysis of murder, of friendship, of loneliness, etc. Nor, indeed, *can* it reach them—and here the old excuse of its extreme youth is of no avail—because it moves in a completely different direction from that which could finally lead it to them in spite of everything. Therefore the foremost battle-cry in the struggle for a *psychological psychology* must be: *Away with sensationalism in psychology!*

The enterprise of characterology in the broader and deeper sense, as described above, primarily involves the concept of *character* itself, understood as the concept of a constant unified being. Just as morphology, which was invoked in the fifth chapter of part 1 for comparison, is concerned with the *form* of organic matter, which remains constant despite all physiological change, so characterology presupposes as its object something that remains constant, and that must be demonstrable by analogy, in every manifestation of the life of the psyche. Thus characterology is primarily opposed to the "theory of actuality" of psychic events, which refuses to recognize the existence of anything permanent, if only because it is based on the outlook of atomistic sensationalism.

Accordingly, character is not something enthroned behind the thoughts and feelings of the individual, *but something that reveals itself in his* ***every*** *thought and* ***every*** *feeling.* "All that a man does is physiognomical of him." Just as every cell holds the properties of the *whole* individual, *every* psychic impulse of a person contains not merely a few individual "traits," but *his whole being,* even though at any one moment only one or another of his peculiarities becomes more prominent.

There is no such thing as an isolated sensation, and the object facing the subject is always a field of vision and a totality of sensations, the *world* of the self, from which now this item, and now that, stands out in sharper relief. *Furthermore, one never associates "concepts" but only moments of one's life,* that is, various states of consciousness filled in manifold ways from a past (each, again, fixed to a specific point in one's field of vision). *Thus every moment in the life of the psyche contains the* ***whole*** *person,* even though at any one time the emphasis is placed on a different aspect of his character. *This* ***being****, which is demonstrable everywhere in the psychic state of every moment, is the object of characterology.* Therefore characterology would be the essential complement of empirical psychology, which, in strange contradiction to its name, ***psycho****logy,* has so far almost exclusively concentrated on changes in the field of the sensations, the motley *world,* while completely neglecting the richness of the self. Used in that way, characterology could have a fertilizing and regenerating effect on general psychology as the theory of the whole that results from the complexity of the subject and the complexity of the object (both of which could only be isolated from this whole by means of a strange abstraction). Many contentious issues in psychology—perhaps the most fundamental ones—may in fact only be decided by a characterological examination, which would show *why* one person advocates this opinion and another that, which would explain why they differ when they are talking about the same topic, and which would demonstrate that the only reason why they have different views on the same event and the same psychic process is that with each of them the event or process has received an individual coloring, the *stamp* of the person's own character. Thus it is only the theory of psychological *differences* that makes *agreement* in the area of *general* psychology possible.

The formal self would be the ultimate problem of a dynamic psychology, the material substance of the self the ultimate problem of a static psychology. And yet the very existence of character is questioned; or should, at any rate, be denied by an all-out positivism in the sense of Hume, Mach, or Avenarius. It is therefore easy to see why we as yet have no characterology, understood as the theory of the specific character.

The worst damage, however, has been done to characterology by linking it closely to psychology. The mere fact that characterology has been *historically* connected with the fate of the concept of the self is no justification for connecting it to the same *factually.* The absolute skeptic differs from the absolute dogmatist by nothing more than a word, and only those who dogmatically adopt the point of view of absolute phenomenalism, in the belief that this alone releases them from all the burdens of proof to which all other points of view are subject simply as a result of entering this field, will reject out of hand the *being* which is asserted by characterology and which by no means needs to be identical to a metaphysical *essence.*

Characterology is obliged to maintain its position against two great enemies. One takes character for granted and denies that science can capture it as artistic presentation does. The other accepts only the sensations as being real; for him reality and sensations have become one, sensation is the building block of both the world and the self, and there is no such thing as character. What then is characterology, the science of character, to do? "De individuo nulla scientia," "individuum est ineffabile," it is told by one side, which clings to the individual; and the other side, which is exclusively dedicated to being scientific and which has not secured "art as the organ of comprehending life" for itself, informs it again and again that science knows nothing about character.

It is in such a crossfire that characterology would have to hold its own. Who, then, is not overcome by the fear that it will share the fate of its sisters and remain an eternally unfulfilled promise like physiognomy, or a divinatory art like graphology?

This is also a question that later chapters must try to answer. It will be their task to examine the simple or multiple meaning of the being asserted by characterology. But why this question is generally so closely connected with the question of the psychic differences between the *sexes* in particular will only become evident from their ultimate findings.

II Male and Female Sexuality

Woman does not betray her secret.

—Kant

Mulier taceat de muliere.

—Nietzsche

PSYCHOLOGY AS SUCH is usually understood to mean the psychology of the psychologists, and psychologists are exclusively men: never in recorded history has a *female* psychologist been heard of. That is why the psychology of woman is usually dealt with in a chapter appended to general psychology in the same way as the psychology of the child. And since psychology has been regularly, albeit unconsciously, written with exclusive reference to man, general psychology has become the psychology of "men," and the problem of a psychology of the sexes is brought up only when the idea of a psychology of woman arises. Thus Kant says: "In anthropology the nature of feminine characteristics, more than those of the masculine sex, is a subject for study by philosophers." The psychology of the sexes will always coincide with the psychology of W.

The psychology of W, however, is also written by men only. It may therefore easily be regarded as impossible really to write such a psychology, which is obliged to make such statements about strangers as have not been verified by their own self-observation. Assuming that W could ever describe herself with the necessary precision it is still not certain that she would show the *same* interest in those aspects that primarily interest us; and even assuming that she would be able and willing to recognize herself as accurately as at all possible, the question still remains whether it would ever be possible to bring her to talk about herself. It will be seen in the course of this investigation that these three improbabilities point toward a common source in the nature of woman.

The investigation can be carried out only on the premise that it is possible to make correct statements about Woman without being a woman. Thus for the time being the first objection stands, and as we shall not be able to refute it till a later stage all we can do now is to ignore it. I will only supply one example. So far—is this just another consequence of oppression by man?—no pregnant woman has ever given expression to her sensations and feelings, whether in a poem, in memoirs, or in a gynecological treatise. This cannot be due to excessive bashfulness, for—as Schopenhauer has rightly pointed out—there is nothing so remote from a pregnant woman as shame about her condition. Moreover it would be possible for her to confess her psychological experiences at that time from memory after the end of her pregnancy. If bashfulness had prevented her from communicating then, it would no longer do so thereafter, and the interest aroused in many quarters by such revelations would probably be sufficient reason for many women to break their silence. But nothing of the kind has happened. Just as in other areas we owe any really valuable revelations about the psychological processes in woman solely to men, the sensations of pregnant women have also been described only by men. How were they able to do that?

Although in recent times the statements of three-quarter women and half women about their psychic lives have been increasing in number, they still tell more about the Man than the actual Woman in them. We can therefore rely on one thing only: *on what is feminine in men themselves.* Here the principle of intermediate forms proves to be in a certain sense the prerequisite for any true judgment by a man about a woman. Nevertheless, it will be necessary later to restrict and amplify this meaning of that principle. For its unqualified application would suggest that the most feminine man is in the best position to describe a woman, with the further logical consequence that a genuine woman is in the best position to see through herself clearly, which has just been very strongly questioned. At this point we already realize that a man may have a certain measure of femininity in him without therefore representing an intermediate sexual form in the same degree, and it appears all the more remarkable that a man should be able to make valid statements about the nature of woman. Indeed, as we seem unable to deny this ability even to M, given the extraordinary masculinity of many obviously excellent judges of women, the problematic nature of the right of Man to have a say about Woman[1] remains all the more remarkable, and we shall later be all the less able to shirk resolving the fundamental methodological doubt about this right. For the time being, however, we shall, as I have said, regard the objection as not having been made and proceed to investigate the matter itself. We ask without further ado: *What is the essential psychological difference between Man and Woman?*

It has been thought that the primal difference between the sexes, from which all other differences can be derived, lies in the greater intensity of the sex drive in Man. Quite apart from whether this statement is correct and whether the word "sex drive" denotes something unambiguous and really measurable, the

1. In what follows man always means the type M and woman the type W, and not men or women as individuals.

legitimacy in principle of such a derivation is surely very questionable at this stage. There may be some truth in all those ancient and medieval theories about the influence of the "unsatisfied womb" in woman and the "semen retentum" in man, and there was no need for the slogan that "everything" is nothing but "sublimated sex drive," which is so popular today. However, no systematic account can be built on a suspicion of such vague connections. There have so far been no attempts whatsoever to ascertain that the degree of any other qualities is determined by the greater or lesser strength of the sex drive.

However, the assertion that the intensity of the sex drive is greater in M than in W is *in itself wrong.* In fact the opposite has also been asserted, and is *just as wrong.* The truth is that even among men of equally strong masculinity the strength of the need for the sexual act varies, as it does, at least to all appearances, among women with the same proportion of W. Here, particularly in the case of men, in attempting a classification one has to consider the contribution of quite different factors, which I have been able to discover in part and with which I will perhaps deal in detail in another publication.

Contrary to a widespread popular view, then, there is *no* difference between the sexes as far as the intensity of the sex drive is concerned. On the other hand, we do notice a difference if we apply to Man and Woman respectively each of the two analytical aspects of the sex drive as defined by Albert Moll: the *detumescence drive* and the *contrectation drive.* The former is the result of a sense of unpleasure arising from the accumulation of a large quantity of mature germ cells, the latter is the need to make physical contact with an individual used as a sexual complement. While M has both the detumescence drive and the contrectation drive, in W a genuine detumescence drive is not present. At one level this is a direct consequence of the fact that in the sex act only M gives something to W, while W gives nothing to M: W *retains* both the male and the female secretions. In anatomical terms the same is expressed through the prominence of the male genitals, which makes the man's body entirely devoid of the character of a vessel. At any rate it is possible to see in this morphological fact a suggestion of the maleness of the detumescence drive, without immediately attaching to it any of the conclusions that are characteristic of the philosophy of nature. That W lacks the detumescence drive is also proved by the fact that most of those who contain more than ⅔ M invariably become addicted in their youth for longer or shorter periods to masturbation, a vice which among women is only practiced by those most like men. To W herself masturbation is something alien. I know that in so saying I am making a claim that is opposed by many robust assertions to the contrary. But a satisfactory explanation of these apparently contradictory observations will follow presently.

First, however, the contrectation drive of W must be discussed. This drive plays an exclusive, and therefore the most important, role in the case of Woman, but even so it cannot be said to be greater in one sex than in the other. For the concept of the contrectation drive does not imply the act of touching but only the need for physical contact as such with another person in close proximity, and says nothing about which of the parties is touching or being touched. The confusion in these matters, where the *intensity of the desire* is always lumped together with the *desire for activity,* comes from the fact that in the whole animal kingdom it is M who *seeks out* and adopts an *aggressive* stance toward W, which is also seen microcosmically in the behavior of every animal or vegetable spermatozoon in respect of the ovum. This can easily result in the error of assuming that an *enterprising behavior* for the purpose of achieving an aim, and the *desire* to achieve it, follow from each other regularly and in a constant proportion, and of inferring the absence of an urge where no obvious motor efforts are made to satisfy it. That is how the contrectation drive has come to be regarded as specifically masculine and to be denied, of all things, to Woman. It is clear, however, that at this point a distinction must be made *within* the contrectation drive. It will be found that, where sexual relations are concerned, M has the need to *attack*[2] and W the need to *be attacked,* and there is clearly no reason why the female need, merely because its aim is passivity, should be less great than the male need for activity. It would be necessary to make these distinctions in the many debates in which time and again the question is raised as to which sex has the stronger urge toward the other.

What has been described as masturbation in Woman springs from a cause other than the detumescence drive. W is, and now we are talking for the first time about a real difference, *much more easily sexually aroused than Man;* her *physiological irritability* (not sensitivity) in the sexual sphere is much greater. The fact of this capacity for easy sexual arousal can manifest itself in Woman either as the *desire* for sexual excitation or in a peculiar, very irritable, apparently very insecure and therefore uneasy and intensive fear of arousal by being touched. The desire for sexual excitation is a real sign of a capacity for easy arousal in that it is not one of those desires that can never be fulfilled by the *destiny* based on the nature of a person but, on the contrary, signifies that the entire constitution of a person can easily and willingly enter a state of sexual arousal, which Woman desires to be as intensive and as perpetual as possible, and which does not naturally end, as it does with Man, in the detumescence achieved through contrectation. Those phenomena that have been made out to be masturbation on the part of Woman are not actions with the immanent tendency to put an end to the state of sexual arousal, as they are in Man; rather, they are all attempts to precipitate, intensify, and prolong it. From the fear of sexual arousal, the analysis of which sets the psychology of Woman a far from easy, if not even the most

2. Translator's note: German *angreifen* means both "to attack" and "to touch."

difficult, task, it is therefore possible to infer with certainty a great weakness in this respect.

For Woman the state of sexual arousal only means the greatest intensification of her whole existence, *which is always and absolutely sexual. W's existence revolves entirely around her sexual life, the sphere of copulation and reproduction, i.e., in her relationship with a man and with children,* and her existence is totally absorbed by these things, while M is *not only* sexual. This then is in reality the difference that has been sought in the differing *intensity* of the sex drive. One should therefore beware of confusing the *force* of sexual desire and the strength of sexual affects with the *breadth* of the sexual desires and apprehensions that engross a human male or female. *Only the greater extension of the sexual sphere across the whole person in W* makes a specific difference of the utmost significance between the sexual extremes.

While W, then, is fully occupied and absorbed by sexuality, M knows a dozen other things: fighting and playing, socializing and feasting, discussions and learning, business and politics, religion and art. I am not talking about whether this was always the case. That need not concern us. It is like the Jewish Question: people say that the Jews have only become what they are, and once upon a time were quite different. That may be so, but we here do not know. Let those who believe evolution to be capable of so much believe it, but these things have not been proven, and one historical tradition is immediately contradicted by another. What matters is the way women are today. And if we come across things that cannot possibly have been implanted in a being from outside, we can safely assume that it has always been the same. Today, at least, this is certainly true: apart from a seeming exception (chapter XII), W concerns herself with extrasexual matters only for the sake of the man she loves or the man by whom she would like to be loved. She has no interest at all in these matters *as such.* There have been cases of a genuine woman learning Latin; but she has only done so, for instance, in order to be able, in this respect as in others, to help and supervise her son, who is attending a grammar school. The enjoyment of something and a talent for it, an interest in something and ease in mastering it, are always directly proportional. Those who have no muscles have no inclination to exercise with dumbbells or to lift weights; only those with a talent for mathematics will choose to study it. Thus even *talent* seems to be more rare or less intensive in genuine Woman (although this matters little, because even if the opposite were the case her sexuality would be too strong to admit any other serious occupation); and that is probably also why Woman lacks the prerequisites for the development of interesting combinations which in Man can mold, albeit not constitute, an individuality.

Accordingly, only the more feminine men are constantly chasing women and interested in nothing but love affairs and sexual relations. However, this remark is by no means meant to solve, or even begin to solve, the Don Juan problem.

W is nothing but sexuality, M is sexual and something else beyond. This shows particularly clearly in the entirely different ways in which Man and Woman experience their entry into the period of sexual *maturity.* In the case of a man the time of puberty is always a time of crisis, when he feels that something alien enters his existence, something is added to his thoughts and feelings, without his *wanting* it. It is the physiological erection, over which the will has no power; the first erection is therefore felt to be mysterious and unsettling by every man, and many men remember the particular circumstances with the greatest accuracy all their life. A woman, on the other hand, not only comes to terms with puberty easily, but feels that her existence has, as it were, been raised to a higher power, her own importance infinitely increased. Man, as a boy, feels no need whatsoever for *sexual* maturity. Woman, already as a quite young girl, expects *everything* from that time. In a man the symptoms of his physical maturity are accompanied by unpleasant, even hostile and anxious feelings. A woman observes her somatic development during puberty with the greatest suspense, with the most feverish, impatient expectation. This proves that Man's sexuality is not situated along the straight line of his development, while in Woman puberty only brings an enormous intensification of her *previous* form of existence. There are not many boys of that age who do not find the idea that they will fall in love or marry (marry in a general sense, not with regard to one girl in particular) extremely ridiculous and who do not reject it with indignation, while the youngest girls already seem to be keen on love and marriage as the fulfillment of their existence. That is why Woman attributes a positive value only to the time of sexual maturity, both in herself and in others, and has no real relationship with either childhood or old age. To her the recollection of her childhood is only a recollection of her stupidity, and the prospect of her old age fills her with fear and loathing. From her childhood her memory singles out the sexual moments alone by means of a positive evaluation, and even those are at a disadvantage against the incomparably greater later intensifications of her life—which is precisely a sexual life. Finally, the wedding night, the moment of defloration, is the most important, I would say, the half-way point of the whole life of Woman. In Man's life the first sexual intercourse plays absolutely no part compared to the significance that it possesses for the opposite sex.

Woman is *only* sexual, Man is *also* sexual: this difference can be further developed in terms of both space and time. In Man's body those points from which he can be sexually aroused are few in number and strictly localized. Woman's sexuality is spread diffusely over her whole body, and every touch, at whatever point, arouses her sexually. Therefore the assertion, in the second chapter of the first part, that the *whole* male as well as the *whole* female body is sexually determined should not be understood to mean that both Man and Woman can undergo a uniform sexual stimulation from every point. In Woman's capacity for arousal there are also some local differences, but there is no sharp division, as there is in Man, between the genital tract and all the other areas of the body.

The morphological protrusion of the male genitals from Man's body could, again, be regarded as a symbol of this situation.

Just as the sexuality of Man stands out *spatially* against the asexual elements in him, the same inequality also marks his behavior at different *times.* Woman is *constantly,* Man only *intermittently sexual.* In Woman the sex drive is always present (the apparent exceptions that are always brought up by those who would deny the sexuality of Woman will be discussed in considerable detail later), in Man it always *rests* for longer or shorter periods. This also explains the *eruptive* nature of the male sex drive, which makes it appear so much more striking than the female, and which has contributed to the proliferation of the error that Man's sex drive is more intensive than Woman's. The real difference is that for M the sex drive is, as it were, an itch with intervals, for W an incessant tickle.

The exclusive and continuous physical and psychic sexuality of Woman has even more far-reaching consequences. The fact that sexuality in Man is not everything, but only an appendage, enables Man *psychologically* to set it against a background and thus to *become conscious* of it. Therefore Man can confront his sexuality and contemplate it in isolation from other things. In Woman sexuality cannot be contrasted to a *non*-sexual sphere either through a temporal limitation of its eruptions or through the presence of an anatomical organ in which it is visibly localized. That is why Man is *conscious* of his sexuality, while Woman is completely unable to become conscious of, and thus in good faith to deny, her sexuality, if only *because she is nothing but sexuality, because she is sexuality itself,* as may be added immediately in anticipation of further explanations. Because *Woman* is *only* sexual, she lacks the *duality* which is a prerequisite of *noticing* sexuality, or indeed noticing anything; while in *Man,* who is always more than merely sexual, sexuality is in contrast to everything else, not only anatomically but also *psychologically.* That is why he has the ability to take up an independent attitude to sexuality. If he faces it, he can limit it or allow it more scope, negate it or affirm it. He has an equal potential to be a Don Juan or a saint, and he can choose the one or the other. To put it bluntly: Man has the penis, but the vagina has Woman.

As a result of these deductions it appears likely that Man becomes conscious of his sexuality and confronts it in an autonomous manner, while Woman seems to lack the ability to do so, and this claim is based on the greater differentiation of Man, in whom the sexual and asexual elements have separated. However, the possibility or impossibility of comprehending a single specific object is not related to the concept commonly associated with the word consciousness, which implies, rather, that *if* an organism has any consciousness, it can become conscious of *any* object. This raises the question about the *nature of female consciousness as such* and the discussion of that topic will involve a long detour before we can return to the point which has just been touched on so cursorily.

III Male and Female Consciousness

Before we can deal in more detail with one of the main differences between the male and female psyche and the extent to which it transforms the objects of the world into its own contents, it will be necessary to take some psychological soundings and define some concepts. As the views and principles of the prevailing psychology have developed without regard to this particular topic it would be surprising if the theories of that psychology could readily be applied to it. Furthermore, as yet there is no *psychology* but only *psychologies,* and a decision to join any one school and treat the entire topic on the basis of that school's dogmas would seem much more arbitrary than the procedure adopted here, which attempts to re-examine the phenomena as independently as necessary, albeit with the closest possible reference to existing achievements.

Attempts to regard all psychic life in a unified manner, and to trace it back to a single fundamental process, have expressed themselves in empirical psychology mainly in the relationship assumed by different researchers between *sensations* and *feelings.* Herbart derived feelings from ideas, while Horwicz claimed that feelings developed from sensations. The leading modern psychologists have emphasized the hopelessness of these monistic efforts. Nevertheless, there was some truth in them.

To find that truth, one must make a distinction that is, strangely enough, missing in today's psychology, even though it seems obvious. One must separate the first awareness of a sensation, the first thought of a thought, the first feeling of a feeling, from later repetitions of the same process, where there is the possibility of recognition. This distinction seems to be of great significance in respect to a number of problems, but unfortunately it is not made in today's psychology.

Every plain, clear, vivid *sensation,* as well as every sharply defined and distinct thought, before it is put into words *for the first time,* is *preceded by a stage of indistinctness,* although this may often be extremely *brief.* Likewise, every unfamiliar *association* is preceded by a more or less short period of time in which there is only a vague sense of direction toward what is to be associated, a general presentiment of an association, a sense of something belonging with something else. Leibniz in particular must have had in mind related processes which, having been more or less well described, gave rise to the above theories of Herbart and Horwicz.

Since only pleasure and unpleasure, and possibly, as Wundt suggested, relaxation and tension, repose and stimulation, are generally considered the simple basic forms of *feelings*, the division of psychic phenomena into sensations and feelings is too narrow for those phenomena which are part of the stages preceding clarity, and consequently useless for the purpose of describing them, as will shortly become more evident. In the interests of a precise definition I will therefore use what is probably the most general classification of psychic phenomena that could be made: Avenarius's division into "elements" and "characters" (where "character" has nothing in common with the *object of characterology*).

Avenarius has made it difficult to use his theories, not so much by his entirely *new* terminology (which contains many excellent elements and is practically indispensable for certain things that he was the first to notice and name), but rather by his unfortunate obsession with deriving psychology from a system of a physiology of the brain *which he himself only gained from the psychological facts of inner experience* (with the external addition of the most general biological knowledge of the balance between nutrition and work), and which is the greatest obstacle to the acceptance of many of his discoveries. In his *Kritik der reinen Erfahrung* [Critique of pure experience] the foundations on which the hypotheses of the physiological first part evolved in his own mind were provided by the psychological second part, but his account reverses these steps and therefore the first part strikes the reader like a report on a journey to Atlantis. Because of these difficulties I must take this opportunity to explain briefly the meaning of Avenarius's classification, which has proved most suitable for my purpose.

An *"element,"* for Avenarius, is what in standard psychology is simply called "sensation," "content of a sensation," or simply "content" (in connection with both "perception" and "reproduction"), and what is described by Schopenhauer as "idea," by the English as both "impression" and "idea," and in everyday life as "thing," "fact," or "object"—*regardless of whether or not a sensory organ has undergone any external stimulation, which was a very important and new notion.* In this context, for Avenarius's purposes as well as ours, it is of minor importance where the so-called analysis stops and whether one regards a *whole* tree as a "sensation" or only accepts a single leaf, a single stalk, or indeed only its color, size, consistency, smell, or temperature (which is where a halt is most often called) as really "simple." For one could go even further down this road and, on the assumption that the green color of the leaf is itself complex, that is, a result of its quality, intensity, brightness, saturation, and expansion, accept only these latter as elements. This would be similar to what has often happened to atoms: at one time they had to give way to "ameras," now again to "electrons."

If "green," "blue," "cold," "warm," "hard," "soft," "sweet," "sour" are elements, then *character,* according to Avenarius, is any "coloring" or "emotional tone" that accompanies them, and this *applies* ***not only*** to "pleasant," "beautiful," "agreeable" and their opposites, but also to "strange," "reliable," "uncanny," "constant," "different," "certain," "familiar," "actual," "doubtful," etc., etc., which Avenarius was first to recognize as belonging psychologically in the same category. *What* I, for example, assume, believe, or know is an *"element,"* while the fact *that* it is just *assumed,* but not *believed* or *known,* is *psychologically* (not logically) a "character," *in* which the "element" is set.

There is a stage in the life of the psyche at which even this most comprehensive classification of psychic phenomena *cannot yet* be carried out and would be *premature.* For *in their beginnings all "elements" appear to form a blurred background,* a "rudis indigestaque moles," with *waves of characterization* (*roughly = emotional accentuation*) *swirling around the whole.* This resembles the process that takes place when one approaches a feature of the environment, such as a shrub or a pile of wood, from a long distance: in order to understand what follows, the reader is asked to think above all of the original impression created by such a feature, the first moment when one is a long way from knowing what "it" really is, that moment of the first and greatest vagueness and uncertainty.

At that particular moment "element" and "character" are absolutely indistinguishable (while, according to Petzold's, no doubt commendable, modification of Avenarius's account, they are always *inseparable*). For instance, in a crowd of people I notice a face that is *immediately* hidden from me by the heaving mass. I have no idea what this face looks like and would be completely unable to describe it or to name even *one* distinguishing mark of it; and yet it excites me a great deal and I ask myself with anxious and nagging agitation: Where have I seen this face before?

If a man, in "the twinkling of an eye," sees a woman's head that makes a very strong sensuous impression on him, he often cannot tell himself what he has really seen, and may not even accurately remember the color of her hair. The prerequisite for this is always, to put it in entirely photographic terms, that the retina should be *exposed* to the object for a sufficiently *short* time, that is, for *fractions* of a second.

If one approaches any object from a long distance, initially one always discerns only quite vague outlines, but one has very vivid feelings, which recede in the same measure as one approaches more closely and becomes more sharply aware of the details. (This, as should be stated expressly, is not a matter of any "feelings of expectancy.") Imagine, for example, the first sight of a human sphenoid detached from its sutures; or of many pictures and paintings as soon as they are seen from a position half a meter this side or that side of the right distance. I remember in particular the impression made on me by some passages of demisemiquavers in Beethoven piano excerpts and by a treatise full of triple integrals before I could read music or had any conception of integration. This is what Avenarius and Petzold *overlooked:* that *whenever the elements stand out in greater relief the characterization* (emotional emphasis) *is to some extent removed* from them.

Some facts established by experimental psychology can also be linked to these results of self-observation. If, in a dark-room, an eye adapted to the darkness is exposed to a momentary or very brief stimulus of *colored* light, the observer will only have an impression of a flash without being able to indicate its exact chromatic quality; what he senses is a "something" lacking any further definition, and what he reports is a "mere impression of light"; and even if the duration of the stimulus is extended (of course not beyond a certain degree) he will find it difficult to give a precise indication of the color.

In exactly the same way every scientific discovery, every technological invention, every artistic creation is preceded by a cognate stage of darkness, a darkness like that from which Zarathustra summons to the light his doctrine of eternal recurrence: "Up, abysmal thought up from my depths! I am your cockerel and dawn, sleepy worm: up! up! My voice shall soon crow you awake!"—The process in its entirety, from total confusion to radiant brightness, is comparable to the sequence of images we receive passively as the many moist cloths wrapped round a sculpted group or a relief are removed one by one; a spectator at the unveiling of a monument has a similar experience. But when I remember something, for instance a melody I once heard, the same process is experienced *again,* albeit often in an extremely shortened and therefore less easily noticeable form. Every new thought is preceded by a stage of what I would like to call "*pre-thought,*" where fluid geometrical structures, visual phantasms, misty images emerge and dissolve, and "uncertain shapes," veiled pictures, mysteriously beckoning masks appear. The beginning and the end of the sequence, which as a whole I will briefly call a process of "*clarification,*" in a certain sense relate to each other like the impressions received by a very short-sighted person of distant objects with and without correcting lenses.

As in the life of the individual (who may die before he has run through the whole process), so in the history of scientific research: "*surmises*" always precede clear insights. It is the same process of clarification, *spread over generations.* Think, for example, of the many Greek and modern anticipations of the theories of Lamarck and Darwin whose "precursors" today are receiving fulsome praise, or of the many forerunners of Robert Mayer and Helmholtz, or of all the points where Goethe and Leonardo da Vinci, perhaps the most versatile men ever, anticipated the later progress of science, etc., etc. Whenever it is discovered that some idea is not at all new and can already be found in this or that thinker, we are faced with such preliminary stages. A similar development, from uncertain groping and cautious balancing to great victories, can be observed with all artistic styles, in painting as in music. Likewise, the intellectual progress of mankind in the sciences is also based almost exclusively on a better and better description of the *same* things: it is the process of *clarification extended across the whole of human history.* Compared with *this,* our new discoveries are not very significant.

How many degrees of clarity and differentiation an impression can pass through on its way to becoming a completely distinct thought, without any fuzziness blurring its contours, can be observed whenever one tries to study and comprehend a difficult new topic, for instance the theory of elliptical functions. How many *degrees of understanding* does one recognize in oneself (particularly in mathematics and mechanics) before one finds everything laid out in beautiful order, organized right through, with perfect and undisturbed harmony between the parts and the whole, open to being effortlessly grasped by the attentive mind. These individual degrees correspond to the stages on the road of clarification.

The process of clarification can also take place in *reverse,* from complete clarity to the greatest vagueness. This *reversal* of the process of clarification is none other than the process of *forgetting,* which generally extends over a lengthy period and is generally noticed only by chance at one or other point of its progress. This resembles the decay of well-established roads which have not been properly maintained or, as it were, "reproduced." Just as the youthful "pre-thought" turns into the most intensively sparkling "thought," so the "thought" turns into the senile "post-thought," and just as a forest path that has not been walked on for a long time begins to be overgrown right and left by grass, herbs, and bushes, the clear outlines of a thought that is no longer thought becomes more blurred day by day. This also explains a practical rule that a friend of mine[1] has very often found to be the case: if somebody wants to *learn* something, be it a piece of music or a chapter of the history of philosophy, he will usually be unable to devote himself to this study without interruptions and will have to go through every single part of the material several times. The question then arises as to the most appropriate length of the pauses between one attempt and the next. It has been discovered—and is probably true in general—that the attempt must be repeated *before one becomes again interested* in the work, that is, as long as one *believes* that one still more or less *knows* the material under study. The reason is that as soon as one has forgotten enough of it to be once again interested, curious, or eager to learn about it, the results of the first practice round have receded, so that the second cannot immediately reinforce the first and one must undertake a large part of the labor of clarification afresh.

Perhaps one must assume, in accordance with Siegmund Exner's theory of the "breaching" of a very popular view, that the physiological parallel to the process of clarification is really the need for the nerve fibers, possibly their fibrils, to be affected (either for a lengthy period or in frequent repetition) in order to become *pathways* for the conduct of stimuli. In the same way, naturally, in the event of forgetting, the result of this "breaching" would be cancelled, and the morphological structural elements developed by it in the individual neuron would atrophy owing to lack of practice. Avenarius's theory of some phenomena

1. Dr. Hermann Swoboda in Vienna.

related to those above—he would have assumed differences of "articulation" or "structuring" in the cerebral system (the "independent oscillations of the C system")—transfers properties from the "dependent series" (i.e., the psychic area) to the "independent" (physical) too simplistically and too literally to be of any benefit, in particular, to the question of psycho-physical correspondences. Nevertheless, the terms "articulated" and "structured" seem well suited to describing the degree of distinctness of the individual psychic data and will be used for that purpose later on.

It was necessary to trace the process of clarification in its entirety to understand the extent and content of that new concept. For what follows now, however, only the initial stage, or starting point, of clarification is important. At the moment when the contents of the subsequent process of clarification present themselves for the very first time, Avenarius's distinction between "element" and "character," as noted above, *cannot yet be applied* to them. Thus, whoever accepts this classification for all the data of the *developed* psyche will have to introduce a specific name for the contents of that stage *in which such a dualism cannot yet be discerned.* For psychic data in that most primitive state of their infancy I offer, without making any claims whatsoever beyond the confines of this study, the word "*henid*" (from ἕν, because they show neither sensation and feeling as *two* analytical elements that can be isolated by abstraction nor indeed any duality at all).

In this context the concept of the absolute henid must be regarded merely as an ideal. How often *real* psychic experiences in the *adulthood* of human beings are undifferentiated enough to justify calling them by that name cannot easily be established with any certainty, but this does not invalidate the theory as such. A common occurrence, experienced by different people in different degrees of frequency in conversation, may well be called a henid: one has a particular feeling and was going to *say* something quite specific, at which point, for example, the other person makes a remark, and "it" has gone and cannot be recaptured. Later on, however, an association reproduces something that one immediately knows to be exactly the *same* thing that one was unable to get hold of beforehand. This is a proof that it was the *same* content, only in a different *form, at a different stage of development.* Clarification, then, not only occurs in this direction in the life of an individual as a whole, but must also be completed anew in respect of each content.

I fear that I could be asked to provide a more accurate and detailed description of what I mean by henid, for instance, what a henid looks like. That would be a complete misunderstanding. It is integral to the concept of the henid that it can only be described as one hazy whole. *As certain as it is that in due course the henid will be identified with a fully articulated content, it is equally certain that it is not yet that articulated content itself,* from which it differs somehow, by the degree of consciousness, the lack of relief, the fusion of background and principal object, the absence of a "focal point" within the "field of vision."

Thus, one can neither observe nor describe any individual henids: *one can only take note of their having been there.*

Incidentally, *in principle* it is just as easy to think and live in terms of henids as in terms of elements and characters; every henid is an individual and can be distinguished perfectly well from every other henid. For reasons that will be explained later, it must be assumed that the experiences of early childhood (and this probably applies without exception to the first fourteen months of *all* human beings) are henids, albeit perhaps not in the absolute sense of the word. In any case, the psychic events of early childhood never stray far from the henid stage, while in the adult there are many contents that develop beyond that stage. The henid clearly represents the sensations of the lowest bionts, and perhaps many plants and animals. In *humans,* on the other hand, a development from the henid toward fully differentiated, vivid sensations and thoughts is possible, even though it is only an ideal that they may never completely reach. While the absolute henid precludes language altogether, since the structure of speech can only arise from the structure of thought, even at the highest intellectual level accessible to humans there are things that are unclear and therefore inexpressible.

The henid theory as a whole, then, is intended to help mediate in the dispute about whether the honor of seniority is due to sensation or feeling, and to try to replace the notions of "element" and "character," which Avenarius and Petzold singled out from the middle of the process of clarification, by describing the facts in terms of *developmental history,* on the strength of the fundamental observation that "elements" cannot be distinguished from "characters" until they have become distinct. That is why people are only inclined to "moods" and all kinds of "sentimentalities" when things do not present themselves in sharp outlines, and by night rather than by day. When night gives way to light people's way of thinking also changes.

But what is the connection between this investigation and the psychology of the sexes? How do—for obviously this lengthy laying of foundations was undertaken for that purpose—M and W differ in respect to the various stages of clarification?

The answer is as follows:

Man has the same psychic contents as woman, in a more articulated form; while she thinks more or less in henids, he thinks in clear, distinct concepts linked to definite feelings which can always be removed from their objects. In W "thinking" and "feeling" are one, undivided, for M they can be separated. That is, W still experiences many things in henid form, when in M clarification has long since taken place.[2] That is why W is sentimental, and women can only be moved but not shocked.

2. At the same time one must think neither of absolute henids in Woman nor of absolute clarification in Man.

The greater articulation of the psychic data in Man corresponds to the sharper outlines of his physique and face, as opposed to the softness, roundness, and indeterminacy of the genuine female figure and physiognomy. A further correspondence exists between this view and the results of comparative measurements of the sensory sensibility of the sexes, which, counter to popular opinion, have constantly demonstrated greater sensibility in men, even if assessed on *average,* and which would certainly have shown much greater differences if account had been taken of the *types.* The only exception is the sense of touch: in this area women are more sensitive than men. This fact is interesting enough to demand an interpretation, which will indeed be attempted later on. It should also be noted here that men are incomparably more sensitive to pain than women, which is of importance for physiological investigations into the "sense of pain" and its distinction from the "sense of touch."

A weak sensibility will certainly favor the contents remaining near the henid stage; however, a lower degree of clarification cannot be proven to be its necessary consequence, but can only be regarded as having a very likely connection with it. A more reliable proof of the lesser articulation of the female imagination is provided by the more *decisive judgment* of men, although this cannot be *derived* exclusively and entirely from the less distinct nature of the thought processes of women (perhaps both go back to a common, deeper root). But this at least is certain: as long as we are near the henid stage, we tend only to know precisely what something is *not* like, which we always know long before we know what something is like: this, the possession of contents in henid form, is probably also the basis of what Mach has called "instinctive experience." While we remain near the henid stage we still talk around the subject, correcting ourselves at every attempt to name it, and saying: "This is still not the right word." From this, uncertainty of judgment naturally follows. Only with complete clarification does our judgment also become clear and firm. *The act of judgment itself requires a certain distance from the henid stage,* even where it is meant to pronounce an analytical judgment that will not increase mankind's intellectual assets.

However, the conclusive proof of the correctness of attributing the henid to W and the differentiated content to M, and seeing this as a fundamental difference between the two, is that, whenever a new judgment is to be made, and not a judgment made long ago expressed once more in the form of a sentence, *it is always W who* ***expects*** *the clarification of her vague ideas,* ***the interpretation of her henids****, from M.* Where Woman has vague, unconscious ideas, she *actually expects, desires, and demands* to see in Man's speech the structuring of thought, *which she regards as a (tertiary) male sexual characteristic and which affects her in that way. That* is why so many girls say that they would only marry, or at least could only *love,* a man *who is more intelligent than they are,* and why they may be surprised, or indeed sexually *repelled,* by a man who simply agrees with what they say and does not immediately say it better than they do. In short, that is why a woman *feels it to be a criterion of masculinity* that a man should also be her intellectual superior, and why she is powerfully attracted to a man who impresses her with his thought, and at the same time, without realizing it, delivers the decisive vote against all theories of equality.

M lives consciously, W lives unconsciously. That is the conclusion we are now entitled to draw with regard to the extremes. *W receives her consciousness from M:* the function of making the unconscious conscious is the sexual function of typical Man with regard to typical Woman, who ideally complements him.

Thus our account has arrived at the *problem of talent:* almost the entire theoretical dispute concerning the Woman Question today is about who has the higher intellectual potential, "men" or "women." At the popular level the question is asked without reference to types, while the views developed here about the types are bound to have an impact on the answer to that question. What must now be discussed is the nature of that connection.

IV Endowment and Genius

SINCE SO MUCH has been written in so many places about the nature of the predisposition to genius, it will prevent misunderstandings if I make some preliminary statements before embarking on a detailed discussion of the matter.

First we must draw a line of demarcation from the concept of talent. In the popular view, genius and talent are almost always connected in such a way as if the former were a higher, or the highest, degree of the latter and capable of being derived from it by intensifying or concentrating the various talents of a person to a maximum, or as if at least there were some transitions mediating between the two. This view is totally wrong. Although there are certainly many different degrees and intensities of genius, these gradations have nothing at all to do with so-called "talent." A person may have a talent, e.g., a talent for mathematics, to an extraordinary degree from birth. He will then be able to master the most difficult chapters of this science with ease, but that does not mean that he has any genius, which is the same as originality, individuality, and the condition of productivity. Conversely, there are supreme geniuses who have not developed any specific talent to a particularly high degree. Novalis or Jean Paul may serve as examples. Genius, then, is by no means a highest superlative of talent. The two are separated by a whole world; they are absolutely heterogeneous in nature, not to be measured against, or compared to, each other. Talent is hereditary and may be the common possession of a family (the Bachs): genius is not transferable, it is never generic, but always individual (Johann Sebastian).

To many easily dazzled, mediocre minds, particularly *women,* wit and genius generally amount to the same thing. Although external appearances may suggest the opposite, in truth women are unable to appreciate genius. For them, any extravagance of nature that makes a man visibly stand out from the common crowd is as able as any other to satisfy their sexual ambition; they mistake the actor for the dramatist and make no distinction between the virtuoso and the artist. Accordingly, they regard a clever man as having genius, and Nietzsche as the prototype of genius. And yet those who merely juggle ideas, who follow all the French fashions of the intellect, have not the remotest affinity to a true elevation of the mind. Great men take themselves and the things around them too seriously to be "clever" more often than once in a while. People who are nothing but clever are impious people; they are people who are not really overcome by things, who never take a sincere and profound interest in things, in whom there is nothing struggling long and hard toward being born. Their only concern is that their thought should glitter and sparkle like a brilliantly cut diamond, not that it should also illuminate anything. And that is because their thinking is above all focused on what others will "say" about these thoughts—a consideration which is by no means always "considerate." There are men who are able to marry a woman who in no way attracts them—merely because *other men* fancy her. And such marriages also exist between many people and their ideas. I am thinking of the malicious, loutish, offensive writings of a certain living author, who thinks that he is roaring when he is only barking. Unfortunately Friedrich Nietzsche too in his later writings (although he is incomparably superior to that other writer) sometimes seems to have been interested mainly in those aspects of his ideas which he suspected would quite shock people. It is often precisely where he *seems* most ruthless that he *is* at his vainest. It is the vanity of the mirror that fervently begs for recognition by what it reflects: look how well, how *ruthlessly*, I reflect!—In our youth, before our character has become firmly established, we probably all try to acquire firmness by attacking others, but really great men are never passionately aggressive except out of dire necessity. It is not they who resemble the new member of the university dueling fraternity in search of his first bout, or the girl who is delighted with her new dress chiefly because it will *so* annoy her "friends."

Genius! The gift of genius! What disquiet and intellectual discomfort, what hate and envy, what resentment and belittlement has this phenomenon provoked in the majority of people, how much incomprehension and how much desire to imitate—to be the "spit and image"—has it brought to light!

We gladly take leave of the imitations of genius, in order to turn to genius itself and its genuine embodiments. But truly, given the infinite abundance of elements merging into one another, any starting point at which we may choose to begin our investigation will be an arbitrary one. All those qualities that must be described as appertaining to genius are so closely connected that examining them in isolation, with the intention of rising only gradually to a higher level of generality, proves to be the most difficult task imaginable, since such an examination runs a constant risk of being seduced into rounding things off prematurely and is in danger of failing to achieve its aim through the isolating method.

All the discussions of the nature of genius so far have been either biological and clinical in kind and have declared with ludicrous presumptuousness that what little knowledge we possess in this area is sufficient to answer the most difficult and most profound psychological questions, or else they have *descended* from the heights of a metaphysical standpoint in order to *absorb* the quality of genius in their system. If the road to be followed here does not lead to all goals *at once,* it is because of the nature of roads.

Let us bear in mind how much better than the average person a great poet is at putting himself in the position of other people. Consider the extraordinary number of characters depicted by Shakespeare or Euripides, or think of the enormous diversity of persons appearing in Zola's novels. Heinrich von Kleist, after Penthesilea, created her diametrical opposite, Käthchen von Heilbronn, and Michelangelo embodied Leda and the Sybil of Delphi from his own imagination. There are probably not many men who had so little of the visual artist in them as Immanuel Kant and Joseph Schelling, and yet it was they who have written the most profound and truest things about art.

In order to recognize and depict a person one must *understand* him. But to understand a person, one must have some similarity to him, one must be like him; in order to recreate and to appreciate his actions, one must be able to reproduce the psychological prerequisites of his actions in oneself: *understanding a person means having him in oneself.* One must resemble the mind one is trying to grasp. That is why only a rogue will always understand another rogue correctly, while a totally harmless person can only understand a good nature equal to his own, and never a rogue. A poseur almost always interprets the actions of another person as poses, and he is more liable to see through another poseur than is a simple person, in whom the poseur in his turn is never quite able to believe. *Understanding a person, then, means being that person.*

But according to this argument, everybody would be understood best by himself, which is certainly not true. Nobody can ever understand himself, because in order to do so he would have to step outside himself: the subject of cognition and volition would have to be capable of becoming the object, just as, in order to understand the universe, it would be necessary to find a standpoint outside the universe, which is not possible, given the very concept of a universe. A person who would be able to understand himself would be able to understand the world. That this statement is not only valid in a relative sense, but harbors a very profound significance, will gradually emerge from this treatise. For the moment, it is certain that we cannot understand our own deepest and most personal nature. And it is in fact true that we are understood, if at all, only by others and not by ourselves. To the other person, who has a similarity to us and yet in other respects is by no means identical to us, this similarity can become an object of contemplation: he can *recognize,* depict, *understand* himself in us, or us in him. *Understanding a person, then, means being* ***also*** *that person.*

The man of genius has revealed himself in the above examples as a man who understands incomparably more than the average person. Goethe is supposed to have said that there was no vice and no crime for which he had not felt a predisposition in himself and which, at one point or another in his life, he had not fully understood. The man of genius, then, is more complex, more multifarious and richer; *and a man must be regarded as having the more genius, the more human beings he unites in himself* and, it must be added, *the more vividly,* the more *intensely* he has the other human beings in himself. If his understanding of his fellow-humans were only like a feeble flicker, he would not be able to set the life in his heroes ablaze like a mighty flame, and his characters would be devoid of strength and substance. The ideal of a genius, in particular of the artistic kind, is to live in all human beings, to lose himself in all, and to *emanate* into the multitude, while the philosopher has the task of finding all the others again *in himself* and to *absorb* them into a unity, which will always be *his* unity alone.

This protean nature of genius must not be understood, any more than the bisexuality I discussed earlier, as simultaneity: not even the greatest genius has the gift of understanding the nature of all human beings at the same time, for example on one and the same day. The more comprehensive and substantial intellectual potential that a man possesses can reveal itself only step by step, in a gradual unfolding of his entire nature. It would seem that this occurs in a process of regular *periods.* These periods, however, do not repeat themselves in the same way in the course of a life, as if each were just a repetition of the one preceding it, but they do so, as it were, in an ever higher sphere. No two moments of an individual life are completely identical, and the similarity between the later and the earlier periods is only that between points on a higher segment of a spiral and those on the homologous lower segment. That is why exceptional individuals so often conceive the plan of a work in their youth, then put it to one side for years before reworking it in their maturity, and finally complete it, after yet another postponement, in their old age: these are the different periods which they enter alternately and which constantly present them with different objects. Such periods exist in every person, but in different strengths, with different "amplitudes." Since a genius comprises the largest number of human beings with the *greatest* amount of life, *the amplitude of the periods will be the more pronounced, the greater a mind a man has.* Accordingly, many outstanding men, from their earliest youth, are accused by their teachers of constantly going "from one extreme to the other." As if they felt particularly comfortable in that situation! In men of excellence in particular, such transitions generally take the form of out-and-out crises. Goethe once spoke of the "recurrent puberty" of artists. What he meant is closely connected with this topic.

It is due precisely to his highly periodic nature that in a genius the fruitful years are always preceded by sterile ones and very productive phases are followed time and again by barren ones—phases in which he thinks nothing of himself and indeed, *psychologically* (not logically), thinks less of himself *than of any other person:* for he is tormented by the memory of his creative period and, above all, by how *free* those who are not plagued by such memories seem to him.

Just as his ecstasies are more powerful than those of the others, so his depressions are also more terrible. Every exceptional individual has such periods, whether shorter or longer, in which he may totally despair of himself and think of committing suicide; periods in which he may be struck by many things and even accumulate many things for a later harvest, but in which nothing appears with the tremendous tension of the productive period, in other words, in which *the storm fails to break.* If in these periods he nevertheless tries to go on creating, people will say: "How low he has sunk," "How spent he is," "How he is copying himself," etc., etc.

In a man of genius his other qualities—not only whether he produces anything at all, but also the material and the spirit in which he produces—are subject to change and a powerful periodicity. At one time he inclines more to reflection and science, at other times to art (Goethe); first his interest is concentrated on human civilization and history, then again on nature (compare Nietzsche's *Untimely Meditations* with his *Zarathustra*); now he is mystical, then naïve (Bjørnson and Maurice Maeterlinck being the most recent examples). Indeed, in an exceptional individual, the periods in which the various sides of his character—and the many people who have an intensive life in him—succeed one another with so great an "amplitude" that this periodicity also reveals itself clearly in physiognomical terms. This is how I would explain the striking phenomenon that the expressions on the face of more endowed people change much more frequently than on that of people without any endowment, and indeed that at different times they can have incredibly different faces; one needs only to compare the pictures that have been preserved of Goethe, Beethoven, Kant, or Schopenhauer in different epochs of their lives. *The number of faces an individual has can actually be regarded as a physiognomical indicator of his endowment.*[1] People who always show the same *totally* unaltered face exist at a very low intellectual level. On the other hand, physiognomists will not be surprised to find that more endowed people, who constantly reveal new sides of their character in their contacts with others and in their conversation so that it is not easy to arrive promptly at a firm judgment about them, also demonstrate this quality through their external appearance.

The *provisional* idea of genius that has been developed here will perhaps be rejected with indignation because, in postulating that a Shakespeare necessarily also had all the vulgarity of a Falstaff, all the villainy of an Iago, all the coarseness of a Caliban in him, it demeans the moral standing of great individuals by imputing to them the most intimate understanding of everything despicable and trivial. Indeed, it must be admitted that, according to this view, men of gen-

1. I use the word "endowment" to avoid the word "genius" as often as possible, and I mean by it a predisposition of which the highest degree is genius. Accordingly, a strict distinction is made here between endowment and talent.

ius are full of the most copious and most violent passions and are not spared even the most revolting urges (which, incidentally, is confirmed everywhere in their biographies).

Nevertheless, that objection is unjustified, as will be seen later, when we go more deeply into the problem. For the time being it should be pointed out that only a superficial method of reasoning can regard that objection as an unavoidable inference from the premises expounded so far, which in themselves suffice to make its opposite more than likely. Zola, who knows the urge for sexual murder so well, would never have committed a sexual murder, *because there are also so many* ***other*** *things in him.* The real sexual murderer is at the mercy of his urge; in the writer describing him, the whole wealth of a manifold disposition acts counter to that impulse. It allows Zola to *know* the sexual murderer much better than any real sexual murderer knows himself, but it ensures precisely that he will *recognize* him if the temptation really approached him; and thus he is already in opposition to it, eye to eye, and able to defend himself against it. That is how the criminal instinct in a great individual is turned into an *intellectual* notion, becoming an artistic motif in Zola or the philosophical conception of the "radically evil" in Kant, and therefore does not lead him to the criminal deed.

The wealth of possibilities that exist in every exceptional individual has important consequences, which take us back to the theory of henids developed in the previous chapter. *We* ***notice*** *sooner what we have in ourselves than what we do not understand* (if this were otherwise there would be no possibility for people to engage with each other—as it is, they usually do not know how *often* they misunderstand each other); thus the genius, who *understands* so much more than the run-of-the-mill person, will also *notice* more than the latter. An intriguer will easily recognize a person who resembles him; a passionate gambler will immediately realize when another betrays a great desire to gamble, while people who are different will miss this for a long time in most cases: "his kind you understand better," we hear in Wagner's "Siegfried." I established above that a more complex person can understand every other person better than that person himself can, provided that he is that person and at the same time something more or, *to put it more accurately, provided that he has both that person* ***and the opposite of that person*** *in himself. Duality is always the prerequisite of noticing and understanding.* If we ask psychology about the most fundamental prerequisite for anything to become conscious, that is, for the process of "differentiation," we receive the answer that the necessary prerequisite is *contrast.* If there were only a monotonous gray, nobody would have any consciousness, let alone any concept, of color, and the absolute *mono*tony of a sound promptly puts people to ***sleep****: duality (the* ***light*** *that separates and distinguishes things) is the cause of wakeful consciousness.*

Therefore nobody can understand himself, even if he were to reflect on himself uninterruptedly all his life. One can only understand another person if one resembles him without being totally identical to him, and if one has in oneself an equal amount of both the other person and his opposite. It is this distribution that creates the most favorable conditions for understanding: see the case of Kleist, mentioned above. *Ultimately, then, understanding a person means having him* ***and*** *his opposite in oneself.*

As a general rule, *pairs* of opposites must always come together in the same person in order to allow him to become conscious of just *one* member of each pair. The study of the eye's sense of color supplies several physiological proofs of this. I will only mention the well-known phenomenon that color-blindness always extends to *both* complementary colors: those blind to red are also blind to green, and there are people blind to blue-and-yellow, but nobody could perceive blue if he were unreceptive to yellow. This law is valid everywhere in the intellectual realm: it is the fundamental law of any formation of consciousness. For instance, a person who is predisposed to cheerfulness will also be more predisposed to sudden swings to melancholy than a person with a permanently even temper, while many a melancholic can only keep himself above water through a forcible mania; and anybody who appreciates every refinement and subtlety as much as Shakespeare will also sense and understand the extremes of crudeness and uncouthness most accurately because they exist, so to speak, as a danger in himself.

Since understanding leads to noticing, the more human types together with their opposites an individual unites in his personality, the less he will *miss* of what people do and do not do, the sooner he will *see through* what they feel, think, and really want. *There is no man of genius who is not a great judge of human character;* the exceptional individual often gets the complete picture of simpler people at the first glance and is often able to characterize them fully at once.

The majority of people have a more or less one-sidedly developed sense for this or that. One person knows all birds and is able to distinguish their voices most clearly, while another from childhood has a loving and assured eye for plants; one feels deeply moved by layers of tellurian sediments and takes the heavenly bodies for a friendly greeting, but often for no more than that (Goethe), while another, full of submissive forebodings, trembles with the coldness of the nocturnal sky and its fixed stars (Kant); one feels that mountains are dead and is mightily attracted only to the sea with its eternal motion (Böcklin), while another is unable to relate to that never-ending restlessness and returns under the sublime power of the mountains (Nietzsche). So every person, even the simplest, finds something in nature to which he is drawn, and for which his senses become more acute than for anything else. How then should the greatest genius, who, in the ideal case, contains all these people, fail to collect in himself their relationships with, and their loving inclinations toward, the outside world together with their inner lives? Thus, not only the generality of all things human, but also of all things natural, grows into him: *he is the man who has the closest rapport with the largest number of things;* who is struck by the most things and misses the fewest; who understands the most things, and understands them most deeply, simply because he is in a position to make the most diverse comparisons and the most numerous distinctions, and knows best how to measure and to define. *The man of genius becomes* ***conscious*** *of the largest number of things, and he becomes most strongly conscious of all of these.* That is why his sensibility will without doubt also be the most subtle. However, this must not be interpreted, as has been done with an obviously one-sided reference to the artist, merely in favor of a refined sensory perception, such as the more acute vision of the painter (or poet) or the more acute hearing of the composer (Mozart). The measure of genius must be sought in his mental, rather than sensory, responsiveness to differences, although the latter will also frequently be turned toward the inside.

Thus the consciousness of genius is *farthest* from the henid stage: on the contrary, it is of the greatest, most dazzling clarity and brightness. *At this point the quality of genius already reveals itself as a higher kind of masculinity;* ***and that is why W cannot be a genius.*** This follows from the logical application of the insight gained in the previous chapter—that M lives more consciously than W—to the essential result of the present chapter, which culminates in the proposition that *genius is identical to a higher, because more general, consciousness.* Such a more intense consciousness of everything, however, is made possible only by the enormous number of opposites that exist together in an exceptional individual.

That is why universality is at the same time the mark of genius. There are no special geniuses, no "mathematical" or "musical geniuses," and no "chess geniuses" either. *There are* ***only*** *universal geniuses. The man of genius can be defined as the man who knows* ***everything*** *without ever having learnt it.* "Knowing everything" naturally does not refer to the theories and systems imposed on the facts by science and learning, neither the history of the Spanish War of Succession nor the experiments in diamagnetism. The artist does not acquire his knowledge of the colors of water when the sky is dull or bright by studying optics, and there is no need to delve into characterology in order to depict people consistently. The more endowed a man is, the more things he *has* always reflected on *independently,* and the more things he relates to personally.

The theory of special geniuses, which makes it possible, for example, to speak of a "musical genius" who is "of unsound mind in every other respect," once again confuses talent with genius. If a musician is truly great, he may, in the language to which his special talent directs him, be just as universal, just as adept at traversing the whole inner and outer world, as the poet or the philosopher: Beethoven was such a genius. Conversely he may move in as limited a sphere as does a mediocre scientific or artistic mind: such a mind was Johann

Strauss, and it is strange to hear him being called a genius, however beautiful flowers his lively but very limited imagination may have produced. To come back to that point once more, there are *many kinds of talents, but there is only* ***one*** *kind of genius,* which may choose and take up any one talent to work with. There is something that all men of genius, as *men of genius,* have in common, however profound a difference there may otherwise be between the great philosopher and the great painter, the great musician and the great sculptor, the great poet and the great founder of a religion. The talent through which the real intellectual predisposition of a man reveals itself is less relevant than is generally believed, and its importance is unfortunately greatly overrated as a result of the close proximity from which an aesthetic examination is often undertaken. Not only the differences in endowment, but the mentality and *weltanschauung* of a man also care little about the dividing lines between the arts. They leap over them, and thus the more unprejudiced eye often discovers surprising similarities: rather than searching for analogies *within* the history of music, or the history of art, literature, or philosophy, it will, say, confidently compare Bach with Kant, place Karl Maria von Weber next to Eichendorff, link Böcklin with Homer, and the rich stimulation and great fruitfulness that thus accrue to the powers of observation will ultimately also benefit the psychological insight, from the lack of which all the histories of art and philosophy have suffered most severely. The question of what organic and psychological conditions make a genius either a mystical visionary or perhaps a great draughtsman must be put to one side, as they are irrelevant for *this* treatise.

From that quality of genius, however, which remains one and the same despite all, often very deeply rooted, differences between individual geniuses, and which, according to the concept established here, can be manifested anywhere, *W is excluded.* Although it will not be decided until a later chapter whether there can be purely scientific geniuses and geniuses of nothing but action, rather than only artistic and philosophical geniuses, there is every reason to be more cautious in awarding the predicate of genius than has been the case so far. In due course it will clearly be seen that if one wants to form an idea of the nature of genius as such, and to arrive at any idea of the same, then Woman *must* be described as incapable of having genius. Nevertheless, it will not be possible for anybody to accuse my exposition of first constructing an arbitrary concept that could not apply to the female sex, and then presenting this retrospectively as the essence of genius, merely in order to avoid having to allow women a place *within* it.

Here we can fall back on the initial reflections of this chapter. While woman does not understand genius, with the possible exception of a living person possessing it, man has a profound relationship with this phenomenon as such, which Carlyle, in his book that is still so little understood has called hero-worship and described so beautifully and captivatingly. The hero-worship of man once more demonstrates that *genius is linked to masculinity and represents an ideal masculinity raised to a higher power.*[2] Woman has no original consciousness, only a consciousness bestowed on her by man. Woman lives unconsciously, man lives consciously, but a genius lives most consciously.

2. *Endowment* (not *talent*) and *sex* are the only two things *that are not inherited,* but are *independent* of "genetic material" and seem to come into being, as it were, spontaneously. This fact alone makes it likely that genius, or the lack of it, must be connected to the masculinity or femininity of a person.

V | Endowment and Memory

To start with the henid theory, I would like to report the following observation. I have just noted, *half* mechanically, the page number of a passage in a botanical treatise from which I intended to copy out an extract later. At the same time I was thinking something in henid form, but what I was thinking, and how I was thinking it, what was knocking on the door of my consciousness, I could no longer remember at the very next moment, although I tried very hard to do so. However, that is precisely why this instance—a typical one—is particularly instructive.

The more sharply defined, the more fully formed, a complex of perceptions is, the easier it is to reproduce. Clarity of consciousness is the first prerequisite of memory, and the *memory* of the stimulation is proportional to the *intensity* of the stimulation of consciousness. "I shall never forget this," "I shall remember this all my life," "This will never again slip my mind," is what people say about events that have greatly excited them, about moments that have made them wiser by an insight or richer by an experience. If, then, the ability of the contents of consciousness to be reproduced is in direct proportion to their organization, it will be clear *that the absolute henid cannot be remembered at all.*

Since the endowment of a human being grows in line with the articulation of all his experiences, *the more endowed an individual is, the better he will be able to remember his* **whole** *past, everything that he has ever thought and done, seen and heard, perceived and felt,* and the greater the assurance and vividness with which he will be able to reproduce every detail of his life. *The surest, most common, most easily ascertainable characteristic of a genius, therefore, is a universal remembrance of everything he has experienced.* It is a widespread theory, particularly popular among the scribblers killing time in the coffee-houses, that *productive* people (because they create *new* things) have no memory, but obviously only because this is the only condition of productivity which the scribblers themselves fulfill.

Of course one must not try to refute this great expansion and vividness of the memory in the man of genius—which I initially introduce quite dogmatically as an inference from my system, without substantiating it again from experience—by pointing out how quickly they forget all the historical facts they were taught in grammar school, or the Greek irregular verbs. *I am talking about a memory for what has been experienced, not about remembering what has been learnt.*

What has been studied for examination purposes is only ever retained in the smallest part, i.e., that part which corresponds to the special talent of the pupil. Thus a decorator may have a better memory for colors than the greatest philosopher, the most narrow-minded philologist may have a better memory for the aorists he learnt by heart many years ago, than his colleague, who is perhaps a poet of genius. It bears witness to the pathetic helplessness of the experimental branch of psychology (and even more to the incompetence of many people, who—with an arsenal of electric batteries and sphygmographic drums behind them, and based on the "exactitude" of their dull series of experiments—demand to be listened to in *rebus psychologicis* before everybody else) that they believe themselves to be able to test people's memory through tasks such as the learning of letters, multidigital numbers, or unconnected words. These experiments measure up so little to the real memory of a human being, that memory which counts when a human being sums up his life, that one cannot help asking whether these hard-working experimenters know anything at all about the existence of that other memory, or indeed about the *life* of the psyche as such. These experiments place the most diverse people under quite uniform conditions, in which their *individuality* can never express itself. They *abstract,* as if deliberately, precisely from the core of the individual, whom they treat simply as a good or bad recording machine. It shows profound insight that the German words "bemerken" and "merken"[1] are formed from the same root. Only what *catches the eye,* of its own accord and as a result of an innate quality, will be *retained.* To remember something, one must have an original interest in it, and if one forgets something then one's interest in it was not strong enough. A religious person therefore will recall most surely and lastingly religious teachings, the poet verses, the numerologist numbers.

And here we can fall back on the previous chapter in a different way and *deduce* the special fidelity of memory in outstanding individuals by a second route. The more exceptional an individual is, the more people and the more interests have come together in him, and therefore his memory must become the more comprehensive. People in general have an exactly *equal* amount of external opportunities to "perceive," but most people "apperceive" only an infinitely small part of the infinite mass. The ideal genius would be a being whose "perceptions" would without exception also be "*apperceptions.*" Such a being does not exist. However, there is also no human being who has never *ap*perceived, but only ever perceived. This is one of the simplest reasons why there must be all possible *degrees* of genius;[2] at least *no male* being is entirely without genius. But complete genius remains an ideal: *there is no human being without any apper-*

1. Translator's note: both verbs mean "notice," but "merken" can also mean "remember" or "memorize."

2. Which, however, have nothing to do with *talent.*

ception, and no human being with universal apperception (which could be a further definition of complete genius). Memory as a possession, in terms of both extent and strength, is proportionate to apperception as a process of appropriation. Thus there is an uninterrupted gradation leading from the totally discontinuous individual, who lives for the moment and to whom no experience could *mean* anything, because he would not be able to relate it to an earlier one—although such an individual does not exist—to one who lives a totally continuous life, to whom *everything* remains *unforgettable* (because it affects him and is understood by him so intensively), *and who exists as little as the former:* for even the supreme genius is not a "genius" at every moment of his life.

The first confirmation of this view of a necessary connection between memory and genius, and of the deduction of this connection that I have attempted here, is supplied by the extraordinary *memory for seemingly trivial circumstances, for minor details,* which distinguishes more endowed individuals and which often astonishes even its owner. As a result of the universality of their disposition, for such individuals everything has a *meaning,* of which they may often remain unconscious for a long time. Thus these things obstinately cling to their memory and imprint themselves on it inextinguishably of their own accord, generally without the need for such individuals to make the slightest effort to remember these things in particular or to put their attention to the service of that particular memory. Therefore, in a deeper sense which will be elucidated later, we could already define the man of genius as one who does not know, and would not be able to use either to himself or to others, the phrase that one or other event of long ago is "no longer true." On the contrary, for him there is *nothing* that would no longer be true, even though, or perhaps precisely *because,* he has a more distinct sense than anybody else of everything that has changed in the course of time.

Therefore the following may be recommended as the best method of objectively testing the endowment, or intellectual significance, of an individual. If we have not been together with him for a long time, we might start talking about our last meeting and link the new conversation to the topics of the last. We shall notice right away how vividly he has absorbed that conversation and how strong and lasting an effect it has had on him, and we shall soon see how faithfully he has retained the details. Just how much people lacking such an endowment forget about their own lives can be tested, with surprise and horror, by anybody who wishes to do so. It may happen that we were together with them only a few weeks ago, and now it has vanished from their mind. We may find people with whom we had a great deal to do a few years ago for a week or a fortnight, either by chance or in connection with some specific business, and who since then have not been able to remember *anything at all,* although—if one assists them through an exact account of all that happened, a revival of the situation in all its details—it is always possible, provided that this effort is continued long enough, first to throw a faint light on what has been completely extinguished and then gradually to bring about a memory of it. As a result of such experiences I have come to regard it as very likely that the assumption that there is no complete oblivion, which must always be made theoretically, can be proven empirically, and not merely through hypnosis, if one knows how to help the person being questioned with the right ideas.

The point, then, is that there is very little that we can tell an individual about his life, about what he has said or heard, seen or felt, done or suffered, that he himself does not know. Thus we have found for the first time a criterion of endowment which can easily be checked by others, ***without*** *there being any need for the presence of any* ***creative*** *achievements by the individual himself.* How frequently it will be applied in our educational practices will not be discussed here, but it is likely to be of equal importance to parents and teachers.

The extent to which people will be able to notice both differences and similarities, naturally, also depends on their memory. This faculty will be most highly developed among those in whose lives the entire past always reaches into the present, with all the discrete moments of their lives merging into the present and being compared to one another. It is therefore they who are most likely to find opportunities to use *similes, and to do that by means of the appropriate tertium comparationis in each case.* For they will always select from the past what agrees most strongly with the present, since in their case both kinds of experience, that of the new and that of the older which is used for comparison, are *articulate* enough to ensure that no similarity and no difference remains concealed from their eyes; which is also why in their case things long past have been able to stand up to the impact of the years. It is not for nothing that people have long regarded a poet's wealth of beautiful and perfect images and similes as a particular merit of the genre, looking up their favorite similes in Homer, Shakespeare, and Klopstock again and again, or waiting for them impatiently while reading. Today, when Germany has no great artist or great thinker for the first time in 150 years, whereas it is hardly possible to get hold of anybody who has not "written" something, all this seems to have gone: there is no demand for such things, and if there were they would not be found either. An age which believes that its character is best expressed in vague, indistinctly shifting moods, and the philosophy of which has become the unconscious in more senses than one, shows only too clearly that there is no truly great man living in it; for greatness is consciousness, before which the mist of the unconscious dissolves as before the rays of the sun. If a single individual were to bestow a consciousness on this time, how willingly would it give up all the atmospheric art on which it still prides itself today. Only in full consciousness, in which all the experiences of the past merge most intensely into the experience of the present, does imagination, the prerequisite of both philosophical and artistic creation, find a place. Accordingly, it is also not true that women have more imagination than men. The experiences, on the basis of which people have tried to attribute a more lively imagination to Woman, derive without exception from the sexual fantasies of women, but the conclusions which alone could justifiably be drawn from this cannot be treated as yet in this context.

The absolute insignificance of women in the *history of music* may be explained by much deeper reasons, but what it proves in the first place is that Woman is deficient in imagination. For musical productivity requires infinitely more imagination than that possessed even by the most masculine woman, much more than is needed for any other artistic or any scientific activity. Nothing real in nature, nothing given in the empirical realm of the senses, corresponds to a musical image. Music, so to speak, bears no relation to the world of experience. In music the human being must independently create even the most basic elements, since in nature there are no notes, no chords, and no melodies. All the other arts have more distinct relations with empirical reality than music, and even architecture, which is *related* to it, no matter what people may say, works with some material throughout, although it shares with music (or has even more than music) the quality of being free of any concrete *imitation.* That is why architecture is also a thoroughly male occupation, and the idea of a female master builder arouses hardly anything but pity.

Likewise, the "stultifying" effect of music (in particular purely instrumental music) on composers and performers, which one often hears about, comes from the fact that even the sense of smell can serve as a better guide for people to find their bearings in the empirical world than the contents of a musical work. It is precisely this total absence of any connections with the world that we can see, touch, or smell that makes music unsuitable for the expression of the nature of Woman. At the same time this characteristic of the art of the creator of music explains why he needs the highest degree of imagination and why an individual to whom melodies occur (indeed who is perhaps swamped by them against his will) is viewed with much more astonishment by his fellow-humans than the poet or sculptor. The "female imagination" must be entirely different from the male, given that there is no female composer who, in the history of music, would deserve even a place like that of Angelika Kauffmann in painting.

Wherever there is a clear need to create a solid form, women have not the slightest achievement to show: neither in music, nor in architecture, nor in sculpture, nor in philosophy. Where a little effect can still be achieved by vague and soft transitions of sentiment, as in painting and literature or in a certain hazy pseudo-mysticism and theosophy, they have most readily sought and found a field for their activities. The lack of productivity in those areas, then, is also related to the lack of differentiation in Woman's psyche. In music in particular what matters is the most articulate sensibility imaginable. There is nothing more definite, more characteristic, more *urgent* than a *melody,* nothing that would suffer more from being blurred. That is why one *remembers* what has been sung so much more easily than what has been spoken, arias always better than recitatives, and that is why the *sprechgesang* takes so much studying by the singer of Wagner.

It was necessary to dwell on this at some length because in music the excuse made elsewhere by male and female champions of women's rights—that it has been accessible to women for too short a time to demand mature fruits from them—does not apply. Female singers and virtuosos have always existed, even in classical antiquity. And yet . . .

The practice of having women paint and draw was already widespread in earlier times and has significantly increased in the last 200 years or so. It is well known how many girls today learn to draw and paint without being obliged to do so. Thus here too there has long been no narrow-minded exclusion, and the *external* opportunities would be plentiful. If nevertheless so few women have any importance in the history of art, what is probably lacking is the *inner* prerequisites. Female painting and etching can only mean a kind of more elegant, more luxurious *handicraft* for women. In this field, it seems, they find the sensual, physical element of color more easily reachable than the intellectual, formal element of the line, which is without doubt the reason why we know some female painters, but as yet no draughtswoman of any significance. The ability to impose form on chaos is in fact the ability of the individual who owes the most universal apperception to the most universal memory: it is the quality of the male genius.

I regret having to operate constantly with this word "genius," which strictly separates the "geniuses" as a specific caste from those who are not at all meant to be "geniuses," just as only people above a certain annual income have to pay a specific tax to the state. Perhaps the name "genius" was invented precisely by a man who himself only deserved it to a very small degree. Greater men probably considered "being a genius" too much as a matter of course, and they probably took too long to realize that it is also possible not to "have genius." As Pascal remarks most aptly: the more original a man is, the more original he also thinks the others to be. And compare this with Goethe's saying that perhaps only a genius can understand a genius.

There are perhaps very few people who have never had a moment of "genius" in their entire lives. If there are, perhaps they only lacked the opportunity, such as a great passion or a great pain. Although the capacity for experience is initially marked by subjectivity, all they would have needed was to experience something intensively enough once, in order to have had genius, at least temporarily. Writing poetry during one's first love is a case in point. And true love is entirely a matter of chance.

Finally one must not overlook the fact that quite ordinary people in a state of great excitement, such as anger over some wickedness, find words of which one would never have thought them capable. Most of what is commonly called *"expression,"* in the arts as in prosaic speech, however, is based (if one recalls what was said earlier about the process of clarification) on a more endowed individual exhibiting clarified, structured contents at a time when in another, less highly endowed, individual they are still at the henid stage or close to it. The process of clarification is greatly *abbreviated* by an expression that some other person has managed to coin, and that is why we feel pleasure even when we see *others* finding a "good expression." If two unequally endowed people experience the same thing, in the more endowed person the intensity will be great enough to reach the "speech threshold."[3] In the other person, however, this will only facilitate the process of clarification.

If, as popular opinion has it, the genius were separated from the man without genius by a thick wall that did not allow any sounds to penetrate from one realm to the other, the non-genius would be *totally* precluded from any understanding of the achievements of the genius, whose works would be unable to produce the slightest impression on him. *Any cultural hopes therefore can only be founded on the demand that this not be so. Nor is it. The difference lies in the lesser intensity of consciousness: it is a quantitative, rather than fundamental or qualitative, one.*[4]

Conversely, it is rather pointless to deny younger people the right to express an opinion and to value their judgments less because they have less experience than older people. There are people who might live a thousand years and more without having a single *experience.* Only among equally endowed people would that kind of talk make sense and be fully justified.

The man of genius, even as a child, leads a more intensive life than all the other children, and the more exceptional he is, the earlier the part of his youth that he can remember. Indeed in extreme cases the memory of his entire life from the third year of his childhood will always remain present to him. Other people, however, date their first memories of their youth from a much later point. I know some whose earliest reminiscence only goes back to their eighth year and *who know nothing of their earlier life except what they have been told,* and there are certainly many people whose first intensive experience must be dated even later. I do not wish to maintain, nor do I believe, that the endowments of two persons can without exception be measured against each other merely according to whether one of them remembers everything from his fifth year and the other only from his twelfth, whether the earliest youthful memory of one dates from the fourteenth month after his birth and that of the other only from his third year. But generally, and without imposing too narrow limits, the rule will probably always be seen to apply.

3. Term coined by Dr. H. Swoboda in Vienna.

4. On the other hand, the *moment* of genius, psychologically speaking, is very significantly separated from the moment without genius, *even in one and the same person.*

Even in an outstanding individual, a longer or shorter period of time passes from the point of his first youthful memory to the moment from which he remembers *everything,* that is, to the day on which he finally became a genius. The majority of people, on the other hand, have simply forgotten the largest part of their lives. Indeed all that many people know is *that no other person has lived for them all that time:* of their whole life only certain moments, some firm points, some prominent stations, are present to them. If one asks them about anything else, they only know—that is, they swiftly calculate—that in such and such a month they were that age, held this or that job, lived here or there, and had such and such an income. If one shared an experience with them years ago, it may take an enormous effort to resurrect the past in them. In such a case a person can be described with certainty as having no endowment, or at least can be regarded as insignificant.

The overwhelming majority of people would be highly embarrassed if they were asked to write an autobiography: very few can even give a full explanation if they are asked what they did yesterday. The memory of most people is merely a disjointed, occasionally associative one. In the man of genius any impression he has received *endures;* more accurately, *he alone actually has impressions.* Connected with this is the fact that probably all outstanding individuals, at least from time to time, *suffer from fixed ideas.* If one compares the psychic make-up of people with a system of bells arranged in close proximity, then it is true of ordinary people that each bell rings only if the next strikes it with its vibrations, and does so only for a few moments; while it is true of the genius that a single bell, if struck, vibrates mightily, producing a full sound rather than a soft one, and making the whole system move and reverberate, often for the rest of his life. But since this kind of movement often begins as a result of quite trivial, indeed ridiculous, impulses, and sometimes persists with the same unbearable intensity for weeks, it is really analogous to madness.

For related reasons, *gratitude* is just about the rarest virtue among human beings. They may sometimes remember how much money they have been lent, but they don't want, and are unable, to think themselves back to the trouble they were in and the relief they felt. If a lack of memory certainly leads to ingratitude, even an excellent memory alone is not enough to make a person grateful. That requires another special condition, which cannot be discussed here.

From the connection between endowment and memory—which has so often been misjudged and denied because it was not sought where it could have been found, that is, *in remembering one's own life*—it is possible to derive a further fact. A poet who has been *compelled* to write his works, without intending to do so, without reflecting and without having to push the pedal to get himself into the mood, or a musician who has ever been forced by the onslaught of the moment of composition to create against his own will, and was unable to resist, even though he would have preferred to rest and sleep—such a man will carry in his head what was born in these hours, all that was not in the least *made,* his whole life. We can be sure that a composer who knows none of his songs and none of his movements, a poet who knows none of his poems, by heart—without having "no doubt, memorized" them, as Sixtus Beckmesser imagines Hans Sachs doing—has never produced anything truly significant.

Before we try to apply these suggestions to the problem of the intellectual differences between the sexes, we must make a distinction between memory and memory. An endowed person's memory receives the individual moments of his life not as discrete points, as pictures of completely separate situations, as different single instants, each of which shows a specific index cut off from that of the next, like the number one from the number two. Rather, self-observation reveals that despite all sleep, all narrowness of consciousness, all gaps in the memory, the individual experiences appear as being mysteriously *connected:* the events do not follow one another like the ticking of a clock, but run together in a unified flow in which there is no discontinuity. In people without genius these moments, which thus unite to form the discrete original diversity into a closed continuum, are few in number. Their lives resemble a small stream rather than —as in the case of a genius—a mighty river, in which *all* the small rivulets from the widest possible area have run together and from which, as a result of *universal apperception,* no experience is *excluded,* but in which, on the contrary, all the individual moments are *absorbed* and received. This *essential* continuity, which alone can fully assure a human being that he is *alive,* that he exists, that he is in the world—which is all-embracing in a genius and restricted to a few important moments in mediocre persons—*is* ***totally*** *absent in women.* When a woman contemplates her life, looking back and reviving her feelings, it does not appear to her under the aspect of an inexorable, incessant thrusting and striving, but she continually gets *stuck* at individual points.

What kind of points are those? They can only be those in which W has an interest by virtue of her nature. I began to consider the exclusive direction of this interest of her constitution in the second chapter. Those who remember the results of that chapter will not be surprised by the following fact.

W has *only one* class of memories: they are memories connected with the sexual drive and reproduction. She remembers her lover and suitor; her wedding night; all her children and her dolls; the flowers she received at every ball, with the number, size, and price of the bouquets; every serenade that was given for her; every poem that (she imagines) was written to her; every saying of a man who has impressed her; but above all—with an accuracy that is as despicable as it is uncanny—*every single compliment* that has ever been paid her in her life.

That is ***all*** that *genuine* Woman remembers of her life.

However, what a person never forgets, and what he is unable to remember, makes it easiest to know his nature, his character. Later it will be necessary to examine more precisely just *what* is indicated by the fact that W has *these* of all memories. A great deal of information can be expected from the incredible fidelity with which women remember every homage and flattery, every proof of gallantry offered to them from their earliest childhood. I am of course aware of the objections that can be made to this restriction of female memory to the area of sexuality and the life of the species, and I must be prepared for a parade of all girls' schools and all their certificates. However, these difficulties cannot be resolved until later. Here I would only like to suggest once more that, in order to be seriously considered with regard to the psychological understanding of individuality, any memory of things learnt can be relevant only if what has been learnt has been really experienced.

The fact that the psychic life of women lacks continuity (which has been introduced here merely as a psychological fact that cannot be ignored, as an appendix, so to speak, to the theory of memory and not as a spiritualistic or idealistic thesis) cannot be elucidated, nor the nature of the continuity explored with reference to the most controversial problem of all philosophy and psychology, until later. As a proof of that lack I will, for the time being, cite only the fact—which has often been regarded with astonishment, and which has been expressly emphasized by Lotze—that women find it much easier to fall into line with, and accommodate sooner to, new circumstances than men, who will long be recognized as parvenus when nobody is any longer able to distinguish a middle-class woman from a noblewoman, or a woman who grew up in straitened circumstances from a patrician's daughter. However, this too is something I shall have to return to in more detail later.

Incidentally, it will now be understood why (if not driven by vanity, desire for gossip, or craving for imitation) only better people write down memories of their life, and why I see this as a main proof of the connection between memory and endowment. Not that every man of genius composes an autobiography: to proceed to write an autobiography, certain *special*, very deeply rooted psychological preconditions are needed. But on the other hand the writing of a *complete* autobiography, if it is the result of an original need, is always a sign of a superior human being. For *reverence* is also rooted in a really *faithful* memory. An exceptional individual would refuse any suggestion that he give away his past for the sake of some advantages of an external material or internal hygienic nature, even if he were promised the greatest treasures of the world, indeed *happiness itself*, in return for forgetting. The desire to drink from the waters of Lethe is a trait of mediocre and inferior natures. And while, as Goethe said, a truly outstanding individual may be very hard and fierce on any errors he has recently overcome in himself, even when he sees others hold on to them, he will never smile about his past actions, never ridicule his earlier way of thinking and living. The abundance of those today who claim to have "overcome" things, in fairness, deserve anything but that predicate: anybody who derisively tells others what he once believed, and how he had "overcome" all that, was never serious about the old things and cares equally little about the new. Such people are only interested in the instrumentation, never in the melody, and none of those stages that they have "overcome" was really deeply rooted in their being. In contrast, it should be observed with what solemn care great men in their autobiographies attribute a value even to the seemingly most trivial things: for them the present and the past are equal, for the others neither the present nor the past is true. The outstanding individual feels how *everything,* even the smallest and most minor detail, acquired an importance in his life, and how it has contributed to his development: *that* is the reason for the extraordinary *reverence* of his memoirs. Surely such an autobiography is not written down abruptly, on the spur of the moment, like any other idea, and the thought of doing so does not occur suddenly: for the great man who writes it, his autobiography is, so to speak, always finished. He feels that his new experiences are meaningful precisely because his previous life is always completely present to him, and that is why he, and really he alone, has a *destiny.* And that is also why the most exceptional individuals in particular will always be much more *superstitious* than mediocre ones. Thus I may sum up:

An individual is the ***more exceptional****, the more all things* ***mean*** *to him.*

In the further course of this investigation it will gradually become possible to attribute an even deeper meaning to this statement, in addition to the universality of relationships of understanding and a comparison by remembrance.

The situation of Woman in this respect is not difficult to describe. A genuine woman never arrives at any consciousness of a destiny, her destiny. Woman is not heroic, because she fights at best for her possessions, and she is not tragic, because her fate is decided together with the fate of these possessions. Since Woman has no continuity she is also incapable of reverence: in fact reverence is an exclusively male virtue. One starts with reverence *for oneself,* and reverence for oneself is the precondition of all reverence for others. But a woman needs very little effort to condemn her own past. If the word irony were appropriate, one might say that a man will not easily contemplate his past self in such an ironic and superior manner as women are often—and not only after their wedding night—in the habit of doing. There will be opportunities to point out that women really want the opposite of everything that is expressed by reverence. As far as the reverence of widows is concerned—but I would rather be silent on that topic. And finally the superstition of women is psychologically completely different from the superstition of outstanding men.

The relationship with one's own past, as it is expressed in reverence and founded on a continuous memory, which in its turn is made possible through apperception alone, can be demonstrated in further contexts and at the same time analyzed more deeply. *Whether or not a person has any relationship with his past is very closely connected with whether he feels a desire for immortality or is indifferent to the thought of death.*

The desire for immorality is generally treated today in a very mean and patronizing way. The problem arising from it, not merely as an ontological but also as a psychological one, is taken shamefully lightly. Some try to explain it, together with the belief in metempsychosis, by saying that in many people some situations, in which they certainly find themselves for the first time, awaken a feeling of having lived through them once before. The other derivation of the belief in immortality, the derivation from the *cult of souls,* which is generally adopted today and found in Tylor, Spencer, and Avenarius, would have been a priori rejected by any age but that of *experimental* psychology. In my view it should appear impossible to any thinking person that something that so many people have cared about, that has been fought and argued about so much, could be only the conclusion of a syllogism based on the premise of, say, the nocturnal dream appearances of dead people. And what are the phenomena that Goethe and Bach intended to explain by conceiving a rock-solid belief in their continuing life after death, and to what "pseudo-problem" can we attribute the desire for immortality that speaks to us from Beethoven's last sonatas and quartets? The desire for the continuation of a personal existence must have sprung from mightier sources than that rationalistic fountain.

This deeper source is intensely connected with the relationship between human beings and their past. *Feeling and seeing oneself in the past provides a powerful reason for wanting to continue to feel and see oneself.* An individual who values his past, who honors his inner life more than his physical life, *will not be prepared to abandon it even to death.* That is why a primary, original desire for immortality occurs most strongly and persistently in the greatest geniuses of mankind, in individuals with the richest past. That this connection between the demand for immortality and memory *really* exists is demonstrated by what people who have been saved from mortal danger unanimously report about themselves. Even if they have never thought much about their past, they now suddenly relive their entire life history at breakneck speed, and in the space of a few seconds remember things which had not returned to their consciousness for decades. For a sense of what awaits them—again by means of contrast—brings to their consciousness all that is now about to be destroyed forever.

Of course we know very little about the mental state of the dying. It takes a more than ordinary individual to recognize what is going on in a dying person. On the other hand, for the reasons that I have explained, it is precisely the better people who usually avoid the dying. But it is probably completely wrong to attribute the sudden religious feeling that arises in so many critically ill people merely to the well-known consideration of "who knows, perhaps, better be on the safe side," and it is very superficial to assume that the traditional doctrine of hell, which they have never before contemplated, will suddenly gain so much force at the precise hour of death that it becomes impossible for a person to die with a lie.[5] For this is the most important thing: Why do people who have persistently led a life of lies feel a sudden urge for the truth? And why does it make such a terrible impression even on those who do not believe in *punishments* in the beyond to hear that a person has *died with* a lie, *with* a wicked deed that he did not repent, why have both the obduracy until the very end and the reversal before death frequently had such a powerful appeal for poets and writers? Therefore the question about the "euthanasia of atheists," which was so often asked in the eighteenth century, is not quite pointless and not just a historical curiosity, as it was treated by Friedrich Albert Lange.

I mention all this not merely to discuss a possibility which hardly deserves the status of a supposition. It does not seem unimaginable to me, since there are so many more people with some of the qualities of genius than there are real "geniuses," that the quantitative differences in endowment find expression above all at the moment at which people become geniuses. For a large number of individuals this moment would coincide with their natural death. If earlier we had reason not to regard geniuses, like taxpayers above a certain annual income, as being separated from all other people by a sharp dividing line, these new reflections unite with those older ones. The first childhood memory of an individual is not linked to any *external* event interrupting the earlier course of things. Rather, sooner or later, suddenly, inconspicuously, *as a result of an inner development,* a day comes for everybody *when his consciousness becomes so intense* that a memory remains. From then on, in proportion to the individual's endowment, more or less numerous memories persist—*a fact that alone reverses the whole of modern psychology*—and thus *different individuals* would *need a different number of impulses* to make them geniuses. People, then, could be classified, in accordance with their endowment, *by the number of these impulses of consciousness, the last of which would occur at the hour of death.* I want to take this opportunity to point out how wrong today's psychology (which considers the human individual as nothing but a superior recording machine with no ontogenetic intellectual development coming *from within*) is in believing that the largest number of impressions is retained at a young age. Impressions that have been experienced must not be confused with the external and alien material held in the memory. Children can absorb the latter so much more easily precisely because they carry such a small burden of felt impressions. A psychology that contradicts empirical observation in such fundamental points has every reason to take stock and retrace its steps. What I have tried to give here is scarcely even a hint

5. I also venture to remind the reader how often pure scientists begin to concern themselves with religious and metaphysical problems shortly before their death: Newton, Gauß, Riemann, Wilhelm Weber.

of the *ontogenetic psychology* or *theoretical biography* which is destined sooner or later to displace today's science of the human mind. Every program contains an implicit conviction, and every goal of the will is preceded by specific ideas about real conditions. The name "theoretical biography" is intended to distinguish its territory from that of *philosophy* and *physiology* better than before, and to *expand* that biological approach which has been one-sidedly paraded and, in part, greatly exaggerated by the most recent school of psychology (Darwin, Spencer, Mach, Avenarius). Such a science would have to account for the *mental life as a whole* as it progresses from the birth of an individual to his death according to certain laws, just as it does for the coming into being and passing away, and all the discrete phases in the life of a plant. And it is to be called *biography,* not *biology,* because its task is to explore the unchanging laws of the *mental* development of the *individual.* So far the history of all species has only known individuals, βίοι. But here the task would be to develop general points of view, to establish types. *Psychology would have to make a start at becoming* ***theoretical biography.*** All existing psychology could and would be absorbed in such a science and only then provide a really fruitful foundation for the humanities, as demanded by Wilhelm Wundt. It would be a mistake to despair of this possibility just because today's psychology, which has not yet realized that its real task is to achieve this goal, is totally incapable of offering the smallest contribution to the humanities. This may justify the retention of Mill's division of natural sciences and humanities *alongside* the new classification of learning into sciences of "laws" and "events," into "nomothetic" and "idiographic" disciplines, despite the great clarification brought about by Windelband's and Rickert's examinations of the relationship between the natural sciences and the humanities.

It is in total agreement with the deduction of the desire for immortality, which connected that desire with the continuous form of memory and reverence, that *women entirely lack a desire for immortality.* We can also gather from this with certainty how wrong are those who regard the postulate of the continuation of a personal existence merely as a product of the fear of death and physical egoism, and who thus really express the most popular opinion about all belief in eternity. For the *fear* of dying is present in women as in men, but the *desire for immortality* is restricted to the latter.

So far my attempt at explaining the psychological desire for immortality has demonstrated a connection that exists between that desire and memory, rather than a really rigorous *deduction* from a higher principle. That there is such an affinity will always be found to be true: the more a man lives in his *past—not,* as one might believe at a superficial glance, in his *future*—the more intense his desire for immortality will be. Likewise, in women the lack of a desire for a life after death agrees with their general lack of reverence for their own person. Nevertheless, just as this lack in Woman calls for a deeper explanation and derivation of both from *one* more general principle, in Man too the combination of memory and the desire for immortality seems to indicate for both a *common* root still to be uncovered. What I have achieved so far is only to prove that, and how, life in one's own past and its valuation in the hope of a beyond are found together in the same person. As yet I have not considered it my task to explore the deeper reason for this connection. But now it is time to undertake the solution of that task.

* * *

Let us take as our starting point our formulation of the universal memory of the exceptional individual. We said that to him everything, that which lost its reality long since as well as that which has vanished only recently, is *equally true.* This implies that an individual experience does not disappear and perish with the moment in time at which it is set, as that atom of time itself does, and that it does not remain *bound* to a specific instant in time, but is *wrested* from it, precisely by means of memory. *Memory renders events timeless:* it is, by definition, the *overcoming of time.* Human beings can remember things past only because memory liberates them *from the influence of time and raises events, which in nature are normally* ***functions*** *of time,* ***above*** *time in the mind.*

But here we seem to run into a difficulty. How can memory imply a negation of time if, on the other hand, it is certain that we would know nothing about time if we had no memory? Surely it is only ever by remembering things past that we become conscious of the fact that there *is* a progression of time. How then can one of two things that are so closely connected represent the opposite and the cancellation of the other?

This difficulty is easy to resolve. It is precisely *because* any living—not necessarily human—being, *if* equipped with memory, is not *simply slotted into the progression of time,* that such a being is able to oppose the progression of time and thus *grasp* it and turn it into an object of contemplation. If the individual experience were bound into the progression of time as a whole, if it became time's slave beyond redemption by memory, it would have to change with time, as a dependent variable changes with the independent. If the human being stood in the *midst* of the temporal flow of events, it could not *strike* him and enter his *consciousness—since the prerequisite of consciousness is duality*—and it could never be an object, a thought, a human idea. One must *somehow* have *overcome* time in order to be able to *reflect* on it, somehow *stand outside time* in order to be able to *contemplate* it. This applies not only to any specific point in time—in the grip of passion itself one cannot think *about* passion, to do so one must have gone beyond it in time—but equally to the *general concept of time. If something timeless did not exist, there would be no conception of time.*

In order to explore this timeless entity, let us first reflect on *just what* is released from time by memory. We have seen that it is anything that is *of any in-*

terest or has any significance to the individual or, to put it briefly, *anything that has a* ***value*** *for the individual.* One remembers only those things that have had a ***value***, albeit often for a long time an unconscious one, for a person: ***it is this value that makes them timeless.*** *One forgets everything that has not somehow, albeit often unconsciously, been* ***attributed value*** *by the person.*

Timelessness, then, is value. And vice versa: a thing has the more value, the less it is a function of time, the less it changes with time. Everything in the world, so to speak, is irradiated by value only to the extent to which it is timeless: ***only timeless things are attributed a positive value.*** *This,* I believe, while not yet the most profound and most universal definition of value, nor an exhaustive account of its nature, is *the first* ***special*** *law of any theory of value.*

A hurried survey will suffice to demonstrate this everywhere. We are always inclined to think little of the convictions of those who have only recently arrived at them, and we will not attach much importance to the comments of an individual whose views are still in flux and constantly changing. On the other hand, an unyielding determination will always inspire respect, even if it manifests itself in the ignoble form of vindictiveness and obstinacy. Indeed, it does so even if expressed through inanimate objects: the "aere perennius" of poets and the "quarante siècles" of the Egyptian pyramids may serve as examples. The fame or good reputation left behind by a man would immediately be devalued by the idea that they were to last only for a short period, rather than for a long time or possibly forever. Further, a man can never attribute a positive value to the fact that he is constantly changing. Assuming that he did this in a certain respect, and he were then told that he is showing himself from a different side each time, he might even be pleased and proud of this quality, and yet it would only be the constancy, regularity, and certainty of these differences in which he is rejoicing. Those tired of life, for whom there are no values left, in fact have *no* interest left in *any constancy.* The fear of the extinction of a family and the dying out of its name is a case in point.

Any social evaluation, which appears, for example, in legal statutes or contracts, although it may be modified by custom or everyday life, lays claim from the outset to timeless validity even if its legal force expressly (according to its wording) only covers a specific period of time: for here time is specifically *chosen* as a constant and not regarded as a variable, depending on which the agreed conditions could change steadily or unsteadily. In fact here too we find that the longer anything lasts, the more highly it will be valued. If two legal parties come to an agreement of very short duration, nobody believes that either of them sets great store by their contract. In this case both contracting parties, feeling the same way, will be on their guard and distrust each other, right from the outset, despite all documents.

The law I have formulated also contains the true explanation of the fact that human beings have *interests beyond their own death.* The desire for value expresses itself in the general striving to emancipate things from time, and this urge extends even to conditions which, "given time," will sooner or later change *in any case,* for example wealth and possessions and anything answering the common description of "earthly goods." Here lies the deep psychological motive for making a *will* and leaving an *inheritance.* This phenomenon did not originate from concern for relatives, since men without families and relatives also make wills, and in general it is precisely they who proceed to do so with far greater seriousness and commitment than a father of a family, who knows that his death will not erase his traces so totally from the lives and thoughts of the others.

A great politician and ruler, and in particular a despot or a man staging a coup d'état, whose rule ends with his life, tries to endow it with value by linking something timeless to it: for example a code of law or a biography of Julius Caesar, all kinds of great intellectual enterprises and collaborative works of learning, museums and collections, buildings made of hard rock (*saxa loquuntur*), and most characteristically, the creation or regulation of a calendar. But he also tries to secure the longest possible duration for his power, even in his own lifetime, not only by mutual safeguards through contracts or the creation of everlasting family relationships through diplomatic marriages, but above all by removing everything that could ever challenge the eternal continuation of his rule merely by virtue of its free existence. That is how the politician becomes the conqueror.

The existing psychological and philosophical investigations into the theory of value have paid no attention whatsoever to the law of timelessness. To a large extent they have been influenced by the requirements of economics, on which they have tried to encroach in their turn. Nevertheless, I do not believe that the new law that I have developed has no validity in political economy just because in that area it is much more frequently blurred by complications than it is in psychology. In economics also the more durable anything is, the more value it has. At a late hour, for example before nightfall, I am able to obtain any goods that can only be preserved for a very limited period—which would, say, perish within a quarter of an hour if I did not buy them—for less money, wherever it is not intended to raise the moral *value* of the business enterprise above fluctuations in time by means of fixed prices. Think also of the many installations for protection from the effects of time and for the preservation of value (warehouses, depots, cellars, réchauds, all collections with curators). Even here it is totally incorrect to define value as that which is suited to satisfying our needs, as is commonly done by psychological value theorists. For even people's moods are part of their (momentary) needs, and yet there is nothing more opposed to any possession of value than *mood.* Moods know *no* value and at most demand it in order to smash it at the next moment. *Thus the element of duration cannot be eliminated from the concept of value.* Even those phenomena that people have tried to explain with the help of Menger's theory of "marginal utility" conform to my view (which in itself by no means naturally presumes to contribute anything to economics). According to this view, the reason why air and water have no value is that a positive value can be attributed *only to things that are somehow individualized and given form:* for whatever has form can be made formless, can be destroyed, and need not *last as such.* A mountain, a forest, a plain, can be given a form by enclosure and limitation and is therefore an object of value even in its wildest state. The air of the atmosphere and the water on and above the earth's surface are dispersed diffusely, without limits, and nobody would be able to enclose them within limits. If a magician were able to compress the atmospheric air surrounding the globe to a relatively small area of the earth, like the genie in the oriental tale, or if somebody succeeded in locking up the earth's masses of water in a large reservoir and prevent it evaporating, both would have immediately acquired *form* and would thus be subject to valuation. Therefore value is only predicated of a thing where there is reason, however remote, to fear that it could in time change: *for value is only acquired in relation to time and established in contrast to it.* Value and time therefore mutually demand each other like two correlative concepts. To what depths such a view may lead, to what extent such a view in particular can even constitute a *weltanschauung,* I would rather not pursue any further *at this point.* For our purposes it suffices to know that any reason to speak of value ceases precisely where time can no longer present a threat. Chaos, even if it is eternal, can only be given a negative value. *Form* ***and*** *timelessness, or individuation* ***and*** *duration,* are the two analytical factors that initially create, and provide the foundation for, value.

After this thorough exposition of the fundamental law of the theory of value in the areas of individual psychology and social psychology, I can gradually resume the central objects of my investigation and deal with what is still outstanding despite being the special task of this chapter.

The first conclusion that may be drawn from the above is that in all areas of human activity there is *a desire for timelessness, a* ***will to value.*** And this will to value, which should not fear any comparison of its depth with that of the "will to power," is utterly lacking in individual women, at least in the shape of the will to timelessness. The fact that women have no desire for immortality is connected with the habit of old women to leave instructions concerning their inheritance only in the rarest of cases. For a person's bequest is sanctified by something higher and more universal, which is also the reason why it is *respected* by others.

The desire for immortality is itself only a specific case of the general law that only timeless things are attributed a positive value. This is where this desire is connected to memory. The persistence of the experiences in a human being is proportional to the significance that they are able to gain for him. As paradoxical as it may sound: ***it is value that creates the past.*** Only what has been attributed a positive value is protected by the memory from the ravages of time, *and thus the psychic* *life of the individual, too, if it is to be attributed a positive value, must not be a function of time, but must be raised above time by an eternally continuing existence beyond death.* This has brought us incomparably closer to the innermost motive of the desire for immortality. It is the total loss of significance which would result if a fulfilled life, a life lived to the full, were to end completely and forever with death, and the *senselessness* of *everything* in that event—as Goethe also put it, albeit in different words, to Eckermann (4 February 1829)—that lead to the demand for immortality.

The genius has the strongest desire for immortality. This coincides with all the other facts that have so far been uncovered about his nature. *Memory is a total victory over time only if it appears in a universal form in a universal human being. Thus the genius is the truly timeless human being,* or at least that, and nothing else, is his ideal of himself. As his deep and urgent longing for immortality proves, he is the human being with the strongest desire for timelessness, *with the most powerful will to value.*[6]

And now a possibly even more miraculous coincidence appears before the dazzled eye. The timelessness of genius reveals itself not only in relation to the individual moments of his life, but also in his relationship with what is singled out from the calendar as his generation and called "his time" in the narrower sense. *With the latter he has de facto no relationship at all.* A genius is not created by the time that needs him. He is not its product, he cannot be explained by it, and one does not honor him if one uses it to make excuses for him. Carlyle has rightly pointed out how many epochs were short of nothing but an exceptional individual, and how urgently they needed him, and yet he failed to appear. The coming of a genius remains a mystery, and we should have enough reverence to refrain from trying to fathom it. Just as the *causes* of his appearance cannot be found in his time, *neither are its* ***consequences*** *bound to any particular time*—and this correspondence is the second mystery. *The deeds of a genius live forever and are in no way changed by time.* The exceptional individual is granted immortality on earth through his works, and thus he is *timeless in a threefold sense:* his universal apperception, or the value he attributes to every single experience, preserves these experiences in his memory and saves them from being destroyed with the passing moment; he is not the product of the time which precedes his appearance; and what he has created does not fall victim to the time in which he is active or indeed any other time which may follow sooner or later.

This is the most opportune point to insert the discussion of a question that must be answered, even though, strangely enough, it seems to have been raised by hardly anybody so far. It is none other than whether what deserves to be

6. One is often surprised to see how people of ordinary, indeed common, nature have no fear whatsoever of death. But this clearly demonstrates that *it is not the fear of death that creates the desire for immortality, but the desire for immortality that creates the fear of death.*

called genius is also found among animals (or plants). Quite apart from the criteria of endowment, which I have already expounded and the application of which to animals is hardly likely to reveal the presence of such distinguished individuals among them, we have sufficient reason to assume—as will be explained later—that there is nothing remotely similar among those beings. *Talents* may exist in the animal kingdom, as they do in humans who are not-quite-geniuses. But we have every reason not to extend to animals what was always regarded as the "divine spark," before Moreau de Tours, Lombroso, and Max Nordau came along. This restriction is not the result of jealousy or the anxious protection of a privilege, but something that can be defended with good reasons.

For the first emergence of genius *in humankind* explains countless things. It explains the whole "objective spirit," in other words, the fact *that humans alone among all living beings have a **history***!

Cannot the whole of human history (naturally in the sense of the history of the mind and not, for example, the history of wars) best be understood through the appearance of a genius, the inspirations emanating from him, and the imitation of what a genius has done by more *pithecoid* creatures? Take house-building, agriculture, and above all *language*! Every word was first created by *one* individual, by an individual above the average, and the same is still the case today (with the sole exception of the names for new technical inventions, which must be ignored in this context). How else should it have been created? The primal words *were* "onomatopoeic" and they incorporated without the will of the speaker, through the sheer intensity of the specific excitement, something similar to the cause of the excitement, while all the other words were originally tropes, as it were, second-order onomatopoeias, metaphors, similes: all prose was once poetry. *Thus most geniuses have remained unknown.* One only needs to think of proverbs, including the most trivial ones today, like "one favor deserves another." Indeed, even that was said for the first time many years ago by *one* witty man. On the other hand, how many quotations from the most widely read classical authors, like many sayings of Christ, appear to us today entirely as impersonal proverbs, and how many times must we remind ourselves that in this case we know the author! Therefore one should not speak of the "wisdom of the language," or of the advantages and felicitous expressions of "French." Language was no more created by a crowd than the "folk song." If we use such phrases we are being ungrateful to so many *individuals* in order to give excessive gifts to a people. The genius himself who has created language belongs, as a result of his universality, not only to that nation from which he stems and in whose language he has expressed his own nature. A nation takes its bearings from its geniuses and models its ideal conception of itself on them, so that this conception cannot be the guiding star of the great individuals, but can indeed be that of all the others. For similar reasons, more caution would also be advisable when, as is often the case, the psychology of language and the psychology of nations are treated, without any critical preliminary studies, as belonging together. The reason why so much astonishing wisdom is really concealed in language is that language is created by great individuals. The fact that an ardently profound thinker such as Jacob Böhme concerns himself with etymology certainly means a little more than many a historian of philosophy seems able to understand. From Bacon to Fritz Mauthner all *blockheads* have been *critics of language.*[7]

A genius, on the other hand, does not criticize language but has created it and is ever creating it afresh, as he does all the other products of the mind which represent the basis of culture in the narrow sense, the "objective spirit," insofar as it really is *spirit.* Thus we see *that the timeless individual is the individual who creates history: history can be created only by individuals who stand outside its causal connections.* For they alone enter that indissoluble relationship with the absolutely timeless, with value, that endows their productions with an eternal content. And any event that finds a place in culture does so under the aspect of eternal value.

If we apply the yardstick of threefold timelessness to the genius, we shall also have the safest guide to the—by now not very difficult—decision as to who should be attributed the predicate of genius and who must be disallowed it. The view which is doubtless the correct one on this occasion, even though it is found in the middle, is situated *between* the popular opinion held, for instance by Türck and Lombroso, who are prepared to apply the concept of genius to any above-average intellectual or practical achievement, and the exclusiveness of the teachings of Kant and Schelling, who recognize the activity of genius in the creative artist alone. *The title of genius can only be justified in the case of the great artists and the great philosophers* (among whom I also count the rarest geniuses, the great *creators of religions*[8]). Neither "the great man of action" nor "the great man of science" has any claim to it.

The *"men of action,"* the famous politicians and generals, may have individual characteristics reminiscent of a genius (e.g., an excellent ability to judge character or an enormous memory for people). *Their* psychology will be discussed later,[9] but they can be mistaken for geniuses only by somebody who is completely dazzled by the mere external appearance of greatness. A genius is distinguished in more than one sense precisely by his ability to *do without* any *external greatness,* and his *pure inner greatness.* The truly exceptional individual has the strongest sense of *values,* while the general and politician understand little more than *forces.* The former may seek to attach power to value, the latter, at best, to attach and bind value to power (remember what I said above about the

7. However, I hasten to ask the good spirits of Bacon for forgiveness for this juxtaposition.
8. They are briefly discussed in chapter XIII.
9. P. 201.

enterprises of leaders). The great general and the great politician rise phoenix-like from the chaos of *circumstances* in order to disappear as that bird does. The great leader or great demagogue is the only man who lives entirely in the present. He does not dream of a more beautiful, better future and does not think back to a lost past. He attaches his existence to the moment, and he does not try, in one of the two ways possible for a human being, *to transcend time.* The authentic *genius,* on the other hand, does not make himself dependent in his work on the concrete temporal conditions of his life, which for the general and politician always remain the thing-in-itself, that which ultimately gives him the direction to follow. Thus the great leader becomes *a phenomenon of nature,* while the great philosopher or artist stands outside nature as an embodiment of the spirit. Accordingly, the works of the man of action usually end with his death, if not sooner and never very much later, leaving no trace apart from the reports of the chronicle of the time about what was created for the sole purpose of being destroyed. The leader creates no works that express the timeless, eternal *values* with tremendous visibility for all the millennia: for those are the deeds of genius. *The* ***latter****, not the former,* ***creates*** *history,* because he is not bound up *in it,* but stands *outside it. The exceptional individual has a history, the leader is had by history.* The exceptional individual creates time, the leader is created—and killed—*by* it.

The great *man of science,* if he is not at the same time a great philosopher, has as little right to the name of genius as the great man of will, unless he is called Newton or Gauß, Linnaeus or Darwin, Copernicus or Galileo. Men of science are not universal, for science deals only with a discipline or, at best, disciplines. The reason for this is not, as is generally believed, "progressive specialization," which "makes it impossible to know everything." Even in the nineteenth and twentieth centuries there are scholars with such astonishingly wide-ranging knowledge as that of Aristotle or Leibniz: I recall Alexander von Humboldt or Wilhelm Wundt. The deficiency, rather, is deeply rooted in the nature of all science and scientists. I shall attempt to uncover the ultimate difference that exists in this respect in chapter VIII. Meanwhile, however, it may already be accepted that the most distinguished man of science is still not as comprehensive a character as even those philosophers on the extreme borderline of what may still be called genius. (I am thinking of Schleiermacher, Carlyle, Nietzsche). What mere scientist could feel that he has an immediate understanding of *all* human beings and *all* things, or even just the possibility of ever achieving such an understanding within, and out of, himself? Indeed, what purpose would the scientific work of millennia have if not that of *replacing* this direct understanding? That is the reason why all scientists are *necessarily* always "experts" in specific areas. Nor does any scientist who is not a philosopher, however great his achievements may be, ever know anything about that continuous life in which nothing is ever forgotten and which distinguishes the genius. This is due precisely to his lack of universality.

Ultimately, the researches of a scientist are always confined to the state of knowledge that prevails in his own time: he receives a certain number and certain kinds of experiences, increases or alters this fund to a smaller or larger extent, and passes it on. But *his* achievements are also subject to being reduced or amplified in many respects, and although they continue to exist as books in libraries, they are not eternal creations beyond the reach of correction in even *one* single point. On the other hand, through the famous philosophies as well as the great works of art, we are addressed by something that cannot be shaken or lost, by a *weltanschauung* that is not altered by the march of the times and that will *always* find adherents with an affinity to the distinctive individuality of its creator that is visibly expressed in it. Even today there are Platonists and Aristotelians, Spinozists and Berkeleyans, Thomists and followers of Bruno, but nowhere do we find any followers of Galileo or Hemholtz, of Ptolemy or Copernicus. It is therefore nonsense, and it distorts the meaning of the word, to speak of "classics of exact science" or "classics of pedagogy" in the same way as one rightly speaks of classical philosophers and classical artists.

The great philosopher, then, bears the name of genius with merit and honor. If it is the philosopher's greatest regret in all eternity that he is not an artist, the artist envies the philosopher no less for the toughness and power of his abstract systematic thought. That is the only reason why a philosopher becomes an aesthetician, and it is not for nothing that the artist is exercised by Prometheus and Faust, Prospero and Cyprian, the Apostle Paul and "Il Penseroso." Consequently, it seems to me, both must be regarded as equals, and neither has too great an advantage over the other.

Nevertheless, in philosophy also it is important not to use the concept of genius as lavishly as is commonly the case, otherwise my exposition would rightly be accused of being biased against "positive science," which is of course the last thing I want, since I would have to regard such an attack as being directed in the first place against me and a large part of this work. It will not do to describe Anaxagoras, Geulincx, Baader, or Emerson as men of genius. Neither unoriginal depth (Angelus Silesius, Philo, Jacobi) nor original shallowness (Comte, Feuerbach, Hume, Mill, Herbart, Locke, Carneades) should be able to obtain a right to be described by that term. Today the history of art is as full of the most erroneous evaluations as the history of philosophy; quite unlike the history of science, which is constantly correcting its own results and which evaluates the phenomena according to the *extent* of these *corrections.* The history of science dispenses with the biography of its most valiant protagonists; its aim is a system of supra-individual experience from which the individual has disappeared. Devotion to science therefore is the *greatest* renunciation: for in so doing the individual as such renounces *eternity.*

VI Memory, Logic, Ethics

THE TITLE I HAVE given to this chapter runs the immediate risk of being easily and gravely misunderstood. Judged by it, the author could appear to hold the view that logical and ethical valuations are exclusively the objects of empirical philosophy, or psychic phenomena just like sensation and feeling, and that logic and ethics therefore are special disciplines or sub-sections of psychology and can be explained in terms of, and within, psychology.

I declare at once and without reservation that I regard this view—"psychologism"—as totally wrong and pernicious: wrong because such an enterprise can never succeed, as we shall see; pernicious because it destroys not so much logic and ethics, on which it hardly impinges, but psychology itself. To exclude logic and ethics from the *foundation* of psychology, and to relegate them to an appendix of the latter, is the correlative of the hypertrophy of sensationalism and, together with it, is responsible for all that today presents itself as "empirical psychology": that pile of dead bones which no amount of sensitivity and diligence can inspire with life and in which, above all else, no real *experience* can be recognized. Thus, with regard to the unfortunate attempts to place logic and ethics, as the delicate youngest child of psychic life, on top of a hierarchical psychological edifice, bonded by whatever kind of mortar, I do not hesitate at least to oppose Brentano and his school (Stumpf, Meinong, Höfler, Ehrenfels), as well as T. Lipps and G. Heymans and the related opinions of Mach and Avenarius, and to join, as a matter of principle, that other direction which today is defended by Windelband, Cohen, Natorp, F. J. Schmidt, and most notably Husserl (who was himself initially a psychologist but has since become most firmly convinced of the untenability of that position). It is the direction which asserts, and is able to uphold, the transcendental critical thought of Kant against the psychological and genetic method of Hume.

However, the present study is not concerned with the generally valid, supra-individual norms of action and thought and the conditions of knowledge. In both its starting point and its goal, it attempts to identify *differences* between human beings, rather than claiming to be valid for any beings (even the "dear little angels" in heaven), as do the basic tenets of the philosophy of Kant. Therefore it could, and indeed had to, be psychological (not *psychologistic*) up to now and will continue in the same vein, although it will not hesitate, when necessary, to attempt a formal reflection and to point out that here and there only the logical, critical, transcendental method is warranted.

The justification for the title of this chapter is somewhat different. My investigation in the previous chapter, which was so laborious because it had to be conducted in an entirely new manner, demonstrated that human memory has a close relationship with some things to which so far it has apparently not been deemed worthy of being related. Time, value, genius, immortality—my investigation was able to show that all these had a remarkable connection with memory, which had not even been suspected beforehand. There must be a deeper reason for the almost complete absence of any such indications. It seems to be the inadequacy and slovenliness of which the theories of memory have time and again been guilty.

Here we are first struck by a theory which was founded as early as the middle of the eighteenth century by Charles Bonnet and given momentum in the last third of the nineteenth century in particular by Ewald Hering (and E. Mach). This theory saw human memory as nothing more than a "general function of organized matter," that is, the ability to react differently, more easily, and more quickly to new stimuli that to some extent resemble previous stimuli than to a first-time irritation. It holds that the phenomena of human memory do not go beyond the capacity for practice found in living beings, and it regards memory as an instance of adaptation on the Lamarckian model. There is certainly something in common between human memory and those facts, for example a greater excitability of the reflexes resulting from a frequent repetition of stimuli. The identical element lies in the fact that the first impression continues to have an effect beyond the moment, and chapter XII will return to the deepest reason for this affinity. But there is a vast difference between the strengthening of a muscle by habituation to repeated contractions or the adaptation of an arsenic eater or morphinist to ever larger quantities of the poison, on the one hand, and somebody's recollection of his earlier experiences, on the other. In the first instance it is only possible to recognize traces of the old in the new, while in the second instance situations experienced earlier emerge into consciousness, entirely in their *old* form, as they themselves were, equipped with all their individual features, and are not merely used to have an after-effect on the new moment by means of a residue. To regard the two phenomena as identical would be so nonsensical that I can dispense with any further discussion of this general biological view.

The theory of association as a theory of memory is connected with the physiological hypothesis *historically* through Hartley and *factually* through the *concept of habituation*. It derives all memory from the mechanical linking of ideas in accordance with one to four laws. *In so doing, it overlooks the fact that memory (the continuous memory of the human being) is basically a manifestation of the will.* If I really want to, I can remember things, for example, in spite of being sleepy, provided that I am truly determined to suppress my somnolence. *Under hypnosis, through which a remembrance of anything past can be achieved, the will of a stranger replaces the all too weak will of the subject,* proving again that it is the *will that seeks out the appropriate associations and that all association is brought about through deeper apperception.* Here I had to anticipate a later section, in which I will try to clarify the relationship between the psychology of association and the psychology of apperception, and to assess the validity of both.

A third confusion, which—despite the objections so rightly raised at about the same time by Avenarius and in particular Høffding—still lumps *memory* together with *recognition,* is closely connected with the psychology of association, which first breaks up the life of the psyche and then believes that it will be able to stick it together again in a dance of the fragments holding hands. Recognition of an object by no means needs to rest on the isolated reproduction of an earlier impression, even though in some cases the new impression seems to have the tendency immediately to reawaken the older one. But *in addition to this* there is a *direct* recognition which occurs at least equally frequently. In this case the new sensation does not *lead away from itself* as if it were connected to something else by a brace, but what has been seen, heard, etc. merely appears in a specific *coloring* (James would say "*tinge*"), with the "character" that Avenarius calls "*notal*" and Høffding "the quality of familiarity." To a man returning to his homeland every inch of the landscape seems "familiar," even if he can no longer put a name to anything, has difficulty finding his way around, and does not recall any particular day he walked there. A tune can "sound familiar" to me without my knowing when and where I have heard it. Here the "character" (in Avenarius's sense) of *familiarity,* of being *intimately known,* etc., hovers above the sensory impression itself, as it were. The analysis knows nothing about associations and their "fusion" with my new sensation which, according to a presumptuous pseudo-psychology, is supposed to *create* that immediate feeling in the first place, and it is perfectly able to distinguish between these cases and those others in which the older experience indeed begins to be faintly and almost imperceptibly associated (in henid form).

This distinction also needs to be made in the psychology of the individual. A superior individual's consciousness of an uninterrupted past is so continually alive that if, for example, he encounters an acquaintance in the street, he will immediately reproduce their last meeting as an independent experience, while in a less endowed individual the simple sense of familiarity that makes recognition possible often appears *on its own* even if he could easily recall the earlier meeting in detail.

If in conclusion we ask whether any organisms apart from humans also possess the ability—which must be distinguished from anything similar—*to revive* earlier moments of their lives *in their entirety,* then this question must in all probability be answered in the negative. Animals would not be able to remain motionless and quiet on the same spot for hours, as they do, if they could recall their past life or anticipate a future in their thoughts. Animals have qualities of familiarity and feelings of expectation (the dog greeting the return of its master after twenty years' absence, the pigs in front of the butcher's gate, the mare in heat being taken to be covered), but they have no recollection and no hope. *They are capable of recognition* (with the help of the "*notal*"), *but they have no memory.*

If memory has thus been shown to be a special quality which is not to be confused with the low areas of psychic life, and if it further seems to be an exclusively human possession, it will not be surprising that it is connected to higher things, such as the concepts of value and time; the desire for immortality, which is not found in any animal; and genius, which is only possible for humans. And if there is an integrated concept of the human being, a deepest *essence* of humanity manifested in all the specific qualities of the human individual, then one will actually have to *expect* the logical and ethical phenomena—which, like memory, are most probably missing in other beings—to be connected with memory at some point. I must now track down this relationship.

To this end I may set out from the well-known fact that *liars* have a bad memory. "Pathological liars" are known to have almost "no memory" at all. I will return to the male liar later, but he is not the rule among men. On the other hand, considering what was earlier said about the memory of women, the many warnings about the untruthfulness of Woman, expressed in proverbs and stories, in literature and popular sayings, may be juxtaposed to the lack of memory in mendacious men. It is clear that any being whose memory is so minimal that its recollection of what it said, did, and suffered on an earlier occasion carries the lowest degree of consciousness is bound to find lying easy, if it has the gift of speech; and an individual of this kind, who is not fully and intensely aware of the true event, will find it hard to resist the impulse to lie when the need to achieve some practical aim arises. This temptation must assert itself even more forcefully if the memory of the being in question is not of that continuous nature which is only known to men; if this being, like W, lives only in moments, so to speak, in a discrete, discontinuous, incoherent fashion, *absorbed by* temporal events rather than rising *above* them, or at least elevating the passing of time to a *problem;* if the being in question does not, like M, relate all its experiences to an integrated *bearer who takes them upon himself;* if a *"center" of apperception,* to which everything past is attributed in an integrated way, *is missing; if this being does not feel and know itself to be one and the same in all the situations of its life.* It probably happens to every man that once in a while he "does not understand" himself. Indeed very many men, if they look back on their past—and this must not be connected with the phenomena of psychic periodicity[1]—find it difficult as a rule to substitute their current personality for the bearer of their earlier ex-

1. Which are known to an individual who always understands himself as well as to one who never does.

periences and are unable to understand how they could think or do this or that at that time. *Nevertheless, they feel and know very well that they have thought and done those things, and do not have the slightest doubt about it.* Genuine Woman totally lacks this sense of identity in all the situations of her life, since her memory, even if it is conspicuously good, as happens in isolated cases, *is always devoid of any continuity.* In Man, who often does not understand his past self, the sense of unity manifests itself in the *desire to understand himself,* and *immanent* in this desire is *the **presumption*** that he has always been *one and the same* despite the fact that he does not understand himself now. Women, looking back on their earlier life, *never* understand themselves, and *have no desire to understand themselves,* as can immediately be seen from the scanty interest they show in the words of a man who tells them something about themselves. *Woman is not interested in herself*—that is why there are no female psychologists and there is no psychology of woman by a woman—and she would be *completely* unable to comprehend Man's desperate, genuinely masculine efforts to interpret his own past as a *logical* sequence of *continuous,* causally linked, totally coherent events, and to establish a connection between the beginning, middle, and end of his individual life.

From here it is possible to build a bridge to logic by means of a border crossing. A being like W, absolute Woman, who is unaware of remaining identical to itself at successive points in time, would have no evidence either of the object of its thoughts remaining identical at different times: for, if both parties are subject to change, there is, so to speak, no absolute system of coordinates to which the change could be related and through which alone the change could be noticed. Indeed a being whose memory reached not even far enough to afford it the psychological possibility of judging that an object or a thing has remained identical with itself despite the passing of time, and to enable it, for example, to enter, fix, and use a given mathematical quantity as the same in a lengthy calculation—*such a being, in the extreme case, would also not be able to use its memory to overcome the supposedly infinitesimal time that is (psychologically) needed in any case for saying that A is still A at the next moment, that is, for making the judgment of identity A = A, or for pronouncing the principle of contradiction, which requires that an A should not immediately vanish from the sight of the thinker, who would otherwise be unable really to distinguish A from non-A, which is not A, and which the thinker cannot envision at the same time owing to the narrowness of consciousness.*

This is not a mere intellectual joke, no mischievous sophism of mathematics, no astonishing conclusion from underhand premises. Surely—this must be stated in advance of the following investigation in order to meet possible objections—the judgment of identity always refers to *concepts* and never to sensations or complexes of sensations, and concepts as logical concepts are timeless: they keep their constancy whether or not I, as a psychological subject, think of them as constant. However, a human being never thinks of a concept as a purely logical concept, *because he is not a purely logical being but also a psychological one,* a being "affected by the conditions of sensuality." Instead, he can only think of a general idea (a "typical," "connotative," "representative" idea) which evolves from his individual experiences through the mutual extinction of differences and intensification of similarities, *but which can, nevertheless, acquire the abstract character of conceptuality and miraculously be put into practice in that sense.* So he must also have the ability to keep and preserve the idea with which he thinks of the *de facto abstract* concept in a *concrete* way: but he is only guaranteed this ability by memory. If, then, he lacked memory he would also be deprived of the ability to think logically, the ability, as it were, that only ever *incarnates* itself through a *psychological* medium.

Thus I have conclusively proved that the extinction of memory is accompanied by the extinction of the ability to carry out the logical functions. This does not affect the propositions of logic: it only demonstrates that the power to apply them is bound to that condition. The proposition A=A always has a *psychological* connection with time, insofar as it can be *stated* only in *contrast* to time: $A_{t1}=A_{t2}$. *Logically,* the proposition does not contain this connection, and later on we shall find out why, in purely logical terms, *as a* ***specific*** *judgment* it has *no* ***specific*** *meaning* and so badly needs this *psychological* foil. In psychological terms therefore that judgment can only be made in *relation to time* and actually turns out to be the *negation* of time.

However, I demonstrated earlier that constant memory is the overcoming of time and thus the psychological *precondition of the conception of time. Therefore the fact of continuous memory presents itself as the* ***psychological*** *expression of the* ***logical*** *principle of identity.*[2] Absolute Woman lacks a continuous memory and therefore this proposition cannot be the axiom of her thinking. ***For absolute Woman the principium identitatis (and contradictionis and exclusi tertii) does not exist.***

But not only these three principles are most closely connected with memory: so is the fourth law of logical thinking, *the principle of sufficient reason,* which demands a rationale for every judgment, a rationale that will reveal the necessity of the judgment to all thinking persons.

The principle of sufficient reason is the vital nerve, the foundation of syllogism. Psychologically, however, the premises of a conclusion are always earlier *judgments,* which precede the conclusion in time and which must be captured by the thinking person, just as the *concepts* are, so to speak, *protected* by the principles of identity and contradiction. The reasons of a human being must always be sought in his past. That is why the maxim of continuity, which entirely domi-

2. By this I also hope to have justified the boldness of my totally new transition from memory to logic.

nates human thinking, is so closely connected with causality. Whenever the principle of sufficient reason comes into effect *psychologically,* it requires a continuous *memory* which preserves all identities. Since W knows neither this kind of memory nor any other continuity, *the principium rationis sufficientis does not exist for her.*

It is therefore correct to say that Woman has no logic.

Georg Simmel described this old insight as untenable because women were often capable of the most extreme and most rigorous consistency when drawing conclusions. Woman may draw relentless conclusions in a *concrete case* where she regards it as appropriate and imperative *in order to achieve some purpose,* but this does not prove that she is able to relate to the principle of sufficient reason; nor does the fact that she so often stubbornly repeats the same thing, and keeps returning to her first contention long after it has been refuted, prove that she is able to relate to the principle of identity. *The question is whether or not one recognizes logical axioms as the criteria of the validity of what one thinks and as the judges of what one says, whether one makes them the constant guiding principle and norm of one's judgment.* A woman never realizes *that a reason must be given for everything;* as she has no continuity she feels no desire for a logical support of everything that is thought: *hence the gullibility of* ***all*** *women.* In isolated cases they may be consistent, but in such cases logic is not their yardstick but their tool, not a judge but usually an executioner. On the other hand, if a woman expressed a view and a man were stupid enough to take it seriously and to demand a proof from her, she would regard such a request as annoying and tiresome, as something directed against her nature. *Man feels ashamed of himself and guilty, if he has omitted to give a reason for an idea, whether or not he has voiced it,* because he feels an obligation to abide by the logical norm that he has set above himself once and for all. A woman feels incensed by the imposition of having to make her thinking *totally* dependent on logic. *She lacks intellectual conscience.* In her case one could speak of "logical insanity."

If one were really to test the logicality of female speech (something that all men tend to avoid, demonstrating by that mere fact their contempt for female logic) the most common mistake one would find would be *quaternio terminorum,* the dislocation which arises from woman's inability to stick to *definite* ideas and to relate to the principle of identity. Woman does not realize by herself that she must adhere to this principle, and it is not the supreme criterion of her judgments. Man feels an obligation to logic, Woman does not. But nothing else matters, for that sense of obligation alone can guarantee that a person will forever strive to think logically. Perhaps the most profound thought ever uttered by Descartes—which is probably the reason why is has been so little understood and most of the time represented as a perniciously false doctrine—is *that all error is guilt.*

The source of all error in life, however, is also invariably a lack of memory. Thus both logic and ethics, which converge in the demand for truth and coincide in the supreme value of truth, are again connected with memory. And here it dawns on us that Plato was not so wrong when he linked insight to remembering. Memory is not a logical and ethical *act* but at least a logical and ethical *phenomenon.* For example, a man who has had a truly deep sensation feels that he is doing wrong if he thinks of something quite different half an hour later, even if he is forced to do so by an external cause. Man regards himself as unscrupulous and immoral if he finds that he has not thought of any one point of his life for a long time. Further, memory is moral for the simple reason that it alone makes *remorse* possible. *All forgetfulness, on the other hand, is in itself immoral.* That is why *reverence* is also a *moral* precept: it is a ***duty*** to forget ***nothing;*** and for that reason alone one must in particular remember the dead. For the same reason Man, motivated by logic and ethics in equal measure, also endeavors to apply logic to his past and organize all its points into a unity.

Thus, as if with one blow, we have hit upon the profound connection between logic and ethics, which Socrates and Plato surmised and which Kant and Fichte had to rediscover, only to become once more neglected and entirely lost to the living.

A being that does not understand or acknowledge that A and non-A mutually exclude each other will be prevented from lying by nothing; or rather, for such a being the *concept* of the lie simply does not exist because the yardstick provided by the opposite, the truth, is missing. If such a being, nevertheless, has the gift of language, it can *lie without knowing it,* indeed without having the ability to realize that it is lying, because it lacks the criterion of truth. "Veritas norma sui et falsi est." There is nothing more shattering for a man than asking a woman he has found to be lying, "Why are you lying?" and then realizing that *she does not understand his question at all* and either gapes at him without understanding or tries to soothe him with a smile—or even bursts into tears.

For with memory alone the problem is not solved. Lying is also common enough among men. And it is possible to lie despite *remembering* the true facts, which are replaced with something else for some purpose. Indeed, only a person who falsifies the facts despite his better knowledge and consciousness can *justifiably* be said to be lying. A person must *be* aware of the idea of truth as the supreme value of both logic and ethics to make it possible to speak of a suppression of this value in favor of some ulterior motives. Where this awareness is absent it is not possible to speak of *error* and *lie,* but at the most of *disorientation* and *mendacity;* not of being ***anti-*** *moral* but only ***a****moral. Thus Woman is* ***a****moral.*

That total lack of understanding for the *value of truth in itself* must therefore lie deeper. Since Man also lies, or indeed Man *alone* actually *lies,* the *demand* for truth, the *desire* for truth, the real basic phenomenon of ethics and logic, cannot be *derived* from, but is only closely *connected* with, continuous memory.

That which enables a human being, a man, to relate sincerely to the idea of truth, and which alone is therefore able to prevent him from lying, can only be something independent of all time, something totally unchangeable, something that *posits* the old deed at the new moment as no less real than it was at the earlier moment, because it has remained *itself* and neither allows the fact that *it* carried out that deed in that way to be changed, nor does it wish to alter it. It can only be the same thing that provides a point of reference for all experiences and thus creates a continuous existence in the first place. It is the same thing that drives a man toward a sense of *responsibility* for his own deeds and makes him strive to be able to *take responsibility* for all his actions, the most recent as well as the oldest. That is what produces the phenomenon of *remorse* and a *sense of guilt*, and what makes Man *relate things past to something that is eternally the same and thus eternally present.* The relationship established in this way is much more subtle and far-reaching than could ever be achieved by public judgment and the norms of society, because it is executed on the individual by the individual himself quite independently of anything social. That is why all moral psychology that tries to base morality on the social coexistence of humans, and to trace the origin of morality back to this coexistence, is fundamentally wrong and untruthful. Society knows the concept of *crime*, but not that of *sin;* it enforces *punishment* without trying to bring about *remorse.* Lying is prosecuted by the criminal code only in its solemn, *publicly damaging* form of perjury, and error has never been listed among the offences against written law. Therefore social ethics, which is afraid that with any kind of ethical individualism a fellow-human would get less than his fair share, and which *for that reason* drivels about the duties of the individual toward society and all the 1,500 million living human beings, does not, as it believes, *extend* the scope of morality, but *restricts* it in an inadmissible and reprehensible fashion.

What then is that thing beyond time and change, that "center of apperception"?

"It can be nothing less than what elevates a human being above himself (as a part of the sensible world), what connects him with an order of things that only the understanding can think and that at the same time has under it the whole sensible world. . . . It is nothing other than *personality.*"

An *"intelligible"* ***self***, which is different from any empirical consciousness, has been defined as the origin and legislator of morality by the most sublime book in the world, the *Critique of Practical Reason*, from which these words are taken.

This brings my investigation to the problem of the subject, which is its next topic.

VII Logic, Ethics, and the Self

It is common knowledge that David Hume has criticized the concept of the self as a mere "bundle" of different "perceptions" in constant flux and motion. No matter how much he thought that this compromised the self, he presents his view in relatively moderate terms, and he covers himself impeccably by his choice of words. He declares that some metaphysicians, who believe that they have a different self, must be ignored: for his part, he is quite certain that he has none, and he assumes (naturally, taking care not to talk about those few oddballs) that the rest of humanity are also nothing but bundles. That is how the man of the world expresses himself. The next chapter will tell how his irony rebounds on him. The reason why it has become so famous is the general overestimation of Hume, for which Kant is to blame. Hume was an excellent empirical psychologist, but he can by no means be called a genius, as he usually is. It does not take much to be the greatest English philosopher, but Hume has no overriding claim to be described even as that. Kant (despite the "paralogisms") rejected Spinozism *a limine* because it regarded human beings not as substances but as mere "accidents," and he thought that he had demolished it together with this "illogical" idea underlying it. Therefore, to say the least, I would not like to swear that he would not have significantly toned down his praise of the Englishman, had he also known his *Treatise,* and not only his later *Inquiry,* in which, of course, Hume did not include his critique of the self.

Lichtenberg, who went to battle against the self after Hume, was considerably bolder than Hume. He is the philosopher of impersonality, and he soberly amends the *phrase* "I think" to the factual "it thinks"; thus the self, for him, is really an invention of *grammarians.* Incidentally, Hume had actually anticipated him in this respect by declaring, at the end of his disquisitions, that all arguments about the identity of the person were a mere battle of words.

In most recent times E. Mach has interpreted the universe as a coherent mass and the selves as points at which the coherent mass has greater consistency. According to him, the only reality lies in the perceptions, which cohere strongly within one individual, but more faintly with those of another individual, who is distinguished from the first precisely *for that reason.* What matters, he argues, is the content, which is also preserved in others, with the exception of the worthless [*sic*] personal memories. The self, he claims, is no real unity, but only a practical one, and it is *unsalvageable:* therefore we can (gladly) do without it. However, he sees nothing reprehensible about behaving from time to time as if we had a self, particularly for the purposes of the Darwinian struggle for existence.

It is strange that a researcher such as Mach—who has not only achieved exceptional things as a historian of his particular science and as a critic of its concepts, but who is also extremely knowledgeable about biological matters and has had a stimulating effect, both direct and indirect, on their theory—should take no account whatsoever of the fact that every organic being is *indivisible* from the outset, that is, some kind of atom or monad (cf. part 1, chapter III, p. 38). After all, the main difference between organic and inorganic matter is that the former is *always* differentiated into heterogeneous parts that are dependent on each other, while even a fully formed crystal is homogeneous throughout. Therefore it should at least be regarded as a possibility that the very phenomenon of individuation, the fact that organic beings generally do not cohere like Siamese twins, also has psychic implications and is likely to have greater consequences in the psychic realm than the Machian self, that mere *waiting room* for perceptions.

There is reason to believe that such a psychic correlate exists even among animals. Everything that an animal feels and perceives is likely to have, for each individual, a different note or coloring, which is not only peculiar to its class, genus, and species, its race and family, but which differs in each individual from every other. The physiological equivalent of this *specificity* of all the perceptions and feelings of every particular animal is the idioplasm, and on grounds which are analogous to those of the theory of idioplasm (cf. part 1, chapter II, p. 20 and part 2, chapter I, p. 72) we must assume that among animals too there is an *empirical character.* The hunter, the breeder, and the keeper, who deal with dogs, horses, and monkeys respectively, will confirm not only the singularity but also the constancy in the behavior of every single animal. Thus, at this point already the existence of something that goes beyond a mere rendezvous of the "elements" is extremely *likely.*

Although this psychic correlate of the idioplasm exists, and animals surely have a peculiar nature of their own, the latter still bears no relation to the intelligible character, the presence of which we have no reason to assume in any being other than the human. The intelligible character of the human being, *individuality,* relates to the empirical character, mere *individuation,* in the same way as memory does to simple immediate recognition. Ultimately we are dealing with identity: in both cases the foundation is structure, form, law, cosmos, which remains the same even when the contents change. The reflections on the basis of which the existence of such a noumenal, trans-empirical subject may be deduced must now be briefly set forth. They are the product of logic and ethics.

Logic is about the true meaning of the principle of identity (and of contradiction; the many controversies about which of them takes precedence over the other, and what is the most correct form of their expression, are not very relevant here). *The proposition A = A is immediately certain and self-evident.* At the same time it is the original standard for the truth of all other propositions. If any proposition ever contradicted it—that is, if at any time a specific judgment contained a predicate that made a statement about a subject which contradicted the concept of that subject—we would regard it as false; and on reflection, the proposition A = A would finally emerge as the maxim of our judgment. It is the principle of true and false, and whoever, as happens so often, regards it as a tautology, which says nothing and which does not advance our thinking, is entirely right, but has misunderstood the nature of the proposition. This applies to Hegel and almost all *empiricists* who came later—nor is it the only point of contact between these apparently irreconcilable opposites. A = A, the *principle of all* truth, cannot itself be a *specific* truth. Whoever finds the principle of identity, or the principle of contradiction, devoid of meaning has himself to blame. He expected to find specific ideas in them, and he hoped to add to his fund of positive knowledge. But those principles in themselves are no insights, no specific acts of thought, but the *standard applied to all acts of thought. This cannot itself be an act of thought which could be compared in any way to the others. The norm of thought cannot be situated in thought itself.* The principle of identity adds nothing to our knowledge. Rather than increasing a fortune, it provides the complete *foundation* for that fortune in the first place. *The principle of identity is either nothing, or it is everything.*

What do the principle of identity and the principle of contradiction refer to? It is generally believed that they refer to judgments. Sigwart, for example, formulates the latter only as follows: "The two judgments, A is B, and A is not B, cannot be true at the same time." He maintains that the judgment "an unlearned man is learned" involves a contradiction, "because the predicate 'learned' is allocated to a subject who, when he was described by the subject words 'unlearned man,' was said not to be learned; it is therefore based on two judgments, X is learned and X is not learned," etc. The psychologism in this reasoning is obvious. It has recourse to a judgment that precedes the formation of the concept of an unlearned man *in time.* However, the above sentence—A is not non-A—claims to be valid, regardless of whether there are, have been, or will be, any other judgments. It refers to the *concept* of the unlearned man. It *secures* this concept by ruling out all those features that contradict it.

This is the true function of the principle of contradiction and the principle of identity. *They constitute conceptuality.*

It is true that this function concerns only the logical concept and not what has been called the "psychological concept." *Psychologically,* the concept is always represented by a concrete general idea; there is, however, a sense in which the element of conceptuality is immanent to this idea. The general idea, which psychologically represents the concept and around which human conceptual thinking revolves, is not the same as the concept. For example it can be richer (if I think of a triangle) or it can poorer (the concept of the lion implies more than my idea of the lion, while the opposite is true in the case of the triangle). The logical concept is the guiding principle followed by the attention when it selects only certain elements from an *idea* which represents a concept to the individual. These elements are *precisely those indicated by the concept,* and the logical concept is the goal and desire of the psychological concept, the polar star to which the attention looks up when it creates the concrete surrogate of the concept: *it is the law which directs the attention in making its choice.*

There is certainly no thought that occurs purely logically and not also psychologically: *for that would be* **the** *miracle.* By definition, only the deity thinks purely logically. A human being is always bound to think psychologically as well as logically, because he possesses not only reason but also sensuality, and because his thought proceeds psychologically in time, even though it aims at logical, i.e., timeless, results. However, logicality is the sublime standard applied to the psychological thought processes of the individual, both by himself and by others. When two people discuss something they talk about the concept and not about the different individual ideas which represent the concept to either of them: *thus the concept is a value, by which the individual idea is measured.* Therefore, how the general idea comes into being *psychologically* has *nothing at all* to do with the nature of the concept and has no significance whatsoever for it. The concept does not acquire its logical character—the source of its *dignity* and *rigor*—from experience, which only ever shows uncertain shapes and which at best could create vague general ideas. *Absolute constancy* and *absolute unambiguity,* which *cannot* derive from experience, are the essence of *conceptuality,* that "hidden art in the depths of the human soul, whose true operations we can divine from nature and lay unveiled before our eyes only with difficulty," as the *Critique of Pure Reason* puts it. That absolute constancy and unambiguity does not refer to metaphysical entities: things are not real insofar as they have a share in the concept, but their qualities, logically, are their qualities only insofar as they are contained in the concept. *The concept is the norm of the essence, not of the existence.*

My logical justification in saying that a circular thing is curved derives from the concept of the circle, which contains the curve as a characteristic. But to define the concept as the essence itself is wrong: "essence" here is either a psychological contrast or a metaphysical thing. And to equate the concept with its definition is forbidden by the nature of definition, for a definition only ever refers to the content of the concept and not to its extent; that is, it only indicates the *wording,* and not the *remit,* of that norm which constitutes the nature of conceptuality. The concept as norm, as a norm of the essence, cannot itself be an essence: the norm must be something else, and as it is not an essence, it can only be—there is no third option—*existence:* nor is it an existence that reveals the presence of any objects, but an existence that reveals the being of a *function.*

In any intellectual debate between human beings, when in the final analysis an appeal is made to definition, the *norm of the essence* is none other than the propositions $A = A$ or $A \neq A$. The concept obtains its conceptuality, that is its *constancy* and *unambiguity,* through the proposition $A = A$, and through nothing else. The roles of the logical axioms are distributed in such a way that the permanent immovability and uniformity of the concept *itself* is guaranteed by the *principium identitatis,* while the *principium contradictionis* clearly delimits it against all possible *other* concepts. *This proves, for the first time, that the conceptual function can be expressed through the two supreme logical axioms, and is itself none other than these.* The proposition $A = A$ (and $A \neq$ non-A) is what makes any concept at all *possible,* it is the *vital nerve* of the conceptual nature, or conceptuality, of the concept.

If I utter the proposition itself, $A = A$, clearly the meaning of this proposition is not that a *specific* A, which *exists,* or even that *every* specific A, which is *really* experienced or *really* thought, is equal to itself. The judgment of identity *does not depend on whether an A actually exists,* which of course is not to say that the proposition does not have to be thought by an existing person; *but the proposition is* ***thought*** *independently of* ***whether*** *something or somebody exists.* It means that if there is an A (there may or may not be one, *even* if there is perhaps none), $A = A$ is valid in any case. Thus a position is irrevocably given, a *being* is posited, namely the being $A = A$, even though it remains hypothetical whether A itself *exists* at all. The proposition $A = A$ therefore maintains that something *exists,* and this existence is that norm of the essence which is sought for. It cannot derive from empirical knowledge, from a few, or however many, *experiences,* as Mill believed: for it is completely independent of experience and is certainly valid, whether experience will show it an A or not. This proposition has not been denied by anybody so far; nor could it be denied, because the denial itself would again presuppose it by trying to deny *something specific.* Since *the proposition asserts a being without depending on the existence of any specific objects or saying something about such an existence, it can only express a being that is different from the being of any real or possible objects. In other words, it can only express the* ***being*** *of something that, by definition, can never become an object.*[1] *Thus the evidence of the proposition will reveal the existence of the subject, and this being which is expressed through the principle*

1. It must be noted that this proof rests on the identification of any *logical* A with the *epistemological* object as such, but the legitimacy of this identification cannot itself be demonstrated. At this juncture, however, for methodological reasons, I will ignore *being as such,* which alone could, strictly speaking, be inferred from the validity of the identity principle. Incidentally, this proof of a being *beyond* experience, a being *independent* of any experience, should have sufficed to refute positivism (which was my purpose). That this being is the being of the self cannot be explained purely *logically,* but really only *psychologically* by the *empirical fact* that the logical norm does not come to man from outside, but is given to him by his own deepest essence. That is the only reason why *absolute being* or the *being of the absolute,* as it manifests itself in the proposition $A = A$, can be equated to the being *of the self:* the absolute self is the absolute.

of identity lies neither in the first A nor in the second A, but in the sign for identity, A ≡ A. This proposition, then, is identical with the proposition: I am.

This difficult but unavoidable deduction can be explained more easily in psychological terms. Clearly, if we are to be able to say A = A, if we are to be able to establish the immutability of the concept in normative fashion and maintain it in opposition to the ever changing individual phenomena of experience, there must be something immutable, and that can only be the subject. If I were part of the circle of change, I would not be able to recognize that an A has remained the same. If I were constantly changing and losing my identity, if my self were functionally tied to change, I would have no possibility of facing and recognizing change. I would lack the absolute mental system of coordinates, through which alone an identity could be defined and preserved as such.

The existence of the subject cannot be *derived:* in this respect Kant's critique of rational psychology is entirely correct. But it is possible to demonstrate where this existence also finds its rigorous and unambiguous expression in logic; and there is no need to portray intelligible being as a mere logical *possibility,* which the moral law alone can in due course turn into a certainty, as Kant did. Fichte was right when he also found a guarantee of the existence of the self in pure logic, insofar as the self coincides with intelligible *being.*

The logical axioms are the principle of all truth. They establish a *being,* and it is this that knowledge is guided by and strives for. Logic is a law which must be obeyed, and *the human being* ***is*** *completely himself only when he is* ***completely*** *logical;* indeed he does not *exist* until he is nothing but logic, throughout and absolutely. *In knowledge he finds himself.*

All error is felt to be guilt. This implies that the individual does not *have* to err. He is *meant* to find the truth: therefore he *can* find it. From the duty of knowledge follow the possibility of knowledge, *freedom* of thought, and hope for the victory of knowledge. The *normativity* of logic contains the proof that *human thought is* ***free*** and *able* to reach its goal.

* * *

I can treat ethics more briefly and in a different way, since this investigation is based throughout on *Kantian moral philosophy* and, as was seen, the preceding logical deductions and postulates were also conducted in a certain analogy to it. The most profound nature of man, his intelligible essence, is that which is not subject to causality and which freely chooses good or evil. This is always manifested in exactly the same way, through the sense of guilt, through *repentance.* Nobody so far has been able to explain these facts differently: and nobody can be persuaded that he *had* to commit this or that deed. Here too the obligation bears witness to the ability. A man may be fully conscious of the causal factors, the low motives, which have pulled him down, and yet—*or indeed all the more readily*—he will attribute his behavior to his intelligible self, which he sees as a free self that *could* have acted differently.

Truthfulness, purity, fidelity, sincerity toward oneself: that is the only conceivable ethic. There are only duties to oneself, duties of the empirical self to the intelligible self, which appear in the shape of those two imperatives that will always defeat psychologism: in the shape of the logical law and the moral law. The normative disciplines, the psychic fact of the inner demand that calls for much more than any bourgeois morality ever wants to have—that is what no empiricism will ever be able to explain adequately. Empiricism finds its true opposite in a critical-transcendental *method,* not in a metaphysical-transcendent one, since all metaphysics is merely a hypostasizing kind of psychology, while transcendental philosophy is the logic of evaluative judgments. Any empiricism and skepticism, any positivism and relativism, any psychologism and any purely immanent way of looking at things feels instinctively that its main difficulty arises from ethics and logic. Hence the constantly renewed and always futile attempts to place these disciplines on an empirical and psychological foundation; and there is hardly anything but an attempt to test and prove the *principium individuationis* experimentally that is still lacking.

Logic and ethics are fundamentally one and the same thing—duty to oneself. They celebrate their union in the supreme value of truth, which is confronted on one side by error and on the other by the lie: truth itself, however, is only one. Any ethics is only possible in accordance with the laws of logic, and any logic is at the same time an ethical law. *Man's* duty and *task is not solely virtue, but also insight, not solely holiness, but also wisdom: only the two together provide the foundation for* ***perfection****.*

However, ethics, whose propositions are optatives, cannot supply a strictly logical proof of *existence,* as logic can. Ethics is not a logical demand in the same sense as logic is an ethical demand. Logic enables the self to set eyes on its full realization as absolute being; on the other hand, it is only ethics that demands this realization. Logic is absorbed by ethics and becomes its essential content, its command.

With reference to that famous passage of the *Critique of Practical Reason* where Kant introduces the human being as part of the intelligible world ("Duty! Sublime and mighty name . . ."), one will therefore be right to ask how Kant can know that the moral law emanates from the personality. The only answer Kant gives is that no other origin, worthy of it, could be found. He gives no further reason why the categorical imperative is the law given by the noumenon: as far as he is concerned, they obviously belong together from the outset. This is in the nature of ethics. Ethics demands that the intelligible self *act* freely, unadulterated by the impurities of the empirical self. *Thus the same being* that *logic presages to us, full of promise, as something already present in one form or another, can only be completely realized in its purity through ethics.*

The omission mentioned above shows clearly what the *theory of monads,* the *theory of the soul,* meant to Kant in his *heart.* It demonstrates how he always clung to it as the only thing of value, and how his theory of the "intelligible" character, which is so often mistaken for a new discovery or invention, or a *medium of information,* of Kantian philosophy, was only intended to pinpoint those elements of it which were scientifically tenable.

The only *duty* there is is duty to oneself: Kant must have become certain of this in his earliest youth (perhaps once he had felt the impulse to lie).

Apart from some affinities to Kant which can be read into the Hercules legend, some passages of Nietzsche and, even more, of Stirner, only Ibsen (in *Brand* and *Peer Gynt*) has, almost independently, discovered the principle of Kantian ethics. Occasionally one comes across statements like Hebbel's epigram "Lie and Truth":

> What do you pay for more dearly, the lie or the truth?
> The former costs you your self, the latter at the most your happiness.

or Suleika's world famous words from Goethe's *Poems of the West and the East* [translated by John Whaley (Bern, New York, 1998), p. 281]:

> Nations, rulers, slaves subjected,
> All on this one point agree:
> Joy of earthlings is perfected
> In the personality.
>
> Every life is worth the choosing
> If oneself one does not miss;
> Everything is worth the losing
> To continue as one is.

It is certainly true that most people somehow need Jehovah. There are very few—they are the men of genius—whose lives are devoid of any *heteronomy.* The others always justify their actions, their thoughts, and their existence, at least in their minds, to somebody *else,* be it a personal Jewish god or a loved, respected, or feared human being. *That* is their only way of acting, formally and externally, in accordance with the moral law.

Kant, whose life was entirely self-directed, and independent down to the last detail, was so convinced that the human being is responsible to none but himself that he regarded that particular point of his doctrine as most obvious and least open to objections. And yet it is in part due to Kant's silence in this particular respect that his ethics has in fact been so little *understood*—although it is *the only kind of ethics which is tenable precisely on the grounds of introspective psychology* and which does not try to drown the hard and stern voice of the single individual in the noise of the many.

As can be inferred from a passage in his *Anthropology,* there was a phase in Kant's own life that preceded the "establishment of a character." But there was a moment when it came to him with awesome, dazzling clarity: I am accountable only to myself, I need not serve anybody else, I cannot become oblivious of myself in work, I stand *alone,* I am *free,* I am *my own master.* That moment marks the birth of the Kantian ethic, the most heroic act in world history.

> Two things fill the mind with ever new and increasing admiration and reverence, the more often and more steadily one reflects on them: *the starry heavens above me and the moral law within me.* I do not need to search for them and merely conjecture them as though they were veiled in obscurity or in the transcendent region beyond my horizon; I see them before me and connect them immediately with the consciousness of my existence. The first begins from the place I occupy in the external world of sense and extends the connection in which I stand into an unbounded magnitude with worlds upon worlds and systems of systems, and moreover into the unbounded times of their periodic motion, their beginning and their duration. The second begins from my invisible self, my personality, and presents me in a world which has true infinity but which can be discovered only by the understanding, and I recognize that my connection with that world (and thereby with all those visible worlds as well) is not merely contingent, as in the first case, but universal and necessary. The first view of the countless multitude of worlds annihilates, as it were, my importance as an *animal creature,* which after it has been for a short time provided with vital force (one knows not how) must give back to the planet (a mere speck in the universe) the matter from which it came. The second, on the contrary, infinitely raises my worth as an *intelligence* by my personality, in which the moral law reveals to me a life independent of animality and even of the whole sensible world, at least so far as this may be inferred from the purposive determination of my existence by this law, a determination not restricted to the conditions and boundaries of this life but reaching into the infinite.

Having reached this conclusion, we now understand this *Critique of Practical Reason.* The human being is *alone* in the universe, in eternal, tremendous *loneliness.*

He has no purpose outside himself, nothing else to live for—he has flown far beyond wanting-to-be-a-slave, being-able-to-be-a-slave, having-to-be-a-slave: all human society has vanished, all *social* ethic has sunk, far beneath him; he is alone, ***alone.***

But now for the first time he is *one* and *all;* and that is why he has a *law* within him, that is why he himself *is* all the law and no capricious willfulness. *He* demands *from himself* that he obey this law *within* him, the law of his own self, and that he be *nothing but* law, without consideration for what is either behind or before him. This is what is so horrifying and at the same time so great: his obedience to duty has *no* ***further*** *purpose.* There is nothing *above* him, above him alone, above him *all-one.* But he must fulfill the inexorable, non-negotiable, i.e., *categorical,* demand *within him. Redemption!* he cries out,[2] rest, just rest from the enemy, peace, not this endless struggle—and he *takes fright:* even in the desire for redemption there was still some cowardice, in the soulful "*just*" there was still some desertion, as if he were too small for this battle. *Why!* he asks, he cries out into the universe—and *blushes;* for he has again wanted *happiness,* recognition for his struggle, somebody to reward him, the ***other.*** Kant's loneliest human being does not laugh and does not dance, he does not roar and he does not cheer: he has no need to make a noise as if the silence of the universe were too deep for him. He does not derive his duty from the meaninglessness of an "accidental" world, but his duty, to him, is *the meaning of the universe.* To say *yes* to ***this*** loneliness is the "Dionysian" element in Kant; that, and nothing less, is morality.

2. Cries Schopenhauer, cries Wagner.

VIII The Problem of the Self and Genius

In the beginning, the Atman alone was this world in the form of man. He glanced around himself; then he saw nothing else than his own self. In the beginning, he then exclaimed: "That I am!" Out of that arose the name "I"—Therefore, even today, when one is called or summoned, he first says: "That I am!" and after that he utters the other names which he bears.

—Brihadâranyaka Upanishad

MANY ARGUMENTS ON principles in psychology arise from the individual characterological differences between the contestants. Thus, as mentioned before, characterology could have an important role to play: while one person claims that he has found this in himself, and another that he has found that, characterology would have to teach *why* the self-observation of the first turns out to be different from that of the second; or at least to show in what *further* respects the persons in question differ. In fact I see no other way of resolving the most controversial psychological issues in particular. Psychology is an empirical science, in which the general does not precede the particular as it does in the supra-individual normative sciences of logic and ethics, and therefore the starting point in psychology must be the individual human being. There is no such thing as an empirical general psychology, and it was a mistake to embark on it without *simultaneously* putting a differential psychology into operation.

The cause of this miserable state of affairs is the dual position of psychology between philosophy and the analysis of sensations. No matter which of the two areas psychologists came from, they have always claimed that their own results were generally valid. However, without any characterological distinctions it may not be possible to give a complete answer even to fundamental questions such as whether or not there is a positive *act* of perception, a *spontaneous* consciousness, already in the sensations.

It is one of the main tasks of this study to use characterology in order to resolve a small fraction of these amphibolies in relation to the psychology of the sexes. However, the different treatments of the problem of the self arise not so much from the psychological differences between the sexes, but, at least initially if not exclusively,[1] from the individual differences in *endowment.*

The choice between Hume and Kant in particular can also be made in *characterological* terms, just as I can choose, for example, between two persons, one of whom has the highest regard for the works of Makart and Gounod and the other for those of Rembrandt and Beethoven. Initially I shall distinguish such people in terms of their endowment. In this case too it is therefore permissible, and indeed necessary, to rate the judgments about the self which come from two very differently endowed persons somewhat unequally. *There is no truly exceptional individual who is not convinced of the existence of the self:* an individual who denies the self can never be a truly exceptional one.[2]

In what follows, this thesis will prove to be absolutely compelling, and an explanation for the higher esteem in which it holds the judgments of a genius will also be sought, and found.

There is, and there can be, no exceptional individual in whose life—generally, the more exceptional he is, the sooner (cf. chapter V)—a moment will not come when he becomes absolutely certain that he has a self of a higher kind.[3] Compare the following statements by three very different men of extreme genius.

Jean Paul, in his autobiographical sketch "A True Story from My Life," relates:

> Never shall I forget that which I have never yet related to a human being—the inward experience of the birth of self-consciousness, of which I well remember the time and place. I stood one afternoon, a very young child, at the house door, and looked at the logs of wood piled on the left, when, at once, that inward consciousness *I am a Me* came like a flash of lightning from Heaven, and has remained ever since. Then was my existence conscious of itself, and for ever. Deceptions of memory are here scarcely imaginable, for no exterior occurrence could mingle with a consciousness so concealed in the holy sanctuary of man, whose novelty alone has given permanence to the every-day circumstances that accompanied it.

Novalis clearly has the same experience in mind when he remarks in his *Fragments on Miscellaneous Topics:*

> This fact cannot be demonstrated, everybody must experience it for himself. It is a fact of a higher kind, *which will only be encountered by the higher man,* but men should strive to induce it in themselves. Philosophy is a way of speaking about oneself in the above manner; it is essentially a self-revelation, the arousal

1. Cf. p. 127, on people who do and who do not understand themselves.
2. Which is not to say that everybody who recognizes the self is a genius.
3. How this is connected with the fact that exceptional individuals can *love* very early (e.g., at the age of four) will become clear later (pp. 216ff.).

> of the real self through the ideal self. Philosophy is the foundation of all other revelations. The decision to philosophize is a challenge to the real self to reflect, to awake, and to be spirit.

Schelling, in the eighth of his *Philosophical Letters on Dogmatism and Criticism,* a little known work of his youth, discusses the *same* phenomenon in the following profound and beautiful words:

> In us all . . . resides a mysterious, miraculous ability to withdraw from the changes of time into our innermost self, which is free of all external trappings and in which we contemplate the eternal within us in the form of immutability. *This contemplation is the deepest, most fundamental experience, on which depends absolutely everything we know and believe about a suprasensory world. This experience is the first to convince us that something actually* ***is****, while everything else to which we apply that word only* ***appears*** *to be.* It differs from every sensuous experience in that it is produced by *freedom* alone, and it is alien and unknown to everybody else, whose freedom, overwhelmed by the power issuing from the objects, hardly suffices to produce consciousness. Nevertheless, even for those who do not possess this freedom of self-contemplation, there is at least an approximation to it, there are indirect experiences, through which they can have an inkling of its existence. There is a certain profoundness, of which we are not conscious and which we strive to develop in ourselves to no avail. It has been described by Jakobi. . . . This intellectual experience occurs when we cease to be an *object* to ourselves, when the experiencing self is identical to the experienced self. *At this moment of experience, time and duration fade away: it is not* ***we*** *who are in time, but rather time—or not really time, but pure, absolute eternity—is* ***in us****.* It is not we who are lost in the experience of the objective world, but the objective world is lost in our experience.

The immanentist and the positivist may only smile at the deceived deceiver, the philosopher who pretends to have such experiences. Well, nothing much can be done about that. Nor is it necessary. But I am not at all of the opinion that the "fact of a higher kind" occurs in *all* men of genius in that mystical form of the subject and the object becoming one, in an integrated experience, as Schelling describes it. This is not the place to discuss whether there are any undivided experiences, in which the dualism is already overcome *in life,* as is testified to by Plotinus and the Indian mahatmas, or whether they are simply the highest intensification of experience, but in principle the same as all other experiences. Nor shall the concurrence of subject and object, of time and eternity, and the visible appearance of God to a living man, be either maintained as a possibility or denied as an impossibility. Epistemologically, an *experience* of one's own self is useless, and nobody so far has ever tried to utilize it for a *systematic* philosophy. I will therefore not call the fact of a "higher kind," which takes one form in one individual and a different form in another, an *experience* of one's own self, but only the *event of the self.*

The event of the self is familiar to every exceptional individual. He may first find, and become conscious of, his self through love for a woman,[4] for an exceptional individual always loves more intensely than a less exceptional one. Again with the help of a contrast, he may arrive at an awareness of his own higher nature—to which he has become unfaithful through an action that he regrets—thanks to a sense of guilt, for the sense of guilt is also more severe and more subtle in an exceptional individual than in an unexceptional one. He may be led by the event of the self to become one with the universe, to see all things in God, or rather to recognize the terrible dualism between nature and spirit in the universe, which may awaken his desire for redemption, his desire for the *inner* miracle. In all such cases, the core of a *weltanschauung* is *given* together with the event of the self, quite automatically, without any involvement of the thinking individual. A *weltanschauung* is not the great synthesis accomplished on the doomsday of science by some particularly industrious man, who has worked his way through one discipline after the other at his desk in the middle of a great library. A *weltanschauung* is something that has been experienced, and it can be *clear and unambiguous as a whole,* even if, for the time being, so many details are wrapped in darkness and contradictions. The event of the self is the root of all *weltanschauung,* that is, of all *experience of the world* as a *whole,* for the artist no less than for the philosopher. And however radically the kinds of *weltanschauung* differ from one another in other respects, they have one thing in common, if they deserve the name of *weltanschauung.*[5] This is precisely what is mediated through the event of the self, the belief *possessed by every exceptional individual: the conviction of the existence of a self or a soul,* which is lonely in the universe, which confronts the whole universe, which *experiences* the whole *universe.*

Reckoning from the event of the self, the exceptional individual will generally live *with a soul,* even though there may be frequent intervals, filled with the most terrible of feelings, a feeling of *being dead.*

This, and not only their elation over something that they have just created, is the reason why I want to add here that exceptional individuals will, always and in every respect, have the greatest self-assurance. Nothing is so wrong as all the talk about the "modesty" of great men, who supposedly did not know what they had in them. There is no exceptional individual who does not know how much he differs from others (apart from periods of depression, in the face of which even his resolution to take pride in himself, made in better times, may remain fruitless) and none who did not regard himself as an exceptional indi-

4. This case will need to be investigated later (pp. 323ff.).

5. Which therefore does not include Darwinism and the monistic systems that center on the "idea of evolution." The rage for genuses and genital intercourse in our time could not have exposed itself more clearly than it has through the fact that the theory of descendence has been linked to the word *weltanschauung* and placed in opposition to pessimism.

vidual, once he had *created* something—although there is also no exceptional individual whose vanity or ambition was so slight that he did not always overrate himself. Schopenhauer believed that he was much greater than Kant. If Nietzsche declares that his Zarathustra is the most profound book in the world, his disappointment over the silence of the journalists and the desire to annoy them—certainly not very noble motives—also play a part.

But one element in the theory about the modesty of exceptional individuals is correct: exceptional individuals are never arrogant. Arrogance and self-assurance are probably the most extreme opposites there can be, and they should not be confused, as they usually are. An individual's arrogance is always in proportion to his lack of self-assurance. Arrogance is surely only a means of forcibly enhancing one's self-assurance by artificially lowering one's fellow-human, and indeed of becoming conscious of having a self. Naturally this applies to unconscious, as it were, physiological, arrogance: sometimes even a superior individual may be obliged, for the sake of his own dignity, to treat some despicable characters with deliberate rudeness.

A firm and utter conviction that they possess a soul is common to all men of genius and requires no *proof* as far as they are concerned. It is about time to dispose of the ludicrous suspicion that a proselytizing theologian is lurking behind anybody who speaks of the soul as a hyper-empirical reality. A belief in the soul is anything but superstition. Nor is it a means of seduction used by every member of the clergy. Artists also talk about their soul without having studied philosophy or theology, and even the most atheistic among them, like Shelley, are convinced that they know what they mean by it. Or does anybody believe that "soul," for them, is merely an empty, beautiful word, which they repeat after others without feeling, and that a great artist uses any terms without being clear about what they signify, which in this case is the most real thing imaginable? The immanentist empiricist, the mere physiologist, is bound to regard all that as meaningless prattle, and Lucretius as the only great poet. Nevertheless, no matter how much the word has been misused, if *great* artists bear witness to their soul they know very well what they are doing. They, like the great philosophers, have a certain *boundary feeling* of the supreme reality. Hume certainly did not know this feeling.

The scientist ranks *below* the philosopher and *below* the artist, as has already been emphasized and will soon be proved. The latter deserve the predicate of genius, the mere scientist never. But if greater importance is attached to a genius's view of a certain problem than to that of a scientist, merely because it is his view, he is given a further, as yet unexplained, preference over science, which is what has been done here. Is this preference justifiable? Can a genius explore things that are denied to the man of science as such, and can his eye reach any depths which the scientist may not even notice?

The idea of genius, as has been shown, includes universality. A man of utter genius, who is a necessary fiction, would have an equally vital, infinitely close, fateful relationship with everything in the world. We have defined genius as universal apperception and thus perfect memory, absolute timelessness. But in order to be able to apperceive something, one must have something akin to it in oneself. One can only notice, understand, and grasp something to which one bears some kind of resemblance (p. 96). As if in defiance of all complexity, the genius was ultimately seen to be the individual with the most intensive, most live, most continuous, most integrated self. The self, for its part, is the center point, the unity of apperception, the "synthesis" of all diversity.

Accordingly, the self of the genius must itself be universal apperception, the point must comprise the infinite space: *the exceptional individual has the* ***whole*** *world* ***in him, genius is the living microcosm.*** He is not a mosaic of many pieces, not a chemical compound made up of a *large* but always *finite number* of elements, and this is not what was meant by the account I gave in the fourth chapter of his closer affinity to more human beings and things: *rather, he is everything.* All psychic phenomena are connected in the self and through the self, where the connection is experienced directly—without having to be laboriously introduced into psychic life through a science (which is expected to do just that in all external matters[6])—and where the whole exists before the parts. So the genius, in whom the self lives like the universe, or indeed as the universe, gazes into nature and the hustle and bustle of all beings as a whole, he *sees* the *connections* and does not construct an edifice from fragments. That is why an exceptional individual cannot begin to be a mere empirical psychologist, for whom there are only details which he tries to cement together through associations, breaches, etc. by the sweat of his brow, or a mere physicist for whom the world is *assembled* from atoms and molecules.

The genius recognizes the **meaning** of the parts from the idea of the whole, in which he constantly lives. Consequently he **evaluates everything**, both within and outside him, according to this idea; and for that reason alone everything in his view, rather than being a function of time, represents a great and eternal idea. Thus a genius is the profound individual, and the profound individual alone is a genius. That is why his opinion is indeed more valid than that of the others. Because he creates out of the whole of his self which contains the uni-

6. That is why *within* the individual human being there is no concept of *coincidence,* and indeed none can even arise. A heated rod is made to expand by a supply of thermal energy and not by a comet that is visible in the sky at the same time: I know this by virtue of long-standing experience and induction, and only on the strength of these. Here the *correct* connection does not arise *directly* from experience. On the other hand, if I am annoyed about my own behavior in certain company, then I *know* the *reason* for my dissatisfaction *immediately,* even assuming that this is happening for the first time, and regardless of how many other psychic events intervened simultaneously. I am at once completely certain of it, or at least I can reach such a certainty the first time it happens, if I do not try to deceive myself.

verse, while others never arrive at a consciousness of this their true self, all things make sense to him, mean something to him, and he always sees symbols in them. To him, breathing is more than an exchange of gases through the thinnest walls of the capillaries, the blue of the sky is more than partly polarized sunlight diffusely reflected by the opaqueness of the atmosphere, and snakes are more than just reptiles without feet, shoulder girdle, and extremities. Imagine collecting together all the scientific discoveries that have ever been made—every excellent contribution to science by Archimedes and Lagrange, Johannes Müller and Karl Ernst von Baer, Newton and Laplace, Konrad Sprengel and Cuvier, Thucydides and Niebuhr, Friedrich August Wolf and Franz Bopp, and so many others—and letting one single individual find all of them: even if **one** single individual had achieved all this in the course of **one** short human life, he would still not deserve to be called a genius.

None of this reaches any depths. The scientist takes the phenomena for what they *are* to the senses, the exceptional individual or genius for what they *mean.* To him, sea and mountains, light and dark, spring and autumn, cypress and palm, dove and swan are *symbols,* in which he does not merely suspect, but recognizes, something deeper. The ride of the Valkyries does not take place on shifts in atmospheric pressure, and the magic fire does not refer to any processes of oxidation. All this is possible for the man of genius only because the *outer* world *in* him coheres as richly and firmly as the *inner,* because the outer life appears to him to be merely a special case of his inner life, because the world and the self have become one in him and he does not need to clamp experience together bit by bit according to laws and rules. On the other hand, even the greatest body of polyhistoric knowledge only adds subjects to subjects and represents no whole. That is why the great scientist is inferior to the great artist or philosopher.

A true infinity in the breast of a genius corresponds to the infinity of the universe. A genius holds within him chaos and cosmos, all particularity and all totality, all multiplicity and all unity. These definitions say more about the quality of genius than about the way a genius *creates.* Therefore the state of artistic ecstasy, of philosophical conception, of religious illumination remains as mysterious as ever, and only the *conditions,* rather than the *process,* of truly exceptional production have become clearer. Nevertheless, the following may be offered as the ultimate definition of genius:

A human being may be called a genius if he lives in a conscious connection with the whole universe. Thus genius alone is the really divine element in humans.

The great idea of the human soul as the microcosm, the most profound creation of the philosophers of the Renaissance—although its first traces are already found in Plato and Aristotle—seems to have been entirely lost to more recent thought since the death of Leibniz. Whereas so far in this study its validity has only been asserted with regard to the genius, those masters claimed that it was the true essence of humanity as such.

However, this discrepancy is only an apparent one. All human beings have genius, and no human being is a genius. Genius is an *idea* that one individual approaches more closely while another remains a long distance from it, and toward which one individual advances fast, but another perhaps not until the end of his life.

An individual to whom we attribute the possession of genius is merely one who has already begun to see, and who opens the eyes of the others. The fact that they can then see with his eyes proves that they were standing at the gate. Even a mediocre individual, as such, can relate to everything *indirectly,* but his idea of the whole is only guesswork and he does not succeed in identifying with it. However, this does not mean that he is unable to follow others in this identification and thus form a picture of the whole. He can connect with the universe through a *weltanschauung* and with all the most individual things through education. Nothing is totally alien to him and he is linked to all things in the world by a bond of sympathy. This is not true of animals or plants. They are limited, they do not know all the elements, but only one, they do not populate the entire earth, and where they are generally in evidence, it is in the service of humans, who have allocated to them a function which is evenly distributed everywhere. They may relate to the sun or the moon, but they certainly lack the "the starry heavens" and the "moral law." The moral law comes from the human soul, which holds all totality, and *which can contemplate everything because it* **is** *everything:* the starry heavens and the moral law, they too are basically one and the same thing. The universalism of the categorical imperative is the universalism of the universe, the infinity of the universe is only a symbol of the infinity of the moral will.

Empedocles, the mighty magus of Agrigento, has already taught this, the microcosm in the human being, as follows:

Γαίῃ μὲν γὰρ γαῖαν ὀπώπαμεν, ὕδατι δ' ὕδωρ,
Αἰθέρι δ' αἰθέρα δῖον, ἀτὰρ πυρὶ πῦρ ἀίδηλον,
Στοργῇ δὲ στοργήν, νεῖκος δέ τε νείκεϊ λυγρῷ.

And Plotinus: "Οὐ γὰρ ἂν πώποτε εἶδεν ὀφθαλμὸς ἥλιον ἡλιοειδὴς μὴ γεγενημένος," which Goethe adapted in the famous lines:

Were they not sun-akin, our eyes,
To sunlight's glory they'd be blind;
Were they not in us, God's own energies,
How could divine things move our kind? [J. W. Goethe, *Poems and Epigrams,* translated by Michael Hamburger (London 1983), p. 90]

The human being is the only entity in nature, he is ***that*** *being in nature, which has a relationship with* ***all*** *the things in it.*

An individual in whom this relationship with all things—and not with many, or just a few, isolated ones—has reached clarity and a most intensive consciousness, and who has thought about everything independently, is called a genius. An individual in whom it is present only as a possibility, and in whom a certain interest in anything can be awakened, but who of his own accord is only interested in a few things, is called an ordinary human being. The same fact is expressed by Leibniz's rarely understood theory according to which the low monad is also a mirror of the world, but does not become conscious of this activity. The man of genius lives in a state of universal consciousness, which is a consciousness of the universal, while the whole of the universe is also present in ordinary people, but is not brought to a creative consciousness. One person lives in a conscious and active connection with the universe, the other in an unconscious, virtual connection. *The man of genius is the actual microcosm, the person without genius is the potential microcosm.* Only the man of genius is a complete human being. What is contained in every individual as a possibility of being human, as humanity (in the Kantian sense), as δυνάμει, is alive and fully developed, as ἐνεργεία, in the genius.

The human being is the universe and therefore not a mere part of it that depends on other parts. He is not *locked* into the laws of nature at a particular point, *but he is himself the quintessence of all laws and* ***therefore free,*** just as the universe itself, being everything, is not conditioned by anything, but is independent. The exceptional individual forgets *nothing,* because he does not forget *himself,* because to forget is to be functionally under the influence of time, and therefore unfree and unethical. He is not thrown up as the child of one historical movement and swallowed again by the next, because *everything, all the past and all the future,* is already enfolded in the *eternity* of his spiritual sight. He has the strongest sense of immortality, because he is not cowed by the thought of death. He enters into the most passionate relationship with symbols or values, by assessing, and thereby interpreting, not only everything in himself, but everything outside himself. He is at one and the same time the *freest* and the *wisest,* ***he*** is the *most moral* individual; and that is the only reason why ***he,*** of all, suffers most from anything that even in him is still unconscious, still chaos, still fate.

Now what of the morality of exceptional individuals in their treatment of others? For this is the only way in which morality can manifest itself, according to popular opinion, which can think of immorality only in connection with the penal code. Have famous men not revealed the most dubious traits precisely in this respect? Have they not often given grounds for accusations of despicable ingratitude, cruel hardness, wicked ruses in seduction?

Great artists and thinkers have had the reputation of being immoral, because the greater they are, the more ruthlessly they keep faith with themselves, shattering the expectations of many with whom they temporarily shared some intellectual interest and who, unable to follow them any further in their high flight, try to chain the eagle to the earth (Lavater and Goethe). The fate of Friederike in Sesenheim surely affected Goethe much more deeply than Friederike herself, although this by no means exonerates him. Fortunately he kept *silent* about so many things that those moderns who believe that they *entirely* possess the happy-go-lucky Olympian in fact hold only the flakes that surround Faust's immortal part, but we can be sure that he himself examined most accurately how much guilt he bore, and regretted it to its full extent. And when jealous detractors, who have never grasped Schopenhauer's theory of redemption and the meaning of nirvana, reproached the philosopher for insisting to the utmost on his *right* to his property, their mean yaps are not worthy of an answer.

It should therefore be clear that the exceptional individual is most moral toward himself. To him, the self of another and its views remain something entirely separate from his own, and he will not allow any view of another to be imposed on him and to repress his own self. He will not passively accept the opinion of another, and if he has ever done so, he will find the thought of it painful and frightening. If he has ever consciously told a lie, he will *carry* it with him all his life and be unable to *shake it off* in a light "Dionysian" manner. However, men of genius will suffer most acutely if in retrospect they realize that they have told a lie, of which they were not aware when they were telling it to others, or with which they deceived themselves. Other people, who have no such desire for truth, always remain more deeply enmeshed in lies and error, which is why they have so little understanding for the true opinion of great personalities and the fierceness of their struggle against the "*life-lie.*"

A superior individual, that is, one in whom the timeless self has seized power, seeks to raise his own value in the estimation of his intelligible self, his moral and intellectual conscience. His vanity, in the first instance, is also addressed to himself: *he develops a desire to impress himself* (with his thoughts, actions, and creations). This vanity is the vanity of the genius, whose value and reward is in himself, and who does not need the opinions of others in order to gain a higher opinion of himself by such a roundabout route. Nevertheless, it is by no means laudable, and ascetically disposed natures (Pascal) will suffer greatly from it, without ever being able to overcome it. Inner vanity will always be joined by vanity in front of others, *but the two are in conflict.*

Does this strong emphasis on duty toward oneself not impair one's ability to do one's duty to others? Is there not a reciprocity between the two, which ensures that whoever keeps faith with himself must necessarily break it with others?

Not at all. Just as there is only one truth, there is also only one *desire* for truth—Carlyle's "sincerity"—which one has, or has not, toward *both* oneself and the world, but never separately, never one of the two, no observation of the world without observation of the self, and no observation of the self without observation of the world. Thus there is only one duty, one kind of morality. We act either *altogether* morally or *altogether* immorally, and whoever is moral toward himself is also moral toward the others.

However, nothing is beset with so many wrong ideas as the definition of our moral duty toward our fellow-humans and the possible ways of fulfilling it.

If, for the time being, I ignore those theoretical systems of ethics which regard the advancement of human society as the principle on which all actions must be based—systems high above any morality of sympathy, because at least they are concerned with the rule of a general moral point of view rather than with concrete feelings in the course of an action or with the empirical aspects of an impulse—then the only thing that remains is the popular opinion which defines the morality of an individual mainly according to the degree of his compassion, his "goodness." Those philosophers who saw the essence and source of any ethical behavior in compassion include Hutcheson, Hume, and Smith, and this theory was subsequently deepened to an extraordinary degree by Schopenhauer's morality of compassion. However, Schopenhauer's essay *On the Basis of Morality* in its very motto—"To preach morality is easy, to found it is difficult"—gives away the fundamental mistake of all ethics of sympathy, which is the failure to recognize that ethics is not an objective descriptive science, but one that sets norms for action. Those who ridicule the attempts to hear accurately what the inner voice in human beings really says, and to discover with certainty what a human being *ought* to do, renounce all ethics, for ethics by definition is the theory of the demands that a human being makes on himself and on all others, and not an account of what he actually achieves by giving scope to these demands or drowning them out. The object of moral science is not what happens, but what *ought* to happen, and everything else belongs in psychology.

Any attempt to dissolve ethics into psychology overlooks the fact that every psychic movement in human beings is *evaluated* by a human being, and that the standard for the appraisal of any event cannot itself be an event. This standard can only be an *idea* or a *value,* which can never be fully realized or deduced from experience, because it remains constant even if all experience were to run counter to it. *To act morally, then, can only be to act in accordance with an idea.* Therefore the choice can only be between moral doctrines that posit ideas, or maxims of action, and of those only two are ever worth considering: on the one hand ethical socialism or "social ethics," founded by Bentham and Mill respectively and later brought by assiduous importers to the Continent, even as far as Germany and Norway, and on the other hand ethical individualism, as taught by *Christianity* and *German idealism.*

The *second* mistake of the ethics of compassion in all its varieties is that it tries to explain and *deduce* morality. Morality by definition should be the ultimate cause of human action and therefore must not itself be explicable and deducible. Morality is a purpose in itself and must not be attached to anything that is external to it, as means and ends are. Insofar as this claim of the morality of sympathy agrees with the principle underlying any merely descriptive and therefore necessarily relativist ethic, both mistakes are basically one, and this enterprise must always be met with the objection that nobody, even if he were to pace out the whole domain of causes and effects, would discover anywhere in it the idea of a supreme *purpose,* which alone is relevant to moral actions. The idea of purpose cannot be explained by cause and effect: on the contrary, it is ruled out by the relationship of cause and effect. Purpose lays claim to creating action. The success and outcome of any action is measured by the purpose, and will always be found wanting even when all the factors that have determined it are well known and however forcefully they assert themselves in the consciousness. Alongside the realm of causes there is a realm of purposes, and that realm is the realm of human beings. The perfect science of existence is a totality of causes which strives to rise to the supreme cause, and the perfect science of moral obligation is a totality of purposes which culminates in one final, supreme purpose.

Whoever attaches an ethically positive value to compassion has passed a moral judgment about something that was not an action but only a feeling, not a deed but only an affect (which by its nature does not come under the aspect of purpose). Compassion may be an ethical *phenomenon,* an expression of something ethical, but it is no more an ethical *act* than the sense of shame or pride. *One must clearly distinguish between an ethical act and an ethical phenomenon.* The former must be understood exclusively as a *conscious affirmation of the idea through action: ethical phenomena are involuntary, spontaneous signs of a constant direction of the mind toward the idea.* It is only in the struggle of motives that the idea intervenes time and again, in an attempt to influence and to decide it: the mere mixture of ethical and unethical feelings, compassion and gloating, self-assurance and exuberance contains nothing of a *decision. Compassion may be the surest sign of a disposition, but not the purpose behind any action.* Only *knowing* the purpose, a *consciousness* of value as opposed to worthlessness, constitutes morality. In this respect Socrates is right, in contrast to all the philosophers who came after him (only Plato and Kant followed him in this). An alogical feeling such as compassion has never any claim to *respect,* but at best arouses *sympathy.*

Accordingly, we must first answer the question in what sense a human being can behave morally toward other human beings.

Not by giving unrequested assistance, which *forces its way* into the solitude of another and breaks through the boundaries that our fellow-humans draw around themselves, but by showing respect by *observing* these boundaries. Not by *compassion,* but by *respect.* As was first articulated by Kant, the only being in the world that we *respect* is the human. It was his tremendous discovery that no human being can use himself, his intelligible self, humanity (not the human society of 1,500 million, but the *idea* of the *human soul*) in his own person or in the person of another, as a means to an end. "In the whole of creation everything one wants and over which one has any power can also be used *merely as a means;* a human being alone, and with him every rational creature, is an *end in itself.*" [*Critique of Practical Reason,* translated by Mary Gregor (Cambridge, 1997), p. 74.]

But how do I show my contempt and my respect for other human beings? The first by *ignoring* them, the second by *taking notice* of them. How do I use them as means to an end, and how do I honor something in them that is its own purpose? In the first case by regarding them as mere links in the chain of circumstances with which my actions must reckon, in the second by trying to *recognize* them. *Only* by being interested in them, thinking of them, attempting to understand their actions, empathizing with their fate, trying to *understand* them as themselves, and without actually letting them see all this, can one *honor* one's fellow-humans. Only an individual who has not become selfish as a result of his own troubles, who forgets all petty quarrels with his fellow-humans, who suppresses his anger with them, and who tries to *understand* them, is truly unselfish toward them; and he acts in a moral way, because it is precisely then that he *conquers* the *most powerful* enemy that makes it hardest to understand one's fellow-human: *self love.*

How does the outstanding individual behave in this respect?

The outstanding individual—who understands the largest number of human beings because his disposition is the most universal, and who lives in the closest contact with the universe, which he strives most passionately to recognize in an objective manner—will also act more morally toward his fellow-man than anybody else. Indeed nobody thinks as much and as intensively about other human beings (in many cases even if he has only had a fleeting glimpse of them) and nobody tries as hard to achieve a clear understanding of them if he does not have them in himself with sufficient distinctness and intensity. Just as he has a past filled with the continuity of his self behind him, he will also wonder about what the fate of the others was before he met them. He follows the strongest inclination of his inner nature in thinking about them, for through them he is trying to obtain clarity and the truth about himself. It is here that all human beings are seen to be members of an intelligible world, in which there is no narrow-minded egoism or altruism. This is the only possible way of explaining how great men enter into a more vital, more understanding relationship, not only with the people *around* them, but also with all the personalities in history who lived *before* them, and *this* is the only reason why the great artist can grasp historical individuality better and more intensively than the mere professional historian. There is no great man who has no personal relationship with Napoleon, Plato, or Mohammed. *For that is how he shows his respect and his true reverence for those who have lived before him.* If many people who have had dealings with artists have been embarrassed by subsequently recognizing themselves in one of their creations, and if therefore there are so many complaints about writers using everything as a model, the unpleasant feeling in such situations is only too understandable. But the artist, who does not reckon with the pettiness of people, has not committed a crime. He has, in his own unreflecting way of representing and recreating the world, *performed the creative act of understanding, and there is no relationship between human beings that is purer than this.*

This should have made Pascal's very true remark, which has been mentioned before, somewhat clearer: "A mesure qu'on a plus d'esprit, on trouve qu'il y a plus de différence entre les hommes. Les gens du commun ne trouvent pas de différence entre les hommes." It is further connected with the fact that the higher the standing of a man, the higher will be the demands that he makes on himself in respect of *understanding* the manifestations of *others.* On the other hand, a man who lacks endowment will soon believe that he understands something, often without even feeling the presence of something that he does not understand, and being hardly aware of *another* mind that addresses him from a work of art or a philosophy. As a result he may at best establish a relationship with things, but he will never rise to reflecting about the creator himself. The exceptional individual, who reaches the highest degree of consciousness, will not easily identify something that he has read with himself and his own opinion, while at a lower degree of intellectual lucidity very different things may merge into one another and look identical.

A man of genius is an individual who has become conscious of his *self.* That is why he is struck most forcibly by the otherness of the others, *that is why he senses the self of another, even before it has become strong enough to make itself known to the other. But only a man who feels that the other* ***is also a self, a monad, a center of the world in his own right****, with his particular way of thinking and feeling and his particular past, will be* ***automatically immune*** *to using his fellow-human merely* ***as a means to an end.*** In accordance with the Kantian ethic, he will also *sense, intuit, and therefore* **honor**, the *personality* of his fellow-human (as part of the *intelligible* world), *and not merely* ***be annoyed*** *by him.* ***Therefore the psychological prerequisite of any practical altruism is a theoretical individualism.***

Here then is the bridge leading from moral behavior toward oneself to moral behavior toward others, the link which was wrongly regarded by Schopenhauer as missing in Kantian philosophy and the apparent absence of which was therefore interpreted by him as a mistake unavoidably arising from the essential principles of that philosophy.

This link can easily be tested. Only the brutalized criminal and the insane have *no* interest *whatsoever* in even one of their fellow-humans, and live as if they were alone in the world, without the slightest *feeling* of the *presence of the other.* Therefore there is no such thing as *practical solipsism:* whoever has a self in him also recognizes a self in his fellow-human, and it is only when a human being has lost the (logical and ethical) core of his own personality that he will react to another as if the latter were no longer human, a being with a personality all his own. *"I" and "thou" are reciprocal terms.*

An individual arrives at the strongest consciousness of his own self when he is together with others. That is why he is prouder in the presence of others than when he is on his own, and it is left to his hours of solitude to dampen his high spirits.

Finally: he who kills himself kills the whole world at the same time; and he who murders another commits the worst crime because he has murdered himself in the other. Therefore all solipsism in practice is preposterous and would better be called *nihilism.* If there is no "thou" then surely there is never an "I," and what is left then is—nothing.

What matters is the psychological *state of mind* which makes it *impossible* to use the other human being as a means to an end. And here it was found: *he who feels his own personality also feels it in others.* For him the Tat-tvam-asi is not a beautiful hypothesis, but a *reality. The highest individualism* ***is*** *the highest universalism.*

Therefore Ernst Mach, who denies the subject, makes a grave mistake in believing that an ethical behavior, "which rules out the disregard of the alien self and an overestimation of one's own," cannot be expected until the self has been renounced. It has just been shown what consequences the lack of a self may have for an individual's treatment of a fellow-human. *The self is also the precondition for all social morality.* For *purely psychological* reasons I shall never be able to behave ethically toward a mere *knot* of "elements." Such conduct can be *affirmed* as an ideal, but it is entirely removed from any practical behavior, for which it can never serve as a norm, *because it* ***eliminates*** *the psychological condition for any fulfillment of the moral idea, whereas the moral demand is psychologically* ***present.***

On the contrary, the important thing is to make every human being conscious of the fact that he possesses a higher self, a soul, and that other human beings also possess a soul (although, in order to achieve that, the majority will always need a *soul shepherd*). Nothing less can ensure that an ethical relationship with one's fellow-human is present, *really present.*

This relationship is realized in a genius in the most unique fashion. Nobody will *suffer* as much as he with, and therefore through, the people with whom he lives. For there is certainly a sense in which a human being can *only* achieve "knowledge through compassion." Although compassion itself is no clear knowledge, whether abstract and conceptual or graphic and symbolic, it is the strongest impulse to attain all knowledge. The genius comprehends things only through suffering *from* them, and he understands human beings only through suffering *with* them. A genius suffers most because he suffers with all and in all; and he suffers most intensely from his compassion.

In an earlier chapter I tried to demonstrate that genius is the one factor which really raises humans above animals, and I made a connection between this and the fact that only humans have a history (which, I argued, is explained by the quality of genius that exists in all human beings, albeit in different degrees). I must now return to the same topic. Genius coincides with a lively activity of the intelligible subject. History reveals itself only in the social domain, in the "objective spirit," while the individuals in themselves eternally remain the same and do not progress as that spirit does (they are *the ahistorical* as such). So we see how our threads join together in order to produce a surprising result. For if—and here I do not believe that I am mistaken—the timeless human personality is also the precondition of any truly ethical behavior toward our fellow-humans, and if *individuality* is the ***prerequisite*** of a *social* mentality, this also explains why the "animal metaphysicum" and the "ζῷον πολιτικόν," the creature with genius and the bearer of history, are *one,* the selfsame being, ***that is,*** *the human being.* And this also resolves the long-standing argument as to which existed *first,* the *individual* or the *community:* ***for both are present, at the same time and together.***

Thus I have demonstrated in every respect that genius is the *higher morality* as such. The exceptional individual is not only one who is most faithful to himself, who forgets nothing about himself, who detests nothing more and can tolerate nothing less than errors and lies: he is also the most social, the most lonely, and at the same time the most sharing of human beings. *Genius is an altogether higher form of existence, not only in an intellectual but also in a moral sense. A genius completely reveals* **the idea** *of humanity. He manifests what a human being is—the* ***subject*** *whose* **object** *is the* **whole** *universe—and he establishes that fact for all eternity.*

Let there be no mistake. *Consciousness,* and *consciousness alone,* is in itself moral. Everything unconscious is immoral, and everything immoral is unconscious. Therefore the "immoral genius," the "great evil-doer," is a mythical animal. He was invented by great individuals at certain moments of their lives as a possibility, and he became, much against the will of his creators, a "bow-wow" with which timid and feeble natures frighten themselves and other children. There is no criminal who is equal to his own crime, and who thinks and speaks like Hagen over Siegfried's body in *The Twilight of the Gods:* "Yes, then! I slew him: I—Hagen—I struck him dead!" Napoleon and Bacon of Verulam, who are cited as examples to the contrary, are far overrated with regard to their intellect, or misinterpreted. And Nietzsche—when he begins to talk about the Borgias—can be trusted least of all in such matters. The conception of the diabolical, the anti-Christ, Ahriman, the "radically evil in human nature," is extremely powerful, but it concerns genius only insofar as it is precisely its opposite. It is a fiction, born in those hours in which great individuals have fought the decisive battle against the criminal within them.

Universal apperception, general consciousness, total timelessness is an ideal, even for men of "genius." *Genius is an inner imperative,* not a fact that is ever fully accomplished in any human being. Therefore a "genius," and he in particular, will be least able to say about himself: "I am a genius." For genius is, by definition, nothing but a complete fulfillment of the idea of humanity, and therefore genius is something which every human being *ought* to be and which *must in principle be possible for every human being to become.* Genius is the highest morality and therefore everybody's duty. A human being becomes a genius through a supreme *act of the will, by affirming the whole universe in himself.* Genius is something that "individuals endowed with genius" *have taken on themselves:* it is the greatest task and the greatest pride, the greatest misery and the greatest elation possible for a human being. However paradoxical this may sound: a human being is a genius if he *wants* to be one.

Now it will be objected that very many people would like to be "original geniuses," but for all their wishing are unable to achieve this. However, if these people, who "would very much like to," had a clearer idea of just *what* this object of their desire *means,* if they realized that genius is identical to *universal responsibility*—and before something is quite clear to us we can only *desire,* but not *will* it—the overwhelming majority would probably *decline* to become geniuses.

For no other reason—fools in such cases think of the effects of Venus or of the spinal degeneration of the neurasthenic—do so many individuals with genius succumb to *madness.* They are those for whom the burden of carrying the whole world on their shoulders, like Atlas, has become too heavy, and who are therefore always the smaller, the less outstanding, and never the greatest, never the strongest minds. But the higher a man stands, the lower he may fall. All genius is an overcoming of a nothingness, of a gloom, of a darkness, and if it degenerates and runs to seed, the night will be the blacker, the brighter the light was previously. A genius who goes mad *no longer wants to be a genius;* instead of morality he wants—*happiness.* For all madness is the consequence of the insupportability of the pain attached to all consciousness; and therefore it was Sophocles who suggested most profoundly the motives of a man in being able to *want* even his *madness,* when he made Ajax say, before his mind finally succumbs to the night:

> ἐν τῷ φρονεῖν γὰρ μηδὲν ἥδιστος βίος

I close this chapter with the profound words of Giovanni Pico de Mirandola, which recall the most sublime elements of Kant's style, and which I have perhaps helped to be better understood here. In his speech "On the Dignity of Man," he makes the divinity speak to man thus:

> Nec certam sedem, nec propriam faciem, nec munus ullum peculiare tibi dedimus, o Adam: ut qual sedem, quam faciem, quae munera tute optaveris, ea pro voto, pro tua sententia, habeas et possideas. Definita caeteris natura intra praescriptas a nobis leges coercetur: tu nullis angustiis coercitus, pro tuo arbitrio, in cuius manus te posui, tibi illam praefinies. Medium te mundi posui, ut cir-

cumspiceres inde commodius quicquid est in mundo. Nec te caelestem, neque terrenum, neque mortalem, neque immortalem fecimus, ut tui ipsius quasi arbitrarius honorariusque plastes et fictor in quam malueris tute formam effingas. Poteris in inferiora quae sunt bruta degenerare, poteris in superiora quae sunt divine, ex tui animi sententia regenerari.

O summam Dei Patris liberalitatem, summam et admirandam hominis felicitatem: cui datum id habere quod optat, id esse quod velit. Bruta simul atque nascuntur id secum afferunt e bulga matris, quod possessura sunt. Supremi spiritus aut ab intio aut paulo mox id fuerunt, quod sunt futuri in perpetuas aeternitates. *Nascenti homini omniferaria semina et omnigenae vitae germina indidit Pater;* quae quisque excoluerit, illa adolescent et fructus suos ferent in illo: si vegetalia, planta fiet, si intellectualia, angelus erit et Dei *filius. Et si nulla creaturarum sorte contentus in unitatis centrum suae se receperit, unus cum Deo spiritus factus, in solitaria Patris caligine qui est super omnia constitutos omnibus antestabit.*

IX | Male and Female Psychology

IT IS TIME to return to the real task of this investigation in order to see how far it has been advanced by my lengthy digressions, which often seemed to distract from it rather substantially.

The principles I have developed are of such radical consequences for a psychology of the sexes that even those who have agreed with my deductions so far may shy away from *these* conclusions. We have not yet reached the point where we can analyze the reasons for this alarm, but in order to protect the thesis which now follows against all the objections that it will provoke, I will substantiate it in this section as fully, and with as many conclusive arguments, as possible.

Briefly, this is what it is all about. I found that the phenomenon of logic and that of ethics, which join together to form the highest value in the concept of truth, force us to assume the existence of an intelligible self, or a soul, as an entity of the highest, hyper-empirical reality. *In the case of a being which, like* **W**, *lacks both logic and ethics, there is no reason to make that assumption.* The complete female knows neither a logical nor a moral imperative, and the words "law," "duty," "duty to oneself" are the words that sound most alien to her. Therefore the conclusion that she lacks a suprasensory personality is perfectly justified.

Absolute Woman has no self.

There is a sense in which this concludes my investigation, having reached the final point to which any analysis of Woman leads. Although this insight, articulated so tersely, seems hard and intolerant, as well as paradoxical and too starkly novel, given such a subject matter, the author is unlikely to have been the first to arrive at this view, even if he was obliged to find his way to it independently before he could grasp the aptness of similar statements made by others before him.

The Chinese have denied Woman a soul of her own from the earliest times. If a Chinese is asked how many children he has, he will only count the boys, and if he only has daughters he will say that he is childless.[1] It was probably for

1. Cf. also Ecclesiastes, 7:28: "One man among a thousand have I found; but a woman among all those have I not found."

a similar reason that Mohammed excluded women from Paradise and thus is partly to blame for the degrading position of the female sex in Islamic countries.

From the ranks of philosophers it is above all Aristotle who must be named here. According to him, in the process of procreation the male principle is the formative, active element, *logos,* while the female element represents passive matter. If one considers that for Aristotle the soul is identical with form, entelechy, primal motive force, it becomes clear how close he is to the view expressed here, even though his opinion only comes to the fore when he talks about the act of impregnation. Elsewhere, in common with almost all Greeks apart from Euripides, he does not seem to think about women and therefore never adopts any position on the properties of Woman as such (and not only with regard to her role in the act of copulation).

Among the Fathers of the Church, Tertullian and Origenes in particular seem to have had a very low opinion of women, while St. Augustine must have been prevented from sharing their views at least by his close relationship with his mother. In the Renaissance the Aristotelian view was frequently taken up again, for instance by Jean Wier (1518–1588). At that time this view seems to have been better understood at both an emotional and an intuitive level, and not regarded as a mere curiosity, as is common in today's science, which will certainly be obliged one day to bow to the anthropology of Aristotle in various ways.

In recent decades the same view has been expressed by Henrik Ibsen (through the characters of Anitra, Rita, and Irene) and August Strindberg (*The Creditor* [translated by Mary Harned, Boston 1911]). But what made the idea of the soullessness of Woman most popular was the wonderful fairy tale of Fouqué, the romantic writer, who owed the subject matter to his assiduous study of Paracelsus, and through E. T. A. Hoffmann, Girschner, and Albert Lortzing, who set it to music. *Undine, soulless Undine, is the Platonic idea of Woman;* and the reality, despite all bisexuality, usually comes very close to her. Nor does the widespread saying "Woman has no character" mean anything fundamentally different. Personality and individuality, (intelligible) self and soul, will and (intelligible) character—all these signify one and the same thing, to which in the human domain only M is entitled, and which W lacks.

Since the human soul is the microcosm and exceptional individuals are those who live throughout *with* their soul—that is, in whom the *whole* world is *alive—the disposition of W must be entirely* ***without*** *genius. Man* has *everything* within him and, according to Pico de Mirandola, it is up to him to encourage one or other of his innate properties to develop. He can reach the greatest heights or degenerate most profoundly, he can become an animal, a plant, *he can even become a woman, and that is why there are female, effeminate men.*

But a woman can never become a man. This is where the most important qualification must be added to the assertions of the first part of this study. *While*

I know a large number of men who, psychically, are almost completely—and not just half—women, I have seen many women with male traits, but never a single woman who was not basically still a woman, even though her femininity was often enough hidden from the eyes of the person herself, and not only from those of others, by many different disguises. One is (cf. part 2, chapter I) *either* a man *or* a woman, regardless of how many peculiarities of both sexes one may have, and this form of being, which has been the problem under investigation from the outset, can now be defined by a person's relationship with ethics and logic. But while there are anatomical men who psychologically *are* women, there are no persons who *are* physically women and yet psychically men, notwithstanding that in many external regards they present a male aspect and create an unfeminine impression.

Therefore the following *final* answer can certainly be given to the question of endowment in the sexes: *there are women with some of the characteristics of genius, but there is no female genius, there never has been one* (even among the masculine women named in history and discussed in the first part) *and there never can be one.* If anybody, wishing to be lax on principle in such a matter, tried to open and expand the concept of genius far enough for women to find however small a space within it, he would have *destroyed* that concept right at the outset. If we are to gain and preserve a rigorous and consistent concept of genius, I do not believe that any definitions other than those developed here are possible. Given these definitions, how could a soulless being have any genius? Genius is identical to *depth.* Just try to connect the words deep and *woman* as an attribute and a noun, and everybody will hear the contradiction. *A female genius, then, is a contradiction in terms,* for we saw that genius was nothing but an intensified, fully developed, higher, universally conscious kind of masculinity. A genius has everything, including Woman, completely within him, but Woman herself is only a part of the universe, and as the part cannot contain the whole, woman cannot contain genius. *Woman's lack of genius* unavoidably follows from the fact that Woman is no monad and therefore no mirror of the universe.[2]

Most of what I may have managed to establish in the previous chapters adds up to prove the *soullessness* of Woman. The third chapter showed that Woman thinks in henids and Man in structured forms, and that the female sex lives less *consciously* than the male. Consciousness is *one* concept of epistemology and at the same time *the* fundamental concept of psychology. Epistemological consciousness and the possession of a continuous self, or the transcendental subject and the soul, are synonymous and interchangeable concepts. Every self exists

2. It would be easy at this point to pick up the creations of the *most famous* women and show, by means of a few examples, how little question there can be of any genius in them. But I was unable to bring myself to undertake such a lengthy piece of research into historical and philological sources, which would not only be hard to execute without any pedantry, but which could also be easily carried out by anybody who enjoys such things.

only insofar as it has a sense of itself and becomes conscious of itself in its thought: all being is consciousness. But now an important explanation must be added to the henid theory. The articulated contents of Man's thought are not simply the contents of female thought, unscrambled and structured. They are not just the actuality of what was merely potential in female thought, but they contain something *qualitatively different* right from the outset. The psychic contents of Man, even at the first henid stage, which they always strive to overcome, are disposed to *conceptuality,* and it is even possible that *all* the sensations of Man, from a very early stage, have a tendency to become *concepts.* Woman has an entirely non-conceptual disposition, both in her perceptions and in her thinking.

All concepts are necessarily based on the logical axioms, which are lacking in women. Women neither regard the principle of identity, which alone can impart an unambiguous clarity to a concept, as their guide, nor do they adopt the *principium contradictionis,* which alone delimits a concept as a totally independent entity against all other things, possible or real, as their own norm. This lack of conceptual clarity in all female thought is the prerequisite of that "sensitivity" in women which grants unlimited rights to vague associations and which so often makes comparisons between quite dissimilar things. Even women with the best and least limited memories never overcome this affectation of *synesthesia.* For example, if a word reminds them of a certain color, or a person of a certain dish—as indeed frequently happens to women—they are completely *satisfied* with their subjective associations, and will neither try to discover why it was precisely that comparison which occurred to them and how far it was actually suggested by the real facts, nor make any further and more concerted efforts to achieve some clarity about the impression which that word or that person made on them. This self-sufficiency and complacency is related to what I described earlier as Woman's lack of intellectual conscience, which will be discussed below and explained in terms of her deficiency in conceptual thinking. This habit of wallowing in purely emotional resonances, of dispensing with conceptuality and comprehensibility, of *drifting* without *striving* for any depth, characterizes the iridescent style of so many modern writers and painters as an eminently *feminine* one. Male thinking fundamentally differs from female thinking by its desire for solid forms, and thus any "atmospheric art" is necessarily a *formless* "art."

For these reasons the psychic contents of Man can never simply be the henids of Woman in a more highly developed, "explicit" form. Woman's thinking is a sliding and flitting through things, a nibbling at their shallowest surface, which Man, "seeking the depths of things," often does not even notice; it is a sampling and tasting, a *feeling with the fingertips,* rather than a *grasping* of the right thing. Therefore, because Woman's thinking is primarily a kind of *tasting, taste* in the *broadest* sense remains the prime female property, the acme of what a woman can achieve unaided and to a certain perfection. Taste requires a restriction of the interest to the surface of things; it seeks the harmony of the whole and never dwells on sharply defined parts. If a woman "understands" a man—the possibility or impossibility of which will be dealt with later—she will, as it were, have an *aftertaste* of the ***thoughts*** *he has placed before her,* however tasteless this particular expression may be. Since she is incapable of sharp distinctions for her part, it is clear that she will often believe that she has understood him, when in fact there are only very vague analogies between their sensations. What must be regarded as the decisive factor in these incongruencies is that the contents of Man's thinking are not situated, albeit at a more advanced point, in the same sequence as those of Woman, but that there are two different sequences which cover the same object, a conceptual male one and a non-conceptual female one. Therefore the identification implied in the term "understanding" may not occur *only* between a highly developed and differentiated later content and an inchoate, unstructured earlier content, both of which belong to the same sequence (as in the case of "expression," discussed on p. 107): rather, when it comes to understanding between Man and Woman in particular, a *conceptual* thought in one sequence is equated with a *non-conceptual* "feeling," a "henid," in the other.

The non-conceptual nature of Woman, no less than her lower degree of consciousness, is a proof of the fact that she possesses no self. For it is only the concept that transforms a mere complex of sensations into an *object,* making it independent of whether or not I perceive it. The existence of a complex of sensations always depends on the will of the individual: he may close his eyes and block his ears and cease to see or hear, or he may get drunk or go to sleep and forget. The concept alone is able to emancipate us from the eternally subjective, eternally psychological, and eternally relative *sensations,* and to create *things.* The intellect actively *produces* objects through its conceptual function. Conversely, it is only when a conceptual function is present that we can speak of a subject and an object, and distinguish between them. In all other cases there is only a heap of similar and dissimilar images that blend and merge without any rule or order. It is the concept that transforms the freely floating *impressions into objects,* producing out of sensation an object, which is confronted by the subject, an enemy against which the subject measures his strength. Thus all reality is constituted by the concept. This is not to say that the object itself is real only insofar as it has a share in an idea that resides beyond experience, in a τόπος νοητός, and that it is only an incomplete projection or unsuccessful likeness of reality. On the contrary, *things become real only insofar as the conceptual function of our intellect affects them.* The *concept* is the "*transcendental object*" of Kant's critique of reason, which can only correspond to a "*transcendental subject.*" The subject in its turn is the sole source of that mysterious objectivizing function which *produces* the Kantian "object X," the *goal* of all *cognition,* and which has been shown to be identical to the logical axioms that, again, only manifest the existence of the subject. The *principium contradictionis* sets the concept apart from everything that is not the concept itself, and the *principium identitatis* makes it possible to contemplate the concept as if it were alone in the world. I can never say about a raw complex of sensations that it is equal to itself: the moment I apply to it the judgment of identity, it has already become a concept. Thus it is the concept that bestows *dignity* and *rigor* on any perceptual construct and any tissue of thoughts: *the concept* ***liberates*** *any content by* ***binding*** *it.* There is such a thing as the *freedom of the object,* no less than the freedom of the subject, and the two correspond to each other. And here it becomes evident once more that all freedom is a voluntary binding of the self, in logic as in ethics. Human beings become free only by becoming the law: that is their only chance of avoiding heteronomy, of being determined by other things and other human beings, which is unavoidably attached to anything arbitrary. That is also why human beings *honor themselves* through the conceptual function: they honor *themselves* by granting their object freedom and autonomy, and turning it into the universally valid *object of knowledge,* to which reference is made whenever two men may argue about something. Only Woman never *confronts* things, but treats them, and herself at the same time, just as she pleases. She cannot give any freedom to the object, because she herself has none.

The process in which sensations achieve independence by becoming concepts is not so much a detachment from the *subject* as a detachment from *subjectivity.* A concept is what *I* think, write, and speak about. This implies a belief that I have a relationship with it, and *that* belief is the essence of ***judgment.*** While the immanentist psychologists, Hume, Huxley, Mach, Avenarius, at least tried to come to terms with the *concept* by identifying it with the notion of a general idea and by dispensing with any distinctions between a logical and a psychological concept, it is quite typical of them that they simply ignore the phenomenon of *judgment* and are indeed obliged to pretend that it does not exist. From their own point of view they cannot afford to show any understanding for that element contained in the act of judgment which is *alien to the monism of sensationalism.* A judgment contains acceptance or rejection, approval or disapproval for certain things, and the standard of approval—*the idea of truth*—cannot be situated in the complexes of perceptions which are being judged. To those who only accept sensations, all sensations must necessarily be of *equal value,* and no sensation has a better prospect than any other of becoming a component of the real world. Thus it is *empiricism,* of all things, that destroys the reality of *experience,* and *positivism* turns out to be the true *nihilism* despite its apparently "sound" and "honest" trademark—just as many a respectable business enterprise proves to be a fraudulent castle in the air. The idea of a *standard* for experience, the *idea of truth,* cannot be situated in *experience* itself. *However, every judgment contains this very claim to truth.* Regardless of how many subjective restrictions are applied to it, it implicitly demands objective validity precisely in the restricted form given to it by its originator. Whoever makes a statement in the manner of a judgment will be treated as if he expected general recognition for what he is saying, and if he claims that he had no such hope he will rightly be accused of abusing the form of judgment. Accordingly, it is true that the function of judgment contains a claim to *knowledge*, that is, *to the truth of the judgment.*

This claim to knowledge means nothing more, nor less, than that the subject is *capable* of making a *judgment* about the object and of making a *correct* statement about it. The objects being judged are *concepts:* the concept is the object of knowledge. The concept *confronted* the subject with an object: *the judgment, in turn, asserts the possibility of a connection* and affinity *between them.* The demand for truth means that the subject is *able* to pass a correct judgment on the object. *Thus the function of judgment implies the* ***proof*** *of a connection between the self and the universe,* and indeed the possibility of their complete unity. This unity and nothing else, not the *correspondence* but the *identity* of being and thought, is *truth,* and it is never actually attainable by humans as humans,[3] but is only an eternal demand. The freedom of the subject and the freedom of the object are ultimately the one and only *freedom.* Therefore the ability to judge—given the most common assumption underlying it, the assumption that a human being is *capable* of making judgments on everything—is only the dry *logical expression of the theory of the human soul as the microcosm.* And the answer to the vexed question whether the concept or the judgment comes first will probably have to be that neither takes priority over the other but each necessarily determines the other. All knowledge aims at an object and takes the form of judgment, its object being a concept. The conceptual function has split the subject and the object apart and rendered the subject lonely: thus the longing in the drive to knowledge, like all love, seeks to reunite what has been separated.

If a being such as genuine Woman lacks the conceptual function, she will necessarily also be deficient in the function of judgment. This assertion will be regarded as ludicrously paradoxical, because women *talk* enough (at least nobody has complained of the opposite) and all talk is said to be an expression of judgments. But this is not correct. The *liar,* for example, who is usually brought up in evidence against the deeper meaning of the phenomenon of judgment, *does not judge at all* (there is an "inner form of judgment,"[4] just as there is an "inner form of language") because, in the act of lying, he does not apply the standard of truth to what he says, and because, however universal a recognition he tries to enforce for his lie, he excludes his own person and thus destroys any objective validity. On the other hand, a person who lies to himself does not ques-

3. Therefore it must not be *assumed* by any philosophy, but only aspired to as a final border mark.

4. Dr. W. Jerusalem's term.

tion his thoughts about their legal cause before an internal tribunal, but would take care not to represent them before an external one. It is therefore possible to keep to the external verbal form of judgment without doing justice to its internal prerequisite. This internal prerequisite is a sincere recognition of the truth as the supreme judge of whatever one says, and an earnest desire to pass muster before that judge with every remark one makes. But any relationship with the truth must be all-inclusive and enduring, and only such a relationship can give rise to truthfulness toward people, toward things, and toward oneself. That is why the distinction I have just made between lying to oneself and lying to others is a false one, and whoever is *subjectively untruthful*—like Woman, as I have already stressed and will explain in great detail later—can have no interest in *objective* truth either. Woman has no enthusiasm for the truth. That is why she is not serious, and that is why she is not interested in *ideas.* There are many female writers, but one looks in vain for *thoughts* in anything ever created by women artists, and their love of (objective) truth is so slight that most of the time they regard thoughts as not even worth *borrowing.*

No woman has any real interest in science, even though she may successfully pretend that she has, both to herself and to many good men who are bad psychologists. We can be certain that behind every woman who has been able to claim an independent scientific achievement that was not *totally* insignificant (Sophie Germain, Mary Somerville, etc.) there was always a man, to whom she was trying to get closer in that way. "Cherchez l'homme" applies much more broadly to women than "cherchez la femme" to men.

The reason why there have been no significant achievements by women, even in the sphere of science, is that the capacity for truth can only arise from the will to truth, and its force is always commensurate to that will.

That is why women's sense of reality is much slighter than men's, no matter how often the opposite has been asserted. Women always subordinate knowledge to an external purpose, and when their intention to achieve this purpose is firm enough their sight can be very sharp and unwavering. But what value truth in itself and for its own sake may have will never be understood by a woman. Therefore, where deception *suits* her (often unconscious) wishes, a woman will become totally uncritical and lose all control over reality. This explains the firm belief of many women that they have been threatened with sexual attacks, and the frequency of their tactile hallucinations, which seem more intensely real to them than a man could ever imagine. For the imagination of Woman consists of errors and lies, but the imagination of Man, if he is an artist or a philosopher, is made up of a higher truth.

The idea of truth is the foundation of anything that deserves the name of *judgment.* To know anything is to judge, and thinking as such is the same as making judgments. The norm for any judgment is the principle of sufficient reason, just as the concept (being the norm for the essence) is constituted by the principle of contradiction and the principle of identity. I have already indicated that Woman does *not* recognize the principle of sufficient reason. To think is to turn diversity into unity. The idea of the *unifying function* of our thinking, both *in relation* to the diversity and *in spite* of it, is based on the principle of sufficient reason, which makes any judgment conditional on a logical cognitive reason, while the other three logical axioms are only an expression of the *existence* of unity, without any reference to diversity. The two phenomena therefore cannot be derived from each other: *the fact that they are two different things should, rather, be seen as a formal logical expression of the dualism in the universe, the existence of diversity alongside unity.* Leibniz was certainly right to distinguish between them, and any theory that denies Woman's possession of logic must prove that she does not understand and obey either the principle of contradiction (and the principle of identity), which refers to the concept, or the principle of sufficient reason, to which judgment is answerable. The proof is found in Woman's lack of intellectual conscience. If a woman ever happens to have a theoretical idea she fails to follow it up or to connect it with other things: she *does not think matters* ***through***. That is why a female philosopher is the most unlikely notion. Woman lacks the stamina, the tenacity, the perseverance in thinking, as well as any motivation to think, and it is entirely out of the question that a woman should *suffer from problems.* Let there be no talk about women at their wits' end. The man with problems wants to know, the woman with problems wants only to be known.

A *psychological* proof of the *masculinity of the function of judgment* is that *Woman perceives the act of judgment as masculine and is attracted by it as by a (tertiary) sexual characteristic.* A woman always *demands* firm convictions from a man, so that she may adopt them. She has no time at all for the *doubter* in a man. Furthermore, she always expects the man to *speak,* and she regards the man's discourse as a sign of masculinity. Women have the gift of language, but not the gift of discourse. A woman converses (flirts) or chatters, but she does not speak. She is most dangerous, however, when she is dumb, for the man is only too inclined to take dumbness for silence.

It has, then, been demonstrated that W lacks not only the logical norms but also the functions regulated by these principles, that is, the capacity for forming concepts and judgments. However, since conceptuality by its very nature consists in confronting a *subject* with its object, and since judgments reveal the primal kinship and the deepest essential unity of the subject and its object, we must once more deny the possession of a subject by Woman.

Having proved that absolute Woman is alogical, I must proceed to supply detailed proof of her amorality. The profound falseness of Woman, which can already be seen to follow from her inability to understand the idea of the truth, and indeed to understand any values at all, will be discussed at length later, but first I will highlight some other aspects. In so doing exceptional ingenuity and extreme caution are constantly called for, because there are so many imitations of ethical behavior, such seemingly accurate copies of morality, that women will probably always be regarded by many as being more moral than men. I have already emphasized the necessity of distinguishing between *a*-moral and *anti*-moral behavior, and I repeat that where genuine Woman is concerned there can only be a question of the former, which involves neither a sense of morality nor even a tendency toward it. It is well known, both from the statistics of crime and from everyday life, that incomparably fewer crimes are committed by women than by men. It is this fact that the busy apologists of the moral purity of women always invoke in support of their case.

But in trying to solve the problem of female morality the crucial issue is not whether a person has objectively sinned against the idea, but only whether he has a subjective core that could have formed a relationship with the idea, and the value of which he has called into question by committing a crime. A male criminal is certainly born with his criminal urges, but he feels, despite all the theories of "moral insanity," that by his deed he has forfeited his own value and his right to live. All criminals are cowards and there is none whose pride and self-respect would have been enhanced rather than diminished by his evil deed, and who would take on the responsibility of justifying it.

The male criminal has the same innate appreciation of the idea of value as a man who almost completely lacks the criminal urges that dominate the former. Woman, on the other hand, often claims to be entirely in the right even if she is guilty of the meanest imaginable deed. While a genuine male criminal responds to all accusations with vacant *silence,* a woman may indignantly voice her surprise and resentment at any doubts cast on her perfect right to act as she pleases. Women are convinced of their "rights" without ever sitting in judgment *over* themselves. The male criminal does not take stock of himself either, but rather than demanding his rights he hastens to avoid thinking of the idea of right, because doing so would remind him of his guilt. This also proves that he once *had* a relationship with the idea and does not want to be reminded of his infidelity to his better self. *No male criminal has ever believed that his punishment was unjust.*[5] A woman, on the other hand, is convinced of the malice of her accusers, and nobody will be able to prove to her against her *will* that she has done anything wrong. If an attempt is made to persuade her, she will often burst into

5. The male criminal in his own way feels guilty even without actually having done anything wrong. He always expects to be accused by others of fraud, theft, etc., even if he has not really committed the crime, because he knows himself to be capable of it. That is also why he feels that he himself has been caught out whenever another malefactor is arrested.

tears, ask for forgiveness, "recognize her wrong" and indeed sincerely believe that she feels it, but only when she is in the mood and because dissolving into tears gives her a certain sensual pleasure. The male criminal is obdurate and cannot be turned round as promptly as a woman whose spurious defiance can give way to an equally spurious sense of guilt if her accuser knows how to handle her. No woman knows the lonely pain of guilt, the torture of sitting on her bed, crying and wishing to die of shame over the disgrace she has brought upon herself, and an apparent exception (the penitent woman, the devotee who chastises her body) will also show in due course that *a woman only ever feels sinful if she is in company.*

Therefore I am not saying that Woman is evil and anti-moral. I maintain *that, quite on the contrary, she can never be evil,* but is only amoral and *mean.*

Female compassion and female modesty are the two other phenomena generally cited by the champions of female virtue. Female kindness and female sympathy above all have given rise to the beautiful myth of woman's soul, and the ultimate argument to which any belief in the higher morality of Woman resorts is Woman as a nurse, as a sister of mercy. I do not enjoy mentioning this point and I would not have raised it, but I am forced to do so by an objection that has been made to me orally and that will probably be followed by others.

It is short-sighted to regard women's nursing as a proof of their compassion, because it indicates the precise opposite. A man would never be able to watch the torments of the sick. He would be so worn down by suffering with them that he would be totally unable to care for them. If one observes female nurses one is astonished to see how calm and "gentle" they remain, even when faced with the most terrible spasms of the dying, and this is just as well, because men, who cannot stand pain and death, would make bad nurses. A man would want to alleviate the agony, delay death, in a word, *help.* Where no help is possible he has no place: that is where nursing comes into its own, and for nursing only women are suitable. Nevertheless, it would be quite wrong to appreciate the activities of women in this area from any point of view other than a utilitarian one.

There is the further fact that for Woman the *problem* of solitude and society simply does not exist. She is particularly well suited to being a companion (a reader, a nurse) because she never finds herself in a position of having to step out of solitude into company. *For a man solitude and company will always be a problem, even though often only one of the two will be a possibility.* A woman does not give up any solitude in order to nurse a patient, as she would have to do if her action were really to be called moral: *for a woman is* ***never*** *solitary,* she knows neither the love nor the fear of solitude. This is one proof of the fact that she is no monad, because all monads have *boundaries.* Women by nature are boundless, but not boundless in the same way as a genius, whose boundaries are at the same time the boundaries of the world. Rather, they are never *separated* by anything real either from nature or from human beings.[6]

This fusion is an eminently *sexual* one, and accordingly all female compassion manifests itself in *physical contact with the object of her compassion.* It is an animal tenderness, which needs to stroke and to comfort. Here we have another proof of the absence of the sharp line which always separates two personalities. Woman does not honor the suffering of her fellow-human by being silent, but believes that she can put an end to it by talking: so strong is her sense of a bond between them as natural, not spiritual, beings. Where sexuality has ceased to exist all compassion is absent: in an old woman there is not even a spark of that alleged kindness, and thus the old age of Woman indirectly proves that all her compassion was only a form of sexual fusion, even when it concerned a person of the same sex.

Living in *fusion,* one of the most important and most far-reaching facts of female existence, is also the reason for the sentimentality of all women, their vulgar and shameless readiness to shed tears with the greatest ease. It is not for nothing that there are only female professional mourners and that a man who cries in company is not thought of very highly. If some people cry, Woman will cry with them; if others laugh, except at her, she will laugh with them; and this takes care of a very large part of female compassion.

Only Woman really directs her laments and her tears *at* others, *demanding* their pity. This is one of the most conclusive proofs of the psychic shamelessness of Woman. Woman provokes the pity of strangers in order to be able to cry *with them* and to pity herself even more than she has done already. Indeed, it is no exaggeration to say that Woman, even when she is crying alone, always cries *with* others, to whom she tells her woes in her mind, and greatly moves herself in the process. "Self-pity" is an eminently female attribute: first a woman joins the ranks of the others *in making herself the object of the others' pity,* and then, deeply moved, begins to cry with them about the "poor woman," that is, herself. For the same reason a man may never be more ashamed than when he catches himself in the act of being impelled toward self-pity, *in which the subject actually becomes an object.*

Female compassion, in which even Schopenhauer believed, is sobbing and wailing for its own sake, at the slightest provocation and without the slightest attempt to suppress the impulse out of shame. Like all suffering, true compassion, which is a suffering with others, must be modest, if it is real suffering: in fact no suffering can be as modest as compassion and love, because these two impulses make us *conscious* of the insurmountable *boundaries* of any individu-

6. Because Woman does not perceive the other human being as a *separate* being she never suffers from her neighbor, and for that reason alone she can always feel *superior* to all human beings.

ality most powerfully. Love and its modesty will be discussed later, but in *compassion,* in genuine male empathy, there is always shame and a sense of guilt, because my plight is not as bad as that of the other man, because I am not he but a *separate* being, who is also kept apart from him by external circumstances. *Male sympathy is the principium individuationis blushing at itself: that is why all female compassion is intrusive, while male sympathy hides from view.*

This has partly uncovered the nature of women's modesty. The rest can only be discussed later in connection with hysteria. Given the naïve zeal with which all women wear low-cut dresses, wherever social conventions allow, it is hard to see how anybody can still believe in the virtue of an innate internal modesty in the female sex. One is or one is not modest, and a modesty that is regularly dispensed with at certain moments is no modesty.

The absolute proof of women's shamelessness (and an indication of *where* the demand for external modesty, which women often observe so scrupulously, may come from) is the fact that women among themselves always undress completely without any embarrassment, while men always try to hide their nakedness from each other. When women are alone they eagerly compare each other's charms, and all those present are often subjected, not without a certain lasciviousness, to a precise and thorough examination, with the main consideration unconsciously always remaining the value that a man will attach to this or that attraction. A male individual is not interested in the nakedness of any other male individual, while every woman always undresses every other woman in her mind and thus demonstrates the general inter-individual shamelessness of the sex. A man finds it embarrassing and unpleasant to imagine the sexuality of his fellow-man. A woman searches in her mind for the sexual relations that another woman may be having, as soon as she meets her. Indeed she evaluates the other woman exclusively in terms of her sexual partner.

I shall return to this in great detail. Meanwhile we have reached a point where our current investigation once more touches on an issue that was discussed in the second chapter of this part. In order to be ashamed of anything one must be *conscious* of it, and a sense of shame, like consciousness, always requires differentiation. Woman, who is purely sexual, may *seem to be asexual because she is sexuality itself* and because, in her, sexuality does not *stand out,* either physically or psychically, either in space or in time, as it does in man. Woman, who is always immodest, can give the impression of being modest, *because she has no modesty that could be violated.* Thus Woman is never naked or always naked, whichever one prefers: never naked because she never really attains a genuine sense of nakedness, always naked, because she lacks the other thing which would need to be present to make her *conscious* of being (objectively) naked and which could give her an internal impulse to cover herself. The fact that one can be naked even when dressed is something not understood by simple minds, but it would reflect badly on a psychologist if he were to infer the slightest lack of nakedness from the presence of a robe. And a woman, objectively, is always naked, even under her crinoline and her bodice.[7]

All this is connected with what the word "self" really means to Woman. If one asks a woman what she understands by her self, she will be unable to imagine anything other than her body. The self of Woman is her external appearance. Mach's "sketch of the self" in his "Introductory Remarks. Antimetaphysical" therefore represents quite correctly the self of perfect woman. If E. Krause says that the self-observation implied in the word "I" is easy to carry out, this is not quite as ridiculous as Mach believes, with the approval of many others who seem to have taken the greatest liking to this particular "jocular illustration of the philosophical 'much ado about nothing'" in Mach's books.

Women's specific vanity is also rooted in women's self. Male vanity is an emanation of the *will to value,* and its *objective* manifestation, *sensitivity,* is the desire that the accessibility of value should not be questioned by anybody. What endows a man with value and timelessness is nothing but his *personality.* This supreme value, which is not a *price,* because, according to Kant, it cannot be "replaced by something else as its *equivalent,*" but which "is raised above all price and therefore admits of no equivalent," is the dignity of man. Women, despite what Schiller says, have no dignity—the idea of a *lady* was merely invented to fill this gap—and their vanity will be guided by what they regard as their supreme value; that is, it will strive for the preservation, enhancement, and recognition of physical beauty. The vanity of W therefore is on the one hand a certain enjoyment of her own body, which is peculiar only to herself and which is *alien* even to the man with the greatest (masculine) beauty.[8] It is a pleasure which even the ugliest girl seems to derive from touching herself or contemplating herself in the mirror, as well as from many organic sensations. However, even in these instances it is the thought of the man to whom these charms will one day belong that asserts itself with full force and a most exciting sense of anticipation, thus proving once more that woman can be alone, but never lonely. On the other hand, then, female vanity is the need to feel that her body is admired or, rather, *desired, and indeed desired by a sexually aroused man.*

This need is so strong that there are really many women for whom this admiration—lustful on the part of man, envious on the part of other women—is enough to live for. They can manage on this, and have hardly any other needs.

Female vanity, then, always involves consideration of others. *Women live only in their thoughts of others.* The sensitivity of Woman concerns this same point. A woman will never forget it if another person has thought her ugly, for a woman on her own never regards herself as ugly, but merely as *inferior,* and

7. I am fully aware of the objections that could be made to this and the reasons that will be asserted time and again for the modesty of Woman. They will be discussed in the twelfth chapter.

8. NB. Many so-called "handsome men" are half women.

even that only when she remembers the victories of other women over her in relation to men. There is no woman who does not think that she is beautiful and desirable when she contemplates herself in the mirror. To woman her own ugliness will never become a painful reality, as it does to a man, but she will try to deceive herself and others about it till the very end.

What then may be the only source of the female kind of vanity? It coincides with her lack of an intelligible self, of something that can be regarded as *permanent and absolutely positive,* and it follows from her deficiency in any *intrinsic value.* As women have no *intrinsic value* in their own eyes, they strive to become objects of evaluation by others, to acquire a value in the eyes of others who desire and admire them. The only thing in the world that has an absolute, infinite value is the soul, which is why Christ has reminded human beings that they "are of more value than many sparrows." But Woman does not evaluate herself by the extent to which she has been faithful to her own personality, or to which she has been free, although that is the only way in which any being with a self can evaluate himself. There is no doubt whatsoever that a genuine woman only values herself as highly as she does the man who has chosen her, and that she depends on marriage not only socially and financially, but in her deepest essence, because she only acquires a value through her husband or lover. *Therefore Woman can have no real value, because she lacks the intrinsic value of the human personality.* Women always derive their value from extraneous things such as their wealth and their possessions, the number and splendor of their dresses, the position of their box in the theatre, their children, and above all their admirers and their husbands. If one woman quarrels with another she will in the last resort always know how to hurt and humiliate her adversary most deeply and most unfailingly by referring to the higher social position, the greater wealth, the reputation and the titles, and also the greater youthfulness and the more numerous female admirers, of her husband. For a man, on the other hand, the greatest disgrace, above all in his own eyes, is to rely on anything alien to him, instead of defending *his intrinsic value* ***in itself*** against any attacks on it.

A further proof of the soullessness of W is the following. While (according to Goethe's famous recipe) being ignored by a man is an extreme provocation for W to try to make an impression on him—since the ability to do so is the whole purpose and value of her life—M will find a woman who treats him unkindly and rudely *eo ipso* unappealing. Nothing makes M as happy as being loved by a girl, and in that event the risk of his being smitten is very great even if she does not captivate him right from the outset. For W the love of a man whom she does not like amounts only to a gratification of her vanity or an irritation and awakening of slumbering desires. A woman always lays equal claim to all the men in the world, and the same is true of her affection for friends of the same sex, which also involves some sexuality at all times.

The behavior of the intermediate sexual forms, which alone are empirically given, must be determined in such cases in accordance with their position between M and W. To provide an example in this part of my study, while M is easily enraptured and inflamed by *every smile* on a girl's lips, feminine men often take proper notice only of women and men who ignore them, much as W promptly ditches any admirer of whom she feels certain and who therefore can no longer increase her intrinsic value. This is also the reason why women are only attracted by, and remain faithful in marriage, to a man who is successful with other women: for *they* cannot confer any new value on *him* and set their judgment *against* that of all the others. In the case of a genuine man the exact opposite is true.

The shamelessness as well as the heartlessness of Woman is manifested by the fact *that,* and *the way in which,* she can talk about being loved. A man feels ashamed when he is loved, because he feels that, instead of being the active and free donor, he has received a gift which makes him passive and which binds him, and because he knows that as a whole he never entirely deserves love; consequently he will observe the most profound silence, even if he has not had an intimate relationship with the girl and would have no reason to be afraid of compromising her by talking about it. A woman *boasts* of being loved, and she brags about it to other women in order to be envied by them. She does not, as a man does, perceive the love of another as an appreciation of her *real* value and a deeper *understanding* of her personality. Rather, she feels that this love *confers* on her a value that she would not have otherwise, and that it endows her with an existence and an essence *which thus* become *hers for the first time* and which she uses to prove herself to others.

This also explains women's incredible *memory* for *compliments,* even if they received these in their earliest youth, as discussed in a previous chapter. It is above all through compliments that women *acquire* a value, and *that is why they demand* that man should be "*gallant.*" Gallantry is the cheapest way of conferring value on a woman, and while it costs a man very little, it is something momentous for a woman, who *never* forgets a tribute and who sustains herself by the most insipid flattery as long as she lives. One remembers only what one regards as a value, and if this is so, it is worth considering just *what* it means that women have the most exceptional memory for compliments in particular. Compliments are something that can confer value on women only because they have no natural standard of value and do not feel that they have within them any absolute value that spurns everything apart from itself. And thus the very phenomenon of courtesy and "chivalry" proves that women have no soul: indeed, it is when a man treats a woman in the most gallant manner that he is least prepared to attribute to her a soul or an *intrinsic value,* and *he scorns and belittles* her most profoundly precisely when she feels *most elevated.*——

Just how amoral Woman is can be seen from the fact that she immediately forgets an immoral deed that she has committed, and that a man who makes an effort to educate a woman is obliged to remind her of it time and again. In that event, as a result of the specific kind of female falseness, she may really seem to realize for a moment that she has done wrong, and thus deceive both herself and the man concerned. In contrast, a man remembers nothing as deeply as any guilt he has incurred. This again reveals memory as an eminently moral phenomenon. Forgiving and forgetting, not forgiving and understanding, are the same. *Whoever remembers a lie reproaches himself with it.* The reason why a woman does not blame herself for a mean action is that she *never really becomes conscious* of it—since she has no relationship with the moral idea—and *forgets* it. That is why it is perfectly understandable that she *denies* it. Foolishly, women are regarded as *innocent,* and indeed as more moral than men, because for them ethical issues never become *problematic.* But all this is only due to the fact that they do not even know what is immoral. After all, a child can take no credit for being innocent either: only an old man could take credit for his innocence—which does not exist.

Self-observation is also an eminently masculine trait—a seeming exception, the hysterical self-observation of some women, cannot be examined at this point—and so is a sense of guilt and remorse. The self-chastisements of women, these strange imitations of a genuine sense of guilt, will be discussed together with the female form of self-observation. *For the subject of self-observation is identical with the moral subject: it can only grasp psychic phenomena by evaluating them.*

It is perfectly acceptable, and in line with positivism, for Auguste Comte to declare that self-observation is a contradiction in terms and an "abysmal absurdity." Given the narrowness of consciousness, it is obvious and hardly needs emphasizing that it is not possible for a psychic event and a separate perception of it to take place at the *same* time: it is the "primary" memory image (Jodl) that is observed and evaluated, and what is judged is a kind of after-image. But given a range of phenomena of the *same value,* it would not be possible to select any one to be made an object and either affirmed or denied, as happens in any act of self-observation. The entity that observes, judges, and evaluates all the contents in such a case cannot be contained in the contents themselves and be one content among others. It is the timeless self that takes account of both the past and the present and thereby *creates* the "unity of self-awareness," the continuous memory, which woman lacks. For it is not memory, as Mill assumes, or continuity, as Mach does, that produces the belief in a self which they claim has no existence apart from memory and continuity. On the contrary, memory and continuity, as well as reverence and the desire for immortality, are brought forth from the value of the self, none of whose contents must be a function of time and allowed to be annihilated.[9]

If Woman had any intrinsic value and the will to maintain it against any

9. This has at last made quite clear what is meant by that particular *value* which *negates time by creating the past,* as was postulated in chapter V.

challenges, or if at least she had a *desire* for *self-respect,* it would not be possible for her to be *envious.* All women are probably envious, but envy can exist only where those qualities are missing. The envy felt by mothers when the daughters of other women get married sooner than their own is a symptom of real meanness and presupposes, as does any envy, a total lack of a sense of justice. It is in the idea of *justice,* which is the practical application of the idea of truth, that logic and ethics are as closely associated as they are in the theoretical value of truth itself.

Without justice there can be no society. Envy, on the other hand, is *the* absolutely anti-social quality. Woman is indeed totally *anti-social,* and if in earlier times the formation of any society was rightly linked to the possession of an individuality, here is the test of that fact. Woman does not care for the state, for politics, for cozy companionship, and any associations of women which do not admit men soon disintegrate. Finally, the family, far from being a social arrangement, is *the downright anti-social* one: when men get married they promptly withdraw from any societies which they had hitherto frequented either as visitors or as members. I wrote this before the publication of Heinrich Schurtz's valuable ethnological researches, which demonstrate with a wealth of material that the beginnings of society are found in *associations of men* and not in the family.

Pascal explained marvelously how human beings seek society only because they do not want to suffer loneliness and wish to forget themselves. This also shows the complete congruency between my earlier position, which denied Woman's ability to be lonely, and my current position, which maintains that she is anti-social by nature.

If Woman had a self, she would also have a sense of property, her own and that of others. But the urge to steal is much more highly developed in women than in men: so-called kleptomaniacs (thieves *without necessity*) are almost exclusively women. Woman appreciates power and wealth, but not property. Female kleptomaniacs, when found guilty of stealing, usually explain that they had had a sense of everything belonging to them. Lending libraries are frequented mainly by women. Many of these would be affluent enough to buy several libraries, but they lack a closer appreciation of what belongs to them and what they have merely borrowed. Here too the connection between individuality and a social disposition is clearly visible: just as one must have a personality in order to comprehend the personality of another, one must be interested in acquiring property of one's own if one is not to touch the property of others.

A necessary part of every *personality,* even more than property, is a *name* and a close *relationship* with it. And here the facts speak so loud that one is astonished to note how rarely their language is heard. Women have no attachment *whatsoever* to their name. This is *proved* by the simple fact that they abandon their own name and lightly adopt that of the man they marry, without ever feeling that this change of name is in itself significant, and without lamenting the loss of their old name for one moment; and there is also a profound reason, inherent in the nature of Woman, why the woman's property (at least until not very long ago) was usually transferred to the man. Nor is there any sign of a struggle on women's part against that particular separation: on the contrary, at the courtship stage they already allow their lover or suitor to give them names that *he* likes. And even if they very reluctantly marry a man they do not love, no woman has ever complained in particular about having to take leave from her name, and every woman abandons and surrenders her name without showing the slightest reverence for the fact that she was once called by it. In fact she generally *demands* new names from her suitor while she impatiently *awaits* her husband's surname, if only for novelty's sake. However, the name is thought to be a symbol of individuality. Apparently, only the members of the lowest races on earth, for example the bushmen of South Africa, have no personal names, because the natural need to distinguish one person from another is not sufficiently developed in them. The reason why Woman is basically *nameless*[10] is that, for reasons inherent in the very idea of her, she *has* no *personality*. An important observation which, having once made it, one will never fail to repeat is connected with this. If a man enters a room and a woman sees him, hears his step, or simply suspects his presence, *she will immediately become a completely different person*. Her expression and her movements change incredibly suddenly. She adjusts her hair, pulls her skirts together and lifts them or fiddles with her clothes, and her whole being is filled with a half-shameless, half-anxious expectation. The only thing that may be open to question in each case is whether she blushes more about her shameless smile or smiles more shamelessly about her blush.

It is an infinitely profound and lasting insight of Schopenhauer that the soul, the personality, the character is identical with free *will*, or at least that the will coincides with the self insofar as the self is thought of in relation to the absolute. As women lack a self they cannot possess a will either. Only those who have no will of their own, no character in the higher sense of the word, can be as easily *influenced* as a woman by the mere presence of another person and become as functionally *dependent* on, rather than freely *comprehend*, that other person. Woman is the best medium, and M is her best hypnotist. For that reason

10. Cf. Klingsor's words to Kundry in Wagner's *Parsifal*, at the beginning of Act II [translated by Andrew Porter (London, 1986), p. 101]:

> Arise! Arise! To me!
> Your master calls you, nameless woman,
> First she-devil! Rose of Hades!
> Herodias were you, and what else?
> Gundryggia, then, Kundry here!
> Come here! Come here now, Kundry!
> Your master calls: arise!

alone it is a mystery why women are supposed to be particularly fit to be doctors, since the more discerning doctors themselves admit that most of what they have achieved to this day—and it is likely to remain so—is due to their suggestive effect on their patients.

Throughout the animal kingdom W is more easily hypnotized than M, and how closely related hypnotic phenomena are to the most everyday events will be evident from the following. Note how easily W is "infected" by laughter or tears (as I have already indicated in the context of female compassion). Note also how impressed she is by everything that is reported in the papers, how easily she falls prey to the most stupid superstitions, how promptly she tries any miraculous cure a neighbor has recommended to her.

Whoever lacks character will also be short of convictions. That is why W is gullible, uncritical, and unable to understand Protestantism. Nevertheless, although it is certain that every Christian, even before being baptized, *is born either* a Catholic *or* a Protestant, nobody has the right to regard Catholicism as feminine simply because it is more accessible to women than Protestantism. For this classification it would be necessary to consider different characterological principles, which cannot be discussed in this treatise.

Thus it has been comprehensively proven that W is soulless and has neither self nor individuality, neither personality nor freedom, neither character nor will. *The importance of this conclusion with regard to psychology can hardly be overrated.* It actually means that *the psychology of M and the psychology of W must be dealt with separately. The psychic life of W can be described in purely empirical terms, while any psychology of M must target the self as the topmost gable of the building, as Kant realized.*

Hume's (and Mach's) view that there are only "*impressions*" and "*thoughts*" (A B C . . . and $\alpha\ \beta\ \gamma$ . . .) has generally led to the banishment of the psyche from psychology. This view proclaims that the entire world can only be understood as an image in an angled mirror or a kaleidoscope; it turns everything into a meaningless and groundless dance of "elements"; it destroys the possibility of establishing a firm foundation for thought; it annihilates the concept of truth and with it the very reality of which it claims to be the sole philosophy. But in addition to all this it also bears the main responsibility for the miserable state of today's psychology.

This present-day psychology proudly calls itself "psychology without a soul," as the much overrated Friedrich Albert Lange first put it. I believe my investigation to have shown that without the assumption of a soul it is not possible to deal with psychic phenomena, either in the case of M, who must be granted to have a soul, or in that of W, who is soulless. Our psychology today is an eminently female psychology. That is why a comparative examination of the sexes is particularly instructive, and why I have taken special care to carry it out so thoroughly. For it is here that we can see most clearly why we are obliged to assume the existence of the self, and how the confusion between the psychic life of man and the psychic life of woman (in the widest and deepest sense) may be regarded as the single most misleading factor in the attempt to create a general psychology, even though (or indeed precisely *because*) it has not been consciously asserted.

The question that now arises is whether *a psychology of M* ***as a science*** *is at all possible. And the answer, for the present, must be no.* Here I must expect to be referred to the studies of experimental psychologists, and even those who have remained more sober amid the frenzy for experiments may be surprised by what I have said and ask whether these studies count for nothing. But experimental psychology has not produced one bit of information about the deeper elements of the psychic life of man, nor can anybody think of more than sporadic references to these innumerable series of experiments, which have never been systematically analyzed. As I have shown, it is above all the *method* of beginning on the outside and trying to penetrate to the core from there that is mistaken, and that is why experimental psychology has not produced *a single* explanation for the deep internal connections between psychic phenomena. Furthermore, as the psychophysical measurement technique has demonstrated, the true nature of psychic phenomena, as opposed to physical ones, implies that the very functions which might perhaps reveal the connections and transitions between those phenomena must even at the best of times prove *discontinuous* and therefore *closed to differential analysis.* With the loss of continuity, however, the theoretical possibility of achieving the absolutely mathematical ideal of any science is also lost. Incidentally, those who know that space and time are created exclusively by the psyche will never expect geometry and arithmetic to be able to give an exhaustive account of their creator.

There is no scientific psychology of man; for it is in the nature of psychology that it tries to deduce the undeducible, and its ultimate aim, to put it more clearly, would have to be *to prove, i.e., deduce, the existence and essence of every human being.* But in that case all human beings, even in their deepest nature, would be determined and the effects of a cause, and no human being would owe any respect to any other human being as a member of a realm of freedom and infinite value: *once I could be fully deduced and fully subsumed I would have lost all my* ***value*** *and would in fact be soulless.* The assumption of a constant determinacy, with which any psychology begins its task, is incompatible with the *freedom of the will* and (as must be added) of *thought.* Therefore, anybody who believed in a free subject, as did for instance Kant and Schopenhauer, was obliged to deny the possibility of psychology as a science, while anybody who believed in psychology—such as Hume or Herbart (the founders of modern psychology)—could no longer regard the freedom of the subject even as a theoretical possibility.

This dilemma explains the sad plight of today's psychology with regard to all questions of principle. The efforts to banish the *will* from psychology, the constantly repeated attempts to derive the will from sensations and feelings, are basically right in suggesting that the will is not an *empirical* fact. The will can never be found and demonstrated in experience because it is in itself the prerequisite of any empirical psychological data. Assume that a person who likes to sleep in in the mornings tries to observe himself at the moment when he decides to rise from his bed. *A decision contains the entire, undivided self* (as does the act of paying attention), and therefore the duality that would be needed in order to perceive the will is missing. The process of *thinking* is as little as the process of willing a palpable fact that could be grasped by scientific psychology. Thinking is judging, but what is judgment to internal perception? Nothing. It is an entirely alien element, which is added to any receptivity and which cannot be derived from the building blocks dragged in by the psychological Fasolts and Fafners: every new act of judgment destroys afresh the labors of the sensational atomists. The same applies to the *concept.* Nobody thinks in concepts, and yet concepts exist, just as judgments exist. Ultimately, Wundt's opponents are also absolutely right in saying that *apperception* is neither an empirical psychological fact nor a perceptible act. Wundt is more profound than his adversaries—only the shallowest fellows can be association psychologists—and he certainly has reason to link apperception with the will and attention. But apperception is no more an empirical fact than will and attention, or judgment and concept. If all these things, including thinking and willing, are nevertheless present, and if they cannot be demonstrated and defy any attempt at analysis, we only have the choice of accepting or not accepting something that alone makes any psychic life possible.

Therefore we should put an end to all the nonsensical talk about an empirical apperception and realize how right Kant was in solely accepting *transcendental apperception.* If we do not penetrate behind experience we are left with nothing but the infinitely attenuated, pitifully barren discipline of sensational atomism with its laws of association, or else psychology becomes a *methodological* annex of physiology and biology, as it does with Avenarius, whose subtle treatment of a rather limited segment of the whole of psychic life has only been followed by a few, and rather unfortunate, attempts at further development.

Thus psychology without philosophy has proved totally unsuitable for initiating a true understanding of human beings, and no promises for the future can give a firm guarantee that it will ever succeed in so doing. The better one is at psychology, the more one will be bored by all these psychologies of today that insist throughout on ignoring the unity on which all psychic events are founded, until at the very end we are regularly given an unpleasant surprise by a closing paragraph about the development of a harmonious personality. "Psychology as an empirical science" tried to build up that *unity,* which alone is the true *infinity,* from a larger or smaller number of component parts, and to derive the condition of all experience *from* experience. The enterprise will fail, and be renewed, in all eternity, because the intellectual movement of positivism and psychologism is bound to persist as long as there are mediocre minds and indolent natures unwilling to think things through to the finish. Those who, like the philosophers of Idealism, do not wish to sacrifice the psyche must abandon psychology: those who uphold psychology kill the psyche. Psychology always tries to deduce the whole from the parts and to present it as being conditional on something else, while any more profound reflection shows that the partial phenomena flow from the whole as their ultimate source. *Thus psychology denies the psyche, and the psyche by definition denies any study of itself: the psyche denies psychology.*

My account has taken the side of the *psyche* against the ludicrous and useless *psychology without a soul.* Indeed it remains doubtful whether psychology can ever be compatible with the soul, or a science that tries to find causal laws and norms created by itself for thinking and willing, compatible with freedom of thought and the will. Nor is the assumption of a specific "psychic causality"[11] likely to alter the fact that psychology, by ultimately demonstrating its own impossibility, will supply the most brilliant proof of the rights of the concept of freedom, however broadly these are ridiculed and maligned at present.

This is by no means designed to inaugurate a new era of rational psychology. On the contrary, my intention, following Kant, is to ensure that the transcendental *idea* of the soul, right from the start, should serve us as a guide in our ascent through the succession of conditions to the absolute, but in no way "regarding descent to the conditioned." What I had to reject were the attempts to make the absolute leap out of the conditional (at the end of a book of 500–1500 pages). The soul is the regulative principle that must be kept in mind and followed by any truly psychological examination, as opposed to the sensationalist analysis, of individual phenomena. Otherwise any account of the psychic life, however detailed, loving, and sympathetic it may be, will reveal a great black hole gaping at its center.

It is hard to understand how some researchers, who have never tried to analyze such phenomena as shame and guilt, faith and hope, fear and repentance, love and hate, longing and loneliness, vanity and sensitivity, ambition and the desire for immortality, can have the temerity to deny the self out of hand, because they are unable to find it like the color of an orange or the flavor of soapy water. Or how would Mach and Hume explain the simple fact of *style,* if not by individuality? Further: animals are never startled when they see themselves in

11. It is only too understandable that people may easily be led to such an erroneous assumption. Who, for example, when reading *this* book, will not have the feeling at the transition between the first part and the second part that the two are about quite different things, the first about external connections, the second about internal ones?

a mirror, but no human being would be able to spend all his life in a room of mirrors. Or can this fear, the fear of the *doppelganger* (of which, characteristically, woman is free[12]), also be explained in "biological" or "Darwinist" terms? One only needs to pronounce the word *doppelganger* in order to make most men's heart beat faster. Here any purely empirical psychology necessarily reaches its end, and *profoundness* is required. For how could *these* things be traced back to an earlier savage or animal stage without the protection of civilization, which Mach believes explains the fear of young children as an ontogenetic reminiscence. Incidentally, I have hinted at this only in order to remind the "immanentists" and "naïve realists" that in them also there are things of which . . .

Why is nobody pleased and in full agreement if he is *classified* as a Nietzschean, a Herbartian, a Wagnerite, etc.? If, in a word, he is *subsumed*? Mach must also have had the experience of being subsumed by one dear friend or another as a positivist, an idealist, or something else. Would he think that he has been adequately described if somebody were to say that the feeling one has about being thus subsumed by others was merely related to a person's almost complete certainty of the *unique* combination of the "elements" in him, or was only hurt calculus? And yet, strictly speaking, this feeling has nothing to do with disagreement in the sense in which one might disagree with some scientific hypothesis. It is also quite different from, and must not be confused with, somebody describing himself as a Wagnerite. Such a statement ultimately always implies a positive assessment of Wagnerism, because the speaker himself is a Wagnerite. Assuming that we are or can be sincere, we shall admit that in so saying we are *also* elevating Wagner. Conversely, when other people speak about us we are usually afraid that they intend to do the opposite. That is why a man can say a great deal about himself that would be most painful for him to hear from others. As Cyrano de Bergerac confesses about the maddest gibes against him:

> Je me les sers moi-même, avec assez de verve,
> Mais je ne permets pas qu'un autre me les serve.

Where then does that feeling, which even people of low quality have, come from? It comes from a consciousness, however dim, of their own self, their individuality, which gets less than its fair share in being subsumed. *This revulsion is the archetype of any indignation.*

Finally, it will not do to regard a Pascal or a Newton on the one hand as thinkers of extreme genius and on the other hand as being tainted with a host

12. Nobody has ever heard of female *doppelgangers*. Women are called the timid sex, because the distinction commonly made between different kinds of fear is insufficient. There is a fear known only to men.

of narrow-minded prejudices, which "*we*" have long since left behind. Are we really so superior to that age, because of our electric trains and empirical psychologies? If there are such things as cultural values, can *culture* really be measured by the state of science, which has only a *social* and never an *individual, non-demonstrable* character, or by the number of public libraries and laboratories? Is culture something external to humans? Is it not, rather, something mainly *within* humans?

Some people may feel far superior to Euler, surely one of the greatest mathematicians of all times, who once said, when he was writing a letter, that he would be doing it in exactly the same way if he happened to find himself in the body of a rhinoceros. I do not wish at all costs to defend Euler's statement, which may be characteristic of a mathematician and would never have been made by a painter, but what seems quite unjustifiable to me is simply to poke fun at Euler or to excuse him with the "limited intelligence of his time," without understanding his words or at least making an effort to understand them.

Thus, even in psychology, it is not possible in the long run to manage *without* the concept of self, at least with regard to human beings. Whether that concept is compatible with a nomothetic psychology in Windelband's sense, i.e., with psychological laws, seems very doubtful, but it must nevertheless be recognized as being necessary. Perhaps psychology will follow the course that I felt able to outline in an earlier chapter, and become theoretical biography. But in that case it will be most likely to become conscious of the limitations of any empirical psychology.

The fact that in *men* there always remains something ineffable and insoluble as far as any psychology is concerned agrees wonderfully with the further fact that *downright cases of "duplex" or "multiplex personality," that is, a duplication or multiplication of the self, have been observed* ***only in women****. Absolute Woman can be dismantled.* Man, in all eternity, can never be completely dismantled even through the best kind of characterology, let alone through experiments. He contains a core of being which admits no dissection. W is an aggregate, and hence dissociable and fissionable.

Therefore it is extremely comical and amusing to hear modern grammar-school boys talk about the soul of Woman (as a Platonic idea), about women's hearts and their mysteries, about the psyche of modern woman, etc. One of the necessary qualifications of a popular obstetrician also seems to be a belief in the soul of Woman. At least many women like to hear people talk about their soul, even though they know (in henid form) that the whole thing is a swindle. *Woman as the sphinx! A worse nonsense has hardly ever been articulated, a worse swindle never perpetrated. Man is infinitely more mysterious, incomparably more complex.* One only needs to step out into the street to find that there is scarcely a woman whose face does not promptly give her away. So infinitely poor is the register of women's feelings and moods, while the face of many a man demands long and hard scrutiny.

At this point we are also brought closer to a resolution of the question whether we are faced with parallelism or interaction between the psychic and the physical. In the case of W psychophysical parallelism, the full coordination of the two sequences applies: the senile involution of Woman is accompanied by the extinction of her capacity for intellectual exertion, which only tags along with, and is made to serve, sexual purposes. A man never grows completely old in the same sense as a woman. In his case intellectual atrophy is not absolutely unavoidable, and is linked to physical atrophy only in isolated cases. Least of all is senile debility to be observed in an individual whose intellectual masculinity is fully developed, that is, in a genius.

It is not for nothing that the strictest parallelists among philosophers, Spinoza and Fechner, were also the strictest determinists. With M, the free, intelligible subject, we must rule out any psychophysical parallelism, which would demand that every mental phenomenon, in precise analogy to mechanics, be determined by a chain of causalities.

By and large, then, the question of the point of view that should be adopted in dealing with the psychology of the sexes would seem to be settled. However, this view encounters an extraordinary difficulty in a series of strange facts which play an absolutely decisive part in the actual soullessness of W, but which, strangely enough, hardly anybody so far seems to have treated as a serious problem. These facts demand an explanation for a very peculiar kind of behavior displayed by women.

It was noted a long time ago that Woman regards the clarity of male thought, as opposed to female vagueness, as a *sexual characteristic* of Man, and the same thing was pointed out later with reference to the male function of structured speech expressing firm logical *judgments.* What sexually stimulates Woman must be a property of M. The resoluteness of a masculine character makes a similar sexual impression on a woman, and she despises a man who gives in to another man. In such cases people often talk about a moral influence of Woman on Man, although she is only trying to secure for herself the sexual complement among his complementary properties in its entirety. Women demand masculinity from men and they feel entitled to show the highest degree of indignation and contempt if a man disappoints their expectations in this respect. Thus a woman, however flirtatious and however untruthful she is, will become bitter and angry if she sees any traces of flirtatiousness or untruthfulness in a man. However cowardly she may be, the man must be brave. It is all too often overlooked that this is only a sexual egoism, which tries to protect its own unalloyed enjoyment of its complement. And thus there is hardly a more conclusive proof of the soullessness of Woman to be found in experience than the fact that *women demand a soul from man,* and that goodness can have an effect on them, even though they themselves are not really good. The soul is a sexual characteristic, which is demanded in no other way and to no other purpose than great muscular strength or the tickling end of a pointed moustache. The crass expression may cause offence, but the fact cannot be altered. Finally, the strongest impact on Woman is made by the male *will.* And she has a remarkably subtle sense of whether a man's "I want" is mere exertion and bluster or real determination. In the latter case the effect is enormous.

But how can Woman, who in herself is soulless, perceive a soul in Man? How can she judge his morality, since she is amoral? How can she comprehend his strength of character, without having a character herself? How can she feel his will, even though she has no will of her own?

By these questions I have formulated the extremely difficult problem that my investigation will have to confront from now on.

However, before attempting the solution, I must fortify the positions that I have achieved on all sides, and protect them against any attacks which, in the view of some people, might be capable of shaking them.

X | Motherhood and Prostitution

THE MAIN OBJECTION to my account so far will be that it cannot be valid for *all* women. It will be argued that what I have said may apply to some, or even many, but that there are others . . .

I did not set out with the intention of dealing with any specific forms of femininity. Women can be classified according to various points of view, and one must certainly beware of claiming that what is true of an extreme type, which can be proved to exist everywhere but which is frequently almost entirely hidden by the predominance of its precise opposite, is true of the generality of women. Women can be classified in *a number* of ways, and there are many *different* female characters, even though in this context the word "character" must only be used in an empirical sense. All the characteristics of Man have remarkable analogies with those of Woman, which often give rise to amphibolies (an interesting comparison of this kind will be made later in this chapter). However, *in addition,* Man's character is always immersed, and firmly anchored, in the sphere of the intelligible, making the confusion between the theory of the soul and characterology, which I censured earlier (p. 73), more understandable. The characterological differences between women are never rooted in the primal soil deeply enough to result in the development of an individuality, and there is perhaps not one single property of Woman that could not be modified, suppressed, or indeed annihilated in the course of life by the will of Man.

I have so far deliberately ignored the question of what *further* differences there might be between *equally male* or *equally female* individuals. Even though the method of explaining psychological differences in accordance with the principle of intermediate sexual forms provided me with only *one* guide among thousands to this most complex of all areas, I have concentrated on it to the exclusion of others for the simple reason that the introduction of any other principle, the expansion of my linear reflections into a plane, would have disrupted this first attempt at a thorough characterological orientation, which was designed to advance beyond the determination of temperaments or types of mentality.

The development of a specific characterology of women must be held over for a separate study, but my treatise also takes some account of individual differences between women, and I trust that I have avoided the mistake of making false generalizations and drawn only such conclusions as apply in the same form and in the same degree to all equally feminine women without exception. Up to this point I have been concerned solely with W in general. However, as my arguments will be primarily contradicted with reference to *one* type of Woman, I must begin by selecting *one* pair of opposites from the many.

All the bad and hateful things that I have said about women will be countered with the notion of Woman as a mother. It is therefore necessary to discuss Woman as a mother, but she cannot be understood without consideration being given at the same time to her antipole, which shows the realization of the other, diametrically opposed, potential within Woman. It is only in this way that the type of the mother can be clearly defined and the properties of the mother made to stand out sharply against everything alien to them.

The polar opposite of the type of the mother is the type of the prostitute. The inevitability of this distinction is no more *deducible* than the fact that Man and Woman are opposites. Just as the latter is only *seen,* and not proven, the former must also be *seen,* or an attempt must be made to find it in reality, in order to ascertain whether the reality readily fits into the pattern. I shall deal with the qualifications that must be made in due course. For the time being, let us assume that women always have something of two types in them, sometimes more of one, sometimes more of the other. *These types are the mother and the prostitute.*

This dichotomy would be misunderstood if it were not distinguished from a popular distinction. It is often said that Woman is *both mother and lover.* I cannot see any point in this distinction. Is the quality of lover meant to denote the stage that must necessarily precede motherhood? If so, it cannot be a permanent characterological trait. And what does the term "lover" tell us about the woman herself beyond the fact that she is involved in a love affair? Does it add an essential, rather than a completely external, attribute to her? It is possible to love both the mother and the prostitute. At most, the word "lover" could be intended to describe a group of women halfway between the two poles, that is, an intermediate form between the mother and the prostitute, unless it were felt to be necessary to state explicitly that a mother's relationship with the father of her children is different from her relationship with the children themselves, and that she is a lover insofar as she allows herself to be loved and gives herself to the man who loves her. But nothing is gained as a result, because this can be done in the same form by both the mother and the prostitute if the occasion arises. The concept of "lover" says nothing about the qualities of the person involved in the love affair, and this is quite natural, because it is only meant to indicate the first chronological stage in the life of *one* and *the same* woman, which is later followed by motherhood as the second stage. Moreover, since the condition of the lover is only an accidental feature of her person, the distinction between her and the mother becomes quite illogical, because motherhood includes an internal element and does not merely indicate the fact that a woman has given birth. What constitutes the deeper nature of motherhood will now be the subject of our investigation.

The fact that motherhood and prostitution are polar opposites can probably be gleaned from the simple observation that good housewives and mothers have more children, while the cocotte never has more than a few, and the streetwalker is mostly sterile. It must be noted that the type of the prostitute includes not only women who sell themselves, but also many so-called nice girls and married women, some of whom never commit adultery not because the circumstances are not favorable, but because they themselves do not allow things to reach that point. Therefore no exception should be taken to my using the term "prostitute," which is yet to be analyzed, in a much broader sense than that of women who sell themselves. The streetwalker is distinguished from the more prestigious cocotte and the more genteel hetaira only by an absolute lack of differentiation and a total absence of memory, which makes her live from one hour to the next or one minute to the next, without the slightest connection between one day and another. Moreover, the prostitute type could manifest itself even if there were only one man and one woman in the world, because it expresses itself in a specific kind of behavior toward a male individual.

The mere fact of lower fertility would release me from the obligation to discuss a commonly held view which tries to attribute prostitution, a phenomenon deeply rooted in the innate nature of a person, to *social* abuses, such as women's lack of employment, and which then blames today's society in particular, alleging that it is the economic greed of the male leaders that makes it so difficult for unmarried women to lead honest lives, or that bachelorhood, also said to be exclusively the product of economic factors, demands prostitution as its necessary complement. However, I should add that prostitution is not only found among poor streetwalkers, but affluent girls also sometimes forgo all the advantages of their reputation, preferring to loiter openly in the street—for *real* prostitution *belongs* in the *street*—rather than having hidden love affairs; and that women are preferred for many jobs in shops, offices, and the postal, telegraphic, and telephone services, where a purely mechanical activity is required, because W is much less complex and therefore has simpler needs than M, and because capitalism discovered long before science that women could be paid less because of their inferior lifestyle. Incidentally, even young prostitutes usually find it hard to make ends meet, because they have to pay high rents, to wear unusual clothes, and to keep their pimps. The frequent phenomenon of prostitutes returning to their earlier occupation after being married demonstrates how deeply rooted the inclination to their way of life is in them. Further, for reasons that are unknown but obviously located in their innate constitution, prostitutes are often *immune* to various infections, to which "decent women" are usually vulnerable. Finally, prostitution has *always* existed and has by no means grown in proportion to the achievements of the capitalist era; in antiquity it was even part of the *religious* institutions of certain peoples, e.g., the Phoenicians.

Thus prostitution can by no means be regarded as something forced upon Woman by Man. Often enough a man is certainly to blame if a girl has to leave domestic service and finds herself unemployed. But the ability to resort to prostitution in such a case must lie in the nature of the human female herself. One cannot build on air. To genuine men, who suffer financial blows more often and who feel poverty more intensely than women, prostitution is still something alien, and male prostitutes (found among waiters, hairdressers' assistants, etc.) are always advanced intermediate sexual forms. Thus the suitability and inclination to prostitution, just as the capacity for motherhood, is organically present in Woman from birth.

This is not to say that every woman who becomes a prostitute does so exclusively as a result of an inner need. Most women perhaps have *both* possibilities in them, the mother as well as the prostitute; only the virgin—with apologies, because I know this will upset *men*—only the virgin does not exist. Given these ambivalent cases, the decisive factor can only be a man, who is able to make a woman a mother through his personality, not only by sexual intercourse but even by a single *look*. Schopenhauer said that a human being must, strictly speaking, date his existence back to the moment when his father and mother fell in love. This is not correct. Ideally, the birth of a human being should be dated from the moment *a woman first sees, or just hears the voice of,* ***him***, the father of her child. For more than sixty years, under the influence of Johannes Müller, T. Bischof, and C. Darwin, biological and medical science, the theory of breeding and gynecology, have adopted an entirely negative attitude to the question of "maternal impression." Later on I will try to develop a theory of maternal impression. Here I would only like to note that it may not be the case that the phenomenon of maternal impression cannot exist, merely because it does not agree with the view that a sperm and an egg alone help to create a new individual. Maternal impression exists, and science should strive to explain it, rather than simply denying it as something impossible and pretending that there could ever be enough empirical scientific evidence to justify such an assertion. In an a priori discipline such as mathematics I may exclude the possibility of $2 \times 2 = 5$ on the planet Jupiter, but biology only knows propositions of "comparative generality" (Kant). At the same time, by writing in *support* of the concept of maternal impression, and considering its denial as narrow-minded, I do not wish to claim that all malformations, or even just a large number of them, result from it. For the moment I am only interested in the possibility of influencing the progeny without having sexual intercourse with the mother. And here I venture to say[1] that just as Schopenhauer and Goethe, with their *unanimous* view about the theory of color, are likely to be *a priori* right against all the physicists of the

1. Cf. the discussions in chapter VIII about the greater respect due to the more profound insight of a great mind than to the state of science at any particular time (p. 149).

past, present, and future, so something that is *true* for Ibsen (in *The Lady from the Sea*) and Goethe (in *Elective Affinities*) will not simply be proved *false* by the expert opinion of all the medical faculties in the world.

Incidentally, a man whose impact on a woman could be expected to be great enough to make her child resemble him, even if the child had not developed from his sperm, would have to complement the woman sexually to an extremely high degree. The very *rare* occurrence of such cases is due to the unlikelihood of a meeting between such perfect complements, and must not be regarded as a valid objection to the *theoretical* possibility of the facts put forward by Goethe and Ibsen.

Whether a woman will meet a man who can make her the mother of his child through his mere presence is a matter of chance. *To that extent* it is *imaginable* that the destinies of *many* mothers and prostitutes could have turned out the opposite of what they have actually become. On the other hand, there are not only countless examples of women remaining true to the type of the mother even without such a man, but there are also doubtless cases in which this man *does present himself* and even *his* presence fails to prevent the woman from finally and irrevocably turning to prostitution.

Therefore we have no alternative but to assume *two* innate, contrasting predispositions, distributed between different women in different proportions: the absolute mother and the absolute prostitute. The reality is found *between* the two: there is certainly no woman completely without the instincts of a prostitute. (Many people will deny this and ask how it is possible to recognize the prostitute element in many women who seem to be anything but cocottes. For the time being I will answer this only by pointing out how ready and willing women are to allow a stranger to touch them indecently and to brush against them. If one applies this standard one will find that there is no absolute mother.) However, there is also no woman completely without any maternal impulses, although I must admit that I have much more often found extraordinary approximations to the absolute prostitute than such degrees of motherliness as to eclipse all the qualities of the prostitute in them.

As even the first and most superficial conceptual analysis of the nature of motherhood shows, the main purpose of the *mother's* life is to achieve a *child,* while in the absolute *prostitute* this purpose of copulation seems to be completely missing. A more detailed examination will have to consider, above all, how the prostitute and the mother relate to *two* things: the relationship of each with the child, and the relationship of each with sexual intercourse.

To begin with, the mother and the prostitute are distinguished by the relationship of the former with the child. The absolute prostitute's sole concern is the man, that of the mother can only be the child. The surest touchstone is her relationship with her daughter: a woman can only be called a mother if she never envies her daughter's greater youth or beauty, if she never in the slightest grudges her daughter the admiration of men, *but completely identifies with her* and is as pleased about her daughter's admirer as if he were her own.

The absolute mother, whose sole concern is her child, will become a mother through any man. It will be found that women who in their childhood played more eagerly with dolls, and who even as young girls very much loved and enjoyed looking after children, are not very particular in their choice of men and readily take any husband who can more or less provide for them and who is acceptable to their parents and relatives. If such a girl has become a mother, no matter by whom, she ideally ceases to be interested in any other man. The absolute prostitute, on the other hand, abhors children even in her own childhood, and later on she uses a child, at most, to lure a man to herself by a pretended idyll of mother and child, calculated to move him. She is the woman who has a desire to attract all men, and since there is no absolute mother, it will be possible to discover in every woman at least a *trace* of this universal vanity, which will never renounce its claim to all the men in the world.

Here a *formal similarity* between the absolute mother and the absolute cocotte is noticeable. *Both* are essentially *undemanding* with regard to the *individuality* of their sexual complement. The former takes any man who can serve her to have a child, and needs no other man as soon as she has the child: *this is the only reason for calling her "monogamous."* The latter gives herself to any man who can provide her with erotic pleasure, which, for her, is an end in itself. This is the point where the two extremes meet, and where we may therefore hope to obtain an insight into the nature of Woman *as such.*

In fact I must declare that the common view of *Woman* being monogamous and *Man* polygamous, which I myself shared for a long time, is entirely wrong. *The opposite* is the case. One must not be misled by the fact that women often wait for, and if possible choose, that man who is able to confer the greatest value on them—the most magnificent and most famous man, the "first among all." This desire distinguishes women from animals, because animals do not strive to acquire any value, either in their own eyes and through themselves (as do men) or through others and in the eyes of others (as do women). But only fools could have seen any cause for praise in this, since it shows most unmistakably that Woman has no *intrinsic value* whatsoever. This desire indeed demands to be satisfied, but it definitely does not involve the moral *idea* of monogamy. Man is in a position to donate and to transfer value to Woman. He *can give* and he *wants* to give, but he can never receive his own value, as Woman does, from others. A woman, then, seeks to acquire as much value as possible by pressing ahead to be chosen by a man who can give her *most* value, while a man's motives for getting married are completely different. He regards marriage, at any rate initially, as the culmination of ideal love, as a fulfillment, even though it is very doubtful whether marriage can ever really achieve so much. Marriage, for him, is further permeated by the utterly male idea of *fidelity* (which presupposes continuity and an intelligible self). It is often said that Woman is more faithful than Man, because fidelity, for a man, is a *coercion* which he has imposed on himself, albeit of his own *free* will and with full *consciousness*. He will often pay no heed to this self-denying ordinance, but he will always believe or somehow feel that he is in the wrong if he infringes it. If he commits adultery he has not listened to his intelligible self. For Woman, adultery is a titillating game, in which only the motives of security and reputation play a part, and the idea of morality never arises. There is no woman who has never been unfaithful to her husband in her thoughts *without* reproaching herself for this. Women enter marriage trembling and full of unconscious desire, and commit adultery with the same expectancy and thoughtlessness, because they have no self that is beyond the reach of time. The motive force of loyalty to a *contract* can be found only in Man; Woman has no understanding of the binding force of the given word. The examples commonly adduced for the fidelity of Woman do little to prove the contrary. The fidelity of Woman is either the lasting after-effect of an intensive relationship of sexual obedience (Penelope) or that slavish relationship itself, doglike, abject, full of tenacious instinctive devotion, and comparable to the physical proximity which is the precondition of any feminine compassion (*Kate of Heilbronn*).

The monogamous marriage, then, was created by Man. It is rooted in the idea of male individuality, which persists unaltered through the ages and which, consequently, can only be fully complemented by one and the same person. In that sense the project of *monogamous marriage* undeniably contains something elevated, and its inclusion among the sacraments of the Catholic Church has a certain justification. Nevertheless, I do not wish to take sides in the debate about "marriage or free love." Based on any deviations from the strictest moral law—and such a deviation is implied in every empirical marriage—a *fully* satisfactory solution of that problem is no longer possible: *at the same time* as marriage *adultery* came into the world.

Nevertheless, marriage can only have been introduced by Man. There is no legal institution of female origin. Every *law* comes from Man, and only a great many *customs* from Woman. (For that reason alone it would be totally wrong to derive law from custom or custom from law; they are quite different things.) Only Man—*la donna è mobile*—could have had the desire and the strength to introduce *order* into the chaos of sexual relationship, as indeed to introduce order, *rules,* and laws as such (in both practical and theoretical matters). There really seems to have been a time when women were allowed to exert great influence on social developments in many peoples, but at that time marriage was unheard of: the age of *matriarchy* was an age of *polyandry.*

The unequal relationship of the mother and the prostitute with their respective children provides many more insights. A woman who is mainly a prostitute will first of all perceive the masculinity of her son, and will always have a sexual relationship with him. However, since no woman is exclusively maternal, it cannot be denied that every son has a residual sexual effect on his mother. That is why earlier on I described the relationship of a woman with her daughter as the most reliable standard of maternal love. On the other hand, it is certain that there also exists a sexual relationship between every son and his mother, however much this is hidden from both of them. This relationship, which is repressed in waking consciousness, appears through sexual fantasies about the mother during sleep (the "oedipal dream") in the early stages of puberty in the case of most men, and now and then even later in the case of some. But the presence of a profoundly sexual element of fusion even in the most strictly maternal relationship of a genuine mother with her child seems to be indicated by the sensual pleasure a woman undoubtedly feels in the process of lactation, and by the anatomical fact that under a woman's nipple there is some erectile tissue which, according to the investigations of physiologists, can be used to trigger contractions of the womb. Both the passivity,[2] brought about in woman by the active sucking of the child, and the condition of close physical contact during the delivery of mother's milk create a perfect analogy to the behavior of woman during sexual intercourse. They make it appear understandable that her monthly periods pause during lactation, and they justify to some extent the man's vague but profound jealousy of her baby. But breastfeeding a child is a thoroughly maternal activity: the more a woman is a prostitute, the less will she want to breastfeed her child, and the less will she be able to do so. Thus it cannot be denied that the relationship between mother and child in itself is akin to that between Woman and Man.

Motherliness is as universal as sexuality, and it differs in degree toward its objects as sexuality does. If a woman is motherly, her motherliness is bound to reveal itself not only toward her own child but also earlier and toward everybody, although later her interest in her own child will absorb everything else and, in the event of a conflict, make her thoroughly narrow-minded, blind, and unfair. The most interesting phenomenon in this context is the relationship of a motherly girl with the man she loves. A motherly woman, already as a girl, adopts the stance of a mother toward the man she loves and even toward the man who later becomes the father of her child: *in a certain sense he is already her child.* This common feature of the mother and the woman in love[3] reveals the

2. The child's thoughtless movements, its urge to get hold of anything for which it feels a momentary craving, its stubborn and blind manner of demanding and grabbing, is sufficiently connected with the passivity revealed by woman in the (more narrowly) sexual sphere.

3. Which has been recognized by the greatest poets. Remember the identification of Aase and Solveig at the close of Ibsen's *Peer Gynt* and the combination of Herzeleide with Kundry in the seduction of Wagner's Parsifal.

most profound nature of *this* type of woman: it is the enduring root-stock of the species formed by the mother, the never-ending rhizome grown into the soil, against which *man* as an individual stands out and becomes aware of his own transience. It is this thought that allows man, more or less consciously, to see in the motherly individual, even as a girl, a certain eternity,[4] which transforms the pregnant woman into a lofty idea (Zola). It is the tremendous *confidence* of the species, albeit nothing else, that underlies the silence of these beings, who may even make man feel small for some moments. At such moments he may be overcome by a certain peace, a great calm, in which all his higher and deeper longings are silent, and he may briefly believe that he has really achieved the most profound connection with the universe through woman. The reason is that to the woman he loves he becomes a *child* (Siegfried with Brünnhilde, Act III), whom the mother contemplates with a smile, for whom she *knows* an infinity of things, whom she tends, and whom she tames and keeps under control. But only for seconds (Siegfried tears himself away from Brünnhilde). For a man is only a man by virtue of what distinguishes him from the species by raising him above it. That is why fatherhood by no means satisfies his deepest emotional need, and why the thought of being absorbed and extinguished within the species horrifies him. The most terrible chapter in the most comfortless of the great books in human literature, *The World as Will and Idea,* is "On Death and Its Relation to the Indestructability of Our True Nature," where the infinite will of the species is represented as the only real immortality.

It is the confidence of the species that makes the mother brave and fearless, in contrast to the prostitute, who is always cowardly and fearful. It is not the courage of individuality, the moral courage arising from the respect for truth and the resoluteness of an inwardly free being, but the will to live permeating the species, that uses the mother as an individual to protect the child and even the man. Like the conflicting concepts of courage and cowardliness, the opposites hope and fear have fallen to the mother and the prostitute respectively. The absolute mother is always and in every respect, as it were, "pregnant with hope": being immortal within the species, she knows no fear of death, which the prostitute dreads even though she has not the slightest desire for individual immortality—one more proof of how wrong it is to try to explain the wish for personal survival merely by the fear and awareness of physical death.

The mother always feels superior to man, knowing that she is his anchor. While she, secure in the unbroken chain of the generations, in a manner of speaking, represents the harbor from which every ship sets sail afresh, man roams far out on the high seas alone. The mother, even at the most advanced age, is prepared to welcome and shelter the child. While this factor, as will be

4. "Ever was I, ever . . . beset by sweet-yearning bliss—but ever working for your own weal" (Brünnhilde to Siegfried) [*Wagner's Ring,* translated by Stewart Spencer (London, 2000), p. 272].

shown, is already psychically present at the conception of the child, the other, aimed at protecting and nourishing, is clearly revealed in pregnancy. This superiority also comes to the fore in relation to her lover: the mother appreciates the naïve and childlike quality of the man, his *simplicity,* while the hetaira appreciates his subtleties and his refinement. The mother has a desire to teach, and to give everything to, her child, even if this child is the man she loves. The hetaira longs for the man to *impress* her, and she wants to *owe* everything to him. The mother, as representative of the species which is at work in all its members, is kind to every member (*in this sense every daughter is still the mother of her father*). It is only when the interests of her children, in the narrower sense, are at stake that she becomes exclusive, and then in an extraordinary degree. The prostitute is never as loving and never as unkind as the mother can be.

The mother is entirely subject to the purposes of the species; the prostitute stands outside them. In fact the species only really has this one advocate, this one priestess, the mother. It is only in her that the will of the species expresses itself in a pure form, while the mere phenomenon of the prostitute proves that Schopenhauer's theory, according to which sexuality serves only to compose the next generation, cannot possibly be generally valid. That the mother's sole concern is the life of her species is also shown by the fact that motherly women in particular treat animals most harshly. One only needs to observe the imperturbable calm and the conviction of carrying out a praiseworthy duty, with which a good housewife and mother slaughters one chicken after another. The reverse side of motherhood is stepmotherhood, and every mother of her own children is the stepmother of all other creatures.

An even more striking proof of the mother's association with the preservation of the species is her peculiarly close relationship with whatever serves as *nourishment.* She cannot bear to see anything that could have been eaten, the smallest leftover, go to waste. It is quite different with the prostitute, who, on a whim and for no good reason, piles up large quantities of food and drink at one moment, only to leave most of it untouched at the next. The mother is avaricious and petty, the prostitute wasteful and capricious. The mother lives to *preserve* the species, which is why she does her best to ensure that her charges eat their fill, and nothing gives her as much pleasure as seeing a healthy appetite. This is connected to her association with bread and anything known as housekeeping. Ceres is a good mother, which is clearly expressed by her Greek name Demeter. Thus the mother looks after the body, but not the soul of her child.[5] The

5. Cf. in Ibsen's *Peer Gynt,* Act II, the conversation between Solveig's father and Aase (one of the best drawn "mothers" in literature) during their search for her son [translated by John Northam (Oxford, 1993), pp. 35–36]:

> Aase: "We must find the lad!"
> Father: "Rescue his soul."
> Aase: "Limbs too!"

relationship between mother and child, on the mother's part, always remains physical, from kissing and hugging the little one to the care surrounding and enfolding the adult. Likewise, her totally irrational delight in every manifestation of the little infant's life can only be understood in terms of this sole duty to preserve and protect earthly existence.

This also explains why maternal love cannot really be held in high moral esteem. Let anybody ask himself whether he sincerely believes that his mother would not love him just as much if he were quite different, and whether her affection for him would become smaller if he were not himself but a completely different person. *This* is the crux of the matter, and this is where those who refuse to abandon their moral respect for Woman on account of maternal love must be challenged. *Maternal love is totally indifferent to the individuality of the child.* It is satisfied by the mere fact of the child, *and this is what is immoral about it.* Every other kind of love between a man and a woman, and even between members of the same sex, involves a particular person with quite specific physical and psychic properties; only maternal love indiscriminately encompasses everything that the mother has ever carried in her womb. It is a cruel admission to make to oneself, as well as to the mother and the child, that this is precisely what reveals the totally unethical nature of maternal love, the love that persists regardless of whether the son becomes a saint or a criminal, a king or a beggar, whether he remains an angel or degenerates into a monster. However, the belief of many children that they are entitled to their mother's love, simply because they are her children (this applies in particular to daughters, although sons are usually also negligent in this respect) is equally base. Maternal love is immoral because it does not relate to another self, but represents a fusion right from the outset: like any immoral behavior toward others, it *crosses a border.* An ethical relationship can only exist *between one individual and another.* Maternal love, which is *indiscriminate* and *intrusive, rules out* individuality. *The relationship between a mother and her child is in all eternity a system of near-reflexes linking the two.* If the child suddenly calls out or cries while the mother is sitting in the next room, the mother will jump up as if stung by a bee and hurry to the child (incidentally, a good opportunity to tell at once whether a woman is more a mother or a prostitute), and later on, when the child has grown up, every wish and every complaint of that adult is also immediately communicated or, so to speak, conducted and transplanted to her, and becomes, unquestioned and unchecked, her own wish and complaint. The nature of motherhood is that of *an unbroken conduit between the mother and anything that was ever connected with her through the umbilical cord.* Therefore I am unable to join in the general admiration of maternal love and cannot help thinking that its most reprehensible feature is precisely what is so often praised about it: its lack of discrimination. Incidentally, I believe that this has been recognized, and only kept quiet about, by many outstanding thinkers and artists. The once so widespread overestimation of Raphael has subsided, and there are no other singers of maternal love above the modest rank of Fischart or Richepin. Maternal love is instinctive and driven: it exists in animals no less than in humans. This alone would be enough to prove that this kind of love cannot be genuine love, this kind of altruism cannot be true morality, for all morality stems from the intelligible character, which animals lack, since they are totally unfree. The ethical imperative can only be obeyed by a rational being: there is no instinctive, but only conscious, morality.

In a certain respect the hetaira is *superior* to the mother as a result of her position outside the purposes of the species, that is, of the fact that she does not serve merely as a habitation and a container or, as it were, an eternal passageway for new beings, and is not consumed by nourishing these—if it is at all possible to talk about a higher ethical level where two women are concerned. The intellectual level of a woman who is completely absorbed by taking care of, and dressing, her husband and child, or by carrying out or supervising the chores of her house and kitchen or her garden and field, is almost always very low. The women with the most highly developed intellects, all those who can in any way become *muses* for men, belong to the category of the prostitute. It is to this, the Aspasia type, that the women of Romanticism must be allocated, above all the most outstanding among them, Karoline Michaelis-Böhmer-Forster-Schlegel-Schelling.

It is connected with this fact that only men without any desire for intellectual production feel sexually attracted to the mother. Those men whose fatherhood is restricted to bodily children must be expected to choose the fertile woman, the mother, rather than the other type. *Exceptional individuals have only ever loved prostitutes.*[6] They choose sterile women, and they themselves, if at all, only produce children who are unfit to live and die early—for which there may be a profound ethical reason. Earthly fatherhood is as deficient in value as motherhood. It is immoral, as will be shown later (chapter XIV), and it is illogical, because it is in every respect an illusion, for nobody ever knows for certain to what extent he is the father of his child. And it is also of short duration and ephemeral, for every human line and race has died and become extinct.

Accordingly, the widespread and exclusive esteem, not to say reverence, accorded to the maternal woman, who then is often made out to be the one and only genuine type of Woman, is quite unjustified, even though almost all men doggedly cling to it and indeed claim that no woman can find fulfillment except as a mother. I confess that I am far more impressed by the prostitute, not as a person but as a phenomenon.

There are various reasons why the mother is generally held in higher esteem. Above all, she seems more suited to comply with the ideal of virginity,

6. Naturally all this does not only refer to streetwalkers who sell themselves.

because she does not care for man as such, or does so only insofar as he is her child. This ideal is merely attached to Woman by Man out of a certain need, as we shall find. In fact, chastity is basically alien to Woman, to the mother desiring children as much as to the prostitute obsessed by men.

Man rewards the mother for the illusion of great morality by raising her above the prostitute in moral and social terms, for absolutely no good reason. The prostitute is the woman who has never conformed to the values of Man and to the ideal of chastity that he seeks in her, but who has always *rejected* these, be it through the hidden reluctance of the woman of the world, the gently passive resistance of the demi-mondaine, or the open demonstration of the streetwalker. *This alone* can explain the special situation, the position outside any social respectability, indeed almost outside any law and order, that the prostitute holds almost everywhere today. The mother has found it easy to submit to the moral will of Man, because she only cares for the child and the survival of the species.

The prostitute is very different. She at least lives her own life fully,[7] even if—in extreme cases—she is punished for this by being excluded from society. Rather than being brave as the mother is, she is a coward through and through, but she always possesses the correlative of cowardice, which is impudence, and thus she is at least brazenly shameless. She is polygamous by nature and always attracts more men than just the one founder of a family. She gives free rein to her urges and satisfies them as if in defiance. She feels that she is a queen, and the most obvious thing to her seems to be her power. The mother is easily offended or outraged. The prostitute cannot be hurt or insulted by anybody. While the mother, as the guardian of the species and of the family, has a certain *honor,* the prostitute has renounced any claim to be honored by society, and this is what fills her with pride and allows her to hold her head high. What she would be unable to grasp is having no power ("the mistress"). She expects everybody to pay attention to her, to think only of her, *to live for her,* and she is incapable of believing anything else. And indeed it is she—Woman as the lady—who has the greatest power among human beings and who exercises the greatest, indeed the only, influence over any aspect of human life that is not regulated by male associations (from the gymnastics club to the state).

In this respect she is analogous to the great conqueror in the sphere of politics. Like the great conqueror, say Alexander or Napoleon, the utterly great, utterly enthralling prostitute is perhaps only born once every thousand years, but then she bestrides the world in triumph, as he does.

Every man of this kind is to some extent related to the prostitute (there is a sense in which every politician is a *tribune of the people,* and the tribunate con-

7. There may well be a connection between this and the fact, which will surprise many, that the prostitute pays more attention to physical *cleanliness* than the mother.

tains an element of prostitution). Like the tribune, the prostitute, who is aware of her power, is never embarrassed when she meets a man, while every man is always embarrassed when he meets the prostitute or the tribune. Like the great tribune, she believes that she makes everybody to whom she speaks *happy.* One only needs to watch such a woman asking a policeman for information, or entering a shop. No matter whether the shop employs men or women, and no matter how small her purchase is, she will believe that she is *handing out* gifts left, right, and center. The same elements will be discovered in every born politician. And the other people, all the other people, faced with *either* of them—even the self-confident Goethe when he met Napoleon in Erfurt—will actually and irresistibly feel that they have received a *gift* (take the myth of Pandora or the birth of Venus, who rises from the sea, already looking around and offering herself).

As promised in chapter V,[8] I have returned for a moment to the "men of action." Even somebody as profound as Carlyle held these in very high esteem and finally placed "the hero as king" highest among all heroes. I already showed in that chapter why this cannot be true. I may now proceed to point out that no great politicians, not even the greatest such as Caesar, Cromwell, Napoleon, or Bismarck, shrink from using lies and deceit, and Alexander the Great even committed murder, before readily allowing a sophist to talk him into believing that he was innocent. But untruthfulness is incompatible with genius. Napoleon in St. Helena wrote memoirs full of lies and oozing with sentimentality, and in his very last words he still assumed the altruistic pose of having only ever loved France. Napoleon, the greatest phenomenon of all, also shows most clearly that the "great men of will" are criminals and therefore no geniuses. He can only be understood in terms of the *tremendous intensity with which he tried to escape from himself:* this is the only possible explanation of any conquest, large or small. Napoleon was never inclined to reflect on himself. He could not live one hour without having some great objective outside him to absorb him completely. That is why he had to conquer the world. Because he had great gifts, greater than any leader before him, he needed more in order to silence all the dissenting voices within him. The tremendous driving force behind his ambition was to drown out his better self. The superior, exceptional individual may share the common desire for admiration or fame, but he does not have the ambition to connect all the things in the world with his own empirical person, to make them dependent on himself, in order to *pile* all the things in the world over his own name like a pyramid reaching into infinity. But this is also why the leader is gradually abandoned by his unfailing sense of reality (that is why he becomes epileptic): he ***takes away*** all the *freedom*[9] of the *object* and enters into a criminal *relationship* with *things* by using them merely as

8. P. 121f.
9. Cf. chapter IX, p. 166f.

means, as pedestals and stirrups for his own small person and its selfish, greedy ends. The great individual has *boundaries,* because he is the monad of monads, and—this is that ultimate fact—he is at the same time the conscious microcosm. He *encompasses all knowledge* and he has the whole universe within him. In the most complete case, as soon as he experiences something he clearly sees all its connections in the cosmos, and he therefore needs *experiences,* but no *induction.* The great tribune and the great hetaira are the absolutely *boundless* beings, who use the whole world to embellish and elevate their *empirical* self. That is why both of them are incapable of any love, affection, and friendship, why they are heartless and unfeeling.

Remember the profound fairy tale about the king who wanted to conquer the stars, which reveals the idea of the leader in a brilliant and glaring light. The true genius confers his own honor on himself and he never enters into a relationship of mutual dependency with the rabble, as the tribune does. The great politician has not only a speculator and a multimillionaire in him, but also a mountebank; he is not only a great chess player, but also a great actor; he is not only a despot, but he also courts favors; he not only prostitutes others, but he is a great prostitute himself. There is no politician, no general, who does not "solicit," and his famous "solicitations" are his sexual acts. *The setting of the true tribune,* like that of the prostitute, *is the street.* A complementary relationship with the rabble is what actually constitutes the politician. Only the rabble is really of any use to him. As far as the others, the individuals, are concerned, he eliminates them if he is unwise, or he tries to disarm them by pretending to appreciate them, if he is as cunning as Napoleon. In fact Napoleon had a most accurate sense of his dependence on the rabble. A politician can by no means do whatever he likes, even if he is a Napoleon, and even if he wanted to realize *ideals,* which he would not want to do if he were Napoleon. If he did, he would soon be taught a lesson by the rabble, his true master. Any "economies of the will" apply only to the *formal act of initiative:* the will of a power-hungry man is never *free.*

All leaders feel the necessity of this reciprocal relationship with the masses, and *that is why* they are without exception *in favor* of constituent assemblies, whether civilian or military, and of the most universal suffrage (Bismarck 1866). The genuine politician appears not in the shape of Marcus Aurelius or Diocletian, but in that of Cleon, Mark Antony, Themistocles or Mirabeau. *Ambitio* literally means going about, and that is what both the tribune and the prostitute do. According to Emerson, Napoleon in Paris "listened after the hurrahs and the compliments of the street, incognito." We read very similar things about Wallenstein in Schiller.

The unique phenomenon of the great man of action has always had a powerful attraction for artists in particular (but also for philosophical writers). The surprising unanimity displayed in this respect will perhaps make it easier to approach the phenomenon by means of conceptual analysis. Mark Antony (Caesar) and Cleopatra are not altogether unlike each other. Initially, most people will probably regard this parallel as quite fanciful, and yet the existence of a close analogy seems to me to be beyond any doubt, however different the two persons may at first sight appear. The "great man of action" *renounces any inner life* in order to *express* himself (the term is appropriate here) fully in the external world, and to suffer the fate of everything that *ex*pires, rather than achieving the permanence of everything that is *in*ternalized. He tosses his whole value behind him and *keeps it at arm's length* with all his might. Similarly, the great prostitute flings the value that she would be able to obtain from being a mother into the face of society, not in order to take stock of herself and to embark on a life of contemplation, but in order to give completely free rein to her sensual urges. Both the great prostitute and the great tribune are like firebrands which, when lit, illuminate vast expanses, pile corpses on corpses as they pass, and fade out like meteors, without contributing anything worthwhile and meaningful to human wisdom, without leaving anything permanent behind, without any sign of eternity—while the mother and the genius quietly work for the future. Both the prostitute and the tribune, therefore, are perceived as "scourges of God," as anti-moral phenomena.

This shows again that I was right earlier on to exclude the "great man of will" from the concept of genius. The genius, and not only the philosophical but also the artistic genius, is always distinguished by the predominance in him of conceptual or representational *knowledge* over anything *practical.*

However, the motive driving the prostitute still needs investigating. The nature of the mother was relatively easy to recognize: she is eminently a tool for the preservation of the species. Prostitution is much more mysterious and difficult to explain. All those who have reflected at any length on this phenomenon must have experienced some moments when they completely despaired of ever being able to throw any light on it. Certainly, what matters most here is the different attitude of the mother and of the prostitute to sexual intercourse. I hope that there is no great risk of anybody regarding the discussion of this topic, and indeed of prostitution itself, as being unworthy of the philosopher. It is the spirit in which they are treated that must endow many subjects with dignity. The sensations of Leda or Danae have often enough caused problems for sculptors and painters, and those writers who have chosen the prostitute as their theme—I am aware of Zola's *Claude's Confession,* Hortense, Renée and Nana, Tolstoy's *Resurrection,* Ibsen's Hedda Gabler and Rita, and finally Sonia by one of the greatest minds, Dostoevsky—never really wanted to portray individual cases, but always universal ones. And for universal things it must be possible to develop a theory.

For the mother, sexual intercourse is a means to an end. The prostitute finds herself in a special situation insofar *as sexual intercourse for her becomes an end in itself.* Throughout nature, sexual intercourse has a further role beyond reproduction, which is indicated, among other things, by the fact that many organisms reproduce without sexual intercourse (*parthenogenesis*). On the other hand, *copulation* among animals is always seen to serve the purpose of producing progeny, and nothing suggests that sexual intercourse is sought *exclusively* for the sake of lust, as it only occurs at certain times, in the mating season. As a result, lust has been regarded as the very means used by nature to achieve *its* aim of preserving the species.

If sexual intercourse is an end in itself for the prostitute, this is not to say that it means nothing to the mother. There is a category of "sexually anesthetic" women, who are usually called "frigid," but such cases are much less frequently believable than is assumed. Often the man alone must be blamed for not being able to bring about the opposite of this coldness through his own person, and the remaining cases cannot be attributed to the type of the mother. Frigidity can occur in both the mother and the prostitute: it will later be explained as a hysterical phenomenon. Nor must the prostitute be considered sexually insensitive because streetwalkers (i.e., that contingent of prostitutes which is on the whole supplied only by the peasant population, chambermaids, etc.) may often have disappointed their clients' high expectations through a lack of liveliness. Just because the prostitute is obliged to put up with the advances of men who sexually have nothing to offer her, it must not be regarded as part of her nature to remain cold in any act of sexual intercourse. This illusion results only from the fact that it is precisely she who makes the highest demands on sensual enjoyment, and her association with her pimp must abundantly compensate her for all the deprivations she suffers otherwise in this respect.

That sexual intercourse, for the prostitute, is an end in itself is also apparent from the fact that she, and she alone, goes in for *coquetry*. Coquetry is never without a connection to sexual intercourse. Essentially, it pretends that the woman has already been conquered by the man, using the *contrast* with the reality, which does not yet show this fulfillment, as an incentive for him to carry out the conquest. It is a challenge to the man, whom she presents with one and the same task in constantly changing forms while *at the same time* giving him to understand that she does not believe him capable of ever fulfilling it. There is a sense in which the game of coquetry as such, even at that early stage, achieves its purpose for the woman, which is sexual intercourse: by arousing the desire of the man the prostitute feels something analogous to the sensations of being the object of sexual intercourse and thus obtains the gratifications of lust at any time and from any man. Whether she will then go all the way, or draw back if events progress too fast, probably only depends on whether the form of real sexual intercourse which she practices at that time, i.e., her current man, already satisfies her to such an extent that she expects nothing *more* from another. And perhaps the only reason why the streetwalker in particular tends not to be coquettish is that she is in any case constantly tasting the sensations at which coquetry aims in their highest measure and their most massive form, so that she can easily do without the thrill of its more subtle variations. Coquetry, then, is a method of bringing about an active sexual attack on the part of the man, to increase or reduce the intensity of that attack at will, and to direct it, without the attacker himself realizing, to where the woman wants it. It is a method of either provoking such glances and words as will make her feel pleasantly tickled and caressed, or of letting things go as far as "rape."[10]

In principle, the sensations of sexual intercourse are the same as any other sensations known to Woman, only in their most intensive form. Woman's ***whole*** *being reveals itself, raised to the highest* ***power****, in sexual intercourse.* That is why the differences between the mother and the prostitute are most pronounced in this area. The mother does not experience sexual intercourse any *less* than the prostitute, but *differently.* The mother's behavior is mainly receptive and accepting, while the prostitute feels and savors the pleasure to the extreme. To the mother (and indeed to every woman, if she becomes pregnant) the man's sperm appears, so to speak, as a *deposit:* the element of absorption and protection is already present to her in the sensation of sexual intercourse, for she is the guardian of life. The prostitute, on the other hand, does not want to feel, as the mother does, that existence itself has been elevated and intensified, when she rises after sexual intercourse: *on the contrary, by engaging in sexual intercourse, she wants to cease to exist as a reality, to be crushed and annihilated, to become nothing and to lose consciousness through lust.* For the mother sexual intercourse is the *beginning of* ***a series,*** while the prostitute wants to *end* and *fade away* in it. The cry of the mother therefore is brief and breaks off suddenly, while that of the prostitute is long drawn-out, because she wants all the life that she possesses to be *concentrated* and *condensed* in that moment. Since this can never happen, the prostitute is *never* satisfied as long as she lives, and could never be satisfied by all the men in the world.

This, then, is a fundamental difference in the nature of the two types of Woman. But every woman equally feels that she is the *object of sexual intercourse,* incessantly and all over her body, everywhere and always, with anything and anybody, without exception, because Woman is exclusively and entirely sexual,

10. The author is in no better position than the reader if the latter is not satisfied by this analysis of coquetry. What the analysis has revealed is rather superficial. The mysterious part of coquetry seems to me more and more to be a peculiar act whereby a woman makes herself the *object* of a man and *links* herself to him *functionally.* In this respect coquetry is quite like the other female aspiration to become the *object of the compassion* of her fellow-humans: *in both cases the subject turns itself into the object, into the sensation of another,* whom it sets up as judge over itself. *Coquetry* is the same specific fusion of the prostitute with things outside her as that represented by the *care* of the mother, which first takes the form of pregnancy, later that of lactation, etc.

and because this sexuality covers her whole body, except that, in the language of physics, it is more *dense* at some points than at others. What is commonly described as sexual intercourse is only a *special case* of the utmost intensity. The prostitute wants *to be subjected to sexual intercourse by everything*—that is why she engages in coquetry even when she is *alone* and *even in front of inanimate objects,* in front of every stream and every tree. The mother is *impregnated* by everything, incessantly and all over her body. *This explains the fact of maternal impression.* The effect of everything that has ever made an impression on a mother persists in proportion to the force of the impression—where the sexual intercourse leading to conception is only the most intensive of these experiences and has a greater influence than all the others—and *all this becomes the father of her child,* the beginning of a *development* the result of which shows later in the child.

That is why fatherhood is a pathetic delusion, for it must always be shared with an infinity of things and human beings, and the *natural, physical* right is the *mother's right.* Some white women who have once had a child by a Negro subsequently often bear a white man children who still carry unmistakable marks of the Negro race. Through the pollination of blossoms with a disparate type of pollen not only the germs but the maternal tissue as well undergoes changes which can only be regarded as an approximation to the forms and colors of that alien pollen. And Lord Morton's mare which, after giving birth to a hybrid by a quagga, was impregnated by an Arab stallion long after, but produced two foals with obvious characteristics of the quagga, is famous.

There has been a great deal of speculation about these cases, and it has been argued that they would be bound to occur much more often if such a process were at all possible. For this so-called "infection" (Weismann has suggested the excellent term *telegony, i.e., conception over a distance,* while Focke spoke about *xeniae,* i.e., gifts brought by guests) to reveal itself clearly, the fulfillment of all the laws of sexual attraction and an exceptionally great sexual affinity between the first father and the mother is required. From the outset there is little likelihood of a meeting of two people in whom sexual affinity is powerful enough to overcome the lack of racial affinity, and yet only when racial difference is present will there be any prospect of recognizing obvious and generally convincing divergences. At the same time a very close family relationship makes it impossible to establish any unambiguous deviations from the type of the father in a child who is supposed to be under the influence of an earlier impregnation. Incidentally, the only explanation of the fierce resistance against the idea of germinal infection is that nobody has been able to accommodate the phenomena within a system.

The theory of telegony has fared no better than the theory of infection. The objections to maternal impression and to telegony would not have become so vociferous, if it had been understood that telegony is simply the most intensive special case of maternal impression, and if it had been recognized that the urogenital tract is not the only, but merely the most effective, *route* to having sexual intercourse with a woman, who may feel *possessed* through a mere *glance* or *word.* A being that has *sexual intercourse* everywhere and with everything can also be impregnated everywhere and by everything: *the mother is conception all over. In her all things acquire life,* because all things make a physiological impression on her and become part of the child that they create. In this sense, in her lowly physical sphere, she can again be compared to the genius.

Things are different with the prostitute. Just as she wants to be annihilated in sexual intercourse, all her other actions also aim at destruction. The mother favors whatever promotes human life and well-being on earth. She holds all debauchery at bay, and she inflames the diligence of her son and the industry of her husband. The hetaira, on the other hand, tries to claim all of man's time and energy *for herself.* But she is not alone in being destined to abuse man, as it were, right from the outset: there is also something in every man that desires this type of woman and that can find no satisfaction by the side of the plainer, always busy mother with her tasteless clothes and her lack of intellectual elegance. Something in him *seeks* pleasure, and he finds it easiest to forget himself with the *fille de joie.* The prostitute represents the principle of recklessness. She does not provide for the future like the mother. She, and not the mother, is the good dancer. She alone demands entertainment and high living. She alone wants to be seen on the promenade and in the night club, at the beach resort and the spa, at the theatre and the concert. She alone always expects new clothes and jewelry, money to blow, luxury instead of comfort, noise instead of quiet. Not for her the armchair in the midst of her grandsons and granddaughters, but the triumphal march through the world on the conquering chariot of the body beautiful.

Thus the prostitute as seductress appears to man directly through the feelings that she arouses in him: she alone, the unchaste woman par excellence, the "sorceress." She is the female "Don Juan," that entity in woman which knows, teaches, and guards the art of love.

But this is linked to things that are even more interesting and lead to even greater depths. The mother wants respectability from Man, not for the sake of an idea, *but because she affirms life on earth.* Just as she herself works, instead of being lazy like the prostitute, and just as she always seems busy preparing the future, so she also appreciates Man's active mentality and does not try to divert him to pleasure. In contrast, the prostitute is most tickled by the idea of a ruthless, roguish man who is averse to work. A man who has been in prison is abhorrent to the mother, and an attraction to the prostitute. There are women who are unhappy if their son does not do well at school, and other women who are actually pleased, even though they pretend the opposite. Whatever is "sound and respectable" appeals to the mother, whatever is "unsound and raffish" appeals to the prostitute. The former abhors a man who drinks, the latter loves him. It would be possible to list many other differences of a similar kind, which are found even among the wealthiest classes. I will only mention as a single example that the streetwalker feels most attracted to those men who are overt criminals: the *pimp* always has a violent, criminal disposition, and he is often also a robber or swindler, if indeed not a murderer.

This suggests—although Woman herself must not be called *anti*-moral, for she is merely amoral—that prostitution has a profound *connection* with the *anti*-moral, while motherhood never carries any such suggestion. Not that the prostitute herself represents the female equivalent of the male criminal. Although she is as work-shy as the male criminal, the existence of a female criminal must not be admitted for the reasons discussed in the previous chapters: women are too low to be criminals. *But that Woman has a relationship* with the anti-moral, with evil, is undeniably felt by man, even if he is not sexually involved with her and cannot be accused of merely fending off a lustful thought of his own by such a projection. Man experiences prostitution right from the outset as something dark, nocturnal, horrifying, uncanny, and its impression weighs more heavily and painfully on him than the impression produced by the mother. The strange analogy between the great hetaira and the great criminal, i.e., the conqueror; the intimate relationship between the small-time prostitute and that paragon of morality, the pimp; the feeling that she evokes in Man and the designs that she has on him; finally, and chiefly, the difference between her way of experiencing sexual intercourse and that of the mother—all these things combine to confirm that view. *Just as the mother represents a life-affirming principle, so the prostitute represents a life-denying one.* But just as the mother's affirmation concerns not the soul but the body, so the prostitute's negation, unlike that of the devil, does not extend to ideas, but only to empirical matters. She wants to be annihilated and to annihilate, she wreaks havoc and she destroys. *Physical life and physical death, so mysteriously joined in sexual intercourse* (see the next chapter), *are distributed between Woman as mother and Woman as prostitute respectively.*

For the time being I can give no more conclusive answer to the question about the significance of motherhood and prostitution. I find myself in a completely dark territory, where no wanderer has set foot so far. The religious imagination of myth may be bold enough to try to illuminate it, but the philosopher is advised not to encroach on metaphysics too soon. Nevertheless, some things need greater emphasis. The anti-moral significance of the phenomenon of prostitution corresponds to the fact that prostitution is restricted to humans. Among animals the female is entirely subject to reproduction, and there are no sterile females. One might even believe that among animals it is the males that prostitute themselves, if one thinks of the peacock fanning out his tail, the shining of the glow-worm, the call of singing birds, or the courtship display of the capercaillie. But these shows of secondary sexual characteristics are mere *exhibitionistic* acts of the male, just as it also happens among humans that rutting men uncover their genitals in front of women as an invitation to sexual intercourse.

However, these acts on the part of animals must be interpreted with caution insofar as it must not be believed that their psychological effect on the female is intended and calculated by the male in advance. They amount to an instinctive *expression* of the male's *own* sexual desire rather than a means of increasing that of the female, an approach to the female *in a state* of sexual arousal, while in *human beings* who expose themselves the idea of arousing the opposite sex is always likely to play a part.[11]

Prostitution, then, is something that occurs only among humans. Animals and plants, which are completely amoral and have no connection of any kind with the anti-moral, know nothing but motherhood. *This is where one of the most profound mysteries of the nature and the origins of* ***human beings*** *lies hidden.* And now I must correct what I said earlier, because the longer I think about it, the more prostitution *seems to be a possibility for* ***all*** *women, just as motherhood, a mere physical fact, is another.* Perhaps prostitution is something that permeates every woman, that tinges the animal mother,[12] and that is ultimately precisely what corresponds in the human woman to those qualities which raise the human man above the male animal. Here, concurrently with the anti-moral element in Man, and not without remarkable connections to it, a factor that completely and fundamentally distinguishes the human female from the animal has been added to the mere motherhood of the animal. The *special* significance that Woman, precisely as *prostitute,* has been able to gain for Man will be discussed toward the end of this investigation. Nevertheless, the origin and the ultimate cause of prostitution may forever remain a profound mystery wrapped in total darkness.

In this broad, but by no means exhaustive study, which has not even touched on all the phenomena, I had no intention whatsoever to set up an ideal of the prostitute, as seems to have been done fairly openly by many gifted writers of recent times. But I *had* to divest the other, the seemingly non-sensual girl of the aura with which every man would dearly like to surround her, and so I had to explain that she is in fact the most motherly creature and that therefore, by definition, virginity is as alien to her as to the prostitute. And even maternal love has been unable to stand up to closer analysis as a moral achievement. Finally, the idea of immaculate conception, and of Goethe's or Dante's pure virgin, contains the truth that the absolute mother would never wish for sexual intercourse as an end in itself, as a matter of lust. Only an illusion could sanctify her for that reason. On the other hand, it is understandable that both motherhood and

11. Nor is the male animal motivated by vanity as a manifestation of the will to value.
12. If one considers how almost all women, given their great freedom today, move about in the streets, how they make all their forms visible by pulling their clothes around them more tightly, and how they use every rainy day for such a purpose, one will not find this an exaggeration.

prostitution, as symbols of profound and mighty mysteries, have been treated with religious veneration.

Having demonstrated the untenability of a view which still tries to defend one particular female type and to claim her as proof of the morality of women in general, I will now set about exploring the reasons why Man will never abandon his attempts to transfigure Woman.

XI Eroticism and Aesthetics

With the exception of a few points still in need of consideration, I have now examined the arguments that are used time and again in an attempt to justify the high esteem in which woman is held and refuted them from the point of view of the critical philosophy on which, for the reasons given, my investigation is based. There is, of course, little hope that the debate will be carried out on such a solid ground. I cannot help thinking of Schopenhauer, whose low opinion of the sex, in his essay "On Women," is still commonly attributed to the fact that a Venetian girl he was walking out with had fallen for the more physically attractive Byron as he was galloping past: as if the worst opinion of women were formed by the man who was least successful, rather than the man who was most successful, with them.

The method of simply describing a person as a misogynist, instead of refuting reasons with reasons, has a great deal in its favor. Hatred never transcends its object, and therefore calling an individual a hater of what he condemns will easily expose him to the suspicion of being insincere, impure, and uncertain, and of trying to compensate for his lack of inner justification through the fervor of his hostility. This kind of answer therefore never fails in its *purpose* of releasing the defenders of women from the obligation to address the question properly. It is the most ingenious and accurate weapon of the enormous majority of men who *never **want** to gain a clear understanding* of Woman.

There are no men who think a great deal about women and still hold them in high esteem. There are only those who despise Woman and those who have never thought about Woman at length or in any depth. In a theoretical controversy it is obviously a bad habit to refer to the psychological motives of one's opponent and to use such a reference instead of proofs. Nor do I wish to embark on a theoretical lecture about the need for both opponents in an objective debate to serve the supra-personal idea of truth and to try to reach a result, irrespective of whether, or how, they both exist as concrete individuals. However, if one party has reached a certain result through a consistently logical argument, while the other simply rejects his conclusions without following his reasoning, then he is surely allowed to take the liberty of clearly confronting the other with the motives of his obstinacy, in order to punish him for the indecency of his refusal to respond to a rigorous deduction. If the other party were conscious of these motives he would weigh them objectively against the reality which conflicts with his wishes. It is only because he was unconscious of them that he was unable to arrive at an objective position in relation to himself. Therefore, after my own rigorously logical and objective deductions, I will now turn the tables and examine the feeling which gives rise to the passionate partisanship of the defenders of women, and the extent to which this is rooted in a sincere or in a dubious mentality.

Emotionally, the objections raised to those who despise women derive, without exception, from the *erotic* relationship of a man with a woman. This relationship is *fundamentally different* from the purely *sexual* one, which accounts for all the interaction between the sexes in the world of animals, and which quantitatively also plays the greatest part among humans. It is totally wrong to say that sexuality and eroticism, the sexual drive and love, are basically one and the same thing, and that the second is a disguise, a refinement, a befogging, a "sublimation" of the first, even though all medical men are likely to swear to this, and even intellects such as Kant and Schopenhauer believed nothing else. Before discussing the reasons for this stark distinction, I would like to say something about these two men. Kant's opinion can carry no weight because he must have known less about either love or the sexual drive than any other man who ever lived in this world. He was so deficient in eroticism that he did not even have the wish to *travel*.[1] Therefore he is too exalted and too pure to take a stand

1. Some readers, whose surprised questions I have had to face, cannot see the connection between erotic desire and the urge to travel which is claimed here. It is clear, however, that this desire must spring from a certain deficiency, a kind of *vague longing*. In attempting a more profound conceptual analysis of this, I am anticipating the theory of eroticism, which will be explained in due course. Just as time is extended into infinity because all temporal existence is finite and human beings strive to escape finiteness, the other mode of sensory experience, space, is thought to be infinite for the same reason. But liberation from time does not consist in an extension of linear time, however great, or indeed infinite, this extension may be, but in the negation of linear time. Eternity is not the longest time, but rather the shortest: it is a total abolition of time. In human beings the discontent with any specific period of time, with temporality, corresponds to a discontent with any specific space. The desire for *eternity* in the first instance is answered in the second by the desire for our true *home*, which we know is not located anywhere, at any concrete point, in the universe, but which we nevertheless continue to seek there, even though we can never find it: this is the origin of the infinity of space, since there is no boundary at which to rest and stop. It is only for this reason that we never stay at any one place but constantly embark on pilgrimages to new territories, just as we overcome every single period of time through our will to live. However, here also our striving is in vain. Space widens into infinity and yet remains space, and all our travels only take us from one restricted place to another.

Human bondage consists in being determined by space no less than by time; both are nothing but the will to escape from functionality, the will to freedom. But no matter how heroic a life of freedom is, even when it takes the form of a striving to overcome space, it must still have a tragic ending if it manifests itself in externals, such as the desire to travel—this love is also as unhappy as it is heroic.

as an authority on this question: his only love, on which he took his revenge, was metaphysics. As for Schopenhauer, he had very little appreciation of a higher kind of eroticism, and only really appreciated sexuality. This can easily be deduced as follows. Schopenhauer's face shows little kindness and a great deal of cruelty (from which he himself must have suffered most terribly: one does not devise an ethic of compassion if one is very compassionate. The most compassionate individuals are those who most resent their own compassion: Kant and Nietzsche). But it may already be indicated at this point that *only* those who have a strong tendency toward *compassion* are capable of a fervent *eroticism.* Those who "couldn't care less" are incapable of love. They are not necessarily satanic natures. On the contrary, they can be highly moral, but they fail to realize what their fellow-humans think or what goes on inside them, and they have no appreciation of a supra-sexual relationship with woman. The same holds for Schopenhauer. He was a man who suffered extremely from the sexual drive, but he never loved. There is no other explanation for the one-sidedness of his famous "Metaphysics of the Love of the Sexes," the most important message of which is that the unconscious ultimate purpose of all *love* is nothing but "the composition of the next generation."

I believe that I can prove this view to be *false.* It is true that no love that is completely devoid of sensuality exists in the world of *experience.* However elevated a human being may be, he is invariably *also* a sensual being. What matters, and what irresistibly demolishes the opposite view, is that every love in itself—even without any ascetic principles joining it—is *hostile* to all those elements in a relationship which drive at sexual intercourse, and which *it actually perceives as its own negation.* Love and desire are two different, mutually exclusive, indeed diametrically opposed states, so much so that at those moments when a person *loves,* the idea of a physical union with the loved one seems completely unthinkable to him. There is no hope entirely without fear, but this does not alter the fact that hope and fear are exact opposites. The same applies to the sexual drive and love. The more erotic an individual is, the less he will be troubled by his sexuality, and vice versa. If there is no adoration entirely free of desire, it does not follow that we can regard the two things as identical. They may at best be *opposite phases* that a more richly endowed individual is able to enter in succession. A man who still claims to love a woman once he actually desires her is either lying or has never known what love is: so great is the difference between love and the sexual drive. That is why it is almost always felt to be hypocritical if somebody talks about love in marriage.

Dull minds that nevertheless continue to cling to the identity of the two, as if obeying a cynical principle, should consider this: sexual attraction grows with physical proximity, while love is strongest when the loved one is absent, and it requires separation, that is, a certain distance, in order to survive. Indeed, where all the journeys to faraway countries have been unable to make true love die, where all the passing of time has been unable to bring *oblivion,* an accidental, involuntary physical contact with the loved woman may awaken the sexual drive and manage to kill love on the spot. And in the case of the more differentiated man, the exceptional individual, the girl whom he desires, and the girl whom he can only love but never desire, surely have different figures, different ways of walking, different characters: *they are two completely different beings.*

Thus there is indeed such a thing as "platonic" love, even if the professors of psychiatry do not think much of it. I would even say that *there is only "platonic"* ***love.*** Whatever else is called love is smut. There is only one love: it is the love for Beatrice, the worship of the Madonna. For sexual intercourse there is the whore of Babylon.

If this were to prove correct, Kant's list of transcendental ideas would need to be extended. Pure, elevated, desireless love, the love of Plato and Bruno, would be a *transcendental idea,* which would not become any less significant as an *idea* just because experience never shows it to be fully realized.

That is the problem of *Tannhäuser.* On the one hand Tannhäuser, on the other hand Wolfram; on the one hand Venus, on the other hand Mary. The fact that two lovers who have found each other for ever—Tristan and Isolde—go to their death instead of the bridal bed proves the existence of something higher, perhaps something metaphysical, in human beings, just as conclusively as the martyrdom of Giordano Bruno does.

> Love pure and holy,
> beckon me onwards to my goal.
> In your celestial beauty
> You have possessed my soul!
> You come to us from heaven,
> I follow from afar:
> Lead me into love's kingdom,
> O shining, blessed star!

[Richard Wagner: *Tannhäuser,* translated by Rodney Blumer (London, 1988), p. 80]

* * *

Who is the object of such a love? The same woman who has been described in this study, the woman without any qualities that can confer value on a being, the woman without the will to a value of her own? Hardly: the woman who is loved like that is a woman who is beautiful beyond measure and as pure as an angel. The question is where that woman's beauty and chastity come from.

There has been a great deal of argument about whether the female sex is really the more beautiful one, and the description of it as the "fair sex" has been disputed even more often. It will be advisable to begin by asking precisely who regards Woman as beautiful and in what sense.

It is well known that Woman is not most beautiful when naked. When reproduced in a work of art, as a statue or a painting, a naked woman may be beautiful. But nobody can consider a naked woman in real life beautiful, if only because the sexual drive makes contemplation without desire, which is the absolutely necessary prerequisite of regarding anything as beautiful, impossible. But even apart from this, a completely naked living woman gives the impression of being unfinished, of reaching for something *outside* herself, and this is incompatible with beauty. A naked woman is more beautiful in her details than as a whole; as a whole she unavoidably awakens a feeling that she is in search of something, and thereby causes the beholder displeasure rather than pleasure. This element of intrinsic purposelessness, of having a purpose *outside* herself, is most evident in a naked woman when she *stands upright;* it is naturally reduced in a recumbent position. Artists portraying the naked woman have probably felt this, and if they depicted her either standing up or floating on air, they never showed her on her own, but always in relation to other figures, from whom she could then try to hide her nakedness with her hand.

But nor is Woman beautiful in every detail, even when she represents the physical type of her sex as completely and as perfectly as possible. The most important element for our theory is her genitals. It has been suggested that all the love a man has for a woman is the detumescence drive, risen to the brain, and Schopenhauer said that "it is only the man whose intellect is clouded by his sexual impulses that could give the name of *the fair sex* to that under-sized, narrow-shouldered, broad-hipped, and short-legged race; *for the whole beauty of the sex is bound up with this impulse*" ["Of Women," in *The Pessimist's Handbook: A Collection of Popular Essays,* translated by T. Bailey Saunders (Lincoln, Nebraska, 1976), p. 205]. If this were true it would have to be the genitals that men love most passionately and find most beautiful about Woman's whole body. I will not mention a few repulsive loudmouths of recent years, whose importunate publicity for the beauty of the female genitals not only proves that this would never be believed without their agitation, but also reveals the insincerity of their arguments, of which they pretend to be convinced. Apart from these, it can be said that no man finds the female *genitals* as such beautiful, but that every man actually finds them *ugly.* In base men sensual desires can be aroused by this particular part of Woman, but these are precisely the men who will perhaps find them very *pleasant,* but never *beautiful.* Therefore the beauty of Woman cannot be merely an effect of the sexual drive; in fact it is the very opposite. Those men who are completely dominated by the sexual drive do not appreciate any beauty in Woman. A proof of this is that they indiscriminately desire every woman they see, merely in response to the vague outlines of her body.

The reason for the phenomena I have described, the ugliness of the female genitals and the unsightliness of her living body *as a whole,* can only be that they offend Man's modesty. The canonic stupidity of our time has made it possible to derive modesty from the fact that we wear clothes and to assume only unnatural urges and hidden lewdness behind the revulsion from female nudity. But a man who has become lewd has ceased to object to nudity, because it no longer strikes him as such. He only desires, and does not love. True love, like true compassion, is modest. There is only one immodest act: a declaration of love that an individual believes to be sincere at the moment of delivering it. This would represent the greatest objective immodesty imaginable. It would be rather like saying: I am longing. The former would be the *idea* of an immodest action, the latter the idea of an immodest speech. Neither is ever realized, because all truth is modest. There is no declaration of love that is not a lie; and just how stupid women really are is shown by how often they believe protestations of love.

Consequently, the standard of what is considered beautiful and what is considered ugly about Woman is to be found in the love of Man, which is always modest. Things here are *not* as they are in *logic,* where truth is the standard of thought and the value of truth is its creator, *nor* as they are in *ethics,* where good is the criterion of what ought to be done, and where the value of the good is vested with the *claim* of directing the will to the good. *Here, in aesthetics, beauty is created by love.* In aesthetics there is no inner norm compelling us to love what is beautiful, and the beautiful does not approach us with the demand that we love it. (*That* is the only reason why there is no supra-individual, exclusively "correct," taste.) *Rather, beauty itself is a projection, or emanation, of the desire to love.* Therefore, the beauty of Woman is not something different from love, not an object to which love is directed. The *beauty of Woman* ***is*** *the love of Man.* Love and beauty are not *two different* facts, but *one and the same.* Just as ugliness derives from hate, beauty derives from love. The fact that beauty has as little to do with the sexual drive as love, and that both love and beauty are alien to desire, expresses the same thing. Beauty is something untouchable, inviolable, which cannot be mixed with other things. It can only be seen as if it were near from a long distance, and it retreats before any approach. The sensual drive, which seeks union with Woman, destroys her beauty. A woman who has been handled and possessed is no longer worshipped by anybody for her beauty.

This leads us to the *second* question: What is the innocence and what is the morality of Woman?

We shall do best to start with some facts that accompany the beginning of every love. As already suggested, physical cleanliness in a man is generally a sign of morality and sincerity; at least those individuals whose bodies are dirty rarely have very pure minds. Now it can be observed that some individuals who generally do not pay much attention to the cleanliness of their bodies wash more often and more thoroughly whenever they make an effort to improve the morality of their character. Likewise, some individuals who have never been clean suddenly develop an inner urge for cleanliness for the duration of a love, and this brief span of time is often the only one in their whole life when they do not look grubby under their shirts. Moving on to the realm of the mind, we see that love, in many individuals, starts with self-accusations and attempts at self-chastisement and atonement. A moral stock-taking begins, and the loved woman seems to radiate an inner purification, even if the man who loves her has never spoken to her and has only seen her a few times from afar. *This* process therefore cannot possibly be rooted in the loved woman herself: she is only too often an immature young girl, only too often a cow, only too often a lascivious flirt, and nobody, except the man who loves her, will normally see any celestial qualities in her. Who can believe that this concrete person is really the object of such a love? Does she not, rather, serve as the *starting point* of an incomparably greater movement of the soul?

Whenever a man loves, he only loves himself. Not his subjectivity, not what he actually represents as a being tainted with every weakness and baseness, every gracelessness and pettiness, but what he wants to be completely and what he ought to be completely, his most personal and most profound intelligible nature, free from any scrap of necessity and from any residue of his earthly nature. In his pursuits in time and space this being is subject to the impurities and limitations of the world of the senses, and he does not exist as a pure, radiant archetype. However deep he may delve into himself, he will find himself turbid and stained, and what he seeks will present itself to him nowhere in white, immaculate purity. And yet there is nothing that he needs more urgently, nothing that he longs for more fervently, than being *himself* and only himself. But as he does not see the one thing he strives for, his goal, shining brightly and standing immovably firm in the depth of his own nature, he must make it easier to emulate by *imagining it outside himself. He projects his ideal of an absolutely valuable being,* which he is unable to isolate within himself, on another human being, and that alone is meant by saying that he *loves* that human being. Only an individual who has done wrong, and who feels that wrong, is capable of this act: that is why a child cannot love. Love represents the highest, never attained, goal of all longing, as if it actually existed somewhere in the world of experience rather than merely in the world of ideas, and, by localizing this goal in a fellow-human, it reveals that in the lover himself the ideal is far from being fulfilled. That is the only reason why love is accompanied by a new awakening of the *striving* for purification, of the desire to reach a goal which is of the highest spiritual nature and which therefore tolerates no physical pollution through any approach to the loved one in *space.* That is also why love is the highest and strongest expression of the will to value, and that is why it reveals, more than anything in the world, the true nature of *human beings,* who are caught between mind and body, between sensuality and morality, and who have a part in both the god and the animal. *A human being is himself, entirely and in every way, only when he loves.*[2] This explains why many people do not begin to believe in their own self and in that of others—the I and the Thou, which long since turned out to be complementary concepts not only in grammar but also in ethics—until they love. It also dispels the mystery of why the *names* of the two persons involved play such an important part in any love affair; why many people need to love before they become aware of their own existence and are overcome by the conviction that they have a soul;[3] why a man in love would on no account wish to soil his loved one through his proximity, but often tries to see her from a distance, in order to reassure himself of her—his—existence; why even many obdurate empiricists, when they love, turn into rapturous mystics, an example of which was supplied by the father of positivism, Auguste Comte himself, whose thought underwent an out-and-out revolution when he met Clotilde de Vaux. Psychologically, *Amo ergo sum* applies not only to the artist, but to the human being as such.

So love, like hate, is a result of a *projection* and not, like friendship, of an *equation.* The prerequisite of friendship is the equal value of both individuals, while love always *posits inequality, unequal value.* To love is to pile on one individual everything that we would like to be but never can be completely, and to make that individual a carrier of all values. The symbol of this supreme perfection is beauty. That is why a lover is so often surprised and even horrified when he realizes that a beautiful woman is not also a moral one, and he accuses nature of deception because "so beautiful a body" can contain "so much depravity." He does not stop to think that the only reason why that woman still seems beautiful to him is that he still loves her: otherwise the incongruity between the external and the internal would no longer hurt him. The common *streetwalker never* seems beautiful, because right from the outset it is impossible to project any value on her. She can only satisfy the taste of an utterly common individual, she is the mistress of the most immoral man, the pimp. Here we *clearly* see a *relationship that is diametrically opposed* to morality. In general, however, Woman's relationship with anything ethical is one of indifference. She is amoral, and therefore, unlike the anti-moral male criminal, whom instinctively nobody loves, or the devil, whom everybody imagines to be ugly, she can provide a foundation for the act of transferring value. Since she neither does good nor commits any sins, nothing in her or about her *resists* such a collocation of the ideal in her person. The beauty of woman is nothing but a morality that has become visible, *but the morality itself is that of man,* which he has transposed in its highest degree and perfection to woman.

2. Not when he *plays* (as Schiller says).

3. Cf. p. 145f.

Since beauty represents nothing if not a renewed *attempt to embody the supreme value,* everything beautiful creates a sense of having found what one seeks, which silences every desire and self-interest. All forms that seem beautiful to a human being are as many attempts on his part to make the supreme value visible through his aesthetic function, which translates moral and intellectual objects into sensual ones. *Beauty is the symbol of perfection in the world of appearances.* That is why beauty is invulnerable, that is why it is static and not dynamic, that is why any *change* in our behavior toward it annuls it and destroys the concept of it. The love of intrinsic value, the longing for perfection, engenders beauty in matter. This is what gives birth to the beauty of nature, which the criminal never perceives, because *nature is created by ethics alone.* This is why nature, always and everywhere, in the largest and smallest of its forms, gives the impression of perfection. Just as the beauty of nature is the nobility of the soul made visible, the laws of nature are the concrete symbols of the moral law, and logic is ethics realized. Just as love, for man, creates a new woman in place of the real one, so art, the eroticism of the cosmos, creates the wealth of forms in the universe out of chaos; and just as there is no natural beauty without form, or without natural laws, there is no art without form, no artistic beauty, that does not obey the rules of art. For natural beauty shows the realization of moral beauty in the same way as the natural laws show the realization of the moral law, and as the purposefulness of nature shows the harmony the archetype of which is enthroned above the mind of man. Indeed, nature, described by the artist as his eternal teacher, *is nothing but the norm which he himself creates for his own work,* and which is not concentrated in a concept, but seen graphically in infinity. To give one example, the propositions of mathematics are music *realized* (and not vice versa), and mathematics is the *true portrayal* of music, transferred from the realm of freedom to the realm of necessity, which makes the *goal* set for musicians a mathematical one. *Thus it is art that creates nature, and not nature that creates art.*

After these hints about art, which, at least in part, are an exposition and further development of the profound ideas of Kant and Schelling (and Schiller, who was influenced by them) I return to my central topic. For the purposes of that topic it has now been established that the belief in the morality of Woman, in other words, the *"introjection" of Man's soul into Woman,* and the beautiful external appearance of Woman are *one and the same fact,* the latter being the visible expression of the former. It is therefore understandable, but still an inversion of the real state of affairs, to talk about a "beautiful soul" in the moral sense, or to follow Shaftesbury and Herbart in subordinating ethics to aesthetics. One may regard τὸ καλόν and τἀγαθόν as being identical, as do Socrates and Antisthenes, but one must not forget that beauty is only a bodily image, in which morality presents itself as a reality, and that aesthetics nevertheless always remains a *creation* of ethics. All these *individual* and temporally *limited* attempts at incarnation are illusory by their very nature, because they only simulate the perfection that is supposed to have been reached. That is why every individual beauty is transient, and any love for woman must endure being refuted by the old woman. The idea of beauty is the idea of nature, which is everlasting, even though every individual beauty and every natural phenomenon perishes. To see perfection itself in what is limited and concrete can only be an illusion, and to see it in the loved woman can only be an error. The love of beauty ought not to be forfeited to Woman to serve as a cover for sexual desire. If all love for specific persons is based on the confusion of those two phenomena, there *can* only be unhappy love. But all love *clings* to this error. It is the most heroic attempt at asserting values where there are none. Only love for infinite value, that is, for the absolute or for God, even if it merely manifested itself in love for the infinite visible beauty of the totality of nature (pantheism), could be described as the transcendental idea of love, if there were such a thing. Love for any individual thing, including a woman, is a fall from the idea, a *transgression*.

Why human beings transgress in this way is already contained in what I have said before. Just as *hate* projects our own bad qualities on our fellow-humans only in order to make that combination appear as a more effective deterrent, and just as the devil was invented only in order to portray all our evil urges *outside* us and to lend us the pride and strength of the fighter, the only purpose of love is to assist us in our fight for the good, which we are not yet strong enough to grasp as an idea *within* us. Therefore both hate and love are forms of cowardice. When we hate we delude ourselves into believing that we are being threatened by somebody else, and we pretend that we are purity itself under attack, instead of admitting to ourselves that we must weed out the evil in ourselves, since it lurks in our own hearts and nowhere else. We construct the evil one in order to have the satisfaction of throwing an inkwell at him. The only reason why the belief in the devil is immoral is that it is an unacceptable method of making our struggle easier, and that it shifts the blame. When we love we transpose the idea of our own *value* into an individual who seems suited to receive it, just as we transfer the idea of our own lack of value when we hate: Satan becomes ugly, the loved woman becomes beautiful. In either case we find it *easier* to get excited about moral values by setting up a contrast and allocating good and evil to *two* different persons. But if any love for individuals, rather than for the idea, is a moral weakness, this must also come to light in the feelings of the lover. Nobody can commit a crime without being made aware of it through a sense of guilt. It is not for nothing that love is the most modest feeling: it has even more reason to be modest than compassion. An individual I pity receives something from me, and in the act of pitying him I give him part of my imagined or real wealth; my help is thus only a visible embodiment of what was already implied in my compassion. If I love an individual, it is *I* who want something, or at least I do not want him to disturb my love through any ugly gestures or base characteristics. Through love I want to find myself, instead of continuing to seek and to strive. From the hand of a fellow-human I want to receive nothing less, and nothing other, than myself. What I want from *him* is *myself*!

Compassion is modest because, by making others appear as my inferiors, it humiliates *them*. Love is modest because, by loving, I place *myself* below others. Love makes the individual most forgetful of his pride, and that is the weakness of which it is ashamed. Therefore compassion is related to love, which is why only those who know compassion know love. And yet the two exclude each other: we cannot love those we pity, and we cannot pity those we love. In compassion I myself am the fixed pole, in love it is the other: the directions, or algebraic signs, of the two affects are diametrically opposed. In compassion I am the giver, in love I am the beggar. Love is the most modest of all requests, *because it begs for the most, the highest.* That is why it turns so promptly into the most brusque, most vindictive pride if a careless or insensitive response of the loved one makes it conscious of what it really begged for.

All eroticism is replete with a sense of guilt. Jealousy reveals the uncertainty of the ground on which love is built. Jealousy is the reverse side of any love, and it brings all its immorality to light. Through jealousy we usurp power over the free will of our fellow-humans. Jealousy is understandable, particularly in the light of the theory that I have developed here, since love localizes *the pure self* of the lover in the loved one, and human beings, as a result of a wrong but not inexplicable conclusion, tend to believe that they have an enduring and ubiquitous claim to their own self. Nevertheless, jealousy reveals that an attempt has been made to achieve through love something that should not have been demanded in that manner: it does so through the simple fact that it is full of fear, and fear, like the cognate sense of shame,[4] always relates to a wrong done in the *past.*

The guilt a human being incurs through love is the wish to *free himself* from the sense of guilt which I described earlier as the prerequisite and precondition of any love. Instead of accepting all the wrong he has done and atoning for it through the rest of his life, he uses love as an attempt to escape from his own guilt, to forget it, and to be happy. Instead of actively realizing the idea of perfection, love tries to show the idea as if it had already been realized. By the most subtle ruse, it pretends that the miracle has happened in the other person, but the fact remains that the lover hopes to achieve his own liberation from evil *without a struggle. This* is the explanation of the profound connection between love and the desire for redemption (Dante, Goethe, Wagner, Ibsen). Love *itself* is only a desire for redemption, and any desire for redemption is immoral (chapter VII, conclusion). Love vaults over time and ignores causality; it tries to achieve

4. The two meet in the concept of *awe* (Latin: *vereri*).

purity suddenly and immediately, without any contribution of its own. That is why, being a miracle from outside instead of within, it is in itself impossible and can never fulfill its purpose, least of all in the case of those individuals who alone would have an immeasurably great capacity for it. It is the most dangerous self-deception, precisely because it seems to advance the struggle for the good most vigorously. Mediocre individuals may be ennobled by it. Those with a more subtle conscience will beware of succumbing to its deception.

The lover seeks his own soul in the loved one. To that extent love is *free* and not subject to the laws of a merely sexual attraction, which were discussed in the first part. The psychic life of woman acquires influence and encourages love when it is most susceptible to idealization, even though the woman's physical charms may be slight and her complementarity limited, and it destroys the possibility of love when it contrasts too blatantly with the "introjection." Nevertheless, despite the opposition between sexuality and eroticism, there is an unmistakable analogy between them. Sexuality uses Woman as a means of obtaining pleasure and a child of the body, eroticism as a means of achieving value and a child of the mind, that is, productivity. It is an infinitely profound, although apparently little understood, saying of Plato's Diotima that love serves not beauty itself, but the creative and productive process inherent in beauty, or the immortality in the mind, in much the same way as the low sexual drive serves the continuing existence of the species. What every father, be it the father of a child of the body or the father of a child of the mind, seeks to find in his child is himself: the concrete realization of his idea of himself, which constitutes the essence of love, is in fact the *child.* That is why the artist so often seeks out woman in order to be able to create the work of art. "We would all choose children of this kind for ourselves, rather than human children. We look with envy at Homer and Hesiod, and the other great poets, and the marvelous progeny they left behind, which have brought them undying fame and memory. . . . In your city, Solon is highly thought of, as the father of your laws, as are many other men in other states, both Greek and foreign. They have published to the world a variety of noble achievements, and created goodness of every kind. There are shrines to such people in honor of their offspring, but none to the producers of ordinary children."

It is not a mere formal analogy, nor an overestimate of a purely accidental linguistic correspondence, if we try to talk about conception and fertility in connection with the mind, about products of the mind, or, as in those words of Plato, about children of the mind in a deeper sense. Just as physical sexuality is an attempt on the part of an organic being to place its own form on an enduring foundation, so every love, basically, is an attempt to create a permanent form of the soul, that is, individuality. This is the bridge that connects the will to achieve eternity for oneself (as one might describe the common factor between sexuality and eroticism) with the child. Both the sexual drive and love are attempts to realize the self. The former seeks to perpetuate the individual through a physical likeness, and the latter to perpetuate individuality through its mental image. But only a man of genius knows a love that is entirely devoid of sensuality, and he alone seeks to beget timeless children in whom the most profound essence of his mind expresses itself.

The parallel can be carried further. It has often been repeated after Novalis that the sexual drive is always akin to cruelty. There is a profound reason for this "association." All that is *born* of woman must *die*. Conception, birth, and death are inseparably linked. Before an untimely death the sexual drive awakens most violently in every being, revealing the desire to reproduce while there is still time. Thus sexual intercourse, not only as a psychological act, but also from the point of view of ethics and natural philosophy, is related to murder: it negates the woman, but also the man; in the ideal case it robs both of consciousness, in order to give life to the child. Those with an ethical outlook will understand that anything that has come into being in this way must perish. But even the highest kind of eroticism, not only the lowest kind of sexuality, never uses Woman as an end in herself, but only as a means to an end, that is, as a way of representing the self of the lover in a pure form: an artist's works are always his own self, which he fixes at various stages, but which he has usually localized beforehand in one woman or another, even if she is merely a woman of his imagination.

However, the real psychology of the loved woman is always *ignored* in the process: as soon as a man *loves* a woman he ceases to *see through* her. Loving a woman is not entering into a relationship of *understanding*, which is the only moral relationship between human beings. One cannot love a human being whom one completely recognizes, because in that case one would be bound to see all the imperfections attached to him as a human being, *whereas love always aims at perfection*. Therefore love for a woman is possible only if this love, instead of taking any notice of her real qualities and considering her own wishes and interests insofar as they run counter to the localization of any higher values in her person, exercises no restraint in *substituting a completely different reality* for the psychic reality of the loved one. A man's attempt to find himself in a woman, rather than simply seeing Woman in a woman, necessarily presupposes a neglect of her empirical person. Such an attempt, therefore, is extremely *cruel* to the woman; and this is the root of the selfishness of all love as well as the selfishness of jealousy, which regards Woman as a completely dependent possession and does not consider her inner life at all.

This is where the parallel between the cruelty of eroticism and the cruelty of sexuality becomes complete. Love is murder. The sexual drive negates woman both as a physical and as a psychic being, and eroticism[5] negates her as a psy-

5. *Suckling* on the part of the mother is *sucking* on the part of the *child*. That is how far the equivalence of motherhood and sexuality goes. The mother *constantly dies* for the child.

chic being. The coarsest kind of sexuality sees Woman only as a device for masturbation or as a bearer of children. The vilest treatment that can be meted out to a woman is to reproach her with her infertility, and the most shameful statute book is one that lists the sterility of the wife as a legal ground for divorce. The higher kind of eroticism, on the other hand, mercilessly demands from Woman that she should satisfy Man's need to adore, and that she should be as easy to love as possible, in order to enable her lover to see his ideal of himself realized in her and to have a child of the mind with her. Thus love is not only anti-logical because it pays no heed to the objective truth of Woman and her real nature, as it deliberately clings to an intellectual illusion and clamors for the deception of reason, but it is also anti-ethical because it tries to force Woman into pretence, delusion, and utter compliance with a command that is alien to her.

Eroticism needs Woman only to make Man's struggle smoother and shorter. It only wants her *to provide the branch on which* ***he*** *can swing himself up to redemption* ***more easily***. Thus Paul Verlaine confesses:

Marie Immaculée, amour essentiel,
Logique de la foi cordiale et vivace,
En vous aimant qu'est-il de bon que je ne fasse,
En vous aimant du seul amour, Porte du Ciel?

And Goethe teaches, perhaps even more clearly, in *Faust:*

Though inviolate, exempted
In thy peerless glory,
Thou mayst listen to their story
Whom sweet sin has tempted.

They were weak, in thee they trust;
Who shall save them now?
Who can break the chains of lust
Who will help but thou?

[*Faust, Part Two,* translated by David Luke (Oxford, 1994), pp. 236–237].

Far be it from me to misjudge the heroic greatness inherent in this highest form of eroticism, the *cult of the Madonna.* How could I close my eyes to the uniqueness of the phenomenon called Dante! The life of this greatest worshipper of the Madonna signals such an immeasurable transfer of value to Woman that even the Dionysian defiance with which he presents this gift, counter to all the reality of Woman, can hardly fail to create an impression of the utmost sublimity. This embodiment of all longing in *one* limited, earthly person—who, moreover, was a girl the poet had seen *once* when he was nine years old, and who may subsequently have turned into a Xanthippe or a lump of fat—implies such an apparent self-abnegation, such a projection of all the values transcending the temporal limitations of the individual on a woman of no intrinsic value, that I hesitate to expose the true nature of the process and to argue against it. *Nevertheless, all eroticism, even the most sublime, remains a threefold immorality:* a selfish intolerance for the real empirical woman, *who is merely used as a means to an end, which is the lover's own improvement,* and who is therefore denied an independent life of her own; further, a felony against the lover himself, a running away from himself, a flight of value to an alien land, a desire for redemption, and therefore a cowardice, a weakness, an indignity, indeed the very opposite of heroism; and thirdly, a fear of the truth, which the lover does not want, because it is an affront to the very intention of his love, and which he cannot bear because it would deprive him of the possibility of a comfortable redemption.

This last immorality is what *prevents* any enlightenment about Woman, because it deliberately *avoids* enlightenment and therefore is likely to foil the recognition of the worthlessness of Woman as such forever. The Madonna is a creation of Man, and nothing corresponds to it in reality. The cult of the Madonna cannot be moral, because it closes its eyes to reality, because the lover of the Madonna lies to himself. The cult of the Madonna of which I speak, the great artist's cult of the Madonna, is a *total* transformation of Woman, which can occur only if the empirical reality of women is completely ignored. The introjection is carried out with exclusive reference to the beautiful body, and it has no use for anything that would stand out in a stark contrast against what that beauty is meant to symbolize.

I have now analyzed the purpose of this re-creation of Woman, or the desire from which love springs, in sufficient detail. It is mainly for the same reason that people refuse to listen to any truth that sounds detrimental to Woman. They prefer to swear by female "modesty," to revel in female "compassion," and to interpret the young girl's lowering of her eyes as an eminently moral phenomenon, instead of abandoning this lie and with it the possibility of using Woman as a means of indulging in their own raptures, and of ceasing to keep this road to their own redemption open.

This, then, is the answer to the question I asked at the beginning, as to why men cling so doggedly to their belief in the virtue of Woman. They persist in making Woman a vessel for the idea of their own perfection and in imagining that this perfection is realized in Woman, in order to make it easier for themselves to realize their children of the mind and their better selves through Woman, whom they have turned into a carrier of the highest value. It is no coincidence that the condition of the lover is so similar to that of the creator. An exceptionally great kindness toward all living things and a disregard for all small concrete values, common to both, are conditions which distinguish both the lover and the productive individual and which always make them appear incomprehensible and ridiculous to the philistine, for whom material trifles are the only reality.

Every great eroticist is a genius and every genius is basically erotic, even though his love for *value,* that is, for *eternity,* for the *universe as a whole,* cannot be accommodated in the body of a woman. *To a certain extent, the relationship between the self and the universe, the relationship between the subject and the object, is a repetition of the relationship between Man and Woman in a higher and wider sphere, or, more accurately, the latter is a special case of the former.* Just as a complex of emotions is transformed into an object, but only by the subject and out of the subject, so the empirical woman is translated into the Woman of eroticism. Just as the drive for knowledge is the longing and love for things in which a human being never finds anything but himself, so the object of love in the narrower sense is only created by the lover, and he always discovers his own deepest self in it. Thus for the lover love is a parabola: it is indeed the focus, but what is conjugated is infinity.

The question that now arises is *who* knows this love, whether *Man alone* is supra-sexual, or whether *Woman* is also capable of the higher kind of love. Let us try to glean a new answer from experience, quite apart from, and uninfluenced by, what I have established so far. Experience shows quite unequivocally that W, with one *seeming* exception, is never anything more than just *sexual.* Women want either sexual intercourse more, or they want a child more (but in any case they want to be married). The "love poetry" of modern women is not only totally unerotic, but extremely sensual; and although it is not long since women began to venture forth with such products, they have been bolder in this respect than men have ever dared to be, and their products are likely to satisfy even the most mouth-watering expectations of the devotees of "reading matter for bachelors." In these products there is not a word about a pure and chaste inclination, which is afraid of soiling the loved one through its own proximity. We find nothing but the most riotous orgies and the wildest lust, so that this literature seems eminently suitable to open our eyes to the thoroughly sexual, and by no means erotic, nature of Woman.

Love alone engenders beauty. Do women have any relationship with beauty? It is not a mere figure of speech if one often hears women say: "O, why should a man be beautiful?" It is no mere flattery, calculated to catch a man by his vanity, if a woman asks him what colors in a dress become her most: she cannot choose them by herself so that they will have an *aesthetic* effect. Even in her attire a woman will at best achieve an arrangement that reveals taste, but no sense of beauty, without the help of a man. If Woman as such had any intrinsic beauty, or if she carried at least an original standard of beauty deep inside her, she would not constantly want to be assured by a man that she *is* beautiful.

Women, then, do not think Man really *beautiful,* and the more they bandy the word about, the more they give away how far they are from having any relationship with the idea of beauty. The most accurate measure of the modesty of an individual is how often he uses the word "beautiful," which is a declaration of love to nature. If *women* longed for beauty they would utter its name less often. But they have no desire for beauty and they can have none, because they are only affected in that way by the socially accepted external appearance of things. Beauty is not what pleases. Although that definition is constantly being put forward, it is utterly wrong, and it runs directly counter to the meaning of the word itself. What pleases is *pretty; beauty* is what *the individual loves.* Prettiness is always general, beauty is always individual. That is why any true recognition of beauty is modest, for it is born of longing, and longing is born of the imperfection and the neediness of the lonely individual. Eros is the son of Poros and Penia, the offspring of the union of wealth and poverty. In order to regard something as beautiful, one needs, as one does for the objectivity of love, an individuality and not only individuation. Mere prettiness is social currency. Beauty is something that one *loves,* prettiness is something that people *fall in love with.* Love is always reaching out beyond itself, it is transcendent, because it stems from the inadequacy of the subject chained to subjectivity. Anybody who thinks that he can detect such a discontent in women is bad at interpreting and making distinctions. W is at most in love, M loves. The claim made by lamenting women that Woman is more capable of true love than Man is stupid and untrue: on the contrary, Woman is *incapable* of true love. Being *in love* resembles not the image of a parabola, as love does, but that of a closed circle, particularly in the case of Woman.

When a man has an individual effect on a woman it is not due to his beauty. Beauty, even if it manifests itself in a man, is appreciated only by a man: Was the conception of beauty, masculine as well as feminine, not obviously created by man? Or is that also supposed to be the result of "oppression"? The only concept that owes its physical content and its lively associations to women, even though it cannot actually stem from women because women have never created a single concept, is that of the "dish" or "hunk," as the slang terms describe it. What these compliments indicate is a strong and highly developed sexuality in Man; for Woman ultimately regards anything that diverts Man from sexuality and procreation—his books and his politics, his science and his art—as her enemy.

Only the sexual aspect of Man, not the asexual or transsexual, has any real effect on Woman, and she demands not beauty but absolute sexual desire from him. *It is never the Apollonian element in Man that makes an impression on her, nor the Dionysian, but always, and to the greatest extent, the element of the faun in him;* never the man, but always "le mâle" (the male animal); it is above all—and a book about Woman as she is cannot keep silent about this—his sexuality in the narrowest sense, *it is his phallus.*[6]

People have either not seen or not wanted to say, or indeed not pictured

6. In a wider sense and for a deeper reason than is perhaps believed, the effect of a man's beard on a woman is psychologically a complete, and only somewhat less intensive, *copy* of the effect of the male member itself. But I cannot develop this any further at present.

quite correctly, what Man's penis psychologically means to Woman, whether she is an adult or even a young virgin, and how it dominates her whole life, although she is often totally unconscious of this. I do not mean to say that a woman thinks a man's penis beautiful, or even just pretty. Rather, it has the same effect on her as the head of Medusa on human beings, or a snake on a bird: it hypnotizes, entrances, fascinates her. She perceives it as that thing for which she does not even have a name: *it is her destiny,* it is what she cannot escape from. The reason why she is so afraid to see Man in the nude, and why she never shows him any desire to do so, is because she feels that she would be lost straightaway. *The phallus is what* ***enslaves*** *Woman absolutely and forever.*

Thus it is the *very* part which thoroughly spoils the look of a man's body, which alone makes a naked man ugly—and which sculptors therefore often cover with an acanthus or fig leaf—that excites women most profoundly and rouses them most powerfully, in particular when it represents the most unpleasant thing of all, in its erect state. And this is the last and most conclusive proof of the fact that what women want from love is not beauty but—something else.

This new experience, which has now been permanently added to my investigation, could have been predicted from what I said earlier. Since logic and ethics are found exclusively in Man it was likely from the outset that women would be on no better terms with aesthetics than with its normative sister sciences. The relationship between aesthetics and logic manifests itself in all the systematic and architectonic aspects of the various philosophies, but also in the demand for rigorous logic in the work of art and, most closely, in the edifice of mathematics and in the musical composition. Just how difficult many people find it to separate aesthetics and ethics has already been mentioned. According to Kant, not only the ethical and logical function, but the aesthetic function also is exercised by the subject in freedom. *But Woman possesses no free will,* and therefore she cannot have the ability to project beauty into space.

This also implies that Woman cannot love. As the precondition of love there must be individuality, not necessarily pure and perfect, but willing to rid itself of any dust and dirt. Eros is an intermediate entity between having and not having. He is no god, but a demon, and he alone corresponds to the position of humankind between mortality and immortality. This was recognized by the greatest thinker, the divine Plato, as he was called by Plotinus (who alone really, that is *inwardly,* ***understood*** him; while many of his commentators and historiographers today understand little more of his teaching than earwigs do of shooting stars). Love, then, is not really a "transcendental idea," for it alone corresponds to the idea of a being that is not purely transcendental and a priori, but also sensual and empirical: *the idea of the human being.*

On the other hand, Woman has no soul, does not long to find a soul, cleansed of all the alien elements adhering to it and in a state of perfection, wherever and whenever that might be. Women have no ideal of Man that would be comparable to the Madonna. Woman does not want the pure, chaste, moral Man, but—somebody else.

I have now proved that Woman *cannot wish* for virtue in Man. If she had a pledge of the idea of perfection within her, if she were in any way an image of God, she would necessarily want man to be holy and divine, just as he wants Woman to be. The fact that this is the last thing she wants again signals that she completely lacks the will to a value of her own, and that she does not imagine such a value somewhere outside herself, as Man prefers to do, in order to make it more easily reachable.

The only mystery that still remains insoluble is why Woman in particular, and not some other being, inspires such idolatry, the only exception being pederasty, where, however, the boy who is the object of the love also becomes a woman. Would the following hypothesis be too bold?

When humankind was created, Man perhaps kept the soul to himself by means of a metaphysical, *extra-temporal* act, although we cannot as yet see why this might have happened. It is this wrong against Woman that he now *atones* for through the pangs of love, *whereby he tries to return to Woman the soul that he stole from her,* or indeed to give her a soul, because he feels guilty of robbing her. For it is precisely in relation to the woman he *loves,* in fact only in relation to her, that he is troubled most by a mysterious sense of guilt. The hopelessness of the attempt to atone for this guilt through such a restitution might then explain why there is no such thing as a *happy love.* This myth would not be a bad subject for a mystery play. But it would go far beyond the limits of a scientific, or even a scientific and philosophical, examination.

I have clarified above what Woman does not want. Now I shall show what she most profoundly wants, and how this, her innermost will, is the direct opposite of the Will of man.

XII The Nature of Woman and Her Purpose in the Universe

Only man and woman together constitute the human being.

—Kant

As my analysis has progressed, my esteem for Woman has sunk lower and lower, and I have been obliged to deny her an increasing number of lofty and noble, great and beautiful qualities. As I am about to take one more step in the same direction in this chapter—in fact the decisive and most extreme step—I hope to avoid any misunderstanding by remarking at this stage, although I shall return to the same point later, that the last thing I wish to do is to support the Asiatic approach to the treatment of women. By now anybody who has carefully followed my earlier discussions of the wrong done to women by sexuality and even by eroticism will have realized that my book does not plead for the harem and that I am on my guard against invalidating the harshness of my judgment by demanding such a problematic punishment.

But it is quite possible to demand *legal equality* for Man and Woman without believing in their *moral* and *intellectual equality.* Nor is it necessarily a contradiction to condemn any barbarism of the male sex against the female sex and yet at the same time to recognize the colossal, cosmic contrast and difference between their natures. There is no man who has not something *supra*sensory, something *good,* in him, and there is no woman of whom the same is really true. ***The most inferior man is still infinitely superior to the most superior woman,*** so much so that it seems hardly permissible to compare and rank them. Nevertheless, nobody has the right to belittle or oppress in any way even the most inferior woman. The fact that the demand for equality before the law is totally *justified* will not shake the conviction of any perceptive judge of human character that the two sexes are the most polar opposites imaginable. The shallow psychological understanding of materialists, empiricists, and positivists (not to mention the profound insights of social theorists into human nature) can again be gleaned from the fact that the champions of the *congenital psychological equality* of Man and Woman have primarily come from those circles and are still recruited from there.

But I hope my standpoint in assessing woman is also safe from being confused with the pedestrian opinions of P. J. Moebius, who deserves praise only for his courageous reaction against the prevailing tide. Woman is not "physiologically feeble-minded." Nor can I share the view that women of outstanding achievement are degenerates. From a *moral* point of view, these women, who are always more masculine than the rest, can only be warmly welcomed and credited with the opposite of degeneration, that is, with having made progress and overcome handicaps. From a *biological* point of view, they are no more and no less degenerate than a feminine man (if he is not judged in ethical terms). Among all the organisms, the intermediate sexual forms are not pathological, but the norm, and therefore their presence is no proof of physical decadence.

Woman's mind is neither deep nor high, neither acute nor direct, but the precise opposite of all this. As far as we can see at present, she has no "mind" at all: woman as a whole is mind*less*, or mind*lessness* itself. But that is not being *feeble-minded* in the customary sense of the word, that is, lacking the simplest practical purchase on everyday life. When it comes to achieving obvious, selfish aims, cunning, calculation, *cleverness* are found much more regularly and constantly in W than in M. A woman is never as stupid as a man can sometimes be.

Has Woman no significance at all? Does she really serve no universal purpose? Has she no vocation and does she fulfill no specific intention in the universe despite all her mindlessness and nothingness? *Does Woman carry out a mission, or is her existence an accident and an absurdity?*

In order to understand the purpose of Woman we must start with a very old and well-known phenomenon, which has never been seriously considered, let alone properly recognized. *It is none other than the phenomenon of* ***matchmaking****, which can lead us to the deepest, most important, insight into the nature of Woman.*

The analysis of matchmaking first reveals the element of *bringing about* and *supporting* a relationship between two people who are capable of entering into a sexual union, whether or not in the form of marriage. This urge to bring two people together *is present in every woman, without exception, from her earliest youth:* little girls already act as go-betweens for their older sisters' lovers. The matchmaking instinct cannot reveal itself fully until a woman has secured her own position, that is, until she has provided for herself through marriage. Nevertheless, it is also present throughout the period between her puberty and her wedding, although it is counteracted by her *envy* of her competitors and her *fear* of their better chances in the struggle for a man, until she has happily conquered her own husband, or he has been brought to heel and trapped by her money, his new relationship with her family, etc. That is the only reason why women do not embark with the greatest enthusiasm on marrying off the daughters and sons of their acquaintances before they themselves are married. And how zealously old women, who are no longer worried about their own sexual satisfaction, engage in matchmaking is so well known that, very unjustly, the old woman has been branded as the *only* real matchmaker.

Women's efforts to make marriages extend to men as well as women, even if they are the mothers of the men concerned, in which case they pursue their aim with particular vigor and persistence. The desire and indeed obsession of every mother is to see her son married, without the slightest regard to his character as an individual—a desire which many have been blind enough to regard as a superhuman quality, that is, as another aspect of maternal love, of which I conceived such a low opinion in a previous chapter. There may be many mothers who are convinced right from the outset that they can only help their son achieve lasting happiness through marriage, even if he is totally unfit for it. But it is certain that many do not believe even this, and that the *strongest motive* is always and everywhere Woman's matchmaking *urge,* her emotional aversion to bachelorhood in men.

At this point it can already be seen that women also *obey a purely instinctive, innate impulse* in trying to marry off *their daughters.* The endless efforts mothers make in order to achieve that purpose do not arise from any logical considerations and only to the smallest degree from material ones; nor do they comply with any explicit or unspoken wishes of their daughter (which their specific choice of a man often contradicts). Given that matchmaking is never restricted to the woman's own daughter but includes all human beings, there can be no question of it being an "unselfish" or "moral" act of *maternal* love, even though most women, if reproached for their matchmaking activities, would surely answer that it is their duty to think in good time of their precious child's future.

A mother marries off her own daughter in exactly the same way as she likes to find a man for any other girl, once she has completed that task within her own family. *It is the same in both cases, it is matchmaking: psychologically, procuring for her own daughter is no different from procuring for somebody else's daughter.* In fact I maintain that no mother has only unpleasant feelings if her daughter is desired and seduced by a stranger, however base his intentions and however despicable his calculations may be.

I have often been able to use the attitude of one sex to certain traits of the other as a helpful criterion for determining which peculiarities are restricted to one sex and which also belong to the other.[1] So far it has always been Woman who had to bear witness to the fact that certain qualities, which many people like to attribute to her, belong exclusively to Man. Now, for once, Man's behavior can demonstrate that matchmaking is genuinely and exclusively feminine. The exceptions are either *very* feminine men, or one particular case which will be discussed in detail later.[2] Every true man treats the marriage-brokering activities of women with revulsion and contempt, even if these concern his own daugh-

1. A list is found in chapter IX, on p. 186f.
2. Chapter XIII.

ter whom he would like to be provided for, and he generally leaves the worries of matchmaking to Woman as her proper province. At the same time it can be seen here most clearly that *man* is not really attracted to the *true psychic* sexual characteristics of Woman, but is actually repelled when he becomes aware of them. While the purely male properties *as such,* and as they really are, *suffice* to attract *Woman,* Man must first transform Woman before he can love her.

However, matchmaking goes far deeper and pervades the nature of Woman to a much larger extent than one might be led to believe by these examples, which only correspond to the common use of the term. First I would like to point out how women sit in the theatre, always wondering *whether,* and *how,* the two lovers will "get each other." *This is also matchmaking,* and does not differ from it, psychologically, by a hair's breadth: *it is the wish for Man and Woman to come together, wherever that may be.* But it goes even further: *reading sensual or obscene poems or novels, and the enormous suspense with which women await the moment of sexual intercourse as they read, is nothing but matchmaking between the two characters of the book,* a tonic excitation by the thought of copulation and a positive evaluation of sexual union. This should not be regarded as a logical and formal analogy, but it should be felt, if possible, how for Woman the two things psychologically ***are** the same.* The mother's excitement on the day of her daughter's wedding is none other than that of a woman reading Prévost or Sudermann's *Regine.* It does happen that men like to read such novels for the purposes of detumescence, but that is something fundamentally *different* from women's way of reading: a man's reading aims at a more vivid imagination of the sexual act; he does not follow every decrease in the distance between the two characters with bated breath right from the outset; and his excitement does not, as in the case of Woman, grow continually and in a very high inverse proportion to that distance. Breathless assent to any reduction of the distance from the goal, disappointment and depression at any frustration of sexual satisfaction, are eminently feminine and unmanly, and they are awakened in Woman equally by any move that may lead to the sexual act, regardless of whether the persons concerned are real or imaginary.

Has nobody ever wondered *why* women so gladly, so "unselfishly," bring other women together with men? The pleasure they derive from this is *the result of a peculiar excitement at the thought of sexual intercourse even between others.*

But even by extending my discussion to the main object of Woman's reading I have not covered the full breadth of matchmaking. When courting couples seek refuge on summer evenings on benches or near the walls of dark parks, a passing woman will always become *curious* and *look* at them, while a man who is obliged to take the same route will turn away in disgust, feeling that his modesty has been offended. Likewise, women passing a courting couple in the street will almost always turn round and follow them with their eyes. This habit of *looking* and *turning back* is matchmaking, as much as anything that I have subsumed under that term so far. If one does not like to see something and does not wish it to happen, one turns away and does not stare at it. Women like to see courting couples and most of all to surprise them as they are kissing and fondling each other, *because women want intercourse* ***as such*** *(and not just for themselves) to take place. One only pays attention to something that one regards in some way as a positive value,* as I showed a long time ago. A woman who sees two lovers always waits for what is to happen, that is, she expects it, anticipates it, hopes for it, and wishes it. I knew a long-married housewife whose maid had once allowed her lover into her room. For a considerable while the housewife listened at the door with great interest, before she went in to give the maid her notice. She had *internally affirmed* the whole process, and then she threw the girl out, passively obeying the traditional concepts of propriety, if not indeed out of unconscious envy. I believe that the latter motive often plays a part and envy contributes its own share to the condemnation of the other woman, who is begrudged those hours that she enjoys on her own.

The idea of sexual intercourse is vividly entertained and never rejected by Woman whenever and in whatever form it takes place[3] (even if it is carried out by animals). She does not repudiate it, she is not disgusted by the disgusting nature of the process, and she does not immediately try to think of something else. The idea takes complete possession of her and continues to exercise her until it is replaced by other ideas of an equally sexual character. This is surely a correct description of a large part of the psychic life of women, which seems to be so mysterious to many. *The desire to be the object of sexual intercourse is the strongest desire of woman, but it is only a* ***special instance*** *of her deepest interest, indeed* ***her only vital interest, which aims at sexual intercourse as such****—her wish that there should be as much sexual intercourse as possible, no matter by whom, where, and when.*

This, more universal, desire may have a stronger leaning either toward the act itself or toward the child. In the first instance a woman is a prostitute and matchmaker, and her aim is to imagine the act. In the second instance she is a mother but does not only wish to be a mother herself: the closer she approaches the type of the absolute mother, the more exclusively she is interested in the creation of the child in *every marriage* that she knows or brings about. The true mother is also the true grandmother (even if she has remained a virgin; think of Jørgen Tesman's incomparable "Aunt Julle" in Ibsen's *Hedda Gabler*). Every complete *mother* labors for the species as a whole, she is the mother of all mankind, and she welcomes *every* pregnancy. The *prostitute* wants other women not to be pregnant but only *prostitutes* like herself.

How women's own sexuality is subordinated to their matchmaking, and can only really be regarded as a special instance of the latter, is clearly revealed

3. The *one* seeming exception that exists will be thoroughly discussed later in this chapter.

by their relationship with married men. Since all women are matchmakers nothing is more repugnant to them than the single status of man, and that is why they all try to marry him off. But once he *is* married they lose a great deal of their interest in him, however much they fancied him beforehand. *Even* if they are already married and therefore do not consider every man primarily as a match for *themselves*—in which case one would expect them to pay no less attention to a married man than to a single one—unfaithful wives hardly ever flirt with another woman's husband, unless they want to lure him away from the latter in order to triumph over her. This finally confirms that women are interested only in matchmaking itself: the reason why they so rarely commit adultery with *married* men is that *these men already satisfy the idea behind matchmaking.* Matchmaking is the most universal property of the human female: the will to become a mother-in-law is even more common than the will to be a mother, the intensity and extent of which is generally much overrated.

The particular emphasis I place here on Woman's *matchmaking* may still not be fully understood, which may make the importance I attribute to it appear exaggerated and the vehemence of my reasoning unwarranted. But it is essential to recognize what all this is about. Matchmaking is that phenomenon which explains the nature of Woman most fully and therefore one must try to analyze and comprehend it, rather than simply noting it and moving on to something else. Certainly, most people know that "every woman likes to do a little matchmaking." *But what really matters is that Woman's* ***essential nature*** *is to be found here and nowhere else.* After careful consideration of the different types of women, and taking account of some more specific classifications in addition to those already put into effect here, I have come to the conclusion that it is *absolutely impossible to predicate as a positive and universal property of Woman anything other than matchmaking, that is, her activities in the service of sexual intercourse* ***as such***. Any definition that tried to restrict Woman's nature to the desire to be the object of sexual intercourse, and that regarded the desire to be raped as the only genuine thing in genuine Woman, would be too *narrow.* Conversely, any definition that suggested that the content of Woman is the child, or the man, or both, would be too *wide.* The most universal and essential nature of Woman is expressed *completely* and *exhaustively by matchmaking, i.e., by her* ***mission in the service of the idea of physical union****. Every woman is a matchmaker,* and this property of Woman, the need ***to be the envoy, the mandatary, of the idea of sexual intercourse****,* is the *only* one that is present in her at *all* ages and that *outlasts even menopause:* an old woman still persists in matchmaking, albeit no longer for herself, but for others. I have already given a reason for the popular image of the old woman as matchmaker. The occupation of the old matchmaker is not something that is *added on.* Rather, it is what now *comes to the fore,* having been *left over* on its own from earlier complications caused by her own desires: a pure devotion to the service of an impure idea.

Here I may be allowed briefly to recapitulate the positive results that my investigation has gradually brought to light about the sexuality of Woman. She proved to be exclusively interested in sexuality, and that not just intermittently but continually: her entire *being,* both physically and psychically, was nothing but sexuality itself. She was caught unawares in the process of feeling engaged in *sexual intercourse* with every single thing, everywhere, over her whole body, and incessantly. And just as Woman's whole body was an annex to her *genitals,* we have now reached the point where the central position of the *idea of sexual intercourse* in her *thinking* manifests itself. *Sexual intercourse is the only thing to which Woman always and everywhere attributes an exclusively* ***positive*** *value: Woman is the bearer of the communal idea as such.* Woman's attribution of the highest value to sexual intercourse is not restricted to any one individual, not even to the individual who attributes value. It concerns *all* beings; it is not individual, but *inter*-individual and *supra*-individual; it is—if I may be forgiven at this point for desecrating the word—***the transcendental*** *function of Woman. For if femininity is matchmaking, femininity is* ***universal sexuality****. Sexual intercourse is Woman's highest value, which she seeks to realize always and everywhere.* ***Her own sexuality is only a limited part of this limitless will.***

Man's utmost elevation of innocence and purity, which would be manifested in the higher kind of virginity that Man desires and demands from Woman as a result of his own erotic need, this exclusively *male* ideal of chastity, is the polar opposite of Woman's striving to create community. This would certainly have been recognized by Man even in the throes of idolatrous erotic illusion, but the intervention of one *further* factor has regularly prevented such a clarification. The time has now come to explain this circumstance, which persistently obstructs the way to Man's understanding of the universal and essential nature of femininity, the most complex problem of Woman, her abysmal *falseness.* However difficult and risky this enterprise may be, it must eventually lead us to *one* ultimate principle which throws a shining light on the deepest root of *both the matchmaking* (in its widest sense, of which a woman's own sexuality is only the most striking special instance) *and the falseness,* which continually *hides*—even from Woman's own eyes—the desire for the sexual act.

* * *

Now everything that may have seemed firmly established is once more called into question. I did not credit women with any self-observation, but there are certainly women who very sharply observe many things that occur inside them. I denied that they have any love of truth, and yet I know women who most scrupulously avoid uttering an untruth. I claimed that a sense of guilt is alien to them, although there are women who bitterly blame themselves even for trivialities, and although we have certain knowledge of penitent women and women who chastise their bodies. I granted modesty to men only, but is the assertion of the modesty of Woman, indeed of the bashfulness that Hamerling saw *only* in woman, not bound to have some foundation in experience which made it possible, indeed easy, to interpret things in that way? And further: can Woman lack religiousness, despite all the *religieuses,* and should she be denied strict moral purity, regardless of all the virtuous women reported by poetry and history? Can Woman be merely sexual and attribute value to sexuality alone, if it is common knowledge that women may be offended by the slightest allusion to sexual matters, that rather than matchmaking they often turn away with resentment and disgust from any place of fornication, that they are often much more indifferent to sexual intercourse than any man, and also loathe it as far as their own person is concerned?

It is probably obvious that all these antinomies revolve round one and the same question, and that the ultimate and final judgment about Woman depends on the answer. Clearly, if a *single* very feminine woman were *internally asexual,* or if she could truly relate to the idea of intrinsic moral value, ***everything*** that I have said about women would immediately and irredeemably lose its universal validity as a psychic characteristic of her sex, and the *entire* case I make in my book would be demolished with one blow. *Those seemingly contradictory phenomena must be explained satisfactorily and it must be shown that their real cause, which is also a ready source of equivocations, corresponds to the* **same** *nature of Woman that I have so far been able to demonstrate everywhere.*

In order to arrive at an understanding of those treacherous contradictions, one must first remember how very easily women are *influenced* or, to put it more accurately, *impressed.* This extraordinary accessibility to alien elements and this ready acceptance of the views of others has not yet been sufficiently recognized in this book. Generally, W clings to M as tightly as a jewel case does to the jewels inside it. *His* views become *her* own, she adopts both his preferences and his most personal dislikes, and she perceives every word that he utters as an exciting *event,* which affects her the more powerfully, the greater his sexual effect is on her. Woman does not perceive this influence of Man as a diversion from the course of her own development. She sees it neither as an alien disruption to be fended off nor as an intrusion into her inner life of which she should try to free herself, and *she is not ashamed of her receptivity.* On the contrary, she feels *happy* only when she can be receptive, and she *demands* that Man *force* her to be so, even in matters of the mind. She only really likes to follow, *and as she waits for a man she is only waiting for the moment when she can be* ***completely passive.***

But women *borrow* their beliefs and their ideas not only from their "own" man (although they would like that best), but also from their fathers and mothers, their uncles and aunts, their brothers and sisters, their near relatives and distant acquaintances, and they are glad if an opinion is *created* for them. Even grown and married women, and not only immature children, copy each other in every respect, *as if that were quite natural,* from a more tasteful dress and hair style, or a striking posture, down to the shops they frequent and the recipes they use for cooking. *Nor* do they feel that by copying each other in this way they are *demeaning* themselves, as they would be bound to feel if they had an individuality intent on following none but its own laws. Thus the theoretical stock behind a woman's thoughts and actions consists mainly of a random collection of received elements, which she seizes all the more avidly and to which she adheres all the more dogmatically, because she never arrives at any conviction of her own by way of an independent and objective contemplation of things. Nor does she ever freely abandon any conviction as a result of a change of perspective, since she never rises above her own ideas and always wants to be taught an opinion, which she can then obstinately continue to hold. That is why women react most intolerantly when a breach of approved customs and traditions occurs, regardless of the content of these institutions. With the women's movement in mind I would like to cite from Herbert Spencer a case of this kind which is particularly amusing if one thinks of the women's movement. As with many Indian tribes of North and South America, among the Dakotas also the men are only interested in hunting and warfare and they have hived off all the low and onerous tasks to their women. The women, rather than feeling in any way oppressed, have gradually become so convinced of the naturalness and legitimacy of this procedure that the greatest affront and worst insult one Dakota woman can inflict on another is to say: "Infamous woman! . . . I have seen your husband carrying wood to his lodge to make the fire. Where was his squaw, that he should be obliged to make a woman of himself?"

This extraordinary propensity of Woman to be determined by factors outside her is in essence identical to her suggestibility, which is much greater and more comprehensive than man's, and both characteristics correspond to the fact that Woman only wishes to play the passive part, and never the active, in the sexual act and the stages leading up to it.[4] *It is the* ***universal*** *passivity of the nature of women that ultimately also makes them accept and adopt Man's valuations, with which they have no original relationship whatsoever.* This ability to be *impregnated* by Man's views, this *penetration* of the intellectual life of Woman by an alien element, this *false* acceptance of morality, which cannot even be called hypocritical because it is not designed to veil anything *anti*-moral, this absorption and use of an imperative that in itself is quite *heteronomous* to Woman, will generally take a smooth and straightforward course *and easily create the most misleading appearance of a higher morality,* as long as Woman herself does not begin to value. Complications can arise only when these traits collide with the *one innate,* genuine, and universally feminine value, *the supreme value that she attributes to sexual intercourse.*

4. The stationary, inert, large egg is sought out by the agile, fast, small spermatozoon.

Woman's affirmation of community as the supreme value is quite unconscious. This affirmation is not opposed, as it is in Man, by its negation, so that the duality, which could lead her to notice things, is lacking. No woman knows, has ever known, or indeed has ever been able to know, what she is doing when she is matchmaking. *Femininity itself is identical with matchmaking,* and Woman would have to step out of herself in order to realize that she is matchmaking. Thus Woman's deepest desire, that which constitutes her very existence, is never recognized by her. Therefore nothing prevents Man's negative valuation of sexuality from completely hiding Woman's positive valuation of it from her own consciousness. *Woman's receptivity goes so far as to make it possible for her to deny her very being, the* ***only*** *really* ***positive*** *thing that she* ***is****.*

But the lie Woman perpetrates in *absorbing* the male social judgments on sexuality, on shamelessness, indeed on the lie itself, and in adopting the male standard for all actions, is a lie of which she never becomes conscious. *She acquires a second nature without the slightest suspicion that it is not her genuine nature.* She takes herself seriously, she believes that she is something and that she believes in something, and she is convinced of the sincerity and authenticity of her moral behavior and judgments: *so deeply ingrained in her is the lie, the* ***organic*** *or—as I would be happiest to say, if it were permitted—the* ***ontological*** *falseness of Woman.*

Wolfram von Eschenbach tells of his hero:

> He lay with such restraint as would not suit many women nowadays, were they so treated. Consider, that to torment a man with desire they offset their modest behavior by dressing provocatively! In the presence of strangers they behave demurely, *but their inward desires clash with their outward show.*

Wolfram hints at the deepest concerns of the female heart clearly enough, but he does not tell everything. In this respect women lie not only to strangers *but also to themselves.* However, one cannot suppress one's own nature, or even the merely physical side of it, in such an artificial and extraneous manner without any consequences. The hygienic punishment for Woman's denial of her true nature is *hysteria.*

Of all the neuroses and psychoses, the *hysterical* phenomena surely present the psychologist with the most attractive task, which is much more difficult and therefore more tempting than a relatively easily understandable *melancholy* or a simple *paranoia.*

Almost all psychiatrists have an irresistible distrust of psychological analyses. They consider any explanation in terms of pathologically altered tissues or intoxication by way of nutrition *a limine* believable, but they are not prepared to accept that psychic factors can have a primary effect. But since it has never been proved that the secondary role must fall to the psychic rather than the physical factors—all references to the "preservation of energy" having been discredited by the most competent physicists themselves—this prejudice can safely be ignored. An enormous amount—indeed there is no reason[5] why not possibly *everything*—may depend on uncovering the "psychic mechanism" of hysteria. That this approach is most probably the right one is also indicated by the fact that the few true insights into hysteria so far have been gained in no other way: I mean the researches linked to the names of Pierre Janet and Oskar Vogt, and in particular J. Breuer and S. Freud. Any further explanation of hysteria must be sought in the direction taken by these men, that is, by reconstructing the *psychological* process that led to the illness.

I believe that the development of hysteria, assuming a "traumatic" *sexual* experience as its most frequent (according to Freud, its *sole*) cause, must schematically be pictured as follows. A woman has had a sexual observation or idea, which she *understood*, either at the time or in retrospect, as relating to herself. Under the influence of a male judgment, which has been forced on her and totally adopted by her, which has become *part of her*, and which exclusively dominates her *waking consciousness*, she *indignantly and unhappily rejects* that observation or idea *as a whole, but, given her nature as Woman, at the same time affirms, desires, and attributes a positive value to it in her deepest unconscious.* This conflict festers and ferments in her, until it bursts out from time to time in a fit. Such a woman shows the more or less typical picture of hysteria, and that is why she feels as if the sexual act, which she *believes* she abhors, but which something in her—her original nature—actually *desires*, were a "foreign body in her consciousness." *The colossal intensity of the desire, which is only heightened by any attempt to suppress it, and the increasingly ferocious and indignant rejection of the thought*—this is the interchange that takes place in the hysterical woman. The *chronic* falseness of Woman becomes *acute*, when it reaches her *main concern*, when she has even absorbed Man's ethically negative valuation of sexuality, and the fact that hysterical women are *most suggestible* by men is well known. ***Hysteria**, then, is the **organic crisis of the organic falseness of Woman**.* I do not deny that there are also hysterical *men*, although these are *relatively rare*, since one of the infinite number of possibilities in the psyche of Man is to become a woman, and consequently to be *hysterical* if the occasion arises. Admittedly, there are also false *men*, but in their case the crisis takes a different course (just as their falseness is always different and never completely *hopeless*): it often leads to *reformation*, albeit often only of a temporary kind.

This insight into the organic falseness of Woman, her inability to see the truth about herself—which alone makes it possible for her to think in a way that is not at all appropriate for her—seems to me in principle to provide a satisfactory resolution of the difficulties presented by the etiology of hysteria. If

5. Apart from the fact that nobody has as yet seen any *tissue* altered by hysteria.

Woman's virtue were genuine she would not be able to suffer from it: she is only atoning for the *lie* against her own constitution, which in reality remains as strong as ever. This said, various details now need to be explained and documented.

Hysteria shows that this falseness, however deep, is not ingrained firmly enough to repress *everything* else. Through education or social interaction, Woman has adopted a whole system of ideas and values that are alien to her, or rather, she has obediently allowed these to influence her throughout. A very powerful impulse is needed to dislodge this great, firmly embedded psychic complex and to reduce Woman to the state of intellectual helplessness, the "abulia," which is so characteristic of hysteria. An immense *fright,* for example, can knock down the whole artificial edifice and turn a woman into a battleground between her unconscious, repressed *nature* and her conscious but, for her, unnatural *mind.* The tug-of-war which now begins explains her extraordinary psychic discontinuity during a hysterical illness, her constant changes of mood, none of which can be captured and held firm, observed, and described, recognized and contested by a dominant core of consciousness. The excessive readiness of hysterical women to be startled is related to this. We may assume that many occurrences, however far removed from the sexual sphere they may *objectively* be, are apperceived by them in sexual terms, but who can tell just *what* they have connected *internally* with that startling external experience of a seemingly quite *a*sexual nature?

The simultaneous existence of so many contradictions in hysterical women has always seemed extremely miraculous. On the one hand they have eminently critical intellects and very sure judgment, they resist hypnosis, etc., etc. On the other hand they can become highly excited by the most trivial things, and it is possible to induce the greatest depths of hypnotic sleep in them. Seen from one angle, they are abnormally chaste: seen from another, they are enormously sensual.

All this is no longer difficult to explain. The thorough honesty, the scrupulous love of truth, the strict avoidance of anything sexual, the considered judgment and the strength of will—*all these are only part of the pseudo-personality* that Woman, *passive as she is, has assumed as a role to play to herself and to the world at large.* Everything that belongs to, and is in line with, her *original* nature constitutes the "split-off person," the "unconscious psyche," which can indulge in obscenities and is so accessible to suggestive influence *at one and the same time.* The facts described as "duplex" and "multiplex personality," "double consciousness" and "double self" have been adduced as one of the strongest arguments against the assumption of the *one* soul. In reality these phenomena give the most significant hint as to why and when we can speak of a soul. *"Splits in the personality" are possible only where there is no personality right from the outset, as in Woman.* All the famous cases described by Janet in his book *L'automatisme psy-*

chologique refer to *women,* and not one to a man. Only Woman—who has no soul and no intelligible self, and who therefore lacks the power to become conscious of everything that is in her and to shed the light of truth on her inner world—can be so duped both by passively allowing herself to be completely infiltrated by an alien consciousness and by following the impulses inherent in the purpose of her own nature, and thus fulfill the precondition of the hysterical states described by Janet. Only she can assume such heavy disguises, portray the *hope* for sexual intercourse as *fear* of the act, *put on an internal mask to deceive herself,* and, as it were, spin an impenetrable cocoon round her real will. Hysteria itself is the bankruptcy of the superficially imposed pseudo-self. At times it almost turns Woman internally into a "tabula rasa," seemingly eradicating all her own drives ("anorexia"), until her true femininity asserts itself and finally prevails against its untruthful denial. If that "nervous shock" or "psychic trauma" is ever really an asexual fright, then that very fact reveals the inner weakness and untenability of the adopted self by chasing and scaring it away and thus creating an opportunity for the eruption of Woman's genuine nature.

The *emergence* of *this* nature is Freud's "counter-will," which the hysterical woman perceives as something alien and which she fends off by taking refuge in her old, but by now brittle and disintegrating, pseudo-self. She tries to repress the "counter-will." Earlier on, the external coercion, which she perceived as a *duty,* relegated her own nature to a level beneath her consciousness, condemning it and putting it in chains. Now, faced with the forces that have been released and are gushing up in her, she once more tries to resort to that system of principles in order to shake off and suppress the unaccustomed temptations, but meanwhile the system has at least lost its exclusive rule.

The "foreign body in the consciousness," the "depraved self," is in reality Woman's very own female nature, while what ***she*** *regards as her true self is precisely the person that she became through the influx of all the* ***alien*** *elements.* The "foreign body" is *sexuality,* which she does not *acknowledge* and which she does not accept as belonging to her, but which she can no longer *banish,* as she was able to do when her drives silently and as if forever retreated before the invasion of morality. Even now the sexual ideas that she has repressed through a supreme effort may "*convert*" into all possible kinds of conditions and produce that protean illness, those leaps from one part of the body to another, that propensity to imitate anything, and that lack of any constancy, which have always made it so difficult to define hysteria by its symptoms. But now no "conversion" completely absorbs the *drive,* which longs to express itself and which is not *exhausted* by any transformation.

Women's incapacity for truth—which for me, basing my arguments as I do on Kant's indeterminism, follows from their lack of a *free will to truth*—is the cause of their *falseness.* Anybody who has had any dealings with women knows how often, *if they are forced to answer a question on the spot,* they will extemporize no matter what false reasons for what they have said or done. It is true that hysterical women most scrupulously (but never without a certain demonstrative deliberateness in front of strangers) try to avoid any untruth: *but this, however paradoxical it may sound, is precisely what constitutes their falseness.* For they do not know that the entire demand for truth has gradually been implanted in them from outside. They have submissively accepted the postulate of morality and therefore, like good slaves, they take every opportunity to demonstrate how faithfully they follow it. It is always suspicious to hear a certain individual being repeatedly described as exceptionally respectable: in that event he has certainly made sure that this is what is generally known about him, and we can bet that in secret he is a scoundrel. It does not enhance our confidence in the authenticity of the morality of hysterics if doctors (naturally in good faith) place such frequent emphasis on the high-mindedness of their patients.

I repeat that hysterics do not consciously dissimulate. They can only realize under the influence of hypnotic suggestion that they have actually been dissimulating, and this alone explains all their "confessions" of play-acting. ***Otherwise** they believe in their own honesty and morality.* Nor are the pains that torture them imaginary. Rather, the fact that they really feel these pains—and that the symptoms do not disappear until Breuer's "catharsis" gradually makes them *conscious* of the true causes of their illness under hypnosis—*proves* the *organic* character of their falseness.

The noisy self-accusations of hysterical women are also nothing but unconscious hypocrisy. A sense of guilt cannot be genuine if it extends *equally* to the smallest and the largest things. If the hysterical self-torturers had the standard of morality within them, and if they had developed this standard out of themselves, they would not be so indiscriminate in their self-accusations and would not blame themselves *equally* for the most trivial omission and for the greatest misdeed.

The decisive sign of the unconscious *falseness* of their self-reproaches is their habit of telling others how bad they themselves are and what sins they have committed, and of asking the others whether they (the hysterics themselves) are not totally depraved creatures. Nobody who is really weighed down by his conscience can talk like that. It is a *delusion,* to which notably Breuer and Freud fell victim, to present hysterics in particular as eminently moral individuals. All that hysterics have done is to allow morality, which was originally alien to them, to take them over from outside more completely than other people. Now they slavishly obey this code, without examining anything independently and reflecting on anything in detail. This can easily create the impression of the greatest moral rigor, and yet it is as immoral as can be, for it is the highest achievable degree of *heteronomy.* Perhaps the moral goal of a *social* ethic, for which a lie can hardly be an offence if it benefits society or the development of the species—in other words, the human ideal of such a *heteronomous* morality—is more closely approached by hysterics than by any other individual. *The hysterical woman is the model of the ethics of success and social ethics,* both genetically, because the moral precepts have really reached her from outside, and practically, because she will most easily seem to act in an altruistic way, given that in her case duties to others are not a special instance of her duty to herself.

The more closely hysterical women believe themselves to be adhering to truth, the more deeply rooted is their falseness. Hysterical women never reflect on themselves. They only want others to think about them and to be *interested* in them. Their utter incapacity for a truth of their own, the truth about themselves, is shown by the fact that they are the best mediums for hypnosis. But whoever allows himself to be hypnotized is committing the most immoral act imaginable. He submits to the most complete slavery: he relinquishes his own will and his own consciousness, so that another individual gains power over him and creates in him whatever consciousness he sees fit to create. Thus hypnosis proves that any *possibility* of truth depends on *wanting* truth, which is the same as wanting oneself: if somebody is given an instruction under hypnosis he will carry it out when awake and, if asked about his reasons, will immediately invent some arbitrary motive for it. Indeed he will try to justify his conduct, not only to others, but even to himself, by any figment of the imagination. Here we have, as it were, an experimental confirmation of Kant's ethics. If a hypnotized person had merely no memory he would be startled by not *knowing* why he is doing something. But he readily invents a new motive, which has nothing at all to do with the true reason why he is carrying out that action. He has renounced his own will, and therefore he no longer has the capacity for truth.

All women can, and want to be, hypnotized, the hysterical ones most easily and most deeply. It is even possible to delete and destroy women's memory of specific events of their lives—for it is the self, the will, that *creates* memory—by simply suggesting that they no longer know anything about them.

Breuer's "abreaction" of psychic conflicts by patients under hypnosis proves conclusively that their sense of guilt was not an original one. Nobody who has ever sincerely felt guilty can be freed from that feeling as easily as hysterics can be by the mere influence of another person's words.

But even this specious imputation that women of a hysterical constitution carry out on themselves loses its validity at the very moment when nature, that is, sexual desire, threatens to prevail against the seeming restraint. What happens to a woman in a hysterical paroxysm is that she keeps assuring herself, even though she no longer quite believes it: this is not something that *I* really want, this is something that *somebody else* wants, something that a *stranger wants from me,* but *I do not want* it. She now relates any move of another person to the demand that she believes to have been made on her from outside, but that really stems from her own nature and fully corresponds to her deepest wishes. That is why women in a hysterical fit are so easily incensed by the smallest thing. Their reaction is always their last untruthful defense against the tremendous eruption of their own constitution: the *attitudes passionnelles* of hysterical women are nothing but this demonstrative rejection of the sexual act, which must be so loud because it is not genuine, and so much noisier than before, because the danger is now greater.[6] The fact that sexual experiences from the time before puberty so often play the greatest part in acute hysteria is therefore easy to understand. The child could relatively easily be influenced by the moral views of others, which did not have to overcome any strong resistance in the child's as yet almost completely dormant sexual desires. But now nature, having been repressed but not defeated, *resumes* the old experience—to which it attributed a *positive* value at the time, even though it did not have the strength to raise it into, and assert it against, waking consciousness—and at last it presents that experience with all its seductive power. Now the true desire can no longer be kept apart from waking consciousness as easily as before, and the crisis ensues. The reason why the hysterical fit itself can take so many different forms and constantly transmute into new symptoms may perhaps simply be that the individual fails to *recognize* the origin of the illness, and rather than *admitting* that a sexual desire is present, and *facing* the fact that this desire emanates from her, attributes it to a second self.

The fundamental mistake of all the medical observers of hysteria is that they have always allowed the hysterics to lie to them, although admittedly the hysterics are also taken in by themselves:[7] *the true and original nature of hysterics is not the self that repulses, but the self that is repulsed,* no matter how hard they pretend both to themselves and to others that the latter is an alien self. If the repulsing self were really their own they would be able to *confront* the impulse as something extraneous to them, to *evaluate* it *consciously* and to *reject* it quite decisively, to *fix* it in intellectual terms and to *recognize* it again. As matters stand, they mask it, because the repulsing self is merely borrowed and they therefore lack the courage to countenance their own desire, which they nevertheless vaguely feel to be the authentic, innate, and only powerful one. That is why that desire cannot remain identical to itself where a subject that is identical to itself is lacking; and as it is threatened with suppression, it leaps, so to speak, from one part of the body to another. For lies have many forms and constantly assume new shapes. This explanation will perhaps be considered a myth, but

6. That is why (according to Janet) women can so easily be transposed into somnambulism from a hysterical fit, because at that moment they are already under the most compelling outside influence.

7. The old view that the hysterical woman dissimulates and tells tall tales *consciously* is quite superficial. The falseness of woman lies entirely in her unconscious. In fact woman is not capable of a real lie, which is the opposite of the possibility of truth.

at least it seems certain that what first appears as contracture, then as hemianesthesia, and then even as paralysis is always one and the same thing. This is the one thing that the hysterical woman refuses to accept as belonging to herself and what, *for that very reason,* gains power over her: for if she attributed it to herself and assessed it, just as she has on all other occasions attributed even the most trivial things to herself, she would somehow find herself both outside and above her experience. The raving and raging of hysterical women against something *that they perceive as an alien will, even though it is their very own,* shows that they are in fact as much the slaves of sexuality as non-hysterical women and that, being equally obsessed by their fate, they possess nothing that transcends it: no timeless, intelligible, *free* self.

Now it will rightly be asked why, if all women are false, not all are hysterical. This question is none other than that of the hysterical constitution. If the theory I have developed here is correct, it must be able to provide an answer that corresponds to reality. According to my theory, the hysterical woman is a woman who has simply accepted the complex of male and social valuations in passive obedience, instead of wishing to give free rein to her sensual nature in the highest possible degree. *The disobedient woman, then, will be the opposite of the hysterical woman.* I do not want to spend a great deal of time on this, because it is really a matter for the specific characterology of Woman. The hysterical woman becomes hysterical as a result of her bondage and she is identical to the mental type of the *maid.* Her opposite, the absolutely unhysterical woman (who, being an idea, does not exist in the world of experience) would be the absolute *termagant.* This in fact is another possible criterion for the classification of all women. The maid serves, the termagant rules.[8] A woman can, and indeed must, be born to be a maid, and many women are very well suited to that occupation, even if they are rich enough never to have to take it up. And there is a sense in which the maid and the termagant always complement each other.[9]

The conclusion from my theory is fully confirmed by experience. The Xanthippe is the woman who really resembles the hysteric least. She takes out her fury (which is probably only rooted in a lack of sexual satisfaction) on others, while the hysterical slave takes it out on herself. The termagant "hates" the others, the maid "hates" "herself." The termagant makes her fellow-humans suffer for anything that troubles her. She weeps just as easily as the maid, but she al-

8. Analogies to this can also be found among men: there are born male servants, and there are also male termagants, e.g., policemen. It is noteworthy that a policeman generally finds a maid as his *sexual* complement.

9. The absolute termagant will never ask her husband what to do, e.g., what to cook, while the hysterical woman is always helpless and needs inspiration from without. I only mention this in order to indicate an extremely banal distinguishing mark of each type.

ways weeps in order to make an impact on others. The slave can also sob alone, *but without ever being lonely*—for loneliness would be identical with morality and as such the precondition of any true community of two or more individuals. The termagant cannot bear being alone, because she must vent her fury on somebody else, while the hysterical woman persecutes herself. The termagant lies openly and impudently, although she does not realize this because she naturally believes herself to be always in the right, and she will even hurl abuse at anybody who may contradict her. The maid meekly obeys the demand for truth, which is equally alien to her nature, and the *falseness* of this docile acquiescence reveals itself in her hysteria, as soon as it conflicts with her own sexual desires. This receptivity and general susceptibility were the reasons why I had to discuss hysteria and the hysterical woman in such detail: it is this type, and not the termagant, that could ultimately have been used as an argument against me.[10]

However, both types, and therefore all women, are characterized by falseness, organic falseness. It is quite incorrect to say that women *lie.* That would presuppose that sometimes they tell the truth. *As if sincerity, pro foro interno et externo,* were not precisely the virtue of which women are *absolutely incapable,* which they find *utterly impossible.* It should be realized *that a woman, throughout her life,* ***is never*** *truthful, even, or* ***precisely*** *when, as with the hysteric, she slavishly follows the demand for truth, which is* ***hetero****nomous to her, and when she therefore* ***does*** *tell the truth in an* ***external*** *sense.*

A woman can laugh, cry, blush, or even look bad at will: the termagant when she wants to do so for some purpose; the maid when this is demanded by an external force, which dominates her without her knowledge. Man clearly lacks even the organic and physiological prerequisites of such falseness.

If the ***truthfulness*** *of this type of woman has been uncovered as* ***the falseness peculiar to her,*** her other much vaunted properties can be expected to be in an equally bad way right from the start. Woman's modesty, her self-observation, her religiousness are singled out for praise. But Woman's modesty is nothing but prudishness, that is, a demonstrative denial of, and defense against, her *own* unchastity. Wherever anything interpreted as modesty is detected in a woman, hysteria is present in exactly the same degree. The totally unhysterical woman, who cannot be influenced at all, that is, the absolute termagant, will not blush even if a man has very good reasons to accuse her of something. She shows the beginnings of hysteria if she blushes under the immediate impact of a man's

10. The maid, not the termagant, is also the woman who, despite chapter XI, might be believed capable of love. However, the love of this woman is only the process of being *intellectually* saturated by the masculinity of a specific man, and therefore it can only occur in the hysteric. It has, and can have, nothing to do with true love. Even Woman's modesty implies such an obsession by one man: this is what makes her inaccessible to all other men.

censure, but she is completely hysterical only if she blushes even when she is alone, with no other person present, because it is only then that she is fully *impregnated* by the other, that is, the male values.

Those women who come close to what has been called sexual anesthesia or frigidity are always hysterical, as I can stress in agreement with the observations of Paul Sollier. Sexual anesthesia is merely *one* of the many hysterical, that is, untrue or false, anesthesias. It is well known, particularly as a result of Oskar Vogt's experiments, that such anesthesias are not a sign of any real lack of sensation, but only of a compulsion that distances and excludes certain sensations from consciousness. If the anesthetized arm of a person under hypnosis is jabbed a given number of times and she has been instructed to call out a number that occurs to her at the same time, she will call out the number of jabs that she was forbidden by a specific order to perceive in her ("somnambulistic") condition. Likewise, sexual frigidity comes about as the consequence of a *command,* that is, of the compelling force of impregnation by an asexual outlook that has been transferred to the receptive woman from her environment. But, like any other anesthesia, this can also be *cancelled* by a sufficiently strong *command* to the contrary.

As with Woman's physical insensitivity to the sexual act, so with her abhorrence of sexuality in general. Such an abhorrence, such an intensive dislike, of anything sexual is really felt by some women, and this might be thought to disprove the idea that matchmaking is universal and identical with femininity. But all those women who can be made ill by surprising a couple in the act of sexual intercourse are hysterical. This actually confirms my theory that matchmaking is the essence of Woman and that her own sexuality is only a specific instance of it. A woman can become hysterical not only if she is subjected to a sexual attack on herself, which she resists *externally* while failing to reject it *internally,* but just as much if she sees any other couple engaging in sexual intercourse. She believes that she is attributing a negative value to their sexual intercourse, while her innate affirmation of it is already breaking through all the received and artificial opinions, all the ideas imprinted and foisted on her, which usually control her perceptions. For even the sexual union of others always makes her feel as if she herself were the object of the intercourse.

Something similar is true of the hysterical "sense of guilt" that I have already criticized. The absolute termagant *never* feels guilty, the slightly hysterical woman only feels guilty in the presence of a man, and the completely hysterical woman feels guilty when faced with the man whom she has totally absorbed. It is no good invoking the religious hypocrites and penitents in order to prove that women can have a sense of guilt. In such cases the extreme forms of self-punishment are precisely what makes them look suspicious. Most of the time the self-chastisement probably only proves that an individual has not risen *above* his deed and has not accepted it by feeling guilty in the first place. Rather, it seems much more an attempt to enforce from without a remorse that is not fully felt internally, and thus to give it the power that it does not have in itself.

What sets this hysterical sense of guilt apart from the truly male way of taking stock of oneself, and how the self-reproaches of the hysterical woman come into being, is very significant and makes a clear distinction necessary. If such a woman happens to perceive that she has in some way transgressed against morality, she will correct herself in accordance with the code, and she will try to obey and become acceptable to it, by striving to replace the immoral desire in herself with the feeling prescribed by the code. The thought that she herself has a deep, inner, and permanent inclination to vice does not occur to her. She is not horrified by it and she does not take stock of herself in order to become clear about it and to sort things out in her own mind, but instead she clings to morality point by point. What takes place here is not a complete transformation under the impact of the idea, but an improvement from point to point, from case to case. In Woman a moral character is produced piecemeal: in Man, if he is good, a moral action arises from a moral character. In the latter instance the whole man is remade through a vow, and what happens is something that can only happen from within, a transition to a mentality which alone can lead to a holiness that is not the holiness of good works. *That is why the morality of Woman is not* ***productive***, which in turn proves that it is immoral, because only ethics can be productive and a creation of something eternal in the human being. That is also why hysterical women have no real genius, even though they are most likely to produce that illusion (St. Theresa). For genius is nothing but a supreme goodness and morality which perceives any limitations as weakness, guilt, imperfection, and cowardice.

There is also a connection between this and the error that women have a religious disposition, which is being repeated parrot-fashion by one person after another. Where the mysticism of Woman goes beyond simple superstition it is *either* a thinly disguised sexuality, as with the many female spiritualists and theosophists—this identification of the loved man with the divinity has been portrayed by various writers, in particular by Maupassant, in whose best novel the wife of Walter, the banker, recognizes Jesus Christ in the features of "Bel-Ami," and after him by Gerhart Hauptmann in *Hannele—or* alternatively she has also adopted her religiousness passively and unconsciously from man and tries to hold on to it the more desperately, the more it is contradicted by her own natural desires. Sometimes the lover becomes the Savior, and sometimes (as has been observed with many nuns) the Savior becomes the lover. All the great female visionaries of history (see part 1, p. 61) were hysterical, and it is not for nothing that the most famous one, St. Theresa, has been called "the patron saint of hysteria." Incidentally, if the religiousness of women were genuine and rooted in their inner being, they could, and indeed should, have shown some religious creativity, but they have never done so in the slightest degree. The reader will understand what I mean if I formulate the real difference between the creed of Man and that of Woman as follows: the religiousness of Man is a supreme faith *in himself,* the religiousness of Woman is a supreme faith *in others.*

This only leaves self-observation, which is often said to be extremely highly developed in hysterical women. However, in this event the observer is still a man who has thoroughly permeated the woman, as is demonstrated by the way self-observation was enforced *under hypnosis* by Vogt, who applied, more widely and precisely, a procedure first used by Freud. The alien influence of man's will *creates a self-observer within the hypnotized woman* by means of a "systematic restriction of the waking state." But even outside hypnotic suggestion, in the healthy life of hysterical women, the observer within them is the man with whom they have been impregnated. Accordingly, women's understanding of human character is also nothing but impregnation with a correctly judged man. During the hysterical paroxysm, their artificial self-observation fades before the violent breakthrough of nature.

Exactly the same is true of the *clairvoyance* of hysterical mediums, which doubtless occurs and which has as little to do with "occult" spiritualism as the hypnotic phenomena. Just as Vogt's patients were perfectly able to observe themselves under the strong will of the hypnotist, so the clairvoyant becomes capable of telepathic feats under the influence of the threatening voice of a man who knows how to force her to do anything, for example obediently reading, blindfolded and from a long distance, some documents in the hands of strangers, as I once had the opportunity to see clearly in Munich. For in Woman the will to the good and the true is not *opposed* by very strong and ineradicable passions, as it is in Man. The male will has more power over Woman than over Man: it can realize in Woman something that in himself is *resisted* by too many things. In *him* an anti-moral and anti-logical element is at work *against* clarification. He never wants knowledge alone, but always something more. *But over Woman Man's will can gain such complete power that he can even endow her with second sight,* so that *she* is freed from all the limitations of the senses.

That is why Woman is more telepathic than Man, why she is more likely to seem sinless than he, and why she can achieve more than he as a *seer,* albeit not before she has become a medium, that is, an object in which *Man*'s will to the good and the true is most easily and completely realized. The Vala can become *knowing,* but not until she has been *overcome* by Wotan. In this she meets him halfway, for the only passion she has is for being forced.

The topic of hysteria, as far as it had to be touched on for the purposes of this investigation, is now exhausted. *Those women who are cited as proof of the morality of Woman are always hysterical,* and the falseness and untruthfulness of their morality consists precisely in their compliance with morality, in their habit of behaving as if the moral law were the law of their own personalities, rather than something that had unceremoniously taken *possession* of them without asking for their consent. The hysterical constitution is a ludicrous mimicry of the male soul, a parody of the freedom of will, which Woman assumes as a pose in front of herself at the same moment as the influence of Man takes the strongest hold of her. Nevertheless, the most outstanding women are hysterical, even though they do not achieve the repression of the compulsive sexuality which raises them above other women by their *own* strength and in a brave struggle against an adversary whom they have brought to a *halt.* But the falseness of hysterical women at least takes *revenge* on them, and to that extent they can be accepted as a *surrogate,* however *adulterated,* of the *tragic,* for which Woman otherwise lacks any capacity.

Woman is *not free:* ultimately, she is always defeated by her desire to be *raped* by Man, both in her own person and in that of others. She is under the spell of the phallus and she irretrievably succumbs to her fate even if she does not achieve a complete sexual union. At most, Woman can reach a vague sense of this captivity, a dark *foreboding* of a destiny hanging *over* her, and since there is no absolute Woman in reality, this can only be the last glimmer of the *free* intelligible subject, the meager residue of innate masculinity, in her, which allows her to *feel* the *necessity,* however faintly, *through the contrast.* It is also *impossible* for Woman to arrive at a clear consciousness of her fate and of the coercion acting on her: *only the free individual* **recognizes** *a fate,* because he is not *included* in the necessity, but at least a part of him—an observer and a fighter—stands outside and above his fate. No further proof of human freedom is needed than the fact that the human individual *has been able to form* the concept of *causality.* Woman usually regards herself as being completely *unbound* precisely because she is *completely* bound, and she does not suffer from passion because she *is* herself nothing but passion. *Only Man* has been able to speak of the "dira necessitas" within him, to conceive of a Moira and a Nemesis, to create the Parcae and the Norns, because he is not only an empirical, *determined* subject, but also an intelligible, *free* one.

But, as I have said, even if a woman begins to have an inkling of her own determined nature, this still cannot be called a clear *consciousness* or an assessment and understanding of it, because that would require the *will* to a self. Rather, she is left with a dark, oppressive feeling, which makes her rear up in despair, but which does not lead her to embark on a determined struggle that holds out the possibility of victory. Women are incapable of overcoming their sexuality, which will always enslave them. We have seen that hysteria is such a helpless attempt on the part of Woman to ward off her sexuality. If her struggle against her own desire were honest and genuine, if she *sincerely wanted* to defeat it, she would be able to do so. But what hysterical women want is hysteria itself: they do not really *try* to be *cured. It is the falseness of this demonstration against slavery that makes it so hopeless.* The most noble specimens of the sex may feel that they are enslaved precisely because they wish to be—remember Hebbel's Judith and Wagner's Kundry—but even this does not give them the strength to resist the coercion in actual fact: at the last moment they will still kiss a man who is violating them, or try to make a man their master if he hesitates to rape them. *It is as if Woman were laboring under a curse.* At some moments she may feel weighed down by it, but she can *never* escape from it, because the burden seems too sweet. Basically, all her screaming and raging is a *fake.* It is precisely when she pretends to be recoiling from her curse with the greatest horror that she wishes to succumb to it most passionately.

* * *

I have not been obliged to withdraw, or even to qualify, any of my numerous earlier statements about Woman's lack of an innate and inalienable relationship with *values.* My arguments have not been overturned even by what people generally call Woman's love, Woman's piety, Woman's modesty, and Woman's virtue, and they have withstood the most powerful onslaught by a whole army of hysterical imitations of all male assets. Woman, that is, the receptive woman who alone matters in this context, is filled, impregnated, and transformed *from her earliest youth* by male *consciousness* and also by the *social climate,* and not merely by the power of the male sperm, which is actually capable of telegony with Woman, and which is certainly the prime cause of the incredible mental changes in all married women. That is why all those properties of the male sex that do not belong to the female sex as such can be so slavishly copied by women, which makes it easier to understand the errors that are rife about the higher morality of Woman.

But this astonishing receptivity of Woman still remains an isolated empirical fact that I have not yet connected to the other positive and negative qualities of Woman, as seems desirable from a theoretical point of view. What has Woman's malleability to do with her matchmaking, and her sexuality with her falseness? *Why is all this found precisely in this combination* ***in Woman****?*

It is also still necessary to explain *why* Woman can absorb everything. What are the causes of that falseness which makes Woman imagine that she really believes what she has only heard from others, that she actually possesses what she has only received from others, and that she truly is what she has only become through others?

In order to answer this I must digress one last time. It may be remembered how I distinguished *recognition among animals,* the psychic equivalent of the general organic capacity for practice, from *human memory,* describing it as something completely different and yet similar. I argued that both represented, as it were, an eternal after-effect of a single impression of limited duration, but that remembrance, as opposed to immediate passive recognition, was characterized by the active reproduction of past events.[11] Later on, I distinguished mere indi-

11. P. 125.

viduation, as a property of all organic matter, from individuality, which was only found in human beings.[12] And finally I had to make a clear distinction between the sexual drive and love, of which again only the first could be attributed to non-humans,[13] even though they were seen to be related to each other, in both their sordid and their sublime manifestations (as efforts aiming at self-perpetuation).

I also repeatedly showed the will to value to be characteristic of humans, while animals only know a striving for lust, and the concept of value is alien to them.[14] There *is* an *analogy* between *lust* and *value, but the two phenomena are completely different.* Lust *is* desired, while value *ought to be* desired, even though they are still mixed up for no acceptable reason, with the result that the greatest confusion continues to reign in both psychology and ethics. But such a muddle has not only occurred between the concept of lust and the concept of value. The distinctions between personality and person, recognition and memory, the sexual drive and love, have fared no better. All these opposites are constantly being lumped together and, what is even more typical, almost always by the same people, with the same theoretical views, and as if with the intention of blurring the difference between humans and animals.

Some other distinctions that I have hardly touched on so far are also usually neglected. The *narrowness of consciousness* is characteristic of animals, while *active attention* is purely human: anybody can see clearly that the two have something in common, but are also different. The same applies to the way *instinct* and *will* are so frequently lumped together. Instinct is common to all living beings, but in humans it is joined by the will, which is free and not a psychological fact, because it underlies all the specific psychological experiences. Incidentally, the fact that instinct and will are almost always regarded as identical is due not only to the influence of Darwin, but almost as much to Arthur Schopenhauer's unclear concept of the will, which makes it appear to belong to a general philosophy of *nature* on the one hand, and to be eminently *ethical* on the other.

I would offer the following table:

Found also in animals, i.e., generally organic:	***Found only*** in humans, i.e., peculiar to the human male:
Individuation	Individuality
Recognition	Memory
Lust	Value
Sexual drive	Love
Narrowness of consciousness	Attention
Instinct	Will

12. P. 134.
13. Pp. 211, 221.
14. Pp. 118f., 151.

It can be seen how in *human beings every* property that belongs to *all* living beings is overlaid by *another,* which in a certain respect is *related to it but is situated at a higher level.* The tendentious, age-old identification of the two columns and, conversely, the constant desire to keep them apart indicates that the members of each column have something in common which links them to each other and which separates them from all the members of the other column. It seems as if in humans a *superstructure* of higher properties had been erected above the correlative lower ones. One could feel reminded of *Indian esoteric Buddhism* and its theory of the *"human life-wave."* It is as though in humans a quality, related to it but belonging to a higher sphere, were *superimposed* on every merely animal property, in the same way as one vibration is added on to another: those low properties are by no means missing in humans, but something else has joined them. What is this new element? How does it differ from, and how does it resemble, the first? My table shows unmistakably that each member of the left-hand column has a similarity to each member of the right-hand column at the same level, and that, on the other hand, all the members of *each* column belong closely together. What is the cause of this strange correspondence in spite of such a profound difference?

The items listed on the left are fundamental properties of all animal and vegetable *life.* All such life is a life of individuals, not of unstructured masses, and it manifests itself in drives that serve to satisfy certain needs, particularly the sexual drive, the aim of which is reproduction. Thus, individuality, will, memory, love can be regarded as properties of a *second* life, which will be related to organic life to a certain extent, and yet differ from it *toto coelo.*

What confronts us here is the profound justification of the idea of an eternal, higher, ***new*** *life, found in the different religions, and particularly in Christianity.* Apart from organic life, humans also have a share in another life, the ζωὴ αἰώνιος of the New Covenant. Just as the former life feeds on earthly nourishment, so the latter requires spiritual sustenance (symbolized by the *Communion*). Just as in the former there is birth and death, the latter also knows a beginning—the *moral rebirth* of the human individual, *"regeneration"*—and an end: the *final* surrender to madness or crime. Just as the former is governed from without by the causal laws of nature, so the latter binds itself from within by normative imperatives. The former is *functional* in a limited way, the latter is *perfect* in its infinite limitless glory.[15]

15. The analogies between the higher and the low life could be multiplied. It was not, as is commonly believed today, merely a superficial and wrong conclusion to posit a perennial and ubiquitous special relationship between *breath* and the human *soul.* Just as the human soul is the microcosm and lives in conjunction with the universe, so breath, in an even more general way than the sensory organs, supplies a connection between every organism and the universe as a whole, and when breath is extinguished, the low life is also at an end. Breath is the principle of earthly life, as the soul is that of eternal life.

The properties listed in the left-hand column are common to all low life: the characteristics in the right-hand column are the corresponding signs of eternal life, heralds of a higher existence, in which human beings, and only human beings, have an additional share. The eternal confusion, and the constantly renewed separation, of the two columns, of the higher and the low life, is the main topic of the entire history of the human mind: *it is the theme of world history.*

This second life may be regarded as something that has developed in human beings in addition to the other, earlier, properties. I will not try to decide this question here. But if we take a more profound view we shall probably not believe that the sensual and visible mortal life is the creator of the higher, spiritual, eternal life, but on the contrary, as suggested in the previous chapter, that the former is a projection of the latter onto the senses, its image in the world of necessity, its *descent* and *reduction* to that world, its *fall from grace.* For nothing but the *last pale reflection* of the higher idea of an eternal life falling on an irritating fly can prevent me killing it. If I have now succeeded in finding a precise expression for the most profound idea of humanity, the idea in which humanity has truly captured its own nature, the idea of *original sin*—given that what loses itself and throws itself away, the essential living being, still to some extent *remains itself* in the process of becoming an empirical reality and an organic vitality, as my table shows—then the question arises as to *why* this sin is committed. And here my investigation is faced with the ultimate problem, the only problem that truly exists, the only problem that no human being has dared to answer, the problem that no human being alive will ever be able to solve. It is the mystery of the world and of life, the urge of the spaceless toward space, the timeless toward time, the spiritual toward matter. It is the relationship between freedom and necessity, the relationship between something and nothing, the relationship between God and the devil. The *dualism* in the world is the incomprehensible thing, the motive force of the *fall from grace,* the primal mystery, the cause and meaning and purpose of the headlong descent from eternal life to a transitory existence, from timelessness to earthly temporality, and the never-ending lapse of the totally innocent into guilt. I can never understand why I committed the original sin, why the free could become unfree and the pure dirty, and why perfection could do wrong.

What can be proved, however, is that neither I nor any other human being will ever understand this. *I can only understand a sin when I have ceased to commit it,* and I cease to commit it the moment I recognize it. That is why I cannot understand life as long as I live, and time is the riddle on which I founder as long as I live in it and continue to posit it.[16] It is only when I have overcome it

16. Cf. chapter V, p. 116. Time can become problematic if one stands to some extent outside it. It can become clear only if one is completely outside it.

that I shall understand it, and therefore only death can teach me the meaning of life. There has never been a moment when I have not longed, *among other things,* for non-existence: How then could I have experienced this longing as an object of contemplation or an object of knowledge? If I had understood a thing I would already be standing outside it, and I cannot comprehend my sinfulness because I am still sinning. The eternal life and the low life do not follow each other but exist *side by side,* and the pre-existence of good is one of value.

Now we can say that *absolute Woman,* who lacks both individuality and will, who has no share in value and in love, is *excluded from the higher, transcendent, metaphysical existence.* The intelligible, hyper-empirical existence of Man is beyond matter, space, and time. In *him* there is more than enough mortality, but also some immortality, and he has the possibility of choosing between them: between the life that ends with earthly death and the life which death alone restores to full purity. The deepest will of Man is directed toward this perfect timeless existence, toward absolute value, and it is the same as the desire for immortality. This at last shows *quite* clearly why Woman has no wish for the continuation of her personal existence: in her there is no trace of the eternal life that Man wants and ought to assert against its cheap copy in the world of the senses. A certain relationship with the idea of the highest value, the idea of the absolute, the idea of *total* freedom—which he does not yet possess, because he is always to some extent *determined,* but which he is able to attain because the spirit has power over nature—a relationship of this kind with the idea as such, or with the divinity, is inherent in every man: his life on earth has separated and detached him from the absolute, but his soul longs to escape from this taint, this *original sin.*

Just as the love between his parents was not a pure love for the idea, but more or less sought an embodiment in the world of the senses, so the son, the result of that love, will want not only the eternal life but also the temporal one, as long as he lives. We are horrified by the idea of death, we resist it, we cling to earthly existence and we prove that we *wanted* to be born when we were born by *still* longing to be born into this world.[17] An individual who completely ceased to be afraid of earthly death would die at that very moment, for he would be left with nothing but the pure will to eternal life, which a human being ought and is able to realize in himself in an autonomous manner: *the eternal life creates itself,* as *all life* does.

But since every man has a relationship with the idea of highest value, without being entirely in possession of it, no man is *happy. Only women are happy.* No

17. That is how, I believe, the chain of the sexual drive, birth, and original sin can be understood. Earlier on (p. 220), I called the specific form in which the low life tries to assert itself a fall from the idea, a transgression. However, the sin is not the *infinite individuality* but the *limited individual.*

man feels happy, because every man has a relationship with freedom and yet is always to some extent in bondage while he is on earth. Only a totally passive being, such as genuine Woman, or a totally active being, the deity, can feel happy. Happiness would be a sense of perfection, which a man can never have, although some women really think that they are perfect. Man always has problems behind him and tasks ahead of him: all problems are rooted in the past, and the land of tasks is the future. For Woman time has no *direction,* no *meaning.* There is no woman who wonders about the purpose of her life, *but the unidirectionality of time is a manifestation of the fact that this life should and can acquire a meaning.*

Happiness, for Man, could only be total, pure *activity,* complete freedom, not even a small degree of bondage, let alone the highest: for the further he departs from the idea of freedom, the more guilty he becomes. To him, life on earth is *suffering* and *must* be so, if only because human beings in the process of receiving sensations are *passive,* because they are affected by external factors, and because experience needs not only form but also matter. There is no human being who does not need any sensory perception. Even a genius would be nothing without it, despite the fact that he fills and penetrates his perceptions with the contents of his self more powerfully and more rapidly than others, and requires no full induction in order to recognize the idea of a thing. *Receptivity* cannot be abolished by any Fichtean surprise action: in his sensations the human individual is *passive,* and his spontaneity, his freedom, can only assert itself in his *judgment* and in the form of that universal *memory* which is able to reproduce all his experiences as prompted by his *will.* To man, love and intellectual creation offer approximations to the highest level of spontaneity, where total freedom already appears to be a reality. That is why they are most likely to give him an intimation of what *happiness* is and, if only momentarily, to make him feel, trembling with excitement, that it is hovering close above him.

To Woman, who can never be profoundly unhappy, happiness is really an empty word *for that very reason.* The concept of happiness was created by Man—the *unhappy* man—even though it is never adequately realized in him. Women never shrink from showing their unhappiness to others, because it is no genuine unhappiness backed by guilt, least of all the guilt of life on earth as original sin.

The final, absolute, proof of the total worthlessness of Woman's life, of its total lack of higher *being,* is supplied by the way women commit suicide. A woman probably always commits suicide thinking of other people, wondering what they would think, how they would pity her, how sorry—or how annoyed—they would be. This is not to suggest that Woman, at the moment of killing herself, is not firmly convinced of her unhappiness, which in her view is *always un*deserved. On the contrary, before her suicide she pities herself most intensively, but in fact, following the pattern of self-pity that I explained earlier, she merely joins the others in weeping over the object of their compassion, and she completely ceases to be a subject. How could a woman regard her unhappiness *as being her own,* if she is incapable of having a destiny? The terrible fact, which is decisive for the *emptiness and nothingness of women,* is that even *in the face of death* they fail to confront the *problem* of life, *their* life, because no higher life of the personality has ever wanted to be realized in them.

Now it is possible to answer the question which was formulated as the central problem at the beginning of this second part, the question about what it means to be Man and to be Woman. Women have no existence and no essence, they ***are*** *not and they are* ***nothing. One IS Man or one IS Woman, depending on whether or not one IS somebody.***

Woman has no share in ontological reality, and that is why she has no relationship with the thing-in-itself, which, in any more profound view, is identical with the absolute, with the idea or with God. Man in his actuality, the genius, believes in the thing-in-itself. For him it is either the absolute embodied in his supreme concept of essential value, in which case he is a philosopher, or it is the miraculous fairy-tale world of his dreams, the realm of absolute beauty, in which case he is an artist. *But both things mean the same.*

Woman has no relationship with the idea, which she neither affirms nor denies. She is neither moral nor anti-moral. Mathematically speaking, she has *no algebraic sign.* She has no direction and is neither good nor bad, neither an angel nor a devil. She is not even selfish (which is why it has been possible for her to be regarded as altruistic). She is *amoral,* just as she is *alogical.* But all being is moral and logical. *Therefore Woman* ***is*** *not.*

Woman is false. Animals have as little metaphysical reality as genuine Woman, but they do not speak and therefore do not lie. To be able to speak the truth one must *be* something, for truth is about *being,* and nobody who is not something himself can have a *relationship* with being. Man wants the whole truth, that is, he *only* wants *to* ***be.*** Ultimately, the urge for knowledge is *identical* to the desire for immortality. However, an individual who makes a statement about a fact without having the courage to assert a being, to whom the external form of judgment is given without the internal one, who is as untruthful as Woman, *must* necessarily *always* be lying. *That is why Woman always lies, even when objectively she is telling the truth.*

Woman is a matchmaker. The units of the low form of life are individuals, organisms. The units of the higher form of life are individualities, souls, monads, or "meta-organisms," to use Hellenbach's apt term. Every monad is different from every other monad, and as separate from it as any two things can ever be. Monads have no windows: instead they have the whole universe in themselves. Man as the monad, whether potential or actual, that is, individuality endowed with genius, wants difference and separation, individuation and divergence, both for himself and *everywhere else:* naïve monism is exclusively female. Every monad is a closed unit, a whole; but it also treats the self of another as such a perfect totality, on which it does not encroach. Man ***has boundaries,*** and he *affirms* and *wants* boundaries. Woman, who knows no solitude, is unable to notice and to understand, to respect, or to honor the solitude of her fellow-humans, nor can she accept it without breaking into it. Since she knows no solitude, she knows no company, but only an indistinct state of fusion with others. Because Woman has no I, she perceives no Thou, and *consequently she believes that I and Thou belong* **together** *as a* **couple**, *as an indistinguishable unity: that is why Woman is capable of bringing others together, that is why she is capable of matchmaking.* The goal of her love is the same as the goal of her compassion: the community, the fusion of everything.[18]

Woman knows no *boundaries* to her self, which could be penetrated and which she would need to guard. This accounts in the first instance for the main difference between male and female *friendship.* Every *male* friendship is an attempt to join together under the sign of one and the same *idea,* which each of the friends pursues separately and on his own, but nonetheless united with the other. *Female* "friendship" means *sticking* together and that, as must be emphasized, with *matchmaking* in mind. For matchmaking is the only possible foundation of a close and sincere interaction between women, assuming that they are not looking for female company merely in pursuit of gossip or some material interests.[19] If one of two girls or women is generally regarded as much more beautiful, the ugly one will derive *a certain sexual satisfaction* from the admiration bestowed on the more beautiful one. The prime condition of any friendship between women, then, is the impossibility of any rivalry between them, and there is no woman who does not immediately compare her body with that of every other woman she meets. The ugly woman can admire the more beautiful woman only if the *in*equality between them is very great and any competition on her part is *hopeless,* in which case, without either of them being in the least conscious of it, the more beautiful woman provides the most direct route to *her own*

18. Individuality is always the enemy of the community, and where it manifests itself most visibly, as in a man of genius, this is particularly noticeable in relation to sexuality. There can be *no other explanation* why all men of genius, if their sexuality is sufficiently developed, suffer without exception from the most powerful sexual perversions (either "sadism" or, in the case of the greatest, "masochism"). This certainly applies to all exceptional individuals, whether they are able to express it in a veiled form, as do artists, or whether they are obliged to keep silent about an infinity of things, as are philosophers, which causes them to be regarded as dry and passionless. What all those inclinations have in common is an instinctive *avoidance* of complete physical union, a *desire to bypass sexual intercourse.* For there will, there can, never be a truly exceptional individual who would see sexual intercourse as more than a bestial, filthy, disgusting act, let alone idolize it as the most profound, most sacred mystery.
19. Male friendship shrinks from tearing down walls between friends. Female friends always *demand* confidences *on account* of their friendship.

sexual satisfaction: in fact, she feels, so to speak, that it is herself who is engaged in sexual intercourse ***in the person*** of the other.[20] The totally *impersonal* life of women, as well as the supra-individual purpose of their sexuality—matchmaking as their fundamental characteristic—is clearly reflected by this fact. Women act as matchmakers for themselves as they do for others, and they act as matchmakers for themselves *in* the others. *The least that even the ugliest woman demands, and that gives her a certain satisfaction, is for any one member of her sex to be admired and desired.*

There is a close connection between this total fusion in the life of Woman and the fact that women are *never really jealous.* However vile jealousy and vindictiveness may be, they nevertheless have a certain greatness, of which women are as *in*capable as they are of any greatness, whether good or evil. Jealousy implies a desperate claim to a supposed right, and the concept of right transcends women. But the most important reason why a woman can never be completely jealous of any particular man is somewhat different. If a man, even one with whom she is madly in love, embraced and possessed another woman next door to her, the thought of this would sexually arouse her to such a degree that there would be no room left in her for jealousy. If a man became aware of such a scene he would be revolted and repelled by it and he would find it nauseating to remain in the vicinity. A woman is either almost frantic with internal affirmation of the whole process, or she becomes hysterical if she refuses to admit to herself that in her deepest being she has also *desired* this union.

Furthermore, a man is never completely overpowered by the thought of the sexual intercourse of others. He stands outside and above such an experience, which, strictly, is not even an experience, as far as he is concerned. A woman, on the other hand, follows the event almost *passively,* with *feverish excitement* and as if *entranced* by the thought of what is happening so close to her.[21]

Man's interest in his fellow-humans, who are mysteries to him, often extends to their sexual lives, but the kind of *curiosity* which, so to speak, *forces* others into sexuality is peculiar to women and is practiced by them quite generally, on women and men in equal measure. What interests a woman about other individuals is first and foremost their *love affairs,* and intellectually she ceases to be intrigued and fascinated by them once she has become clear about this particular point.

20. In such cases the prettier woman treats the less good-looking or less noticed one with a mixture of pity and contempt, which, in addition to her need for a foil to offset her own attractions, encourages her to keep up such relationships for long periods.

21. And here is also the difference between the matchmaking of Woman and the matchmaking of the criminal. The criminal too can be a matchmaker, but for him matchmaking is only a special case. He supports crime and sensuality, wherever they may occur. He is pleased about any murder, any death and disaster, any conflagration and destruction: *for he is everywhere in search of a justification for his own surrender to non-being, to the low life.*

All this again clearly suggests that femininity and matchmaking are identical, and a purely *immanent* examination of the topic would have to end with this statement. However, I set out to do more than that, and I think I have already given a hint of how Woman as something positive, as matchmaker, is connected with Woman as something negative, as a being totally devoid of the higher life of a monad. Woman realizes only one idea, of which therefore she can never become conscious, and which is the diametrical opposite of the idea of the soul. Whether she is a mother who longs for the marriage bed or a prostitute who prefers the bacchanal, whether she wants to found a family with a man or whether she seeks the tangled masses of the *Venusberg,* she always acts *in accordance with the idea of community,* the idea that goes furthest in obliterating the *boundaries* of the individuals by *mixing them all together.*

So one thing here makes the other possible: only a being without individuality, without boundaries, can be the emissary of sexual intercourse. It was not without good reason that I presented my arguments at such length, as has certainly never been done in any treatment of this subject or in any other characterological study. The topic is so fertile because here the connection between all the higher life on the one hand and all the low life on the other must reveal itself. Here every psychology and every philosophy finds an excellent touchstone by which to test itself. That alone is why the problem of Man and Woman remains the most interesting chapter of characterology, and why I chose it as the object of such a comprehensive and wide-ranging investigation.

At this point in the discussion some readers will no doubt openly ask a question which they may so far only have contemplated as a possible objection in their own minds: whether, seen in this light, women are in fact human beings, or whether, according to the author's theory, they would not really have to be classified as animals or plants. It will be pointed out that, in the author's view, women are no less deficient in any supra-sensory existence than animals or plants, and that their share in eternal life is as small as that of any other organisms which have neither the desire for, nor the possibility of, personal continuation after death. Both kinds are equally bereft of any metaphysical reality, and none, neither women, nor animals, nor plants, really *exist*—all are mere appearance and have none of the thing-in-itself about them.

The human individual, according to the deepest understanding of his nature, is a mirror of the universe, the microcosm, but Woman has absolutely no genius and does not live in a profound nexus with the universe.

In a beautiful passage of Ibsen's *Little Eyolf,* the woman speaks to the man:

Rita: We are creatures of the earth, after all.
Allmers: We have some kinship with sea and heavens too, Rita.
Rita: You, perhaps. Not I.

This passage tersely reveals the realization of the dramatist (who, astonishingly, is so often taken to be a worshipper of Woman) that Woman has no relationship with the idea of infinity, with the deity, because she has no soul. According to the Indians, the *Brahman* is reached only through the *Âtman*. Woman is not a microcosm, she was not created in the image of God. Is she, then, still a human being? Or is she an animal? Or a plant?

Anatomists must think these questions rather ridiculous and they will regard a standpoint that can throw up such problems as erroneous right from the outset. For them, Woman is *homo sapiens*, clearly distinguished from all the other species, and assigned to the human male just as the females of every other genus and species are assigned to their males. And the philosopher certainly must not say: What do I care about the anatomists? Although he can expect very little understanding of what moves him from that quarter, he is talking here about anthropological matters, and if he finds the truth, the morphological facts must also have been given their due.

Indeed! Women are closer to nature in their unconscious than Man. The flowers are their sisters, and they are less far removed from animals than Man, as is proved by the fact that they are surely more strongly inclined to bestiality than he is (remember the myths of Leda and Pasiphae; and women's relationship with their lapdog is also much more sensual than is generally believed).[22] Nevertheless, women are human beings. Even W, whom we imagine to be without a trace of intelligible self, is at least the complement of M, and the fact that the human woman is the specific *sexual* and *erotic* complement of the human man—while it is not the moral phenomenon that the advocates of marriage blather about—has an enormous significance for the problem of Woman. Furthermore, animals are mere individuals, while women are persons (although not personalities). Women are endowed with the external form of judgment albeit it not with its internal form, with language albeit not with coherent speech, with a certain memory albeit not with a continuous and homogeneous consciousness of themselves. For everything in Man they have peculiar *surrogates*, which persist in promoting the confusions to which the devotees of femininity are so prone. The result is a certain *amphisexuality* of many terms (vanity, shame, love, imagination, fear, sensitivity, etc.) which have a male as well as a female meaning.

This seems to raise anew the question about the *ultimate nature of the difference between the sexes.* The roles played by the male and the female principle in the animal and vegetable kingdom will not be considered here: we are only concerned with human beings. That such principles of masculinity and femininity must be treated as theoretical concepts, and not as metaphysical ideas, has been

22. This must not be confused with the ability to embrace the whole of nature, which belongs to Man because he is *not only* nature. Women stand in nature as a *part* of nature, and they are causally interrelated with all other parts: they are much more *dependent* than Man on the moon and the sea, the weather and thunderstorms, electricity and magnetism.

demonstrated by my entire examination right from the outset. The further course of the investigation has shown the enormous differences that exist between male and female, far beyond the merely physiological and sexual difference, without doubt at least in *humans.* Therefore the view that the dualism of the sexes is nothing more than a mechanism for the distribution of different functions to different beings resulting in a physiological division of labor—a view which I believe owes its exceptional popularity to the zoologist Milne-Edwards—appears totally unacceptable, and nothing more needs to be said about its superficiality, which verges on the ridiculous, and its intellectual poverty. Darwinism has been particularly favorable to the popularization of this view, and there has even been a fairly general assumption that the sexually differentiated organisms evolved from an earlier stage of sexual uniformity, as a result of the victory of those beings that had thus shed some of their functions over the more primitive, overburdened, asexual, or bisexual species. However, Gustav Theodor Fechner, long before the modern churchyard beetles of Darwin, demonstrated with irrefutable arguments that such an "origin of sex" by means of the "advantages of the division of labor," or "load-shedding in the struggle for existence," is a *totally unworkable proposition.*

The purpose of Man and Woman cannot be explored in isolation: their significance can only be recognized in comparison with, and determined in contrast to, each other. The key to the nature of *both* must be found *in their relationship with each other.* I already referred to this briefly when I tried to explain the nature of eroticism. *The relationship between Man and Woman is none other than the relationship between* ***subject*** *and* ***object. Woman seeks her fulfillment as an object.*** She is the *chattel,* either of the man or of the child, and all she wants to be taken for is a *chattel,* despite all her attempts to hide this. There is no surer way to misunderstand what Woman really wants than by being interested in what goes on inside her and sympathizing with her emotions and her hopes, her experiences and her inner nature. Woman *does not want* to be treated as a *subject. All she ever wants—and that is what makes her Woman—is to remain passive and to feel a will directed toward her. She does not want to be treated either timidly or gently. Nor does she want to be* ***respected****. Rather, she needs to be desired merely as a body and to be the sole possession of another. Just as a mere sensation only assumes reality when it becomes a concept—that is, an object—so Woman only acquires her existence, and a sense of her existence, when she is elevated by a man or a child—a subject—to his* ***object****, and thus has an existence bestowed on her.*

The epistemological contrast between the subject and the object corresponds to the ontological opposition between ***form*** and ***matter***. The latter opposition is only a translation of the former contrast from the transcendental into the transcendent, from the critique of experience into metaphysics. Matter, that which is absolutely unindividualized, that which can assume any form but has no definite and permanent qualities of its own, lacks essence in the same degree as mere sensation, the raw material of experience, in its turn lacks existence. While therefore the contrast between subject and object is a contrast of existence (since sensation only acquires reality as an object facing the subject) the contrast of form and matter is a difference of essence (unformed matter is absolutely devoid of qualities). That is why Plato was able to describe materiality—the malleable mass, the in itself formless ἄπειρον, the kneadable dough of ἐκμαγεῖον, that which receives the form, its place, its χώρα, the ἐν ω, the eternal second and eternal other, the θάτερον—also ***as non-being***, as μὴ ὄν. Those who, often enough, make it appear as if this most profound thinker believed that non-being is space drag him down to the lowest level of superficiality. It is certain that no great philosopher will attribute a metaphysical existence to space, but nor can he regard it as non-being in itself. To take empty space to be "air" or "nothing" is characteristic of the naïve, impudent windbag. It is only on deeper reflection that space acquires some reality and becomes a problem. Plato's non-being is precisely what to the philistine appears as the most real thing imaginable, as the sum total of existential values: it is none other than matter.

Plato himself described his conception of that which is capable of assuming any form whatsoever as the *mother* and *wet-nurse* of all becoming, while Aristotle, discussing the *act of procreation* in his natural philosophy, allocated the *material* role to the female principle and the *formative* role to the male principle. Can I then be accused of an arbitrary act of blatant discontinuity if, following and extending the views of both Plato and Aristotle, I suggest that *the significance of Woman for humankind consists in her being the representative of matter*? Man, the microcosm, is composed of both the higher and the lower life, of what exists in a metaphysical sense and what has no essence, of form and matter: *Woman is nothing, she is merely matter.*

This insight finally provides the keystone of the edifice. From here everything that has still been uncertain becomes clear and forms a coherent, rounded whole. The sexual desire of Woman aims at *physical contact*, it is only the *contrectation drive* and not the *detumescence drive.*[23] Accordingly, her most refined sense, in fact the only one that is more highly developed in her than in man, is the *sense of touch.*[24] The eye and the ear lead to the boundless and convey intimations of infinity. The sense of touch requires the closest physical proximity in order to function. One mingles with what one touches: the sense of touch is the eminently dirty one and seems almost expressly designed for a being that was made for physical proximity. What it communicates is a sensation of resistance, a perception of the palpable; and, as Kant has shown, *matter* is precisely what we can only describe as a space-filler that offers a certain *resistance* to anything that tries

23. Cf. p. 77.
24. Cf. p. 89.

to penetrate it. The experience of "obstacles" has created both the psychological (not the epistemological) concept of the *thing* and the excessive degree of reality that most people attribute to the data supplied by the sense of touch, which they regard as more solid, "primary" qualities of the world of experience. But the reason why Man emotionally never *entirely ceases* to look upon matter as the true reality is none other than the last remnant of femininity still clinging to him. If there were such a thing as absolute Man, he would not attribute any kind of being to matter, even psychologically (and not just logically).

Man is form, Woman is matter. If this is correct it must also find its expression in the interrelation between their individual psychic experiences. The structured contents of Man's psychic life, as opposed to the inarticulate and chaotic imagination of Woman, which I discussed a long time ago, proclaim the same contrast between form and matter. Matter wants to be formed: *that is why Woman demands* from Man a *clarification* of her confused ideas, an *interpretation of her henids.*[25]

Women are matter capable of assuming any form. The results of those investigations which demonstrated that girls have a better memory than boys, in particular for subjects taught at school, can be explained by nothing but the inanity and nullity of women, who can be *impregnated* with anything, while men only remember what really interests them and *forget* everything else (cf. part 2, pp. 102, 115f.). But, above all, what I called the *clinging* of Woman, her extraordinary *susceptibility* to the judgments of others, her *suggestibility,* her total *transformation* by Man, derive from the fact that she is only matter, from her lack of any *original form* of her own. *Woman is nothing, and that is the reason, the* ***only*** *reason, why* ***she can become everything****, while Man can only ever become what he* **is**. A woman can be turned into *whatever one wants:* a man can at most be helped to become what *he* wants. That is why it really only makes *sense,* in the true meaning of the word, to *educate women,* not men. In Man nothing essential is ever changed by any kind of education; in Woman even her most basic nature, her high esteem for sexuality, can be totally repressed through external influence. Woman may seem everything and deny everything, but she is never really anything. Women do not have this or that quality: their peculiarity is *having no qualities at all.* That is all the complexity and all the mystery of Woman, and that is what constitutes all her superiority and incomprehensibility in the eyes of Man, who seeks a firm core even in her.

Even those readers who may have agreed with my deductions so far will complain that they give no indication of ***what*** Man really *is.* Is it possible to predicate any general quality for him, as *matchmaking* and the *lack of essence* could be predicated of Woman? Is there an actual *concept* of Man, as there is one of Woman, and can this concept be defined in a similar manner?

25. Cf. pp. 88, 89.

The answer must be that masculinity consists precisely in the *fact* of individuality, the essential monad, and coincides with it. But every monad is *infinitely* different from every other monad, and therefore no monad can be subsumed in a more comprehensive concept containing anything common to several monads. *Man* is the *microcosm* and he contains *all* the possibilities that exist. This must not be confused with the *universal* ***susceptibility*** of Woman, who can become everything *without being anything,* while Man *is* everything and *becomes* more or less of that, depending on his endowment. Man also has elements of Woman, of matter, in him, and he can allow that part of his nature to develop, i.e., he can deteriorate and degenerate. Or he can recognize it and fight it—and *that is why he,* and he *alone,* can arrive at the truth about Woman (part 2, p. 75f.). *Woman, on the other hand, has no possibility of developing, except through Man.*

The significance of Man and Woman will only ever become quite clear if we examine their *sexual* and *erotic* interrelations. The most profound desire of Woman is to be *formed,* and *thus created,* by Man. Woman wishes man to teach her opinions that are *totally different* from the ones she has had before, she wants him to overthrow everything that she has previously regarded as right (the opposite of reverence, p. 111), she wants to be *proved wrong* and *reformed* by him altogether. The will of Man alone *creates* Woman, *rules* her and *changes her completely* (hypnosis). Here at last we can also find the explanation of the relationship between the physical and the psychic in Man and Woman. Earlier on, I assumed for Man an interaction between the psychic and the physical, albeit only in the sense that the body was one-sidedly created through the projection of the transcendent soul onto the world of appearances, and for Woman a parallelism of merely empirical psychic and physical factors. Now it is clear that an interaction is also effective in Woman. But while in *Man,* in accordance with Schopenhauer's most true theory that a human being is his own work, it is his *own* will that *creates* and *recreates* a body for itself, *Woman* is physically *influenced* and *transformed* by the will of *another* (hypnotic suggestion, maternal impression). Thus Man forms not only himself but also Woman, and her more easily. The myths of Genesis and other cosmogonies, in which Woman is created from Man, proclaimed a deeper truth than the biological theories of descendency, according to which the male evolved from the female.

At this point I may also try to answer the most difficult question that I left open in chapter IX (p. 187), the question how Woman, who has no soul and no will of her own, can nevertheless discover the extent to which Man possesses these things. In order to do so, all one needs to have realized is that what Woman notices, and is able to appreciate, is not the *specific* nature of a man but only the *general fact,* and possibly the *degree,* of his *masculinity.* It is quite incorrect, and *either hypocritical or wrongly derived from subsequent impregnation by the nature of a man,* to claim that woman has an innate *understanding* of Man's *indi-*

viduality.[26] A man in love, who is easily taken in by the unconscious simulation of a deeper understanding on the part of Woman, may believe that a girl understands him. But no man who is less easily satisfied will be able to ignore the fact that women only have a sense of the *presence* of the soul, but not of *what* it is, and of the *formal general fact* of the personality, but not of its *specificity.* In order to perceive and apperceive a *specific* form, matter itself would need to have a *form,* but since the relationship between Woman and Man is the same as that between matter and form, Woman's understanding of Man is nothing but a willingness to be formed as forcefully as possible, or the instinctive attraction to existence of that which has none. This "understanding," then, is not a theoretical one. It is no sharing, but a desire to have a share. It is intrusive and selfish. Woman has no relationship with Man and no appreciation of Man, only an appreciation of *masculinity,* and if she can be regarded as more sexually demanding than he, this great demand is nothing but a strong desire to be formed most extensively and most powerfully: *it is the expectation of the largest possible quantity of existence.*

Finally, *matchmaking* also is nothing but this. The sexuality of women is *supra*-individual, because women are not clearly distinguished, formed, individualized entities in the higher sense. The supreme moment in the life of a woman —at which her *primal* being, the *primal lust,* manifests itself—is the moment the man's semen flows into her. At that moment she passionately embraces the man and presses him to her. This is the supreme lust of passivity, even more powerful than the feeling of happiness under hypnosis, it is matter in the process of being formed, refusing to let the form go and straining to bind the form to itself forever. That is why Woman is so excessively *grateful* to man for sexual intercourse, whether this sense of gratitude is restricted to the moment, as with streetwalkers who have no memory, or whether it has a longer after-effect, as with more differentiated women. The deepest foundation of matchmaking is this endless striving of poverty to unite with wealth, the totally formless and therefore supra-individual aspiration of the *un*structured to acquire an existence by making contact with, and permanently retaining, a form. The fact that Woman is no monad and has no boundaries makes matchmaking merely *possible:* the reason why matchmaking becomes a *reality* is that she represents the idea of *nothingness,* of *matter,* trying incessantly and in every possible way to seduce form into mixing with it. Matchmaking is the eternal striving of nothingness for something.

This is how the duality of Man and Woman has gradually developed into dualism as such, the dualism of the higher and the low life, the subject and the object, form and matter, the something and the nothing. All metaphysical, all

26. Cf. also p. 165.

transcendental being is logical and moral: *Woman is alogical and amoral.* But she does not imply a rejection of logic and morality, she is not *anti*-logical or *anti*-moral. She is not *negation,* but *nothingness.* She is *neither yea nor nay. Man* holds the possibility of being absolutely something and absolutely nothing, and that is why all his actions are *directed* toward either the one or the other. *Woman* does not *sin, because she is sin* ***itself****, which is one* ***possibility*** *in Man.*

Unadulterated Man is the image of God, of the absolute ***something****. Woman, including Woman in Man, is the symbol of* ***nothingness****: that is the significance of Woman in the universe, and that is how Man and Woman complement and condition each other.* As the *opposite* of Man, Woman has a purpose and function in the universe; and just as the human man reaches beyond the animal male, so the human *woman* reaches beyond the female of zoology.[27] In *humans* it is not a *limited being* that struggles against *limited non-being* (as in the animal kingdom): *the opponents here are limitless being and limitless non-being. That is why* only Man and Woman *together* constitute the human being.

The *purpose* of Woman, then, is to be *non-purpose.* She represents *nothingness,* the opposite pole to the divinity, the *other possibility* in humankind. That is why, quite rightly, nothing is regarded as more contemptible than a man who has become a woman, and why such a man is respected even less than the most dim-witted and coarsest criminal. And this also accounts for the deepest *fear* in Man: the *fear of Woman,* that is, the *fear of meaninglessness,* the fear *of the tempting abyss of nothingness.*

It is the *old woman* who wholly reveals what Woman is in reality. As experience also shows, the beauty of Woman is only *created* by Man's *love:* a woman becomes more beautiful when a man loves her, *because she passively complies with the will involved in his love.* However mystical this may sound, it is a simple everyday observation. The old woman demonstrates that Woman never *was* beautiful: if Woman *existed* there would be no witches. But Woman is nothing, she is a hollow vessel covered for a while in makeup and whitewash.

All the qualities of Woman depend on her non-existence, her *lack of essence:* it is because she has no true, immutable life, but only an earthly one, that she assists procreation in *this* life by her matchmaking, and that she can not only be transformed by a man who has a sensual effect on her, but is receptive to all possible influences. Thus the three fundamental qualities of Woman, which have been uncovered in this chapter, join together and unite in her non-existence.

Of those three qualities, two *negative* ones, which can be *directly* deduced from the concept of non-existence, are mutability and falseness. Only matchmaking, the only *positive* quality of Woman, does not follow from this concept equally promptly through a simple analysis.

27. Cf. the conclusion of chapter X.

This is quite understandable. The *existence* of Woman herself is *identical* with matchmaking, with the affirmation of sexuality as such. *Matchmaking is nothing if not universal sexuality,* and the fact that Woman *exists* means precisely that there is a radical inclination to universal sexuality in the world. *To trace matchmaking even further back in* ***causal*** *terms is the same as* ***explaining the existence of Woman.***

If we approach this from my table about dual life (p. 253), we find a movement from the highest life toward the earthly life, a resort to the non-existent instead of the existent, a will to nothingness, negation as such, evil in itself. The anti-moral is the affirmation of nothingness: the desire to turn form into formlessness and into matter, the desire to destroy.

But negation is related to nothingness, and that is why there is such a profound connection between everything criminal and everything feminine. The anti-moral and the amoral, which I explicitly separated earlier on in this investigation, meet in the common concept of the immoral, so that the customary confusion of the two now proves to have a certain justification. For nothingness alone is really—nothing. It is not, and it has neither existence nor essence. It is only a means of negation, it is that which, through the negation, is opposed to something. Woman does not acquire an existence until Man assents to his own sexuality, denying the absolute, and turning from the eternal life to the low. ***Only if something comes to nothing can nothing come to something.***

To *affirm the phallus* is to affirm the *anti*-moral. That is why the phallus is perceived to be the ugliest thing. That is why it was always imagined in a connection with Satan: the center of Dante's *hell* (the inner center of the earth) is *Lucifer's sexual organ.*

This is the explanation of the absolute power of male sexuality over Woman.[28] It is only when Man becomes **sexual** that Woman acquires an existence and a meaning: her existence is linked to the phallus, and **that** is why the phallus is her supreme master **and** her absolute ruler. When Man becomes sex, he becomes the fate of woman: Don Juan is the only man who makes her tremble all over.

The curse that we suspected to hang over Woman is the ill-will of man: *nothingness* is only a tool in the hand of *negation.* The fathers of the church expressed the same thing more dramatically when they called Woman the instrument of the devil. For matter in itself is *nothing until form tries to give it an existence.* The form's fall from grace is the contamination that it brings upon itself through its urge to act on matter. *When Man became* ***sexual*** *he* ***created*** *Woman.*

The existence of Woman, then, means precisely that Man has affirmed sexu-

28. Cf. the conclusion of chapter XI. That is also why superior women must be bisexual, i.e., not *exclusively* dominated by the rule of the phallus (part 1, p. 58f.). On the other hand, *hysteria* seems to play a considerable part in lesbian love.

ality. Woman is merely the **result** of this affirmation, she is sexuality itself (p. 81).

Woman's existence *depends* on Man: by becoming Man, as the opposite of Woman, by becoming sexual, Man *posits* Woman and calls her into being. That is why it is of supreme importance to Woman to *ensure that Man remains sexual:* for the degree of her existence corresponds to the degree of Man's sexuality. *That* is why Woman wants Man to *become a phallus all over, **that is why Woman is a matchmaker**.* She is incapable of using another being as anything but a means to an end, the end being sexual intercourse, because the ***sole purpose*** for which she herself is used is ***to make Man guilty***. And she would be *dead* the moment Man overcame *his* sexuality.

Man created Woman and will always create her afresh, so long as he remains sexual. Just as he gave Woman *consciousness* (part 2, end of chapter III), he gives her *existence.* By failing to renounce sexual intercourse he calls forth Woman. ***Woman is the guilt of man.***

Man wants love to help him make amends for his guilt. This throws light on the meaning of the obscure myth I introduced at the end of the previous chapter. It shows clearly what was still hidden from us at the time: that Woman does not exist before and without the fall of Man, that she has no prior wealth that he steals from her, and that it is he who posits Woman as poverty itself right from the outset. Man *as an eroticist apologizes to Woman* for the crime that he has committed, and is still continually committing, by creating her, that is by endorsing sexual intercourse. Where else would the inexhaustible *generosity* of all love come from? Why else would love be so eager to give Woman, and no other being, a soul? Why does love, of which the child is not yet capable, first appear together with sexuality in the period of physical maturity, when Woman is once more posited and the guilt renewed? Woman, all the way through, is only an object created by the drive of Man as its own goal, as a hallucination that his delusion is eternally laboring to capture. She is the objectivization of male sexuality, *the embodiment of sexuality, Man's guilt made flesh.* Every man, by incarnating himself, also creates a woman for himself, since everybody also has a sexual side. Woman for her part exists not through her own guilt but through that of another: whatever she can be accused of is the guilt of Man. Man's *love* is designed to *cover* up his guilt instead of *overcoming* it: it *elevates* Woman instead of *eliminating* her. A something embraces a nothing, in the belief that in so doing it is ridding the world of negation and reconciling all contradictions, while in fact the nothing could only disappear if the something kept away from it. Just as Man's hatred against Woman is only a hatred against his own sexuality that he has not yet learnt to see, so Man's love is only his boldest, his final attempt to save Woman as Woman for himself, instead of denying her as Woman. The reason why this love is accompanied by a sense of guilt, is that the love is intended to *clear away,* not to *atone for,* the guilt itself.

For woman IS only Man's guilt and is only THROUGH Man's guilt; and if femininity means matchmaking, this is only because all guilt of its own accord strives to multiply. What Woman accomplishes through her mere existence, through her whole nature, without being able to do anything else and without ever becoming conscious of it, is only *one inclination in* ***Man,*** his second, ineradicable, *low* inclination: she is, like the Valkyrie, the "blindly elective tool" [Richard Wagner, *The Valkyrie,* in *Ring of the Nibelung,* translated by Stewart Spencer, London 2000, p. 155] of the will of *another.* Matter seems to be no less an inexplicable mystery than form, Woman as infinite as Man, nothingness as eternal as existence. But *this* eternity is only the eternity of guilt.

XIII Judaism

> Here we must clearly articulate *something* that really exists, rather than trying to give an artificial life to something that does not exist by means of some fantasy.
>
> —Richard Wagner

It would not be surprising if some readers felt that in my entire investigation so far "men" had been given too good a deal and collectively placed on too high a pedestal. Perhaps my investigation will be spared any cheap objections and I shall not be asked, for example, how surprised this philistine or that rascal would be to hear that he has the whole universe in him, but my treatment of the male sex might still be considered too lenient, and my treatise accused of a tendentious neglect of all the revolting and paltry sides of masculinity in favor of its highest peaks.

Such an accusation would be unjustified. I have no intention to idealize men in order to disparage women more easily. Regardless of how much inanity and meanness may be rife in the empirical representatives of masculinity, what we are dealing with are the better *possibilities* which exist in every man and of which he becomes aware, either with a painful clarity or with a vague hatred, if he neglects them—possibilities which, as such, are of no account to Woman either in reality or in her thoughts. Nor could I essentially be concerned with distinctions *between* men, even though my mind is far from being closed to the importance of such distinctions. I wanted to establish what Woman is *not,* and she has indeed proved to lack an infinitely great deal of what is never *completely* missing in even the most mediocre and most plebeian man. What Woman *is,* the positive qualities of Woman (if it is possible to speak about any being, anything positive, in Woman), will also be found in many men. As I have repeatedly stressed, there are *men* who have *become women,* or who have *remained women,* but there is no woman who could transcend certain moral and intellectual limits which are clearly circumscribed and not set particularly high. I will therefore repeat: *the most superior woman is still infinitely inferior to the most inferior man.*

However, the objections could go further, and my theory would be open to criticism, if it ignored a certain point. In some peoples and races the men, although they cannot be interpreted as intermediate forms, so slightly and so rarely approach the idea of masculinity, as it is portrayed here, that the principles, indeed the whole foundation, on which this study rests could seem to be severely shaken. For, example, what are we to think of the *Chinese,* with their feminine lack of any needs and any form of aspiration? *Here* one might even be tempted to believe in the femininity of a whole nation. At least it cannot be a mere whim of a whole nation that the Chinese wear pigtails, and they also have a very sparse growth of beard. And what about the *Negroes*? There has probably never been a genius among Negroes, and their morality is generally so low that the Americans, as we know, are beginning to fear that it was an ill-considered move to emancipate them.

Even if the theory of intermediate sexual forms had any prospects of proving significant in a racial anthropology (given that a larger overall quantity of femininity seems to have been distributed among some peoples than among others), I must admit that my deductions so far have primarily concerned *the Aryan man and the Aryan woman.* How far the conditions that produce the pinnacles of humankind are found in the other great tribes, and what has so long held those tribes back from approaching these, would still need to be elucidated through a most detailed, and extremely rewarding, psychological study of racial characteristics.

Judaism—which I have chosen to discuss primarily because, as will be seen, it is the hardest and most formidable enemy not only of the views that I have developed and even more of those that I shall develop here, but of the entire standpoint that makes those views possible—seems to have a certain anthropological relationship with the two races that I have mentioned, both the Negroes and the Mongols. The Jews' readily curling hair points to the Negro, and the Chinese or Malayan shape of the facial skull, regularly accompanied by a yellowish complexion, so often found among Jews, suggests an admixture of Mongol blood.

This insight is no more than the result of everyday experience, and my remarks should not be understood in any other way. The *anthropological* question of the origin of Jewry is an extremely difficult one, and even such an interesting attempt at resolving it as that undertaken by H. S. Chamberlain in his famous *Foundations of the Nineteenth Century* has come in for a very great deal of opposition in recent times. I do not have the knowledge that is required to deal with this question: what I want to analyze here briefly, but as profoundly as possible, is only the psychic peculiarity of Judaism.[1] That is the task of psychological ob-

1. The mentality of the Jewish race indeed seems to me to be quite peculiar, uniform, and very distinct from any tendency of the mind and the heart that we find in the other peoples of the earth, or such at least will be the final result of my investigation. That is also why I do not believe that the Jewish character can be explained, in terms of racial chemistry, as a cross

servation and analysis. It can be solved without resorting to any hypotheses about historical processes which are no longer verifiable. All that is needed is objectivity, all the more as one may almost say that the most important and most conspicuous question in the official forms that everybody is obliged to complete for public use today is that asking whether or not he is a Jew, and that this seems to have become the most common criterion of classification used by civilized people. Nor can it be claimed that the store generally set by an honest statement in this respect is inappropriate to its seriousness and significance and exaggerates its importance. The fact that we encounter this question in every sphere, whether cultural or economic, religious or political, artistic or scientific, biological or historical, characterological or philosophical, must have a profound, indeed the most profound, cause in the nature of Judaism itself. No effort to discover this cause must seem too great: for the rewards are bound to be infinite.[2]

First, however, I will explain exactly what I mean by Judaism. I do *not* mean either a *race* or a *nation*, and even less a legally recognized religious faith. *Judaism must be regarded as a cast of mind, a psychic constitution, which is a* ***possibility*** *for* ***all*** *human beings and which has only found its most magnificent* ***realization*** *in historical Judaism.*

That this is so is proved by nothing if not by *antisemitism.*

The most genuine, most Aryan, most confident Aryans are not antisemitic. Generally, they cannot even *understand* the *hostile* form of antisemitism, however unpleasant an impression conspicuous Jewish characteristics certainly make on them. They are those whom the defenders of Judaism like to call "philosemites," and whose surprised and disapproving remarks about Jew-hatred are quoted when Judaism is disparaged or attacked.[3] The *aggressive* antisemite, on the other hand, always exhibits certain Jewish peculiarities; sometimes this can even show in his physiognomy, while his blood may be entirely free of any Semitic admixture.

Nor could this possibly be otherwise. *Just as we* ***love*** *in others only what we would like to be completely but never are completely, so we* ***hate*** *in others only what we never want to be, but always are in part.*

and mixture of different peoples, for any such components would have to be psychologically traceable. Judaism is probably something completely uniform, and any attempt at deriving and assembling it empirically seems hopeless. One can be anything but a philosemite and yet admit that in this respect there is some truth in the Jews' belief that they are a "chosen people."

2. At this point the author must remark that he is himself of Jewish origin.

3. Such a man, almost free from Judaism, and therefore a "philosemite," was Zola. As a rule, however, the more exceptional individuals have almost always been antisemites (Tacitus, Pascal, Voltaire, Herder, Goethe, Kant, Jean Paul, Schopenhauer, Grillparzer, Wagner) because, having far more things in them than others, they also understand Judaism better (cf. chapter IV).

We do not hate anything with which we have no affinity at all. Often the other person only makes us realize the ugly and mean features we have in ourselves.

This explains why the most rabid antisemites are found *among the Jews.* For only the completely Jewish Jews, like the totally Aryan Aryans, have no antisemitic disposition whatsoever. Among the rest, the baser natures apply their antisemitism only to others and pass judgment on them without ever examining themselves in this matter. Very few begin with their antisemitism on themselves.

Nonetheless, one thing remains certain: whoever hates the Jewish character hates it first in himself. By persecuting it in the other, he is only trying to separate himself from it, and by trying to localize it entirely in his fellow-human, in order to dissociate himself from it, he can momentarily feel free of it. Hatred, like love, is the result of projection: we only hate those who remind us *un*pleasantly of ourselves.[4]

The antisemitism of *the Jew,* then, proves that nobody who knows the Jew regards him as lovable—not even the Jew himself. The antisemitism of *the Aryan* supplies the no less significant insight that Judaism must not be confused with *the Jews.* There are Aryans who are more Jewish than many Jews, and there are really some Jews who are more Aryan than certain Aryans. Of those non-Semites who had a great deal of Judaism in them, I do not want to list either the lesser ones (such as the well-known Friedrich Nicolai in the eighteenth century) or the middling ones (where Friedrich Schiller can hardly be ignored) and analyze them with regard to their Judaism. But even the most profound antisemite —Richard Wagner himself—cannot be cleared of having a Jewish element, even in his art. This is true, even though the impression that he is the greatest artist in the history of humankind cannot be deceptive, and his Siegfried is without doubt the most *un-Jewish thing* that could ever have been imagined. However, nobody is an antisemite for nothing. Just as Wagner's aversion to grand opera and the theatre is rooted in the strong attraction that he himself felt toward them, an attraction that is clearly recognizable even in *Lohengrin,* so his music, the most powerful in the world as far as its individual motifs are concerned, cannot be entirely cleared of a certain flashiness, loudness, and brashness which is connected with his efforts at the external instrumentation of his works. Nor can it be overlooked that Wagner's music makes the strongest impression on both the Jewish antisemite, who is never able to escape from Judaism completely, and the antisemitic Indo-European, who is afraid of falling under the spell of Judaism. The music of *Parsifal,* which will always remain almost as inaccessible to the thoroughly genuine Jew as the *Parsifal* poem, the pilgrims' chorus and

4. Cf. chapter XI, p. 220.

the journey to Rome in *Tannhäuser*, and no doubt many other examples, must be *entirely* disregarded in this context. It is also certain that no individual who is *nothing but* a German could ever become as conscious of the nature of Germanness as Wagner does in *The Mastersingers of Nuremberg*.[5] Finally, one should remember that side of Wagner which felt drawn to Feuerbach, instead of Schopenhauer.

I am not planning to belittle that great man by the minutiae of psychology. Judaism was a great help to him in clearly understanding and affirming the other pole in him, in fighting his way through to Siegfried and Parsifal within him, and in giving the Germanic spirit the most elevated expression that it has probably ever found in history. An even greater man than Wagner had to overcome Judaism in himself before finding his mission, and, as I may put it at this stage, *the world-historical significance and the immense merit of Judaism is perhaps none other than that it persists in making the Aryan conscious of his own individuality and reminding him of* ***himself***. That is what the Aryan *owes* to the Jew. Thanks to the Jew he knows what he must beware of: *Judaism as a possibility within himself.*

This example will have demonstrated clearly enough what must be understood by Judaism in my estimation. Judaism is neither a nation nor a race, and neither a faith nor a body of writing. From now on, when I speak of the Jew I mean neither a specific individual nor a collective, *but every human being as such, insofar as he participates in the Platonic idea of Judaism.* And my only concern is to grasp the significance of this idea.

For purposes of differentiation, this investigation must be conducted in the present context of a psychology of the sexes. If one thinks about Woman and the Jew one will always be surprised to realize the extent to which Judaism in particular seems to be steeped in femininity, the nature of which I have so far only tried to explore in contrast to masculinity *as a whole without regard to any differences* within it. One could well be inclined to attribute to the Jew a larger share of femininity than to the Aryan, and ultimately to assume that even the most masculine Jew has a Platonic μέθεξις in Woman.

This view would be erroneous. However, since some of the most important points in which the deepest nature of femininity seemed to manifest itself are, strangely enough, also found in the Jew as if for the second time, it is essential to establish the agreements and divergences between them as accurately as possible.

The agreements strike the eye at first sight, wherever it looks. Indeed, the analogies seem likely to be traceable to such exceptional lengths that we may expect both confirmations of our earlier results and many interesting new contributions to our main topic. And it seems quite immaterial what we start with.

5. Cf. p. 96.

Thus, to begin with an analogy to Woman, it is most remarkable how Jews favor movable goods—even in these days, when they are free to acquire others—and how, in spite of their acquisitiveness, they have no real desire for *property,* least of all in its most solid form, landed property. *Property* is indissolubly linked to a personal identity, to individuality. The fact that Jews are turning to communism in such large numbers is connected with this. *Communism* as a tendency toward *community* should always be distinguished from *socialism* as an aspiration to social *cooperation* and to the recognition of humanity in every human being. Socialism is Aryan (Owen, Carlyle, Ruskin, Fichte), communism is Jewish[6] (Marx). The reason why the ideas of modern social democracy have moved so far away from Christian, Pre-Raphaelite socialism is that the Jews play so large a part in it. The Marxist strand in the workers' movement (in contrast to Rodbertus), its collectivist inclinations notwithstanding, has no relationship with the idea of the *state,* and this can certainly only be attributed to the Jew's total incomprehension of that idea. The state is too intangible, the abstraction involved in it is too remote from all concrete purposes, for the Jew to warm to it. The state is the totality of all those purposes which can be realized only by a partnership of rational beings behaving as such. *But this Kantian reason, the spirit, is what both the Jew and Woman seem to lack most.*

That is why Zionism is so hopeless, even though it has assembled the most noble emotions among Jews: Zionism is the negation of Judaism, the *idea of which* implies its expansion over the whole earth. The concept of the citizen totally *transcends* the Jew. That is why there has never been a Jewish *state* in the strict sense of the word, and there can never be one. The idea of the state implies something positive, a hypostatization of inter-individual purposes, a voluntary decision to join a self-imposed legal order, of which the head of state is a *symbol* (and nothing else). That is why the opposite of the state is anarchy, to which communism even today is closely related as a result of its lack of understanding of the state, however much most other elements in the socialist movement contrast with this. Although the idea of the state is not nearly realized in any historical form, any historical attempt to form a state contains something, albeit perhaps only a minimum, that raises such an entity above being a mere association for the purposes of business or power. A historical examination of how a certain state came into being says nothing about the *idea* underlying it, *insofar* as it is in fact a state and not a barracks. To grasp that idea, it will be necessary to do more justice to Rousseau's much maligned theory of social contract than has been the case. A state, if it is a state, can only be the expression of an alliance of ethical personalities for the pursuit of common tasks.

6. And Russian. However, the Russians typically have only a slight social disposition and among all European peoples the least sympathy for the state. This, in the light of the above, agrees with the fact that they are without exception antisemites.

The fact that the Jew has been a stranger to the state, not only since yesterday, but more or less since the beginning of time, suggests *that the Jew, like Woman, has no personality, and this will indeed gradually prove to be the case.* For the unsociability of the Jew, like that of Woman, can only be derived from their lack of an intelligible self. Jews like to stick together, as do women, but they do not *interact* as independent, separate beings under the sign of a supra-individual idea.

Just as in reality there is no such thing as the "dignity of women," it is equally impossible to imagine a *Jewish* "gentleman." The genuine Jew is deficient in the inner nobility that generates the dignity of the self and respect for the self of another. *There is no Jewish nobility,* which is all the more remarkable as Jews have practiced inbreeding for thousands of years.

What is called Jewish arrogance is also explained by the Jew's lack of a *conscious* self and his violent desire to increase the value of his own person by humiliating his fellow-humans. *The genuine Jew has no self and therefore no intrinsic value.* This, despite his incompatibility with anything aristocratic, is the source of his feminine obsession with titles, which is in line with his tendency to show off, be it his box in the theatre or the modern paintings in his drawing room, his Christian acquaintances or his erudition. This, in fact, is also the prime reason for the Jew's inability to understand anything aristocratic. The Aryan has a desire to know who *his* ancestors were. He respects them and is interested in them *because they were his ancestors,* and he appreciates them because he always regards his own past more highly than does the rapidly changing Jew, who is irreverent because he cannot endow life with value. The Jew totally lacks the pride in his ancestors that even the poorest, most plebeian Aryan possesses to a degree. He does not, as the Aryan does, honor his ancestors because they are *his* ancestors, he does not honor *himself* in them. It would be wrong to counter this by pointing out the extraordinary extent and strength of Jewish tradition. To the Jewish descendant, the history of his people, even if it seems to mean a great deal to him, is not the sum of what happened in former times, but only a ready source of new hopeful dreams: the Jew's *past* is not really his past, but at all times only his *future.*

It has often enough been attempted, not only by Jews, to attribute the Jews' faults to the brutal oppression and enslavement that they had undergone from the Middle Ages until the nineteenth century. It is argued that obsequiousness was bred into the Jew by the Aryans, and there are many Christians who therefore seriously consider the Jew as their own guilt. But such self-reproaches go too far: it is not permissible to speak of changes brought about in human beings through *external* influences in the course of generations, *without* taking into account that there must be something *within* them that has met the external opportunities part of the way and has willingly lent them a helping hand. So far it has not been proved that *acquired* properties can be inherited, and in *humans,* despite all their pseudo-adaptations, the character of both the individual and the race is more certain to remain constant than in any other living being. It is a sign of the shallowest superficiality to believe that humans are formed by their environment, and it is degrading to be forced to devote even one line to arguing with such a view, which takes away the breath of any free insight. A human being can only change from within; otherwise there is never anything real in him and, as with Woman, it is his being nothing that forever remains the same. Incidentally, how can anybody think that the Jew was created by history, given that the Old Testament already reports with obvious approval how Jacob, the patriarch, lied to his dying father Isaac, deceived his brother Esau, and cheated his father-in-law Laban?

However, the defenders of the Jews are *right* in saying that Jews commit serious crimes more rarely than Aryans, as is also shown by the relevant statistics. The Jew is not really *anti*-moral, but, it should be added, nor does he represent the highest ethical type. Rather, he is relatively *a*moral, never very good and never very bad, basically neither of the two but, more exactly, *mean. That is why Judaism lacks both the concept of angels and that of the devil,* the personification of good as well as that of evil. This assertion cannot be refuted by reference to the Book of Job, the figure of Belial or the myth of Eden. I do not feel qualified to join in the debates of modern source criticism in an attempt to separate the genuine elements from borrowed ones, but what I know full well is that in the psychic life of today's Jew, be he "enlightened" or "orthodox," neither a diabolical nor an angelic principle, neither heaven nor hell, plays the smallest religious part. If, then, the Jew never reaches the greatest moral heights, he is also certain to commit murder and other violent crimes much more rarely than the Aryan. And it is this that fully explains his lack of any fear of a diabolical principle.

The advocates of *women* cite the lower level of criminality no less often than the champions of the *Jews* as proof of women's more perfect morality. The homology between the two types seems more and more complete. There is no female devil, just as there is no female angel: only love, the defiant denial of reality, can make Man see Woman as a heavenly being, and only blind hatred can make him declare her corrupt and villainous. *In fact, what both Woman and the Jew completely lack is* ***greatness****,* greatness in any respect, either as outstanding victors in the moral sphere or as magnificent servants of the anti-moral. In the Aryan man the good and the evil principles of Kantian religious philosophy are *both together and yet as far apart as possible,* and he is fought over by his good and his evil demon. In the Jew, in almost the same way as in Woman, good and evil are not yet differentiated: there is no Jewish murderer, but neither is there a Jewish saint. Therefore it is probably true that the few elements of a belief in the devil in the Jewish tradition derive from Parsism and come from Babylon.

The Jews, then, do not live as free, autonomous individuals who choose between virtue and vice, as do the Aryans. The Aryans are automatically pictured by everybody as *an assembly of individual men,* the Jews as a coherent plasmodium spread over a wide area. Antisemitism has wrongly turned the latter into a stubborn, conscious closing of ranks and called it "Jewish solidarity." This is an understandable confusion of different things. If some accusation is leveled against an individual who belongs to the Jewish race and all the Jews, without actually knowing him, inwardly support him, wishing, hoping, and trying to prove him innocent, *it must on no account be believed that he interests them in any way as a Jewish individual and that his fate, because it is the fate of a Jew, will arouse more pity in them than that of any Aryan who is unjustly persecuted.* This certainly is not the case. *It is only the threat to Juda**ism**, the fear that a shameful shadow might fall on Jewry as a collective, or, more accurately on anything Jewish as such, on the **idea** of Juda**ism**, that produces those symptoms of involuntary partisanship.* It is exactly the same as when women are delighted to hear every individual member of their sex being disparaged, and indeed help to belittle her, so long as Woman herself is not shown in a bad light, no man is deterred from desiring women *in general,* nobody loses faith in "love," but marriages continue to take place and the number of old bachelors does not increase. What is defended is only the *species,* what is protected is only the *sex* or the *race,* not the individuals, who are considered only insofar as they are members of the group. *Both the genuine Jew and the genuine Woman live only in the species, not as individualities.*[7]

This explains why the *family* (as a biological, not a legal, unit) is of greater importance to the Jews than to any other people in the world, with the English, who are the Jews' distant relatives, following next, as will be seen. The family in this sense has a female, maternal origin and has nothing to do with the state or the formation of society. A sense of belonging together that unites the members of a family, although it is only the result of a shared atmosphere, is strongest among Jews. It is characteristic of all Indo-European men—of the more endowed in a higher degree than of the mediocre, but found even in the most commonplace—that their relations with their *fathers* are never entirely harmonious. Each of them, however slightly, feels a conscious or unconscious *anger* against the individual who forced him to live and gave him the name that he saw fit to give him at his birth, on whom he was *dependent* at least in these respects, and who must be regarded even in the deepest metaphysical sense as being *connected* to the fact that he wanted to enter life on earth. It is only among Jews that the son is deeply *embedded* in the family and feels comfortable in close community with his father, while it is almost only among Christians that father and son relate to each other like friends. Even the daughters of Aryans are more detached from their families than Jewesses and often take up careers that will

7. The belief in Jehovah and the teaching of Moses is merely a belief in this Jewish species and its vitality. Jehovah is the personification of the idea of Juda*ism.*

distance them from, and make them independent of, their relatives and their parents.

Here we can also test the arguments of the previous chapter, which suggested that living without any individuality and without being separated from other individuals by the boundaries of solitude was the indispensable prerequisite of matchmaking (p. 259). Male matchmakers always have an element of Judaism in them, *and this is where we reach the point of closest correspondence between femininity and Judaism.* The Jew is always more lecherous, more lustful, than the Aryan man, although, strangely enough and possibly in connection with the fact that he is not really of an *anti*-moral disposition, he is less sexually potent and certainly less capable of any *great lust* than the latter. Only Jews are genuine marriage-brokers, and marriage-brokering by men is nowhere as widespread as among Jews. Of course, Jews have a more urgent need for this kind of activity, because, as I have already noted (part 1, p. 41), there is no other nation in which marrying for love is as rare as among them: one more proof of the soullessness of the absolute Jew.

That matchmaking is an organic disposition of the Jew is also suggested by the Jew's lack of understanding of any kind of asceticism. It is substantiated by the fact that Jewish rabbis like to speculate in particularly great detail about the business of procreation and maintain an oral tradition with regard to the begetting of children. Indeed it could hardly be expected otherwise from the supreme representatives of a people whose moral duty, at least according to its tradition, is "to go forth and multiply."

Finally, matchmaking is a blurring of boundaries, *and the Jew is the blurrer of boundaries* κατ' ἐξοχήν. He is the opposite pole of the aristocrat. The principle of any aristocratism is the strictest *observation* of all *boundaries* between human beings, but the Jew is the born communist and always wants community. The informality of the Jew in company and his lack of social tact are the results of this. Manners are nothing but a subtle way of emphasizing and protecting the boundaries of the personal monads, but the Jew is no monadologist.

Although it should be obvious, I want to stress once more that despite my unfavorable appraisal of the genuine Jew by these remarks, or any that are yet to follow, nothing could be further from me than wishing to play into the hands of a theoretical, let alone, practical persecution of the Jews. I am talking about Judaism as a Platonic idea—*the absolute Jew exists no more than the absolute Christian*—and not about any individual Jews, many of whom I would be sorry to have hurt and some of whom would suffer a great injustice if what I have said were applied to them. Slogans such as "Buy only from Christians" are *Jewish,* because they regard and assess the individual merely as a member of a species, in much the same way as the Jewish term "goy" simply describes and immediately subsumes the Christian as such.

I do not support boycotting, expelling, or disqualifying the Jews from any office and dignity. The Jewish question cannot be solved by such means, which do not comply with morality. But neither is "Zionism" equal to that task. Zionism is an attempt to collect the Jews, who, as H. S. Chamberlain shows, long before the destruction of the temple in Jerusalem, had in part chosen the diaspora as their natural life, the life of a root-stock crawling all over the world and eternally thwarting individuation. Zionism, then, wants something *un*-Jewish. *The Jews would have to overcome Judaism before they could be ripe for Zionism.*

To this end, however, it would above all be necessary for the Jews to understand themselves, to get to know themselves, to fight themselves, and to ***want*** *to conquer Judaism* ***in themselves***. But so far the self-knowledge of Jews has only extended to making and thoughtfully appreciating jokes about themselves—and to nothing more. *Unconsciously,* the Jew respects the Aryan more than himself. Only a firm and unshakeable determination to make it possible for himself to feel the greatest self-respect could liberate the Jew from Judaism. But such a decision can only be made and carried through by the individual and not by a group, however strong and honorable it may be. Thus the Jewish question can only be solved at the *individual* level, and *every single Jew must seek to answer it for his own person.*

There is no other solution to the question, and there can be none. Zionism will never be able to solve it.

On the other hand, a Jew who would have overcome, a Jew who would have become a Christian, would have every right to be taken by the Aryan for an individual and no longer to be judged as a member of a race that he has long since transcended through his moral efforts. He could rest assured that nobody would wish to contest such a well-founded claim on his part. The superior Aryan always has the desire to respect the Jew, and his antisemitism neither pleases nor amuses him. That is why he does not like it if a Jew makes any confessions about Jews, and any Jew who nevertheless does so may expect even fewer thanks from him than from the Jews, who are always extremely touchy in this respect. Least of all does the Aryan want the Jew to concede that antisemitism is right by converting. But a Jew intent on his *internal* liberation must not allow even this danger of his sincerest efforts being utterly misunderstood to daunt him. He must stop trying to achieve the impossible, that is, to esteem himself as a *Jew*—which is what the Aryan wants him to do—and strive to gain the right to honor himself as a *human being.* He will long to achieve the *inner* baptism by the spirit, which may only then be followed by the symbolic external baptism of the body.

An understanding of ***what*** *Jewish and Judaism really is,* which the Jew needs so badly, would solve one of the most difficult problems. Judaism is a much more profound mystery than is imagined in many antisemitic catechisms, and will in the final analysis probably remain shrouded in a certain darkness forever. Even the parallel with Woman will soon let us down, although for the time being it is still able to assist us.

In the Christian, pride and humility, in the Jew, superciliousness and groveling are in conflict with each other, as are self-assurance and contrition in the former, and arrogance and devotion in the latter. The Jew's lack of understanding of the idea of mercy is connected with his total lack of humility. His slavish disposition is the source of his heteronomous ethics, the Ten Commandments, the most immoral book of laws in the world, which promises well-being on *earth* and the conquest of the world as a reward to those who meekly obey the powerful will of *another.* The Jew's relationship with Jehovah, the *abstract* idol which he fears like a *slave* and the name of which he does not even dare to *enunciate,* characterizes him, in analogy to Woman, as a being in need of domination by an alien force. Schopenhauer once wrote: "The word God means a human being who has made the world." This is indeed true of the God of the Jews. Of the divine in humanity, the "God who lives in my breast," the genuine Jew knows nothing. He has no understanding of what Christ or Plato, Meister Eckhart or St. Paul, Goethe or Kant, and every Aryan, from the Vedic priests to the magnificent closing lines of Fechner's *Three Motives and Grounds of Belief,* meant by the divine, or of the words "I am with you always, even to the end of the world." What is given to a human being by God is his soul, *but the absolute Jew is soulless.*

Thus it is inevitable that the Old Testament should lack the belief in immortality. How could those who have no soul have a desire for the immortality of the soul? The Jews, just as women, quite generally have no *desire for immortality:* "Anima naturaliter christiana," says Tertullian.

For the same reason—as H. S. Chamberlain correctly recognized—the Jews are also devoid of any real mysticism, apart from a terrible superstition and magical interpretation, called "Kabbala." Jewish monotheism has nothing whatsoever to do with a genuine belief in God. Indeed it is the negation of such a belief, a travesty of the true service of the principle of good, and the homonymity of the Jewish God and the Christian God is the worst mockery of the latter. This is no religion based on pure reason, but rather an old woman's belief arising from squalid fear.

But why does the orthodox slave of Jehovah so easily and promptly turn into a materialist, a "free thinker"? Why does a well-known pun by Lessing, identifying enlightenment with rubbish, seem to be tailor-made for Judaism, despite the objections of Dühring, who was an antisemite and probably for good reasons? Here the *slave mentality* has given way to its perennial reverse side, *impudence:* the two are alternating phases of one and the same will in the same individual. *Arrogance toward things* that are not perceived, or not even dimly felt, to be symbols of something more profound, the lack of *verecundia* in relation to natural processes, also leads to the Jewish, materialistic type of science, which today has unfortunately acquired a certain dominance and become intolerant of any kind of philosophy. If, as is the necessary and only correct way, Judaism is regarded as an *idea* in which the Aryan can also have a smaller or larger *share,* there can be little objection to wishing to substitute for the "history of materialism" the "nature of Judaism." Wagner has discussed the "Jews in music." Here something needs to be said about the "Jews in science."

Judaism in the broadest sense is that movement in science which regards science above all as a *means to the end* of ruling out anything transcendent. The Aryan perceives the striving to understand and explain *everything* as a devaluation of the world, because he feels that it is precisely the unfathomable that gives existence its value. The Jew has no respect for mysteries, because he does not sense any anywhere. His aspiration is to make the world seem as flat and commonplace as possible, not in order to secure through clarity the eternal rights of the eternally dark, but in order to make the universe drearily obvious and to remove anything that obstructs the free movement of his elbows even in matters of the mind. *Anti*-philosophical (not aphilosophical) science is basically Jewish.

The Jews have also been least averse to a mechanistic and materialistic worldview, because their worship of God has nothing to do with true religion. Just as it was *they* who most eagerly took up Darwinism and the ridiculous theory of the descent of human beings from monkeys, so they became almost creative when they established the *economic* conception of human history, which deletes the role of the spirit in the development of humankind most completely. Having been the most rabid adherents of Büchner, they are now the most enthusiastic champions of Ostwald.

Nor is it a coincidence that such a large part of *chemistry* today is in Jewish hands, as it was once in the hands of their racial relatives, the Arabs. A total absorption in matter, and a desire for the total absorption of everything in matter, implies the lack of an intelligible self and therefore is essentially Jewish.

O curas Chymicorum! o quantum in pulvere inane!

Admittedly, this hexameter was written by the *most German* scientist of all times: his name is Johannes Kepler.[8]

It is certainly also connected with the influence of the Jewish mentality that medicine, to which hordes of Jews are now turning, has taken its present course. From the savages to today's naturopathy, which the Jews, characteristically, have totally avoided, the art of healing has always contained a religious element, and the medicine man has always been the priest. The exclusively *chemical* approach in medicine—that is Judaism. However, it will certainly never be possible to explain the organic by the inorganic, but at most the latter by the former. There is no doubt that Fechner and Preyer are right to believe that the lifeless has evolved from the living, and not the other way round. What we see daily in the life of the *individual*—that organic matter becomes inorganic (death is already pre-

8. Here I was concerned to assign a place to the Jews' urge for chemistry. I have no intention to offend the other kind of chemistry, the science of Berzelius, Liebig, or van t'Hoff.

pared in old age by various forms of sclerosis, such as senile arteriosclerosis and atheromatosis), while nobody has ever seen anything living arising from anything dead—should also be applied to the *totality* of inorganic matter, in accordance with the "biogenetic" parallelism between ontogeny and phylogeny. If the theory of abiogenesis from Swammerdam to Pasteur has been obliged step by step to abandon so many of its positions, it will also have to let go of the last foothold that it seems to have in the widespread desire for monism, if that desire can be satisfied in a different and better way. The equations describing lifeless, inorganic processes may one day become *liminal* cases of the equations describing living organic processes, if certain time values are inserted, but it will never be possible to represent the living through the dead. In Goethe's great work, Faust had no truck with the *attempts to create a homunculus:* it is no coincidence that these attempts were reserved for his apprentice Wagner. Truly, chemistry can only cope with the excrements of living matter: after all, dead matter itself is only an excretum of life. The chemical way of looking at things places the organism at the same level as its emissions and excretions. How else could we account for such things as the belief that it is possible to influence the sex of an embryo by feeding it more or less sugar? The *brazen treatment* of those things that the Aryan, in the depth of his soul, has always perceived as *providence* was first introduced to the natural sciences by the Jews. The time of those deeply religious scientists for whom their objects always had a share, however small, in a supra-sensory dignity, for whom there were secrets, who could hardly get over their astonishment at what they felt *blessed* to be discovering—the time of Copernicus or Galilei, Kepler or Euler, Newton or Linnaeus, Lamarck or Faraday, Konrad Sprengel, or Cuvier—seems long gone. Today's free spirits, who are free from any spirit and therefore no longer able to believe in the immanent revelation of anything higher in the totality of nature, perhaps for precisely that reason, are unable to match and take the place of those men even in their own scientific specialisms.

This *lack of depth* also explains why the Jews are unable to produce any really great men and why *Judaism,* like Woman, *is denied the highest degree of genius.* The most outstanding Jew of the last 1,900 years, about whose purely Semitic descent there is no doubt and who is certainly more important than either Heine, a poet devoid of almost any *greatness,* or Israels, an original but by no means profound painter, is the philosopher Spinoza. However, even he is hugely overrated everywhere, owing less to a deeper study of his works than to the accidental circumstance that he is the only thinker whom Goethe read in some detail.

For Spinoza himself, strictly speaking, *problems* did not exist. This shows that he was a genuine Jew, or else he could not have chosen the "mathematical method" which seems calculated to make everything appear *obvious.* Spinoza's system was his refuge, into which he withdrew because he avoided thinking about himself more than anybody. That is why this system was able to soothe and refresh Goethe, who probably thought about himself most extensively, and more painfully than anybody else. For the truly exceptional individual, no matter what he is thinking about, is basically only thinking about himself. Furthermore, although Hegel was certainly wrong to treat logical opposition as real repugnance, in a *more profound* thinker, *psychologically,* even the driest *logical problem* is certain to arise from a fierce *inner conflict.* Spinoza's system, with its unconditional monism and optimism, and with its perfect harmony that Goethe found so hygienic, is undeniably not the philosophy of a powerful individual: it is the seclusion of an unhappy man who seeks the idyll but is not really capable of it because he totally lacks a sense of humor.

Spinoza repeatedly proves the genuineness of his Judaism and clearly reveals the perennial limitations of the purely Jewish mind. I mean less his incomprehension of the idea of the state and his adherence to the Hobbesian allegation that the original human condition is "war of all against all." Rather, what testifies to the relatively low level of his philosophical views is his utter incomprehension of the *freedom of the will*—the Jew is always a slave and therefore a determinist—and, above all, the fact that to him, as a *genuine Jew,* individuals are merely accidents, not substances, merely non-real modes of an infinite substance, which alone is real and which is alien to any individuation. The Jew is no monadologist. That is why there is no greater contrast than that between Spinoza and his far more important and universal contemporary Leibniz, the representative of the theory of *monads,* and the even greater creator of that theory, Bruno, whose similarity to Spinoza has been exaggerated by superficial observers in a manner verging on the grotesque.[9]

Just as the Jew (*and Woman*) lacks both the "radically good" and the "radically evil," so he lacks both *genius* and the "radically stupid" element in the nature of the human male. The specific kind of intelligence which is praised in both the Jews and women is, on the one hand, only a *greater vigilance due to their greater selfishness* and, on the other hand, a result of the infinite adaptability of both to any external purposes whatsoever, *because they have no original standard of value, no kingdom of purposes in their own breast.* Conversely, they have more unadulterated natural instincts, which do not recur in the Aryan man in the

9. Spinoza was not a genius. There is no intellectually poorer and more unimaginative philosopher among all the *singular* figures in the history of philosophy, and Spinozism is *totally* misunderstood by those who—misled by the thought of Goethe—may see it as the modest expression of an extremely profound relationship with nature. If one wants to embrace the universe one cannot start with definitions. Spinoza's relationship with nature was actually an exceptionally loose one. This tallies with the fact that he never encountered art in his whole life (cf. chapter XI, p. 219).

same way to help him out when the supra-sensory element in his intelligence has abandoned him.

This is also the place to remember the similarity between the Englishman and the Jew, which has often been emphasized since Richard Wagner first noted it. Among all the Germanic peoples the English are most likely to have a certain affinity to the Semites. This is suggested by their orthodoxy, including their strictly literal interpretation of the Sabbath. The religiousness of the English often involves hypocrisy, and their asceticism a great deal of prudery. Like women, they have never been productive either in music or in religion. There may be irreligious poets—who cannot be *very* great—but there is no irreligious musician, and there is also a connection between religion and the fact that the English have never produced a significant architect and even less an outstanding philosopher. Berkeley is an Irishman, as are Swift and Sterne, while Erigena, Carlyle and Hamilton, like Burns, are Scots. Shakespeare and Shelley, the two greatest Englishmen, are still far from the pinnacles of humanity and come nowhere near Dante or Aeschylus. If we consider the English "philosophers," we see it was they who have supplied the reaction against any depth ever since the Middle Ages, from William of Occam and Duns Scotus, through Roger Bacon and the Chancellor of the same surname, Spinoza's spiritual relative Hobbes and the shallow Locke, to Hartley, Priestley, Bentham, the two Mills, Lewes, Huxley, and Spencer. This list contains all the important names from the history of English philosophy, for Adam Smith and David Hume were Scots. *Let us never forget that psychology without the soul has come to us from England.* The Englishman has impressed the German as an efficient empiricist and as exponent of *Realpolitik* in both practical and theoretical terms, but this is all that can be said about his importance for philosophy. There has never yet been a profound thinker who stopped at empiricism, and never an Englishman who transcended it on his own.

Nonetheless, the Englishman must not be confused with the Jew. The Englishman has much more of the transcendent in him than the Jew, but his mind is directed from the transcendent to the empirical, rather than from the empirical to the transcendent. Otherwise he would not have such a *sense of humor,* while the Jew, who has no sense of humor, is in fact the most productive target of any wit, and in this respect second only to sexuality.

I know how difficult a problem laughter and humor is: as difficult as anything that is found only in humans and not in animals, and so difficult that Schopenhauer has nothing much, and even Jean Paul nothing entirely satisfactory, to say about it. Humor contains many different things. To some it seems to be a more subtle form of self-pity or of pity for others, but this does not tell us what is exclusively characteristic of humor itself. It may be the expression of a conscious "pathos of distance"—in an individual who is impervious to any pathos—but again nothing has been gained with regard to the decisive factor for humor in particular.

The most important thing about humor seems to me to be an *excessive emphasis on the empirical,* with the aim of making its *unimportance* more visible. Basically, anything that is realized is ridiculous. This is the foundation of humor, and this is what makes it the antithesis of eroticism.

Eroticism brings the human being and the world together, and directs everything in them toward the *goal:* humor makes them follow opposite directions, and dissolves all syntheses in order to show what the world is without any nuances. One might say that humor and eroticism relate to each other as do unpolarized and polarized light.[10]

While eroticism tries to move from the limited to the unlimited, humor settles on the limited, which it pushes into the limelight and exposes by observing it from all sides. The humorist has no desire to travel.[11] He alone appreciates small things and the inclination toward them. His realm is neither the sea nor the mountains, but the flat land. That is why he likes to seek out the idyll and why he delves into every *individual thing,* but only in order to reveal the *disproportion* between it and the *thing-in-itself. He shows up immanence by totally detaching it from transcendence,* and no longer even mentioning the name of the latter. Wit seeks out the contradiction in experience, while humor hurts it more by representing it as a closed whole, but *both show all that is possible* and thereby compromise the world of experience most thoroughly. The tragic, on the other hand, demonstrates what is *impossible* in all eternity, and thus both the comic and the tragic, each in its own way, negate the empirical world, even though each seems to be the opposite of the other.

The Jew—whose starting point is not the supra-sensory as it is of the humorist, and whose goal is not the supra-sensory as it is of the eroticist—has no interest in belittling that which is given. That is why life, to him, never becomes either a fantasy or a madhouse. Humor, which knows values that are *higher* than any concrete thing but which cunningly keeps quiet about them, is essentially *tolerant,* while satire, its opposite, is essentially *intolerant* and therefore a better match for the true nature of the Jew and of Woman. Both Jews and women are humorless, but inclined to mockery. In Rome there was even a female writer of satires, called Sulpicia. Because satire is intolerant it most readily makes an individual unacceptable to society. The humorist, who knows how to prevent himself and others being seriously worried by the trivialities and meannesses of the world, is the most welcome guest in any society. Humor, like love, can move mountains. It is the kind of conduct that is very favorable to a social ex-

10. To explain this to oneself, one might think of the difference between Shakespeare and Beethoven, which is one of the greatest contrasts in psychology.
11. Cf. p. 212.

istence, that is, to a community united by a *higher* idea. The Jew has no social disposition, while the Englishman has it in a high degree.

The comparison between the Jew and the Englishman thus fails even sooner than the comparison between the Jew and Woman. The reason why I felt obliged to go into such detail in both respects was the heated debate that has long raged about the value and the nature of Judaism. In this context I might also mention Wagner, who was exercised most intensively by the problem of Judaism throughout his life, and who thought that he could rediscover a Jew not only in the Englishman, but unmistakably the shadow of Ahasverus also falls on his Kundry, the most profound female figure in all art.

No woman in the world represents the *idea* of Woman as perfectly as the Jewess, and that not only in the eyes of the Jew. This seems to confirm the parallel between the Jew and Woman and leads all the more to a rash acceptance of it. Even the Aryan feels that way: remember Grillparzer's *The Jewess of Toledo.* This illusion is so easily created because the Aryan woman demands a metaphysical element as one of the sexual characteristics of the Aryan man and is as open to being imbued with his religious convictions as she is with his other qualities (cf. chapter IX, toward the close, and chapter XII). In reality, of course, there are only male Christians and no female Christians. But the Jewess can seem to represent more fully both poles of femininity, as a housemother with many children and as a lustful odalisque, as Cypris and as Cybele, because the man who is her sexual complement and whose mind impregnates hers, who has created her for himself, contains so little that is transcendent in himself.

The congruency between Judaism and femininity *seems* to become complete as soon as one begins to reflect on the Jew's infinite capacity for change. The Jews' great talent for journalism, the "agility" of the Jewish mind, the lack of any deeply rooted and original *convictions*—Do these things not prove that both the Jews and women ***are** nothing and therefore can become **everything***? The Jew is an individual but has no individuality. Being entirely committed to the low life, he has no desire for any personal continuation after death. He lacks true, immutable, metaphysical *being,* and he has no share in the higher, *eternal* life.

And yet it is precisely here that Judaism and femininity *diverge* in a decisive manner. *The Jew's lack of being and his ability to become everything are different from woman's.* Woman is matter, which *passively* assumes any form. In the Jew there is undeniably a certain *aggressiveness.* His receptivity is not the result of any great impression made on him by others, and he is no more suggestible than the Aryan. Rather, he actively adapts to different circumstances and requirements, to any environment and any race, like a parasite that changes and assumes a completely different appearance with any given host, so that it is constantly taken for a new animal, even though it always remains the same. The Jew assimilates to everything and thereby assimilates everything to himself. In so doing he is not subjected by the other, but subjects the other to himself.

The Jew has an *eminently conceptual* disposition, which Woman *totally lacks.* This conceptual disposition accounts for the Jew's inclination to jurisprudence, for which Woman will never develop a taste, and it also manifests the Jew's *activity,* although it is activity of a very peculiar kind and definitely not the activity of the freedom that creates itself in the higher life.

The Jew is eternal, as is Woman, albeit not as a personality, but as a species. *He is not direct like the Aryan man, but his indirectness is different from that of Woman.*

The essentially Jewish character is most profoundly revealed by the Jew's *lack of religiousness.* This is not the place to examine the concept of religion, which would demand long-winded explanations and divert us far from our topic. Therefore religion may be understood, for the time being, as the *affirmation* ***by*** *a human being of all the higher life* ***in*** *a human being, which is eternal and which can never be derived from, nor proved by, the data of the low life. The Jew is the human being* ***without belief.*** *Belief* is the action by which a human being enters into a relationship with a *being. Religious belief* is specially directed to ***absolute*** *being. And the Jew* ***is*** *nothing, ultimately because he* ***believes*** *in nothing.*

But belief is everything. One may or may not believe in God, and it does not matter too much, so long as one at least believes in one's atheism. But the point is precisely that the Jew does not believe in anything. He does not believe in his belief, and he doubts his doubt. He is never completely overwhelmed by joy, but he is no less incapable of being entirely overcome by misery. He never takes himself seriously and therefore he does not really take any other human being or any other thing seriously. It is internally *comfortable* to be a Jew, and he must put up with some external discomfort in return.

I have finally identified the essential difference between the Jew and Woman. Their similarity is most deeply rooted in the fact that the Jew believes *in himself* no more than Woman believes in herself. But *she* believes in *others,* in her man, in her child, in "love." She has a center of gravity, even though it is situated outside her. *The Jew, on the other hand, believes in nothing, either within himself or outside himself.* He finds no support and puts down no roots in others, as Woman does. His profound incomprehension of any landed property and his preference for mobile capital are symbols of his utter rootlessness. And his lack of a profound and immutable appreciation of nature is also connected with this.

Woman believes in Man, whether the man outside her or the man within her, that is, the man who has impregnated her mind, and consequently she can even take herself seriously.[12] The Jew never really regards anything as genuine, unshakable, sacred, and inviolable. That is why he is always frivolous and makes a joke of everything. He does not believe in the Christianity of any Christian, let alone the sincerity of the baptism of a Jew. But nor is he really realistic

12. Cf. chapter XII, pp. 237, 242.

and a genuine empiricist. This is where I must add the most important qualification to my earlier statements, which partly followed H. S. Chamberlain. The Jew is not really an immanentist like the English philosophers of experience. The positivism of the mere empiricist believes that all possible human knowledge is contained within in the world of the senses, and he hopes for the completion of the system of exact science. The Jew does not believe in knowledge either, although this by no means makes him a skeptic, because he is no more convinced by skepticism. In contrast, even the entirely ametaphysical system such as that of Avenarius is dominated by a solemn care, and even the relativist views of Ernst Mach are enveloped by a confident *piety.* Empiricism may not be profound, but that is no reason to call it Jewish.

The Jew is irreligious in the widest sense. Religiousness is not something *beside* and *outside* other things: it is the grounding of *everything,* the foundation on which everything else is built. The Jew is unjustly regarded as prosaic, simply because he is not enthusiastic and does not long for a primal source of being. Any genuine internal culture—whatever an individual regards as truth, so that there may be culture for him, truth for him, values for him—is deeply founded in belief and requires piety. Nor is piety something that only reveals itself in mysticism and religion: it also lies at the heart of any science and any skepticism, of *anything that a human being seriously means within himself.* There is no doubt that piety can express itself in a variety of ways: passion and clear-headedness, high enthusiasm and profound seriousness are the two most noble forms in which it appears. The Jew is never in raptures, but nor is he really sober. He is not ecstatic, but nor is he dry. He is not intoxicated either by base or by elevated things, and he is neither an alcoholic nor capable of higher ecstasies, but this does not make him cool and still leaves him a long way from calm and persuasive reasoning. His heat perspires and his coldness steams. His limitations always turn into meagerness, his wealth into bombast. If he tries to reach the heights of boundless enthusiasm he never gets beyond histrionics, but if he decides to remain within the narrowest confines of the intellect he still does not refrain from noisily rattling his chains. And even though he hardly feels impelled to kiss the entire world, he does not molest it any the less.

All separation and all embracing, all severity and all love, all detachment and all fervency, every true and genuine emotion of the human heart, be it serious or joyous, is ultimately based on piety. Religion is the positing of the self and of the world together with the self. Therefore belief need not always relate to a metaphysical entity, as it does with the genius, the most pious individual. It may concern something empirical and seem to be fully absorbed in this: ultimately, it is one and the same belief in a being, a value, a truth, an absolute, a god.

This *most comprehensive* concept of religion and piety could easily be misinterpreted in various ways. I would therefore like to add a few more remarks to explain it. Piety is not merely *possession,* but also the struggle to *gain possession.* Not only the convinced *prophet of God* (such as Händel or Fechner) is *pious,* but also the erring, doubting *seeker of God* (such as Lenau or Dürer).[13]

Piety need not face the universe as a whole in eternal contemplation (as Bach does): it may manifest itself as a religious feeling *accompanying* all *individual* things (as with Mozart). Finally, it is not bound to the appearance of a founder: the *Greeks* were the most pious people in the world and therefore had the highest culture known so far, but there was certainly never an outstanding founder of a religion among them (nor did they need one, cf. p. 299).

Religion is the creation of the cosmos, and whatever is in a human being is in him only as a result of *religion.* Therefore, the Jew is not the religious individual that he is so often falsely claimed to be, but the irreligious individual κατ' ἐξοχήν.

Do I need to give reasons for this? Do I need to explain at length that the Jew has no zealous belief and that therefore the Jewish faith is the only one which does not proselytize, so that converts to Judaism are the cause of the greatest puzzlement and the greatest merriment among the Jews themselves?[14] Do I need to elaborate on the nature of Jewish prayer, stressing its purely formal character and its lack of the kind of fervor which the moment alone can produce? Finally, do I need to repeat what the Jewish religion is: no doctrine of the meaning and purpose of life, but a historical tradition, which can be summed up in the one crossing of the Red Sea, and which therefore culminates in the thanks of a fleeing coward to his powerful rescuer? It would in any case be clear that the Jew is totally irreligious and as far from any belief as can be. He does not posit himself and, with himself, the world, which is the essence of religion. All belief is heroic, but the Jew knows neither courage nor fear as a sensation of threatened belief. He is neither sun-like nor demonic.

Therefore it is not mysticism, as Chamberlain thinks, but *piety* that the Jew ultimately lacks. If only he were an honest materialist, if only he were a narrow-minded worshipper of evolution! However, he is not a critic, but only a fault-finder. He is not a skeptic in the image of Descartes, and he does not doubt in order to progress from the greatest distrust to the greatest certainty. He is an absolute ironist, like—and here I can only name a Jew—like Heinrich Heine.

13. The Jew is not Verrocchio's Thomas (at the church of Or San Michele in Florence), who is not yet inspired and who does not yet see, but who would like nothing more than to believe and who is simply not yet able to do so. Rather, the Jew perceives his own unbelief as a sign of his superiority, as a joke that he alone knows.

14. Jewish intolerance is no valid argument against this. Truly religious people are *always* zealous, but *never* zealots. Rather, intolerance is identical with unbelief. Just as *power* is the most deceptive surrogate of *freedom,* so intolerance only arises from an *individual's* lack of *confidence* in his own belief.

The criminal is also impious and has no support in God, but as a result he sinks into the abyss, because he is unable to *stand beside God,* for which the Jew has a peculiar knack. Therefore the criminal is always *desperate,* but the Jew never. The Jew is no genuine revolutionary (for where would he find the strength and inner zest for rebellion) and this distinguishes him from the *Frenchman:* he is merely subversive, but never really destructive.

Now what is the Jew himself, if he is none of all that a human being can be? What truly goes on inside him, if he lacks anything ultimate, any foundation that the psychologist's plumb line would finally hit loud and clear?

There is a sense in which all the psychological contents of the Jew are twofold or manifold, and *he can never transcend this ambiguity, this duplicity or indeed multiplicity.* He always has *another* possibility, or *many* other possibilities, where the Aryan, who sees just as much, firmly makes up his mind and chooses. I believe that this ambiguity, this lack of the immediate inner *reality* of any psychic process, this deficiency in that being-in-and-for-itself which alone can give rise to the highest form of creativity, must in my view be regarded as the definition of what I have called Judaism as an idea.[15] *It is like a condition* ***before being****,* an eternal wandering back and forth before the gate of reality. There is nothing with which the Jew can truly identify, no cause for which he can risk his life unreservedly.[16] What the Jew lacks is not the zealot but the zeal, because anything undivided, anything whole, is alien to him. It is the *simplicity* of *belief* that he lacks, and it is because he lacks this *simplicity* and stands for nothing *positive* that he seems to be more intelligent than the Aryan and is *supple* enough to wriggle out of any oppression.[17] *Inner ambiguity,* I repeat, *is absolutely Jewish, simplicity is absolutely un-Jewish.* The question of the Jew is the question addressed to Lohengrin by Elsa: the inability to *believe* in any annunciation, even by an inner revelation, the impossibility of simply believing in *any* kind of *being.*

It may be objected that such contradictions are only found in those civilized Jews in whom the old orthodoxy is still effective alongside the modern mentality. That would be far from true. The education of the Jew only reveals his nature even more clearly, because it engages in many things that ought to be given more serious consideration than mere financial transactions. That the Jew is not unequivocal in himself can be proved by the fact that the Jew *does not sing.* This

15. This is really the explanation of the Jew's lack of genius (cf. pp. 158ff.): only belief is creative. And perhaps the Jew's inferior sexual potency reflects the *same* fact in the *low* sphere.

16. It is Man who creates Woman. That is why Jewish women are known not to possess the simplicity of Christian women, who readily give themselves to their sexual complement.

17. But this must not be regarded as a predominance of the will and as an abnormal withdrawal of the intellect, as it was interpreted by Schopenhauer, and subsequently, using Schopenhauer's inadequate psychological distinctions, by H. S. Chamberlain. The Jew has no really strong will, and his inner indecisiveness could easily and *wrongly* be confused with psychic "masochism," that is, inertia and helplessness at the moment of decision.

is not because of any modesty, but because he does not *believe* in his own singing. The Jew's peculiar revulsion from singing, or even from loud and clear words, has as little to do with genuine reserve as his ambiguity has with any real sophistication or genius. Modesty is always proud, while that aversion of the Jew is a sign of his lack of *inner dignity:* he has no understanding of spontaneous being, and the mere act of singing would make him feel ridiculous and compromised. Modesty comprises all those elements that have a close and continuous link with the self, but the Jew's embarrassment extends to things that cannot be sacred to him and that he would not therefore run the risk of defiling if he raised his voice in public. And this again coincides with the impiety of the Jew: for all music is absolute and exists as if detached from any base, which is why of all the arts it has the closest relationship with religion and why a simple song, which fills a single melody with a whole soul, is as un-Jewish as religion itself. This shows how difficult it is to define Judaism. The Jew lacks hardness, but also gentleness—rather, he is tenacious and soft. He is neither crude nor subtle, neither rude nor polite. He is not a king or a leader, but nor is he a subject or a vassal. He cannot be profoundly shaken, but he is equally deficient in equanimity. He never takes anything for granted, but any true astonishment is equally alien to him. He has nothing of Lohengrin in him, but perhaps even less of Telramund (who stands and falls with his honor). He is ridiculous as a member of a student dueling society and yet does not make a good philistine. He is never stolid, but neither is he whole-heartedly reckless. Because he believes in nothing he takes refuge in material things, and that alone is the origin of his avarice: it is here that he seeks a reality and tries to convince himself through "business" that something exists—that is why the only value that he actually recognizes is the money he "earns." Nevertheless, he is not even a true businessman: for the "dishonest" and "dubious" element in the conduct of the Jewish dealer is merely the concrete manifestation of the Jew's lack of an *inner identity* even in this sphere. *"**Jewish**," therefore, is a **category**,* which cannot psychologically be traced back and determined any further. Metaphysically, one may describe it as a *condition before being.* Introspectively, one does not get beyond the inner ambivalence, the absence of any conviction, the incapacity for any kind of love, that is, for any undivided dedication and sacrifice.

The Jew's eroticism is sentimental, his humor is satire. But every satirist is sentimental, just as every humorist is merely an eroticist in reverse. Satire and sentimentality contain the duplicity that basically constitutes Judaism (for satire conceals too little and thus distorts the humor), and both have in common the smile that characterizes the Jewish face: not a blissful, not a painful, not a proud, not a contorted smile, but that vague expression (the physiognomical *correlative* of inner ambiguity) which indicates a *readiness* to *respond to anything* and in which all reverence of the individual for himself is missing, the reverence which alone provides the foundation for all other *verecundia.*

I believe I have now been clear enough not to be misunderstood about what I mean by the true nature of Judaism. Ibsen's King Håkon in *The Pretenders* and his Dr. Stockmann in *An Enemy of the People* may, if necessary, show even more clearly what will be inaccessible to the genuine Jew in all eternity: *immediate being, the divine right of kings, the oak tree, the trumpet, the Siegfried motif, the creation of the self by the self, the word* ***I am***. The Jew is truly "God's orphan child," and there is no (male) Jew who, be it ever so dimly, does not ***suffer*** from his Jewishness, that is, most fundamentally, from his *un*belief.

Judaism and Christianity thus show the greatest, most immeasurable contrast. Of all forms of being, the former is most divided and most lacking in inner identity, while the latter has the firmest belief and the utmost trust in God. Christianity is the highest degree of heroism: the Jew, on the other hand, is never integrated and whole. That is why the Jew is a coward, and the hero is his diametrical opposite.

H. S. Chamberlain has said many true and apt things about the genuine Jew's terrible, uncanny incomprehension of Christ, of his person and his doctrine, of the warrior and the patient sufferer in him, of his life and his death. It would be wrong, however, to think that the Jew *hates* Christ. The Jew is not the anti-Christ: *he simply has no relationship whatsoever with Jesus.* Strictly speaking, there are only Aryans—criminals—who hate Jesus. The Jew only feels *disturbed* and *irritated* by him, as by something that he cannot attack with his wit because it is beyond his understanding.

Nevertheless, the legend of the New Testament, the ripest flower and supreme completion of the Old, together with the artificial adaptation of the latter to the Messianic promises of the former, has stood the Jews in good stead: it has been their strongest external protection. The fact that, despite their polar opposition, Christianity evolved from Judaism of all things is one of the most profound psychological mysteries: the problem with which we are dealing here is none other than the psychology of the founder of a religion.[18]

What is the difference between a genius who founds a religion and all other geniuses? What inner necessity drives him to founding a religion?

It can only be that he himself has not always believed in the God whom he proclaims. Buddha and Christ are reported to have been exposed to much greater temptations than all other human beings. Two more, Mohammed and Luther, were *epileptics. Epilepsy* is *the disease of the criminal:* Caesar, Narses, Napoleon, the "great" criminals all suffered from it, and Flaubert and Dostoevsky, who at least had an inclination toward it, both had an extraordinary amount of the criminal in them, even though, of course, they were not actual criminals.

18. At this point I shall finally deal with what I had to leave out deliberately from the discussions in chapters IV–VIII.

The founder of a religion is the individual who once led a completely godless life and yet struggled through to the highest faith. "How it is possible that a naturally evil human being should make himself into a good human being surpasses every concept of ours. For how can an evil tree bear good fruit," Kant asks in his philosophy of religion, but *nevertheless, in principle, affirms* this possibility: "For, in spite of that fall, the command that we *ought* to become better human beings still resounds unabated in our souls; consequently, we must also be *capable* of it." The incomprehensible possibility of the total *rebirth* of an individual who was depraved through all the years and days of his earlier life, this high mystery, is *realized* in those six or seven individuals who founded the great religions of humankind. This is what distinguishes them from the genius proper, in whom the disposition for good predominates from birth.

The other kind of genius receives the grace before his birth: the founder of a religion does so in the course of his life. In him an older being dies most completely and gives way to an entirely new one. The greater an individual wants to be, the more things there are in him that he must condemn to death. I believe that in this respect Socrates (as the only Greek) comes close to the founders of religions. Perhaps he fought the decisive battle against evil the day he stood up alone for twenty-four hours in one and the same place near Potidaea.[19]

The founder of a religion is the individual for whom *not one single problem has been solved* at his birth. He is the individual with the fewest certainties of his own. In him *everything* is at risk and open to question, and he is obliged to conquer for himself not just this or that, but *everything,* during his life. Generally, one person has to contend with illness and suffers from his physical weakness, while another trembles with fear of crime because it exists in him as a possibility, and everybody does something wrong and burdens himself with some sin at birth. Original sin is only formally the same for everybody, but materially different for all. One person chose one paltry and worthless thing, another person another, when he ceased to will, when his will suddenly became instinct, when his individuality became merely an individual, when his love became lust, when he was born; and it is this, his own specific original sin, this nothingness in his own person, that he perceives during his life as a guilt and a blemish and an imperfection, and that becomes a problem, a riddle, and a task for his thinking mind. In contrast to these, only the founder of a religion must atone for original sin *as a whole:* to him everything, the whole universe, is problematic, but he solves every problem and redeems himself into the whole universe. He answers every problem and he frees himself entirely from guilt. He

19. Nietzsche was probably right in not seeing him as a genuine Hellene, while Plato is again a Greek through and through.

gains the firmest foothold above the deepest abyss, he overcomes nothingness as such and he grasps the thing-in-itself, that is, being as such. In that sense it can be said that he has really been liberated from original sin, and that in him God has completely become a human being, but the human being has also completely become God. For in him everything once was guilt and a problem, but now everything becomes atonement and solution.

All genius is nothing but the highest freedom from natural laws.

"He who overcomes himself frees himself from the force that binds all beings."

If this is true, the founder of a religion is the greatest genius. He has achieved what the most profound thinkers of humankind have only presented as a possibility, with hesitation, in order to preserve their ethical outlook and to avoid having to abandon the *freedom of choice: the complete rebirth of the human being,* his "regeneration," the total reversal of the will. Other great minds also have to fight evil, but in their case the scales are loaded in favor of good right from the outset. Not so with the founder of a religion. In him there is so much evil, so much will to power, so much earthly passion, that he is obliged to struggle with the enemy in himself for forty days in the desert, incessantly, without food, without sleep. It is only then that he has won: he has not entered death, but freed the supreme life in himself. If it were otherwise, there would be no impulse to found a religion. In this respect the founder of a religion is quite the opposite pole to the ruler, the Emperor the opposite of the Galilean. In Napoleon also a reversal took place at a certain point of his life, but instead of turning *away* from earthly life he finally chose its treasures, its power, and its glories. Napoleon is great by virtue of the colossal intensity with which he puts the idea behind him, the enormous tension of his rejection of the absolute, and the magnitude of his *unatoned* guilt. The founder of a religion, on the other hand, cannot and need not bring to humankind anything other than what he, the most burdened individual, has achieved: a covenant with the deity. He knows that he is most laden with guilt, and he atones for the *largest* amount of guilt through his death on the cross.

In Judaism there were two possibilities. Before the birth of Christ these were joined and no choice had yet been made between them. There was a diaspora and concurrently at least a kind of state: negation and affirmation existed side by side. *Christ was the individual who overcame the strongest negation, Judaism, within himself, and who thus created the strongest affirmation, Christianity, as the most extreme opposite of Judaism.* Out of the condition *before* being, being and non-being *separated.* Now the dice were cast: the old Israel divided into Jews and Christians, and the *Jew,* as we know him and as I have described him, came into being ***at the same time*** as the *Christian.* The diaspora now became complete and Judaism forfeited the possibility of greatness: since then *Judaism* has not been able to produce men such as Simson and Joshua, the most un-Jewish Jews in the old Israel.

Christianity and Judaism are interdependent in the history of the world as affirmation and negation. Israel held the highest possibilities ever granted to a nation: the possibility of Christ. *The other possibility is the Jew.*

I hope that I shall not be misunderstood: I do not want to impute to Judaism any relationship with Christianity that is alien to it. *Christianity is the absolute negation of Judaism, but it has the same relationship with Judaism that links all things with their opposites, every affirmation with its negation, which is overcome by it.*[20] Even more than piety and Judaism, Christianity and Judaism can only be defined *through each other* and through their mutual exclusion. Nothing is easier than being a Jew, nothing harder than being a Christian. *Judaism is the abyss over which Christianity is erected, and that is why the Jew is the strongest fear and the deepest aversion of the Aryan.*[21]

I am unable to share Chamberlain's belief that the birth of the Savior in Palestine could have been a mere coincidence. *Christ was a Jew, but only in order to overcome Judaism in himself most completely,* since the firmest *believer* is he who has overcome the most powerful *doubt,* and the most *positive* affirmer he who has risen above the most dreary *negation.* Judaism was the specific original sin of Christ, and it is Christ's victory over Judaism that makes him richer than Buddha and Confucius and all the rest. *Christ is the greatest human being because he struggled with the greatest adversary.* Perhaps he is, and will remain, the only Jew who has succeeded in defeating Judaism. The first Jew would then have been the last to have totally become *Christ,* but perhaps Judaism today still has the possibility of bringing forth Christ, and perhaps the next founder of a religion will also have to pass through *Judaism* in the first place.

This alone makes it possible to understand the prolonged existence of the Jews, who outlast all other nations and races. The Jews could not have persisted and preserved themselves if they had not had at least *one* belief, and this *one* belief is the dim, vague, and yet desperately certain feeling that there must be something, if only one thing, about Judaism and in Judaism. This one thing is the Messiah, the redeemer. The redeemer of Judaism is the redeemer from Judaism. Every other people realizes a certain single, special idea, and that is why every other nation ultimately perishes. Only the Jew realizes no special idea, because if he could realize anything, it would only be the idea-in-itself: from the midst of Judaea the divine human being must issue. The vitality of Judaism

20. The reader may remember my remarks about the psychological significance of pairs of opposites (p. 96f.) and about the role of polarity in characterology (p. 70f.).

21. This is also the cause of the difference and the boundary between the antisemitism of the Jew and the antisemitism of the Indo-European. The Jewish antisemite merely dislikes the Jew. The antisemitic Aryan, on the other hand, however bravely he fights Judaism, in his heart of hearts, is always what the Jew never is: a *Judaeophobe.*

is connected with this: Judaism lives on Christianity in more than just the sense of material exploitation. Metaphysically, the only purpose of the Jewish character is to serve as a pedestal for the founder of a religion. This further explains the strangest phenomenon in the ways of the Jews, their special method of paying homage to their God: never as individuals, but always in a crowd. They can only be "pious" together with others and they need somebody else to "pray with," because their hope is the permanent possibility of seeing the greatest conqueror, the founder of a religion, issuing from their species. This is the unconscious significance of all the Messianic hopes in the Jewish tradition: *the purpose of the Jews is the Christian.* If, then, the Jew perhaps still contains the highest *possibilities,* he certainly contains the lowest *realities.* Of all human beings it is probably he who has the *potential* to achieve the *most* and at the same time the *inner ability* to achieve the *least.*

* * *

Our present age shows Judaism at the highest peak it has climbed since the days of Herod. The *spirit of modernity* is *Jewish,* wherever one looks at it. Sexuality is affirmed and today's species ethic sings the wedding hymn to sexual intercourse. The unfortunate Nietzsche is certainly not responsible for the grand union of natural selection and natural fornication, whose despicable apostle is called Wilhelm Bölsche. He appreciated asceticism and thought its opposite more desirable only because he suffered too much from his own. But women and Jews are matchmakers: their aim is to make humanity guilty.

Our age is not only the most Jewish, but also the most effeminate of all ages; an age in which art only provides a sudarium for its moods and which has derived the artistic urge in humans from the games played by animals; an age of the most credulous anarchism, an age without any appreciation of the state and law, an age of species ethic, an age of the shallowest of all imaginable interpretations of history (historical materialism), an age of capitalism and marxism, an age for which history, life, science, everything, has become nothing but economics and technology; an age that has declared genius to be a form of madness, but which no longer has one great artist or one great philosopher, an age that is most devoid of originality, but which chases most frantically after originality; an age that has replaced the idea of virginity with the cult of the demivierge. *This age also has the distinction of being the first to have not only affirmed and worshipped sexual intercourse, but to have practically made it a duty,* not as a way of achieving oblivion, as the Romans or Greeks did in their bacchanals, but in order to find itself and to give its own dreariness a meaning.

But opposed to the new Judaism a new Christianity is straining toward the light. Humankind is waiting for the new founder of a religion, and the struggle is coming to a head as it did in the year one. Humankind once more has the choice between Judaism and Christianity, between business and culture, between Woman and Man, between the species and the personality, between worthlessness and value, between the earthly life and the higher life, between nothingness and the deity. These are the two poles: there is no third realm.

XIV | Woman and Humanity

Now at last, cleansed and armed, we can once more confront the question of the emancipation of women. Cleansed, because our eye is no longer clouded by the ambiguities swarming around the subject like a thousand midges; armed, because we are in possession of firm theoretical concepts and assured ethical views. A long way from the playground of ordinary controversies and far beyond the problem of differences in endowment, my investigation reached some points that foreshadowed the role of Woman in the universe and the meaning of her mission for humanity. Therefore, I will once more refrain from discussing any overly specific questions, particularly as I am not optimistic enough to expect that my results will have any influence on the conduct of political affairs. Rather than elaborating any suggestions concerning social hygiene, I will deal with the problem in terms of the idea of humanity which dominates the philosophy of Immanuel Kant.

That idea is under considerable threat from femininity. Women are equipped to a high degree with the art of creating the illusion that they are really asexual and that their sexuality is only a concession to Man. For if this illusion were to cease, what would become of the competition of several, or indeed many, men for one woman? However, with the support of men who have believed them, women today have almost succeeded in persuading the opposite sex that the most important, most characteristic, need of Man is sexuality, that he can expect the fulfillment of his truest and deepest desires only from Woman, and that chastity, for him, is something unnatural and impossible. How often are young men who find satisfaction in serious work told by women, to whom they do not seem too ugly and too unpromising as lovers or sons-in-law, not to study too hard, but to "enjoy life." These friendly admonitions reveal Woman's, naturally unconscious, sense of failing in her mission—which is directed solely at copulation—and of *becoming nothing* and losing all her significance together with her entire sex, as soon as a man begins to take an interest in anything other than sexual matters.

That women will ever change in this respect is doubtful. Nor should it be believed that they were ever any different. Today the sensual element may be more prominent than it used to be, because such an infinitely large part of the "women's movement" is only a desire to exchange motherhood for prostitution:

the movement as a whole is an emancipation of prostitutes rather than an emancipation of women, and its main result is certainly the bolder emergence of the cocotte element in Woman. But what seems *new* is the behavior of *men*. Under the influence of Judaism, among other things, men today are close to complying with, and indeed appropriating, women's evaluation of themselves. Male chastity is laughed at and no longer *understood*, Woman is no longer perceived by Man as his sin and his *destiny*, and Man is no longer ashamed of his own desire.

It is now clear *where* the demand for the lack of restraint, the coffee-house concept of the Dionysian, the cult of Goethe insofar as Goethe is Ovid, the whole modern *copulation culture*, comes from. We have reached a point where hardly anybody has the courage to confess his belief in chastity, and almost everybody prefers to behave as if he were a debauchee. Sexual excesses are the most popular topic to *brag* about, and sexuality is so highly rated that the braggart has a hard time trying to make people believe him. Chastity, on the other hand, commands so little respect that the truly chaste man often hides behind the appearance of the roué. It is certainly the case that the modest are even *ashamed* of their modesty: however, today's modesty is not the modesty of eroticism, but the shame of a woman who has not yet found a man and has not yet received her value from the opposite sex. That is why everybody is eager to show everybody else how *faithfully* and with what dutiful *pleasure* he exercises his sexual functions. Thus the decision as to what is masculine is today made by Woman, who by her nature is able to appreciate only the sexual side of Man, and men receive the measure of their masculinity from her hand. And thus the number of copulations and the "sweetheart" or "girlfriend" have become the means whereby *one male individual proves himself in front of another.* But no, because then there would be no men left.

On the other hand, the high esteem in which *virginity* is held *originally* came from men, and still does so where there are any men left: it is Man's projection of his own *immanent* ideal of immaculate purity on the object of his love. One must not be misled either by women's fear and terror of being touched, which so readily turn into trustfulness at the shortest possible notice, or by their hysterical repression of sexual desires, or by their *external compulsion* to fulfill Man's demand for physical purity to ensure that the buyer does not fail to turn up, or indeed by their need to *receive* value, which often makes them wait for so long for the man who can endow them with the greatest value (which is generally quite wrongly interpreted as a high *self*-esteem on the part of such girls). Right from the outset, we can hardly be in any doubt about what *women* think of virginity, if we remember that women's main aim is to bring about *sexual intercourse as such*, which alone can provide them with an existence. That Woman wants sexual intercourse and nothing else, however uninterested in *lust* she seems to be for her own person, has already been proved by her ubiquitous matchmaking.

To convince ourselves of this anew, we must consider how Woman regards virginity in other members of her sex.

Here we notice that the condition of unmarried women is held in very low esteem by women themselves. In fact this is *the one* female condition that is attributed a *negative* value by Woman. Women do not really appreciate any woman until she is married. Even if she is "unhappily" married to an ugly, weak, poor, common, tyrannical, unprepossessing man, she is still married, that is, she has received a value and an existence. And if a woman, however briefly, has tasted the splendors of the life of a mistress, or even if she has become a streetwalker, she is rated more highly than the old maid sewing or darning alone in her room without ever having belonged to a man, whether in a lawful or unlawful union, and whether for a long period or in a rapidly passing frenzy.

Similarly, if a very young girl is distinguished by physical charms she is attributed a positive value by Woman not because of her beauty—Woman lacks the ability to recognize beauty, because she has no value to project—but only because she has a better prospect of captivating a man. *The more beautiful a virgin is, the more reliable a* ***promise*** *she holds for other women, the more valuable she is to woman as a matchmaker destined to be the guardian of the community: this* ***unconscious*** *thought alone causes a woman to take pleasure in a beautiful girl.* I have already discussed how this can appear in an undiluted form only once the female individual passing judgment has herself received an existence (because otherwise those emotions would be outweighed by her envy of her competitor and the feeling that the latter is reducing her own chances in the struggle for value). Women must make matches for themselves before the others can expect them to act as matchmakers on their behalf.

The contempt for the "old maid," which has unfortunately become so common, is entirely of *Woman*'s making. Men will often speak of an aged spinster with respect, but every woman and every girl, whether married or unmarried, will have nothing but the most extreme contempt for her, even though in some cases they may not be conscious of this. I once heard a married lady—who was regarded as having considerable wit and numerous talents, and who had so many admirers thanks to her attractive appearance that there could be no question of envy in her case—make fun of her plain and elderly Italian teacher, who had repeatedly declared: Io sono ancora una vergine (that she was still a virgin).

However, assuming that her remark was correctly reproduced, it must be admitted that the older woman had probably only made a virtue of necessity and would have been very glad to lose her virginity somehow without losing her reputation in society.

This is the most important thing: women not only despise and ridicule the virginity of other women, but they also have an extremely low opinion of their own virginity as a *condition* (which they regard highly only as a much wanted *commodity* of the *highest* value in *men*'s eyes). That is why they look up to any married woman as if she were a superior being. That the sexual act in particular is what ultimately matters most to Woman can be seen from the downright veneration paid by young girls to very recently married women, for it is the latter to whom the purpose of their existence has just been unveiled and who have been led to its summit. On the other hand, every young girl considers every other young girl as an incomplete being who, like herself, is still in search of her vocation.

Thus I believe that I have demonstrated how perfectly my inference from matchmaking—that the ideal of virginity must be of male origin and cannot be of female—corresponds to experience. Man demands chastity both from himself and from others, and he demands it most from the being that he loves. Woman wants to be able to be unchaste and she demands sensuality, not virtue, from Man also. Woman does not appreciate "good boys." On the contrary, it is common knowledge that she always falls into the arms of a man who has the greatest reputation of being a Don Juan. Woman wants man sexually, because it is only through his sexuality that she can gain an existence. The eroticism of Man, a phenomenon which implies *distance,* is incomprehensible to women, who only understand that side of him which relentlessly seizes and appropriates the object of his desire, and who are not impressed by those men in whom any brutal instincts are only slightly developed or not at all. Even Man's higher, platonic love is basically unwelcome to women: it flatters and caresses them, but it ***means*** nothing to them. And if a prayer on bended knees lasted too long, Beatrice would become as impatient as Messalina.

Woman is most profoundly degraded by sexual intercourse, and most highly elevated by love. The fact that Woman demands sexual intercourse and not love signifies that she wants to be degraded and not elevated. **The ultimate opponent of the** *emancipation of women is Woman.*

Sexual intercourse is immoral, not because it is lascivious, not because it is the epitome of all bliss in the low life. An asceticism that declares lust to be the essence of immorality is itself immoral, because it seeks the standard for the wrong that is being done in a *concomitant* and external consequence of the act, and not in the mental attitude: it is *heteronomous.* A human being is *entitled* to strive for lust, and he has every right to try to make his life on earth easier and happier, so long as he does not sacrifice any moral commandment in the process. But in resorting to asceticism a human being tries to *extort* morality by means of self-laceration. He expects morality to *follow from a reason* and, in his own case, to be the result of, and the reward for, having denied himself so much. Therefore, asceticism, both as a matter of principle and as a psychological disposition, is *reprehensible,* for it makes virtue *dependent* on the *success* of something else, turning it into the *effect of a cause,* and failing to aspire to it for its own sake and as an end in itself. Asceticism is a dangerous seducer: so many fall prey to its deception so readily because pleasure is the *most common motive* for abandoning the path of the law and therefore it is easy to succumb to the error that choosing pain instead of pleasure is the surer guide to the right path. But pleasure as such is neither moral nor immoral. *It is only when the will to pleasure has conquered the will to value* that a human being has fallen.

Sexual intercourse is immoral *because* at such a moment there is no man who does not use Woman as a means to an end and who does not put lust before the value of humanity, in both his and her person. In sexual intercourse lust makes Man forget both himself and Woman, whom he no longer regards as having a psychic existence but only a physical one. He expects from her either a child or the satisfaction of his own lust, and in both cases he is using her not as an end in herself, but for an alien purpose. For this reason alone, and none other, sexual intercourse is immoral.

Woman is certainly the missionary of sexual intercourse, and she always uses herself, like everything else in the world, as nothing but a means to this end. She wants Man to be a means to the end of her own lust or child, and she *herself* wants to be used by Man as a means to an end, as a thing, as an object, as his possession, and to be changed and molded by him as he sees fit. However, not only must no human being allow another human being to use him as a means to an end, but nor must the attitude of Man to Woman be determined by the fact that she really desires sexual intercourse and indeed *craves nothing* ***else*** from him, even though she never fully admits this either to him or to herself. It is true that Kundry appeals to Parsifal's ***compassion*** for her longing, but this precisely reveals the whole weakness of the ethics of compassion that would force us to fulfill every wish of our fellow-human, however unjustifiable it may be. An all-out morality of sympathy is as absurd as an all-out social ethic, because both make *what ought to be* dependent on the *will* (whether the will of the individual concerned, the will of another individual, or the will of society) *instead of* making *the will* dependent *on what ought to be.* Both choose as their standard of morality a concrete human destiny, a concrete human happiness, a concrete human moment, *instead of the idea.*

The question is: How should Man treat Woman? *As she herself wants to be treated or as the moral idea demands?* If he is to treat her as she herself wants to be treated, he must engage in sexual intercourse with her, because she wants to be the object of sexual intercourse, beat her because she wants to be beaten, hypnotize her because she wants to be hypnotized, show her by gallantry how little he values her in herself because she wants compliments rather than being respected in herself. If, on the other hand, he wants to encounter Woman as the moral idea demands, he must try to see the human being in her and to respect her. *W is a function of M,* a function that he can posit or cancel, and women want to be no more and nothing other than just this. It is said that in India widows allow themselves to be burnt with pleasure and conviction and even insist on this kind of death, but this does not make the custom any less barbaric.

As with the emancipation of women, so with the emancipation of the Jews and Negroes. The main reason why these peoples have been treated as slaves and always held in low esteem is certainly their own submissive disposition, for they do not have as strong a desire for freedom as Indo-Europeans. Even though in America today the whites have been obliged to segregate themselves fully from the Negroes, who have made a wicked and unworthy use of their freedom, in the war between the Northern states and the Confederates, which resulted in the freedom of the blacks, justice was entirely on the side of the former. In the Jew, more in the Negro, *and to an even greater extent in Woman,* the *disposition to humanity* is burdened with a larger number of amoral urges and is *obliged to struggle with more obstacles* than in the Aryan man, but *even in them the idea of humanity* (that is, not the idea of human society, but the fact of *being human,* the *soul as part of an intelligible world*) must be *honored,* however small its last remnant may be. Nobody but the law must claim any power over even the most degraded criminal, and no human being has the right to lynch him.

The problem of Woman and the problem of the Jew are completely identical with the *problem of slavery* and must be solved in the same way. Nobody should be oppressed, even if he only feels happy under oppression. If I use a domestic animal I do not deprive it of freedom, because it did not have any before I began to use it, but Woman still has an impotent sense of not being able to do otherwise, a last, albeit extremely puny, trace of intelligible freedom, probably because there is no such thing as absolute Woman. Women are *human beings* and must be treated *as such,* even if they themselves would *never* want this. *Woman and Man have equal rights.*

Incidentally, this does not imply that women should immediately be granted a share in political power. From the point of view of *utility* such a concession, for the time being and possibly forever, is certainly inadvisable. In New Zealand, where the ethical principle was held so high as to give women the right to vote, the results have been disastrous. Just as no children, imbeciles, or criminals would rightly be granted any influence over the governance of the community, even if they suddenly achieved a numerical parity or indeed majority, so it is *legitimate,* for the present, to keep women out of matters in which there is every reason to fear that a female influence would do nothing but harm. Just as scientific results are independent of whether or not everybody agrees with them, so the rights or otherwise of Woman can be determined quite accurately without involving women themselves in the decision, and they need not be afraid of being cheated if this decision is made according to the point of view of justice and not of power.

Justice is one and the same for both Man and Woman. Nobody must presume to deny or forbid Woman anything as being "unfeminine," and it is a vile judgment to find a man who has killed his adulterous wife not guilty, as if, legally, she had been his *possession.* Woman must be judged as an individual and in accordance with the idea of freedom, not as one of a species, not according to a standard derived from the empirical world, nor from the needs of Man's love, even if she should never prove worthy of such an elevated judgment.

Therefore this book is the greatest homage ever paid to women. Man can adopt only *one* moral attitude to Woman, as to everything else: not sexuality and not love—both of which use her as a means to *alien* ends—*but only the attempt to understand her.* Most people theoretically pretend to respect ***Woman*** and practically despise ***women*** all the more: I have reversed this relationship. It proved impossible to attribute a high value to ***Woman,*** but ***women*** must not be excluded from any respect once and for all right from the outset.

Unfortunately, some very famous and exceptional men have really had *rather mean* views on this matter. Remember the attitude of Schopenhauer and Demosthenes to the emancipation of women. And Goethe's

> Thus the maiden is always busy and matures in secret
> Toward domestic virtue, to *make an intelligent man happy.*
> If she then finally wishes to read, she will certainly choose a cookbook

is no better than Molière's

> Une femme en sait toujours assez,
> Quand la capacité de son esprit se hausse
> A connaître un pourpoint d'avec un haut-de-chausse.

Man must overcome the aversion against the masculine woman in himself, which is nothing but common selfishness. If Woman were to become masculine, by becoming logical and ethical, she would no longer lend herself so well as a *passive screen* for *projections,* but that is not enough reason to have her educated, as is done today, only for her husband and her child, and to impose a norm on her that forbids her anything that is *masculine.*

Even though *absolute* Woman has no possibility of being moral, it does not follow from recognizing this *idea* of Woman that Man should allow the *empirical* woman to *succumb* to it completely and irredeemably, and even less that he should contribute to making her conform more and more to it. To adopt Kant's terminology, "a germ of good" must theoretically be assumed to be present in the living human woman, and it is this remnant of the free nature that enables her vaguely to feel her destiny.[1] *Theoretically,* it must *never be categorically asserted* that it is impossible to graft something more onto that germ, even though *in practice* this has certainly never been achieved, and even if it were never achieved in the future.

The most profound cause and purpose of the universe is the good, and the

1. Cf. chapter XII, p. 248f.

whole world is subject to the moral idea. Even animals are assessed as *phenomena,* with elephants being attributed a higher moral value than snakes, although they are not *held accountable* as persons, for example, for killing another animal. Woman, however, *is held accountable, and this implies the demand that she should change. And if all femininity is immoral, Woman must cease to be Woman and become Man.*

In this respect in particular the greatest care must be taken to avoid the risk of external imitation, which always throws Woman back most firmly into femininity. The chances of truly emancipating women, that is, giving them a freedom which is not *willfulness* but *will,* are extremely slight. To judge by the facts, women seem to have only two possibilities. They may either falsely accept Man's own creations, by believing that they themselves want something that *contradicts* their own *as yet unweakened* nature, and by becoming falsely indignant about immorality, *as if they were moral,* and about sensuality, *as if* they wanted a chaste love; or they may openly admit[2] that the content of Woman is the man and the child, without realizing what they are in fact admitting, and what shamelessness, what defeat, is implied in this assertion. *Unconscious hypocrisy or cynical identification with natural instinct:* there seems to be no other choice available to Woman.

However, what is needed is *neither the affirmation nor the denial* of femininity, but its *rejection* and its *conquest.* For example, if a woman *really wanted* Man to be chaste, she would have conquered Woman in herself, because sexual intercourse would no longer be her highest value and her ultimate aim. But the trouble is that it is impossible to believe in the authenticity of such demands, even if they are really made from time to time. A woman who demands chastity from Man, apart from being hysterical, is so stupid and so incapable of any truthfulness that she no longer even suspects that she is denying her own self and absolutely and irredeemably destroying her own existence. One hardly knows which to prefer: Woman's infinite falseness in subscribing to the *ascetic* ideal, which is the most alien thing to her, or her shameless admiration of the notorious lecher, to whom she simply gives herself.

But since Woman's true will *in both cases* is equally directed to making Man guilty, *this* is the crux of the Woman Question; and to that extent the Woman Question coincides with the question of humanity.

At one point in his writings, Friedrich Nietzsche says:

> To blunder over the fundamental problem of "man and woman," to deny here the most abysmal antagonism and the necessity of an eternally hostile tension, perhaps to dream here of equal rights, equal education, equal claims and duties: this is a *typical* sign of shallow-mindedness, and a thinker who has proved

2. As does, for instance, Laura Marholm.

> himself to be shallow on this dangerous point—shallow of instinct!—may be regarded as suspect in general, more, as betrayed, as found out: he will probably be too "short" for all the fundamental questions of life, those of life in the future too, incapable of *any* depth. On the other hand, a man who has depth, in his spirit as well as in his desires, and also that depth of benevolence which is capable of hardness and severity and is easily confused with them, can think of woman only in an *oriental* way—he must conceive of woman as a possession, as property with lock and key, as something predestined for service and attaining her fulfilment in service—in this matter he must take his stand on the tremendous intelligence of Asia, on Asia's superiority of instinct, as the Greeks formerly did: they were Asia's best heirs and pupils and, as is well known, from Homer to the age of Pericles, with the *increase* of their culture and the amplitude of their powers, also became step by step *more strict* with women, in short more oriental. *How* necessary, *how* logical, *how* humanly desirable even, this was: let each ponder for himself!

Here Nietzsche, the individualist, is thinking entirely in terms of social ethics: his theory of castes and groups and his theory of seclusion, as so often, disrupt the autonomy of his moral teaching. *In the service of society and of the undisturbed peace of men,* he is trying to submit Woman to a power relationship in which she will as good as cease to voice any desire for emancipation and will no longer even repeat the false and insincere demand for freedom put forward by today's champions of women's rights, *who have no idea of what Woman's bondage really consists in and what its causes are.* However, I did not quote Nietzsche in order to convict him of an inconsistency, but in order to show, with his own words in mind, how the problem of humanity cannot be solved without solving the problem of Woman. Those who think it an unnecessarily high demand that Man should respect Woman for the sake of the idea, of the noumenon, and not use her as a means to an end outside her, and who think that consequently Man must grant to Woman the same rights but also the same duties (to educate herself morally and intellectually) as to himself, should bear in mind *that Man is unable to solve the ethical problem for his own person if he persists in negating the idea of humanity in Woman* by using her merely as a commodity to be consumed and enjoyed. *Given the Asian standpoint, sexual intercourse is the price Man must pay Woman for her oppression.* And however characteristic of Woman her *eagerness to submit even to the worst slavery for this price* may be, Man must not accept the deal, because morally he would thereby also be the loser.

Even *technically,* then, the problem of humanity cannot be solved by Man alone. Even if he wanted to redeem only *himself,* he must *carry* Woman *with him* and try to make her abandon her immoral designs on him. Woman must renounce sexual intercourse *internally* and *truthfully,* of her own *free will.* But this actually means that Woman *as such* must *perish,* and there is no prospect of establishing the Kingdom of God on earth until then. That is why Pythagoras, Plato, Christianity (as opposed to Judaism), Tertullian, Swift, Wagner, Ibsen stood up *for* the liberation and redemption of Woman, that is, *not for the emancipation of woman from Man, but for the emancipation of Woman from Woman.* And in such company it is easy to put up with Nietzsche's anathema.

However, it is hard for Woman to reach such an aim by her own strength. It would have to be possible for the spark that is so weak in her to be kindled again and again by the fire of Man: an *example* would need to be given. Christ gave the example. He redeemed Magdalene by returning to that part of his past and atoning for it as he did for everything else. Wagner, the greatest individual since Christ, understood this most profoundly. Until Woman ceases to exist as Woman for Man, she cannot herself cease to exist as woman: Kundry can only really be freed from Klingsor's spell by Parsifal, the sinless, immaculate man. This *psychological* deduction agrees with the philosophical as completely as it does here with Wagner's *Parsifal,* the most profound work of world literature. It is man's sexuality that gives Woman an existence as Woman in the first place. The degree to which matter exists corresponds to the amount of guilt in the universe, and Woman also will live only until Man has fully expiated his guilt and really overcome his *own* sexuality.

This is the only way to defeat those who counter all anti-feminist tendencies by arguing that it is necessary to come to terms with Woman because she is as she is and cannot be changed, and that there is no point in fighting a losing battle. I have shown that Woman *is* not, and that she *dies* the moment Man wants nothing but to *be.* What is being fought is not a matter of an eternally unalterable existence and essence: it is something that *can* be eliminated and *should* be eliminated.

The old maid is the woman who is no longer encountered by a man who creates her. As a result she perishes, and the old woman is the more evil, the more she is an old maid. If a man and a woman created by him meet again on bad terms, both must die: if they meet again on good terms, the miracle happens.

For those who have *understood* it, the Woman Question can only be solved in this way alone, and in no other. The solution will be considered impossible, its spirit inflated, its claim exaggerated, its demands intolerant. And indeed: our concern has long since ceased to be the Woman Question that women *talk* about. It is what women are *silent* about and *must* eternally be silent about: *the bondage* inherent in *sexuality. This* Woman Question is as old as sexuality itself and no younger than humankind. And the answer is that Man must redeem *himself* from sexuality in order to redeem Woman. He can do so in *no other way,* and his *chastity*—rather than his unchastity, as she believes—is her *only* salvation. In the process she obviously perishes as *Woman,* but only in order to rise again from the ashes, newborn, rejuvenated, as *the pure* ***human being***.

The Woman Question will persist as long as there are two sexes and will not fall silent until the question of humanity does. This is what Christ meant when, according to the testimony of Clemens, the father of the Church, he told Salome, without cheerfully glossing over sexuality, as St. Paul and Luther did after him, that death would hold sway as long as women brought forth and that the truth would not be seen before two were made into a single one, and male and female had become a third, which was the same, but *neither* Man *nor* Woman.

* * *

Thus at last the demand for abstinence on the part of both sexes is fully explained from the supreme point of view of the problem of Woman, seen as the problem of humanity. To derive this demand from the detrimental effects of sexual intercourse on health is shallow and may for ever be disputed by the advocates of the body; to found it on the immorality of lust is wrong, because this introduces a heteronomous motive into ethics. When St. Augustine demanded chastity from all human beings, he was told that humankind would then soon disappear from the face of the earth. This strange fear, which seems to suggest that the most horrifying thing would be the extinction of the *species,* not only reveals an extreme lack of belief in *individual* immortality and in the eternal life of the moral individual, and is not only desperately irreligious: it is also a sign of faint-heartedness and of the inability to live outside the *herd.* Those who think that way cannot imagine the earth without the teeming mass of human beings on it, and they are frightened *not so much of death as of solitude.* If the moral personality within them, which is in itself immortal, had enough strength, they would have the courage to face this consequence: they would not fear the death of the body and they would not resort to the certainty of the continuation of the species as a paltry surrogate for their lack of belief in eternal life. The negation of sexuality kills only the physical human being, and that only in order to give a full existence to the spiritual.

Therefore it cannot be a moral duty to ensure the continuation of the species, as is so frequently argued. This excuse is such an obviously *barefaced lie* that I hesitate to make a fool of myself by asking whether any human being has ever performed sexual intercourse with the thought of having to avert the great danger of the demise of humankind, or whether anybody has ever believed himself justified in accusing a chaste individual of acting immorally. *Fecundity is nothing if not disgusting,* and nobody who asks himself sincerely will feel it to be his duty to ensure the continuing existence of the human species. But what is not felt to be a duty ***is*** not a duty.

On the contrary: it is immoral to turn a human being into the effect of a cause, to produce a conditioned human being, as does parenthood, and the ultimate source of the bondage and determinacy which accompany the freedom and spontaneity of a human being is the fact that he has been created in such an immoral fashion. Reason has no interest whatsoever in the eternal continuation of humankind. Whoever wants to perpetuate humankind wants to perpetuate a problem and a guilt, indeed the only problem and the only guilt that there are, for the aim is the deity and the ending of humankind in the deity, a pure separation between good and evil, between something and nothing. Therefore, the attempts that have sometimes been made to sanctify sexual intercourse (which admittedly it badly needs) by inventing an ideal sexual act in which only the procreation of the human species is envisaged prove to be an affectionate disguise rather than an adequate defense. For the motive that allegedly allows and sanctifies it is not only no commandment and nowhere to be found as an imperative in the human being, but is itself morally reprehensible, since one does not ask a human being whom one fathers or mothers for his agreement. As for the other kind of sexual intercourse, in which the possibility of procreation is artificially prevented, even that extremely feeble justification loses its validity.

Thus sexual intercourse in any case contradicts the idea of humanity; not because asceticism is a duty, but above all because in sexual intercourse Woman wants to become an object, a thing, and Man really does her the favor of regarding her as a thing and not as a living human being with internal psychic processes. That is why Man despises Woman as soon as he has possessed her, and Woman *feels* that she is now despised, even though two minutes earlier she was idolized.

The only thing that a human being can respect in a human being is the *idea,* the idea of humanity. The contempt for Woman (and for Man himself), which follows sexual intercourse, is the surest indication that the idea has been violated. And anybody who cannot understand what is meant by this Kantian idea of humanity might at least consider that the women concerned are *his* sisters, *his* mother, *his* female relatives: it is *for our own sake* that Woman should be treated and *respected* as a human being and not *degraded,* as she always is through sexuality.

However, Man would not be *justified* in ***honoring*** Woman until she *herself* desisted from ***wanting*** *to be an object and matter* for Man, and until she really began to care for an emancipation that would be more than an emancipation of the prostitute. Although nobody has said so openly until now, Woman's bondage must be sought precisely in her worship of the sovereign power of Man's phallus over her. That is why the emancipation of women has only ever been desired sincerely by *men,* men who were not very sexual, who were not in very great need of love, who had no very deep insight, but men who were noble and passionate about justice, as cannot be doubted. I do not want to gloss over Man's erotic motives or make his dislike of "emancipated women" appear less than it actually is: it is easier to allow oneself to be drawn along, as did Goethe, than forever ascend in solitude, as did Kant. But a great deal that is interpreted as Man's *hostility* to emancipation is in truth only distrust and doubt about its possibility. Man does not want Woman as a slave, but often enough primarily seeks a companion who understands him.

The education received by Woman today is not of the kind that would prompt Woman to decide to overcome her true bondage and that would make it easier for her to do so. The ultimate device of a *mother's* pedagogy is to threaten her daughter, who refuses to do this or that, with the punishment *that she will not find a husband.* The intention of the education imparted to women is nothing but matchmaking, and a successful match is its crowning glory. While Man cannot be significantly changed by such influences, Woman is even more *confirmed* by them in her femininity, her lack of independence and her bondage.

The education of Woman must be taken away from Woman and ***the education of humankind as a whole must be taken away from the mother.***

This would be the first prerequisite for putting Woman at the service of the idea of humanity, which she has obstructed more than anybody else right from the outset.

* * *

A woman who had really renounced, a woman who sought peace in herself, would no longer be a woman. She would have ceased to be Woman, and she would have at last received the inner baptism in addition to the outer.

Can that ever happen?

There is no absolute Woman, and yet an affirmative answer to this question seems like the affirmation of a miracle.

Such an emancipation will not make Woman any happier: it can promise her no bliss, and the road to God remains a long one. No being that exists between freedom and bondage knows happiness. But will Woman be able to decide to give up slavery in order to become *unhappy*?

There can be no question of making Woman holy in the near future. The question is only whether Woman can honestly arrive at the problem of her existence, that is, the concept of *guilt.* Will she at least *want* freedom? The only thing that matters is enforcing the ideal, recognizing the lodestar. The crucial question is whether the categorical imperative can come to life in Woman. Will Woman subject herself to the moral idea, the *idea of humanity*?

For *that* alone would be the *emancipation of women.*

Appendix: Additions and References

Introduction to First Part

(P. 9, l. 1) The term "intermediate generalizations" is taken from John Stuart Mill. —On the development of a conceptual system of thinking as described, see E. Mach, Die Analyse der Empfindungen etc., 3rd ed., Jena 1902, pp. 242f. [*Contributions to the Analysis of the Sensations*, translated by C. M. Williams, Bristol 1998].

(P. 10, ll. 23ff.) See Ludwig Boltzmann, Über den zweiten Hauptsatz der mechanischen Wärmetheorie [On the second theorem of mechanical heat], Almanach der k.k. Akademie der Wissenschaften zu Wien, year 36, p. 255: "How striking is the difference between animal and plant, and yet the simple forms continuously merge into one another, so that some are precisely on the borderline, representing both animals and plants. The individual species are usually most sharply distinguished in natural history, but occasionally continuous transitions occur." On the relationship between chemical compounds and mixtures, see F. Wald, Kritische Studie über die wichtigsten chemischen Grundbegriffe [Critical study of the most important fundamental concepts of chemistry], Annalen der Naturphilosophie, I, 1902, pp. 181ff.

(P. 10, l. 10) For example, Paul Bartels's very detailed study Über Geschlechtsunterschiede am Schädel [On sexual differences of the skull], Berlin 1897, arrives at the conclusion (p. 94): "so far we are not aware of any fundamental difference between the male and female skull. . . . Any recognizable differences prove to be characteristics of the respective male and female average and show a larger or smaller number of exceptions." (P. 100): "A conclusive identification of the sex is not currently possible and will, I fear, never be possible."

(P. 11, l. 12) Konrad Rieger, Die Kastration in rechtlicher, sozialer und vitaler Hinsicht [Castration from a legal, social, and vital point of view], Jena 1900, p. 35: "Anybody who has seen a large number of naked people will know from experience that, on the one hand, there are many women whose pelvis is 'male' and that, on the other hand, there are many men whose pelvis is 'female.' . . . As is generally known, it is therefore by no means always possible to identify the sex of a skeleton."

Part 1, Chapter I

(P. 12, l. 8) Before Heinrich Rathke (Beobachtungen und Betrachtungen über die Entwicklung der Geschlechtswerkzeuge bei den Wirbeltieren [Observations and reflections on the development of the sexual organs of vertebrates],

Halle 1825. Neueste Schriften der naturforschenden Gesellschaft in Danzig, vol. I, no. 4), Tiedemann's belief that all embryos were originally female and the testicles had come into being through a further development of the ovaries generally prevailed. (Cf. Richard Semon, Die indifferente Anlage der Keimdrüsen beim Hühnchen und ihre Differenzierung zum Hoden [The indifferent arrangement of the gonads in chicks and their differentiation into the testicle], postdoctoral thesis, Jena 1887, pp. 1f.). Rathke (pp. 121f.) adduced many arguments against the view that the male sex is a more highly developed form of the female, and was the first to arrive at the conclusion: "All . . . observations reported in this work confirm that any recognizable differentiation in respect of the sexes between male and female organisms is entirely missing in the earliest phase of life. At least this is the case in respect to the internal sexual organs, for as far as the external ones are concerned I can for the most part only judge by the experiences of others, not my own. These experiences of others, however, also seem to indicate the identical nature of those external features. It may thus be maintained that originally, at least among vertebrates, the sexes, within the limits of sensory perception, are identical." This view was further examined, confirmed, and finally established in the works of Johannes Müller (Bildungsgeschichte der Genitalien [Developmental history of the genitals], Düsseldorf 1830), Valentin (Über die Entwicklung der Follikel in den Eierstöcken der Säugetiere [On the development of the follicle in the ovaries of mammals], Müllers Archiv 1838, pp. 103f.), R. Remak (Untersuchungen über die Entwicklung der Wirbeltiere [Studies in the development of vertrebrates]), and Wilhelm Waldeyer (Eierstock und Ei [Ovary and ovum], 1870).

(P. 12, l. 10) For plants this has only recently been demonstrated in K. Goebel's treatise "Über Homologien in der Entwicklung männlicher und weiblicher Geschlechtsorgane" [On homologies in the development of male and female sexual organs], Flora oder allgemeine botanische Zeitung, vol. XC, 1902, pp. 279–305). Goebel shows how in plants also male and female organs develop from an original basic form, as in the female organ those cells that in the male lead to the production of spermatozoids become sterile, and vice versa.

(P. 12, ll. 10ff.) The times given refer to the *external* sexual organs. They vary according to different observers, cf. W. Nagel, Über die Entwicklung des Urogenitalsystems des Menschen [On the development of the uro-genital system of humans], Archiv für mikroskopische Anatomie, vol. XXXIV, 1889, pp. 269–384 (especially pp. 375f.). The dates given in the main text are generally taken from Oscar Hertwig, Lehrbuch der Entwicklungsgeschichte des Menschen und der Tiere, 7th ed., pp. 427, 441 [*Text-book of the Embryology of Man and Mammals*, translated from the 3rd German edition by E. L. Mark, London 1892]. The moment of differentiation of the internal gonads is extremely controversial, and even the question whether in their initial phase they are hermaphroditically or sexually determined is as yet contentious. Cf. Nagel's treatise (pp. 299ff.), which also provides the most detailed orientation on this issue.

(P. 12, ll. 2 from bottom ff.) From Oscar Hertwig, Lehrbuch der Entwicklungsgeschichte des Menschen und der Tiere, 7th ed., Jena 1902, pp. 444f.) [*Text-book of the Embryology of Man and Mammals*, translated from the 3rd German edition by E. L. Mark, London 1892, pp. 410f.] I quote the entire table providing "a brief survey (1) of the comparable parts of the outer and inner sexual organs of the male and female, and (2) of their derivation from indifferent fundaments of the urogenital system in Mammals":

Male sexual parts.	*The common form from which both arise.*	*Female sexual parts.*
Seminal ampullae and seminal tubules.	Germinal epithelium.	Ovarian follicle, Graafian follicle.
	Primitive kidney.	
a) Epididymis with rete testis and tubuli recti.	a) Anterior part with the sexual cords (sexual part).	a) Epoöphoron with medullary cords of the ovary.
b) Paradidymis.	b) Posterior part (the real mesonephric part).	b) Paroöphoron
Vas deferens with seminal vesicles.	Mesonephric duct.	Gartner's canal, in some Mammals.
Kidney and urether.	Kidney and urether.	Kidney and urether.
Hyatid of epidydimis. Sinus prostaticus (Uterus masculinus.)	Müllerian duct.	Oviduct and fimbriae. Uterus and vagina.
Gubernaculum Hunteri.	Inguinal ligament of primitive kidney.	Round ligament and lig. ovarii.
Male urethra (pars prostatica et membranacea).	Sinus urogenitalis.	Vestibule of the vagina.
Penis.	Genital eminence.	Clitoris.
Pars cavernosa urethrae.	" folds.	Labia minora.
Scrotum.	" ridges.	" maiora.

(P. 13, l. 5) Ernst Häckel, Generelle Morphologie der Organismen [General morphology of the organisms], vol. II: Allgemeine Entwicklungsgeschichte der Organismen [General embryology of the organisms], Berlin 1866, pp. 60f.: "Every individual (of whatever order) as a hermaphrodite combines in itself both sexual materials, ovum and sperm. The opposite of this is the separation of the genitals, the distribution of the two sexual materials to two individuals (regardless of the order) which we call *separation of the sexes* or *gonochorism*. Every individual of whatever order as a *non-hermaphrodite (gonochoristus)* has only one of the two sexual materials, ovum or sperm." In a note he supplies the etymology: "γονή, ή, genital: χωριστός, separate. We introduce this new word here because strangely enough a *general* term for the separation of the sexes has so far been entirely missing, while for the phenomenon of dual sex there have been several (hermaphroditism, androgyny)."

(P. 13, l. 16) The sexes are probably least dimorphous in echinoderms. Further, according to Weismann, Das Keimplasma, Jena 1892, pp. 466f. [*The Germ-Plasm: A Theory of Heredity*, translated by W. Newton Parker and Harriet Rönnfeldt, London 1893] there are also among volvox, sponges, and hydromedusae some organisms whose male and female specimens differ only by the nature of their sexual cells, that is, without any further sexual characteristics.

(P. 13, l. 19) Normal hermaphroditism among fish: seabass (serranus scriba), gilthead seebream (chrysophrys aurata), and myxine glutinosa (a cyclostoma that lives on other fish as a parasite). See C. Claus, Lehrbuch der Zoologie, 6th ed., Marburg 1897, p. 745 [*Elementary Text-book of Zoology*, translated and edited by Adam Sedgwick, London 1892], and Richard Hertwig, Lehrbuch der Zoologie, 5th ed., Jena 1900, p. 99 [*A Manual of Zoology*, translated and edited by J. S. Kingsley, London 1903].

(P. 13, l. 14 from bottom) Because of inheritance Darwin and particularly Weismann posit the bisexuality of sexually differentiated organisms as an actual necessity. Darwin: (Das Variieren der Tiere und Pflanzen im Zustande der Domestikation, 2nd ed., Stuttgart 1873, vol. II, pp. 59f.) [*The Variation of Animals and Plants under Domestication*, 2 vols., London 1868, vol. 2, p. 52)]: "We thus see that in many, probably all cases, the secondary characters of each sex lie dormant or latent in the opposite sex, ready to be evolved under peculiar circumstances. We can thus understand how, for instance, it is possible for a good milking cow to transmit her good qualities through her male offspring to future generations; for we may confidently believe that these qualities are present, though latent, in the males of each generation. So it is with the game-cock, who can transmit his superiority in courage and vigour through his female to his male offspring; and with man it is known that diseases, such as hydrocele, necessarily confined to the male sex, can be transmitted through the female to the grandson. Such cases as these offer . . . the simplest possible examples of reversion; and they are intelligible on the belief that characters common to the grandparent and grandchild of the same sex are present, though latent, in the intermediate parent of the opposite sex." Weismann (Das Keimplasma, eine Theorie der Vererbung, Jena 1892, pp. 467f.) [*The Germ-Plasm: A Theory of Heredity*, translated by W. Newton Parker and Harriet Rönnfeldt, London 1893, pp. 357–358]: "In the human race we know that all the secondary sexual characters are transmitted by individuals of the opposite, as well as of the corresponding sex. A fine soprano voice, for instance, may be transmitted from mother to granddaughter through a son, and a black beard from the father to the grandson through a daughter. And in other animals, the sexual characters of both sides must be present in every sexually differentiated organism, some of them becoming manifest and others remaining latent. This fact can only be proved in certain cases, for we seldom notice the individual differences of these characters with sufficient accuracy; it can, however, be shown to be true, even in tolerably simply organised species, and we must therefore suppose that *latent characters belonging to the other sex* are always present *in each sexually differentiated organism*. In bees, the males developed from unfertilised eggs possess the secondary sexual characters of the grandfather; and in the water-fleas, in which several generations of females arise from one another, the last of these generations produces males with secondary sexual characters of the species, which must consequently have been present in a latent condition in an entire series of female generations." Compare also Moll, Untersuchungen über die Libido, Berlin 1898, vol. I, p. 444 [*Libido sexualis. Studies in the Psychosexual Laws of Love Verified by Clinical Sexual Case Histories*, translated by David Berger, New York 1933].

(P. 13, l. 10 from bottom) As is generally known, the "Platonic idea" is regarded as the "object of art" in the third book of Schopenhauer's "Die Welt als Wille und Vorstellung" [*The World as Will and Idea*, translated by R. B. Haldane and J. Kemp, 3 vols., London 1883].

(P. 14, l. 5f.) Since 1899 an annual *Jahrbuch für sexuelle Zwischenstufen* [Yearbook of intermediate sexual forms], edited by Dr. Magnus Hirschfeld, has been appearing. This enterprise would be even more commendable than it is, if it did not take into consideration only homosexuals and born hermaphrodites, i.e., those forms situated *midway* between the sexes. See also chapter IV and references.

(P. 14, ll. 23ff.) Also with reference to plants. See August Schulz, Beiträge zur Kenntnis der Bestäubungseinrichtungen und Geschlechtsverteilung bei den Pflanzen [Contributions to our knowledge of the pollination apparatus and distribution of the sexes in plants], part II, Kassel 1890, passim, esp. p. 185. Darwin, Die verschiedenen Blütenformen bei Pflanzen der nämlichen Art, Werke IX/3, Stuttgart 1877, p. 10 [*Different Forms of Flowers on Plants of the Same Species*, London 1877, pp. 11–12], tells us further about the common ash (Fraxinus excelsior): "I examined . . . fifteen trees growing in the same field; and of these, eight produced male flowers alone, and in the autumn not a single seed; four produced only female flowers, which set an abundance of seeds; three were hermaphrodites, which had a different aspect from the other trees whilst in flower, and two of them produced nearly as many seeds as the female trees, whilst the third produced none, so that it was in function a male. *The separation of the sexes, however, is not complete in the Ash; for the female flowers include stamens, which drop off at an early period, and their anthers, which never open or dehisce, generally contain pulpy material instead of pollen. On some female trees, however, I found a few anthers containing pollen-grains apparently sound. On the male trees most of the flowers include pistils,* but these likewise drop off at an early period; and the ovules, which ultimately abort, are very small compared with those in female flowers of the same age." See also the discussion of heterostyly in chapter III.—As far as animals are concerned, and in particular humans, it would be possible to fill whole reams with references from publications related to this topic, but I prefer to refer first to Albert Moll, Untersuchungen über die Libido sexualis, I, pp. 334ff. [*Libido Sexualis: Studies in the Psychosexual Laws of Love Verified by Clinical Sexual Case Histories*, translated by David Berger, New York 1933] (for example, his proofs for the occurrence of secreting mammary glands in men).—Konrad Rieger, Die Kastration in rechtlicher, sozialer and vitaler Hinsicht [Castration from a legal, social, and vital point of view], Jena 1900, p. 21 n. 2: "some nanny-goats have very strong horns that differ only slightly from those of a *billy*-goat; other nanny-goats are completely hornless, and finally there are *uncastrated billy*-goats without horns." P. 26: "If one looks at a large number of pictures of cattle one sees immediately that there are very significant differences in relation to the horns among the bulls themselves." P. 30: "I myself happen to have recently seen a female sheep from an imported race that had the most beautiful ram horns." See further, M., Über Rehböcke mit abnormer Geweihbildung und deren eigentümliches Verhalten [On roebucks with abnormal antlers and their peculiar behavior], Deutsche Jäger-Zeitung, XXXII, p. 363. E. R. Alston, On Female Deer with Antlers, Proceed. Zoolog. Society, London 1879, pp. 296f.—Reports on *local* high frequencies of intermediate forms among beetles and butterflies are found in William Bateson, *Materials for the Study of Variation. Treated with Especial Regard to Discontinuity in the Origin of Species,* London 1894, p. 254: "In all other localities the male Phalanger maculatus alone is spotted with white, the female being without spots, but in Waigiu the females are spotted like the males. This curious fact was first noticed by Jentink." (F. A. Jentink, Notes, Leyd. Mus., VII, 1885, p. 90.) And in a note referring to this: "Compare the converse case of Hepialus humuli (the Ghost Moth), of which, in all other localities, the male are clear and the females are light yellow-brown with spots, but in the Shetland Islands the males are very like the females, *though in varying degrees.* See Jenner Weir, Entomologist, 1880, p. 251 Pl."—Darwin, Das Variieren der Tiere und Pflanzen im Zustande der Domestikation, II, 259 [*The Variation of Animals and Plants under Domestication*, vol. 2, p. 317]: "The atrophied mammae, which, in male domesticated animals, including man, have in some rare cases grown to full size and secreted milk, perhaps offer an analogous case." On this, Moll, Untersuchungen, I, 481 [*Libido Sexualis*, translated by David Berger, New York 1933, passage not found in translation]: "In men we find numerous transitions from the typical character of the male breast to the complete development of female mammary glands."—Darwin deals with *the great variability of the secondary sexual characteristics* in chapter 5 of "Die Entstehung der Arten" (pp. 207ff. in the translation by Haek, Universalbibliothek [*The Origin of Species,* London 1877]), and with "gradations of secondary sexual character" in chapter 14 of "Die Abstammung des Menschen" (vol. II, pp. 143ff. of the same German edition) [*The Descent of Man,* London 1877, vol. 2, p. 135]).—On intermediate sexual forms among cervids, see also Adolf Rörig, Welche Beziehungen bestehen zwischen den Reproduktionsorganen der Cerviden und der Geweihbildung [What relationships exist between the reproductive organs of cervids and their antlers], Archiv für Entwicklungsmechanik der Organismen VIII, 1899, 382–447 (with bibliography); among birds: A. Tichomiroff, Androgynie bei Vögeln [Androgyny in birds], Anatomischer Anzeiger, 15 March 1888 (III, 221–228); in birds and other animals: Alexander Brandt, Anatomisches und Allgemeines über die sogenannte Hahnenfedrigkeit und über anderweitige Geschlechtscharaktere bei Vögeln [Anatomical and general observations on cock feathers in hens and other sexual characteristics in birds], Zeitschrift für wissenschaftliche Zoologie, 48, 1889, pp. 101–190.

(P. 14, l. 12 from bottom) On the virile pelvis of women, cf. W. Waldeyer, Das Becken, Topographisch-anatomisch mit besonderer Berücksichtigung der Chirurgie und Gynäkologie dargestellt [The pelvis, a topographical and anatomical presentation with special reference to surgery and gynaecology] (in G. Joessel, Lehrbuch der topographisch-chirurgischen Anatomie [Textbook of topographical and surgical anatomy], part II, Bonn 1899, pp. 393f.): "We also find female pelves of the male kind. The bones are more massive, the iliae steep, the pubic bone narrow, the pelvic cavity has the shape of a funnel. Generally the women concerned also have something . . . masculine in their further physical make-up (viragoes). But this is not necessarily always the case."

(P. 14, l. 10 from bottom) On *bearded women,* cf. Max Bartels, Über abnorme Behaarung beim Menschen [On abnormal growth of hair in humans], Zeitschrift für Ethnologie VIII (1876), pp. 110–129 (with bibliography), XI (1879), 145–194, XIII (1881), 213–233. Wilhelm Stricker, Über die sogenannten "Haarmenschen" (Hypertrichosis universalis) und insbesondere die bärtigen Frauen [On so-called "wolf people" (hypertrichosis universalis) and in particular bearded women], Bericht über die Senckenbergische naturforschende Gesellschaft, Frankfurt, 1877, pp. 97f. Louis A. Duhring, Case of Bearded Women, Archives of Dermatology III (1877), pp. 193–200. Harris Liston, Cases of bearded women, British Medical Journal of 2 June 1894. Albert Moll, Untersuchungen über die Libido sexualis, Berlin 1989, I, p. 337 (with bibliography) [*Libido sexualis,* translated by David Berger, New York 1933]. Cesare Taruffi, Hermaphrodismus und Zeugungsunfähigkeit. Eine systematische Darstellung der Mißbildungen der menschlichen Geschlechtsorgane [Hermaphroditism and procreative dysfunction. A systematic account of the deformities of the human sexual organs] translated into German by R. Teuscher, Berlin 1903, pp. 164–173: Über Hypertrichosis beim Weibe [On hypertrichosis in women], with extensive bibliography. Alexander Brandt, Über den Bart der Mannweiber (Viragines) [On the beard of amazons (viragines)], Biologisches Zentralblatt 17, 1897, pp. 226–239. Les Femmes à barbe, Revue scientifique VII, 618–622. Gustav Behrend, Hypertrichosis [Hypertrichosis] in Eulenburgs Realenzyklopädie, vol. XI^3, p. 194. Alexander Ecker, Über abnorme Behaarung beim Menschen, insbesondere über die sogenannten Haarmenschen [On abnormal growth of hair in humans, with special reference to so-called wolf people], Braunschweig 1878, with bibliography, p. 21.

(P. 14, ll. 4 from bottom ff.) Compare, e.g., the tables on p. 16 and pp. 24ff. in Livius Fürst, Die Maß-und Neigungsverhältnisse des weiblichen Beckens nach Profildurchschnitten gefrorener Leichen [The proportions and inclinations of the female pelvis according to profile sections of frozen corpses], Leipzig 1875, with the measurements for the dimensions of the pelvis of the two sexes reported by various observers such as Luschka, Henle, Rüdinger, Hoffmann, Pirogoff, Braune, Le Gendre, and Fürst himself.—Further, W. Krause, Spezielle und makroskopische Anatomie [Special and macroscopic anatomy] (vol. II of the 3rd edition of Handbuch der menschlichen Anatomie [Handbook of human anatomy] by C. F. T. Krause), Hannover 1897, pp. 122ff., with tables for the maximum and minimum proportions in both men and women.

(P. 15, l. 2 from bottom) The statement about ophites follows Überweg-Heinze, Grundriß der Geschichte der Philosophie [Outline history of philosophy], part II, Die mittlere oder die patristische und scholastische Zeit [The middle or patristic and scholastic age], 8th ed., Berlin 1898, p. 40.

Part 1, Chapter II

(P. 16, l. 10) Havelock Ellis, *Man and Woman, A Study of Human Secondary Sexual Characters,* London 1894, German: Mann und Weib, Anthropologische und psychologische Untersuchung der sekundären Geschlechtsunterschiede, übersetzt von Dr. Hans Kurella (Bibliothek für Sozialwissenschaft, vol. III), Leipzig 1895. Another relevant work, more one-sided but more original and amplified by valuable psychological examples from creative literature, C. Lombroso and G. Ferrero, Das Weib als Verbrecherin und Prostituierte, Anthropologische Studien, gegründet auf eine Darstellung der Biologie und Psychologie des normalen Weibes, translated into German by Dr. Hans Kurella, Hamburg 1984 [*The Female Offender,* London 1895].

(P. 16, l. 1 from bottom) J. J. S. Steenstrup, Untersuchungen über das Vorkommen des Hermaphroditismus in der Natur, translated into German by C. F. Hornschuch, Greifswald 1846, pp. 9ff. [Studies in the occurrence of hermaphroditism in nature].—For Steenstrup's views cf. the negative judgments of R. Leuckart, article "Zeugung" [Procreation] in R. Wagner's Handwörterbuch der Psychologie [Concise dictionary of physiology], vol. IV, 1853, pp. 743f., and C. Claus, Lehrbuch der Zoologie, p. 117[6] [*Elementary Text-book of Zoology,* translated and edited by Adam Sedgwick, London 1892].

(P. 17, l. 1) Ellis, Mann und Weib, in particular pp. 203ff. [*Man and Woman, A Study of Human Secondary Sexual Characters,* London 1894].

(P. 17, l. 6) On sexual differences in the composition of the blood, Ellis, pp. 204f.—Olof Hammarsten, Lehrbuch der physiologischen Chemie, 4th ed., Wiesbaden 1899, p. 137 [*A Text-book of Physiological Chemistry*, 7th ed. translated by John A. Mandel, New York & London 1911, p. 128]: "In the blood of man there are generally 5 million red corpuscles in 1 cm^3 and in woman 4 to 4.5 million."—Ernst Ziegler, Lehrbuch der allgemeinen und speziellen pathologischen Anatomie, vol. II: Spezielle pathologische Anatomie, 9th ed., Jena 1898, p. 3 [*A Text-book of Special Pathological Anatomy,* translated from the eighth German edition by D. MacAlister and H. W. Cattell, New York 1896 etc., vol. I, p. 3]: "In 100 cubic centimetres of blood there are in men 14.5 grammes of haemoglobin, and in women 13.2 grammes." Cf. esp. Lombroso-Ferrero, pp. 22f. and the literature cited there.

(P. 17, l. 7) v. Bischoff, Das Hirngewicht des Menschen [The weight of the human brain], Bonn 1880.—Rüdinger, Vorläufige Mitteilungen über die Unterschiede der Großhirnwindungen nach dem Geschlecht beim Fötus und Neugeborenen [Preliminary notes on the differences in the convolutions of the cerebrum according to sex in the fetus and newborn baby], Beiträge zur Anthropologie und Urgeschichte Bayerns, I, 1877, pp. 286–307.—Passet, Über einige Unterschiede des Großhirns nach dem Geschlecht [On some differences of the cerebrum according to sex], Archiv für Anthropologie, vol. XIV, 1883, pp. 89–141, and Emil Huschke, Schädel, Hirn und Seele des Menschen und der Tiere nach Alter, Geschlecht und Rasse [The skull, brain, and soul of humans and animals according to age, sex, and race], Jena 1854, pp. 152f., have also affirmed the existence of such differences and supplied precise data.

(P. 17, l. 8) Alice Gaule, Die geschlechtlichen Unterschiede in der Leber des Frosches [The sexual differences in the liver of the frog], Archiv für die gesamte Physiologie, edited by Pflüger, vol. LXXXIV, 1901, no. 1/2, pp. 1–5.

(P. 17, l. 11) I have not been able to ascertain the first occurrence of the term "erogenous" ("Zones érogènes" as the name for those parts of the body that have a particular sexual attraction for the opposite sex). The late Professor Freiherr v. Krafft-Ebing, whom I once asked for information about this, suspected that it came from Gilles de la Tourette. However the latter's great work on hysteria contains nothing relating to this.

(P. 17, ll. 23ff.) Quoted from Steenstrup, op. cit., pp. 9–10.

(P. 18, l. 24) John Hunter, Observations on certain parts of the animal oeconomy, London 1786, reports in his "Account of an extraordinary pheasant," first published in the Philosophical Transactions of the Royal Society of London, vol. LXX/2, 1 June 1780, pp. 527–535, about cock feathers in old hens, comparing it with the beards of grandmothers. On p. 63 (528) he introduces the famous distinction: "It is well known that there are many orders of animals which have the two parts designed for the purpose of generation different in the same species, by which they are distinguished into male and female: but this is not the only mark of distinction in many genera of animals, of the greatest part the male being distinguished from the female by various marks. *The differences which are found in the parts of generation themselves, I shall call the first or principal, and all others depending upon these I shall call secondary.*" If in my main text (pp. 19ff.) the range of the secondary characteristics is described more rigorously than usual as the totality of characteristics first becoming externally visible in sexual maturity, this makes use of Hunter's *original* definition, p. 68: "We see the sexes which at an early period had little to distinguish them from each other, acquiring about the time of puberty secondary properties, which clearly characterise the male and the female. The male at this time recedes from the female, and assumes the secondary characters of his sex." Cf. Darwin, Das Variieren etc, I², p. 199 [*The Variation* etc.] Entstehung der Arten (translated into German by Haek), p. 201 [*The Origin of Species*].

(P. 18, l. 25) The fact that it is necessary to distinguish between primary and "primordial" sexual characteristics is proved by the many cases in which the external sexual organs are somewhat female but the gonads still male. Cf., e.g., Andrew Clarke, A case of spurious hermaphroditism (hypospadia and undescended testis in a subject who has been brought up as a female and married for sixteen years), Middlesex Hospital, The Lancet, 12 March 1898, pp. 718f.— L. Siebourg, Ein Fall von Pseudohermaphroditismus masculinus completus [A case of pseudohermaphroditismus masculinus completus], Deutsche medizinische Wochenschrift, 9 June 1898, pp. 397–368 [*sic*].

(P. 18, l. 6 from bottom) The theory of "inner secretion" in general does not come, as one reads everywhere now, from Brown-Séquard, who was only the first to apply it to the gonad, but from Claude Bernard, preceded by a vague intimation of the matter in C. Legallois in 1801, about which one learns more from Année biologique, vol. I, pp. 315f. Cf. Bernard, Nouvelle fonction du foie considéré comme organe producteur de matière sucrée chez l'homme et les animaux [A new function of the liver considered as the organ producing sweet substance in man and animals], Paris, Baillière, 1853, pp. 58 and 71f. Further Leçons de physiologie expérimentale, vol. I, Paris 1855, from which the following passages may be quoted literally: "On s'est fait pendant longtemps une très fausse idée de ce qu'est un organe sécréteur. On pensait que toute sécrétion devait être versée sur une surface interne ou externe, et que tout organe sécrétoire devait nécessairement être pourvu d'un conduit excréteur destiné à porter au dehors les produits de la sécrétion. L'histoire du foie établit maintenant d'une manière très nette qu'il y a des sécrétions internes, c'est à dire des sécrétions dont le produit, au lieu d'être déversé à l'extérieur, est transmis directement dans le sang"

(p. 107)—"Il doit être maintenant bien établi qu'il y dans le foie deux fonctions de la nature de sécrétions. L'une, sécrétion externe, produit la bile qui s'écoule au dehors; l'autre, sécrétion interne, forme le sucre qui entre immédiatement dans le sang de la circulation générale" (p. 107).—Further (Rapport sur les progrès et la marche de la physiologie générale en France [Report on the progress and course of general physiology in France], Paris 1867, p. 73): "La cellule sécrétoire crée et élabore en elle-même le produit de sécrétion qu'elle verse soit au dehors sur les surfaces muqueuses, soit directement dans la masse du sang. J'ai appelé *sécrétions externes* celles qui s'écoulent en dehors, et *sécrétions internes* celles qui sont versées dans le milieu organique intérieur." (P. 79:) "Les sécrétions internes sont beaucoup moins connues que les sécrétions externes. Elles ont été plus ou moins vaguement soupçonnées, mais elles ne sont point encore généralement admises. Cependant, selon moi, elles ne sauraient être douteuses, et je pense que le sang, ou autrement dit le milieu intérieur organique, doit être regardé comme un produit des glandes vasculaires internes." (P. 84): "Le foie glycogénique forme une grosse glande sanguine, c'est-à-dire une glande qui n'a pas de conduit excréteur extérieur. Il donne naissance aux produits sucrés du sang, peut-être aussi à d'autres produits albuminoïdes. Mais il existe beaucoup d'autres glandes sanguines, telle que la rate, le corps thyroïde, les capsules surrénales, les glandes lymphatiques, dont les foncions sont encore aujourd'hui indéterminées; cependant on regarde généralement ces organes comme concourant à la régénération du plasma et du sang, ainsi qu'à la formation des globules blancs et des globules rouges qui nagent dans ce liquide." It is therefore necessary to correct the common assertion that Brown-Séquard is the founder of the theory of the functions of the glands without exits, as for example in Bunge's "Physiologische Chemie" (Lehrbuch der Physiologie des Menschen ["Physiological chemistry" (Textbook of human physiology)], Leipzig 1901, vol. II, p. 545), Chrobak and Rosthorn (Die Erkrankungen der weiblichen Geschlechtsorgane [The diseases of the female sexual organs], part I, Vienna, 1896/1900, p. 388), Ernst Ziegler (Lehrbuch der allgemeinen und speziellen pathologischen Anatomie, I[9], 1898, p. 80 [*A Text-book of Special Pathological Anatomy*, translated and edited from the eighth German edition by D. MacAlister and H. W. Cattell, New York 1896, etc.]), Oscar Hertwig (Die Zelle und die Gewebe, vol. II, 1898, p. 167 [*The Cell, Outlines of General Anatomy and Physiology*, translated by M. Campbell, London, New York, 1895]) or H. Boruttau (Kurzes Lehrbuch der Physiologie [Concise textbook of physiology], Leipzig and Vienna 1898, p. 138).

Brown-Séquard himself (Effets physiologiques d'un liquide extrait des glandes sexuelles et surtout des testicules [Physiological effects of a liquid extracted from the sexual glands and primarily the testicles], Compte Rendus hebdomadaires des Séances de l'Académie des Sciences, Paris, 30 May 1892, pp. 1237f.) says: "Déjà en 1869, dans un cours à la Faculté de Médecine de Paris, j'avais émis l'idée que les glandes ont des sécrétions internes et fournissent au sang des principes utiles sinon essentiels." Thus the priority without doubt belongs to Bernard; only the application to the gonads is Brown-Séquard's exclusive merit: "Je croyais, dès alors, que la faiblesse chez les vieillards dépend non seulement de l'etat sénile des organes, mais aussi de ce que les glandes sexuelles ne donnent plus au sang des principes qui, à l'âge adulte, contribuent largement à maintenir la vigueur propre à cet âge. Il était donc tout naturel de songer à trouver un moyen de donner au sang des vieillards affaiblis les principes que les glandes sexuelles ne lui fournissent plus. C'est ce qui m'a conduit à proposer l'emploi d'injections sous-cutanées d'un liquide extrait de ces glandes." Brown-Séquard's first publication on this topic is that contained in "Comptes Rendus hebdomadaires des séances et mémoires de la Société de la Biologie," vol. 41, 1889, pp. 414–419 (dated 1 June 1889).

The following may be listed as opponents of the theory of inner secretion, in particular of the gonads: Konrad Rieger in his study of castration (Jena, 1900, p. 71; he is reminded by it of the medieval monks' theories of "semen retentum") and A. W. Johnston, Internal Secretion of the Ovary, 25th Annual Meeting of the American Gynaecological Society, cf. British Gyn. Journal, Part 62, August 1900, p. 63. The question whether the phenomena after castration and involution of the gonads, insofar as they originate in the genitals, are mediated through the nerves or the blood after puberty and in gravidity is left open by Ziegler, Pathologische Anatomie, I^9, p. 80, and O. Hertwig, Zelle und Gewebe, II, p. 162 [vol. I: *Text-book of the Embryology of Man and Mammals*, translated from the 3rd German edition by E. L. Mark, London 1892; vol. II not translated]). The latter says: "If on the one hand the connection between the development of the gonads and the secondary sexual characteristics cannot be denied, on the other hand we lack any profound knowledge of it. Is the correlation between organs that have no direct functional relationship with each other mediated through the nervous system, or are there perhaps some special substances that are secreted by the testicle or ovary and, finding their way into the blood stream, induce the distant parts of the body to grow correlatively? So far there exists no experimental basis at all to decide this alternative."

The last sentence was probably no longer quite correct by the time Hertwig wrote it (1898). F. Goltz and A. Freusberg (Über den Einfluß des Nervensystems auf die Vorgänge während der Schwangerschaft und des Gebäraktes [On the influence of the nervous system on the processes during pregnancy and the act of birth], Pflügers Archiv für die gesamte Physiologie, IX, pp. 552–565) had reported in 1874 (p. 557): "A bitch whose spinal cord had been completely severed at the level of the first lumbar vertebra came on heat, conceived, and gave birth to a viable whelp without any artificial help. During and after these processes the animal displayed all the natural drives (instincts) connected with them just like an intact creature" (i.e., the mammary glands filled and the whelp was treated with the greatest tenderness. Cf. also Brücke, Vorlesungen über Physiologie [Lectures on physiology] II^3, Vienna 1884, pp. 126f.). Goltz himself had already at that time arrived at the following conclusion: "It seems . . . extremely doubtful to me whether the connection between the womb and the mammary should be thought of as involving the nervous system. In this case also the idea that the blood mediates this connection appeals to me more." At the same place he recalls the deficiency symptoms after castration. In their more famous work, "Der Hund mit dem verkürzten Rückenmark" [The dog with the shortened spinal cord] (Pflügers Archiv, 63, pp. 362–400), F. Goltz and J. R. Ewald returned to the topic 22 years after that investigation (cf. pp. 385f. of that treatise).

The main proof that there is *no* nervous mediation is, I believe, that one-sided castration, i.e., the extirpation of only one ovary or testicle, does not change the development of the secondary sexual characteristics in the slightest. The influence of each gonad, however, if it took place through the nerves, would have to be imagined as always having a *stronger* effect on one hemisphere of the body, and indeed a one-sided castration would, at least initially, have to be regarded as decisive for *one* half of the body only. However, with the exception of one reference, which Rieger, Die Kastration, p. 24, rightly suspects of being a tall tale (in Brehm's Säugetiere [Mammals, no English translation of this edition], Leipzig and Vienna 1891, III[3], p. 430: "stags castrated on one side only grow antlers on the undamaged side"), nothing of the kind has been heard anywhere: animals castrated on one side are like those that are not castrated at all. For an early reference see Berthold, Nachrichten von der Universität und Gesellschaft der Wissenschaften zu Göttingen, 1849, no. 1, pp. 1–6. Cf., e.g., Chrobak-Rosthorn, Erkrankungen der weiblichen Geschlechtsorgane, I/2, pp. 371f.: "Sokoloff[1] operated on dogs and observed the changes after both one-sided and double-sided castration. *In the former case rutting occurred normally,* in the latter it regularly stayed away. *One-sided castration of young animals allows the growth of both halves of the womb to continue.* As early as 1½ months after two-sided castration a clear atrophy of the circular muscle layer had occurred."

I regard this proof as even more stringent than the attempts at transplantation (on the basis of which the following rightly opt for inner secretion: J. Halban, Über den Einfluß der Ovarien auf die Entwicklung des Genitales [On the influence of the ovaries on the development of the genital], Monatsschrift für Geburtshilfe und Gynäkologie, XII, 1900, pp. 496–506, esp. p. 505; A. Foges, Zur Lehre von den sekundären Geschlechtscharakteren [On the theory of secondary sexual characteristics], Pflügers Archiv, XCIII, 1902, pp. 39ff.; Emil Knauer, Die Ovarientransplantation, experimentelle Studie [The transplantation of ovaries, an experimental study], Archiv für Gynäkologie, LX, 1900, esp. pp 352–359), because it would still be possible to object to these that mediating nervous pathways had entered the transplanted tissue simultaneously with its vascularization.

(P. 18, ll. 3 from bottom ff.) Havelock Ellis established a different conception of *tertiary sexual characteristics,* Mann und Weib, p. 24 [*Man and Woman, A Study of Human Secondary Sexual Characters*, London 1894, p. 20]: "Thus we have, for instance, the much greater shallowness, proportionately, of the female skull; we have the greater size and activity of the thyroid gland in women and the smaller average proportion of red blood corpuscles; and we have a different average relationship of the parts of the brain to each other. These differences are probably related indirectly to primary and secondary sexual differences; they are not of great importance from the zoological point of view, and occasionally of great interest from the social point of view. They cannot be easily put into the same group as the secondary sexual characters as usually understood; and perhaps it would be convenient if we were to agree to distinguish them as tertiary sexual characters." Ellis himself remarks that "this distinction is difficult to make because of the tendency of these characters to merge into one another." However, not only the theoretical but also the practical value of this classification seems less to me than the value of that proposed in my main text, which describes as

1. Über den Einfluß der Ovarienexstirpation auf Strukturveränderungen des Uterus [On the influence of the extirpation of the ovaries on structural changes of the uterus]. Archiv für Gynäkologie, 51, 1896, pp. 286ff.

the primordial the general biological sexual characteristics, as primary the anatomical in the narrower sense, as secondary the physiognomical in the narrower sense, as tertiary the psychological, and as quaternary the social differences between the sexes.

(P. 19, ll. 15ff.) The assumption strikes me as very probable that *simultaneously with every external secretion* an *internal secretion* takes place, that is, the latter also is not a continuous but intermittent function. The beard, for example, does not grow evenly but in bursts, spasmodically. The most obvious explanation of this seems to be interruptions in inner secretion.

(P. 19, l. 12 from bottom) The term "complementary condition" is taken from Richard Avenarius, Kritik der reinen Erfahrung [Critique of pure experience], vol. I, Leipzig 1888, p. 29.

(P. 19, l. 4 from bottom–p. 20, l. 10) On the idioplasm cf. C. v. Naegeli, Mechanisch-Physiologische Theorie der Abstammungslehre [Mechanico-physiological theory of evolution], 1884, where the concept is introduced on p. 23 in a manner that differs slightly from its development in my main text. Naegeli then continues: "Every perceptible property is present as a predisposition in the idioplasm, so that there are as many kinds of idioplasm as there are combinations of properties. Every individual has its origin in a somewhat different idioplasm, and in the same individual every organ and every part of an organ comes into being as a result of a specific modification or rather a specific condition of the idioplasm. Thus the idioplasm, which at least in a certain period of development is distributed across all parts of the organism, has somewhat different properties at each point and produces, for example, now a branch, now a flower, a root, a green leaf, a petal, a stamen, an embryo, a hair, a sting." The most important passage in this context is pp. 32f.: "Any cell must contain a certain quantity of it [the idioplasm], because this is the precondition of the inherited activity." Furthermore p. 531: "Every ontogeny . . . begins with a tiny germ which contains a small amount of idioplasm. This idioplasm divides, while continually increasing in a corresponding measure, in the course of cell division, as a result of which the organism grows, into the same number of parts, which are allocated to the cells. . . . Every cell of the organism has the idioplasmic potential to become the germ of a new individual. Whether this potential can be realized depends on the nature of the nutritional plasma. In the lower plants every cell has this capacity; in higher plants some cells have lost it; in the animal kingdom generally only those cells normally determined to be non-sexual or sexual germs possess it."—Hugo de Vries, in his book Intracellulare Pangenesis, Jena 1889, pp. 55–60, 75ff., 92ff., 101ff., and esp. p. 120 [*Intracellular Pangenesis*, tr. by C. S. Gager, Chicago 1910]. Oscar Hertwig, Die Zelle und die Gewebe [*The Cell, Outlines of General Anatomy and Physiology,* translated by M. Campbell]. (In respect of biology in general I have found this book the most instructive, apart from Darwin's "Variieren" [*Variation*].) Hertwig substantiates the theory in the first volume (Jena 1893), pp. 277ff. [pp. 347–348]: "When a *Funaria hygrometrica,* is chopped up into very small pieces, and placed upon damp soil, a complete plant grows out of each minute fragment. Similarly, if the fresh water *Hydra* is cut up into small portions, each develops into a complete *Hydra,* possessing all the properties of its species. Buds may be formed from the most different parts of a tree by the growth of the vegetative cells; these buds develop into shoots, which, if separated from the parent, and planted in the earth, can take root and grow into complete trees. . . . if a willow twig is cut off and placed in water, it develops root-forming cells at its lower extremity; thus the cells are here executing functions, very different from their original ones, which proves that they possessed this capacity potentially. Further, on the other hand, shoots can develop from severed roots, and even subsequently can produce male and female sexual products. In this case, therefore, sexual cells proceed directly from the component parts of a root-cell, and hence serve for the reproduction of the whole. . . . Most botanists agree with the theory, recently advanced by de Vries, in opposition to Weismann, which states that all, or at any rate by far the greater number, of the cells of a vegetable body contain all the hereditary attributes of their species in a latent condition, and therefore the whole hereditary mass, whilst the former only contain a part of it."—The theory of idioplasm has been opposed most fiercely by August Weismann in his study "Die Kontinuität des Keimplasmas als Grundlage einer Theorie der Vererbung," 1885 (Aufsätze über Vererbung und verwandte biologische Fragen, Jena 1892, pp. 215ff.) ["The Continuity of Germ Plasma as the Foundation of a Theory of Heredity" (*Essays upon Heredity and Kindred Biological Problems,* 2nd ed., Oxford 1891–92)]. Weismann's main argument (p. 237 [vol. 1, p. 200]), "we have no right to assume that any of them [somatic cells] can form germ-cells until it is proven that somatic idioplasm is capable of undergoing re-transformation into germ-idioplasm," may no longer be tenable in view of the precise investigations of Friedrich Miescher (Die histochemischen und physiologischen Arbeiten von F. M. [The histo-chemical and physiological studies of F. M.] Leipzig 1897, vol. II, pp. 116ff.) of the development of the gonads in salmon at the expense of their principal lateral rump muscle. See incidentally the devastating criticism of Weismann's extremely artificial theories by Kassowitz, Allgemeine Biologie [General biology], vol. II, Vienna 1900, to which Weismann, probably because of their overly sharp tone, did not reply.

The theory of idioplasm is entirely supported by studies such as Paul Jensen, Über individuelle physiologische Unterschiede zwischen Zellen der gleichen Art [On individual physiological differences between cells of the same kind] (Pflügers Archiv, LXII, 1896, pp. 172–200). He writes, for example (p. 191): "If a foraminifer is stimulated by touch, never through its own severed pseudopodia, but always through the pseudopodia of another individual, the protoplasm of the former must differ in a certain way from that of the latter, or, to put it in general terms: the protoplasm of different individuals must be physiologically different. But what is this difference, and what is the stimulus that arises from it? We cannot help assuming differences in the chemical composition of the protoplasm of different individuals."—On the regenerative capability (also of low animals) cf. Hermann Vöchting, Über die Regeneration der Marchantieen [On the regeneration of marchantiae] Jahrbücher für wissenschaftliche Botanik, vol. XVI, 1885, pp. 367–414. Über Organbildung im Pflanzenreich, Physiologische Untersuchungen über Wachstumsursachen und Lebenseinheiten [On the formation of organs in the plant kingdom, physiological investigations into the causes of growth and units of life], part I, Bonn 1878, pp. 236–240, esp. pp. 251–253.—Jacques Loeb, Untersuchungen zur physiologischen Morphologie der Tiere [Investigations into the physiological morphology of animals], Würzburg 1892, pp. 34ff. (on regeneration in ciona intestinalis).

(P. 20, ll. 20ff.) If every cell, and therefore every nerve cell, is (to a certain degree) male or female then there is no reason left to assume a "psycho-sexual centre" for the sex drive in the brain, as postulated in particular by Krafft-Ebing (Psychopathia sexualis, 11th ed., p. 248 n. 1) [*Psychopathia Sexualis, With Especial Reference of the Antipathic Sexual Instinct. A Medico-Forensic Study*, translated by F. J. Rebman, 12th ed., London 1906, p. 348] and his pupils, as well as (after him) Taruffi, Hermaphrodismus und Zeugungsunfähigkeit [Hermaphroditism and procreative dysfunction], translated into German by R. Teuscher, Berlin 1903, p. 190, regardless of Goltz's experiments cited in the note concerning P. 18, l. 6 from bottom.

(P. 20, l. 3 from bottom) Wilhelm Caspari, Einiges über Hermaphroditen bei Schmetterlingen [Some points about hermaphrodites among butterflies], Jahrbücher des nassauischen Vereines für Naturkunde, year 48, pp. 171–173 (Presentation by P. Marchal, Année biologique, I, p. 288), reports how sometimes one side of a butterfly is entirely male and the other entirely female. In saturnia pavonia, the peacock butterfly, the difference between male and female coloring is very great and therefore the contrast between the right and the left half of the body of hermaphrodites of this kind is extremely striking.—Richard Hertwig, Lehrbuch der Zoologie^{5}, 1900, p. 99 [*A Manual of Zoology*, from the fifth German edition, translated by J. S. Kingsley, London & New York 1903] on this "hermaphroditismus lateralis" and those hermaphroditic forms in butterflies such as ocneria dispar (a silk moth) whose male half carries the specific shape of the male antenna, eyes, and wing, and thus substantially differs from the female half.

(P. 21, ll. 23ff.) Aristotle says (Histor. Anim. 5, 14, 545, á 21 [*Generation of Animals*, translated by A. L. Peck, London 1963] :) εἰς τὸ θῆλυ γὰρ μεταβάλλει τὰ ἐκτεμνόμενα. μεταβάλλει δὲ καὶ ἡ φωνὴ ἐπὶ τῶν ἐκτεμνομένων ἁπάντων εἰς τὸ θῆλυ. Erroneous statements of most recent times concerning the regular feminization of an emasculated animal stem mainly from William Yarrell (On the influence of the sexual organ in modifying external character, Journal of the Proceedings of the Linnean Society, Zool. vol. I, 1857, p. 81) and have often been repeated after him (with or without acknowledgment), e.g., by Darwin, Das Variieren etc. II^{2}, p. 59 [*The Variation* etc. II, p. 52]: "the capon takes to sitting on eggs, and will bring up chickens." Weismann, Keimplasma, pp. 469f. [*The Germ-plasm, a Theory of Heredity*, translated by W. Newton Parker and Harriet Rönnfeldt, London 1893, p. 358]: "the secondary sexual characters of one sex may, under special circumstances, become developed susequently in fully-developed individuals. This results in both sexes, especially in the case of castration." Likewise Moll, Die konträre Sexualempfindung, 3rd ed., Berlin 1899, p. 170 n. 1 [*Perversions of the Sex Instinct. A Study of Sexual Inversion*, translated by Maurice Popkin, Newark 1931 etc.]. These theories were *opposed* in particular by Rieger (Die Kastration [Castration], pp. 33f.), and Hugo Sellheim (Zur Lehre von den sekundären Geschlechtscharakteren [On the theory of the secondary sexual characteristics], Beiträge zur Geburtshilfe und Gynäkologie, edited by A. Hegar, vol. I, 1898, pp. 229–255): "We were in no way able to establish [in capons] any change, any development of maternal love which would have expressed itself in care for the chicks placed among them" (p. 234). "The larynx of a castrated animal shows no sign of actively approaching the female animal, as is assumed by some to be one of the changes caused by the removal of the testicles" (p. 241). Finally, Arthur Foges (Zur Lehre von den sekundären Geschlechtscharakteren [On the theory of secondary sexual characteristics], Pflügers Archiv, vol. XCIII, 1902, pp. 39–58) has confirmed Sellheim's results and once more rejected the older assumptions (p. 53). However, the last two authors would seem to go too far in ruling out feminization. Although feminization may not be a necessary consequence of castration and may occur entirely *without* it (see p. 22, ll. 9ff. and note referring to that passage), castration may in many cases facilitate its occurrence.

(P. 21, ll. 8 from bottom ff.) For the assumption of male characteristics by women and female animals after the end of sexual maturity, or menopause, see above all Alexander Brandt's detailed treatise Anatomisches und Allgemeines über die sogenannte Hahnenfedrigkeit und über anderweitige Geschlechtsanomalien bei Vögeln [Anatomical and general observations on so-called cock feathers in hens and other sexual anomalies in birds] Zeitschr.f. wiss. Zool., 48, 1889, pp. 101–190.—First reference to cock feathers in hens in Aristotle, Histor. Animal. 9, 49, 631 b, 7ff. [*Generation of Animals,* translated by A. L. Peck, London 1963].—In the 19th century the phenomenon was discussed in particular by William Yarrell, On the Change in the Plumage of some Hen-pheasants, Philosophical transactions of the Royal Society of London, 10 May 1827 (part II, pp. 268–275); Darwin, Das Variieren, II^2, pp. 58ff. [*The Variation*]; Oscar Hertwig, Die Zelle und die Gewebe, vol. II, Jena 1898, p. 162 [*The Cell, Outlines of General Anatomy and Physiology,* translated by M. Campbell, London & New York 1895].—An interesting case of hypertrichosis, cited from Virchow by Chrobak and Rosthorn, Die Erkrankungen der weiblichen Geschlechtsorgane [The diseases of the female sexual organs], part I, p. 388, "concerning a young woman who fell ill with acute gastritis and enteritis during menstruation and later became amenorrheic, and on whose entire body black hairs grew during the absence of her period," may belong to the same area.

(P. 21, l. 2 from bottom) Does: following Brehm's Tierleben, 3rd ed. by Pechuel-Loesche, Säugetiere, vol. III, 1891, p. 495 [Brehm's life of animals, Mammals, no English translation of this edition]: "Very old does sometimes also develop a short horn bud and weak antlers. . . . Block tells me about one such pair of antlers that it consisted of two horns about 5 cm. in length and even deceived an old huntsman, who took the doe for a buck and shot her."

(P. 22, l. 1) Cf. Paul Mayer, Carcinologische Mitteilungen [Carcinological communications], Mitteilungen a. d. zool. Station zu Neapel, I, 1879, VI: Über den Hermaphroditismus bei einigen Isopoden [On hermaphroditism in some isopods], pp. 165–179. Concerning the genera cymothoa, anilocra, and nerocila, Mayer has established that the same individuals function in their youth as males in which, after shedding their skin, the ovaries which are originally present but dysfunctional later repress the male gonads so that these animals now fulfill the role of females.—The term "protandry" (modeled on botany, cf. Noll's Physiologie [Physiology] in Strasburger's Lehrbuch der Botanik, 3rd ed., 1898, p. 250 [*A Text-book of Botany,* translated by H. C. Porter, London & New York 1903]) is also used by Mayer, p. 177, for this phenomenon. Cf. Cesare Lombroso and Guglielmo Ferrero, Das Weib als Verbrecherin und Prostituierte, translated by Hans Kurella, Hamburg 1894, p. 3 [*The Female Offender,* London 1895]. Incidentally, L. Cuénot was able to demonstrate exactly the same phenomenon in certain starfish: Notes sur les Echinodermes [Notes on echinoderms], III: "L'hermaphrodisme *protandrique* d'Asterina gibbosa Penn. et ses variations suivant les localités" (Zoologischer Anzeiger, XXI/1, 1898, pp. 273–279). He concludes:

"L'hermaphrodisme protandrique est donc ici indiscutable: les Asterina sont fonctionellement mâles . . . puis, elles deviennent exclusivement femelles pour le reste de leur existence."

(P. 22, ll. 9ff.) There are further sporadic reports on sexual transformation. E.g., by L. Janson, Über scheinbare Geschlechtsmetamorphose bei Hühnern [On apparent sexual metamorphosis in hens], Mitteilungen d. deutsch. Gesellschaft für Natur-und Völkerkunde Ostasiens, no. 60, pp. 478–480.—Kob, De mutatione sexus, Berlin 1823.—Anecdotal cases, from writings of very uneven reliability, are collected in Taruffi, Hermaphrodismus und Zeugungsunfähigkeit [Hermaphroditism and procreative dysfunction], Berlin 1903, pp. 296, 307f., 364f. "A duck ten years old has been known to assume both the perfect winter and summer plumage of the drake." Darwin, Das Variieren etc., II^2, p. 58 [The Variation etc., II, p. 51]. Cf. Moll, Untersuchungen über die Libido sexualis, I, p. 444 [*Libido Sexualis*, translated by David Berger, New York 1933].—R. v. Krafft-Ebing, Psychopathia sexualis mit besonderer Berücksichtigung der konträren Sexualempfindung, eine klinisch-forensische Studie [8th ed., Stuttgart 1893, pp. 198f. *Psychopathia Sexualis,* translated by Francis J. Rebman, London 1899] mentions several extremely remarkable cases of men who have experienced a total transformation into women in the course of their lives; a particularly relevant example is the autobiography of a doctor (pp. 203ff.) which, as Krafft-Ebing is obliged to admit on p. 215, is entirely free of any paranoid delusion, even though he introduces that case on p. 203 under the heading "Metamorphosis sexualis paranoica."

(P. 22, l. 13 from bottom) The experiments mentioned here are those carried out by Emil Knauer (Die Ovarientransplantation, Experimentelle Studie, [The transplantation of ovaries, an experimental study], Archiv für Gynäkologie, vol. LX, 1900, pp. 322–376). The transplantation failed in all but two of thirteen cases (ibid., p. 371). "Considering these last two, positive, results I feel able to claim *that the transplantation of the ovaries from one animal to another is also possible*" (p. 372). Foges, who was aware of Knauer's successes and repeated the same experiment, never succeeded in effecting the exchange (Pflügers Archiv, vol. XCIII, 1902, p. 93), and neither were those of Knauer's predecessors cited by himself on pp. 373f. The reason (in addition to inequalities in the perfection of technical execution) is probably that assumed in my main text.—For the success of transplantation within the same animal cf. Knauer, pp. 339ff.

(P. 22, ll. 1 from bottom ff.) On blood transfusion, which has almost fallen into disuse today because of the risks involved, cf. L. Landois's article "Transfusion" in Eulenburgs Realenzyklopädie der Heilkunde, 2nd ed., vol. XX, 1890, which supports transfusion, and Ernst v. Bergmann, Die Schicksale der Transfusion im letzten Dezennium [The fate of transfusion in the last decade], Berlin 1883, as well as A. Landerer, Über Transfusion und Infusion [On transfusion and infusion], Virchows Archiv für pathologische Anatomie und Physiologie und klinische Medizin, vol. CV, 1886, pp. 351–372, which both oppose it.

(P. 23, ll. 15ff.) The most detailed, albeit in principle extremely favorable, report on organotherapy is Georg Buschan's article entitled "Organsafttherapie" [organotherapy] in Eulenburgs Realenzyklopädie, 3rd ed., vol. XVIII (1898), pp. 22–82.

(P. 23, l. 17) According to Foges, Zur Lehre von den sekundären Geschlechtscharakteren [On the theory of secondary sexual characteristics], Pflügers Archiv, vol. XCIII, 1902 (p. 57), the *quantity* of substances secreted by the gonads into the blood would be of the greatest importance, for he attributes the failure of the transplantations of testicles to preserve the normal sexual characteristics in his experimental animals to the fact that, in comparison to the size of the normal testicle, only a very small amount of testicular tissue was properly incorporated.

(P. 23, l. 19) According to Buschan (op. cit., p. 32) a series of experiments carried out in the physiological laboratory of the University of Rome by Ferré and Bechasi (Note préliminaire sur l'etude de l'action du suc ovarien sur le cobaye [Preliminary note on the study of the effect of ovarian juice on the guinea pig] Gazette hebdomadaire, XLIV, 1897, no. 50) clearly show "that the effect of these [organic] preparations on the male sex is very different from that on the female. When these observers injected 5 cm^3 of an ovarial extract . . . into a *female* guinea pig there occurred neither a local nor a general reaction, and only the animal's body weight increased; when the same amount was injected into a *male* animal, there were neither any local nor any general phenomena, but there was weight loss. When 10 cm^3 was injected the local reaction in the *female* animal was quite small, a general reaction was absent, and the gain in weight was significant; in the *male* animal, on the other hand, the local irritation was quite substantial, a temporary increase in temperature followed, and the weight loss became even more marked. Finally, when 15 cm^3 was injected the local reaction in the *female* remained slight, but in the male reached an even more significant level; the temperature of the former also increased by some tenths of a degree during the day of the injection, but the latter displayed very clear hypothermia with nervous trembling and intensive depression; *in addition the male guinea pig suffered a very substantial weight loss and ultimately died within four to six days.*"

(P. 24, ll. 9ff.) This could differ in relation to different organisms. For example, counter to statements to the contrary by Born and Pflüger, Oscar and Richard Hertwig on p. 43 of their "Experimentelle Untersuchungen über die Bedingungen der Bastardbefruchtung" [Experimental investigations into the conditions of illegitimate fertilization] (Oscar and Richard Hertwig, Untersuchungen zur Morphologie und Physiologie der Zelle [Studies in the morphology and physiology of the cell], no. 4, Jena 1885): "Given even the strongest magnification we have not been able to discover any differences in shape and size between the mature spermatozoa of a sphaerechinus or strongylocentrotus or an arbacia." In contrast, L. Weill, Über die kinetische Korrelation zwischen den beiden Generationszellen [On the kinetic correlation between the two generative cells], Archiv für Entwicklungsmechanik der Organismen, vol. XI, 1901, pp. 222–224, assumes the existence of individual differences even between the spermatozoids and ova of the same animals.—Incidentally, the fact that the dimensions of the ova certainly vary, is shown by the measurements cited by Karl Schulin, Zur Morphologie des Ovariums [On the morphology of the ovary], Archiv für mikroskopische Anatomie, vol. XIX, 1881, pp. 472f., and W. Nagel, Das menschliche Ei [The human ovum], ibid., vol. XXXI, 1888, pp. 397, 399.

(P. 24, ll. 14ff.) For the speed of spermatozoids cf. Chrobak-Rosthorn I/2, p. 441.

(P. 24, ll. 17ff.) Purser, The British Medical Journal, 1885, p. 1159 (cf. Moll, Untersuchungen, I, p. 252 [*Libido Sexualis,* translated by David Berger, New York

1933]) and particularly Franz Friedmann, Rudimentäre Eier im Hoden von Rana viridis [Rudimentary ova in the testicle of rana viridis], Archiv für mikroskopische Anatomie und Entwicklungsgeschichte, vol. LII, 1898, pp. 248–261 (with numerous references). Friedmann's case is particularly interesting in that in *both* testicles there were well developed ova with diameters of 225–500 ì (five in one, ten in the other), all of which were located *within the seminiferous tubules* themselves and not only between the testicular tubes. Pflüger, Über die das Geschlecht bestimmenden Ursachen und die Geschlechtsverhältnisse der Frösche [On the causes determining the sex and the sexual circumstances of frogs], Archiv für die gesamte Physiologie, vol. XXIX, 1882, pp. 13–40, also reports on the large Graafian follicles that he found, counter to expectations, in the testicles of common frogs (p. 33). His treatise actually refers to transitional forms from testicle to ovary.—Further reading listed in Frank J. Cole, A Case of Hermaphroditism in Rana temporaria, Anatomischer Anzeiger, 21 September 1895, pp. 104–112. G. Loisel, Grenouille femelle présentant les caractères sexuels secondaires du mâle, Comptes rendus hebdomadaires des Séances et Mémoires de la Société de Biologie, LIII, 1901, pp. 204–206. La Valette St. George, Zwitterbildung beim kleinen Wassermolch [Hermaphroditism in the small newt], Archiv für mikroskopische Anatomie, vol. XLV (1895), pp. 1–14.

(P. 25, l. 8) As early as 1877 the well-known gynaecologist A. Hegar made a start on a theory of intermediate sexual forms, although he did not develop it very far (Über die Exstirpation normaler und nicht zu umfänglicher Tumoren degenerierter Eierstöcke [On the extirpation of normal and not excessively large tumors of degenerate ovaries], Zentralblatt für Gynäkologie, 10 November 1877, pp. 297–307, p. 305:) "The saying 'propter solum ovarium mulier est quod est' is decidedly too pointed if it is understood to mean that the impulse for the production of the specifically female body type and the specifically female sexual characteristics is given exclusively by the ovary. Geoffroy St. Hilaire already argued for the independent development of the individual sections of the sexual apparatus, and more recently Klebs has explained this theory with reference to the conditions of hermaphroditism. At any rate, even assuming that the ovary is the most important moving force, it is necessary to go back still further in search of a factor determining the emergence of a male gonad in one case and a female gonad in the other. [Here the respective arrhenoplasm and thelyplasm of a whole organism were considered as such]. . . . Here, in the context of our reflections, we can simply talk about *one* sexually determining factor. If we now assume that in every individual there are originally two sexually determining factors, and if we further assume that these factors try to create not only the specific gonad but also, at the same time, the other sexual characteristics, there seems to exist a satisfactory explanation of all . . . the facts. One tendency usually predominates in such a way as to create only one specific type, while the other is repressed. This predominance may be so significant that, even in a case of a defective or rudimentary development of the specific gonad, the corresponding further sexual characteristics are produced. [Disharmony in the sexual characteristics of the different parts of *one* organism.] In what way this repression occurs, however, is not easy to say. Probably some partly very simple mechanical processes are involved. [??] The material is used up, or there is simply no space, no room left for the development of the organ of the other type. We actually find an analogous process among birds, where the left ovary, through its more powerful growth, causes the right to atrophy or, as it were, squeezes it to death. . . . If the direction of the movement happens to be weak, chance resistances, even if they are slight, can have a significant effect. In such cases the other sexually determining factor will take effect and thus we see an individual come into being which is of a different sexual type than that which is due to it in accordance with its gonad. Most often, however, we find mixtures of male and female properties in all possible combinations, down to those subtle nuances where we talk about a feminine man and a masculine woman."

(P. 26, l. 1f.) Maupas, Sur le déterminisme de la sexualité chez l'Hydatina senta [On the determinism of sexuality in hydatina senta], Comptes rendus hebdomadaires des Séances de l'Académie des Sciences, 14 September 1891, pp. 388f.: "Au début de l'ovogénèse, l'oeuf est encore neutre et, en agissant convenablement, on peut à ce moment lui faire prendre à volonté l'un ou l'autre caractère sexuel. L'agent modificateur est la température. L'abaisse-t-on, les jeunes oeufs qui vont se former se revêtent l'etat de pondeuses d'oeufs femelles; l'élève-t-on, au contraire, c'est l'etat de pondeuses d'oeufs mâles qui se développe."

(P. 26, l. 5) Cf. M. Nußbaum, Die Entstehung des Geschlechts bei Hydatina senta [The origin of sex in hydatina senta], Archiv für mikroskopische Anatomie und Entwicklungsgeschichte, vol. XLIX (1897), pp. 227–308, p. 235: "The measurements indicated by Plate for male and female summer eggs of hydatina senta suggest of necessity that sex cannot in all cases be predicted from the size of the eggs. One may assume that females always develop from the largest eggs and males from the smallest. However, between these distant borders there are gradual transitions of which one cannot say what they will develop into. . . . One and the same female lays eggs of very different sizes."

(P. 26, l. 6f.) The expressions "arrhenoplasmic" and "thelyplasmic" follow Brandt's treatise (Zeitschrift für wissenschaftliche Zoologie, vol. XLVIII, p. 102), quoted above.

Part 1, Chapter III

(P. 27, ll. 2ff.) Carmen, Opéra-Comique tiré de la nouvelle de Prosper Mérimée par Henri Meilhac & Ludovic Halévy, Paris, Acte I, Scène V, p. 13 [Carmen, translated by Anthony Burgess, London 1986].

(P. 27, l. 12 from bottom) The philosopher is Arthur Schopenhauer in his "Metaphysik der Geschlechstliebe" (Die Welt als Wille und Vorstellung, ed. Frauenstädt, vol. II, chapter 44, pp. 623f. [*The World as Will and Idea,* translated by R. B. Haldane and J. Kemp, London 1883–1886, XXIV, vol. 3, pp. 356–357]: "First: all sex is one-sided. This one-sidedness is more distinctly expressed in one individual than in another; therefore in every individual it can be better supplemented and neutralised by one than by another individual of the opposite sex, for each one requires a one-sidedness which is the opposite of his own to complement the type of humanity in the new individual that is to be produced, the constitution of which is always the goal towards which all tends. Physiologists know that manhood and womanhood admit of innumerable degrees, through which the former sinks to the repulsive gynander and hypospadaeus, and the latter rises to the graceful androgyne; from both sides complete hermaphrodism can be reached, at which point stand those individuals who, holding the exact mean between the two sexes, can be attributed to neither, and consequently are unfit to propagate the species. Accordingly, the neutralisation of two individualities by each other, of which we are speaking, demands that the definite degree of *his* manhood shall exactly correspond to the definite degree of *her* womanhood; so that the one-sidedness of each exactly annuls that of the other. Accordingly, the most manly man will seek the most womanly woman, and *vice versa,* and in the same way every individual will seek another corresponding to him or her in degree of sex. Now how far the required relation exists between two individuals is instinctively felt by them, and, together with the other relative consideration, lies at the foundation of the higher degrees of love." This passage shows much fuller insight than the only other passage worth mentioning where I was able to discover something similar and which is found in Albert Moll, Untersuchungen über die Libido sexualis, Berlin 1897, vol. I, p. 193 [*Libido Sexualis,* translated by David Berger, New York 1933, passage not found in translation]: "We may say that between the typical female sexual urge, which is directed towards fully grown male persons, and the typical male sexual urge, which is directed towards fully grown female persons, there is a whole range of transitions."

I was unfamiliar with either passage when (at the beginning of 1901) I thought I was the first to have found this law, even though my formulation is so close in *content* and sometimes even in *wording* to that of Schopenhauer in particular.

(P. 27, ll. 9 from bottom ff.) The following remark of Blaise Pascal (Pensées 1, 10, 24 [*Pensées and Other Writings,* translated by Honor Levi, Oxford 1995]) may be included here, although its broad validity will become quite clear only gradually in the course of what follows (see first part, chapter V and second part, chapter I): "Il y'a un modèle d'agrément et de beauté, qui consiste en un certain rapport entre notre nature faible ou forte, telle qu'elle est, et la chose qui nous plaît. Tout ce qui est formé sur ce modèle nous agrée: maison, chanson, discours, vers, prose, femme, oiseaux, rivières, arbres, chambres, habits."

(P. 28, l. 2f.) Charles Darwin, Die Abstammung des Menschen und die Zuchtwahl in geschlechtlicher Beziehung, translated into German by David Haek (Universalbibliothek), vol. II, chapter 14, pp. 120–132, chapter 17, pp. 285–290 [*The Descent of Man, and Selection in Relation to Sex,* London 1871]; the cases by no means suggest a "choice" on the part of the female alone, but equally a preference for and a rejection of females by the males. See also: Das Variieren der Tiere und Pflanzen im Zustande der Domestikation, translated by J. V. Carus, chapter 18 (Stuttgart 1873, II^2, p. 186) [*The Variation of Animals and Plants under Domestication,* London 1868, p. 162]: "It is by no means rare to find certain males and females which will not breed together, though both are known to be perfectly fertile with other males and females. . . . The cause apparently lies in an innate sexual incompatibility of the pair which are matched. Several instances have been communicated to me. . . . In these cases, females, which either previously or subsequently were proved to be fertile, failed to breed with certain males, with whom it was particularly desirable to match them." And so on.

(P. 28, ll. 7–8) "Almost without exception," "almost always" because of Oscar and Richard Hertwig, Untersuchungen zur Morphologie und Physiologie der Zelle, Heft 4: Experimentelle Untersuchungen über die Bedingungen der Bastardbefruchtung [Studies in the morphology and physiology of the cell, no. 4: Experimental investigations into the conditions of illegitimate fertilization], Jena 1885, p. 33: *"In the cross-fertilization of two species there is very often no reciprocity.* Here all possible gradations are found. While the ova of echinus microtuberculatus can be fertilized almost without exception by the semen of strongylocentrotus lividus, crossing in the opposite direction will produce development only in a few cases. Fertilization of strongylocentrotus lividus by the semen of arbacia pustulosa remains unsuccessful, while some ova of arbacia pustulosa will develop when the semen of strongylocentrotus lividus is added to them. And likewise in other cases. Currently it is not at all possible to establish any regular relationships between bastardizations in opposite directions."

(P. 29, l. 18) The term "sexual *affinity,*" in analogy with chemical affinity, was first introduced by O. and R. Hertwig (Experimentelle Untersuchungen über die Bedingungen der Bastardbefruchtung [Experimental investigations into the conditions of illegitimate fertilization], Jena 1885, p. 44. In his book "Die Zelle und die Gewebe," vol. I, pp. 240f. [*The Cell, Outlines of General Anatomy and Physiology,* translated by M. Campbell, London & New York 1895], the former restricted the term more narrowly to the interaction between individual cells than has been done here.

(P. 29, l. 5 from bottom) Despite the term "complement," the view of sexual complementation proposed here has nothing to do with the "complemental males" among cirrepedes that mate with hermaphrodites, discovered by Darwin (A Monograph on the Sub-Class Cirripedia: The Lepadidae or Pedunculated Cirrepedes, London 1851, pp. 55, 182, 213ff., 281f., 291ff.; The Balanidae or sessile Cirripedes, The Verrucidae etc., London 1854, p. 29).

(P. 30, l. 16) Wilhelm Ostwald, Die Überwindung des wissenschaftlichen Materialismus (Vortrag auf der Naturforscherversammlung zu Lübeck) [Overcoming scientific materialism (lecture given to the conference of naturalists in Lübeck)], Leipzig 1895, pp. 11, 27.—Richard Avenarius, Kritik der reinen Erfahrung [Critique of pure experience], Leipzig 1888–1890, frequently, e.g., vol. II, p. 299.

(P. 31, l. 1 from bottom) P. Volkmann, Einführung in das Studium der theoretischen Physik, insbesondere in das der analytischen Mechanik mit einer Einleitung in die Theorie der physikalischen Erkenntnis [Introduction to the study of theoretical physics, in particular to that of analytical mechanics with an introduction to the epistemology of physics], Leipzig 1900, p. 4: "Physics is . . . a system of concepts with retrospective corroboration."

(P. 32, l. 4) For heterostyly, in addition to Darwin's fine book, the standard work on the subject, and the wealth of literature quoted in it at every turn, cf.: Oskar Kirchner and H. Potonié, Die Geheimnisse der Blumen, eine populäre Jubiläumsschrift zum Andenken an Christian Konrad Sprengel [The secrets of the flowers, a popular jubilee publication in memory of Christian Konrad Sprengel], Berlin 1893, pp. 21f.; Julius Sachs, Vorlesungen über Pflanzenphysiologie, 2nd ed., Leipzig 1887, p. 850 [*Lectures on the Physiology of Plants,* translated by H. M. Ward, Oxford 1887]; Noll in Strasburger's Lehrbuch der Botanik für Hochschulen, 3rd ed., Jena 1898, pp. 250 [*A Text-book of Botany,* translated by H. C. Porter, London & New York 1903]; Julius Wiesner, Elemente der wissenschaftlichen Botanik [Elements of scientific botany], vol. III: Biologie der Pflanzen [The biology of plants], Vienna 1902, pp. 152–154. Anton Kerner v. Marilaun, Das Pflanzenleben, vol. II, Vienna 1891, pp. 300ff., 389ff. [*The Natural History of Plants,* translated by F. W. Oliver, London 1894–1895]; Darwin himself in "Entstehung der

Arten" [*The Origin of Species*], chapter 9 (pp. 399f., translated into German by Haek) and "Das Variieren etc." [*The Variation* etc.], chapter 19 (II^2, pp. 207ff.).

(P. 32, l. 5) "Persoon, in Usteri's Annalen [Annals] 1794, no. 11, p. 10, provided the first description of long-styled and short-styled forms of primula," says Hugo v. Mohl, Einige Beobachtungen über dimorphe Blüten [Some observations on dimorphous flowers], Botanische Zeitung, 23 October 1863, p. 326.

(P. 32, l. 5) Charles Darwin, *The Different Forms of Flowers on Plants of the Same Species,* London 1877, 2nd ed., 1884, pp. 1–277. (German: Die verschiedenen Blütenformen bei Pflanzen der nämlichen Art, Werke, translated by J. V. Carus, IX/3, Stuttgart 1877, pp. 1–240.) In his first publications on this subject in 1862 and in those that followed, Darwin had used only the ambiguous terms "dimorphism" and "trimorphism." The term "heterostyly" was first suggested for this by Friedrich Hildebrand in his treatise "Über den Trimorphismus in der Gattung Oxalis" [On trimorphism in the genus oxalis] (p. 369), in "Monatsberichte der kgl. preußischen Akademie der Wissenschaften zu Berlin," 1866, pp. 352–374. Cf. also his larger works: Die Geschlechtsverteilung bei den Pflanzen und das Gesetz der vermiedenen und unvorteilhaften Selbstbefruchtung [The distribution of the sexes in plants and the law of avoided and disadvantageous self-fertilization], Leipzig 1867, and Die Lebensverhältnisse der Oxalisarten [The living conditions of the species of oxalis], Jena 1884, pp. 127f.

(P. 32, l. 6) The only monocotyledons with heterostylous flowers are the pontederiae discovered in Brazil by Fritz Müller (Jenaische Zeitschrift für Naturwissenschaft VI, 1871, pp. 74f.).

(P. 32, l. 14) Darwin also comes close to this view once or twice, but immediately loses sight of it, because in his mind the generally valid principle of intermediate sexual forms is always displaced by the idea of a progressive tendency of plants to become dioecic (cf. p. 257 of the English edition). However, at one point (p. 296) he says about rhamnus lanceolatus: "The short-styled form is said by Asa Gray to be the more fruitful of the two, as might have been expected from its appearing to produce less pollen, and from the grains being of smaller size; *it is therefore the more highly feminine of the two.* The long-styled form produces a greater number of flowers. . . . they yield some fruit, but as just stated are less fruitful than the other form, *so that this form appears to be the more masculine of the two.*"

(P. 32, l. 19f.) On lythrum salicaria the English text on p. 137 (in the German translation p. 118[1]) reads literally: "If smaller differences are considered, there are five distinct sets of males."

(P. 32, l. 8 from bottom) William Bateson, Materials for the Study of Variation Treated with Especial Regard to Discontinuity in the Origin of Species, London 1894, pp. 38f. About xylotrupes he actually says: "The form is dimorphic, and has two male normals." The passage is too extensive to be quoted here in full.

(P. 33, l. 16 from bottom) Darwin, p. 148: "It must not however be supposed that the bees do not get more or less dusted all over with the several kinds of pollen."

(P. 34, ll. 2–6) Darwin, p. 186, speaks of this phenomenon as "the usual rule of the grains from the longer stamens, the tubes of which have to penetrate the longer pistils, being larger than those from the stamens of less length." See also pp. 38, 140, and particularly 286ff.—F. Hildebrand, Experimente über den Dimorphismus von Linum perenne und Primula sinensis [Experiments on the dimorphism of linum perenne and primula sinensis], Botanische Zeitung, 1 January 1864, p. 2: "My observations . . . showed that . . . the grains of pollen of the short-styled form are significantly larger than those of the long-styled."

(P. 34, l. 7) Hildebrand, Monatsberichte der königlich preußischen Akademie der Wissenschaften, 1866, p. 370, objects to Lindlay and Zuccarini that short-styled flowers cannot be male, and long-styled female, because the stigma of the short-styled form does not atrophy and the pollen of the long-styled form is neither bad nor ineffectual. However, it is characteristic of plants that among them *juxtapositions* are possible to a much greater extent than among animals.

(P. 34, l. 19) L. Weill, Über die kinetische Korrelation zwischen den beiden Generationszellen [On the kinetic correlation between the two generative cells], Archiv für Entwicklungsmechanik der Organismen, vol. XI, 1901, pp. 222–224.

(P. 35, l. 6 from bottom) Here the t factor plays an important and extremely remarkable part not only in humans and other organisms, but even in the relations of the germ cells. Thus O. and R. Hertwig, Untersuchungen zur Morphologie und Physiologie der Zelle, 4. Heft, Experimentelle Untersuchungen über die Bedingungen der Bastardbefruchtung [Studies in the morphology and physiology of the cell, no. 4, Experimental investigations into the conditions of illegitimate fertilization], Jena 1885, p. 37, report on their observations of echinoderms: "We now found that ova which were illegitimately fertilized immediately after their evacuation from the packed ovaries *rejected* the strange spermatozoon, but 10, 20, or 30 hours later, on the occasion of the second, third, or fourth subsequent fertilization, absorbed it and then continued to develop normally." P. 38: "The later [after the evacuation of the ovaries] that fertilization occurred, whether after 50 or 10 or 20 or 30 hours, the more the percentage of illegitimately fertilized ova increased, until finally an optimum of illegitimate fertilization was reached. We describe as such the stage at which almost the entire quantity of ova, with the exception of a small number, develops normally."

(P. 36, l. 1f.) "Phantasien eines Realisten" [Phantasies of a realist] by Lynkeus, Dresden and Leipzig 1900, part II, pp. 155–162.

(P. 36, l. 11f.) " . . . in general . . . "; k does *not always* simply increase in proportion to generic proximity. See O. and R. Hertwig op. cit., pp. 32f.: "The success or failure of illegitimate fertilization does not exclusively depend on the degree of generic kinship between the crossed species. We can observe that some species which hardly differ from one another in external features cannot be crossed, while this is possible between species belonging to relatively distant and different families and orders. Amphibians supply us with particularly apt examples of this. Rana arvalis and rana fusca are almost identical in appearance, but nevertheless the ova of the latter cannot be fertilized, while in some cases fertilization with the semen of bufo communis and even triton was possible. The same phenomenon could be noted, albeit less clearly, in echinoderms. Nevertheless, it must be remembered that generic kinship is an important factor for the possibility of illegitimate fertilization. For no cross-fertilization has ever been achieved between animals that are as remote from one another as amphibians and mammals, or sea-urchins and starfish." Cf. Julius Sachs, Lehrbuch der Pflanzenphysiologie 2nd ed., Leipzig 1887, p. 838 [*Text-book of Botany. Morphological and Physiological,* Oxford 1882, p. 818]: "This kind of affinity is not always concurrent with the external resemblance of the plants. Thus, for example, hybrids have never been obtained between the apple and pear, *Anagallis arvensis* and *cærulea, Primula officinalis* and *elatior,* or *Nigella damascena* and *sativa,* nor between many other pairs of species belonging to the same genus which are very nearly allied to one another; while in other cases very dissimilar forms unite, as *Ægilops ovata* with *Triticum vulgare, Lychnis diurna* with *L. Flos-cuculi, Cereus speciosissimus* with *Phyllocactus Phyllanthus,* the peach with the almond. A still more striking proof of the difference between sexual and genetic affinity is afforded by the fact that varieties of the same species will sometimes be partially or altogether infertile with one another, as *e.g., Silene inflata* var. *alpina* with var. *angustifolia,* var. *latifolia* with var. *littoralis,* &c." Cf. also Oscar Hertwig, Die Zelle und die Gewebe, vol. I, p. 249 [*The Cell, Outlines of General Anatomy and Physiology,* translated by M. Campbell, London, New York 1895].

(P. 36, l. 9 from bottom) Wilhelm Pfeffer, Lokomotorische Richtungsbewegungen durch chemische Reize [Locomotor movements in response to chemical stimuli], Untersuchungen aus dem botanischen Institut zu Tübingen, vol. I, 1885, pp. 363–482.

(P. 36, l. 1 from bottom) Über die Wirkung der Maleinsäure [On the effect of malic acid] ("which, as far as we know, does not occur in the plant kingdom"), Pfeffer, op. cit., p. 412.

(P. 37, l. 3) The term is introduced in Pfeffer, op. cit., p. 474 n. 2.

(P. 37, l. 9) This is supported, above all, by L. Seligmann's report, Weitere Mitteilungen zur Behandlung der Sterilitas matrimonii, Vortrag in der gynäkologischen Gesellschaft zu Hamburg [Further communications on the treatment of sterilitas matrimonii, lecture given to the Hamburg Gynaecological Society], Zentralblatt für Gynäkologie, 18 April 1896, p. 429: "Arranging the microscopic preparation in such a way that on one side of the cover glass some normal cervical secretion was applied to the glass, and some under the glass, produced the result that, after a while, on one side of the vaginal secretion there were only very few spermatozoa, which were no longer moving, while on the other side of the cervical secretion dense crowds of spermatozoa found themselves in lively motion. Here one can obviously speak of a chemotactical effect of the cervical secretion on the sperm cells."

(P. 37, ll. 10ff.) M. Hofmeier, Zur Kenntnis der normalen Uterusschleimhaut [On the understanding of the normal mucous membrane of the uterus], Zentralblatt für Gynäkologie, vol. XVII, 1893, pp. 764–766. "After the positive observations there can no longer be any doubt that *the cilial current in the uterus actually runs from the top toward the bottom.*"

(P. 37, l. 16) For the migration of salmon, including its fast and its weight loss cf. above all Friedrich Miescher, Die histochemischen und physiologischen Arbeiten von F. M. [The histochemical and physiological works of F. M.], collected and edited by his friends, vol. II, Leipzig 1897, pp. 116–191, 192–218, 304–324, 325–327, 359–414, 415–420.

(P. 37, ll. 19ff.) P. Falkenberg, Die Befruchtung und der Generationswechsel von Cutleria [The fertilization and alternation of generations in cutleria], Mitteilungen aus der zoologischen Station zu Neapel, vol. I, 1879, pp. 420–447. On pp. 425ff. we read: "The attempt at cross-fertilization between the closely related species of cutleria, c. adspersa and c. multifida, which—apart from their different locations—are externally distinguished by only slight habitual differences, produced entirely negative results. Lively swarms of spermatozoids of one species were added to static ova, capable of conception, of the other species. In such cases, under the microscope, spermatozoa were seen wandering about in large numbers, and finally dying without having carried out the act of fertilization on the ova of the related species of alga. Some spermatozoids, which came across the stationary ova by chance, momentarily adhered to them, but just as quickly broke loose again. The picture under the microscope became very different once in such preparations even a single ovum of the same species capable of conception was added to the spermatozoids. It took only a few moments to gather all the spermatozoids from all sides around this one ovum, even if it was several centimeters from the main mass of spermatozoids. The picture now corresponded entirely to the illustrations given for fucus by Thuret (Recherches sur la fécondation des Fucacées [Studies in the fertilization of fucacea], Ann. des Sc. natur., Sér. 4, Tome II, p. 203, pl. 12, fig. 4), and likewise the ovum that had long since become static was now turned this way and that by the united strengths of the many spermatozoids. . . . These experiments demonstrate on the one hand that the attraction between the ova of cutleria and the spermatozoids makes itself felt across relatively significant distances, and on the other hand that this attraction exists only between the sexual cells of the same species. In addition, the reported phenomena show that under the influence of the attraction of the ova the movements of the spermatozoids of cutleria . . . are sufficiently energetic to overcome that force which normally directs them toward the incident light, and to enable them to take the opposite direction. The force that strives for the union of the male and female sexual cells of cutleria and that regulates the direction in which the male swarmers move may be located in the male or in the female cell, or in both—but so much is certain that the force which in cutleria leads the spermatozoa to the ova must be located in the organism itself and acts independently of chance and of currents which may, for instance, occur in water."

(P. 38, l. 3) Cf. Johann Peter Eckermann, Gespräche mit Goethe in den letzten Jahren seines Lebens [*Eckermann's Conversations with Goethe,* translated by R. O. Moon, London 1951] (30 March 1824).

(P. 38, l. 9) The analogies between humans and domestic animals concerning the lack of connection between sexual intercourse and specific points in time are often exaggerated; cf. Chrobak-Rosthorn, Die Erkrankungen der weiblichen Geschlechtsorgane [The diseases of the female sexual organs], Vienna 1900, part I/2, pp. 379f.

(P. 39, l. 13) I mean the extraordinarily true passage: "They exerted, as before, an indescribable, almost magical attraction upon one another. They lived beneath one roof, but even when they were not actually thinking about one another, when they were involved with other things, driven hither and thither by society, they still drew close together. If they found themselves in the same room, it was not long before they were standing or sitting side-by-side. Only the closest proximity to one another could make them tranquil and calm of mind, but then they were altogether tranquil, and this proximity was sufficient: *no glance, no word, no gesture, no touch was needed, but only this pure togetherness. Then they were not two people, they were one person, one in unreflecting perfect well-being,* contented with themselves and with the universe. *Indeed, if one of them had been imprisoned at the far end of the house, the other would have gradually and without any conscious intention have moved across in that direction.*" (Goethe, Die Wahlverwandtschaften, part II, chapter 17 [*Elective Affinities,* translated by R. J. Hollingdale, Harmondsworth 1971, p. 286].)

(P. 39, ll. 12 from bottom ff.) Compare this with the following poetic statements.

Theognis says to the boy Kyrnos (ll. 183ff.):

"Κριοὺς μὲν καὶ ὄνους διζήμεθα, Κύρνε, καὶ ἵππους
εὐγενέας, καί τις βούλεται ἐξ ἀγαθῶν
βήσεσθαι· γῆμαι δὲ κακὴν κακοῦ οὐ μελεδαίνει
ἐσθλὸς ἀνηρ, ἥν οἱ χρήματα πολλὰ διδῷ.
οὐδὲ γυνὴ κακοῦ ἀνδρὸς ἀναίνεται εἶναι ἄκοιτις
πλουσίου, ἄλ' ἀφνεὸν βούλεται ἀντ' ἀγαθοῦ.
χρήματα γὰρ τιμῶσι· καὶ ἔκ κακοῦ ἐσθλὸς ἔγημεν,
καὶ κακὸς ἐξ ἀγαθοῦ· πλοῦτος ἔμιξε γένος." etc.

Shakespeare makes the bastard Edmund utter these well-known lines (King Lear, Act I, Scene 2):

Why brand they us
With base? with baseness? bastardy? base, base?
Who, in the lusty stealth of nature, take
More composition and fierce quality
Than doth, within a dull, stale, tired bed,
Go to th' creating a whole tribe of fops
Got 'tween asleep and wake?

(P. 40, ll. 7ff.) Darwin, Das Variieren der Tiere und Pflanzen, vol. II, chapters 17–19 (e.g., p. 170 of the 2nd ed., Stuttgart 1873 [The Variation of Animals and Plants], but in particular: Die Wirkungen der Kreuz-und Selbstbefruchtung im Pflanzenreich, Stuttgart 1877 (Werke, vol. X), p. 24: [*The Effects of Cross and Self Fertilisation in the Plant Kingdom,* London 1876, p. 27]: "The most important conclusion at which I have arrived is that the mere act of crossing by itself is not good. The good depends on the individuals which are crossed differing slightly in constitution, owing to their progenitors having been subjected during several generations to slightly different conditions, or to what we call in our ignorance spontaneous variation."

Part 1, Chapter IV

(P. 41, ll. 1ff.) From the literature I will only name the few most important books, in which all further references can be found: Richard v. Krafft-Ebing, Pyschopathia sexualis, mit besonderer Berücksichtigung der konträren Sexualempfindung, 9th ed., Stuttgart 1894 [*Psychopathia Sexualis, with Especial Reference to Antipathic Sexual Instinct,* translated by F. J. Rebman, 12th ed. London 1906]. Albert Moll, Die konträre Sexualempfindung, 3rd ed., Berlin 1891 [*Perversions of the Sex Instinct, A Study of Sexual Inversion,* translated by Maurice Popkin, Newark 1931]. Untersuchungen über die Libido sexualis, vol. I, Berlin 1897–1898 [*Libido Sexualis,* translated by David Berger, New York 1933]. Havelock Ellis and J. A. Symonds, Das konträre Geschlechtsgefühl, Leipzig 1896 [*Sexual Inversion,* London 1897].

(P. 41, l. 19) v. Schrenck-Notzing, Die Suggestionstherapie bei krankhaften

Erscheinungen des Geschlechtslebens, mit besonderer Berücksichtigung der konträren Sexualempfindung, Stuttgart 1892 (e.g., p. 193) [*Therapeutic Suggestion in Psychopathia Sexualis (Pathological Manifestations of the Sexual Sense), with Especial Reference to Contrary Sexual Instinct,* translated by Charles Gilbert Chaddock, Philadelphia 1901, p. 191]): "The part played by the accessory factor in the etiology of the habitual impulse to perverse sexual acts is usually more important than that played by hereditary disposition." Ein Beitrag zur Ätiologie der konträren Sexualempfindung [A contribution to the aetiology of contrary sexual instinct], Vienna 1895, pp. 1ff. Kriminalpsychologische und psycho-pathologische Studien [Studies in criminal psychology and psychopathology], Leipzig 1902, pp. 2f., 17f.—Emil Kraepelin, Psychiatrie, 4th ed., Leipzig 1893, pp. 689f. [*Psychiatry. A Textbook for Students and Physicians,* ed. Jacques M. Quen, 2 vols., Canton, Mass. 1991]—Ch. Féré, La descendence d'un inverti [The descent of an invert], Revue générale de clinique et de thérapeutique, 1896, quoted from Moll, Untersuchungen, vol. I, p.651 n. 3 [*Libido Sexualis,* translated by David Berger, New York 1933]. However, in his book L'Instinct Sexuel, Evolution et Dissolution, Paris 1899, pp. 266ff. [*The Evolution and Dissolution of the Sexual Instinct,* translated by H. Blanchamp, London 1900] Féré places the emphasis on congenital disposition.

(P. 42, l. 11f.) "Complementary condition" from Avenarius, Kritik der reinen Erfahrung [Critique of pure experience], vol. I, Leipzig 1888, p. 29; "partial cause" from Alois Höfler, Logik unter Mitwirkung von Dr. Alexius Meinong [Logic, with the assistance of Dr. Alexius Meinong], Vienna 1890, p. 63.

(P. 43, l. 7) Reciprocal sexual attraction between persons situated midway between M and W also seems very likely in view of F. Neugebauer's observations ("Fifty False Marriages between Individuals of the Same Gender with Some Divorces for 'Erreur de Sexe'"), paper in British Gynaecological Journal, 15, 1899, p. 315, cf. 16, 1900, p. 104 of "summary of Gynaecology, including Obstetrics."

(P. 43, l. 12) Cf. Emil Kraepelin, Psychiatrie, 4th ed., Leipzig 1893, p. 690 [*Psychiatry. A Textbook for Students and Physicians,* ed. Jacques M. Quen, 2 vols., Canton, Mass. 1991, vol. 2, p. 422]: "Persons in whom signs of heterosexual instincts *never* existed are relatively rare."

(P. 43, l. 19f.) The American J. G. Kiernan is supposed to have first sought the cause of homosexuality in the lack of sexual differentiation in the embryo (American Lancet, 1884, and Medical Standard, Nov.–Dec. 1888), as Frank Lydston (Philadelphia Medical and Surgical Recorder, September 1888, Addresses and Essays, 1892, pp. 46, 246) did after him: I have had no access to either treatise. The same theory is advanced by a patient in Krafft-Ebing, Psychopathia sexualis, 8th ed., Stuttgart 1893, p. 227 [*Psychopathia Sexualis,* 10th German ed., translated by Francis J. Rebman, London 1899]. Krafft-Ebing himself accepted the theory in a treatise entitled "Zur Erklärung der konträren Sexualempfindung" [On the explanation of sexual inversion], Jahrbücher für Psychiatrie und Nervenheilkunde, vol. XIII, no. 2. It was further adopted by Albert Moll, Untersuchungen über die Libido sexualis, vol. I, pp. 327ff. [*Libido Sexualis,* translated by David Berger, New York 1933], Magnus Hirschfeld, Die objektive Diagnose der Homosexualität [The objective diagnosis of homosexuality], Jahrbuch für sexuelle Zwischenstufen, vol. I, 1899, pp. 4ff. Havelock Ellis, Studies in the Psychology of Sex, vol. I, Sexual Inversion, 1900, pp. 132f. Norbert Grabowski, Die mannweibliche Natur des Menschen [The male-female nature of the human being], Leipzig 1896 etc.

(P. 44, l. 11) The recognition of laws ruling the animal kingdom in respect of sexual attraction has momentous consequences in that it makes the hypothesis of "sexual selection" almost totally impossible.

(P. 44, l. 20) Homosexuality in animals: cf. Ch. Féré, Les perversions sexuelles chez les animaux [The sexual perversions of animals], in L'Instinct Sexuel, Paris 1899, pp. 59–87 [*The Evolution and Dissolution of the Sexual Instinct,* translated by H. Blanchamp, London 1900]. F. Karsch, Päderastie und Tribadie bei den Tieren, auf Grund der Literatur zusammengestellt [Pederasty and tribady in animals, compiled from the literature], Jahrbuch für sexuelle Zwischenstufen, vol. II, 1900, pp. 126–154. Albert Moll, Untersuchungen über die Libido sexualis, vol. I, 1898, pp. 368ff. [*Libido Sexualis,* translated by David Berger, New York 1933].

(P. 44, l. 8 from bottom) It is therefore erroneous to believe, as so many do (even as far back as Plato, Gesetze, VIII, 836c [*Laws,* translated by Trevor J. Saunders, Harmonsdworth 1970, pp. 333–334]) that "paederasty (of either sex)" is an "unnatural" vice, peculiar only to *humans.* Nevertheless, while homosexuality is not restricted to humans, Plato may have been right in respect to pederasty.

(P. 45, ll. 8ff.) Cf. Krafft-Ebing in Alfred Fuchs, Die Therapie der anomalen Vita sexualis, Stuttgart 1899 [The therapy of anomalous sexual life], p. 4.

(P. 46, l. 2) The only really great man who seems to have strictly condemned homosexuality is the apostle Paul (Romans, 1, 26–27), but he admitted that sexuality played a small part in his own disposition, which suffices to explain the somewhat naïve optimism of his remarks about marriage.

(P. 46, l. 16) Moll, Untersuchungen über die Libido sexualis, vol. I, Berlin 1898, p. 484 [Libido Sexualis, translated by David Berger, New York 1933, passage not found in translation].

(P. 46, l. 2 from bottom) According to this nomenclature, men such as Michelangelo or Winckelmann, the former certainly one of the most masculine artists, should be described not as homosexuals but as pederasts.

Part 1, Chapter V

(P. 47, l. 11) If Theodor Gomperz, Griechische Denker, Leipzig 1896, vol. I, p. 149 [*Greek thinkers. A History of Ancient Philosophy,* translated by Laurie Magnus (vol. 1–3), G. G. Berry (vol. 4), London 1901–1912], is correct in his interpretation of some lines of Parmenides preserved in Latin (cf. Parmenides' Lehrgedicht, griechisch und deutsch von Hermann Diels, Berlin 1897, Fragment 18 and Diels's comments, pp. 113ff. [*Parmenides,* translated by Leonardo Tarán, Princeton 1965]), I would have to name the great thinker as my precursor. Gomperz says: "In [this] theory we mark the tendency, so characteristic of a Pythagorean or mathematical training, to derive distinctions of quality from differences of quantity. He followed Alcmæon in using the hypothetical proportions of the male and female generative elements to account for idiosyncrasies of character, and above all for the peculiar sexual inclinations of the male and female products. In precisely the same way he referred the intellectual differences of individuals and their mental condition with its temporary variations to the greater or smaller share of the two primary matters which their bodies contained." Unless Gomperz meant a different fragment than that named above, this interpretation would attribute something to Parmenides that is due to Gomperz. Cf. also Zeller, Die Philosophie der Griechen, I/1, 5th ed., Leipzig 1892, pp. 578f. n. 4 [*Outlines of the History of Greek Philosophy,* translated by L. R. Palmer, London 1931].

(P. 47, l. 7 from bottom) This is an allusion to L. William Stern's programmatic piece, Psychologie der individuellen Differenzen (Ideen zu einer "differentiellen Psychologie") [The psychology of individual differences (ideas for a "differential psychology")], Schriften der Gesellschaft für psychologische Forschung, no. 12, Leipzig 1900.

(P. 48, l. 19) On periodicity in human life, particularly of the male, and indeed in all matters biological, the most interesting and stimulating points are found in a book whose title, which is also unfortunate in various other respects, suggests nothing about such a content, i.e., Wilhelm Fließ, Die Beziehungen zwischen Nase und weiblichen Geschlechtsorganen in ihrer biologischen Bedeutung dargestellt [The biological significance of the connections between the nose and the female sexual organs], Leipzig and Vienna 1897. This is an extremely original work, whose historic importance is likely to be fully recognized one day when research has advanced far beyond it. To date, the extremely remarkable things discovered by Fließ have typically received little attention (cf. Fließ, pp. 117ff., 174, 237).

(P. 51, l. 4) Statements by a variety of authors about this alleged "monotony" of women can be found in the large collection by C. Lombroso and G. Ferrero, Das Weib als Verbrecherin und Prostituierte, Anthropologische Studien, gegründet auf eine Darstellung der Biologie und Psychologie des normalen Weibes, translated into German by Kurella, Hamburg 1894, pp. 172f. [*The Female Offender,* London 1895].

(P. 51, l. 1 from bottom) Greater diversity of males: Darwin, Die Abstammung des Menschen etc. [*The Descent of Man* etc.], translated into German by Haek, chapter 8, pp. 334ff., chapter 14, pp. 132ff, esp. p. 136, chapter 19, pp. 338ff.—C. B. Davenport and C. Bullard, Studies in Morphogenesis, VI: A Contribution to the Quantitative Study of Correlated Variation and the Comparative Variability of the Sexes, Proceedings of the Amer. Phil. Soc. 32, pp. 85–97. Paper in Année Biologique, 1895, pp. 273f.

(P. 52, l. 15) The "actuality theory" of psychic events is that of Wilhelm Wundt (Grundriß der Psychologie, 4th ed., Leipzig 1901, p. 387 [*Outlines of Psychology,* translated by C. H. Judd, Leipzig 1902]). It rejects any substantial and timeless being in psychology, considering this to be its fundamental difference from natural science, which can never transcend the concept of matter (cf. also Wundt's Logik [Logic], vol. II, Methodenlehre [Methodology], 2nd ed., Leipzig 1895).

(P. 52, ll. 10 from bottom ff.) The justification in principle of physiognomy, which despite Lichtenberg's evil prophecy, did not "suffocate in its own fat" but rather died of a wasting disease, and which will be demonstrated in what follows, is in essence already contained in Aristotle's words (περὶ ψυχῆς A 3. 407 b, 13f.): "Εκεῖνο δὲ ἄτοπον συμβαίνει καὶ τούτῳ τῷ λόγῳ καὶ τοῖς πλείστοις τῶν περὶ ψυχῆς· συνάπτουσι γὰρ καὶ τιθέασιν εἰς σῶμα τὴν ψυχήν, οὐθὲν προσδιορίσαντες διὰ τίν' αἰτίαν καὶ πῶς ἔχοντος τοῦ σώματος. Καίτοι δόξειεν ἂν τοῦτ' ἀναγκαῖον εἶναι· διὰ γὰρ τὴν κοινωνίαν τὸ μὲν ποιεῖ τὸ δὲ πάσχει καὶ τὸ μὲν κινεῖται τὸ δὲ κινεῖ, τούτων δ' οὐδὲν ὑπάρχει πρὸς ἄλληλα τοῖς τυχοῦσιν. Οἱ δὲ μόνον ἐπιχειροῦσι λέγειν ποῖόν τι ἡ ψυχή, περὶ δὲ τοῦ δεξομένου σώματος οὐθὲν ἔτι προσδιορίζουσιν, ὥσπερ ἐνδεχομένου κατὰ τοὺς Πυθαγορικοὺς μύθους τὴν τυχοῦσαν ψυχὴν εἰς τὸ τυχὸν ἐνδύεσθαι σῶμα· δοκεῖ γὰρ ἕκαστον ἴδιον ἔξειν εἶδος καὶ μορφήν. Παραπλήσον δὲ λέγουσι ὥσπερ εἴ τις φαίη τὴν τεκτονικὴν εἰς αᾧοὺς ἐνδύεσθαι· δεῖ γὰρ τὴν μὲν τέχνην χρῆσθαι τοῖς ὀργάνοις, τὴν δὲ ψυχὴν τῷ σώματι."

(P. 53, l. 2) P. J. Moebius, Über die Anlage zur Mathematik [On the aptitude for mathematics], Leipzig 1900.

(P. 54, l. 9) While Hume keeps silent about the difference, Mach denies it (cf. Die Prinzipien der Wärmelehre, historisch-kritisch entwickelt, 2nd ed., Leipzig 1900, pp. 432ff. [*Principles of the Theory of Heat, Historically and Critically Elucidated,* Dordrecht, Lancaster 1986]).

(P. 54, l. 17) The view of the problem of time which is rejected here is that of Ernst Mach, Die Mechanik in ihrer Entwicklung historisch-kritisch dargestellt, 4th ed., Leipzig 1901, p. 233 [*The Science of Mechanics. A Critical and Historical Account of its Development,* translated by Thomas J. McCormack, La Salle, Ill. 1960]. J. B. Stallo's remarks about this question in The Concepts and Theories of Modern Physics, 3rd ed., London 1890, p. 204, are infinitely shallow.

(P. 54, l. 7 from bottom) On Aristotle as the founder of correlation theory, see Jürgen Bona Meyer, Aristoteles' Tierkunde, Berlin 1855, [The zoology of Aristotle], p. 468.

(P. 54, ll. 6 from bottom ff.) For the strange correlation in cats, and "correlated variability" as such, see Darwin, Das Variieren der Tiere und Pflanzen, Stuttgart 1873, chapter 25 (vol. II^2, p. 375) [*The Variation of Animals and Plants under Domestication,* 2 vols., London 1868]). Cf. Entstehung der Arten, pp. 36f., 194f. of the German translation by Haek (Universal-Bibliothek) [*The Origin of Species*].

(P. 55, l. 16 from bottom) Ernst Mach, Die Mechanik etc., 4th ed., p. 235 [*The Science of Mechanics,* translated by Thomas J. McCormack, La Salle, Ill. 1960].

(P. 55, ll. 2 from bottom ff.) Here our study coincides with Wilhelm Dilthey, Beiträge zum Studium der Individualität [Contributions to the study of individuality], Sitzungsberichte der kgl. preußischen Akademie der Wissenschaften zu Berlin, 1896 (pp. 295–335), p. 303: "In a type . . . various characteristics, parts, or functions are regularly combined with one another. The relationship between these features, the combinations of which constitute the type, are such that it is possible to infer from the presence of one feature that of the other and from the variations within one feature those within the other. This typical combination of characteristics increases in the universe through an ascending series of life forms, reaching its apex in organic and then in psychic life. This principle of the type can be regarded as the second principle controlling the individuals. It was this law that enabled the great Cuvier to reconstruct the body of an animal from its ossified remains, and the same law in the intellectual and historical world enabled F. A. Wolf and Niebuhr to draw their conclusions."

(P. 56, l. 10) The worms concerned are nereids, artificially deprived of their supraœsophageal ganglion. "If there are several animals which have been operated upon in a vessel, . . . when [they] reach a corner [they] do not turn around but attempt to go through the glass. The worms remained like this for many hours at a time, and then died in consequence of their vain attempt to go forward." Jacques Loeb, Einleitung in die vergleichende Gehirnphysiologie und vergleichende Psychologie mit besonderer Berücksichtigung der wirbellosen Tiere, Leipzig 1899, p. 63 [*Comparative Physiology of the Brain and Comparative Psychology,* London 1901, p. 92] (where a drawing of this process, based on S. S. Maxwell, Pflügers Archiv für die gesamte Physiologie, 67, 1897, is to be found).

(P. 56, l. 17) The expression "watcher" etc. from Schopenhauer, Parerga II, § 350 bis [*Parerga and Paralipomena,* Translated by E. F. J. Payne, vol. II, § 350 a, Oxford 2000, p. 607].

(P. 56, l. 1 from bottom) Konrad Rieger says (Die Kastration [Castration], Jena 1900, Vorwort, p. XXV): "I entirely share the conviction of Gall, Comte, Moebius that the greatest progress would be achieved, both in pure science and in a practical social and political respect, if a method capable of exactly determining the morality, character and will of a human being [by means of physiognomy] were to be found." I cannot agree with this view, which I regard as somewhat exaggerated, but I quote it because at least it shows the importance of the matter in the correct light.

Part 1, Chapter VI

(P. 57, l. 6) My understanding of the Woman Question as developed in this chapter is closest to that of Arduin, Die Frauenfrage und die sexuellen Zwischenstufen [The woman question and the intermediate sexual forms], Jahrbuch für sexuelle Zwischenstufen, vol. II, 1900, pp. 211–223. I am, however, entirely independent of this author.

(P. 58, l. 9 from bottom) Cf. Welcker, Sappho von einem herrschenden Vorurteil befreit [Sappho, freed from a prevailing prejudice], Göttingen 1816, reprinted in his "Kleine Schriften" [Short writings], part II, Bonn 1845, pp. 80–144. Also Q. Horatius Flaccus, erklärt von Hermann Schütz [Horace, explained by Hermann Schütz], part III, Episteln [Epistles], Berlin 1883, comments on Epistles 1, 19, 28. On the same, Welcker, Kleine Schriften [Short writings], vol. V, pp. 239f.

(P. 58, l. 2 from bottom) The information about Laura Bridgman derives from Albert Moll, Untersuchungen über die Libido sexualis, Berlin 1897–1898, vol. I, p. 144 [*Libido sexualis,* translated by David Berger, New York 1933]. However, the passages in Wilhelm Jerusalem, Laura Bridgman, Erziehung einer Taubstummen-Blinden, eine psychologische Studie [Laura Bridgman, Education of a deaf-mute and blind woman], Vienna 1890, p. 60, rather suggest the opposite. On George Sand: Moll, ibid., pp. 698f. n. 4; on Catherine II: Moll, Die konträre Sexualempfindung, 3rd ed., Berlin 1899, p. 516 [*Perversions of the Sex Instinct. A Study of Sexual Inversion,* translated by Maurice Popkin, Newark 1931]; on Christina: Adele Gerhardt and Helene Simon, Mutterschaft und geistige Arbeit [Motherhood and intellectual labor], Berlin 1901, p. 209 ("at any rate a personality put at risk by sexually pathological symptoms").

(P. 59, l. 3 from bottom) Mérimée: according to Adele Gerhardt and Helene Simon, Mutterschaft und geistige Arbeit, eine psychologische und soziologische Studie auf Grundlage einer internationalen Erhebung mit Berücksichtigung der geschichtlichen Entwicklung [Motherhood and intellectual labor, a psychological and sociological study based on an international survey with reference to historical development], Berlin 1901, p. 162. The story about George Sand and

Chopin, ibid., p. 166. I am indebted to this assiduous work for a number of further references and some suggestions about sources.

(P. 59, l. 21) Compare "Briefe Ludwigs II. von Bayern an Richard Wagner" [Letters from Ludwig II of Bavaria to Richard Wagner], published in Die Wage, Wiener Wochenschrift, 1 January–5 February 1899.

(P. 59, ll. 8 from bottom ff.) On George Eliot: Gerhardt and Simon, op. cit., p. 155. On Lavinia Fontana ibid., p. 98. On Droste-Hülshoff, p. 137. On Rachel Ruysch: Ernst Guhl, Die Frauen in der Kunstgeschichte [Women in art history], Berlin 1858, p. 122.

(P. 60, l. 9) On Rosa Bonheur, cf. Gerhardt-Simon, pp. 107f., where the painter's biographer, René Peyrol (Rosa Bonheur, Her Life and Work, London), is quoted as follows: "The masculine vigour of her character, as also her hair, which she was in the habit of wearing short, contributed to perfect her disguise." When R. B. walked about in men's clothes nobody had the slightest suspicion.

(P. 60, l. 13 from bottom) As women produce less than men, their works have rarity value and are regarded rather as curiosities right from the outset. See Guhl, Die Frauen in der Kunstgeschichte [Women in art history], pp. 260f.: "The mere fact that a work stemmed from the hand of a woman was sufficient reason for praise."

(P. 61, l. 15f.) See P. J. Moebius, Über die Vererbung künstlerischer Talente [On the heredity of artistic talents], in "Umschau," IV, no. 38, pp. 742–745 (15 September 1900). Jürgen Bona Meyer, Zeitschrift für Völkerpsychologie und Sprachwissenschaft, 1880, pp. 295–298. Karl Joel, Die Frauen in der Philosophie [Women in philosophy] Sammlung gemeinverständlicher Vorträge, edited by Virchow and Holtzendorff, no. 246, Hamburg 1896, pp. 32, 63.

(P. 61, l. 18f.) Guhl, op. cit., p. 8.

(P. 61, l. 20) Here I should also have mentioned Dorothea Mendelssohn as being very masculine; about her and her extremely feminine husband Friedrich Schlegel, see J. Schubert, Frauengestalten aus der Zeit der deutschen Romantik [Female personalities from the age of German romanticism], Hamburg 1898 (Sammlung gemeinverständlicher wissenschaftlicher Vorträge, edited by Virchow, no. 285), pp. 8f. Mention should also have been made of the highly gifted homosexual countess Sarolta V. from Krafft-Ebing's Pychopathia sexualis (8th ed., 1893, pp. 311–317) [*Psychopathia Sexualis,* translated by F. J. Rebman, 12th ed., London 1906].

(P. 61, ll. 22ff.) Guhl, op. cit., p. 5.

(P. 61, l. 5 from bottom) Anybody who is a keener collector, with greater knowledge of the history of literature, art, science, and politics, than I am, and who knows how to find more abundant sources than I have been able to do, will certainly discover many other remarkable confirmations of this point.

(P. 62, ll. 3 from bottom ff.) Passage about famous women, Darwin, Abstammung des Menschen, translated into German by Haek, vol. II, pp. 344f. [*The Descent of Man,* London 1871, vol. 2, p. 327].

(P. 63, l. 2 from bottom) This statement about Burns, which I have taken from Carlyle, On Heroes etc., London, Chapman & Hall, p. 175, is contradicted by what the "Memoir of Robert Burns," printed at the start of the edition of the Poetical Works, London, Warne 1896, reports on pp. 16f. about his education.

(P. 63, l. 11 from bottom) Quoted from Burckhardt, Die Kultur der Renaissance in Italien, 4th ed. by Ludwig Geiger, Leipzig 1885, vol. II, p. 125 [*The Civilisation of the Renaissance in Italy,* translated by S. G. C. Middlemore, Harmondsworth 1990, pp. 251–252].

(P. 63, l. 8 from bottom f.) Gerhardt and Simon, op. cit., pp. 46f.

(P. 64, ll. 1ff.) Here I am indebted to Ottokar Lorenz (Lehrbuch der gesamten wissenschaftlichen Genealogie, Stammbaum und Ahnentafel in ihrer geschichtlichen, soziologischen und naturwissenschaftlichen Bedeutung [Comprehensive textbook of scientific genealogy, the family tree, and the genealogical table and their historical, sociological, and scientific significance], Berlin 1898, pp. 54f.). He writes: "Nobody familiar with cultural conditions of the past is likely to regard those phenomena that today are called, not very accurately, the emancipation of women as an entirely new thing in all its individual parts. In particular women's drive to acquire the learning of their time was just as great in the 16th and 10th centuries as in the 19th. Today's social idea of securing for women an independent activity also has full analogies in the church and convent life of past ages. If one examines the causes of these phenomena, which recur regularly as the epochs succeed each other, there can be no doubt that those drives, those movements, rooted in the personal qualities of the women striving for so-called emancipation in different forms and different ages must at least have a large share in them. Therefore, the Woman Question, standing out in more or less sharp relief as time passes and generations follow each other, proves a certain recurrence of qualities in women that in some epochs are undoubtedly of a more masculine kind than in others, in which the same characteristics were regarded as downright ugly."

(P. 64, l. 12) Darwin, Das Variieren etc., II^2, p. 58 [Darwin, Variation, II, p. 51]: "It is well known that a large number of female birds, . . . when old and diseased, . . . partly assume the secondary male characteristics of their species. In the case of the hen-pheasant this has been observed to occur far more frequently during certain seasons than during others."

(P. 64, l. 5 from bottom) Werner Sombart (Die Frauenfrage [The Woman Question], in the Vienna weekly "Die Zeit," 1 March 1902, p. 134), discussing the idea that mechanization is responsible for women's labor because it has made muscular strength superfluous, says: "Admittedly, this is true of many industries, e.g., for the important weaving industry. But it is not true of spinning, for one, which was much more exclusively female labor before the invention of mechanical spinning mills: here it was actually technology that created the possibility of male labor, and mechanical spinning mills, of course, employ numerous male spinners. *Nor is it true of most other labor-intensive industries, as is shown by millinery, embroidery, knitting, the tobacco industry, and others, in which machines have driven out, rather than attracted, women.* Nor does it apply to the main area of modern female labor, the clothing industry. For hand-sewing is no less accessible to women than machine sewing. Rather, what was decisive for the development of female labor, what on the side of the production processes determined the differentiation of labor, which was complex from the outset (and therefore always skilled), was not even primarily this process in the production sphere, but certain demographic developments: the emergence of a surplus female population in the country and in the cities as a result of more deeply rooted causes that need not be discussed in detail here. If one needs a slogan one might say: modern female labor in industry (and in all the other spheres of economic life that are not related to agriculture) owes its existence not directly to changes in technology but to transformations in the conditions of settlement."

(P. 65, l. 10) Krafft-Ebing, Psychopathia sexualis, p. 220 [*Psychopathia Sexualis,* translated by Francis J. Rebman, London 1906, passage not found in translation]: "The tendency of nature at today's developmental stage is to produce monosexual individuals."

(P. 65, l. 18) On gephyrea Weismann, Keimplasma, pp. 477f. [*The Germ-Plasm, A Theory of Heredity,* translated by W. Newton Parker and Harriet Rönnfeldt, London 1893, p. 364]: "In various groups of the animal kingdom *species exist in which the males differ from the females in nearly all their characters.* In many Rotifers the males are very much smaller than the females, and exhibit an entirely different structure; the alimentary canal, moreover, is entirely wanting. In *Bonellia viridis,* a marine gephyrean worm, the male differs so much from the female that one might be tempted to class it with an entirely different group—the Turbellaria. The difference in the sizes also of the two sexes is still more marked in this instance, the length of the male being 1–2 mm., and that of the female 150 mm.; the former, moreover, lives as a parasite within the latter." And so forth. Cf. Claus, Lehrbuch der Zoologie, 6th ed., Marburg 1897, p. 403 [*Elementary Text-book of Zoology,* translated and edited by Adam Sedgwick, London 1892]. Several isopods (bopyrides) are also more sexually differentiated than humans, see Claus, op. cit., p. 482.

Part 2, Chapter I

(P. 69, l. 1) Thomas Carlyle, On Heroes, Hero-Worship and the Heroic in History, London, Chapman & Hall, p. 99.

(P. 69, ll. 15 from bottom ff.) Cf. Franz L. Neugebauer, 37 Fälle von Verdoppelungen der äußeren Geschlechtsteile [37 cases of duplication of the external sexual organs], Monatsschrift für Geburtshilfe und Gynäkologie, VII, 1898, pp. 550–564, 645–659, esp. pp. 554f., where a case of "juxtapositio organorum sexualium externorum utriusque sexus" is described. I ignore those individuals who merely seem to be hermaphrodites due to inhibited development.

(P. 70, l. 9 from bottom) Aristotle, Metaphysik A5, 986a, 31 [*The Metaphysics,* translated by Hugh Lawson-Tancred, London 1998]: ί Ἀλκμαίων ὁ Κροτωνιάτης φησὶ εἶναι δύο τὰ πολλὰ τῶν ἀνθρωπίνων.

(P. 70, l. 8 from bottom) Cf. Schelling, Von der Weltseele, Werke, Stuttgart and Augsburg, 1857, section I, vol. II, p. 489 [On the world soul]: "Thus the law of polarity is probably a general law of the world."

(P. 71, ll. 14 from bottom ff.) I mean Wilhelm Dilthey's excellent and deservedly well-known essays, Ideen über eine beschreibende und zergliedernde Psychologie [Ideas about a descriptive and analytical psychology], Sitzungsberichte der kgl. preußischen Akademie der Wissenschaften, 1894, pp. 1309–1407, and Beiträge zum Studium der Individualität [Contributions to the study of individuality], ibid. 1896, pp. 295–335. In the first essay we read, e.g. (p. 1322): "The works of poets, reflections on life as articulated by great writers, contain an understanding of human beings which leaves all psychological explanations far behind." In the second essay (p. 299, note): "I expect a . . . convincing analysis . . . even of a heroic act of will that is able to sacrifice itself and throw sensuous existence away."

(P. 73, l. 6 from bottom) See Heinrich Rickert, Die Grenzen der naturwissenschaftlichen Begriffsbildung. Freiburg im Breisgau 1902, p. 545 [*The Limits of Concept Formation in Natural Science,* abridged ed., translated by Guy Oakes, Cambridge, New York 1986, passage not found in translation]: "Atomizing individual psychology regards all *individuals* as equal and, *being the most general theory of the life of the psyche, is obliged to do so,* while individualistic *historiography* is interested in individual differences."

(P. 73, l. 3 from bottom) Compare the controversies in 1898 and 1899 between G. v. Below and Karl Lamprecht about historical method and the relationship between sociological historiography and individuality.

(P. 73, l. 2 from bottom) "No scientific mind can ever exhaust, no progress of science can ever equal, what the artist has to say about the content of life. Art is the organ for understanding life." Dilthey, Beiträge zum Studium der Individualität [Contributions to the study of individuality], Berliner Sitzungsberichte, 1896, p. 306.

Part 2, Chapter II

(P. 75, ll. 1ff.) The mottos are taken from Kant, Anthropologie in pragmatischer Hinsicht, part II B, aphorism 232 (p. 229 in Kirchmann's edition) [*Anthropology from a Pragmatic Point of View,* translated by Victor Lyle Dowdell, London 1978, p. 216]; Nietzsche, Jenseits von Gut und Böse [*Beyond Good and Evil. Prelude to a Philosophy of the Future,* translated by R. J. Hollingdale, Harmondsworth 1990].

(P. 75, ll. 12ff.) Kant, op. cit. (p. 228) [p. 216].

(P. 75, l. 6 from bottom) I feel justified in having ignored in the text two female psychologists whose works were known to me, for one is an American experimenter and the other the Russian author of a bad history of the concept of apperception.

(P. 76, l. 3) ". . . the remarkable phenomenon that, whereas every woman would die of shame if surprised in the act of generation, she nevertheless bears her pregnancy in public without a trace of shame and even with a kind of pride. For as everywhere else an infallibly certain sign is taken as equivalent to the thing signified, so also does every other sign of the completed coitus shame and confuse the woman in the highest degree; pregnancy alone does not." Schopenhauer, Parerga, II, § 166 [*Parerga and Paralipomena,* translated by E. F. J. Payne, vol. II, § 166, Oxford 2000, p. 317].

(P. 76, l. 11) The best things about the pregnant woman and what goes on inside her have been said in the poem "Geheimnisvolle Kräfte schlingen" [Mysterious forces entwine] (Emil Lucka, Sternennächte [Starry nights], Wigand, Leipzig 1903).

(P. 76, l. 6 from bottom f.) Thus, among others, Guglielmo Ferrero, Woman's Sphere in Art, New Review, November 1893 (taken from Havelock Ellis).

(P. 76, l. 4 from bottom f.) Scientific researchers seem predominantly to adhere to the view that women's "sex drive" is less intense (e.g., Hegar, Der Geschlechtstrieb [The sexual drive], 1894, p. 6), while almost all practical "connoisseurs of women" firmly believe the opposite.

(P. 77, l. 20f.) Moll's distinction in his books, Die konträre Sexualempfindung, 3rd ed., Berlin 1899, p. 2 [*Perversions of the Sex Instinct. A Study of Sexual Inversion,* translated by Maurice Popkin, New York 1976]. Untersuchungen über die Libido sexualis, 1897, vol. I, p. 10 [*Libido sexualis,* translated by David Berger, New York 1933].

(P. 77, l. 18 from bottom) That in women lust cannot be produced, as in men, by some kind of ejaculation is explained by Moll (Untersuchungen, I, pp. 8ff. [*Libido sexualis,* translated by David Berger, New York 1933]). Cf. also Chrobak-Rosthorn, Die Erkrankungen der weiblichen Geschlechtsorgane [The diseases of the female sexual organs], Vienna 1900 (from Nothnagel's Spezielle Pathologie und Therapie [*Nothnagel's Encyclopedia of Practical Medicine,* translated under the editorial supervision of A. Stengel, Philadelphia, London 1902], vol. I, pp. 423f. [translation of relevant volume not found]: "With Moll, we must assume . . . a detumescence (evacuation) drive, more correctly perhaps a depletion drive, and a contrectation (touch) drive. The question is much more difficult with regard to women . . . in whom we have not been able to find any analogy to the process in men, since no *ejaculation* of gametes takes place. . . . It is true that in women also during intercourse an evacuation of fluid from the Bartholin glands takes place, accompanied by movements of the musculi ischio et bulbocavernosi, and there is also a deflation of the vessels (at the corpora cavernosa of the clitoris), which are filled to bursting through the muscular movements and thereby perhaps create a sense of discomfort, but this evacuation on the one hand never affects the germ-producing organs, while on the other hand this so-called ejaculation often enough fails to take place, *without preventing a sense of sexual satisfaction.*"

(P. 79, l. 4) Given the fact that W herself is sexuality, absolutely and everywhere, it is easy to understand that throughout zoology it is not really possible to speak of "secondary sexual characteristics" in the same sense with reference to females as with reference to males. Females "rarely exhibit noticeable sexual characters" (Darwin, Entstehung der Arten, p. 201, ed. Haek. [*The Origin of Species,* London 1861, p. 168].

(P. 81, l. 8) Among animals the males are also subject to a much greater contrast between the rutting season and life at any other time than the females. To cite one example rather than many, compare Friedrich Miescher's description of Rhine salmon before and during spawning time (Die histo-chemischen und physiologischen Arbeiten von F. M. [The histo-chemical and physiological works of F. M.], Leipzig 1897, vol. II, p. 123): "Whenever, say in December, one sees a male so-called winter salmon, with clear scales emitting a bluish sheen, a beautifully rounded body, a short snout . . . without any trace of a hook . . . and if next to him one sees the familiar hooked salmon with a nose twice as long, an entirely changed physiognomy of the anterior head, a skin covered in red and black spots like a tiger and thick with epithelic growth, a flattened body and thin stomach walls hanging loose, one finds it hard to persuade oneself that these are specimens of the same species. The contrast is somewhat less in the female specimen. The length and shape of the snout are not significantly different; the red spots on the head and body, which are completely absent in the winter salmon, are less strongly developed in the female spawning salmon than in the male; the skin is dull and seems dirty, but not as swollen."

(P. 81, l. 11) An outstandingly good but strangely ignored essay by Oskar

Friedländer ("Eine für Viele," eine psychologische Studie ["One for many," a psychological study], "Die Gesellschaft," Münchener Halbmonatsschrift, year XVIII, 1902, no. 15/16, p. 166) is so close in this respect to my own view that I must quote it here and shall do so several more times: "Certainly the sex drive takes a more violent and impetuous form in man than in woman. This is probably due less to the different degrees of intensity than to the fact that in the male mind the most heterogeneous elements from all psychic areas meet, struggling for predominance and trying to oust the sexual instincts, which are felt all the more strongly because of the contrast, while their even distribution across *the whole soul* of woman . . . does not allow them to assume a particularly sharp relief."

Second Part, Chapter III

(P. 82, l. 15) "Desire and emotion are only ways in which our ideas exist in our consciousness." J. F. Herbart, Psychologie als Wissenschaft, neu gegründet auf Erfahrung, Metaphysik und Mathematik, II. (analytischer) Teil, § 104 (Werke VI, p. 60, ed. Kehrbach, Langensalza 1887). [*A Text-book in Psychology. An Attempt to Found the Science of Psychology on Experience, Metaphysics, and Mathematics,* New York 1896, translation of passage not found].

(P. 82, l. 15) A. Horwicz, Psychologische Analysen auf physiologischer Grundlage, Ein Versuch zur Neubegründung der Seelenlehre [Psychological analyses on a physiological basis, an attempt at a new foundation of psychology], II/1, Die Analyse des Denkens [The analysis of thinking], Halle 1875, pp. 177f.: "In our view feeling is the earliest, most elementary product of psychic life, the earliest and only content of consciousness, the mainspring of all psychic development. How does thinking relate to this? . . . Thinking is a phenomenon consequent on feeling, as is also movement, it is the most fundamental dialectic of the urges . . . an urge that is exercised more strongly, and is differentiated from others, results in thought-out, orderly movements, chosen from a number of commonly used movements, that is, thought-out thinking." II/2, Die Analyse der qualitativen Gefühle [The analysis of qualitative feelings], Magdeburg 1878, p. 59: "It [feeling] is the most general elementary form of consciousness, albeit in this simplest shape [in animals and plants] only a very faint, dim consciousness, a brooding intuition rather than cognition and knowledge. However, in order to become a clear and distinct consciousness, it needs no doubtful further ingredients but only multiplication and a considerable intensification in degree." See Wilhelm Wundt, Über das Verhältnis der Gefühle zu den Vorstellungen [On the relationship between feelings and ideas], Vierteljahrsschrift für wissenschaftliche Philosophie, III, 1879, pp. 129–151, and Horwicz's reply: "Über das Verhältnis der Gefühle zu den Vorstellungen und die Frage nach dem psychischen Grundprozesse" [On the relationship between feelings and ideas and the question of the fundamental psychic process], op. cit., pp. 308–341.

(P. 82, l. 5 from bottom) On such "feelings of tendency," see William James, The Principles of Psychology, New York 1890, vol. I, p. 254.

(P. 82, l. 3 from bottom) Cf. especially Leibnitii Meditatones de cognitione, veritate et ideis Acta eruditorum, Lips. [Leipzig] 1684, pp. 537f. (pp. 79f., ed. Erdmann) [*Meditations on Knowledge, Truth and Ideas,* translated by R. N. D. Martin and Stuart Brown, Manchester, New York 1988].

(P. 83, l. 1) Wilhelm Wundt, Grundzüge der physiologischen Psychologie, 5th ed., Leipzig 1902, vol. II, pp. 286ff. [*Principles of Physiological Psychology,* translated from the fifth German edition by E. B. Titchener, London 1904].

(P. 83, l. 8) Richard Avenarius, Kritik der reinen Erfahrung [Critique of pure experience], vol. I, Leipzig 1888, p. 16. Der menschliche Weltbegriff [The human concept of the world], Leipzig 1891, pp. 1f. Cf. Joseph Petzoldt, Einführung in die Philosophie der reinen Erfahrung [Introduction to the philosophy of pure experience], vol. I, Die Bestimmtheit der Seele [The determinacy of the soul], Leipzig 1900, pp. 112ff.

(P. 83, l. 9) On the different meanings of "character" (which also had to be used in this work in three different applications but avoiding all ambiguities), see Rudolf Eucken, Die Grundbegriffe der Gegenwart, historisch und kritisch entwickelt, 1893, pp. 273ff. [Main Currents of Modern Thought. A Study of the Spiritual and Intellectual Movements of the Present Day, translated by Meyrick Booth, London 1912].

(P. 83, l. 22) Avenarius's equation of images from perception and images from memory was accepted among later psychologists only by Oswald Külpe who, albeit in a terminologically far from flawless manner, discusses the theory of memory as the theory of "centrally excited sensations" in his "Grundriß der Psychologie, auf experimenteller Grundlage dargestellt" (Leipzig 1893), pp. 174ff. [*Outlines of Psychology, Based upon the Results of Experimental Investigation,* translated by Edward Bradford Titchener, London, New York 1895, p. 169].

(P. 84, l. 18) Petzoldt, op. cit, pp. 138ff.

(P. 85, ll. 2ff.) Cf. A. Kunkel, Über die Abhängigkeit der Farbenempfindung von der Zeit [On the dependency of color sensation on time], Archiv für die gesamte Physiologie der Menschen und der Tiere, IX, 1874, p. 215. On this further, Fechner, Elemente der Psychophysik, 1st ed., Leipzig 1860, vol. I, pp. 249f. [*Elements of Psychophysics,* translated by Helmut E. Adler, New York, London 1966]; Oswald Külpe, Grundriß der Psychologie, pp. 131, 210 [*Outlines of Psychology,* Bristol 1998]; Hermann Ebbinghaus, Grundzüge der Psychologie [Outlines of psychology], Leipzig 1902, p. 230.

(P. 85, l. 12f.) Quoted from Nietzsche, Also sprach Zarathustra, book III, chapter "Der Genesende" [*Thus Spoke Zarathustra,* translated by R. J. Hollingdale, Harmondsworth 1961, chapter "The Convalescent," p. 232].

(P. 85, l. 15 from bottom) Johann Gottlieb Fichte, Über den Begriff der Wissenschaftslehre (Werke I/1, Berlin 1845, p. 73) [*The Science of Knowledge,* translated by A. E. Kroeger, London 1889, p. 52]: "The human mind makes many attempts; by blindly groping it first discovers dawn, and only from dawn does it emerge to the light of day. At first it is led by dark feelings." Schopenhauer, Parerga, I, § 14 (Werke IV, pp. 159f., ed. Grisebach [*Parerga and Paralipomena,* translated by E. F. J. Payne, vol. II, § 14, Oxford 2000, pp. 132–133): "In general, however, it may be said on this point that, before every great truth has been discovered, a previous feeling, a presentiment, a faint outline thereof, as in a fog, is proclaimed, and there is a vain attempt to grasp it just because the progress of the times prepared the way for it. Accordingly, it is preluded by isolated utterances; but he alone is the author of a truth who has recognized it from its grounds and has thought it out to its consequents; who has developed its whole content and has surveyed the extent of its domain; and who, fully aware of its value and importance, has therefore expounded it clearly and coherently. On the other hand, in ancient and modern times, one has expressed a truth on some occasion, semi-consciously and almost like talking in sleep; and accordingly it can be found there if it is expressly looked for. Yet this does not signify much more than if such a truth were before us *totidem literis,* even though it may exist *totidem verbis.* In the same way, the finder of a thing is only the man who, knowing its value, picked it up and kept it, not he who once accidentally took it up in his hand and dropped it again. Or again Columbus is the discoverer of America, not the first shipwrecked sailor there cast up by the waves. This is precisely the meaning of the saying of Donatus: *pereant qui ante nos nostra dixerunt.*" Kant says even more aptly: "For such general and yet definite principles are not easily learned from other men, who have had them obscurely in their minds. We must hit on them first by our own reflexion, then we find them elsewhere, where we could not possibly have found them at first, because the authors themselves did not know that such an idea lay at the basis of their observations. Men who never think independently have nevertheless the acuteness to discover everything, after it has been once shown them, in what was said long since, though no one ever saw it there before." (Prolegomena zu jeder künftigen Metaphysik, § 3, toward the end [*Prolegomena to any Future Metaphysics,* translated and edited by Gary Hatfield, Cambridge 1997, p. 19].)

(P. 86, l. 9 from bottom) S. Exner, Entwurf zu einer physiologischen Erklärung der psychischen Erscheinungen [Blueprint of a physiological explanation of psychic phenomena], part I, Leipzig, Vienna 1894, pp. 76ff. Cf. H. Høffding, Vierteljahrschr.f. wiss. Philos. 13, 1889, p. 431.

(P. 87, l. 2) Avenarius, Kritik der reinen Erfahrung [Critique of pure experience], vol. I, Leipzig 1888, p. 77; vol. II, Leipzig 1890, p. 57. Incidentally, the same expression is suggested in a similar case by Wilhelm Dilthey, Ideen über eine beschreibende und zergliedernde Psychologie [Ideas about a descriptive and analytical psychology], Berliner Sitzungsberichte, 1894, p. 1387.

(P. 87, l. 9 from bottom) However, the following supposition now seems more likely to me than Exner's theory. The parallelism between phylogenesis and ontogenesis, the "fundamental biogenetic law," is generally asserted without any further thought as to *why* the development of the individual always repeats the history of the species: people are in such a hurry to exploit that fact for the theory of descendence and in particular for its absolute application to humans. But perhaps that phenomenon is paralleled by the development of the henid into a differentiated entity, which could put an end to its current isolation and mysteriousness.

(P. 89, ll. 3ff.) For the erroneous popular assumption of a generally greater receptiveness of the senses in Woman, an assumption that confuses sensitivity with emotivity and irritability, see Havelock Ellis, Mann und Weib, pp. 153f. [*Man and Woman*]. On the more refined sense of touch in men, cf. Lombroso-Ferrero, Das Weib als Verbrecherin und Prostituierte, pp. 48f. [*The Female Offender,* London 1895].

(P. 89, l. 19 from bottom) See Ernst Mach, Die Mechanik in ihrer Entwicklung, historisch-kritisch dargestellt, 4th ed., Leipzig 1901, pp. 1f., 28f. [*The Science of Mechanics. A Critical and Historical Exposition of Its Principles,* translated by T. J. McCormack, London, Chicago 1902]. Die Prinzipien der Wärmelehre, historisch-kritisch entwickelt, 2nd ed., Leipzig 1900, p. 151 [*Principles of the*

Theory of Heat. Historically and Critically Elucidated, edited by Brian McGuinness, Dordrecht, Lancaster, c. 1986].

Second Part, Chapter IV

(P. 91, ll. 1f.) The definitions of the nature of genius reached in this chapter are entirely provisional and can be understood only after reading chapter VIII, when they will be resumed and fully explained by being shown as parts of a much larger whole.

(P. 93, l. 22) About *understanding* human beings and human manifestations there is characteristically little to be found in scientific psychological literature. Wilhelm Dilthey alone remarks (Beiträge zum Studium der Individualität [Contributions to the study of individuality], Berliner Sitzungsberichte, 1896, pp. 309ff.): "Initially we may regard understanding a condition other than our own as inference by analogy, leading from an *external physical process*—by virtue of its *similarity* to *such* processes as we find connected to certain *internal* conditions—to an *internal* condition that is similar to the latter. . . . The links in the process of reproduction are by no means connected through merely logical operations such as, for example, inference by analogy. Reproducing is re-experiencing. This is a mystery. Like a primal phenomenon, it may be explained by the fact that we feel the conditions of others to some extent as if they were our own and are initially able to share their joy or grief, in proportion to the measure of the sympathy, love, or affinity between us and them. The relationship between this fact and reproductive understanding rests on a variety of circumstances. Understanding also depends on the measure of sympathy and we are quite unable to understand people who arouse no sympathy whatsoever in us. The relationship between sympathy and reproductive understanding becomes very clear when we sit in front of the stage. [. . .] In accordance with these circumstances *scholarly exegesis or interpretation* as the art of reproductive understanding always contains an element of genius, that is, it can achieve a high degree of perfection only through internal affinity and sympathy. Thus the works of the Ancients were not fully understood again until the Renaissance, when similar conditions resulted in an affinity between the people concerned. . . . There is no scholarly process that can leave this living reproduction behind as if it were a subordinate element. Here is the maternal soil from which even the most abstract operations of scholars in the humanities must constantly draw their strength. *Here understanding can never be identified with rational comprehension. One tries in vain to explain a hero or a genius in terms of all kinds of circumstances. The most appropriate approach to them is the subjective one.*" (Pp. 314f.): "The old painters strove to assemble the permanent features of a physiognomy at an ideal moment, which was most comprehensive and most characteristic of it. If a new school tries to pin down a momentary impression in order to enhance the impression of life, it delivers the persons to the accidental nature of the moment. However, even then the understanding of the quintessence of impressions at a given moment occurs under the impact of the psychic connections that have been grasped. In this apperception the combination of the features emerges from a point where an impression is felt and which causes the omissions and emphases: thus a momentary image of both the artist's mode of apperception and the object comes into being, and any attempt at seeing without apperceiving or, as it were, dissolving the concrete image into colors on a plate, must fail. What leads to even greater depths, the point of impression, is ultimately determined by the relationship between some vital being outside me and that within me, and my own relationship with life is intimately affected by something that is active in another part of nature; it is from this vital point that I understand the features which converge there. That is how a type comes into being. The original was an individual: every genuine portrait, particularly in a figure painting, is a type. Nor can poetry simply write down what is happening, etc." The only other work worth mentioning is Hermann Swoboda, Verstehen und Begreifen [Understanding and comprehension], Vierteljahrsschrift für wissenschaftliche Philosophie, XXVII, 1903, nos. 2 and 3. Like Dilthey, Swoboda regards identity or kinship as the *sole* prerequisite of understanding: in this respect I differ from both.

(P. 96, l. 14 from bottom f.) Richard Wagner, Gesammelte Schriften und Dichtungen, 3rd ed., Leipzig 1898, vol. VI, p. 128 [Siegfried, *The Ring of the Niblung,* translated by Stewart Spencer, London 2000, p. 233].

(P. 98, l. 2) Thus a more endowed person will feel the effect on his psychological condition of the smallest doses of coffee, tea, and nicotine more intensely than an unendowed one.

(P. 98, l. 22) There are only universal geniuses: "ὃν γὰρ ἀπέστειλεν ὁ θεὸς, τὰ ῥήματα τοῦ θεοῦ λαλεῖ· οὐ γὰρ ἐκ μέτρου δίδωσι τὸ πνεῦμα" (St. John's Gospel, 3, 34).

(P. 98, l. 12 from bottom) The confusion criticized here appears particularly clearly in Franz Brentano, Das Genie, ein Vortrag [Genius, a lecture], Leipzig 1892, p. 11: "Every genius has his own particular field; not only is there no universal genius in the full sense of the word, but even within the individual artistic genres genius usually has more narrow limits. Thus Pindar, e.g., was a lyric poet of genius and nothing more." If this popular view were tenable one would have to place the poet and painter Rossetti above the "mere" poet Dante, regard Novalis more highly than Kant, and consider Leonardo da Vinci as the greatest human being.

(P. 99, l. 15 from bottom) This tallies with Schopenhauer's conviction (Welt als Wille und Vorstellung, vol. II, chapter 31, p. 447, ed. Frauenstädt [*The World as Will and Idea,* translated by R. B. Haldane and J. Kemp, London 1883, vol. 3, p. 159]): "Women may have great talent, but not genius."

(P. 99, l. 1 from bottom f.) On the relationship between other people and the hero, Carlyle, On Heroes, Hero-Worship and the Heroic in History, London, Chapman and Hall, pp. 10ff.

Second Part, Chapter V

(P. 101, l. 17) Some eighteen months after writing these passages I found in Schopenhauer's unpublished Neue Paralipomena [New paralipomena], § 143, the only passage known to me in the entire literature that expresses an inkling of the links between genius and memory. It says: "Is not all genius rooted in the perfection and vividness of our memories of our own life? For it is only through these memories, which integrate our life in one great whole, that we acquire a more comprehensive and more profound understanding of it than others do."

(P. 101, l. 10 from bottom) David Hume once asks (A Treatise of Human Nature, 1st ed., London 1738, vol. I, p. 455): "Who can tell me, for instance, what were his thoughts and actions on the first of January 1715, the 11. of March 1719 and the 3. of August 1733?" A perfect genius would need to have certain knowledge of this with regard to every day of his life.

(P. 104, ll. 15ff.) See Goethe, Dichtung und Wahrheit, part III, Book XIV (vol. XXIV, p. 141 of the Hesse edition [*Poetry and Truth: From My Own Life,* translated by Minna Steele Smith, London 1908, vol. 2, pp. 163–164]): "One feeling which was very strong in me, and for which I could never find adequate expression, was a sense of the past and present as being one; a conception which infused a spectral element into the present. It is expressed in many of my shorter and longer works, and always adapts itself well to poetry, though, whenever it sought directly to interpret itself through and in actual life, it must have appeared to everyone strange, inexplicable, perhaps gloomy."

(P. 106, l. 7f.) "The success of female singers during the seventeenth century had also opened up every opportunity of a theoretical musical education for women. It is therefore not possible to regard inadequate training as a reason for the inferior achievement of women in composition." Thus Adele Gerhardt and Helene Simon, Mutterschaft und geistige Arbeit [Motherhood and intellectual labor], p. 74. This passage also gives me a chance to quote Mill's acute syllogism: "Women are taught music, but not for the purpose of composing, only of executing it: and accordingly it is only as composers, that men, in music, are superior to women." (J. S. Mill, The Subjection of Women, London 1896, p. 134 [Die Hörigkeit der Frau, translated into German by Jenny Hirsch, Berlin 1869, p. 126]).

(P. 106, l. 9f.) The statement about female painters, etc. is based on Guhl, Die Frauen in der Kunstgeschichte [Women in art history], Berlin 1858, p. 150.

(P. 106, l. 14 from bottom f.) "A mesure qu'on a plus d'esprit, on trouve qu'il y a plus d'hommes originaux. Les gens du commun ne trouvent pas de différence entre les hommes." (Pascal, Pensées, I, 10, 1. [*Pensées and Other Writings,* translated by Honor Levi, Oxford 1995]).

(P. 107, l. 18) This corresponds to what Helvetius (according to J. B. Meyer, Genie und Talent, Eine prinzipielle Betrachtung [Genius and talent, a theoretical examination], Zeitschrift für Völkerpsychologie, vol. XI, 1880, p. 298) and Schopenhauer (Parerga und Paralipomena II, § 53 [*Parerga and Paralipomena,* translated by E. F. J. Payne, Oxford 2000]) teach about the fact that the difference between genius and normal minds is only one of degree. Cf. also Jean Paul, Vorschule der Ästhetik, § *8* [*Horn of Oberon. Jean Paul Richter's School for Aesthetics,* translated by Margaret R. Hale, Detroit 1973, p. 30]: "And how could a genius be tolerated or even exalted for so much as a month, not to mention thousands of years, by the multitude so unlike him, if there were not some understood family resemblance?"

(P. 107, ll. 18 from bottom ff.) Compare the autobiographies of significant people with those of less eminent men. The former always go back further (Goethe, Hebbel, Grillparzer, Richard Wagner, Jean Paul, etc.). Rousseau, Confessions, Nouvelle édition, Paris 1875, p. 4 [*Confessions,* translated by Angela Scholar, Oxford 2000]: "J'ignore ce que je fis jusqu'à cinq ou six ans. Je ne sais comment j'appris à lire; je ne me souviens que de mes premières lectures et de leur effet sur moi: *C'est le temps d'où je date sans interruption la conscience de moi-même.*"—Of course not every autobiographer is a great genius (J. S. Mill, Darwin, Benvenuto Cellini).

(P. 109, l. 5f.) Richard Wagner, Die Meistersinger von Nürnberg, Act III (Gesammelte Schriften und Dichtungen, vol. VII, Leipzig 1898, p. 246 [*The Mastersingers of Nuremberg,* translated by Frederick Jameson, revised by Norman Feasey and Gordon Kember, London 1983, p. 109]).

(P. 109, l. 8) Thus Aristotle remarks (while for Plato, apart from Timaeus Dff. [*Timaeus and Critias,* translated by H. D. P. Lee, Harmondsworth 1971], time in the narrower sense does not seem to have been a problem), Physika VI, 9, 239 b, 8 [*Physics,* translated by Robin Waterfield, Oxford 1996]: Οὐ γὰρ σύγκειται ὁ χρόνος ἐκ τῶν νῦν ἀδιαιρέτων.

(P. 109, l. 3 from bottom) Just how shallow the roots of memory are in the nature of Woman is shown by the fact that Woman's ability to remember certain things can be killed under hypnosis by forbidding her ever to think of them again. I cite such a case from a narrative of Freud in his "studien über Hysterie" edited jointly with Breuer, Leipzig and Vienna 1895 (p. 49) [*Studies on Hysteria,* translated by A. A. Brill, Boston 1960, pp. 41–42]: "Here I interrupt her . . . and I then remove all possibilities of her seeing again these sad things by wiping away not only the plastic memories, but also the whole reminiscence, as if it had never been a part of her." In a note on this Freud adds: "This time my energy carried me a little too far. A year and a half later when I saw Mrs. Emmy again in relatively fine health she complained that *it was remarkable that certain very important events of her life she could only recall vaguely.* She saw in this the proof of her failing memory. I had to guard against giving her a special explanation for this amnesia."

(P. 110, l. 19) Lotze: in Mikrokosmus [Microcosm], 1st ed., 1858, vol. II, p. 369.

(P. 112, l. 9) This derivation from the apparent familiarity of new situations is found in Rhys Davids, Der Buddhismus, Leipzig, Universalbibliothek, p. 107 [*Buddhism: Being a Sketch of the Life and Teachings of Gautama,* London 1882].

(P. 112, l. 11) Edward B. Tylor, Die Anfänge der Kultur, Untersuchungen über die Entwicklung der Mythologie, Philosophie, Religion, Kunst und Sitte, translated into German by J. W. Spengel and F. Poske, Leipzig 1873, vol. II, p. 1 [*Primitive Culture. Researches into the Development of Mythology, Philosophy, Religion, Art, and Custom,* London 1871, vol. 2, p. 1]: "Let us . . . call to mind the consideration which cannot be too strongly put forward, that the doctrine of a Future Life as held by the lower races is the all but necessary outcome of savage Animism."—Herbert Spencer, Die Prinzipien der Soziologie, vol. I, Stuttgart 1877, § 100 (p. 225) [*The Principles of Sociology,* London and Edinburgh 1876]. Richard Avenarius, Der menschliche Weltbegriff [The human concept of the world], Leipzig 1891, pp. 35ff.

(P. 112, l. 15f.) For this sudden appearance of all memories before death or when in danger of death and close to death, see Fechner, Zend-Avesta [Zend-Avesta], 2nd ed., vol. II, pp. 203ff.

(P. 113, l. 9f.) On the "euthanasia of atheists," see what F. A. Lange says (Geschichte des Materialismus [History of materialism], 5th ed., 1896, vol. I, p. 358).

(P. 114, l. 5 from bottom f.) For the reasons given I find the Indian theories about life after death, the Greek notion of drinking from Lethe, and the annunciation of Wagner's Tristan [*Tristan and Isolde*, translated by Andrew Porter, London 1981, p. 81] "The boundless realm / Of endless night, / And there we know one thing only: / Endless godlike / All forgetting!" far less comprehensible than the view of Gustav Theodor Fechner, for whom the life to come is a full and complete life of remembrance (Zend-Avesta oder über die Dinge des Himmels und des Jenseits vom Standpunkte der Naturbetrachtung [Zend-Avesta or on the things of heaven and the beyond from the point of view of the contemplation of nature], 2nd ed. by Kurd Laßwitz, Hamburg and Leipzig 1901, vol. II, pp. 190ff., e.g., p. 196): "A full remembrance of our old life will begin when all our old life is behind us, and all our remembering within our old life itself is merely a small foretaste of it." The assumption that our memories of life on earth are totally extinguished by death is *unethical:* it devalues what is valuable, since things without value are in any case forgotten. And then: in remembering as such, man is active and memory is an expression of the will; a fully active life must be thought of as having absorbed all the elements of activity, it is eternal because it is timeless and therefore sees things past and things future side by side. In a fine passage Fechner says (ibid., pp. 197f.): "Imagine therefore that once you have finally closed your eyes and entirely mortified all the ideas and sensations of this world which the spirit has so far acquired through you, not only your memories of your last day will awaken but also, in part, your memories and, in part, your ability to remember your entire past life in a more lively, coherent, comprehensive, bright, clear, and distinct manner than any of your memories that ever awakened while you were still lying half in the bondage of the senses; for just as your own body was an instrument for receiving and processing the experiences of the senses on earth it was also an instrument for binding you to that task. Now the receiving, collecting, and transforming on earth is over. The pail that you brought home opens and you, or rather the higher spirit in you, gains at once all the riches that you gradually accumulated in it. The faded image of all that you did, saw, thought, and achieved in your life on earth now awakens in you, bright and spiritually coherent; count yourself lucky if you are able to rejoice in it. As your entire spiritual being is illuminated you are born into the new life, and from then on you will devote yourself to the higher life of the spirit with a clearer consciousness.

There are those who believe in a future life but are not prepared to believe one particular thing, which is that remembrance of the present life will extend into it. Man, they claim, will be made afresh and reappear as a different person who, in his new life, will know nothing about the earlier man. In so doing they destroy the very bridge that leads them from this world to the other, and they cast a dark cloud between the two realms. Instead of sharing our belief that man is destined after death to regain himself utterly and completely, indeed become more complete than he ever was while alive, they make him lose himself entirely. For them a breath that rises from the water, instead of indicating the future condition of the water as a whole, disappears together with the water. Then they expect it to reappear suddenly as a new water in a new world. But how did it turn into that? How did it get there? They leave us without an answer. And that is also an easy way to be left without a belief in it.

What is the reason for such a view? They say that memories of the present life cannot be expected to extend into the next, because memories of the earlier life do not extend into the present. But let us stop inferring the same thing from different things. Since life before birth contained no memories, nor even the ability to remember, how could memories extend from it into the present life? But since memories, and indeed the ability to remember, have developed in the present life why should memories not extend into the future life, and even be enhanced, since in the future life we can expect a further enhancement of what became enhanced in the transition from the previous life to the present? Death can be understood as a second birth into a new life . . . but can everything therefore be the same between birth and death? After all, nothing else between two things is exactly the same. Death is a *second* birth, while birth is a *first*. And should the second birth throw us back to the point of the first, rather than guide us in a new attempt further ahead on the road to ourselves? And must the dividing line between two lives necessarily be a break? Could it not equally well consist in narrowness suddenly spreading into wideness?" (pp. 199f.).

(P. 116, l. 11) In Döring's, Meinong's, Ehrenfels's, and Kreibig's books on the theory of value I have looked in vain for some definition of the relationship between value and time. What can be found in Alexius v. Meinong, Psychologisch-ethische Untersuchungen zur Werttheorie [Psychologico-ethical investigations into the theory of value], Graz 1894, pp. 46 and 58ff., and in Josef Clemens Kreibig, Psychologische Grundlegung eines Systems der Werttheorie [Psychological foundations of a systematic theory of value], Vienna 1902, pp. 53ff., bears no relation to the theoretical purpose under consideration here. Kreibig's discussion (p. 54) in particular shows how hopelessly Brentano's school has confounded a "sense of value" with pleasure: "In the long run the constant, unchanging, and protracted sound of a steam whistle or foghorn, the monotony of a uniformly grey sky, the endless chatter of a facetious companion arouse displeasure, even if these phenomena were originally felt to be pleasant. Goethe aptly says that nothing is harder to bear than an unbroken series of fine days. In all elevated spheres we are faced with a similar situation: the perennially sweet Mendelssohn, the droning hexameters of Voss, the eulogies of lickspittles eventually become painful. The socialist Fourier demonstrates his powers of observation by varying the duties of each individual in his phalanstery in accordance with the 'butterfly mind' that he recognizes in human beings. On the other hand it is not necessary to demonstrate in detail that an overly speedy sequence of different experiences is tiring and thus has a negative influence on values." Long duration may reduce pleasure but cannot devalue anything that is of value.

Only in two places can I find any views that might recall the arguments of the main text. Harald Høffding, in his "Religionsphilosophie" (translated into German by F. Bendixen, Leipzig 1901, pp. 105, 193ff.) [*The Philosophy of Religion*, translated from the German edition by B. E. Meyer, London 1906], puts forward a thesis of the "conservation of value" which might distantly recall the proposition of the timelessness of value. I am in much closer and more clearly recognizable agreement with Rudolf Eucken, Der Wahrheitsgehalt der Religion, Leipzig 1901, pp. 219f. [*The Truth of Religion*, translated by W. Tudor Jones, Theological Translation Library, edited by Cheyne (T. K.) and Bruce (A. B.), vol. 30, 1911, passage not found in translation]: "It is said that man belongs to bare time but he does so only for a certain stretch of his existence; all spiritual life is an elevation above time, an overcoming of time. Whatever spiritual contents are unfolded they carry within them a claim to being regarded as having no relation to time and being untouched by its flux, that is, as being valid in an eternal order of things. Not only science and learning deliver their truth 'under the aspect of eternity,' but whatever wants to be valuable and essential refuses to drift with the flow of time and to submit to the flux of its fashions and moods: on the contrary, it wants to measure the times and determine their value on its own terms.

This demand for eternity is not content with seeking a refuge from the snarls of time, but joins battle with time on time's own ground: history in the human sense originates and consists above all in this clash of time and eternity. A striving toward something unchangeable beyond all temporal things arises in time itself; thus cultural life fixes, and confers classical status on, certain achievements of the past, which it would not merely like to retain constantly in its consciousness but recognize as providing an unmistakable standard to strive by.... History in the human and spiritual sense is not created through the succession and accumulation of phenomena, but through this succession being thought and experienced. However, even a mere overview and unification of the diversity in a comprehensive picture would be impossible without the observer stepping out of the restless current of time. Nor is contemplation by itself able to produce a historical form of culture, for this materializes only if the essential and the accidental, the enduring and the transient separate in history, which is not possible without vigorous sorting and sifting of the chaotic profusion flowing toward us. Genuinely lasting things, which alone have any value for our own lives, must always be carved out of the phenomena. But who should carry out the sorting and sifting, if not a process of life that is superior to time and that judges by inner necessities? And how should it do this, if not by raising what has been found to be genuine out of the whole flux of time, and fixing it in opposition to time? . . . " Pp. 221f. [in translation by T. K. Cheyne and A. B. Bruce, p. 272]: "It is quite another thing to deny the spiritual nature of man as a participator in eternity. For such a customary notion means not so much the adumbration of earthly views on the future, as of surrendering all Spiritual life to bare Time, and along with this to press it down, fritter it away, and inwardly destroy it. Also, the life of man in Time thus becomes a mere appearance and shadow unless there dwells within him a striving towards eternity; and consequently, through a complete binding to Time, all human experience and all human reality which endeavoured to illumine the mere moment sink back into the abyss of nothingness."

If I wanted to cite any other works I would only be able to refer to the beautiful dream described by Knut Hamsun in his novel "Neue Erde" (translated into German by M. v. Borch, Munich 1894, pp. 169ff. [*Shallow Soil*, translated by C. C. Hyllested, London 1914]), or I would have to fall back directly on Plato's eternal ideas which are enthroned somewhere "beyond the heavens," untouched by time. Plato's *ideas* in their later, more restricted, version are the *values* of the modern philosophy that was founded by Kant. But in the purely psychological discussion of the present chapter this is not yet being considered.

(P. 119, ll. 22ff.) Carlyle, On Heroes etc., pp. 11f.: "He was the 'creature of the Time,' they say; the Time called him forth, the Time did everything, he nothing.... The Time call forth? Alas, we have known Times *call* loudly enough for their great man; but not find him when they called! He was not there; Providence has not sent him; the Time, *calling* its loudest, had to go down to confusion and wreck because he would not come when called.

For if we will think of it, no time need have gone to ruin, could it have *found* a man great enough, a man wise and good enough: wisdom to discern truly what the Time wanted, valour to lead it on the right road thither; these are the salvation of any Time. But I liken common languid Times, with their unbelief, distress, perplexity, with their languid doubting characters and embarrassed circumstances, impotently crumbling down into ever worse distress towards final ruin;—all this I liken to dry dead fuel, waiting for the lightning out of Heaven that shall kindle it. The great man, with his force direct out of God's own hand, is the lightning. His word is the wise healing word which all can believe in. All blazes round him now, when he has once struck on it, into fire like his own. The dry mouldering sticks are thought to have called him forth—!—Those are critics of small vision, I think, who cry: 'See, is it not the stick that made the fire?' *No sadder proof can be given by a man of his own littleness than disbelief in great men.*"

(P. 121, l. 6) Bacon as a critic of language: Novum Organum I, 43.—Fritz Mauthner, Beiträge zu einer Kritik der Sprache [Contributions to a critique of language], vol. I, Sprache und Psychologie [Language and psychology], Stuttgart 1901.

(P. 121, l. 20 from bottom) Hermann Türck, Der geniale Mensch [The man of genius], 5th ed., Berlin 1901, pp. 275f.—Cesare Lombroso, Der geniale Mensch, translated into German by M. O. Fränkel, Hamburg 1890, passim [*The Man of Genius* (New York, London 1910)].—For the entertainment of the reader I will quote the following view from Francis Galton (Hereditary Genius, Inquiry into its Laws and Consequences, London 1892, p. 9, cf. Preface, p. XII): "When I speak of an eminent man, I mean one who has achieved a position that is attained by only 250 persons in each million of men, or by one person in each 4000."

(P. 121, l. 18 from bottom) Kant on genius: Kritik der Urteilskraft, § 46–50 [*The Critique of Judgement,* translated by James Creed Meredith, Oxford 1978]. Cf. Otto Schlapp, Kants Lehre vom Genie [Kant's theory of genius], Göttingen 1902, esp. pp. 305ff. Schelling, System des transzendentalen Idealismus, Werke I/3, pp. 622–624, p. 623 [*System of Transcendental Idealism,* translated by Peter Heath, Charlottesville 1978, p. 228]: "Only what art brings forth is simply and solely possible through genius."—Kant's denial of genius to philosophers is opposed by Jean Paul, Das Kampanertal oder über die Unsterblichkeit der Seele, 503. Stazion [*Das Campaner Thal or, Discourses on the Immortality of the Soul,* translated by Juliette Gowa, London 1857], and Johann Gottlieb Fichte, Über den Begriff der Wissenschaftslehre, 1794, § 7 (Sämtliche Werke herausgegeben von J. H. Fichte, vol. I/1, p. 73, note) [*Science of Knowledge,* translated by Peter Heath, Cambridge 1982].

Second Part, Chapter VI

(P. 124, l. 15 from bottom) *In favor* of psychologism: Karl Stumpf, Psychologie und Erkenntnistheorie [Psychology and epistemology], Abhandlungen der philosoph. philol. kl. königlich bayerischen Akad. der Wissensch., vol. 19, 1892, pp. 465–516. Alois Höfler, Logik [Logic], Vienna 1890, p. 17: "Since psychology has as its immediate object *all* psychic phenomena, and logic only the phenomena of *thinking*, or more accurately of *correct* thinking, the theoretical study of the latter is only a *special part of psychology*." Theodor Lipps, Grundzüge der Logik [Outline of logic], Hamburg 1893, pp. 1.f, 149.

Against psychologism: Edmund Husserl, Logische Untersuchungen, part I, Halle 1900 [*Logical Investigations*, translated by J. N. Findlay, London 2001]. Hermann Cohen, Kants Theorie der Erfahrung [Kant's theory of experience], 2nd ed., Berlin 1885, pp. 69f. and 81f., and Logik der reinen Erkenntnis [Logic of pure knowledge, Berlin 1902 (System der Philosophie [System of philosophy], part I), pp. 509f. Wilhelm Windelband, Kritische oder genetische Methode [Critical or genetic method] (Präludien, 1st ed., 1884, pp. 247ff. [*An Introduction to Philosophy*, translated by Joseph McCabe, London 1921]). Ferdinand Jakob Schmidt, Grundzüge der konstitutiven Erfahrungsphilosophie als Theorie des immanenten Erfahrungsmonismus [Outline of a constitutive philosophy of experience as a theory of empirical monism], Berlin 1901, pp. 16.f., 59f., 69f. Emil Lucka, Erkenntnistheorie, Logik und Psychologie [Epistemology, logic, and psychology], in the Vienna half-monthly journal "Die Gnosis" of 25 March 1903.

(P. 124, l. 4 from bottom f.) If Kant, in formulating his moral law for "all rational beings," had in mind a bearer other than man, and was not merely trying to keep the accidental elements of empirical humanity out of a rigorous formal theory, he might have thought of those inhabitants of other planets discussed in the third part of the "Allgemeine Naturgeschichte und Theorie des Himmels" [*Universal Natural History and Theory of the Heavens*, translated by Stanley L. Jaki, Edinburgh 1981, p. 186] rather than what Schopenhauer (Preisschrift über die Grundlage der Moral, § 6 [*On the Basis of Morality*, translated by E. F. J. Payne, Providence, R.I., Oxford 1995, pp. 63–64]) falsely attributes to him: "We cannot help suspecting that Kant here gave a thought to the dear little angels, or at any rate counted on their presence in the conviction of the reader." For the Kantian ethic would not apply to angels, in whom what ought to be coincides with what is.

(P. 125, l. 9f.) A. Meinong's essay Zur erkenntnistheoretischen Würdigung des Gedächtnisses [An epistemological appreciation of memory], Vierteljahrsschrift für wissenschaftliche Philosophie, X, 1886, pp. 7–33, also has nothing to do with the problems under discussion here.

(P. 125, l. 14f.) Charles Bonnet, Essai analytique sur les facultés de l'âme [Analytical essay on the faculties of the soul], Copenhagen 1760, p. 61: "La souplesse ou la mobilité des fibres augmente par le retour des mêmes ébranlements. Le sentiment attaché à cette augmentation de souplesse ou de mobilité constitue la réminiscence" (quoted from Harald Høffding). See further Max Offner, Die Psychologie Charles Bonnets, Eine Studie zur Geschichte der Psychologie [The psychology of Charles Bonnet, a study in the history of psychology], Schriften der Gesellschaft für psychologische Forschung, no. 5, Leipzig 1893, pp. 34ff.— Ewald Hering, Über das Gedächtnis als eine allgemeine Funktion der organisierten Materie, Vortrag [On memory as a general function of organized matter, a lecture], 2nd ed., Vienna 1876.— Cf. E. Mach, Die Analyse der Empfindungen und das Verhältnis des Physischen zum Psychischen [*Analysis of Sensations and the Relation of the Physical to the Psychical*, translated by C. M. Williams, Bristol 1996], 3rd ed., Jena 1902, pp. 177ff.

(P. 126, l. 1f.) On remembering under the influence of suggestion, see Friedrich Jodl, Lehrbuch der Psychologie [Textbook of psychology], 2nd ed., Stuttgart, Berlin 1903, vol. II, p. 159: "The event in which the process of reproduction is not steered and the attention is not fixed by the subject's own will, but in which the will of another intervenes through the subject's own will in order to achieve certain purposes and provoke certain phenomena of consciousness . . . may be regarded as an intermediate stage between the active and the passive element of representative attention. . . . What comes about through the will of the subject in voluntary reproduction here comes about through an external influence."

(P. 126, l. 9) Richard Avenarius, Kritik der reinen Erfahrung [Critique of pure experience], vol. II, Leipzig 1890, pp. 32, 42ff.—H. Høffding, Über Wiedererkennen, Association und psychische Aktivität [On recognition, association, and psychic activity], Vierteljahrsschrift für wissenschaftliche Philosophie, XIII, 1889, pp. 420f. and XIV, 1890, pp. 27ff. Psychologie in Umrissen, translated into German by Bendixen, 2nd ed., 1893, pp. 163f. [*Outlines of Psychology*, translated by Mary E. Lowndes, London 1891], Philosophische Studien [Philosophical studies] VIII, pp. 86f.

In the first essay Høffding says (pp. 426f.): "What exists in such states of consciousness . . . is an immediate awareness of the difference between the known and familiar and something new and strange. This difference is so clear and simple that it can no more be described in detail as, e.g., the difference between pleasure and displeasure or the difference between yellow and blue. We are faced here with an immediate difference in quality. In what follows I will call that peculiar quality which makes the familiar appear as the opposite of the new the *quality of familiarity*." "[It] must further be emphasized that in the cases discussed above one's self-observation *does not show the slightest trace of any other ideas that would be awakened by the phenomenon which has been recognized* and which could be assumed to play a part in the process of recognition itself. Therefore, if anybody assumes that all recognition requires such ideas, the burden of proof rests with him; and if it is possible to explain immediate recognition, as it occurs in the cases that have been cited, without such an assumption then this explanation will be the only scientific one."

This theory of Høffding has been rejected, for totally inadequate reasons, by Wilhelm Wundt, Grundzüge der physiologischen Psychologie, 4th ed., Leipzig 1893, vol. II, p. 442, note 1 [*Principles of Physiological Psychology*, vol. I, translated from the 5th German edition by E. B. Titchener, London 1904, no translation of vol. II], and William James, The Principles of Psychology, 1890, vol. I, p. 674, note 1. Høffding himself remarks clearly enough: "This reproduction need not imply that what is reproduced should appear as an independent element in consciousness. Nor does this happen in the cases in question, the peculiarity of which consisted, among other things, precisely in their uncompounded character. Apart from the recognized feature or features there is nothing whatsoever in consciousness that has anything to do with recognition. The word '*Les Plans*' sounds familiar, and this quality of familiarity is the *entire phenomenon. . . .*" On the other hand it is not true to say, as Wundt does (op. cit. II^4, p. 445): "The simultaneous process of association *always* turns into a clearly successive one, in which the first existing impression, the intermediate idea which then joins it, and finally the feeling of recognition appear as the links in the chain of association."

(P. 127, l. 5) The same confusion of recognition with memory underlies the examples which led G. John Romanes, Die geistige Entwicklung im Tierreich [Mental development in the animal kingdom], Leipzig 1885, pp. 127f., to credit animals with having a memory.

(P. 129, l. 3) The term "connotative" comes from John Stuart Mill, System der deduktiven und induktiven Logik, translated into German by Gomperz, I², Leipzig 1884, pp. 30f. [*A system of Logic, Ratiocinative and Inductive. Being a Connected View of the Principles of Evidence and the Methods of Scientific Investigation,* London 1843].—The expression "typical idea" is used by Høffding, while the term "representative idea" is common in English and French psychology.

(P. 130, l. 5) A marvelous description of Woman's lack of logic and her total lack of continuity is provided by Fouqué in "Undine" (chapter 5) [La Motte-Fouqué, *Undine* etc., translated by Edmund Gosse, London 1932, p. 28]: "Part of the day he wandered about with an old cross-bow, which he had found in a corner of the cottage and had furbished up, watching for the birds which flew over his head, and, when he could manage to hit them, carrying them back to the kitchen to be roasted. If he brought such booty with him, Undine scarcely ever failed to scold him for so wickedly robbing the dear creatures of the air, sailing up there in the sea of azure, of their innocent lives; she would even burst into bitter tears when she saw the dead birds. But if he came back home and had shot nothing, she scolded him none the less, that through his negligence and want of skill they were obliged to put up with fish and shrimps for dinner."

(P. 130, l. 7) G. Simmel, Zur Psychologie der Frauen [On the psychology of women], Zeitschrift für Völkerpsychologie und Sprachwissenschaft, XX, 1890, pp. 6–46: "This is the place to remember the much criticized logic of women. First, the view that tries to deny logic to women either totally or almost totally must be flatly rejected; that is one of those trivial paradoxes which can certainly be countered by saying that whoever has had any less than superficial dealings with women has often enough been surprised by the sharpness and mercilessness of their conclusions."

(P. 132, ll. 5 from bottom ff.) Kant, Kritik der praktischen Vernunft, p. 105 (Universalbibliothek) [*Critique of Practical Reason,* translated and edited by Mary Gregor, Cambridge 1997].

Second Part, Chapter VII

(P. 133, l. 14f.) The passage on Spinoza in Kant is extremely characteristic (cf. chapter 13); it is found in Kritik der praktischen Vernunft, ed. Kehrbach, p. 123 [*Critique of Practical Reason,* translated and edited by Mary Gregor, Cambridge 1997].—What may rightly have appealed to Kant about Hume was the special position this most intelligent of empiricists allocated to mathematics. Kant's fulsome praise, to which Hume primarily owes his high prestige among post-Kantian philosophers and historians of philosophy, may probably be explained by the fact that Kant had vaguely felt the necessity of replacing the metaphysical stance with the transcendental even before he had become familiar with Hume. Hume's attack struck him as one that he himself should have undertaken long before, and he severely reproached himself for his own lack of robustness in calling to account any unproven speculations. That is the reason why he could place Hume's skepticism above the dogmatism that he still felt in his own bones, and why he took relatively little offence at the shallowness of Hume's empiricism, although he could not of course stop at that point. —As to how unbelievably shallow Hume as a historiographer was also in his judgments about historical movements and historical personalities, see Julius Goldstein's booklet Die empiristische Geschichtsauffassung David Humes mit Berücksichtigung moderner methodischer und erkenntnistheoretischer Probleme, eine philosophische Studie [David Hume's empirical concept of history, with reference to modern methodological and epistemological problems. A philosophical study], Leipzig 1903, e.g., the statements about religion and religious people, and in particular Luther, quoted from Hume's "History of England" on pp. 19f. Those passages reveal Hume's bigotry.

(P. 133, ll. 3ff.) David Hume, A Treatise of Human Nature, Being an Attempt to Introduce the Experimental Method of Reasoning into Moral Subjects, Book I. Of the Understanding, part IV. Of the Sceptical and Other Systems of Philosophy, Sect. VI. Of Personal Identity, vol. I (of the first English edition, London 1739), p. 438f.:

"For my part, when I enter most intimately into what I call myself, I always stumble on some particular perception or other, of heat or cold, light or shade, love or hatred, pain or pleasure. I never can catch myself at any time without a perception, and never can observe anything but the perception. When my perceptions are remov'd for any time, as by sound sleep; so long am I insensible of *myself,* and may truly be said not to exist. And were all my perceptions remov'd by death, and cou'd I neither think, nor feel, nor see, nor love, nor hate after the dissolution of my body, I shou'd be entirely annihilated, nor do I conceive what is farther requisite to make me a perfect non-entity. If any one, upon serious and unprejudiced reflection thinks he has a different notion of *himself,* I must confess I can reason no longer with him. All I can allow him is, that he may be in the right as well as I, and that we are essentially different in this particular. He may, perhaps, perceive something simple and continu'd, which he calls *himself;* tho' I am certain there is no such principle in me.

But setting aside some metaphysicians of this kind, I may venture to affirm of the rest of mankind that they are nothing but a bundle or collection of different perceptions, which succeed each other with an inconceivable rapidity, and are in a perpetual flux and movement."

(P. 133, l. 13 from bottom) Georg Christoph Lichtenberg, Ausgewählte Schriften, ed. Eugen Reichel, Leipzig, Universalbibliothek, pp. 74f. [*Lichtenberg's Reflections,* translated by Norman Alliston, London 1908, pp. 86–87]: "We are conscious of certain impressions which are involuntary; others—at least, so we believe—depend on ourselves; where is the boundary line? We know of nothing but the existence of our impressions, feelings and thoughts. *It thinks,* we ought really to say; just as we now say, it thunders. To say cogito is too much, if you translate this into 'I think.' Still, to assume or postulate this *'I'* is a practical necessity."

(P. 133, l. 10 from bottom f.) Hume, op. cit., pp. 455f.: "All the nice and subtile questions concerning personal identity can never possibly be decided, and are to be regarded rather as grammatical than as philosophical difficulties. . . . All the disputes concerning the identity of connected objects are merely verbal."

(P. 133, l. 7 from bottom f.) E. Mach, Die Analyse der Empfindungen und das Verhältnis des Physischen zum Psychischen, 3rd ed., Jena 1902, pp. 2ff., 6f.,

10f., 18ff., 29f. [*Analysis of Sensations and the Relation of the Physical to the Psychical*, translated by C. M. Williams, Bristol 1996].

(P. 134, l. 23f.) The *idioplasm* is probably the physiological equivalent of the *empirical* self missed by Alois Höfler, Psychologie [Psychology], Vienna, Prague 1897, p. 328.

(P. 135, l. 10) Hegel, Enzyklopädie der philosophischen Wissenschaften im Grundrisse, § 115 (Werke, vollständige Ausgabe, vol. VI, Berlin 1840, pp. 230f. [*The Logic of Hegel*, translated from the Encyclopaedia of the Philosophical Sciences, with Prolegomena by William Wallace, Oxford 1892, pp. 213–214]): "This maxim, instead of being a true law of thought, is nothing but the law of *abstract understanding*. The *propositional form* itself contradicts it: for a proposition always promises a distinction between subject and predicate; while the present one does not fulfil what its form requires. . . . It is asserted that the maxim of Identity, though it cannot be proved, regulates the procedure of *every* consciousness, and that experience shows it to be accepted as soon as its terms are apprehended. To this alleged experience of the logic-books may be opposed the universal experience that no mind thinks or forms conceptions or speaks, in accordance with this law, and that no existence of any kind whatever conforms to it. Utterances after the fashion of this pretended law (A planet is—a planet; Magnetism is—magnetism; Mind is—mind) are, as they deserve to be, reputed silly. That is certainly a matter of general experience."

(P. 135, l. 12f.) Cf. Hermann Cohen, System der Philosophie [System of philosophy], part I, Logik der reinen Erkenntnis [Logic of pure cognition], Berlin 1902, p. 79: "It is said that this identity means nothing but tautology. The word describing the objection betrays the suppression of the principle. Of course identity means tautology: this is because through the Same (ταὐτὸ) thought becomes logos. And this explains why preferably, *and indeed exclusively, identity was established as the law of thinking.*"

(P. 135, ll. 20 from bottom ff.) Both passages from Sigwart, Logik, I^2, Freiburg 1889, pp. 182, 190 [*Logic*, translated by H. Dendy, in Library of Philosophy, ed. Muirhead (J. H.), 1895, pp. 139, 145].

(P. 135, l. 7 from bottom) In this respect my exposition agrees entirely with Heinrich Gomperz, Zur Psychologie der logischen Grundtatsachen [On the psychology of the fundamental facts of logic], Leipzig, Vienna 1897, pp. 21f.: "Nowhere are scientific concepts the objects of psychology, i.e., of psychological experience. . . . We arrive at such concepts through a specific method, namely through synthesis, just as we proceed toward natural laws through the method of induction, and we use these concepts by way of analysis as we use those laws by way of deduction. And therefore there is no more a psychology of the scientific concept of a mammal than there is a psychology of the scientific law of gravity. This cannot be altered by the fact that we denote these laws by specific words, such as mammal and gravitation. For these words denote merely external albeit ideational matters. These are objects, not elements, let alone components, of thought."

(P. 136, ll. 20 from bottom ff.) The passage comes from Kant, Kritik der reinen Vernunft, ed. Kehrbach, p. 145 [*Critique of Pure Reason*, translated by Paul Guyer, Allen W. Wood, Cambridge 1998, p. 273].— I believe that both here and on pp. 164–168 I have made a small contribution to solving the riddle referred to by Kant.

(P. 136, l. 14 from bottom) What I mean by essence therefore rather agrees with the Aristotelian τὸ τί ἦν εἶναι. For Aristotle too at one point the concept is λόγος τί ἦν εἶναι λέγων (Eth. Nicom. II, 6, 1107 a 6 [*The Nichomachean Ethics*, translated by David Ross, Oxford 1980]).

(P. 137, l. 15f.) See Schelling, System des transcendentalen Idealismus, Werke I/3, p. 362 [*System of Transcendental Idealism*, translated by Peter Heath, Charlottesville 1978, p. 22]: "In the judgement A=A there is a total abstraction from the content of the subject A. Whether A as such has reality or not is a matter of entire indifference for this knowledge." "The proposition is evident and certain, quite regardless of whether A is something really existing, or merely imagined, or even impossible."

(P. 137, l. 21f.) John Stuart Mill, System der deduktiven und induktiven Logik, Eine Darlegung der Grundsätze der Beweislehre und der Methoden wissenschaftlicher Forschung, book II, chapter 7, § 5, 2nd ed. translated into German by Theodor Gomperz, Leipzig 1884, vol. I (Gesammelte Werke, vol. II), p. 326 [*A System of Logic, Ratiocinative and Inductive, Collected Works,* Toronto 1973, vol. 7, pp. 277–278]: "I consider [the Principium Contradictionis] to be, like other axioms, one of our first and most familiar generalizations from experience. The original foundation of it I take to be, that Belief and Disbelief are two different mental states, excluding one another. This we know by the simplest observation of our own minds. And if we carry our observations outwards, we also find that light and darkness, sound and silence, motion and quiescence, equality and inequality, preceding and following, succession and *simultaneousness,* any positive phenomenon whatever and its negative, are distinct phenomena, pointedly contrasted, and the one always absent where the other is present. I consider the maxim in question to be a generalization from all these facts."

I will remain silent about the shallowness of this discussion; for to say that John Stuart Mill is the greatest numbskull among the famous numbskulls of the nineteenth century can be regarded as an identical equation. Still, it would be hard to conduct an argument more falsely and carelessly than Mill has done here. For this man Kant was born in vain: he has not even understood that the proposition A=A can never be contradicted by any experience and that we may claim this by rights with absolute certainty, while no induction is ever capable of supplying any propositions of such a degree of certainty.— Furthermore, Mill here mistakes the contrary opposition for the contradictory.— I will ignore his many ignorant insults to the identity principle.

(P. 138, l. 17) Johann Gottlieb Fichte, Grundlage der gesamten Wissenschaftslehre, Leipzig 1794, pp. 5ff. (Sämtliche Werke, ed. J. H. Fichte, part I, vol. I, Berlin 1845, pp. 92ff. [*The Science of Knowledge,* translated by A. E. Kroeger, London 1889, pp. 65–67]:

"A is A.

Everyone admits this proposition, and without the least hesitation. It is recognized by all as completely certain and evident.

If anyone should ask for proof of its certainty, no one would enter upon such a proof, but would say: This proposition is *absolutely* (that is, *without any further ground*) *certain;* and by saying this would ascribe to himself the power of *absolutely positing something.*

In insisting on the in itself certainty of the above proposition, you posit *not* that A *is.* The proposition A is A is by no means equivalent to A *is.* (*Being* when posited without predicate is something quite different from being when posited with a predicate.) Let us suppose A to signify a space enclosed within two straight lines, then the proposition A is A would still be correct; although the proposition A *is* would be false, since such a space is impossible.

But you posit by that proposition: *If* A is, *then* A is. The question *whether* A is at all or not, does not, therefore, occur in it. The *content* of the proposition is not regarded at all: merely its *form*. The question is not whereof you know, but *what* you know of any given subject. The only thing posited, therefore, by that proposition is the *absolutely* necessary connection between the two As. This connection we will call X.

In regard to A itself nothing has as yet been posited. The question, therefore, arises: Under what condition *is* A?

X at least is in the Ego, and posited *through* the Ego, for it is the Ego which asserts the above proposition, and so asserts it by virtue of X as a law, which X or law must, therefore, be given to the Ego; and, since it is asserted absolutely, and without further ground, must be given to the Ego through itself.

Whether and *how* A is posited we do not know; but since X is to designate a connection between an unknown positing of A (of the first A in the proposition A is A) and a positing of the same A, which latter positing is absolute on condition of the first positing, it follows that A, *at least in so far as that connection is posited*, is posited *in* and *through* the Ego, like X. Proof: X is only possible in relation to an A; now X is really posited in the Ego; hence, also, A must be posited in the Ego, in so far as X is related to it.

X is related to that A, in the above proposition, which occupies the logical position of subject, and also to that A which is the predicate, for both are united by X. Both, therefore, are posited in the Ego, in so far as they are posited; and the A of the predicate is posited *absolutely* if the first one is posited. Hence, the above proposition may also be expressed: If A is posited *in the Ego,* then *it is posited,* or then it *is.*

Hence, by means of X, the Ego posits: that A *is* absolutely for the asserting Ego, and *is* simply because it is posited in the Ego; or that there is something in the Ego which always remains the same, and is thus able to connect or posit; and hence the absolutely posited X may also be expressed, Ego=Ego, or I am I.

Thus we have already arrived at the proposition *I am;* not as expression of a deed-fact, it is true, but, at least, as expression of a *fact.*

For X is absolutely posited; this is a fact of empirical consciousness, as shown by the admitted proposition. Now, X signifies the same as I am I; hence this proposition is also absolutely posited.

But Ego is Ego, or I am I, has quite another significance than A is A. For the latter proposition has content only on a certain condition, namely, *if* A is posited. But the proposition I am I is unconditionally and absolutely valid, since it is the same as X; it is valid not only in form, but also in content. In it the Ego is posited not on condition, but absolutely, with the predicate of self-equality; hence, it is posited, and the proposition may also be expressed, *I am.*"

This proof supplied by Fichte is erroneous; for although he initially denies it he finds the existence of that very A of which it is said to be A = A already contained in the proposition itself. The proof that I myself attempted in the text is also inadequate and is based on an inadmissible equivocation which is corrected in the note on p. 137. My views on this changed while the book was in the press. I now believe that it is a hopeless enterprise to pick the I out of the proposition with Fichte and Schelling; but what is indeed expressed in the proposition is the being, the absolute hyper-empirical being that is no longer accidental but being that is in itself *being.* The proof then runs briefly as follows: something (i.e., the equals sign, Fichte's X) is, regardless of whether or not something exists. What exists and is valid is at least the being A = A, independent of any particular A and of whether or not such an A is. And because Woman has no connection with this proposition she *is* not. In this form too the proposition remains of the greatest consequence for chapter XII, where the soullessness of Woman is subsumed in a wider context (pp. 251ff.).

(P. 138, l. 5 from bottom) On repentance, cf. Kant, Kritik der praktischen Vernunft, pp. 218ff. (ed. Kehrbach) [*Critique of Practical Reason,* translated by Mary Gregor, Cambridge 1997, p. 73].

(P. 139, l. 13 from bottom) Kritik der praktischen Vernunft, p. 105, Kehrbach [*Critique of Practical Reason,* translated by Mary Gregor, Cambridge 1997].

(P. 140, l. 10) Ibsen's Brand replies to those questioning him (Act 5) [*Brand. A Version for the English Stage,* translated by Geoffrey Hill, Harmondsworth 1996, p. 145]:

> *How long will the strife last?*
> Till you have sacrificed
> all your earthly good,
> every last farthing;
> till you have understood,
> what the words "All or nothing"
> truly mean; till you control
> Your own strength, your own soul.
> *What will your losses be?*
> Ancient idolatry,
> and servitude that shines
> weighed down by golden chains
> and deep pillows of sloth,
> your thraldom to earth.
> What will the *victor's wreath*
> be? It will be faith
> raised up; it will be joy
> in sacrifice; integrity
> of the soul; Everyman's
> triumph, his crown of thorns.

(P. 140, l. 12f.) Friedrich Hebbels sämtliche Werke [Friedrich Hebbel's complete works], ed. Hermann Krumm, vol. I, p. 214.

(P. 140, l. 1 from bottom f.) Kant, Anthropologie in pragmatischer Hinsicht, § 87 (ed. Kirchmann, p. 216) [*Anthropology from a Pragmatic Point of View,* translated by Victor Lyle Dowdell, edited by Hans H. Rudnick, London 1978, p. 159]: "A man who is conscious of [having] character in his way of thinking does not have it by nature; he must have acquired it. Since the act of establishing character, like a kind of rebirth, is a certain ceremony of making a vow to oneself, we may also assume that the solemnity of the act makes it and the moment when the transformation took place unforgettable to him, like the beginning of a new epoch."

(P. 141, ll. 7ff.) Kant, Kritik der praktischen Vernunft, ed. Kehrbach, pp. 193f. [*Critique of Practical Reason,* translated and edited by Mary Gregor, Cambridge 1997, pp. 133–134].

(P. 141, ll. 9 from bottom ff.) See Kant, Grundlegung zur Metaphysik der Sitten, section 3, where the following simple and yet so profound words are found (ed. Kirchmann, p. 75) [*Groundwork of the Metaphysics of Morals,* translated and edited by Mary Gregor, Cambridge 1998, pp. 52–53]: "Natural necessity was a heteronomy of efficient causes, since every effect was possible only in accordance with the law that something else determines the efficient cause to causality; what, then, can freedom of the will be other than autonomy, that is, the will's property of being a law to itself? But the proposition, the will is in all its actions a law to itself, indicates only the principle, to act on no other maxim than that which can also have as object itself as a universal law. This, however, is precisely the formula of the categorical imperative and is the principle of morality; hence a free will and a will under moral laws are one and the same."

Second Part, Chapter VIII

(P. 143, ll. 1ff.) The passage is taken from "Große Wald-Upanishad" ["Brhdaranyaka Upanishad"] (I, 4, 1) in Paul Deussen's translation (Sechzig Upanishads des Veda, Leipzig 1897, pp. 392f. [*Sixty Upanishads of the Veda,* translated by V. M. Bedekar and G. B. Palsule, Delhi 1980, vol. 1, p. 410]).

(P. 144, ll. 20ff.) The following quotations are taken from Jean Pauls Werke, ed. Hempel, part XLVIII, p. 328 [*Life of Jean Paul Richter,* translated by Eliza B. Lee, London 1849, p. 32].—Novalis, Schriften [Works], ed. Schlegel and Tieck, part II, Vienna 1820, pp. 143f.—Schellings Werke [Works], I/1, p. 318f.

(P. 147, l. 4) Friedrich Nietzsche, Götzendämmerung oder wie man mit dem Hammer philosophiert (Werke, part I, vol. VIII, p. 165) [*Twilight of the Idols,* translated by Duncan Large, Oxford 1998].

(P. 148, ll. 9 from bottom ff.) By this remark I hope to contribute to the clarification of what Wilhelm Dilthey, without being properly understood, discovered as the fundamental difference between psychical and physical processes (e.g., Beiträge zum Studium der Individualität [Contributions to the study of individuality], Berliner Sitzungsberichte, 1896, p. 296): "The fundamental difference between psychological insight and the understanding of nature consists in the fact that coherence in psychic life is primarily given, and therefore this is also where the first and fundamental peculiarity of the humanities lies. Since in the area of external phenomena only juxtaposition and succession are experienced, the idea of coherence could not come into being unless it were given in the subject's own coherent unity."

(P. 149, l. 18) The conscious connection with the cosmos and the consciousness of the microcosm that constitute the man of genius may suffice to explain the fact that most, if not all, geniuses know and undergo telepathic experiences and visions. *A genius has something of a clairvoyant in him.* I did not want to touch on these things in my main text because today anybody who considers telepathy as possible is taken for an obscurantist. The revelations of the dying probably also belong in this context: the dying achieve a deeper union with the cosmos than was possible for the living, and in their hour of death they can therefore appear to people who are far away, and gain influence on their thoughts and dreams.

(P. 149, ll. 4 from bottom ff.) The idea of the microcosm of course also underlies the story of creation in Genesis, which makes man appear as the image of God.

Naturally the same notion is also found among the *Indians*. Bṛihadâraṇyaka-Upanishad 4, 4, 5 (Deussen, Sechzig Upanishads des Veda, Leipzig 1897, p. 476 [Paul Deussen, *Sixty Upanishads of the Veda*, translated by V. M. Bedekar and G. B. Palsule, Delhi 1980, vol. 1, p. 410]): "Indeed, this self is the Brahman consisting of knowledge of Manas (mind), of life-breath, of eyes, of ears, of earth, of water, of wind, of ether, consisting of fire and not consisting of fire, consisting of desire and not consisting of desire, consisting of anger and not consisting of anger, consisting of righteous law and not consisting of righteous law, *consisting of all*." Chândogya-Upanishad 3, 14, 2f. (op. cit. p. 109 [vol. 1, p. 111]): "Mind is his [the human being's] stuff, living (breathing) is his body, light his form, resolution is truth, *his self is infinity*. He is all-doing, all-wishing, all-smelling, all-tasting, encompassing all, silent, unconcerned:— this is my soul in the innermost part of the heart, smaller than a grain of rice, or a grain of barley, or a grain of mustard or a grain of millet or a grain of the grain of the millet; — this is my soul in my innermost heart, greater than the earth, greater than the aerial space, greater than these worlds.

The all-doing, the all-wishing, the all-smelling, the all-tasting, the all-encompassing, silent, unconcerned—this is my soul in the innermost part of the heart, this is the Brahman, into which I shall enter, after departing from here.— He, who becomes this, does not doubt."

Plato first teaches in Menon (81 c.) [The Dialogues of Plato, translated by R. E. Allen, vol. I, Meno (New Haven, London 1984)]: "ἅτε οὖν ἡ ψυχὴ ἀθάνατός τε οὖσα καὶ πολλάκις γεγονυῖα καὶ ἑωρακυῖα καὶ τὰ ἐνθάδε καὶ πάντα χρήματα, οὐκ ἔστιν ὅ τι οὐ μεμάθηκεν . . . ἅτε γὰρ τῆς φύσεως ἁπάσης συγγενοῦς οὔσης καὶ μεμαθηκυίας τῆς ψυχῆς ἅπαντα οὐδὲν κωλύει . . . πάντα . . . ἀνευρεῖν." There are also some echoes of this in Philebos (29 aff.) [Philebus, translated by Robin A. H. Waterfield, Harmondsworth 1982], e.g.: "Τρέφεται καὶ γίγνεται καὶ ἄρχεται τὸ τοῦ παντὸς πῦρ ὑπὸ τοῦ παρ' ἡμῖν πυρός, ἢ τοὐναντίον ὑπ' ἐκείνου τό τ' ἐμὸν καὶ τὸ σὸν καὶ τὸ τῶν ἄλων ζώων ἅπαντ' ἴσχει ταῦτα." More explicitly Aristotle, De anima III, 8, 431, b, 21 [*De anima*, translated by D. W. Hamlyn, Oxford 1993]: "ἡ ψυχὴ τὰ ὄντα πώς ἐστι πάντα." Cf. Ludwig Stein, Die Psychologie der Stoa [The psychology of the Stoa], vol. I: Metaphysisch-anthropologischer Teil [Metaphysical-anthropological part] (Berliner Studien für klassische Philologie und Archäologie, vol. III, no. 1, Berlin 1886), p. 206: "In Aristotle one already encounters a clear reference to the microcosm. Indeed one will not go wrong even if one attributes even this term to the Stagirite (Aristotle, Physika, VIII[2], 252 b, 24 [*Physics*, translated by Robin A. H. Waterfield, Oxford 1996]): "εἰ δ' ἐν ζῴῳ τοῦτο δυνατὸν γενέσθαι, τί κωλύει τὸ αὐτὸ συμβῆναι καὶ κατὰ τὸ πᾶν; εἰ γὰρ ἐν μικρῷ κόσμῳ γίνεται, καὶ ἐν μεγάλῳ . . . although the concept may be older." P. 214: "In the Stoa we are faced for the first time with a clearly stated, sharply outlined and boldly developed microcosm." Further details about the history of the microcosm idea (e.g., in Philo) in Stein, op. cit. It also occurs in St. Augustine according to Überweg-Heinze, Grundriß der Geschichte der Philosophie [*A History of Philosophy, from Thales to the Present Time*, translated from 4th German ed.

by G. S. Morris, in Smith (H. B.) and Schaff (P.), Theological and Philosophical Library, 1872–1874], II^8, p. 128. Pico de Mirandola's view is extensively quoted by me on p. 159f. Cf. also Rudolf Eisler, Wörterbuch der philosophischen Begriffe und Ausdrücke [Dictionary of philosophical concepts and terms], Berlin 1901, sub verbo, and Rudolf Eucken, Die Grundbegriffe der Gegenwart, historisch und kritisch entwickelt, 2nd ed., Leipzig 1893, pp. 188f. [*The Fundamental Concepts of Modern Philosophic Thought, Critically and Historically Considered,* translated by M. Stuart Phelps, New York 1880].

(P. 150, l. 15 from bottom) Probably nothing is so little understood about Kant's ethics as the demand that one should act according to a most general maxim. There is still a sense that this means something social, the Büchnerian ethic ("What you don't want to be done to you," etc.), an instruction for a penal code. The general nature of the categorical imperative only expresses in transcendental terms that metaphysic which was taught, according to Cicero (De natura deorum, II, 14, 37 [*The Nature of the Gods,* translated by Horace C. P. McGregor, Harmondsworth 1978]), by the great stoic Chrysippos: "Cetera omnia aliorum caussa esse generata, ut eos fruges atque fructus quos terra gignat, animantium caussa, animantes autem hominum, ut equum vehendi caussa, arandi bovem, venandi et custodiendi canem. Ipse autem homo ortus est ad mundum contemplandum et imitandum."

(P. 150, ll. 12 from bottom ff.) Empedocles in Aristotle, Metaphysik, 1000 b, 6 [*The Metaphysics,* translated by Hugh Lawson-Tancred, London 1998].—Plotinus, Enneades I, 6, 9 [*The Enneads,* translated by Stephen McKenna, Harmondsworth 1991]—Incidentally, we also find in Plato, Rep. 508 b [*Republic,* translated by Robin A. H. Waterfield, London 1993]: "ἄλ' [ὄμμα] ἡιοειδέστατόν γε, οἶμαι, τῶν περὶ τὰς αἰσθήσεως ὀργάνων."

(P. 151, l. 20 from bottom) The three problems that perhaps reveal most readily how far the depth of an individual reaches are the problem of religion, the problem of art, and the problem of freedom—all three, basically, the one problem of being. The form in which this single problem is understood by the fewest is the problem of freedom. To the lowest people "indeterminism" is obvious, to mediocre people "determinism"; that this is where the dualism reveals itself most intensively—how rarely is that understood!

The most profound thinkers of humanity have certainly thought in terms of indeterminism. Goethe, Dichtung und Wahrheit, part IV, book 16 (vol. XXIV, p. 177, Hesse, ed.) [*Poetry and Truth,* translated by Minna Steele Smith, London 1908, vol. 2, p. 206]: "If anything like reason shows itself in the brute creation, it is long before we can recover from our amazement; for, although the animals stand so near to us, they yet seem to be divided from us by an infinite gulf, and to be entirely subject to the rule of necessity." By the same gulf, however, Goethe is separated from the "modern outlook" and "developmental theory."

Thus also Dante, Paradiso, Canto V, ll. 19–24 [*The Divine Comedy,* translated by Mark Musa, vol. 3, *Paradise,* Harmondsworth 1986]:

Lo maggior don, che Dio per sua larghezza
Fesse creando, ed alla sua bontate
Più conformato, e quel ch'ei più apprezza
Fu della volontà la libertate,
Di che le creature intelligenti
E tutte e sole fûro e son dotate.

Similarly, Plato (in whom every philosophical idea that exists can already be found), anticipates the Schelling-Schopenhauer theory of freedom, when he makes the Parca Lachesis say in his "Republic" (X, 617, D E) [*Republic,* translated by Robin A. H. Waterfield, London 1993]): "Ψυχαὶ ἐφήμεροι . . . οὐκ ὑμᾶς δαίμων λήξεται, ἄλ' ὑμεῖς δαίμονα αἱρήσεσθε . . . αἰτία ἑομένου· θεὸς ἀναίτιος." And likewise all the greatest, Kant, St. Augustine, Richard Wagner ("Siegfried," Act III, Wotan and Erda).

(P. 153, l. 1) Carlyle, On Heroes etc., in several places, especially p. 116 (Chapman and Hall edition, London). What he says is the whole and unadulterated truth: *"The merit of originality is not novelty; it is sincerity."*

(P. 156, ll. 9ff.) Pensées de Blaise Pascal, Paris 1841, p. 184 (Partie I, Article X, 1) [*Pensées and Other Writings,* translated by Honor Levi, Oxford 1995].

(P. 157, ll. 18ff.) Mach, Die Analyse der Empfindungen etc., 3rd ed., 1902, p. 19 [*Contributions to the Analysis of the Sensations,* translated by C. M. Williams, Bristol 1998)].

(P. 157, l. 2 from bottom) I could provide no better evidence for what I have noticed about the strange behavior of more endowed people in the company of others than the highly interesting confession of the poet John Keats, who is relatively little appreciated on the Continent. Although this is stated with special reference to the poet, it is valid, with a few easily applied modifications, to the artist, indeed to genius of any kind. Keats writes to his friend Richard Woodhouse on 27 October 1818 (The Poetical Works and Other Writings of John Keats, edited by Harry Buxton Forman, vol. III, London 1883, pp. 233f.): "As to the poetical character itself (I mean that sort, of which, if I am anything, I am a member; that sort distinguished from the Wordsworthian or egotistical sublime, which is a thing per se, and stands alone), it is not itself—it has no self—it is everything and nothing—it has no character—it enjoys light and shade—it lives in gusto, be it foul or fair, high or low, rich or poor, mean or elevated—it has as much delight in conceiving a Jago or an Imogen. What shocks the virtuous philosopher delights the cameleon poet. It does no harm from its relish of the dark side of things, any more than from its taste for the bright one, because they both end in speculation. *A poet is the most unpoetical of anything in existence,* because he has no identity: he is continually in for, and filling, some other body. The sun, the moon, the sea and men and women, who are creatures of impulse, are poetical and have about them an unchangeable attribute; the poet has none. He is certainly the most unpoetical of all God's creatures. If then, he has no self,[2] and if I am poet, where is the wonder that I should say I would write no more. Might I not that very instant have been cogitating on the character of Saturn and Ops? It is a wretched thing to confess, but it is a very fact, that not one word I ever utter can be taken for granted as an opinion growing out of my identical nature. How can it, when I have no nature? When I am in a room with people, if I ever am free from speculating on creations of my brain, then not myself goes home to myself, *but the identity of everyone in the room begins to press*

2. One would be using a very double-edged sword if one were to understand these words to mean that Keats, like Hume, had declared that he had no soul, since in reality it is rather the existence of the soul that is expressed here.

upon me, so that I am in a very little time annihilated—not only among men; it would be the same in a nursery of children."

(P. 158, ll. 11 from bottom ff.) Richard Wagner, Gesammelte Schriften und Dichtungen, Leipzig 1898, vol. VI, p. 249 [*The Twilight of the Gods,* in *The Ring of the Niblung,* translated by Stewart Spencer, London 2000, p. 346].

(P. 158, ll. 10 from bottom ff.) Thus J. B. Meyer, Genie und Talent. Eine psychologische Betrachtung [Genius and talent, a psychological reflection], Zeitschrift für Völkerpsychologie und Sprachwissenschaft, 1880, XI, p. 289 says: "Cesare Borgia, Louis XI of France, Richard III were villains of genius, and in the ranks of swindlers there is many a genius"—a clear expression of popular opinion.

(P. 159, ll. 13 from bottom ff.) Sophocles, Aias, line 553 [*Ajax,* translated by Herbert Golder and Richard Pevear, Oxford 1999].

(P. 159, ll. 5 from bottom ff.) Joannis Pici Mirandulae Concordiaeque Comitis . . . Opera quae extant omnia Basileae, Per Sebastianum Henricepetri, 1601, vol. I, pp. 207–219: "De hominis dignitate oratio" [*On the Dignity of Man,* translated by Charles Glenn Wallis, Indianapolis 1965]. The passage quoted p. 208.—Mirandola Giovanni Pico, Count of Mirandola (a small town in the southern Po Valley between Guastalla and Ferrara, northeast of Modena, which is also known from Schiller's "Don Carlos") only lived from 1463 to 1494.—"supremi spiritus" are the angels, and the devils the ("paulo mox") fallen angels.— A genius must be regarded as a human being who is not satisfied with the fate of any single creature; if genius is the divine in a human being, a human being who becomes all genius becomes God.

Second Part, Chapter IX

(P. 161, l. 6 from bottom) Theodor Waitz, Anthropologie der Naturvölker, part I, Leipzig 1859, p. 380 [Anthropology of primitive peoples]: "If older Christian authorities only saw the sensual side of marriage and seriously doubted that women also had a soul, we cannot be surprised that the Chinese, Indians, and Moslems actually deny it to them. If a Chinese is asked about his children, he only counts the boys; if he only has girls he says that he has no children." (Duhaut-Cilly, Voyage autour du monde, 1834, II, p. 369 [A Voyage: To California, the Sandwich Islands & Around the World in the Years 1826–1829, translated by August Frugé and Neal Harlow, San Francisco 1999]).

(P. 162, l. 3) Aristotle, De gener. animalium, I, 2, 716 a 4 [Generation of Animals, translated by A. L. Peck, London 1963]: "τῆς γενέσεως ἀρχὰς ἄν τις οὐχ ἥκιστα θείη τὸ θῆλυ καὶ τὸ ἄρρεν, τὸ μὲν ἄρρεν ὡς τῆς κινήσεως καὶ τῆς γενέσεως ἔχον τὴν ἀρχήν, τὸ δὲ θῆλυ ὡς ὕης. I, 20, 729 a 9: τὸ μὲν ἄρρεν παρέχεται τό τε εἶδος καὶ τὴν ἀρχὴν τῆς κινήσεως, τὸ δὲ θῆλυ τὸ σῶμα καὶ τὴν ὕην. 729 a 29: τὸ ἄρρεν ἐστὶν ὡς κινοῦν, τὸ δὲ θὴλυ, ᾗ θῆλυ, ὡς παθητικόν. II, 1, 732 a 3: βέλτιον γὰρ καὶ θειότερον ἡ ἀρχὴ τῆς κινήσεως, ᾗ ἄρρεν ὑπάρχει τοῖς γινομένοις. ὕη δὲ τὸ θῆλυ. II, 4, 738 b 25: ἀεὶ δὲ παρέχει τὸ μὲν θῆλυ τὴν ὕην, τὸ δὲ ἄρρεν τὸ δημιουργοῦν. ἔστι τὸ μὲν σῶμα ἐκ τοῦ θήλεος, ἡ δὲ ψυχὴ ἐκ τοῦ ἄρρενος." See further I, 21, 729 b 1 and 730 a 25. II, 3, 737, a 29. 740 b 12–25. In Metaphysik V, 28 1024 a 34, IX, 1057 a 31f. I, 6, 988 a 2f. [The Metaphysics, translated by Hugh Lawson-Tancred, Harmondsworth 1998], he explains, according to the same principle, why man can beget more children than woman: "οἱ μὲν πὰρ ἐκ τῆς ὕης πολλὰ ποιοῦσιν, τὸ εἶδος ἅπαξ γεννᾷ μόνον, φαίνεται δ' ἐκ μιᾶς ὕης μία τράπεζα, ὁ δὲ τὸ εἶδος ἐπιφέρων εἷς ὢν πολλὰ ποιεῖ. ὁμοίως δ' ἔχει καὶ τὸ ἄρρεν πρὸς τὸ θῆλυ· τὸ μὲν γὰρ ὑπὸ μιᾶς πληροῦται ὀχείας, τὸ δ' ἄρρεν πολλὰ πληροῖ· καίτοι ταῦτα μιμήματα τῶν ἀρχῶν ἐκείνων ἐστὶν."

For this theory of Aristotle, cf. J. B. Meyer, Aristoteles Tierkunde [The zoology of Aristotle], Berlin 1855, pp. 454f.; Hermann Siebeck, Aristoteles, Stuttgart 1899 (Frommanns Klassiker der Philosophie, vol. VIII), p. 69; Eduard Zeller, Die Philosophie der Griechen in ihrer geschichtlichen Entwicklung, II/2, Leipzig 1879, 3rd ed., pp. 325 and 525f. [Outlines of the History of Greek Philosophy, translated by L. R. Palmer, Bristol 1997]; Überweg-Heinze, Grundriß der Geschichte der Philosophie, I^9, Berlin 1903, p. 259 [A History of Philosophy, From Thales to the Present Time, translated from 4th German ed. by G. S. Morris, in Smith (H. B.) and Schaff (P.), Theological and Philosophical Library, 1872–1874]; J. J. Bachofen, Das Mutterrecht. Eine Untersuchung der Gynaikokratie der alten Welt, Stuttgart 1861, pp. 164–168 [Myth, Religion, and Mother Right, selected writings, translated by Ralph Manheim, Princeton 1973, incomplete].—Aristotle's theory of procreation and its relationship with earlier and modern views is treated in particular by Wilhelm His, Die Theorien der geschlechtlichen Zeugung [Theories of sexual procreation], Archiv für Anthropologie, vol. IV, 1870, pp. 202–208.

(P. 162, l. 17) Jean Wier, Opera omnia, Amstelodami 1660, Liber IV, Caput 24. From more recent literature I can only name Oken (Lehrbuch der Naturphilosophie, 3rd ed, Zürich 1843, p. 387, no. 2958 [Textbook of natural philosophy]): "In copulation the male parts are the sensory organ and the female only the receptive mouth. Actually both are sensory organs, but the former is the active one and the latter the passive" (ibid. no. 2962). "Even though the male semen joins in solidifying into the embryo it is not its mass that plays a part, but only its polarizing force."

The discussions of my main text do not aim to provide a theory of procreation in terms of natural philosophy like those of Aristotle and Oken. However, the speculations of these men were without doubt based on the concept of intellectual differences between the sexes, which they even extended to the relationship between the two germs involved in fertilization; I may therefore be allowed to cite them here.

(P. 162, l. 18 from bottom) Cf. Ausgewählte Werke von Friedrich Baron de la Motte-Fouqué, Ausgabe letzter Hand [Selected Works of Baron Friedrich de la Motte-Fouqué, final edition by the author], vol. XII, Halle 1841, pp. 136ff.

(P. 163, l. 10 from bottom f.) Those Kantians who only comprehend the letter of the philosopher will surely deny this; and they would find a certain justification for so doing in the Kantian terminology, according to which the transcendental subject is the subject of the *intellect* and the intelligible character the subject of *reason*, but the latter, as the practical capability in man, is superior to the former, as a merely theoretical one. However, I can quote passages such as the following in the preface to "Grundlegung zur Metaphysik der Sitten" (p. 8, ed. Kirchmann) [Kant: *Groundwork of the Metaphysics of Morals*, translated by Mary Gregor, Cambridge 1998, p. 5]: "I require that the critique of a pure practical reason, if it is to be carried through completely, be able at the same time to present *the unity of practical with speculative reason in a common principle, since there can, in the end, be only one and the same reason,* which must be distinguished merely in its application." Similarly in "Kritik der praktischen Vernunft," pp. 110, 118, 145 (ed. Kehrbach) [Critique of Practical Reason, translated and edited by Mary Gregor, Cambridge 1997]. Incidentally, it was precisely this "unity of the whole pure capability of reason (of the theoretical as well as the practical)" that Kant's planned but not realized major work "The supreme position of transcendental philosophy in the system of ideas: God, the world and man, or a system of pure philosophy in its context" (cf. Hans Vaihinger, Archiv für Geschichte der Philosophie, IV, p. 734f.) was intended to describe.

At this point I would like to note the following:

Strangely enough, in the extensive literature about Goethe's relationship with Kant I find no mention of the most Kantian passage in the whole of Goethe, although admittedly it was written before Goethe had read anything by Kant and is also less characteristic of his relationship with the concrete person Kant and his books than of Goethe's relationship with Kantian thought. It is found in the "Physiognomische Fragmente" [Physiognomical Fragments] (First Essay, Third Fragment: vol. XIV, p. 242 of the Hesse edition) that Goethe wrote while still in Frankfurt, and it runs: "Benign providence has endowed everybody with a certain urge to act in this way or that, which helps all to find their way in this world. It is this same urge that more or less combines the experiences of a human being without himself being aware of it." This clearly states the identity of the intelligible being that is on the one hand the source of the synthetic unity of apperception, and on the other hand the noumenon with its *free* will.

(P. 165, l. 17 from bottom) One of the simplest and clearest discussions of this fact stems from Franz Staudinger, Identität und Apriori [Identity and a priori], Vierteljahrsschrift für wissenschaftliche Philosophie, XIII, 1889, pp. 66f.: "Not only is today's perception of the sun different from yesterday's, today's sun itself is no longer that which was shining yesterday. But I say nevertheless: yesterday's sun and today's is one. This, however, means nothing other than that I must assume an enduring coherence of the object itself to which my ideas, which are entirely separate in temporal terms, refer. What is conceived is an objective existence of the object itself which is supposed to be entirely independent of our fragmented perception. This realization of the endurance of the object itself is the decisive factor constituting our idea of substance. The enigma contained in the fact that we move to the idea of the unity of a single enduring object from entirely separate ideas, which, strictly speaking, each time only describe objects in the present, still receives too little attention, although it has been clearly recognized by Kant. However, whether Kant has solved this enigma, and how it may be solved, is a question concerning the origin of the elements of knowledge. . . . Here we must content ourselves with the fact that we are obliged to relate such ideas as we call perceptions to objects that are unified and that endure at least from our first perception to the present."

This difficulty also seems to disappear in the face of the view explained in my main text, or at least to reveal its identity with another, admittedly no less great, difficulty. Psychologically, A = A, the principle of conceptuality and objectivity, is a negation of time (even though this relationship with time is not contained in the strictly logical *sense* of the proposition) and to that extent conveys the continuity of the object. However, insofar as it expresses the being of the subject, it *posits* the same continuity for the inner life, *despite* the isolation of the psychic experiences, despite the narrowness of consciousness. It is therefore only *one* enigma, the question about the continuity of the object being the same as that about the continuity of the subject.

(P. 165, l. 3 from bottom) Kant, Kritik der reinen Vernunft, 1st ed., Von der Synthesis der Rekognition im Begriffe (p. 119, Kehrbach) [Critique of Pure Reason, On the Synthesis of Recognition in the Concept, translated by Paul Guyer, Cambridge 1998].

(P. 166, l. 18 from bottom) Cf. in particular Huxley, Hume (English Men of Letters, ed. John Morley, No. 5, London 1881), pp. 94f.:

"When several complex impressions which are more or less different from one another—let us say that out of ten impressions in each, six are the same in all, and four are different from all the rest—are successively presented to the mind, it is easy to see what must be the nature of the result. The repetition of the six similar impressions will strengthen the six corresponding elements of the complex idea, which will therefore acquire greater vividness: while the four differing impressions of each will not only acquire no greater strength than they had at first, but, in accordance with the law of association, they will all tend to appear at once, and will thus neutralise one another.

This mental operation may be rendered comprehensible by considering what takes place in the formation of compound photographs—when the images of the faces of six sitters, for example, are each received on the same photographic plate, for a sixth of the time requisite to take one portrait. The final result is that all those points in which the six faces agree are brought out strongly, while all those in which they differ are left vague; and thus what may be termed a *generic* portrait of the six, in contradistinction to a *specific* portrait of any one, is produced."—A similar idea of the origin of concepts through superimposition, resulting in the intensification of similarities and the extinction of dissimilarities, is already known to Herbart (Psychologie als Wissenschaft, II, § 122 [Psychology as science], who excellently understood and explained the difference between logical and psychological concepts.—Avenarius: Kritik der reinen Erfahrung [Critique of pure experience], vol. II, Leipzig 1890, pp. 298ff.—Mach, Die ökonomische Natur der physikalischen Forschung, Populär-wissenschaftliche Vorlesungen [The economic nature of research in physics, lectures on popular science], Leipzig 1896, pp. 217ff. Mach delves more deeply in his "Prinzipien der Wärmelehre, historisch-kritisch entwickelt.," 2nd ed., Leipzig 1900, pp. 415f., 419f. [*Principles of the Theory of Heat, Historically and Critically Elucidated,* ed. Brian McGuinness, Dordrecht, Lancaster c. 1986]).

(P. 167, l. 20) Judgment exists; as a precondition of its existence the assumption that there is a connection between man and the cosmos, or, in epistemological terms, a link between *thinking* and *being,* is immanent to it. Fathoming this connection and this link is the fundamental problem of all theoretical philosophy, just as fathoming the relationship between what *should be* and what *is* is the fundamental problem of all practical philosophy. Being is supposed to be contemplated through thinking and realized through action; and thus ultimately the demands of knowledge and the demands of morality once more coincide: the dualism of sensation and thought, of the resistance of the senses and the moral law, must finally disappear.Therefore, insofar as judgment *exists,* the human being is the microcosm.

(P. 167, l. 8 from bottom) The term "inner form of judgment" is found in Wilhelm Jerusalem, Die Urteilsfunktion, eine psychologische und erkenntnis-kritische Untersuchung [The function of judgment, a psychological and epistemological investigation], Vienna, Leipzig 1895, p. 80.

(P. 167, l. 7 from bottom f.) This was already emphasized by Lotze (cf. note on p. 110, l. 9).

(P. 169, l. 11) Leibniz, Monadologie No. 31 (Opera philosophica, ed. Erdmann, p. 707 [*The Monadology and Other Philosophical Writings,* translated by Robert Latta, Oxford 1898]): "Nos raisonnements sont fondés sur deux grands principes, *celui de la contradiction,* en vertu duquel nous jugeons faux ce qui en enveloppe, et vrai ce qui est opposé ou contradictoire au faux; [no. 32] *et celui de la raison suffisante,* en vertu duquel nous considérons, qu'aucun fait ne serait se trouver vrai ou existant, aucune énonciation véritable, sans qu'il y ait une raison suffisante, pourquoi il en soit ainsi et non pas autrement, quoique ces raisons le plus souvent ne puissent point nous être connues."

(P. 170, l. 11) On the lesser criminality of women, see, e.g., Dr. G. Morache's article Die Verantwortlichkeit des Weibes vor Gericht [The legal responsibility of woman], in "Wage," 14 March 1903, pp. 372–376: "The number of women quite significantly exceeds that of men; in France less than elsewhere, but even here the difference is noticeable. If female criminality equalled the male, the figures expressing it would also have to be fairly equal.

Let us pick three figures at random, say, 1889, 1890, 1891. During this period 2970 men were taken to court for grave crimes (murder, infanticide, sexual offences) while in the same period 745 women were accused of the same crimes. The criminality of woman therefore is expressed by a figure that amounts to a quarter of the male, or, in other words, three crimes in four are committed by men and one by women. Even disregarding the crime of infanticide, for which the man alone is really responsible because he is, after all, the originator, we find that among those accused of common crimes there are only 211 women and 2954 men; thus women are 14 times less criminal than men.

There is no lack of interpretations of these undeniable facts—for it would be impossible to contest them. It is said that the physical constitution of woman is not suited to violence, which is involved in the majority of criminal actions; that she is not made for armed crimes or burglary. It is argued that, although she does not physically commit the crime, she nevertheless suggests it and profits from it; in moral terms she is the originator and all the more guilty because she operates in the dark and strikes through the hand of another. Thus the old word reappears: Cherchez la femme. . . . The Italian school has clearly recognized that from a material point of view woman is less criminal than man, but it offers an interesting explanation for this fact: the male criminal steals and murders in order to obtain without labor the money that affords him idleness and pleasure; woman has a far simpler means of achieving the same purpose, she trades with her body and sells herself; if one adds the number of female criminals to that of prostitutes one arrives at the same number as for male criminality.

The theory seems satisfactory, but is paradoxical. Furthermore, it is fundamentally wrong: for although the number of female criminals brought to court is known, the number of those women who profit from their charms behind some mask and in many different forms cannot be estimated even approximately."

So much for Morache. Apart from the superficiality of the idea that crimes are committed for the sake of profit, we may add that there are enough women of the prostitute type who by no means prostitute themselves for money or jewelry, women from the highest and richest circles, who give themselves to any coachman who arouses their desire, rather than in order to indulge in even greater luxury.—See further Ellis, Mann und Weib, pp. 364ff. [*Man and Woman. A Study of Human Secondary Sexual Characters,* London 1894] and the extensive literature quoted there. Lombroso-Ferrero, Das Weib als Verbrecherin und Prostituierte, Hamburg 1894, part II: Kriminologie des Weibes [The criminology of woman], pp. 193ff. [*The Female Offender,* London 1895, no translation of part II found] and particularly Paul Näcke, Verbrechen und Wahnsinn beim Weibe, mit Ausblicken auf die Kriminal-Anthropologie überhaupt [Crime and madness in woman, with references to criminal anthropology in general], Vienna, Leipzig 1894, with a very complete bibliography on pp. 240–255.

(P. 170, l. 1 from bottom) This is also the reason why Woman is not *ugly,* while the male criminal is ugly.

(P. 171, l. 10 from bottom f.) The nursing of women is dealt with from this point of view by E. Leyden, Weibliche Krankenpflege und weibliche Heilkunst [Female nursing and female medicine], Deutsche Rundschau, XIX, 1879, pp. 126–148, Franz König, Die Schwesternpflege der Kranken, Ein Stück moderner Kulturarbeit der Frau [Female nursing, a part of woman's work in modern civilization], op. cit., LXXI, 1892, pp. 141–146, Julius Duboc, Fünfzig Jahre Frauenfrage in Deutschland, Geschichte und Kritik [Fifty years of the woman question in Germany, history and critique], Leipzig 1896, pp. 18f.—For the *hysterical* character of various instances of nursing (which should be understandable after chapter XII), see Freud's remarks in Breuer and Freud's Studien über Hysterie, Leipzig, Vienna 1895, p. 141 [*Studies on Hysteria,* translated by A. A. Brill, Boston 1960].

(P. 174, l. 6) Mach, Die Analyse der Empfindungen, 3rd ed., 1902, p. 14 [*Contributions to the Analysis of the Sensations,* translated by C. M. Williams, Bristol 1998].

(P. 174, l. 14) It is printed, for example, in Karl Pearson, The Grammar of Science, London 1892, p. 78.

(P. 174, l. 17) Kant: in "Grundlegung zur Metaphysik der Sitten," p. 60, ed. Kirchmann [*Groundwork of the Metaphysics of Morals,* translated by Mary Gregor, Cambridge 1998].

(P. 175, l. 8f.) The term "intrinsic value" is not mine, but was first used, I think, by August Döring, Philosophische Güterlehre [Philosophical theory of values], 1888, pp. 56, 319ff.

(P. 175, l. 5 from bottom f.) Kant, Anthropologie, p. 234, ed. Kirchmann [*Anthropology from a Pragmatic Point of View,* translated by Victor Lyle Dowdell, London 1978, p. 222]: "The man is jealous when he is in love; the woman is also jealous without being in love, because any lover gained by other women is one lost from the circle of her admirers."

(P. 175, l. 3 from bottom) Proof: there is comradeship between several people, but friendship only between two.

(P. 176, l. 3 from bottom) I hope to analyze the phenomenon of gallantry elsewhere. Kant (Fragmente aus dem Nachlaß [Fragments from the estate], ed. Kirchmann, vol. VIII, p. 307) also speaks about the "insult to women in the custom of flattering them."

(P. 177, l. 20) Cf. Auguste Comte, Cours de philosophie positive, 2e éd., par

E. Littré, vol. III, Paris 1864, pp. 538f. [*The Positive Philosophy of Auguste Comte,* translated by Harriet Martineau, London 1853]. He talks about the "vain principe fondamental de l'*observation intérieure*" and the "profonde absurdité que présente la seule position, si évidemment contradictoire, de l'homme se regardant penser." Ethics would be in dire straits if self-observation were not possible. Self-observation is, after all, the precondition for the *possibility* of an ethic, and "Know thyself" is a moral commandment and therefore a possibility: "Thou canst, because thou shalt." The results of self-observation are immediate evidence and possess the character of the most powerful reality. This is where I experience all causal connections, intellectually according to the proposition of sufficient reason, emotionally according to the law of motivation, without being referred to induction, experiment, or construction.

(P. 177, l. 17 from bottom) Friedrich Jodl, Lehrbuch der Psychologie [Textbook of psychology], 2nd ed., vol. II, Stuttgart, Berlin 1903, p. 103.

(P. 177, l. 9 from bottom f.) Mill: in his book against Hamilton (according to Pierre Janet, L'Automatisme psychologique [Psychological automatism], 3e éd., Paris 1899, pp. 39f., where a variety of points, less well-known in Germany, are made on the problem of self). Mach: Die Analyse der Empfindungen, 3rd ed., 1902, pp. 3, 18f. [*Contributions to the Analysis of the Sensations,* translated by C. M. Williams, Bristol 1998].—Incidentally, Hume already says (Treatise, I, 4, 6, p. 454 of 1st ed., vol. I, London 1739): "Memory is to be considered as the source of personal identity."

(P. 178, l. 17) Heinrich Schurtz, Altersklassen und Männerbünde, Eine Darstellung der Grundformen der Gesellschaft [Age groups and men's associations, an exposition of the fundamental forms of society], Berlin 1902.

(P. 178, l. 20) Pascal, Pensées I, 7, l [*Pensées and Other Writings,* translated by Honor Levi, Oxford 1995], "Misère de l'homme."

(P. 178, l. 15 from bottom) On the cleptomania of women, see Albert Moll, Das nervöse Weib [The nervous woman], Berlin 1898, pp. 167f. Paul Dubuisson, Les voleuses des grands magasins, Archives d'Anthropologie criminelle, XVI, 1901, pp. 1–20, 341–370.

(P. 178, l. 10 from bottom) Eduard von Hartmann, Phänomenologie des sittlichen Bewußtseins, Prolegomena zu jeder künftigen Ethik [Phenomenology of moral consciousness, prolegomena to any future ethics], Berlin 1879, pp. 522f., makes the following correct remark:

"Almost all women are born defrauders out of passion. Only a few will decide to return an excess of goods or change they may receive; they console themselves with the thought that the merchant has profited enough from them and that they could not be proved to have been conscious of their misappropriation."

(P. 178, l. 1 from bottom) The opposite seems to have occurred in only *one* case. The husband of Isabella Parasole, a famous woodblock carver, is thought to have adopted his wife's name. (According to Ernst Guhl, Die Frauen in der Kunstgeschichte [Women in art history], Berlin 1858, p. 97.)

(P. 179, l. 13) On bushmen, see Klemm, Allgemeine Kulturgeschichte der Menschheit [General cultural history of humanity], Leipzig 1844, vol. I, p. 336.

(P. 180, l. 11) Here I may call Kant himself as a witness for my view of the soullessness of woman. He says (Anthropologie, p. 234, ed. Kirchmann [*Anthropology from a Pragmatic Point of View,* translated by Victor Lyle Dowdell, London 1978, p. 222]): "'What the world says is *true,* and what it does is *good*' is a feminine principle which is hard to relate with *character* in the narrow sense of the word." But he adds: "However, there have been valiant women who, in connection with their own household, have developed their specific and proper character with honor." In any case, nobody will argue with honor that this qualification can save the "intelligible character" of Woman, which, according to Kant's principal theory is a purpose in itself.—Incidentally, if a Kantian who adhered only to the wording of the master objected to the whole exposition that according to Kant *all* rational beings have a claim to the intelligible character, one could reply that Woman actually has no reason in the Kantian sense. Since Woman has no relationship with values, the conclusion is justified that the legislator who establishes value is absent.

(P. 180, l. 20 from bottom) The significance and consequences of the profound difference between the psychic life of Man and Woman is still underrated, perhaps even in this book. Only rarely do we encounter some inklings, as for instance in Heinrich Spitta, Die Schlaf-und Traumzustände der menschlichen Seele mit besonderer Berücksichtigung ihres Verhältnisses zu den psychischen Alienationen [The human soul's states of sleep and dream with special reference to their relationship with psychic alienations], 2nd ed., Tübingen 1882, p. 301: "A decisive and pervasive influence on the whole of psychic life is primarily based on the difference between the sexes; this dividing line drawn by nature through the entire human world is documented in all areas of psychic life. As a result of the difference between the two sexes all our feelings, wishes, and desires, in a word our entire way of imagining, all our thoughts and endeavors assume a peculiar type, which becomes more and more pronounced in the course of the different stages of our lives, and in so doing, as it were, creates the mold in which each of us comprehends the whole of his own mental world in his own characteristic way. The difference between the psychic life of man and woman is enormous and extends to the smallest details."—Friedrich Nietzsche, Also Sprach Zarathustra, part III (Kapitel von den drei Bösen) [*Thus Spoke Zarathustra,* translated by R. J. Hollingdale, Harmondsworth 1961, Part Three: Of the Three Evil Things, p. 207: "And who has fully conceived *how strange* man and woman are to one another!"

(P. 180, l. 7 from bottom) Friedrich Albert Lange, Geschichte des Materialismus und Kritik seiner Bedeutung in der Gegenwart, book II, 5th ed. Leipzig 1896, p. 381 [*The History of Materialism, and Criticism of its Present Importance,* translated by Ernest Chester Thomas, London 2000, p. 168].

(P. 182, ll. 7 from bottom ff.) Contrast Theodor Lipps, Suggestion und Hypnose [Suggestion and hypnosis], Sitzungsberichte der philosophisch-historischen Klasse der königlichen Akademie der Wissenschaften zu München, 1897/II, p. 520: "Psychologically, the whole is always more than, and in a certain sense always before, the part." See in particular also the characterological treatises of Wilhelm Dilthey, already mentioned on several occasions.

(P. 183, l. 21) Cf. Kant, Kritik der reinen Vernunft, p. 289, ed. Kehrbach [*Critique of Pure Reason,* translated by Paul Guyer, Cambridge 1998].

(P. 183, l. 8 from bottom) A very interesting exposition that touches on mine at certain points is that of Oskar Ewald, Die sogenannte empirische Psychologie und der Transcendentalismus Kants [The so-called empirical psychology and the transcendentalism of Kant], Die Gnosis, half-monthly journal, Vienna, 5 March 1903, pp. 87–91. Ewald's aim is to provide a theory of psychological categories in the form of a table listing those intellectual concepts ("will, strength, and psychic activity") that make psychological experience possible in the first place. He writes that Kant only performed half the work, that is, the scientific part, but left the other half still to be done. I cannot agree with this view because if it were correct there would have to be two kinds of experience, external and, associated with it, internal, whereas in fact the coherence of psychic life is experienced directly and allows empirical rules of greater than merely comparative generality to be drawn from its observation (see p. 148). But I would not wish with these objections to dispose of the problem raised by Ewald. This problem, if pursued far enough, is perhaps the most profound philosophical problem, or identical with it; for the relationship between concept and idea, freedom and necessity, plays a part in it. And ultimately the whole question is most closely connected with the postulate of epistemology's independence of psychology. I cannot go into this in more detail and only wish to have made a reference to that idea which is a significant one even though it was published in a somewhat occult environment.

(P. 184, l. 8) E. Mach, Die Analyse der Empfindungen und das Verhältnis des Physischen zum Psychischen, 3rd ed., Jena 1902, pp. 60f. [*Contributions to the Analysis of the Sensations,* translated by C. M. Williams, Bristol 1998].

(P. 184, ll. 13 from bottom ff.) The French lines come from Edmond Rostand, Cyrano de Bergerac, Act I, Scene IV (Paris 1898, p. 43) [*Cyrano de Bergerac,* translated by Anthony Burgess, London 1985].

(P. 184, ll. 5 from bottom ff.) The views contested here are those of Mach, Die Mechanik, 4th ed., Leipzig 1901, pp. 478ff. [*The Science of Mechanics,* translated by Thomas J. McCormack, La Salle 1960].

(P. 185, l. 18) Wilhelm Windelband, Geschichte und Naturwissenschaft, Rektoratsrede [History and science, rector's address], Strasbourg 1894.

(P. 185, l. 15 from bottom) v. Schrenck-Notzing, Über Spaltung der Persönlichkeit (sogennantes Doppel-Ich) [On split personality (so-called double self)], Vienna 1896, p. 6, following Proust, mentions a case (the only one I have come across in literature) of a male hysteric with "condition prime" and "condition seconde." Some more cases have certainly been observed, but their number is minute in comparison to the mass of women with such changes in their psychic condition. That there are men with a "multiple self" proves nothing against the theses of my main text; for a man can also realize that one among the innumerable possibilities in him, he can also become a woman (cf. pp. 162, 239, 264).

(P. 185, l. 4 from bottom) Thus Heine says in a very bad poem (Letzte Gedichte, with reference to "Lazarus" 12 [*The Lazarus Poems,* translated by Alistair Elliot, Manchester 1990]):

> The figure of the real Sphinx
> Is like a woman's, not a Thing's—
> That's guff about the paws and claws,
> The lion's body, and the wings.
>
> The riddle of this real Sphinx
> Is dead obscure though. There were none
> So hard among the ones unravelled
> By Ms Jocasta's husband-son.

Second Part, Chapter X

(P. 190, l. 5f.) Only 34% of genuine prostitutes give birth (according to C. Lombroso and C. Ferrero, Das Weib als Verbrecherin und Prostituierte, translated into German by H. Kurella, Hamburg 1894, p. 540 [*The Female Offender,* London 1895]).

(P. 190, ll. 19 from bottom ff.) The view being rejected here is above all a well-known theory of social-democratic theoreticians, in particular August Bebel (Die Frau in der Vergangenheit, Gegenwart und Zukunft, 9th ed., Stuttgart 1891, pp. 140ff. [*Woman in the Past, Present and Future,* translated by H. B. Adams Walther, London 1988, pp. 91ff.]): "Prostitution, a necessary social institution of the bourgeois world." "Prostitution becomes a necessary social institution, just as much as the police, the standing army, the church, the capitalist, etc., etc."

(P. 190, l. 1 from bottom) On these honors awarded to prostitution cf. Heinrich Schurtz, Altersklassen und Männerbünde, Eine Darstellung der Grundformen der Gesellschaft [Age groups and men's associations, an exposition of the fundamental forms of society], Berlin 1902, pp. 198f. Also Lombroso-Ferrero, Das Weib als Verbrecherin und Prostituierte, Hamburg 1894, pp. 228ff.; on the Phoenicians, p. 230 [*The Female Offender,* London 1895].

(P. 191, ll. 17ff.) Schopenhauer's idea, corrected here, is stated in "Die Welt als Wille und Vorstellung," vol. II, p. 630, ed. Grisebach [*The World as Will and Idea,* translated by R. B. Haldane and J. Kemp, London 1883].

(P. 191, l. 21) Johannes Müller, Handbuch der Physiologie des Menschen für Vorlesungen [Handbook of human physiology for lectures], vol. II, part 2, Coblenz 1838, pp. 574f.: "In maternal impression . . . something positive is supposed to be produced and the form of the product is supposed to correspond to the form in the imagination. This effect is improbable if only because it is supposed to extend from one organism to the other; the connection between mother and child, however, is nothing but the closest possible juxtaposition of two in themselves totally independent organisms that attract each other with their surfaces and one of which supplies the nourishment and warmth that the other appropriates. [Precisely this, the idea of mere juxtaposition, is wrong. Cf. p. 198 of my main text.] But apart from that, the old and highly popular superstition of maternal impression can be refuted through many other reasons. I have the opportunity to see most deformed infants that are born in the Prussian monarchy. Nevertheless, I may say that despite this great opportunity I do not as a rule come across anything new of this kind, and that these only amount to a repetition of certain forms which range with the large number of inhibited developments, cleavages, fusions of lateral parts with defects of the central ones, etc. . . . If one further considers that surely every pregnant woman is often startled during her pregnancy, and that very many surely have such an impression, at least once if not more often, without this having any consequence, there will surely be no lack of opportunity, if a monster is born somewhere, to explain this in accordance with the popular belief. A reasonable theory of maternal impression is thus reduced to the fact that any intensely passionate state of the mother can have an equally sudden influence on the organic interaction between mother and child and consequently bring about an inhibition of the developments or a stoppage of the formations at certain stages of the metamorphosis without, however, the possibility of the woman's imagination having any influence on the point at which such retentions occur, etc."

T. Bischoff's article "Entwicklungsgeschichte mit besonderer Berücksichtigung der Mißbildungen" [Embryology with special reference to malformations] in Rudolf Wagner's Handwörterbuch der Physiologie [Concise dictionary of physiology], vol. I, Braunschweig 1842, pp. 885–889. To begin with, p. 886: "Meckel was first to point out rightly that the question about maternal impression, as it is commonly asked, usually contains two essentially different questions, firstly: Can the affects of the mother have an influence on the development of the new organism? and secondly: Can any affects of the mother that are caused by a specific object change the development of the new organism in such a way that it becomes identical or similar to that object? Although experience frequently shows that the fetus can develop quite independently of both the physical and the psychic states of the mother, and that therefore there is no absolutely necessary connection between the two, nevertheless thousands of cases have proved that the development of the progeny depends on the physical and psychic states of the mother so decisively that the first question must definitely be answered in the positive. . . . It was true in many cases, and it still happens, that a strong fright or emotion of the mother has caused a malformation, although the shape of that malformation did not correspond to the object of her fright. We see how numerous assertions can be explained by this fact with the aid of the imagination, which creates similarities where there are none. However, we are in a position to give more detailed explanations and information even for these similarities. . . . Thus it is understandable that fear and fright, depressing and debilitating influences can cause disruptions and inhibitions in the development of the embryo which, coincidentally and on isolated occasions, can have a certain similarity to the objects of the emotions." He further names eight objections "that must be raised to the explanation of certain malformations as originating in emotions of the mother caused by objects similar to those malformations." Having listed these well-known arguments—that I cannot repeat here—he concludes: "If we add to all this that we can explain most malformations by developmental laws and other causes that can be scientifically analyzed, *then everybody will probably have to admit that maternal impression can be regarded only as a very rare and limited cause of malformations.*" P. 885: "Hippocrates already defended a princess who had come under suspicion of adultery because she had given birth to a black child, by arguing that a picture of a Negro had been hanging at the foot of her bed. . . . Later it seems that the belief in maternal impressions was primarily strengthened by the unfortunate and pernicious delusion that malformations were the result of divine anger or demonic and sodomistic descent. The unfortunate mothers of such malformations were of course only too ready to divert away from themselves the terrible suspicion falling on them, and the consequent, often cruel punishments, by supporting the assumption of maternal impression as much as possible. This assumption therefore became the most common one, and the imagination had no difficulty in finding external objects to serve as the causes of malformations."

Charles Darwin, Das Variieren der Tiere und Pflanzen im Zustande der Domestikation, translated into German by J. Viktor Carus, vol. II, 2nd ed., Stuttgart 1873, p. 301 (chapter 22) [*The Variation of Animals and Plants under Domestication*, London 1868].

Negative attitude of breeding theorists: Hermann Settegast, Die Tierzucht [Animal breeding], 4th ed., vol. I; Die Züchtunglehre [The theory of selection], Breslau 1878, pp. 100–102, 219–222; p. 219: "The belief in the possibility of maternal impression is ancient. The Bible (1st book of Moses, 30, 37–39) already tells us that the patriarch Jacob knew how to produce artificially a "maternal impression" of the mother ewe and thereby create spotted lambs. He did so by putting into the watering troughs some sticks that had been given a spotted appearance by peeling the bark off in places. It may be left open whether Jacob believed that these spotted sticks produced the maternal impression during the mounting of the mother ewe, which seems to have occurred near the watering troughs, or whether *already pregnant* mother ewes were bound to produce lambs spotted like the sticks, when those striking objects were shown to them as they were drinking. In any case, Jacob achieved his avaricious aim, laying the foundations of his wealth. To this day accounts of this kind find believers." In a note added to this: "As late as 1874, Dr. J. in one of the most widely read and respected newspapers of Germany writes, among other things: 'It is a peculiar experience of the breeder that through the imagination of the mother animal, particularly if she is pregnant, the color of the surrounding objects, and especially the color of animals closest to her, is frequently transferred to her progeny. It has also been very often observed that the repeated and generous use of whitewash has frequently increased the proportion of white or white-spotted calves born in the stables and sheds concerned.' Stories of this and similar kinds bear witness to the careless way in which unfounded assertions, uncritically and out of the desire to titillate the reader, are dressed up as so-called experiences. . . . The circumstances and facts that speak against the possibility of maternal impression are so numerous that it appears to us almost like a residue of superstition if people continue to adhere to this untenable theory for the explanation of striking forms."

Finally I will cite a gynaecologist, Max Runge, Lehrbuch der Geburtshilfe [Textbook of obstetrics], 6th ed., Berlin 1901, pp. 82f.: "The question whether strong psychic impressions undergone by a pregnant woman can have an influence on the development of physical malformations or mental defects in the embryo (maternal impression in pregnant women) exercises many laymen. Modern scientific medicine, up to our own day, has rejected this question and, in particular, most firmly denied the possibility of a causal connection between psychic impression and an existing malformation of the child. Most recently, however, the question has been considered worthy of discussion. If the question may therefore still be scientifically arguable, in practice it is still advisable to oppose firmly the belief in so-called maternal impression among pregnant women and their environment."

Here Runge alludes to the treatises of J. Preuß, Vom Versehen der Schwangeren [On maternal impression in pregnant women], Berliner Klinik, no. 51 (1892), Ballantyne, Edinburgh Medical Journal, vol. XXXVI, 1891, and Gerhard von Welsenburg's study, Das Versehen der Frauen in Vergangenheit und Gegenwart und die Anschauungen der Ärzte, Naturforscher und Philosophen darüber [Maternal impression in women in the past and present, and the views of physicians, naturalists, and philosophers on this matter], Leipzig 1899. Von Welsenburg's detailed list finally leaves the question undecided.

On maternal impression and the certainly exaggerated desire to attribute all malformations to that cause alone, cf. also Ploß, Das Weib in der Natur-und Völkerkunde, 7th ed., 1902, vol. I, pp. 809–811 [*Woman: An Historical, Gynaecological and Anthropologial Compendium,* translated by Eric John Dingwall, London 1985], Benjamin Bablot, Dissertation sur le pouvoir de l'imagination des femmes enceintes [Dissertation on the power of imagination in pregnant women], E. v. Feuchtersleben, Die Frage über das Versehen der Schwangeren [The question of maternal impression in pregnant women], in Verhandlungen der k.k. Gesellschaft der Ärzte zu Wien, 1842, pp. 430f., and others, on whom information can be found in von Welsenburg. Von Welsenburg also cites numerous advocates of maternal impression (including Budge, Schönlein, Carus, Bechstein, Prosper Lucas, G. H. Bergmann, A. von Solbrig, Theodor Roth, Karl Hennig [the last two in Virchows Archiv 1883, 1886], Bichat, and others). In conclusion, I would only like to mention the comment of an outstanding, lucid, and sober researcher such as Karl Ernst von Baer on this question (in Physiologie als Erfahrungswissenschaft [Physiology as an empirical science], 2nd ed., vol. II, Leipzig 1837, p. 127, by another adherent of maternal impression, the admirable Karl Friedrich Burdach):

"A pregnant woman was very much frightened and disturbed by a flame visible in the distance, because she saw it in the region of her home. The consequences showed that she had not been wrong; but since the place was seven miles away it took a long time to be found out for certain, and this long period of uncertainty may have had a particularly strong effect on the woman, so that for a long time afterwards she claimed that she could constantly see the flame before her eyes. Two or three months after the fire she gave birth to a daughter, who had a red spot on her forehead which pointed upward in the shape of a leaping flame and did not fade until the child was seven. *I am reporting this case because I know it only too well, as it concerns my own sister,* and because it was *during her pregnancy* that she complained about the flame in front of her eyes and after the birth the cause of the anomaly was not, as usual, sought in the past."

(P. 192, l. 1f.) Henrik Ibsen, Die Frau vom Meer, Act II, Scene VII. [*The Lady from the Sea,* translated by Peter Watts, Harmondsworth 1965].—Goethe, Die Wahlverwandtschaften, part II, chapter 13 [*Elective Affinities,* translated by R. J. Hollingdale, Harmondsworth 1971, p. 286].— Von Welsenburg also refers to a hunter in Immermann's "Münchhausen" (Book II, chapter 7, pp. 168–175, ed. Hempel) [partly translated as *Der Oberhof. A Tale of Westphalian Life,* London 1879], who, as a result of a bad dream of his mother, was born with a mark shaped like a hunting knife below his heart.

It is interesting to hear the views of two scientists on the well-known episode in "Die Wahlverwandtschaften" [*Elective Affinities,* translated by R. J. Hollingdale, Harmondsworth 1971, p. 286]. H. Settegast, Die Tierzucht [Animal breeding], 4th ed., vol. I: Die Züchtungslehre [The theory of selection], Breslau, 1878, pp. 101f., first talks about the issue of the embryo being influenced by impressions of the mother during gestation, and continues: "It is reported that a foal with a white head was once born as a result of the fact that during the act of mating a boy who had covered his head with a white cloth was within the mating animals' range of vision. A piebald foal was born after the mare in season had been repeatedly led to the mating station in the company of a piebald horse. In another case the piebald skin of the foal is said to have been caused by the sudden appearance of a spotted hound during the act of mating. . . . If the objection were to be made that it is doubtful whether a phenomenon that a *human being* regards as sufficiently striking to occupy the imagination of a mating animal is also considered as such by the animal, one could cite from experience numerous cases in which the imagination of one of the animals engaged in the act must demonstrably have been occupied by a sensuous object. Thus in animal breeding, for example, a fairly common method of inducing a male animal to mate with a female that he does not desire is to place one of his favorites close to the one he scorns. Now he no longer refuses to mount, while the female favored by the male individual is swiftly pushed out of the way and replaced with the scorned one for copulation. *It has never been observed that the child of an animal deceived in this way resembled the object of his inclination, which must have occupied his imagination during the act of mating, and that a process described with poetic mastery by Goethe in his Elective Affinities had taken place. It is to his domain of imagination and poetry that the belief in the influence of psychic impressions on the product of procreation will have to be relegated.*"

Rudolf Wagner's addition to R. Leuckart's Artikel "Zeugung" [Procreation] in Wagner's Handwörterbuch der Physiologie [Concise dictionary of physiology], vol. IV, Braunschweig 1853, p. 1013, says much less dismissively: "As a result of a great fright there can be a miscarriage. Continuous grief can result in a general indisposition of the mother, which can cause a breakdown of her constitution, malnutrition, and illnesses of the fetus. But a specific influence through impressions of external objects on pregnant women must not be admitted, and the development of malformations, birth marks, etc. can never be connected to these. *The view of those who wish to assume that the physical and psychic development of the fetus is influenced by inner thought processes at the moment of sexual intercourse—in the sense of Goethe's Elective Affinities, where this view is expressed with the profoundness characteristic of a good judge of human nature—can be neither proved wrong nor confirmed from a physiological point of view.* Physiology has not penetrated to such depths and it is doubtful that it will ever reach them. *However, if I am to articulate my subjective judgment I must admit that I am inclined to doubt, rather than assume, such an influence of the mere imagination at the moment of the act of procreation.*"

Finally it may be noted that Kant also disputed maternal impression in the treatise Über die Bestimmung des Begriffs einer Menschenrasse [On the definition of the concept of a human race] (Berliner Monatsschrift, November 1785, vol. VIII, pp. 131–132, ed. Kirchmann): "It is clear that if we admitted that the magic power of the imagination or the artificial manipulation of animal bodies by human beings is capable of modifying the procreative power itself and to transform the primeval model of nature, or disfigure it with additions which would nevertheless be persistently preserved in subsequent acts of procreation, we would no longer be able to tell the original from which nature set out or the extent to which it is possible to change, and, given that the human imagination has no bounds, into what grotesque shapes the species and genera might finally degenerate. Bearing this in mind I will not, as a matter of principle, accept any bungling influence of the imagination on nature's business of procreation, nor any ability of man to bring about, through external manipulation, any modifications in the ancient original of the species and genera, to introduce these into procreativity and to make them hereditary. For if I admitted even one case of this kind it would be as if I admitted even one ghost story or magic trick, etc."

(P. 192, l. 4 from bottom f.) For the lack of any maternal feeling in prostitutes, cf. Lombroso-Ferrero, pp. 539f. of the German edition (Das Weib als Verbrecherin und Prostituierte, Hamburg 1894 [*The Female Offender,* London 1895]).

(P. 194, l. 17 from bottom) The moral arguments in favor of marriage are pure sophistry. Attempts to uphold it have even been made from the point of view of Kantian ethic—and there is no other ethic—as, for instance, by G. v. Hippel (Über die Ehe, 3rd ed., Berlin 1792, p. 150 [*On Marriage,* translated by Timothy F. Sellner, Detroit c. 1994, p. 144]): "Man is never a means, but always the end; never the instrument, always the agent, acting upon his own free will; he is never the object, but always the subject of pleasure! In marriage, two persons come together in order to find pleasure in each other: the woman wishes to be an 'object' for the man, and her husband as well takes a legally binding oath to give himself to her. Since both parties are willingly lowering themselves to the level of 'instruments,' however, each of which is in turn played by the other, the two 'null and voids' cancel each other out, and this one single contract for the enjoyment of another human being is permissible, necessary, and divinely ordained." Indeed Kant himself carries out a similar arithmetical operation in his Metaphysische Anfangsgründe der Rechtslehre (§ 25, pp. 88f., ed. Kirchmann) [*Metaphysical Elements of Justice. Part One of The Metaphysics of Morals,* translated by John Ladd, Indianapolis c. 1999, pp. 88–89]: "The natural use that one sex makes of the sexual organs of the other is a *pleasure* for which one party gives itself up to the other. In this act a person makes himself into a thing, which is inconsistent with the right of humanity in one's own Person. This is possible only under one condition, that, while one Person is acquired by the other *as if a thing,* this other [Person] in turn reciprocally acquires the first. For in that way the Person regains himself and once more reestablishes his Personhood. However, for a human being, the acquisition of a body part is at the same time the acquisition of the whole Person, for a Person is an absolute unity. Consequently, one sex's giving itself up and taking on [the other] for the pleasure of the other is not only allowable under the condition of marriage, but it is also *only* possible under that condition."

This justification seems very strange. Morally, two people stealing an equal amount from each other do not cancel each other's action out. This statement can probably only be explained by the small part that women played in Kant's psychic life and the low intensity of the erotic inclinations with which he had to contend.

(P. 195, l. 15f.) Cf. Joseph Hyrtl, Topographische Anatomie [Topographical anatomy], 5th ed., 1865, pp. 559f.: "The compression of the outlets of the individual glandular lobes is prevented by the hardening of the nipple, which becomes the stiffer, the more the mechanical stimulus exerted by the child's jaws on the nipple increases. The numerous touch corpuscles on the surface of the papilla will reward the mother's fulfilment of her duty with a pleasant tickle, which, however, is not sensual enough to win every mother over for the performance of her most sacred duty." (But every mother in the sense of true motherhood as developed in my main text in opposition to a prostitute's mentality.)—On the erection of the nipple itself, see L. Landois, Lehrbuch der Physiologie des Menschen, 9th ed., Vienna and Leipzig 1896, p. 441 [*A Text-book of Human Physiology,* translated by A. A. Eshner, London 1904, vol. 1, p. 424]: "During the release of milk, there is not only the mechanical action of sucking, but also the activity of the gland itself. This consists in the erection of the nipple, whereby its non-striped muscular fibres compress the sinuses on the milk-ducts, and empty them, so that the milk may flow out in streams."—On the contractions of the uterus, Max Runge, Lehrbuch der Geburtshilfe [Textbook of obstetrics] 4th ed., Berlin 1898, p. 180: "The stimulation of the nipples by sucking sets off contractions of the uterus."

(P. 195, l. 14 from bottom) Compare with this the following reflections of J. J. Bachofen, which perhaps deserve to be called profound (Das Mutterrecht, Stuttgart 1861, pp. 165f. [*Myth, Religion and Mother Right,* selected writings, translated by Ralph Manheim, Princeton 1973, passage not found in translation]): "Man appears as the moving principle. With the effect of the male force on the female material the movement of life, the cycle of ὁρατὸς κόσμος begins. While previously everything was in repose, now the first male deed sets off that eternal flow of things which is called forth by the first κίνησις and which, in the well-known image of Heraclitus, is never quite the same at any one moment. Through Peleus's deed the race of mortals is born from Thetis's immortal womb. Man brings death into the world. While the mother enjoys her own immortality, now, awakened by the phallus, her body releases a race of mortals hurrying forever toward death like a river and consuming themselves constantly like the fire of Meleager." On pp. 34f. also Bachofen says many fine things about the kind of immortality based on the "demetrian-tellurian principle."

(P. 196, l. 20f.) Schopenhauer, Die Welt als Wille und Vorstellung, vol. II, book 4, chapter 41 [*The World as Will and Idea,* translated by R. B. Haldane and J. Kemp, London 1883, pp. 249–308].

(P. 197, ll. 16ff.) Schopenhauer, Die Welt als Wille und Vorstellung, vol. II, book 4, chapter 44 [*The World as Will and Idea,* translated by R. B. Haldane and J. Kemp, London 1883, vol. 3, p. 340]: "The ultimate end of all love affairs, whether they are played in socks or cothurnus, is . . . more important than all other ends of human life, and is therefore quite worthy of the profound seriousness with which every one pursues it. That which is decided by it is nothing less than the *composition of the next generation,*" etc.

(P. 198, l. 12f.) For instance, Eduard von Hartmann, who is in any case extremely shallow and unoriginal, and who now seems to be regarded by some as a great thinker merely because he is not a university professor, says in his "Phänomenologie des sittlichen Bewußtseins, Prolegomena zu jeder künftigen Ethik" [Phenomenology of moral consciousness, prolegomena to any future ethics], Berlin 1879, pp. 268f.: "Imagine . . . a woman animated by the most naïve but most ruthless and most shameless selfishness who, from the day she becomes a mother, with the whole naïveté of feminine feeling, expands her self to include the persons of her children, shrinking from no sacrifice for their well-being, but who inflicts her expanded maternal selfishness on the outside world just as ruthlessly and shamelessly as she did her previous egoism, indeed even more unscrupulously, because she believes that her behavior is morally justified by her maternal duties. . . . Although such a one-sided love, which treats everything that lies outside this loving relationship with total disregard, is morally imperfect, it is nevertheless an immeasurable advance in principle beyond unyielding selfishness and plain self-love, showing a fundamental break with the exclusive devotion of the will to the welfare of the individual. One may say that in such a mother, for all the one-sidedness of her morality, an infinitely greater ethical *depth* is found than in the virtuoso of a morality of cleverness, the passive slaves of ecclesiastic moral formulae and the artist of aesthetic morality, all put together, because she has *fundamentally destroyed* the *root of all evil* in at least *one* respect, while the first two of the others are guided by considerations that lie outside the matter itself, and the third only by superficial and external aspects of it. Such a love will therefore inspire moral respect and, in its higher degrees, even awe and admiration, even where its one-sidedness leads to immoral behavior in other directions." All these errors arise from the entirely untenable belief in an instinctive, naïve, unconscious, and therefore perfect morality, which is found everywhere in spite of Kant. It will be necessary to keep repeating that morality and consciousness, just as unconsciousness and immorality, are the same thing. (Thus Hartmann speaks of "unconscious morality," op. cit., p. 311; it must, however, be granted that elsewhere he makes more perceptive judgments about women; e.g., p. 526: "The lack of lawfulness and justice makes the female sex as a whole a moral parasite of the male.")

(P. 199, l. 2) Johann Fischart, Das philosophische Ehzuchtbüchlein [The philosophical booklet of morality in marriage]—Jean Richepin's well-known ballad "La Glu" [Bird glue] from the Breton (in "La Chanson des Gueux" [The song of the beggars]). H. Heine could also have been listed here owing to several of his poems.

(P. 199, l. 7) J. J. Bachofen, Das Mutterrecht, Eine Untersuchung über die Gynaikokratie der alten Welt nach ihrer religiösen und rechtlichen Natur, Stuttgart 1861, p. 10 [*Myth, Religion and Mother Right,* selected writings, translated by Ralph Manheim, Princeton 1973, p. 79]: "At the lowest, darkest stages of human existence the love between the mother and her offspring is the bright spot in life, the only light in the moral darkness, the only joy amid profound misery." "The relationship which stands at the origin of all culture, of every virtue, of every nobler aspect of existence, is that between mother and child; it operates in a world of violence as the divine principle of love, of union, of peace." Bachofen is a much more profound and far-sighted man, with a more universal and more genuine philosophical education, than any sociologist since Hegel; and yet here he overlooks something as obvious as the total absence of differences between maternal love in animals (hens, cats) and humans.

Robert Hamerling, normally a rhetorician rather than a genuine artist, makes a good remark about maternal love, which clearly shows, apparently without his intention to do so, that here there can be no question of morality (Ahasver in Rom [Ahasverus in Rome], canto II, Werke, Volksausgabe, vol. I, p. 59):

> Maternal love, you see, is the legal minimum
> Of happiness in love that mean nature
> Bequeaths to every creature—the rest
> Is illusion and deceit. *It truly delights me*
> *That there is a creature for which*
> *It is an eternal and natural necessity to love me.*

(P. 199, l. 19) On the famous Karoline, see Minna Cauer, Die Frau im XIX. Jahrhundert [Woman in the 19th century], Berlin 1898 (in Am Ende des Jahrhunderts, Rückschau auf hundert Jahre geistiger Entwicklung [At the end of the century, a review of a hundred years of intellectual development], edited by Dr. Paul Bernstein), pp. 32–37.

(P. 200, l. 8 from bottom) In the Renaissance there was no shortage of approximations to those greater hetairas (Aspasia, Cleopatra). See Burckhardt, Die Kultur der Renaissance in Italien, 4th ed. by L. Geiger, vol. I, p. 127 [*The Civilisation of the Renaissance in Italy,* translated by S. G. C. Middlemore, Harmondsworth 1990].

(P. 202, l. 6 from bottom) The story about Napoleon from Emerson, Repräsentanten des Menschengeschlechtes, translated into German by Oskar Dähnert, Leipzig, Universalbibliothek, p. 199 [Representative Men, Cambridge, Mass., London 1987, p. 146].

(P. 205, l. 18) This view of motherhood is closest to that of Aischylus (Eumenides, V, ll. 658f. [*The Oresteia,* translated by Robert Fagles, London 1984]):

Οὐκ ἔστι μήτηρ ἡ κεκλημένου τέκνου
τοκεύς, τροφὸς δὲ κύματος νεοσπόρου.
τίκτει δ' ὁ θρῴσκων, ἡ δ' ἅπερ ξένῳ ξένη
ἔσωσεν ἔρνος, οἷσι μὴ βλάψῃ θεός

(P. 206, l. 12) The illusion of fatherhood gave its name to August Strindberg's powerful tragedy "Der Vater" [*The Father,* translated by Michael Meyer, London 1986]. (With special reference to this point, see p. 34 of this extraordinary work of literature [translated into German by E. Brausewetter, Universalbibliothek].)

(P. 206, l. 15) Bachofen, Das Mutterrecht, p. 9 [*Myth, Religion and Mother Right,* translated by Ralph Manheim, Princeton 1973, pp. 132–133]: "The very word matrimony (literally mother-marriage) is based on the fundamental idea of mother right. One said *matrimonium,* not *patrimonium* (father-marriage, paternal inheritance), just as one originally spoke of a *materfamilias. Paterfamilias* is unquestionably a later term. Plautus uses the word *materfamilias* several times, *paterfamilias* not once. According to mother right there is, to be sure, a *pater,* but no *paterfamilias. Familia* is a purely physical concept, and hence relates at first only to the mother. The transfer to the father is an *improprie dictum* (a derived term), adopted as a legal term but only later prevalent in common nonjuridical sense. The father is always a juridical fiction, the mother a physical fact. Paulus states: 'The mother is always certain, even though she has conceived by all and sundry; the father, on the other hand, is only he who is mentioned in the marriage certificate.' As Paulus puts it, mother right is *natura verum* (true by nature), the father exists only *iure civili* (in civil law)."

(P. 206, l. 17) Herbert Spencer, Die Unzulänglichkeit der natürlichen Zuchtwahl, Biologisches Zentralblatt, XIV, 1894, pp. 262f. [*The Inadequacy of Natural Selection,* London 1893, pp. 60–62]: "I am much indebted to a distinguished correspondent who has drawn my attention to verifying facts furnished by the offspring of whites and negroes in the United States. Referring to information given him many years ago, he says: 'It was to the effect that the children of white women by a black father had been *repeatedly* observed to show traces of black blood, in cases when the woman had previously connection with [*i.e.,* a child by] a negro.' At the time I received this information, an American was visiting me; and, on being appealed to, answered that in the United States there was an established belief to this effect. Not wishing, however, to depend upon hearsay, I at once wrote to America to make inquiries . . . Professor Marsh, the distinguished palæontologist, of Yale, New Haven, who is also collecting evidence, sends a preliminary letter in which he says: 'I do not myself know of such a case, but have heard many statements that make their existence probable. One instance, in Connecticut, is vouched for so strongly by an acquaintance of mine, that I have good reason to believe it to be authentic.'

That cases of the kind should not be frequently seen in the North, especially nowadays, is of course to be expected. The first of the above quotations refers to facts observed in the South during slavery days; and even then, the implied conditions were naturally very infrequent. Dr. W. J. Youmans of New York has, on my behalf, interviewed several medical professors, who, though they have not themselves met with instances, say that the alleged result, described above, 'is generally accepted as a fact.' But he gives me what I think must be regarded as authoritative testimony. It is a quotation from the standard work of Professor Austin Flint, and runs as follows:

'A peculiar and, it seems to me, an inexplicable fact is that previous pregnancies have an influence upon offspring. This is well known to breeders of animals. If pure-blooded mares or bitches have been once covered by an inferior male, in subsequent fecundations the young are likely to partake of the character of the first male, even if they be afterward bred with males of unimpeachable pedigree. What the mechanism of the influence of the first conception is, it is impossible to say; but the fact is incontestable. The same influence is observed in the human subject. A woman may have, by a second husband, children who resemble a former husband, and this is particularly well marked in certain instances by the color of the hair and eyes. A white woman who has had children by a negro may subsequently bear children to a white man, these children presenting some of the unmistakable peculiarities of the negro race.' [*A Text-Book of Human Physiology.* By Austin Flint, M.D., LL.D. Fourth edition. New York: D. Appleton & Co. 1888, p. 797.]

Dr. Youmans called on Professor Flint, who remembered 'investigating the subject at the time his larger work was written [the above is from an excerpt], and said that he had never heard the report questioned.'" (For the same question, see Spencer, Biolog. Zentralblatt, XIII, 1893, pp. 743–748).

(P. 206, l. 20) See Charles Darwin, Über die direkte oder unmittelbare Einwirkung des männlichen Elementes auf die Mutterform ["On the Direct or Immediate Action of the Male Element on the Mother Form"] (Das Variieren der Tiere und Pflanzen im Zustande der Domestikation, chapter 11, vol. I, 2nd ed. Stuttgart 1873, pp. 445f. [*The Variation of Animals and Plants under Domestication,* London 1868, vol. I, pp. 397–405]): "Another remarkable class of facts must be here considered, because they have been supposed to account for some cases of bud-variation: I refer to the direct action of the male element, not in the ordinary way on the ovules, but on certain parts of the female plant, or in the case of animals on the subsequent progeny of the female by a second male. I may premise that with plants the ovarium and the coats of the ovules are obviously parts of the female, and it could not have been anticipated that they would be affected by the pollen of a foreign variety or species, although the development of the embryo, within the embryonic sack, within the ovule, within the ovarium, of course depends on the male element."

Even as long ago as 1729 it was observed ("Philosophical Transactions," vol. 43, 1744–45, p. 525) that white and blue varieties of the Pea, when planted near each other, mutually crossed, no doubt through the agency of bees, and in the autumn blue and white peas were found within the same pods. Wiegmann made an exactly similar observation in the present century. The same result has followed several times when a variety with peas of one colour has been artificially crossed by a differently-coloured variety (Mr. Swayne, in "Transact. Hort. Soc.," vol. 5, p. 234, and Gärtner, "Bastarderzeugung," 1849, pp. 81 and 499). These statements led Gärtner, who was highly sceptical on the subject, carefully to try a long series of experiments: he selected the most constant varieties, and the result conclusively showed that the colour of the skin of the pea is modified when pollen of a differently coloured variety is used. This conclusion has since been confirmed by experiments made by the Rev. J. M. Berkeley ("Gard. Chron.," 1854, p. 404).

(P. 447 [p. 398]): "Turning now to the genus Matthiola. The pollen of one kind of stock sometimes affects the colour of the seeds of another kind, used as the mother-plant. I give the following case the more readily, as Gärtner doubted similar statements with respect to the stock previously made by other observers. A well-known horticulturist, Major Trevor Clarke, informs me (see also a paper by this observer, read before the International Hort. and Bot. Congress of London, 1866) that the seeds of the large red-flowered *biennial* stock (*Matthiola annua; Cocardeau* of the French) are light brown, and those of the purple branching Queen stock (*M. incana*) are violet-black; and he found that, when flowers of the red stock were fertilised by pollen from the purple stock, they yielded about fifty per cent. of *black* seeds. He sent me four pods from a red-flowered plant, two of which had been fertilised by their own pollen, and they included pale brown seed; and two which had been crossed by pollen from the purple kind, and they included seeds all deeply tinged with black. These latter seeds yielded purple-flowered plants like their father; whilst the pale brown seeds yielded normal red-flowered plants; and Major Clarke, by sowing similar seeds, has observed on a greater scale the same result. The evidence in this case of the direct action of the pollen of one species on the colour of the seeds of another species appears to me conclusive."

Here Darwin places special emphasis on the radical alteration of the mother plant by the male pollen. Thus in the English text (2nd ed., London, 1875), vol. II, pp. 430f.): "Professor Hildebrand (Botanische Zeitung, May 1868, p. 326) . . . has fertilised . . . a kind [of maize] bearing yellow grains with the precaution that the mother-plant was true. A kind bearing yellow grains was fertilised with pollen of a kind having brown grains, and two ears produced yellow grains, but one side of the spindle was tinted with a reddish brown; *so that here we have the important fact of the influence of the foreign pollen extending to the axis.*" (P. 449 of the German edition [vol. I, p. 400]): "Mr. Sabine (Transact. Horticult. Soc., vol. 5, p. 69) states that he has seen the form of the nearly globular seed-capsule of *Amaryllis vittata* altered by the application of the pollen of another species, of which the capsule has gibbous angles."

(P. 459 [vol. I, p. 401]): "I have now shown on the authority of several excellent observers, in the case of plants belonging to widely different orders, that the pollen of one species or variety, when applied to a distinct form, occasionally causes the coats of the seeds and the ovarium or fruit, including even in one instance the calyx and upper part of the peduncle of the mother-plant, to become modified. Sometimes the whole of the ovarium or all the seeds are thus affected; sometimes only a certain number of the seeds, as in the case of the pea, or only a part of the ovarium, as with the striped orange, mottled grapes and maize, are thus affected. It must not be supposed that any direct or immediate effect invariably follows the use of foreign pollen: this is far from being the case; nor is it known on what conditions the result depends."

(P. 451 [vol. II, p. 402]): "The proofs of the action of foreign pollen on the mother-plant have been given in considerable detail, because this action [. . .] is of the highest theoretical importance, and because it is in itself a remarkable and apparently anomalous circumstance. That it is remarkable under a physiological point of view is clear, for the male element not only affects, in accordance with its proper function, the germ, but the surrounding tissues of the mother-plant." (Here the English edition I[2], p. 430, continues): "*We thus see, that an ovule is not indispensable for the reception of the influence of the male element.*"

(P. 206, l. 22) I quote the famous report in the original (Philosophical Transactions of the Royal Society of London, 1821, part I, pp. 20f.):

A communication of a singular fact in Natural History, By the Right Honourable Earl of Morton, F.R.S., in a letter addressed to the President.

Read, November 23, 1820

My Dear Sir,

I yesterday had an opportunity of observing a singular fact in Natural History, which you may perhaps deem not unworthy of being communicated to the Royal Society.

Some years ago, I was desirous of trying the experiment of domesticating the Quagga, and endeavoured to procure some individuals of that species. I obtained a male: but being disappointed of a female, I tried to breed from the male quagga and a young chestnut mare of seven-eighths Arabian blood and which had never been bred from: the result was the production of a female hybrid, now five years old, and bearing, both in her form and in her colour, very decided indications of her mixed origin. I subsequently parted with the seven-eighth Arabia mare to Sir Gore Ouseley, who has bred from her a very fine black Arabian horse. I yesterday morning examined the produce, namely, a two-years old filly, and a year-old colt. They have the character of the Arabian breed as decidedly as can be expected, where fifteen-sixteenths of the blood are Arabian; and they are fine specimens of that breed; *but both in their colour, and in the hair of their manes, they have a striking resemblance to the quagga.* Their colour is bay, marked more or less like the quagga in a darker tint. Both are distinguished by the dark line along the ridge of the back, the dark stripes across the fore-hand, and the dark bars across the back-part of the legs. The stripes across the fore-hand of the colt are confined to the withers, and to the part of the neck next to them; those on the filly cover nearly the whole of the neck and the back, as far as the flanks. The colour of her coat on the neck adjoining to the mane is pale and approaching to dun, rendering the stripes there more conspicuous than those on the colt. The same pale tint appears in a less degree on the rump: and in this circumstance of the dun tint also she resembles the quagga . . . [p. 22]. These circumstances may appear singular; but I think you will agree with me that they are trifles compared with the extraordinary fact of so many striking features, which do not belong to the dam, being in two successive instances communicated through her to the progeny, not only of another sire, who also has them not, but of a sire belonging probably to another species; for such we have very strong reason for supposing the quagga to be.

I am, my dear Sir
Your faithful humble servant

Morton.

(P. 206, l. 20 from bottom f.) In particular detail H. Settegast, Die Tierzucht [Animal breeding], 4th ed., vol. I: Die Züchtungslehre [The theory of selection], Breslau 1878, pp. 223–234: Infektion (Superfötation) [Infection (superfetation)]. He relegates everything to the realm of superstition and fantasy. "So we come to the conclusion that the supposed infection of the mother is based on an illusion and that it is inadmissible to try and explain through it those cases in which the child does not correspond to the parents in color and pattern, in shape and characteristics. From our examinations of deviations from parental relationship so far, it is evident that the isolated cases which infection theory interprets in its own favor, and which can at the same time be seen as proven, must be attributed to the emergence of new forms in nature.

We believe that our explanations have refuted the infection theory: we can hardly hope to have succeeded in banishing it forever. The infection theory is the Loch Ness monster of genetics."

(P. 206, l. 18 from bottom) F. C. Mahnke, Die Infektionstheorie [The infection theory], Stettin 1864. On this question, cf. also Rudolf Wagner, addition to R. Leuckart's article "Zeugung" [Procreation] in Wagner's Handwörterbuch der Physiologie [Concise dictionary of physiology], vol. IV, 1853, pp. 1011ff. Oskar Hertwig, Die Zelle und die Gewebe, vol. II, Jena 1898, pp. 137f. [*The Cell, Outlines of General Anatomy and Physiology,* translated by M. Campbell, London, New York 1895].

(P. 206, l. 18 from bottom) August Weismann, Das Keimplasma, Eine Theorie der Vererbung, Jena 1892, pp. 503f. [*The Germ-Plasm. A Theory of Heredity,* translated by W. Newton Parker and Harriet Rönnfeldt, London 1893]. Die Allmacht der Naturzüchtung, Jena 1893, pp. 81–84, 87–91 [*The All-Sufficiency of Natural Selection. A Reply to Herbert Spencer,* Contemporary Review 64 (1893)]. Weismann, as he is bound to do (in accordance with his conviction of the total imperviousness of the plasm to any influence), takes a negative attitude and invokes above all the detailed explanations of Settegast. Similarly Hugo de Vries, Intracellulare Pangenesis, Jena 1889, pp. 206–207 [*Intracellular Pangenesis,* translated by C. S. Gager, Chicago 1910].

In contrast, Darwin is convinced of the "direct action of the male element on the female" (not merely on a single germ-cell), Das Variieren der Tiere und Pflanzen im Zustande der Domestikation, chapter 27 (*The Variation of Animals and Plants under Domestication,* vol. II^2, p. 414, Stuttgart 1873, London 1868, vol. 2, p. 365); as must be anybody who observes the enormous change that occurs in women immediately on marriage, and their extraordinary assimilation to their husband in the course of married life. See in my main text pp. 252, 265. According to Darwin, op. cit., p. 414 [p. 365]: "We here see that the male element affecting and hybridising not that part which it is properly adapted to affect, namely the ovule, but the partially developed tissues of a distinct individual."

Darwin speaks in more detail about telegony in chapter 11 of the same work, where he cites from the literature a large number of cases which supply proof of it (vol. I^2, pp. 453–455 [vol. I, pp. 404–405]):

"With respect to the varieties of our domesticated animals, many similar and well-authenticated facts have been published, and others have been communicated to me, plainly showing the influence of the first male on the progeny subsequently borne by the other to other males. It will suffice to give a single instance, recorded in the 'Philosophical Transactions,' in a paper following that by Lord Morton: Mr. Giles put a sow of Lord Western's black and white Essex breed to a wild boar of a deep chestnut colour; and the 'pigs produced partook in appearance of both boar and sow, but in some the chestnut colour of the boar strongly prevailed.' After the boar had long been dead, the sow was put to a boar of her own black and white breed,—a kind which is well known to breed very true and never to show any chestnut colour,—yet from this union the sow produced some young pigs which were plainly marked with the same chestnut tint as in the first litter. *Similar cases have so frequently occurred, that careful breeders avoid putting a choice female to an inferior male on account of the injury to her subsequent progeny which may be expected to follow.*

Some physiologists have attempted to account for these remarkable results from a first impregnation by the close attachment and freely intercommunicating blood-vessels between the modified embryo and the mother. But it is a most improbable hypothesis that the mere blood of one individual should affect the reproductive organs of another individual in such a manner as to modify the subsequent offspring. The analogy from the direct action of foreign pollen on the ovarium and seed-coats of the mother-plant strongly supports the belief that the male element acts directly on the reproductive organs of the female, wonderful as is this action, and not through the intervention of the crossed embryo."

Wilhelm Olbers Focke, Die Pflanzen-Mischlinge, Ein Beitrag zur Biologie der Gewächse [The hybrid plants, a contribution to the biology of plants], Berlin 1881, pp. 510–518: "I suggest . . . that such deviations from the normal shapes or coloring as are produced in any part of a plant through the influence of strange pollen should be called xeniae, because they are, as it were, gifts from the plant donating the pollen to the plant receiving the pollen" (p. 511).

(P. 206, l. 4 from bottom) For "maternal impression," see notes to p. 191f.

(P. 207, l. 4) Just as I argued for maternal impression by reference to Goethe and Ibsen, I could have argued for the reality of telegony by reference to the work of a great artist, had my attention been drawn to it before I completed this chapter: I mean Madeleine Férat, the little read but very magnificent novel of the young Zola. Judged by this and other works, what Zola thought about women must have been very close to my views. See Madeleine Férat, Nouvelle édition, Paris, Bibliothèque-Charpentier 1898, pp. 173f., particularly pp. 181ff. and 251f. [*Madeleine Férat,* translated by Alec Brown, London 1957], passages that I cannot include here because of their great length.

(P. 208, l. 4) About pimps, cf. Lombroso-Ferrero, Das Weib als Verbrecherin und Prostituierte, Hamburg 1894, pp. 560ff. of the German edition, and about their identity with actual criminals, ibid. pp. 563–564 [*The Female Offender,* London 1895].

Second Part, Chapter XI

(P. 211, ll. 7ff.) Schopenhauer, Parerga und Paralipomena, vol. II, chapter XXVII [*Parerga and Paralipomena,* translated by E. F. J. Payne, Oxford 2000].—The story about Lord Byron is reproduced from R. von Hornstein by Eduard Grisebach in the appendix to Schopenhauer's Sämtliche Werke [Complete works], vol. VI, pp. 191f.

(P. 212, l. 16) Kant, Beobachtungen über das Gefühl des Schönen und Erhabenen, Königsberg 1764, section III (vol. VIII, p. 36 of Kirchmann's edition) [*Observations on the Feeling of the Beautiful and Sublime,* translated by John T. Goldthwait, Berkeley, Los Angeles 1960, p. 86]: "This complete fascination is really overlaid upon the sexual instinct. Nature pursues its great purpose, and all refinements that join together, though they may appear to stand as far from that as they will, are only trimmings and borrow their charm ultimately from that very source."—Schopenhauer in his repeatedly quoted "Metaphysik der Geschlechtsliebe" ["Metaphysics of the Love of the Sexes"] (Die Welt als Wille und Vorstellung, vol. II, chapter 44 [*The World as Will and Idea,* translated by R. B. Haldane and J. Kemp, London 1883, vol. 3, p. 340]).

(P. 213, l. 22 from bottom f.) Schopenhauer, Parerga und Paralipomena, vol. II, § 369 [*Parerga and Paralipomena,* translated by E. F. J. Payne, Oxford 2000].

(P. 214, l. 11) Kant, Kritik der reinen Vernunft, Transcendentale Dialektik, I, 3, System der transcendentalen Ideen (pp. 287ff., Kehrbach) [*Critique of Pure Reason,* translated by Paul Guyer, Cambridge 1998, book I, "The Transcendental Dialectic," section 3, "The System of Transcendental Ideas"].

(P. 214, ll. 18 from bottom ff.) The song is that of Wolfram in Wagner's Tannhäuser, Act II, Scene 4 [*Tannhäuser,* translated by Rodney Blumer, London 1988, p. 80].

(P. 218, l. 20) Plato, Phaedrus, p. 251 A.B. [*Phaedrus,* translated by James H. Nichols, Jr., Ithaca, N.Y., London 1998]: "ὅταν θεοειδὲς πρόσωπον ἴδῃ κάλλος εὖ μεμιμημένον, ἤ τινα σώματος ἰδέαν, πρῶτον μὲν ἔφριξε . . . εἶτα προσορῶν ὡς θεὸν σέβεται, καὶ εἰ μὴ δεδιείη τὴν τῆς σφόδρα μανίας δῆξαν, θύοι ἂν ὡς ἀγάλματι καὶ θεῷ τοῖς παιδικοῖς. ἰδόντα δὲ αὐτόν, οἷον ἐκ τῆς φρίκης, μεταβολή τε καὶ ἱδρὼς καὶ θερμότης ἀήθης λαμβάνει. δεξάμενος γὰρ τοῦ κάλλους τὴν ἀπορροὴν διὰ τῶν ὀμμάτων, ἐθερμάνθη ᾗ ἡ τοῦ πτεροῦ φύσις ἄρδεται. θερμανθέντος δὲ ἐτάκη τὰ περὶ τὴν ἔκφυσιν, ἃ πάλαι ὑπὸ σκληρότητος συμμεμυκότα εἶργε μὴ βλαστάνειν. ἐπιρρυείσης δὲ τῆς τροφῆς ᾤδησέ τε καὶ ὥρμησε φύεσθαι ἀπὸ τῆς ῥίζης ὁ τοῦ πτεροῦ καυλὸς ὑπὸ πᾶν τὸ τῆς ψυχῆς εἶδος. πᾶσα γὰρ ἦν τὸ πάλαι πτερωτή."

(P. 219, l. 19) Cf. Dante, Paradiso, Canto VII, ll. 64–66: "La divina bontà, che da sè sperne Ogni livore, ardendo in sè sfavilla Si che dispiega le bellezze interne" [*The Divine Comedy,* translated by Mark Musa, vol. 3, *Paradise,* Harmondsworth 1986].

(P. 219, l. 12 from bottom) Kant, Kritik der Urteilskraft [*The Critique of Judgement,* translated by James Creed Meredith, Oxford 1978].—Schelling, System des transcendentalen Idealismus, Sämtliche Werke, section I, vol. III. [*System of Transcendental Idealism,* translated by Peter Heath, Charlottesville, Va. 1978].—Schiller, Über die ästhetische Erziehung des Menschen [*On the Aesthetic Education of Man,* translated by Reginald Snell, Bristol 1994].

(P. 219, l. 5 from bottom) Shaftesbury: according to W. Windelband, Geschichte der neueren Philosophie in ihrem Zusammenhange mit der allgemeinen Kultur und den besonderen Wissenschaften, 2nd. ed., Leipzig 1899, vol. I, p. 272 [A History of Philosophy, 2nd ed., translated by James H. Tufts, London 1931].—Herbart, Analytische Beleuchtung des Naturrechts und der Moral [An analytical elucidation of natural law and morality], Göttingen 1836, Sämtliche Werke [Complete works], ed. Hartenstein, vol. VIII, pp. 213ff.

(P. 222, l. 18) Plato's Gastmahl, 206 E [*Symposium,* translated by Tom Griffith, London 1991].

(P. 222, ll. 19 from bottom ff.) Plato, op. cit., chapter 27, l. 209 C–E (German translation by Schleiermacher) [*Symposium,* translated by Tom Griffith, London 1991, p. 50].

(P. 223, l. 5f.) Novalis: "It is miraculous enough that the association of lust, religion, and cruelty has not long since drawn people's attention to their close relationship and common tendency." (Novalis' Schriften [Novalis's writings], ed. Ludwig Tieck and F. Schlegel, part II, Vienna 1820, p. 288.)

(P. 223, l. 7) Bachofen, Das Mutterrecht, Stuttgart 1861, p. 52 [*Myth, Religion, and Mother Right,* selected writings, translated by Ralph Manheim, Princeton 1973, p. 164]: "Death as well as life . . . both are encompassed by material, tellurian being. All personifications of the chthonian power of earth combine these two aspects, coming into being and passing away, the two poles between which, as Plato said, the cycle of all things moves. Thus Venus, goddess of material generation, is also Libitina, the goddess of death. At Delphi there is a pillar named Epitymbia (on the tomb), and hither the departed are summoned to partake of the sacrifices offered up to them. In the Roman mortuary inscription found near Campana's columbarium, Priapus is called *mortis et vitai locus.* And no motif is more frequent in the tombs than Priapus, symbol of material generation. [Sentence missing in translation:] In southern Etruria there is even a tomb at the entrance of which, on the right doorpost, a female sporium is represented."—The cycle of death and life was also a favorite theme of Buddha's speeches. However, it was also taught by the most profound of Pre-Eleatic Greeks, Anaximandros (see Simplicius in Aristot., Physika 24, 18 [*Physics,* books I and II, translated by W. Charlton, Oxford 1970]): "ἐξ ὧν ἡ γένεσίς ἐστι τοῖς οὖσι, καὶ τὴν φθορὰν εἰς ταὐτὰ γίνεσθαι κατὰ χρεών. διδόναι γὰρ αὐτὰ τίσιν καὶ δίκην τῆς ἀδικίας κατὰ τὴν τοῦ χρόνου τάξιν."

(P. 223, l. 15 from bottom f.) Giordano Bruno, Gli eroici furori, 2nd dialogue 13 (Opere di G. B. Nolano, ed. Adolfo Wagner, vol. II, Leipzig 1830, p. 332 [*The Heroic Frenzies,* translated by Paul Eugene Memmo, Chapel Hill 1964]): "Tutti gli amori, se sono eroici, e non son puri animali, che chiamano naturali e cattivi a la generazione come instrumenti de la natura, in certo modo hanno per oggetto la divinità, tendono a la divina bellezza, la quale prima se comunica a l'anime e risplende in quelle, e da quelle poi, o per dir meglio, per quelle poi si comunica a li corpi."

(P. 223, ll. 14ff.) E. v. Hartmann, Phänomenologie des sittlichen Bewußtseins, 1879, p. 699, only echoes the general opinion: "It is time to make it clear to adolescent girls that their vocation, prescribed to them by their sex, can only be fulfilled in their position as wife and mother, that it consists in nothing other than in giving birth to and bringing up children, that the most capable and honorable woman is she who has given humanity the largest number of well brought-up children, and that all so-called vocational training of girls is only a sad makeshift solution for those who are unlucky enough to have missed their true vocation."

(P. 224, ll. 2ff.) Particularly in Judaism, even today, sterile women are sometimes regarded as useless (cf. chapter XIII, p. 281). But according to German law also "a man was entitled . . . to demand a divorce because of his wife's sterility." Jakob Grimm, Deutsche Rechtsaltertümer [German legal antiquities], 4th ed., Leipzig 1899, p. 626.

(P. 224, ll. 15ff.) The French quotation comes from the cycle "sagesse" [Wisdom] (Paul Verlaine, Choix de Poésies, Edition augmentée d'une Préface de François Coppée, Paris 1902, p. 179).

(P. 226, l. 20) See Liebeslieder moderner Frauen [Love songs of modern women] collected by Paul Grabein, Berlin 1902.

(P. 227, l. 8f.) Poros and Penia as parents of Eros: according to the profound fable in Plato's Symposion (p. 203, B–D) [Symposium, translated by Tom Griffith, London 1991]. Cf. pp. 228 and 267.

(P. 227, l. 5 from bottom) On the effect of the male genital on the female sex, cf. an account by Freud (Breuer and Freud, Studien über Hysterie, Leipzig, Vienna, p. 113 [*Studies on Hysteria,* translated by A. A. Brill, Boston 1960]; and above all the magnificent scene in Zola's novel "Germinal" (Quinzième partie, Fin, p. 416) [*Germinal,* translated by Peter Collier, Oxford 1993], where the women catch sight of the genitals of Maigrat, who has been murdered and, after his death, castrated.

(P. 228, l. 6) I did not realize till long after I had written down this passage that in Latin "fascinum" (e.g., Horace, Epod. 8, 18 [*Odes and Epodes,* translated by David Mulroy, Ann Arbor c. 1994]), from which "fascinare" is derived, means none other than the male member.

(P. 228, l. 12 from bottom f.) Plato, Symposion, 202, D–E [*Symposium,* translated by Tom Griffith, London 1991]: "Τί οὖν ἂν εἴη ὁ Ἔρως; . . . Μεταξὺ θνητοῦ καὶ ἀθανάτου, . . . δαίμων μέγας, ὦ Σώκρατες· καὶ γὰρ πᾶν τὸ δαιμόνιον μεταξύ ἐστι θεοῦ καὶ θνητοῦ." E· οὔτε ἀπορεῖ Ἔρως ποτὲ οὔτε πλουτεῖ. σοφίας τε αὖ καὶ ἀμαθίας ἐν μέσῳ ἐστίν."

(P. 228, ll. 8 from bottom ff.) The latest interpreter of Greek thought is a follower of Mill: Theodor Gomperz, Griechische Denker, eine Geschichte der antiken Philosophie, vol. II, Leipzig 1902, pp. 201ff. [*Greek Thinkers. A History of Ancient Philosophy,* translated by Laurie Magnus, London 1901–1912, vol. 2, pp. 335–336]. In some places this author of often outstanding merit seems himself to have felt how far he is from understanding the inner motives of the philosopher's thought. Those passages in the book where the author believes that he understands Plato and feels obliged to praise him are more interesting. Only two passages of the "Republic" find full favor with the spirit of modernity, which achieved the highest syntheses of which it was capable in the game of lawn tennis. ("It is no little to Plato's credit that he did not censure the 'limping' one-sidedness of the mere sportsman and hunter more severely than that of the man who cultivates his mind to the entire neglect of his body. . . . It is no less characteristic that in the choice of rulers he desires comeliness of form to be taken into consideration, so far as possible, as well as mental and moral qualities. . . . The ascetic author of the *Phaedo* has here become a true and complete Hellene once more.") The highest recognition awarded to the dialogue on the statesman is that "a breath of the Baconian, or modern inductive spirit has passed over his soul" (p. 465 [vol. 3, p. 185]). The most praiseworthy thing in "Phaedo" seems to be the anticipation of the psychology of "association" (p. 356 [vol. 3, p. 47]), and in all seriousness a passage of the Sophist (247, D E) is extolled as "Plato's wonderful utterance," which is misunderstood, perhaps out of pure kindness, as an anticipation of "the modern 'energy' school" on the part of the philosopher, who had no similarity whatsoever to John Stuart Mill (p. 455 [vol. 3, p. 173]). What happens to Timaeus in these circumstances can easily be imagined. Incidentally—and this remark is not only directed against an inadequate interpretation of Plato—it is essential to refrain from praising a philosopher or an artist just because those who are nothing-but-scientists are beginning to understand one of their thoughts after a thousand years. Goethe, Plato, and Kant appeared on earth for greater things than empirical science, based on its experience alone, would ever be able to comprehend or substantiate.

(P. 229, l. 1f.) O. Friedländer, in his essay "Eine für viele" [One for many] (cf. note to p. 81, l. 11), pp. 180f., remarks very sharply but correctly: "Nothing can be further from women than the struggle against men's pre-marital unchastity. On the contrary, what they demand from the latter is the most subtle knowledge of all details of the sexual life and the determination also to bring this theoretical superiority to bear in practice. . . . The virgin usually prefers to entrust her untouched charms to the tried and tested hands of the dissolute lecher, who has long since passed the final examination in the ars amandi, rather than to the trembling fingers of the erotic illiterate, who can hardly stammer the ABC of love."

Part 2, Chapter XII

(P. 230, l. 1) I found the motto from Kant quoted somewhere, but cannot remember where, nor have I been able to find it in Kant's works. In the "Fragmente aus dem Nachlass" [Fragments from the estate] (vol. VIII, p. 330, ed. Kirchmann) we read: "If one considers that man and woman constitute a moral whole one must not attribute the same properties to both, but such properties to her as are lacked by him"—a view, incidentally, which could easily make the truth appear in reverse: man has in him all the properties of woman, at least as possibilities; on the other hand, woman is poorer than man, because she is only a part of him. (See the end of this chapter.)

(P. 231, ll. 1ff.) Paul Julius Moebius, Über den physiologischen Schwachsinn des Weibes [On the physiological feeble-mindedness of woman], 5th ed., Halle 1903. Über einige Unterschiede der Geschlechter [On some differences between the sexes], in: Stachyologie, Weitere vermischte Aufsätze [Stachyology, further assorted essays], Leipzig 1901, ll. 125–138.

(P. 235, l. 14) The strength of woman's desire for a child is often exaggerated. E. v. Hartmann (Phänomenologie des sittlichen Bewußtseins [The phenomenology of moral consciousness], 1879, p. 693) remarks, in part correctly: "The instinct for the possession of children in *young* women and girls is by no means as generally and distinctly developed as is generally assumed, and as girls themselves pretend in order to attract men; only at a more mature age do childless women feel their condition to be a painful privation in comparison to their contemporaries with children. . . . In the majority of cases, it is in order to satisfy men, rather than for their own sakes, that young women wish to have children;

the mother instinct does not awaken until the young citizen of the world demanding help *is really there.*" Incidentally, this shows how necessary the division in chapter X is both in respect of this matter and as opposed to the eternally repeated assertions of gynaecologists (for whom Woman theoretically is always a mere institution for breeding).

(P. 236, l. 17)

Woman it is who seeks a *heart,* not *pleasure.*
Woman is chaste in her deepest being,
And only a woman knows what shame is.

Hamerling, Ahasver in Rom [Ahasverus in Rome], canto II: Werke [Works], Volksausgabe Hamburg, vol. I, p. 58.

(P. 238, l. 14) Herbert Spencer, Die Prinzipien der Ethik, vol. I, Stuttgart 1894, pp. 341f. [*The Principles of Ethics,* London 1892–1893].

(P. 238, l. 16 from bottom) Ellis, Mann und Weib, p. 288 [*Man and Woman, A Study of Human Secondary Sexual Characters,* London 1894], puts forward the interesting supposition that there is a connection between the phenomenon of *mimicry* and that of *suggestibility.* This might correspond better to the exposition in my main text than any other interpretation of that phenomenon.

(P. 239, ll. 21ff.) Wolfram von Eschenbach, Parzival, translated into modern German by Karl Pannier (Leipzig, Universalbibliothek), book IV, ll. 698ff. [*Parzival,* translated by A. T. Hatto, Harmondsworth 1980, p. 110].

(P. 239, ll. 6 from bottom ff.) A voice like that of Konrad Rieger, a Würzburg professor, is very isolated among psychiatrists: "What I strive for is the autonomy of psychiatry and psychology. They should both be free from an anatomy that does not concern them; and from a chemistry that does not concern them. A psychological phenomenon is as original as a chemical or anatomical one. It needs no props to support it." (Die Kastration in rechtlicher, sozialer und vitaler Hinsicht [Castration from a legal, social, and vital point of view], Jena 1900, p. 31).

(P. 240, l. 6) Pierre Janet, L'Etat Mental des Hystériques, Paris 1894 [*The Mental State of Hystericals,* translated by Caroline Rollin Corson, Bristol 1998]; L'Automatisme psychologique, Essai de Psychologie expérimentale sur les formes inférieures de l'activité humaine [Psychological automatism, essay in experimental psychology on the inferior forms of human activity], 3rd ed., Paris 1898; F. Raymond and Pierre Janet, Névroses et Idées fixes [Neuroses and obsessions], Paris 1898.—Oskar Vogt: in the essays cited in note to p. 250, l. 7.—J. Breuer and S. Freud, Studien über Hysterie, Leipzig, Vienna 1895 [*Studies on Hysteria,* translated by A. A. Brill, Boston 1960].

(P. 240, l. 11) Sigmund Freud, Zur Ätiologie der Hysterie, Wiener klinische Rundschau, X, l. 379ff. (1896, nos. 22–26) ["The Aetiology of Hysteria," *The Complete Psychological Works,* vol. 3, translated by James Strachey, London 2001, pp. 187–222]. Die Sexualität in der Ätiologie der Neurosen, ibid. XII, 1898, nos. 2–7 ["Sexuality in the Aetiology of the Neuroses" (1898), *The Complete Psychological Works,* translated by John Strachey, vol. 3, London 2001, pp. 263–285].

(P. 240, l. 19 from bottom f.) "Foreign body" according to Breuer and Freud, Studien über Hysterie, p. 4 [*Studies on Hysteria,* translated by A. A. Brill, Boston 1960, p. 3].

(P. 240, l. 16 from bottom) Here one may remember Zola's most perfect female character, Françoise in his most powerful novel, "La Terre" [*The Earth,* translated by Douglas Parmée, Harmondsworth 1980], and her behavior toward Buteau, whom she unconsciously desires and constantly rejects right to the end.

(P. 240, l. 11 from bottom.) Among hysterical *men* there are probably many sexual intermediates. This is suggested by a remark of Charcot (Neue Vorlesungen über die Krankheiten des Nervensystems, insbesondere über Hysterie, translated into German by Sigmund Freud, Leipzig, Vienna 1886, p. 70 [*Clinical Lectures on Diseases of the Nervous System,* translated by Ruth Harris, Tavistock/Routledge 1991, pp. 75–76]): "In men it is not uncommon to find that the testicle, *especially if it presents an abnormality of position or development,* is the seat of a partial hysterogenic zone." See p. 74 about a hysterical boy of effeminate appearance. A passage that I clearly remember reading in the same book, but was unable to find again later, states that the testicle is a particularly hysterogenic zone *if it has remained behind in the inguinal canal.* In women, however, all the hysterogenic points are also those with a strong sexual emphasis (the illial, mammary, and inguinal points, the "ovary," cf. Ziehen's article "Hysterie" [Hysteria] in Eulenburgs Realenzyklopädie [Eulenburg's Encyclopaedia]). A testicle that has not completed its descent is a gonad of a strongly female sexual character (according to part 1, chapter II); it is close to an ovary and can take over its properties, thus becoming hysterogenic.—In a lecture I once saw a psychiatrist demonstrate the incorrectness of the theory of the female nature of hysteria by means of a boy who had himself been struck by the small size of his testicles.

According to Briquet (quoted in Charcot, op. cit., p. 78 [*Clinical Lectures on Diseases of the Nervous System,* translated by Ruth Harris, Tavistock/Routledge 1991]) for every twenty hysterical women there is one hysterical man.

For the rest, even the most manly man, and perhaps he most of all, has the *possibility* of a woman in him. Hebbel, Ibsen, Zola—the three greatest judges of Woman's character in the nineteenth century—are extremely masculine artists, the third so much so that his novels are strikingly unpopular with women *in spite of their often highly sexual content. . . .* The more somebody is a man, the more he has *overcome* of the woman in himself, and in that sense the most masculine man is perhaps at the same time the most feminine. This is probably the most correct answer to the question raised on p. 76.

(P. 241, ll. 5ff.) Pierre Janet once comes fairly close to my conception of the passive adoption of Man's view. Névroses et Idées fixes [Neuroses and obsessions], I, pp. 475f.: "On a vu que le travail du directeur pendant les séances . . . a été un travail de synthèse; il a organisé des résolutions, des croyances, des émotions, il a aidé le sujet à rattacher à sa personnalité des images et des sensations. Bien plus il a échafaudé tout ce système de pensées autour d'un centre spécial qui est le souvenir et l'image de sa personne. Le sujet a emporté dans son esprit et dans son cerveau une synthèse nouvelle, passablement artificielle et très fragile, sur laquelle l'emotion a facilement exercé sa puissance désorganisatrice," p. 477: les phénomènes "consistent toujours dans une affirmation et une volonté c'est-à-dire une direction imposée aux gens qui ne peuvent pas vouloir, qui ne peuvent pas s'adapter, qui vivent d'une manière insuffisante."

(P. 241, l. 11) Abulia: see Janet's description (Un cas d'aboulie et d'idées fixes, Névroses et Idée fixes [A case of abulia, Neuroses and obsessions], vol. I, pp. 1ff.).

(P. 241, l. 20 from bottom f.) Janet speaks about the extraordinary *credulity* of hysterical women, L'Automatisme psychologique, Essai de Psychologie expérimentale sur les formes inférieures de l'activité humaine [Psychological automatism, essay in experimental psychology on the inferior forms of human activity], 3. éd., Paris 1899, pp. 207f. Further, p. 210: "Ces personnes, en apparence spontanées et entreprenantes, sont de la plus étrange docilité quand on sait de quelle manière il faut les diriger. De même que l'on peut changer un rêve par quelques mots adressés au dormeur, de même on peut modifier les actes et toute la conduite d'un individu faible par un mot, une allusion, un signe léger auquel il obéit aveuglement tandis qu'il résisterait avec fureur si on avait l'air de lui commander." Briquet, Traité clinique et thérapeutique de l'hysterie [Clinical and therapeutic treatise on hysteria], Paris 1859, p. 98: "Toutes les hysteriques que j'ai observées étaient extrêmement *impressionables*. Toutes, dès leur enfance, étaient très craintives; elles avaient une peur extrême d'être grondées, et quand il leur arriva de l'être, elles étouffaient, sanglotaient, fuyaient au loin ou se trouvaient mal." (See further on in the main text about the hysterical constitution.) How, on the other hand, the obstinacy of hysterics represents anything but a valid objection to this can be seen from Lipps's brilliant remark (Suggestion und Hypnose [Suggestion and hypnosis], p. 483, Sitzungsberichte der philosophisch-philologischen und der historischen Klasse der Akademie der Wissenschaften zu München, 1897, vol. II): "*In principle blind obstinacy is the same as blind obedience* . . . it is not surprising that . . . both are found . . . in the suggestible person. The highest degree of suggestibility . . . determines the automatism of the will. What is solely or overwhelmingly at work here is the impulse of the will contained in the order. A lower degree of suggestibility, on the other hand, may generate, in addition to automatism of the will, blind contravention of the order."

(P. 241, ll. 13 from bottom ff.) Freud's "Deckerinnerungen" (Monatsschrift für Psychiatrie und Neurologie, VI, 1899) also belong here ["Screen Memories," *The Complete Psychological Works*, vol. 3, translated by James Strachey, London 2001, pp. 299–322]. They are reactions of the pseudo-self to those events to which it responds differently from the real nature.

(P. 241, l. 6 from bottom f.) E.g., T. Gomperz, Griechische Denker, Leipzig 1902, II, p. 353 [*Greek Thinkers. A History of Ancient Philosophy*, translated by Laurie Magnus, London 1901–1912, vol. 3, p. 43]: "It is only in recent times that . . . cases of 'double consciousness' and kindred phenomena have been invoked against the supposed uncompounded nature of the soul."

(P. 241, l. 1 from bottom f.) See also p. 185, ll. 15 from bottom ff. and the note referring to them.

(P. 242, l. 12) The temporary absence of all emotivity, the total indifferentism of hysterics, has been called "anorexia," a lack of striving: this results from the suppression of female drives, in that the only evaluation of which women are capable, and which normally determines their actions, has been driven out of the consciousness.

(P. 242, l. 13) On the "shock nerveux," see Oeuvres complètes de J. M. Charcot, Leçons sur les maladies du système nerveux, Tome III, Paris 1887, pp. 453ff. [*Clinical Lectures on the Diseases of the Nervous System*, translated by Ruth Harris, London 1991].

(P. 242, l. 17) "Counter-will": Breuer and Freud, Studien über Hysterie, p. 2 [*Studies on Hysteria*, translated by A. A. Brill, Boston 1960, p. 2].

(P. 242, l. 18) On "defense": Freud, Neurologisches Zentralblatt, 15 May 1894, p. 364.

(P. 242, ll. 10 from bottom ff.) The terms "conversion" and "to convert" were introduced by Freud, Die Abwehr-Neuropsychosen, Versuch einer psychologischen Theorie der akquirierten Hysterie, vieler Phobien und Zwangsvorstellungen und gewisser halluzinatorischer Psychosen, Neurologisches Zentralblatt, vol. XIII, 1 June 1894, pp. 402ff. ["The Neuro-Psychoses of Defence (1894)," *The Complete Psychological Works,* vol. 3, translated by John Strachey, London 2001, pp. 45–61]. Cf. also Breuer and Freud, Studien über Hysterie, pp. 73, 105, 127, 177ff., 190, 261 [*Studies on Hysteria,* translated by A. A. Brill, Boston 1960]. They mean the transformation of forcibly suppressed psychic agitation into permanent physical symptoms.

(P. 242, l. 7 from bottom) Cf. P. J. Moebius, Über den Begriff der Hysterie [On the concept of hysteria], Zentralblatt für Nervenheilkunde, Psychiatrie und gerichtliche Psychopathologie, XI, pp. 66–71 (1. II. 1888).

(P. 243, l. 19) Breuer and Freud, Studien über Hysterie, p. 6 [*Studies on Hysteria,* translated by A. A. Brill, Boston 1960].

(P. 243, l. 1 from bottom) On hysterical heteronomy, see, e.g., Pierre Janet, Névroses et Idées fixes [Neuroses and obsessions], I, 458: "D. . . . , atteinte de la folie de scrupule, me demande si réellement elle est très méchante, si tous ce qu'elle fait est mal; je lui certifie qu'il n'en est rien et elle s'en va contente."

(P. 244, l. 10) O. Binswanger, article "Hypnotismus" [Hypnotism] in Eulenburg's Realenzyklopädie der gesamten Heilkunde [Complete encyclopaedia of medicine], 3rd ed., vol. XI, p. 242: "Hysterical individuals offer the richest harvest of hypnotic phenomena."

(P. 244, l. 16f.) Breuer and Freud, Studien über Hysterie, pp. 10, 203 [*Studies on Hysteria,* translated by A. A. Brill, Boston 1960).

(P. 244, ll. 17 from bottom ff.) The highly sexual nature of the relationship between the hypnotist and the medium is proved by the strange facts of "isolated rapport," studied in particular by Albert Moll (Der Rapport in der Hypnose, Untersuchungen über den tierischen Magnetismus [Rapport in hypnosis, studies on animal magnetism], Schriften für psychologische Forschung, nos III–IV, Leipzig 1892). Literature in Janet, Névroses et Idées fixes [Neuroses and obsessions], vol. I, Paris 1898, p. 424, see also p. 425: "si le sujet n'a été endormi qu'un très petit nombre de fois à des intervalles éloignées . . . il se réveillera de l'hypnose dans un état presque normal et ne conservera de son hypnotiseur aucune préoccupation particulière . . . Au contraire, si, pour un motif quelquonque . . . les séances de somnambulisme sont rapprochées, il est facile de remarquer que l'attitude du sujet vis-à-vis de l'hypnotiseur ne tarde pas à se modifier. Deux faits sont surtout apparents: le sujet, qui d'abord avait quelque crainte ou quelque répugnance pour le somnambulisme, recherche maintenant les séances avec un désir passioné; en outre, surtout à un certain moment, il parle beaucoup de son hypnotiseur et s'en préoccupe d'une façon évidemment excessive." Hypnotism, then, has the same effect on woman as sexual intercourse: the more it is repeated the more she enjoys it. See pp. 427f. on "passion somnambulique": "Les malades . . . se souviennent du bien-être que leur a causé le somnambulisme précédent et ils n'ont plus qu'une seule pensée, c'est d'être endormis de nouveau. Quelques malades voudraient être hypnotisés par n'importe qui, mais le plus souvent il n'en est pas ainsi, c'est leur hypnotiseur, celui que les a déjà endormis fréquemment, qu'ils réclament avec une impatience croissante." P. 447 on the jealousy of the mediums: "Beaucoup de magnétiseurs on bien décrit la souffrance qu'éprouve une somnambule quand elle apprend que son directeur endort de la même manière und autre personne." Further, p. 451: "si Qe., même seule, laisse sa main griffoner sur le papier, elle voit avec étonnement qu'elle a sans cesse écrit mon nom ou quelque recommendation que je lui ai faite." "si je la laisse regarder [une boule de verre] en évitant de lui rien suggérer, elle ne tarde pas à voir ma figure dans cette boule." Janet himself discusses the question whether hypnotic phenomena are sexual, pp. 456f., but denies it for quite invalid reasons, e.g., because a hypnotized woman is often afraid of the hypnotist or has motherly feelings for him. But it is clear that women's fear of men is only a cover for expectation and desire, and that the maternal relationship is also a sexual one. Moll himself says, p. 131: "Incidentally, a certain kinship between sexual love and suggestive rapport cannot be denied in some cases." Freud, in Breuer and Freud, Studien über Hysterie, p. 44 [*Studies on Hysteria,* translated by A. A. Brill, Boston 1960, p. 38]: "My influence was always already noticeable during the massage, when she became quieter and clearer, and even without hypnosis she always could give reasons for her moodiness," etc. Just as the sexual bonds that attach a woman to a man are loosened through every weakness and every lie of the latter, so the influence of suggestion can also be broken as soon as the will of the hypnotist has proved to be the opposite of what was expected from him in particular. Such a case is reported by Freud (Breuer and Freud, Studien über Hysterie, pp 64f. [*Studies on Hysteria,* translated by A. A. Brill, Boston 1960, pp. 53–54]): "By a train of thought, which I have not investigated, [the mother] came to the conclusion that both of us, Dr. N. and myself, were to blame for her child's illness, because the serious illness of her child was rather lightly presented to her. Through an act of will she abrogated more or less the effect of my treatment and soon lapsed back into the state from which I had freed her." Indeed the relationship between medium and hypnotist, at least on the part of the former, is always and invariably a *sexual* one or quite analogous to a sexual one.

(P. 244, l. 13 from bottom) Breuer in Breuer and Freud, Studien über Hysterie, pp. 6–7. [*Studies on Hysteria,* translated by A. A. Brill, Boston 1960].

(P. 245, ll. 6 from bottom ff.) Conversion of the hysterical attack into somnambulism: Pierre Janet, Névroses et Idées fixes [Neuroses and obsessions], vol. I, Paris 1898, pp. 160f.

(P. 245, ll. 10ff.) It is probably overly risky—and indeed too crude to appeal to me greatly—to interpret any therapeutic successes of ovariotomy in the treatment of hysterical illnesses, which are so frequently reported, in terms of my own theory. Nevertheless, the many available reports of the kind, if they can be relied on, easily fit into the general picture. For the sexuality which opposes a counter-sexual will to impregnation is radically extirpated or at least significantly reduced by that operation (see part 1, chapter II), and thus the cause of the conflict is removed.

(P. 245, ll. 9 from bottom ff.) F. Raymond and Pierre Janet, Névroses et Idées fixes [Neuroses and obsessions], vol. II, Paris 1898, p. 313: "La malade entre à l'hôpital . . . nouvelle émotion en voyant une femme qui tombe par terre: cette émotion bouleverse l'equilibre nerveux, lui rend tout à coup la parole et transforme l'hémiplégie gauche en paraplégie complète. *C'est transformations, ces équivalences sont bien connues dans l'hystérie;* ce n'est pas une raison pour que nous ne déclarions pas qu'elles sont à notre avis très étonnantes et probablement très instructives sur le mécanisme du système nerveux central."

(P. 246, l. 20f.) This agrees with all the information supplied about the character of hysterical women. For example, Sollier, Genèse et Nature de l'Hystérie [The genesis and nature of hysteria], Paris 1897, vol. I, p. 460, notes: "Elles [les hystériques] sentent instictivement qu'elles ont besoin d'être dirigées, commandées, et c'est pour cette raison qu'elles s'attachent de préférence à ceux qui leur imposent, chez qui elles sentent une volonté très-forte." He quotes a remark of one of his female patients: "Il faut que je sois en sous-ordre; . . . je sais bien faire ce qu'on me commande, mais je ne serais pas capable de faire les choses toutes seule, et encore moins de commander à d'autres."

(p. 246, l. 13 from bottom) One might perhaps think that the *mother* is the hysterical woman: for a while this was my view because I believed that the mother was less sensual, and I tried to explain hysteria through the conflict between the desire of an individual for a child and a revulsion from the means necessary to this end, that is, as a clash between the individual will and the generic will within the unconscious mind of a single individual. However, according to Briquet, prostitutes are very often hysterical. In this respect there is no difference between the mother and the prostitute. For hysterical women can also be mothers: Léonie, from whom Pierre Janet collected so many experiences, regarded him, her hypnotist, as her *son* (Névroses et Idées fixes [Neuroses and obsessions], vol. I, p. 447). Since then I myself have had ample opportunity to notice that mothers and prostitutes are equally hysterical.

(P. 248, l. 6) Paul Sollier, Genèse et Nature de l'Hystérie, Recherches cliniques et expérimentales de Psycho-Physiologie [The genesis and nature of hysteria, clinical and experimental researches into psycho-physiology], Paris 1897, vol. I, p. 211: "L'anésthésie et bien plus fréquente chez les hystériques que l'hyperesthésie, et par suite la frigidité est l'etat le plus habituel . . . Il est aussi une conséquence de l'anésthésie des organes sexuels chez l'hystérique qu'il est bon de signaler et que j'ai été à même de constater: C'est l'absence de sensation des mouvements du foetus pendant the grossesse. Quoique ceux-ci soient faciles à démontrer par le palpation, ce phénomène peut cependant donner dans certains cas des craintes non justifiées sur la santé du foetus; ou pousser certaines femmes à réclamer une intervention en niant énergiquement qu'elles sont enceintes." This could well agree with chapter X (p. 195): the denial of sexuality must be accompanied by a denial of the child. See further Sollier, vol. I, p. 458: "Chez celles-ci [les grandes hystériques] il y a de l'anésthésie génitale comme de tous les organes, et elles sont ordinairement complètement frigides . . . Certaines hystériques prennent l'horreur des rapports conjugaux qui leur sont ou absolument indifférents quand elles sont anésthétiques, ou désagréables quand elles ne le sont pas tout-à-fait."

(P. 248, l. 7f.) Oskar Vogt, Normalpsychologische Einleitung in die Psychopathologie der Hysterie [Introduction to the psychopathology of hysteria in terms of normal psychology], Zeitschrift für Hypnotismus, vol. VIII, 1899, p. 215: "On the one hand I suggest to A. that at every touch of his right arm the idea of a red color should arise in him, and on the other hand I make his right arm insensitive. If I now touch his arm A. does not feel the touch in spite of concentrating his attention on it, but nevertheless, every time I touch him, which A. does not feel, the idea of the red color arises in A."

(P. 249, l. 12 from bottom f.) Guy de Maupassant, Bel-Ami, Paris, pp. 389f. [Bel-Ami, translated by Margaret Mauldon, Oxford 2001].

(P. 249, ll. 10 from bottom ff.) Freud recounts such a very instructive case of impregnation through ideas coming entirely from outside, in Breuer and Freud, Studien über Hysterie, 1895, pp. 242f. [*Studies on Hysteria,* translated by A. A. Brill, Boston 1960]. A lady fantasizes in symbols of the theosophists, whose society she has joined. When Freud asks her since when she has been reproaching and feeling dissatisfied with herself, she answers, *since she has been a member of the society and reading the writings published by it.* Women, like children, are also suggestible through books.

(P. 249, l. 4 from bottom f.) The term "patron saint, etc." was coined by Breuer (Breuer and Freud, Studien über Hysterie, p. 204 [*Studies on Hysteria,* translated by A. A. Brill, Boston 1960, p. 173]). Some interesting points are found in a small pamphlet, with an anti-religious tendency, by Dr. Rouby, L'Hystérie de Sainte Thérèse [The hysteria of St. Theresa] (Bibilothèque diabolique), Paris, Alcan 1902, pp. 11f., 16f., 20f., 39f. Gilles de la Tourette, Traité clinique et thérapeutique de l'Hystérie d'après l'enseignement de la Salpétrière [A clinical and therapeutic treatise on hysteria according to the teaching of the Salpétrière], Paris 1891, vol. I, p. 223: "Il n'est pas douteux que sainte Thérèse . . . fût atteinte de cardialgie hystérique, ou mieux d'angine de poitrine de même nature, complexus qui s'accompagne souvent de troubles hyperésthésiques de la région précordiale." Hahn, Les phénomènes hysteriques et les révélations de Sainte-Thérèse [The hysterical phenomena and the revelations of St. Teresa], Revue des Questions Scientifiques, vol. XIV and XV, Bruxelles 1882. Charles Binet-Danglé, Physio-Psychologie des Religieuses [The physio-psychology of nuns], Archives d'Anthropologie criminelle, XVII, 1902, pp. 453–477, 517–545, 607–623.

(P. 250, l. 7) Oskar Vogt, Die direkte psychologische Experimentalmethode in hypnotischen Bewußtseinszuständen [The direct psychological experimental method in hypnotic states of consciousness], Zeitschrift für Hypnotismus V, 1897, pp. 7–30, 180–218. (See in particular pp. 195ff.): "Experience teaches that the exactness of self-observation can be increased through suggestion." P. 199: "self-observation can be strengthened: first through specialized reinforcements of intensity or inhibitions and then through a restriction of the waking state and thus of the attention being paid to the elements of consciousness participating in the experiment." P. 218: "In a human individual high suggestibility can join with the capacity for critical self-observation [that is, in the state of "partial systematic awakeness," created by the hypnotist.]" On the methodology of the aetiological investigation of hysteria, ibid., VIII, 1899, pp. 65ff., particularly p. 70. On the critique of the hypnogenetic investigation of hysteria, ibid. pp. 342–355. Freud as predecessor: Breuer and Freud, Studien über Hysterie, pp. 133ff. [*Studies on Hysteria,* translated by A. A. Brill, Boston 1960].

(P. 253, l. 15 from bottom) The remark about Schopenhauer needs an explanation. The confusion between instinct and will is perhaps the most momentous fault of Schopenhauer's system. As much as it has contributed to popularizing his philosophy, it has to the same extent oversimplified the facts. This explains how Schopenhauer, who rightly considers the will as the intelligible essence of man, can find the same again everywhere in organic nature, and finally also in inorganic nature, as movement. However, as a result, Schopenhauer's system is unavoidably invaded by confusion. He has a profoundly *dualistic* disposition and a *monistic metaphysic;* he knows that the intelligible essence of a *human being* is precisely the will, but he is nevertheless obliged to distinguish humans from animals and plants by means of an unfortunate psychology which very mistakenly separates the will and the intellect, attributing only the latter to human beings. Whatever one may say, he is *ultimately* an optimist, since he *affirms* another form of being, about which he merely refrains from making any positive comments, and therefore another life: and, however paradoxical this may sound to our ears today, it is only his *monism* that gives his system its negative evaluation—since he sees the same will here as there and fails to separate the eternal and the earthly life, so that the only immortality can be that of the will of the species. Thus his identification of the higher concept of will with the lower—the latter of which should always be described as instinct—is revealed as the fatal flaw of his entire philosophy. If he had understood Kant's moral philosophy he would also have recognized the difference between will and instinct: *the will is always free, and only the instinct is unfree. There is no question about freedom, but only a question about the existence of the will.* All the *phenomena* are causally determined; therefore, a will can be of no use to, or admitted by, *empirical* psychology, which acknowledges only psychic *phenomena. For all will, by definition, is free and absolutely spontaneous.* Kant says (Grundlegung zur Metaphysik der Sitten, p. 77, Kirchmann [*Groundwork of the Metaphysics of Morals,* translated by Mary Gregor, Cambridge 1998, p. 54]): "We must presuppose [the idea of freedom] if we want to think of a being as rational and endowed with consciousness of his causality with respect to actions, that is, with a will, and so we find that on just the same grounds we must assign to every being endowed with reason and will this property of determining himself to action under the idea of his freedom." One sees that for Kant too there is no unfreedom of the will: the will can in no way be determined. A human being who *wills,* really *wills,* always wills *freely.* Nevertheless, human beings have not only will but also instincts. Kant, ibid., p. 78 [p. 54]: "this [the moral] 'ought' is strictly speaking a 'will' that holds for every rational being under the condition that the reason in him is practical without hindrance; but for beings like us—who are also affected by sensibility, by incentives of a different kind, and in whose case that which reason by itself would do is not always done—that necessity of action is called only an 'ought,' and the subjective necessity is distinguished from the objective."

***All** will is will to value, and all **instinct** instinct to pleasure;* there is no will to pleasure and also no *will to power,* but only greed and persistent hunger for domination. Plato clearly recognized this in "Gorgias," but he was not understood. 466 D E [*Gorgias, The Dialogues of Plato,* translated by R. E. Allen, vol. 1 (New Haven, London 1984)]: "φημὶ γάρ, ὦ Πῶλε, ἐγὼ τοὺς ῥήτορας καὶ τοὺς τυράννους δύνασθαι μὲν ἐν ταῖς πόλεσι σμικρότατον, ὥσπερ νῦν δὴ ἔεγον· οὐδὲν γὰρ ποιεῖν ὧν βούλονται, ὡς ἔπος εἰπεῖν· ποιεῖν μέντοι ὅτι ἂν αὐτοῖς δόξῃ βέλτιστον εἶναι." And as for the "οὐδεὶς ἑκὼν ἁμαρτάνει" of Socrates—it is likely to be lost many more times, all the shallow and uncomprehending objections to this most certain knowledge will be heard and the even sadder attempts to *forgive* Socrates, so to speak, for this pronouncement will be resumed again and again (e.g., Gomperz, Griechische Denker, Eine Geschichte der antiken Philosophie, Leipzig 1902, pp. 51ff. [*Greek Thinkers. A History of Ancient Philosophy,* translated by Laurie Magnus, London 1901–1912]). It must therefore be repeated all the more often.

The idea of an entirely free being is the idea of God; the idea of a being mixed of freedom and unfreedom is the idea of the human being. *Insofar* as the human being is *free,* that is, wills *freely,* he *is* God. And thus the Kantian ethic in its deepest foundations is mystical and says nothing other than Fechner's credo:

My soul rests in God
It realizes God in itself;
His will is my command.

(Die drei Motive und Gründe des Glaubens [The three motives and grounds of belief] Leipzig 1863, p. 256).

(P. 254, l. 8f.) Cf. A. P. Sinnett, Die esoterische Lehre oder Geheimbuddhismus, 2nd ed., Leipzig 1899, pp. 153–172 [*Esoteric Buddhism,* 1883].

(P. 256, l. 22) This is one of Goethe's finest words (Maximen und Reflexionen, III [*Goethe's Maxims and Reflections,* translated by R. H. Stephenson, Glasgow 1986, passage not found in translation]): *"The idea is eternal and unique; we do not do well to use the plural as well as the singular."*

(P. 256, l. 5 from bottom) I can find a remotely similar remark only in the small but interesting paper by Karl Joel, Die Frauen in der Philosophie [Women in philosophy], Hamburg 1896 (Sammlung gemeinverständlicher wissenschaftlicher Vorträge, no. 246), p. 59: "Woman is intellectually happier, but more unphilosophical, according to the old adage that philosophy is born out of the struggles and doubts of the soul. Schopenhauer's mother was a novelist and his sister a painter of flowers."

(P. 257, l. 4 from bottom) Cf. Taguet, Du suicide dans l'hystérie [On suicide in hysteria], Annales Médico-Psychologiques, V. série, vol. 17, 1877, p. 346: "L'hystérique ment dans la mort comme elle ment dans toutes les circonstances de sa vie."

(P. 258, l. 6 from bottom) Lazar B. Hellenbach, Die Vorurteile der Menschheit [The prejudices of humanity], vol. III: Die Vorurteile des gemeinen Verstandes [The prejudices of common understanding], Vienna 1880, p. 99.

(P. 261, ll. 8ff.) How intimately sexuality and the abolition of borders are related is hinted at by Bachofen, Das Mutterrecht, p. XXIII [*Myth, Religion, and Mother Right,* selected writings, translated by Ralph Manheim, Princeton 1973, p. 102]: "The Dionysian cult . . . loosed all fetters, removed all distinctions, and by orienting people's spirit towards matter and the embellishment of physical existence, carried life itself back to the laws of matter. This sensualization of existence coincides everywhere with the dissolution of political organization and the decline of political life. Intricate gradation gives way to democracy, the undifferentiated mass, the freedom and equality which distinguish natural life from ordered social life and pertain to the physical, material side of human nature. The ancients were well aware of this connection; as they stated in no uncertain terms. . . . The Dionysian religion represented the apotheosis both of Aphroditean pleasure and of universal brotherhood; hence it was readily accepted by the servile classes and encouraged by tyrants—by the Pisistratids, the Ptolemies, and Caesar—since it favored the democratic development on which their tyranny was based" (see chapter X, p. 202). Bachofen calls these phenomena "offshoots of an essentially feminine culture" [p. 103], but he was granted no real insight into their deeper causes. In addition to statements such as this, in his writings also there are enthusiastic hymns to the chaste nature of woman.

(P. 261, ll. 6 from bottom ff.) "Klein-Eyolf," Act 3 (Henrik Ibsens sämtliche

Werke, ed. Brandes, Elias, Schlenther, Berlin, vol. IX, p. 72 [*Little Eyolf*, in *The Master Builder and Other Plays*, translated by Una Ellis-Fermor, Harmondsworth 1958, p. 276]).

(P. 262, l. 2) For the difficult question of the relationship between Âtman and Brahman, see Paul Deussen, Das System des Vedânta, etc., Leipzig 1883, pp. 50f. [*The System of the Vedânta*, translated by Charles Johnston, New York 1973].

(P. 263, l. 7f.) Milne-Edwards, Introduction à la Zoologie générale, I[e] partie, Paris 1851, p. 157. Similarly Rudolf Leuckart, article "Zeugung" [Procreation] in Wagner's Handwörterbuch der Physiologie [Concise dictionary of physiology], vol. IV, Braunschweig 1853, pp. 742f.: "In a physiological respect this distribution of the female and male organs appears to be a division of labor."

Leuckart's negative comments reveal little understanding of the relationship between the male and the female (op. cit.): "One often hears the assertion that the male and female individuals of an animal species, in terms of equipment and activities, are not merely different from, but *opposed* to each other. However, we must most categorically reject such a view. The theory of the contrast between the sexes, which first arose from certain vague and mystical ideas about copulation and fertilization, dates back to a period of research in natural history when it was believed possible to explain life in all its manifestations in terms of polarity, polar behavior, etc. Male and female products, organs, and individuals were supposed to relate to each other like + and –, as if nature handled sex and sexual materials as a physicist handles electricity and Leyden bottles!

An uninhibited and unprejudiced contemplation of nature shows us no difference between male and female genitals other than it does in general between organs and groups of organs that mutually support and complement each other in their work. . . . Generally, the physiological motives of such a division of labor are not difficult to name. They are basically the same as those that we regard as justifying any division of labor, including those in practical life. The advantages connected with it are, above all, savings of energy and time for other new achievements. *In the dualism of sex we see nothing other than a mechanical arrangement which gives rise to certain advantages.*"

This understanding of sexual difference is the most common. Others worth considering are the views of K. W. Brooks (The Law of Heredity, A Study of the Cause of Variation and the Origin of Living Organisms, Baltimore 1883) and August Weismann (Die Bedeutung der sexuellen Fortpflanzung für die Selektionstheorie [The significance of sexual reproduction for the theory of selection], Jena 1886), both of whom regard sexual reproduction as the means "used by nature to produce variation" (Weismann, Aufsätze über Vererbung, Jena 1892, p. 390 [*Essays upon Heredity and Kindred Biological Problems*, authorized translation, edited by E. B. Poulton, S. Schönland, and A. E. Shipley, Oxford 1889, p. 326]); finally, the views of Edouard van Beneden (Recherches sur la maturation de l'oeuf, la fécondation et la division cellulaire [Researches into the maturing of the egg, fertilization, and the division of cells], Gand 1883, pp. 404f.), Viktor Hensen (Physiologie der Zeugung [The physiology of procreation], in Hermann's Handbuch der Physiologie [Handbook of physiology], vol. VI/2, pp. 236f.), Maupas (Le rajeunissement karyogamique chez les Ciliés [Karyogamic rejuvenation in cilia], Archives de Zoologie expérimentale, 2. série, vol. VII,

1890) and Bütschli (Über die ersten Entwicklungsvorgänge der Eizelle, Zellteilung und Konjugation der Infusorien [On the first processes in the development of the ovum, cell division, and conjugation of infusoria], Abhandlungen der Senckenbergischen naturforsch. Gesellschaft, X, 1876), although these refer more to the nature of the *fertilization* process, in which these researchers see the intention of a *rejuvenation* of the individuals.—What Wilhelm Wundt, System der Philosophie [System of philosophy], 2nd ed., Leipzig 1897, pp. 521ff., says about sexual and non-sexual procreation does not go beyond a reception of the prevailing scientific views.

(P. 263, l. 15) The refutation of the theory of descendency in this context in Fechner, Einige Ideen zur Schöpfungs-und Entwicklungsgeschichte der Organismen [Some ideas on the genesis and developmental history of the organisms], Leipzig 1873, pp. 59ff.

(P. 263, l. 13 from bottom) As can be seen, establishing the passivity of Woman in this context is more than just repeating an old triviality, found, for example, in J. Scherr, Geschichte der deutschen Frauenwelt, II (4), 1879, p. 262 [History of German womanhood].

(P. 264, l. 5) Plato in Timaeus, p. 50 B C [*Timaeus and Critias,* translated by H. D. P. Lee, Harmondsworth 1971]: "δέχεται γὰρ ἀεὶ τὰ πάντα, καὶ μορφὴν οὐδεμίαν ποτὲ οὐδενὶ τῶν εἰσιόντων ὁμοίαν εἴηφεν οὐδαμῇ οὐδαμῶς· ἐκμαγεῖον γὰρ φύσει παντὶ κεῖται, κινούμενόν τε καὶ διασχηματιζόμενον ὑπὸ τῶν εἰσιόντων. φαίνεται δὲ δι' ἐκεῖνα ἄλοτε ἄλοῖον· τὰ δὲ εἰσιόντα καὶ ἐξιόντα τῶν ὄντων ἀεὶ μιμήματα, τυπωθέντα ἀπ' αὐτῶν τρόπον τινὰ δύσφραστον καὶ θαυμαστόν, ὃν εἰσαῦθις μέτιμεν. ἐν δ' οὖν τῷ παρόντι χπὴ γένη διανοηθῆναι τριττά, τὸ μὲν γιγνόμενον, τὸ δὲ ἐν ᾧ γίγνεται, τὸ δ' ὅθεν ἀφομοιούμενον φύεται τὸ γιγνόμενον." P. 52 A B: "τρίτον δὲ αὖ γὲνος τὸ τῆς χώρας ἀεὶ, φθορὰν οὐ προσδεχόμενον, ἕδραν δὲ παρέχον ὅσα ἔχει γένεσιν πᾶσιν, αὐτὸ δὲ μετί ἀναισθησίας ἁπτὸν λογισμῷ τινὶ νόθῳ, μόγις πιστόν, πρὸς ὅ δὴκαὶ ὀνειροπολοῦμεν βλέποντες καὶ φαμεν ἀναγκαῖον εἶναί που τὸ ὅν ἅπαν ἔν τινι τόπῳ καὶ κατέχον χώραν τινά, τὸ δὲ μήτε ἐν γῇ μήτε που κατ' οὐρανὸν οὐδὲν εἶναι" etc. See J. J. Bachofen, Das Mutterrecht, Stuttgart 1861, pp. 164–168 [*Myth, Religion, and Mother Right,* selected writings, translated by Ralph Manheim, Princeton 1973].

(P. 264, ll. 8ff.) The most detailed attempt to explain this interpretation of xw/ra as space was made by Hermann Siebeck (Platos Lehre von der Materie, Untersuchungen zur Philosophie der Griechen [Plato's theory of matter, studies in the philosophy of the Greeks], 2nd ed., Freiburg 1888, pp. 49–106).

(P. 264, l. 18) Plato, Timaeus, p. 50 D [*Timaeus and Critias,* translated by H. D. P. Lee, Harmondsworth 1971]: "Καὶ δὴ καὶ προσεικάσαι πρέπει τὸ μὲν δεχόμενον μητρί, τὸ δ' ὅθεν πατρί, πὴν δὲ μεταξὺ τούτων φύσιν ἐκγόνῳ." P. 49 A: "τίνα οὖν ἔχον δύναμιν κατὰ φύσιν αὐτὸ ὑποληπτέον; τοιάνδε μάλιστα, πάσης εἶναι γενέσεως ὑποδοχὴν αὐτό, οἷον τιθήνην." See Plutarch de Is. et Osir. 56 (Moralia 373 E F) ["Isis and Osiris," Moralia, vol. 5, translated by Frank C. Babbitt, London 1927].

(P. 264, l. 22) Aristotle: see note to p. 162, l. 3.

(P. 264, l. 4 from bottom) Kant, Metaphysische Anfangsgründe der Naturwissenschaft, Zweites Hauptstück , Erklärung 1–4 [*Kant's Prolegomena and Metaphysical Foundations of Natural Science, Second Division, Explanations I–IV,* translated by E. B. Bax, London 1883].

(P. 265, l. 9) The inkling of this profound meaning of the contrast between man and woman is very old (see p. 15). Following Aristotle (Metaphysik, A 5,

986 a, 22–26 [*The Metaphysics,* translated by Hugh Lawson-Tancred, Harmondsworth 1998]), the Pythagoreans drew up a "table of contrasts," in which they "τὰς ἀρξὰς δέκα λέγουσιν εἶναι τὰς κατὰ συστοιχίαν λεγομένας, πέρας καὶ ἄπειρον, περιττὸν καὶ ἄρτιον, ἓν καὶ πλῆθος, δεξιὸν καὶ ἀριστερόν, ἄρρεν καὶ θῆλυ, ἠρεμοῦν καὶ κινούμενον, εὐθὺ καὶ κάμπυλον, φῶς καὶ σκότος, ἀγαθὸν καὶ κακόν, τετράγωνον καὶ ἑτερόμηκες."

(P. 265, l. 15) I mean the investigations of Jastrow (A Statistical Study of Memory and Association, Educational Review, New York, December 1891; quoted from Ellis, Mann und Weib, p. 173 [*Man and Woman*]).

(P. 268, l. 18 from bottom) Here I would not like to omit quoting the words of Giordano Bruno (De gli eroici furori [*The Heroic Frenzies,* translated by Paul Eugene Memmo, Chapel Hill 1964], in the introductory letter to Sir Philip Sidney, Opere di Giordano Bruno Nolano, ed. Adolfo Wagner, vol. II, Leipzig 1830, pp. 299f.):

"È cosa veramente . . . da basso, bruto e sporco ingegno d'essersi fatto constantemente studioso, et aver affisso un curioso pensiero circa o sopra la bellezza d'un corpo feminile. Che spettacolo, o dio buono, più vile e ignobile può presentarsi ad un occhio di terso sentimento, che un uomo cogitabundo, afflitto, tormentato, triste, maninconioso, per divenir or fredd, or caldo, or fervente, or tremante, or pallido, or rosso, or in mina di perplesso, or in atto di risoluto, un, che spende il miglior intervallo di tempo e li più scelti frutti di sua vita corrente destillando l'elixir del cervello con mettere in concetto, scritto e sigillar in publici monumenti quelle continue torture, que'gravi tormenti, que'razionali discorsi, que'faticosi pensieri, e quelli amarissimi studi, destinati sotto la tirannide d' una indegna, imbecilla, stolta a sozza sporcaria? . . . Ecco vergato in carte, rinchiuso in libri, messo avanti gli occhi, e intonato a gli orecchi un rumore, un strepito, un fracasso d'insegne, d'imprese, di motti, d'epistole, di sonetti, d'epigrammi, di libri, di prolissi scarfazzi, di sudori estremi, di vite consumate, con strida, ch'assordiscon gli astri, lamenti, che fanno ribombar gli antri infernati, doglie, che fanno stupefar l'anime viventi, suspiri da far esmanire e compatir li dei, per quegli occhi, per quelle guance, per quel busto, per quel bianco, per quel vermiglio, per quella lingua, per quel labro, quel crine, quella veste, quel manto, quel guanto, quella scarpetta, quella pianella, quella parsimonia, quel risetto, quel sdegnosetto, quella vedova finestra, quel'eclissato sole, quel martello, quel schifo, quel puzzo, *quel sepolcro, quel cesso, quel mestruo, quella carogna, quella febre quartana,* quella estrema ingiuria e torto di natura, che con una superficie, un'ombra, un fantasma, un sogno, un circeo incantesimo ordinato al servigio de la generazione, ne inganna in specie di bellezza; la quale insieme viene e passa, nasce e muore, fiorisce e marcisce: et è bella un pochettino a l'esterno, che nel suo intrinseco, vera-e stabilmente è contenuto un navilio, una bottega, una dogana, un mercato di quante sporcarie, tossichi e veneni abbia posuti produrre la nostra madrigna natura: la quale, dopo aver riscosso quel seme, di cui la si serva, ne viene sovente a pagar d'un lezzo, d'un pentimento, d'una tristizia, d'una fiacchezza, d'un dolor di capo, d'una lassitudine, d'altri e d'altri malanni, che sono manifesti a tutto il mondo, a fin che amaramente dolga, dove soavemente proriva . . . Voglio che le donne siano così onorate et amate, come denno essere amate et onorate le donne: per tal causa dico, e per tanto, per quanto si deve a quel poco, a quel tempo e quella occasione, se non hanno altra virtù che naturale, cioè di quella bellezza, di quel splendore, di quel servigio, senza il quale denno esser stimate più vanamente nate al mondo, che un morboso fungo, quel con pregiudizio di miglior piante occupa la terra, e più noiosamente, che qual si voglia napello, o vipera, che caccia il capo fuor die quella?" etc.

(P. 269, l. 17) *Woman* then is the *expression* of the fall of mankind, she is the objectivized sexuality of Man and nothing else. Eve was never in Paradise. On the other hand, I believe, with the myth of Genesis (I, 2:22) and with the apostle St. Paul (I. Timoth. 2:13, and in particular I. Corinth. 11:8: οὐ γάρ ἐστιν ἀνὴρ ἐκ γυναικός, ἄλλὰ γυνὴ ἐξ ἀνδρός) in the priority of *Man,* in the creation of Woman through Man, in her *secondary derivation,* which makes her soullessness possible. It is no objection to this metaphysical posteriority of Woman—which is a posteriority in existential rank and is not located in time, but which rather signifies a creation of Woman at all times by the still sexual Man, a *permanent event,* as it were—that in not very differentiated organisms the male sex is still absent and the functions fulfilled by it at a more advanced stage seem dispensable. Incidentally, I am well aware that this implies a harsh rejection of all descendence-theoretical speculations insofar as they presume to exert an influence on philosophy, but I find it relatively easy to bear the responsibility for this step. Philosophy is not history, but rather its strict opposite: there is no philosophy that would not deny time, no philosopher for whom time would be a reality like other things.

Nevertheless, it is very understandable how the view of the eternity of Woman and the transitoriness of Man could come into being. The absolutely formless seems to be as durable as the pure spiritual form, an idea that is quite unimaginable to mediocre minds. And about the eternity of the mother the most necessary things are said in chapter X. See also Bachofen, Das Mutterrecht, p. 35 [*Myth, Religion, and Mother Right,* selected writings, translated by Ralph Manheim, Princeton 1973, passage not found in translation]: "Woman is the given, man becomes. From the beginning the earth is the maternal basic material. From her womb then issues the visible creation, and it is in this that a double divided sex manifests itself for the first time; it is in this that the male form is revealed for the first time, so that man and woman do not appear simultaneously, and are not of the same order. Woman leads the way, man follows; woman is earlier, man's relationship with her is that of a son; woman is the given, man is that which has come into being out of her. He belongs to visible, but constantly changing, creation; he only comes into existence in mortal form. Woman alone is present, given, unchanging from the beginning; man has become, and therefore is doomed to constant destruction. Hence in the domain of physical life the male principle takes second place, it is subordinate to the female." P. 36: "In the plant which breaks out of the soil the maternal nature of the earth becomes concrete. At this stage no display of masculinity is as yet present: this will only be recognized later in the first child who has developed as a male. Man therefore is not only later than woman, but it is also she who is seen to reveal the great mystery of the procreation of life. For the act that awakens life in the darkness of the earth's womb and unfolds its germ eschews all observation; the first thing that becomes visible is the event of birth; and in this woman alone participates. The existence and development of male strength is first revealed through the formation of the male child; through such a birth the mother reveals to humanity that which was unknown before the birth, and the activity of which was buried in darkness. In countless representations of the old mythology male strength appears as the mystery revealed; woman, on the other hand, appears as that which is given from the beginning, as that which is substantial primal ground, which is material, which can be perceived by the senses, which itself needs no revelation, but which in fact, for its part, brings the existence and form of masculinity to certainty through the first birth."

The μὴ οὔ, which is represented by Woman, is the totally unformed, and unstructured, the amorphous, matter which has no ultimate part in the idea of life, but which seems to be just as eternal and immortal as pure form, guiltless higher life, unembodied spirit. The first because none of it can be changed, no form destroyed in what is formless; the second because it undergoes no incarnation, and does not become finite and therefore destructible.

The concept of eternal life found in the religions is the concept of absolute, metaphysical being (aseity) found in the philosophies.

(P. 253, l. 17 from bottom f.) Dante, Inferno XXXIV, ll. 76f. [*The Divine Comedy,* translated by Mark Musa, vol. I, *Inferno,* Harmondsworth 1984].

(P. 253, ll. 9 from bottom ff.) Tertullian's apostrophe to woman requires the most serious reflection, and deserves the deepest respect of the listener, rather than laughter (which would probably meet him everywhere today) (De habitu muliebri liber, Opera rec., J. J. Semler, Halae 1770, vol. III, pp. 35f.) ["The Apparel of Women," *Disciplinary, Moral and Ascetical Works,* translated by Rudolph Arbesmann, Washington 1977]: "Tu es diaboli ianua, tu es arboris illius resignatrix, tu es divinae legis prima desertrix, to es, quae eum suasisti, quem diabolus aggredi non valuit. Tu imaginem dei, hominem, tam facile elisisti; propter tuum meritum, id es mortem, etiam filius dei mori debuit; et adornari tibi in mente est, propter pelliceas tuas tunicas?" These words are directed at *womanhood* as an *idea;* empirical women would only feel pleasantly tickled by being attributed such importance; women are very satisfied with *anti*-sexual men, and helpless only when faced with *a*-sexual ones.

(P. 269, l. 13f.) How closely Man converges with Woman through his sexuality is demonstrated by the fact that erection is beyond the reach of the will and cannot be revoked by it in the same way as a muscular contraction is cancelled by an order of the will in a healthy person. The state of sensual arousal dominates Woman entirely, but in Man only one part. Nevertheless, lust may be the only sensation that in general is not entirely different in the two sexes; the sensation of sexual intercourse has the same quality for Man and Woman. Otherwise sexual intercourse would be impossible. It is the act that makes two human beings most alike. Nothing therefore can be more erroneous than the popular opinion that Man and Woman *differ,* mainly or even exclusively, in their *sexuality,* as stated, for instance, by Rousseau (Emile, Livre V, beginning [*Emile, or On Education,* translated by Allan Bloom, Harmondsworth 1991]): "En tout ce qui ne tient pas au sexe la femme est homme." Sexuality is precisely the *bond* between Man and Woman and always has a *compensating* effect on them.

(P. 270, l. 13 from bottom) The specific *pity* of Man for Woman—because of her inner emptiness and dependency, her instability and lack of substance—also, like any pity, suggests guilt.

(P. 271, l. 3) This apparently offers three *different* explanations of matchmaking (and consequently three derivations of femininity); but, as can clearly be seen, they all express one and the same thing. The eternally growing guilt of the higher life is the fall of that life into the low life, a fall which is eternally inexplicable to humans and which, for them, is the truly *last* fact: the sudden fall of the entirely guiltless into guilt. The low life, for its part, culminates in that act through which it is newly created; and therefore any encouragement of the low life necessarily includes matchmaking. The same striving to endow earthly life with reality is marked by the seductive drive of all matter toward being shaped, or, as Plato has profoundly suggested, by the treacherous advances of Penia (poverty, emptiness, nothingness) to the drunken, dreaming god Poros (the rich).

Part 2, Chapter XIII

(P. 272, ll. 1ff.) The motto is taken from "Das Judentum in der Musik" (Gesammelte Schriften und Dichtungen von Richard Wagner, 3rd ed., vol. V, Leipzig 1898, p. 66 [*Jews in Music,* translated by H. Ashton Ellis, London 1977, passage not found]).

(P. 273, l. 8) On the deficient growth of beards in the Chinese, Darwin, Abstammung des Menschen, translated into German by Haek, vol. II, p. 339 [*The Descent of Man,* vol. 2, London 1871]. Supposedly the men's *voices* also do not differ so much from those of the women in various human races, e.g., in particular among Chinese and Tartars "the voice of the male is said not to differ so much from that of the female as in most other races" (Darwin, Die Abstammung des Menschen, translated into German by Haek, Leipzig, Universalbibliothek, vol. II, p. 348, according to Sir Duncan Gibb, Journal of the Anthropological Society, April 1869, pp. LVII–LVIII [*The Descent of Man,* vol. 2, London 1871, p. 330]).

(P. 273, l. 9 from bottom f.) Houston Stewart Chamberlain, Die Grundlagen des neunzehnten Jahrhunderts, part I, 4th ed., Munich 1903, pp. 345ff. [*The Foundations of the Nineteenth Century,* translated by John Lees, London, New York 1911].

(P. 274, l. 20 from bottom) Only the very overrated G. E. Lessing and F. Nietzsche are worthy of note as relatively outstanding "philosemites," but the latter probably merely as a result of his need to oppose Schopenhauer and Wagner; and the former recognized his own stature much more clearly and admitted it much more openly than the historians of German literature (cf. Hamburgische Dramaturgie, Stück 101f. [Hamburg Dramaturgy, translated by Helen Zimmern, New York 1962, Sections 101f]). The harshest antisemite of all was probably Kant (according to his note to § 44 of his "Anthropologie in pragmatischer Hinsicht" [*Anthropology from a Pragmatic Point of View,* translated by Victor Lyle Dowdell, London 1978]. On the "consensus ingeniorum," see Chamberlain, Die Grundlagen des 19. Jahrhunderts, 4th ed., Munich 1903, p. 335 [The Foundations of the Nineteenth Century, translated by John Lees, London, New York 1911].

(P. 279, ll. 9ff.) First Book of Moses, chapter 25, 24–34; 27, 1–45; 30, 31–43.

(P. 279, ll. 16ff.) According to M. Friedländer, Der Antichrist in den vorchristlichen jüdischen Quellen, Göttingen 1901, pp. 118ff. [The Anti-Christ in pre-Christian Jewish sources], the Anti-Christ already played a part as "Beliar" in pre-Christian Judaism (e.g., in the book of Deuteronomy, which was admittedly very late). Friedländer's view, as I believe (having to disregard the historical material), culminates in the idea that the Anti-Christ had to exist first, so that Christ could come to destroy him (p. 131). However, this would attribute to evil an autonomous existence prior to good and therefore independent of it, while in fact evil is only a "privation" of good (St. Augustine, Goethe). The devil is thought up by the *good* individual, who fights against him. Only the good individual, not the bad one, *fears* evil, which is served by the criminal. Evil is only a fall from good and has any meaning only in relation to it, while good is in itself and needs no relation to anything.

It has been established that the few elements of the pre-Christian Jewish belief in the devil derive from Parsism. See W. Bousset, Die jüdische Apokalyptik, ihre religionsgeschichtliche Herkunft und ihre Bedeutung für das neue Testament [Jewish apocalyptics, its origin in religious history and its significance for the New Testament], Berlin 1903, pp. 38–51. P. 45: "The conclusion cannot be avoided: the new elements that Jewish apocalyptics brings to the hopeful faith of Judaism are determined and inspired by the Eranic religion." And p. 48: "Now it is possible to claim that the notion of dualism is specifically un-Israelitic. The religion of the prophets and the Old Testament does not know the devil. The figure of Satan, as it appears in the narrative section of the book of Job, in the Chronicle, in Zachariah, has very little in common with the later figure of the devil as it prevails in the New Testament era, indeed not much more than the name. Moreover, all the passages listed here—including the narrative section of the Book of Job—are rather late ones. The belief in the devil and the assumption of an organized demonic realm directly contradict the pious spirit of the prophets and the psalms, their strong and rigid monotheism. On the other hand, in no other religion is dualism so firmly embedded and so deeply rooted as in the Eranic religion. This too immediately suggests the dependency of Jewish apocalyptics."

(P. 280, l. 2f.) These are not only the arguments of the day, but even those of Schopenhauer (Parerga und Paralipomena, vol. 2, § 132 [*Parerga and Paralipomena,* translated by E. F. J. Payne, Oxford 2000, vol. 2, p. 262]): "[The Jewish race] lives parasitically on other nations and their soil; but yet it is inspired with the liveliest patriotism for its own nation. This is seen in the very firm way in which Jews stick together on the principle of each for all and all for each, so that this patriotism *sine patria* inspires greater enthusiasm than does any other. The rest of the Jews are the fatherland of the Jew; and so he fights for them as he would *pro ara et foris,* and no community on earth sticks so firmly together as does this."

(P. 282, l. 3) Houston Stewart Chamberlain, Die Grundlagen des neunzehnten Jahrhunderts, 4th ed., Munich 1903, p. 143, note 1 [*The Foundations of the Nineteenth Century,* translated by John Lees, London, New York 1911]—On the Jewish diaspora of the last pre-Christian centuries, cf. further M. Friedländer, Der Antichrist in den vorchristlichen jüdischen Quellen, Göttingen 1901, pp. 90f. [The Anti-Christ in pre-Christian Jewish sources].

(P. 283, l. 6) The most pertinent and forceful things about the lack of a belief in immortality in the Old Testament were said by Schopenhauer (Parerga und Paralipomena, vol. 1, pp. 151f., ed. Grisebach [*Parerga and Paralipomena,* translated by E. F. J. Payne, Oxford 2000]).

(P. 283, l. 11f.) Schopenhauer, Neue Paralipomena [New paralipomena], § 396 (Manuscripts found in the estate, vol. IV, ed. Eduard Grisebach, p. 244).

(P. 283, l. 16) Gustav Theodor Fechner, Die drei Motive und Gründe des

Glaubens [The three motives and grounds of belief], Leipzig 1863, pp. 254–256. Also in "Tagesansicht gegenüber der Nachtansicht" [The day view as opposed to the night view], Leipzig 1879, pp. 65–68.

(P. 283, l. 22) Tertulliani Apologeticus adversus gentes pro christianis, cap. 17 (Opera, vol. V, p. 47, rec. Semler, Halae 1773) ["Apology," *Apologetic Works*, translated by Rudolf Arbesmann et al., Washington, D.C. 1950, pp. 7–126.]

(P. 283, l. 20 from bottom) Chamberlain, op. cit., pp. 391–400.

(P. 283, l. 5 from bottom) Schopenhauer had the most accurate sense of the character of Jewishness at one point, for it was he who spoke of "the well-known faults attaching to the Jewish national character, of which a surprising absence of all that is expressed in the word *verecundia* is the most conspicuous, although this fault is far more useful in the world than is perhaps any positive quality" (Parerga und Paralipomena, vol. 2, § 132 [*Parerga and Paralipomena,* translated by E. F. J. Payne, Oxford 2000, vol. 2, p. 263]).

I will touch on this lack of *verecundia* and try to connect it to all the rest of the Jewish character later (p. 294).

(P. 284, l. 13 from bottom) Quoted from Kepler's poems according to Johann Karl Friedrich Zöllner, Über die Natur der Kometen, Beiträge zur Geschichte und Theorie der Erkenntnis [On the nature of the comets, contributions to the history, and theory of knowledge], 2nd ed., Leipzig 1872, p. 164.

(P. 284, l. 5 from bottom) Gustav Theodor Fechner, Ideen zur Schöpfungs- und Entwicklungsgeschichte der Organismen [Ideas on the genesis and developmental history of the organisms], Leipzig 1873. Wilhelm Preyer, Naturwissenschaftliche Tatsachen und Probleme, Populäre Vorträge [Facts and problems of natural science, popular lectures], 1880, lecture II: Die Hypothesen über den Ursprung des Lebens ("Kosmozoen-Theorie") [The hypotheses about the origin of life ("cosmozoa theory")].

(P. 286, l. 11) The main objection of Schopenhauer (Über den Willen in der Natur, Werke [Works], ed. Grisebach, vol. III, p. 337 [*On the Will in Nature,* translated by E. F. N. Payne, New York, Oxford 1992]) and Chamberlain (Grundlagen des 19. Jahrhunderts, 4th ed., pp. 170f. [*The Foundations of the Nineteenth Century,* translated by John Lees, London, New York 1911]) to Spinoza, concerning his strange moral doctrines, reflects much less on him and on Judaism, and indicates least of all any immorality in Spinoza himself. Spinoza's ethical doctrine turned out so shallow precisely because he had personally very little criminality to overcome in himself. For the same reason Aristotle's, Fechner's, or Lotze's ethical theories also fall short of the real problem, although, being Aryans, they are more profound than the Jew from the outset.

(P. 286, l. 17) I believe that what Chamberlain says (op. cit., pp. 243f. [p. 241]) is based on a misunderstanding, a confusion of will and willfulness: "The *liberum arbitrium* is decidedly a Semitic conception and in its full development a specifically Jewish one."

(P. 286, l. 20) Quite differently also in Fechner, whom superficial observers have tried to locate very close to Spinoza, although the latter is vastly inferior to him in respect of importance and depth! See, e.g., Zend-Avesta [Zend-Avesta], II^2, p. 197: "The human being, out of whom issues the other-worldly spirit [at death] . . . remains an individual under *all* the influences that he may encounter."

(P. 287, l. 5 from bottom) Schopenhauer, Die Welt als Wille und Vorstellung, vol. II, book 1, chapter 8: Zur Theorie des Lächerlichen [*The World as Will and*

Idea, translated by R. B. Haldane and J. Kemp, London 1883, chapter 8: "On the Theory of the Ludicrous"].—Jean Paul, Vorschule der Ästhetik, § 26–55 [*Horn of Oberon. Jean Paul Richter's School for Aesthetics,* translated by Margaret R. Hale, Detroit 1973].

(P. 289, l. 7) The problem of Judaism is openly formulated in "Der fliegende Holländer" [*The Flying Dutchman,* translated by David Pountney, London 1982], in "Lohengrin" [*Lohengrin,* translated by Amanda Holden, London 1993], in "Parsifal" [*Parsifal,* translated by Andrew Porter, London 1986]; but Wagner conceived Siegfried, the "foolish boy" [*The Ring of the Niblung,* translated by Stewart Spencer, London 2000, p. 253], no less than Parsifal, the "pure fool" [*Parsifal,* translated by Andrew Porter, London 1986, p. 98], in contrast to everything Jewish.

(P. 290, l. 17f.) But how all this is connected will best be understood if one hears the following lines from the Chândogya Upanishad (7, 19–21, p. 184 of Deussen's German translation, Leipzig 1897 [*Sixty Upanishads of the Veda,* translated by V. M. Bedekar and G. B. Palsule, Delhi 1980, vol. 1, pp. 186–187]):

"One thinks, if he believes; there is no thinking without belief or faith; only one who has faith has thinking. One must, therefore, seek to know faith."

"Sir. I would like to know faith!"

"One believes when one grows forth out of something. Without growing forth there is no faith. He has faith or believes in that out of which he has grown forth. One must, therefore, seek to know the growing forth or being rooted in."

"Sir, I would like to know the growing forth!"

"One grows forth out of something when he creates; without creation, there is no growing forth. One must, therefore, seek to know the creative activity."

"Sir, I would like to know the creative activity!"

(P. 292, l. 18f.) The positing of the self by the self remains the most profound idea of Fichte's philosophy. Cf. Grundlage der gesamten Wissenschaftslehre, Sämtliche Werke, ed. J. H. Fichte, I/1, Berlin 1845, pp. 95f. [*The Science of Knowledge,* translated by A. E. Kroeger, London 1889, pp. 68–72] (see note to p. 138, l. 17):

"The proposition A=A is *asserted.* But all asserting is an act of the human mind; for it has all the conditions of such an act in empirical consciousness, which must be presupposed as well known and admitted in order to advance our reflection. Now, this act is based on something which has no higher ground, namely, X or I am.

Hence, that which is *absolutely posited and in itself grounded* is the ground of *a certain* (we shall see hereafter of *all*) acting of the human mind; hence its pure character; the pure character of activity in itself, altogether abstracting from its particular empirical conditions.

The positing of the Ego through itself is, therefore, the pure activity of the Ego. The Ego *posits* its being, by virtue of its mere being. It is both the acting and the product of the act; the active and the result of the activity; deed and act in one; and hence the *I am* is expressive of a deed-act. . . .

If the Ego *is* only in so far as it posits itself, then it is only *for* the positing, and posits only for the being Ego. *The Ego is for the Ego;* but if it posits itself absolutely, as it is, then it posits itself necessarily, and is necessary for the Ego. *I am only for me; but for me I am necessarily.* (By saying *for me,* I already posit my being.)

To posit itself and *to be* is, applied to the Ego, the same. Hence, the proposition I am because I have posited myself, can also be expressed: *I am absolutely because I am.*

Again, the Ego as positing itself and the Ego as being are one and the same. The Ego is as *what* it posits itself, and posits itself as *what* it is. Hence, *I am absolutely what I am.*

The immediate expression of the thus developed deed-act may be given in the following formula: *I am absolutely because I am, and I am absolutely what I am for myself.*

If this narration of the original deed-act is to be placed at the head of a science of knowledge as its highest fundamental principle, it may perhaps be best expressed thus:

The Ego posits originally its own Being."

(P. 292, l. 14f.) Cf. H. S. Chamberlain, op. cit., pp 397f.—The duality of religion and faith, asserted by Chamberlain on pp. 405f., may hardly be tenable.

(P. 293, l. 16 from bottom) Cf. H. S. Chamberlain, Die Grundlagen des 19. Jahrhunderts, 4th ed., Munich 1903, pp. 244, 401 [*The Foundations of the Nineteenth Century,* translated by John Lees, London, New York 1911].

(P. 295, l. 15) Chamberlain, op. cit., pp. 329f.

(P. 295, l. 5 from bottom f.) On the "epileptic genius," see in particular Lombroso, Der geniale Mensch, Hamburg 1890, passim [*The Man of Genius,* New York, London 1984]. Information on Napoleon's epilepsy is supplied by Louis Proal, Napoléon I, était-il épileptique? [Was Napoleon I. an epileptic?], Archives d'Anthropologie criminelle, 1902, pp. 261–266 (with testimonies from Constant and Talleyrand).

(P. 296, l. 20f.) Kant, Die Religion innerhalb der Grenzen der bloßen Vernunft, pp. 46–47, ed. Kehrbach. See pp. 49f. [*Religion within the Boundaries of Mere Reason,* translated by Allen Wood, George Di Giovanni, Cambridge 1998, p. 68]: "But if a human being is corrupt in the very ground of his maxims, how can he possibly bring about this revolution [a transition to the maxim of the sacredness of belief] by his own forces and become a good human being on his own? Yet duty commands that he be good, and duty commands nothing but what we can do. The only way to reconcile this is by saying that a revolution is necessary in the mode of thought but a gradual reformation in the mode of sense (which places obstacles in the way of the former), and that both must therefore be possible also to the human being. That is: if by a single and unalterable decision a human being reverses the supreme ground of his maxims by which he was an evil human being (and thereby puts on a "new man"), he is to this extent, by principle and attitude of mind, a subject receptive to the good."

Kant (Philosophy of Religion [*Religion within the Boundaries of Mere Reason,* translated by Allen Wood, George Di Giovanni, Cambridge 1998]; see in my main text, p. 141 and in the appendix, pp. 370–371), Goethe (quotation on p. 297), Jacob Böhme (De regeneratione ["Of Regeneration or the New Birth," *The Works of Jacob Behmen,* vol. 4, London 1881]) and Richard Wagner (Wotan visiting Erda, Siegfried, Act III) were also less remote from this event of a literal *rebirth* of the *whole* individual than most other great men. But in their case the rebirth is limited to one act, through which they, as it were, already *absorb* the whole future into the present: they also have a *presentiment* of all their *future* relapses into immorality as their guilt, and thus they rise above both the past and the present through a timeless positing of their character, through a vow for all eternity. But in their case this process does not contrast so totally with their earlier life as in the case of the founder of a religion. ***He ascends from the night to the light, and his most ghastly horror is that of the night in which he has so far lived blindly and comfortably, and in which other people still live blindly and comfortably.***

Part 2, Chapter XIV

(P. 301, ll. 3 from bottom ff.) The growing reluctance and inability of mothers to breastfeed their children is much more likely to indicate the predominance in today's women of the prostitute element than the consumption of alcohol, which has remained unchanged in quantity for centuries (cf. p. 180, l. 20 from bottom f.).

(P. 302, l. 10) "All higher culture is founded not on the principle of *sexuality* but, quite the reverse, on the principle of *asceticism*," this (if asceticism is not understood too narrowly in the sense of Jesuitic training) is the truest word in O. Friedländer's excellent article (cf. note to p. 304, l. 10).

(P. 302, l. 17 from bottom) This valuation of men according to their sexual capacity has found its way even into science. "Il ne peut être douteux que les testicules donnent à l'homme ses plus nobles et ses plus utiles qualités" (Brown-Séquard, Archives de Physiologie normale et pathologie [Archives of normal physiology and pathology], 1889, p. 652).

Rieger is much to be commended for opposing these very popular views as vigorously as he has done in his book "Die Kastration" [Castration] (Jena 1900).

(P. 304, l. 10) By a different route and through an analysis of masculinity rather than femininity, Oskar Friedländer ("Eine für Viele, eine Studie" ["One for many, a study"], Die Gesellschaft, Münchener Halbmonatsschrift, 1902, no. 15/16) arrives at the *same* result (pp. 181f.): "The sexes form and influence each other in the direction of the physical and moral ideal which they use as the standard for their reciprocal esteem, and the more or less complete fulfillment of which must be thought of as determining their preference for one person rather than another when choosing a lover. Therefore, if genuine femininity is inseparably linked to the attribute of chastity, the reason must be sought not in the nature of woman, but in the moral disposition of man. For him chastity, and in a wider sense the ability to overcome the limitations of the sensual existence of the individual, is the highest moral value and will remain so despite all the lamentable aberrations in which our age, which pays tribute to an entirely unjustified optimism, is so rich; that is why he transfers it to the opposite sex in the shape of a moral imperative. Woman, less for an ethical than for a sexual purpose, has every interest in fulfilling this demand. That is why she clings to it—in particular to the appearance of chastity and the rules of convention—with such inexorable doggedness.

I may be excused from applying this to the opposite case. It will not be asking too much from the astuteness of my readers if I leave them to decide where the ideal of male unchastity could have originated."

(P. 304, l. 10f.) However, it is well known that the value attached to virginity also differs greatly between the different human races. See Heinrich Schurtz,

Altersklassen und Männerbünde [Age groups and men's associations], Berlin 1902, p. 93.

(P. 304, l. 5 from bottom f.) An individual who punishes himself by crucifying his flesh and mortifying his body wants a victory without a struggle; he eliminates the body because he is too weak to overcome its instincts. He is as cowardly as a suicide who shoots himself because he despairs of a victory over himself. And doing penance is the exact opposite of repentance; for it proves that the individual has not risen *above* his misdeed but is still caught up in it, or else he would not be castigating himself; in spite of allocating the blame he would be making a distinction between the moment of the deed and the moment of repentance, if indeed there were any repentance. For the prerequisite of repentance is the inability to commit a deed at the stage that has been reached, and nobody would wish to punish his own inability to do evil. Kant also saw through this asceticism (Metaphysische Anfangsgründe der Tugendlehre, § 53 [*Ethical Philosophy: The Complete Texts of Grounding for the Metaphysics of Morals,* translated by James W. Ellington, Indianapolis, Cambridge c. 1994]).

(P. 305, l. 22) Richard Wagner, Parsifal, ein Bühnenweihfestspiel, Act II (Gesammelte Schriften und Dichtungen, 3rd ed., Leipzig 1898, vol. X, pp. 360f. [*Parsifal. Stage Dedication Festival Play,* translated by Andrew Porter, London 1986].

(P. 307, l. 12) Schopenhauer: "The mormons are right." (Parerga und Paralipomena, vol. II, end of § 370 [*Parerga and Paralipomena,* translated by E. F. J. Payne, vol. II, § 166, Oxford 2000, vol. 2, p. 625]). Demosthenes 59, 122 [Apollodoros against Neaira, translated by Christopher Carey, Warminster c. 1992]: (Κατὰ Νεαίρας): "Τὰς μὲν γὰρ ἑταίρας ἡδονῆς ἕνεκ' ἔχομεν, τὰς δὲ παλλακὰς τῆς καθ' ἡμέραν θερατείας τοῦ σώματος, τὰς δὲ γυναῖκας τοῦ παιδοποιεῖσθαι γνησίως καὶ τῶν ἔνδον φύλακα πιστὴν ἔχειν."

(P. 307, ll. 13ff.) Goethe, Zweite Epistel [Second epistle]—Molière, Les Femmes Savantes, Acte II, Scène VII. [*The Learned Ladies,* translated by Richard Wilbur, New York, London 1978].—Even Kant could not be exempted from this objection if he were to be judged by a work he wrote in 1764. In "Beobachtungen über das Gefühl des Schönen und Erhabenen" (Section III, vol. VIII, p. 32, ed. Kirchmann) [*Observations on the Feeling of the Beautiful and Sublime,* translated by John T. Goldthwait, Berkeley, Los Angeles, 1960, p. 81] he says: "[Women] do something only because it pleases them, and the art consists in making only that please them which is good. I hardly believe that the fair sex is capable of principles, and I hope by that not to offend, for these are also extremely rare in the male."

(P. 307, l. 9 from bottom f.) Kant, Die Religion innerhalb der Grenzen der bloßen Vernunft, ed. Kehrbach, p. 47 [*Religion within the Boundaries of Mere Reason,* translated by Allen Wood, George Di Giovanni, Cambridge 1998].

(P. 308, l. 6) W. H. Riehl, Die Familie [The family], Stuttgart 1861, p. 7: "One must . . . admire the mad courage of the socialists, who attribute the same political and social vocation to both sexes despite all their physical and psychic differences, and who try quite resolutely to dethrone a law of nature in order to replace it with the law of a school and a system. Périsse la nature plutôt que les principes!"

The standpoint that Riehl calls mad is my own. I cannot see how any other could be adopted so long as one wants to think in ethical rather than utilitarian terms. The old misuse of the words "nature," "natural," and "in keeping with nature" will certainly be renewed as soon as the struggle against this demand is taken up. However, to put it quite unequivocally, a human being's relationship with nature is not destroyed, *but in fact created when the human being rises above nature* and becomes *more* than a mere limb, a mere part of it. For nature is always the *whole* of the material world, which cannot be overlooked from one of its parts.

(P. 308, l. 20f.) The lower a woman's stature, the more she needs emancipating. Normally the opposite is assumed.

(P. 308, ll. 18 from bottom ff.) I am thinking of the literature on "Vera," which raised rather a lot of dust in 1902. The one good thing written about the whole debate is found in Oskar Friedländer's essay "Eine für Viele, eine Studie" ["One for many, a study"], quoted several times earlier (cf. in particular the note to p. 304, l. 10).

(P. 308, l. 6 from bottom) Friedrich Nietzsche, Jenseits von Gut und Böse, aphorism 238 [*Beyond Good and Evil,* translated by R. J. Hollingdale, Harmondsworth 1990, pp. 166–167].

(P. 309, l. 18 from bottom) "Pythagoras appears as the advocate of the female sex, as the defender of its rights, its invulnerability, its elevated calling in the family and in the state. To men he presents the oppression of women as a sin. Woman should not be subjected to her husband but placed next to him with equal rights." (J. J. Bachofen, Das Mutterrecht, Eine Untersuchung über die Gynaikokratie der alten Welt nach ihrer religiösen und rechtlichen Natur, Stuttgart 1861, p. 381 [*Myth, Religion, and Mother Right,* selected writings, translated by Ralph Manheim, Princeton 1973, passage not found].)

(P. 310, l. 10f.) Only one perceptive treatise about Wagner's "Parsifal" has come to my notice: Zur Symbolik in Wagners Parsifal [On the symbolism in Wagner's Parsifal] by Emil Lucka, Wiener Rundschau, V, 16, pp. 313f. (15 August 1901). Unfortunately this excellent essay treats the subject too concisely. I myself hope to have the opportunity to carry out a detailed interpretation of this poetic work that will differ considerably from that author's on many points.

(P. 311, l. 1) Clemens Alexandrinus, Stromata, III 6, vol. I, p. 532, ed. Potter (Oxford 1715) = p. 1149, ed. Migne (Patrologiae Graecae, Tomus VIII, Paris 1857) [*Stromateis,* translated by John Ferguson, Washington 1991]: "Τῇ Σαλώμῃ ὁ Κύριος πυνθανομένῃ μέχρι πότε θάνατος ἰσχύσει οὐκ ὡς κακοῦ τοῦ βίου ὄντος καὶ τῆς κτίσεως πονηρᾶς 'Μέχρις ἄν, εἶπεν, ὑμεῖς αἱ γυναῖκες τίκτετε' ἄλ' ὡς τὴν ἀκολουθίαν τὴν φυσικὴν διδάσκων· γεννήσει γὰρ πάντως ἕπεται καὶ φθορα."—Ibid., III, 13 (I, 553 Potter, p. 1192 Migne) the following words of Jesus are reported from the "Gospel of the Egyptians" according to the testimony of Cassianus (his work Περὶ ἐγκρατείας or περὶ εὐνουχίας): "Πυνθανομένης τῆς Σαλώμης πότε γνωσθήσεται τὰ περὶ ὧν ἤρετο, ἔφη ὁ Κύριος", Οταν τὸ τῆς αἰσχύνης ἔνδυμα πατήσητε, καί ὅταν γένηται τὰ δύο ἕν, καὶ τὸ ἄρρεν μετὰ τῆς θηλείας οὔτε ἄρρεν οὔτε θῆλυ."—Finally ibid., III, 9 (I, 540 Potter, p. 1165 Migne): "ἦλθον καταλῦσαι τὰ ἔργα τῆς θηλείας· θηλείας μὲν, τῆς ἐπιθυμίας· ἔργα δέ, γέννησιν καὶ φθοράν."

This statement is so unprecedented in Greek culture that it must be regarded as genuine, and it may be called extremely fortunate that it did not get lost, as the most glorious statements of Christ certainly have because the synoptic evangelists could not understand and therefore remember them.

Incidentally, the idea that the desire for Woman is always immoral is already stated in: "πᾶς ὁ βλέπων γυναῖκα πρὸς τὸ ἐπιθυμῆσαι ἤδη ἐμοίχευσεν αὐτὴν τῇ καρδίᾳ αὐτοῦ" (Gospel of Matthew, 5, 28).

(P. 311, l. 11) Augustinus, De bono viduitatis [The good of widowhood], Cap. XXIII (Patrologiae Latinae, Tom. XL, pp. 449f., ed. Migne, Paris 1845): "Non vos . . . frangat querela vanorum, qui dicunt: Quomodo subistet genus humanum, si omnes fuerint continentes? Quasi propter aliud retardetur hoc saeculum, nisi ut impleatur praedestinatus numerus ille sanctorum, quo citius impleto, profecto nec terminus saeculi differetur." De bono conjugali, Cap. X (ibid., p. 381) [The good of marriage]: "sed novi qui murmurent. Quid si, inquiunt, omnes homines velint ab omni concubitu continere: unde susistet genus humanum? Utinam omnes hoc vellent, dumtaxat in charitate de corde puro et conscientia bona et fide non ficta (1. Tim, 1, 5): multo citius Dei civitas compleretur, et acceleraretur terminus saeculi." I am indebted for these references to Schopenhauer's "Die Welt als Wille und Vorstellung," vol. II, chapter 48 [*The World as Will and Idea,* translated by R. B. Haldane and J. Kemp, London 1883].

(P. 311, l. 19) This is the real motive for that fear, which Leo Tolstoy (Über die sexuelle Frage [On the sexual question], Leipzig 1901, pp. 16ff., 87f.) sought without being able to find it.

(P. 311, l. 10 from bottom) It may be described as pathological that a man finds a pregnant woman repulsively ugly (although she sometimes sensually arouses him), but this is exactly what distinguishes him from an animal, and whoever tries to talk him out of it is trying to strip him of his humanity. The phenomenon is deep-rooted and shows once more how all aesthetics is only an expression of ethics.—"Toutes les hideurs de la fécondité," Charles Baudelaire once says (Les fleurs du mal, Paris 1857, 5th poem, p. 21 [*The Flowers of Evil,* translated by James McGowan, Oxford, c. 1993]).

(P. 312, l. 18 from bottom) The idea of humanity in the Kantian sense is also expressed by Plato in a famous passage of the Politeia (IX, 589 A B) [*Republic,* translated by Robin A. H. Waterfield, London 1993], which at the same time contains the view of humans as being endowed with all possibilities: "ὁ τὰ δίκαια λέγων λυσι τελεῖν φαίη ἂν δεῖν ταῦτα πράττειν καὶ ταῦτα λέγειν, ὅθεν τοῦ ἀνθρώπου ὁ ἐντὸς ἄνθρωπος ἔσται ἐγκρατέστατος."

(P. 312, ll. 8 from bottom ff.) The whole development described by Herbert Spencer, Die Prinzipien der Ethik, Stuttgart 1892, vol. II, pp. 181f. [*The Principles of Ethics,* London 1892–1893, pp. 163–164]—the development from the "Fijian [who] might kill and eat his wife," from the ancient Germans, among whom the husband "might sell and even kill" his wife, from the earliest times in England, when the bride was bought and her will was not considered in the deal, up to the present day, when women are at least legally entitled to own some property of their own—this whole development was by no means caused by any movements on the women's side but occurred gradually as men brought the legal institutions closer to perfection.

Here I would like to end by quoting Oskar Friedländer, who says, op. cit., pp. 182f. (Die Gesellschaft, 1902, no. 15/16): "Incidentally, the scarce moral elements contained in the emancipation movement—and this is the best indication of the inner meaning of the whole fuss—originated, as little as the ideal of chastity, in the heated brains of the women who championed above all else the emancipation of the flesh. It was *men* who brought these elements to bear in order to end the unworthy 'bondage of women,' nor did women appear on the battlefield until the frontline attack had been decided in their favor and they could no longer honorably absent themselves. It is indicative enough that the most bitter opponents of the new direction appeared precisely in their ranks. The apparent readiness to take the altered circumstances into account and the aggressive attitude of some women must not be allowed to obscure the true facts. In these circles university studies do not hold a higher position than cycling or lawn tennis: the requisite minimum of scholarly education is regarded today as one of the secondary sexual characteristics. The ethical core of the tendency toward emancipation, the raising of women to the moral level of men, has always been regarded by women as a troublesome coercion, of which they will certainly rid themselves once they can do so without damaging their reputation and disavowing the good opinion of their advocates too openly."

Index

To assist the reader in following up Weininger's references, this name index was added to the original by the editor and the translator. Where only surnames are listed it was not possible to amplify Weininger's own usage.

AUDREY HARTFORD was born in Schwetzingen, Germany. She has recently completed a study of the Austrian writer Hermann Bahr and French literature.

LADISLAUS LÖB, who was born in Cluj, Romania, and grew up in Switzerland, is Emeritus Professor of German at the University of Sussex. He has written extensively on German literature (particularly drama from the Enlightenment to the present) and translated numerous works from German and Hungarian, including Krisztián Ungváry's *Battle for Budapest* and Béla Zsolt's *Nine Suitcases.* He is currently preparing a book about the rescue of 1700 Hungarian Jews from Bergen-Belsen concentration camp during World War II, and a translation of writings by Nietzsche.

LAURA MARCUS was born in London, England, and is Professor of English at the University of Sussex. She has published widely on nineteenth- and twentieth-century literature and culture. Her publications include *Auto/biographical Discourses: Theory, Criticism and Practice; Virginia Woolf;* and *Sigmund Freud's The Interpretation of Dreams.* She has co-edited *The Cambridge History of Twentieth-Century English Literature* (forthcoming 2005) and is currently working on a book on cinema and modernism.

DANIEL STEUER was born in Bad Homburg, Germany, and is Senior Lecturer in German at the University of Sussex. His publications include books and articles on Goethe, Wittgenstein, Thomas Bernhard and others. He is co-editor of a volume on *Metaphor and Rational Discourse.* His research centers on the relationship between science, philosophy, and literature, and he is currently writing a monograph on the idea of natural history in twentieth-century authors such as Benjamin, Adorno, and W. G. Sebald.